MEADOW LANE MEN
The Complete Who's Who
of
Notts County F.C.

By Garth Dykes

Published by
Yore Publications
12 The Furrows,
Harefield,
Middx. UB9 6AT

British Library Cataloguing-in-Publication Data.
A catalogue record for this book
is available from the British Library.

ISBN 0954783069

Printed and bound by
Cromwell Press Ltd.
Trowbridge

DEDICATION

To Daniel Dykes, of Wurzburg, Germany,
with love from his Grandpa.

ABOUT THE AUTHOR

Garth Dykes was born at Mellor, near Blackburn, and was educated at Chadderton Grammar School. Qualifications in cotton spinning followed and a career in yarn sales eventually took Garth to Leicester, where he has lived since 1961. A member of the Football Writers' Association, Garth's lifelong love of football – he attended his first match in season 1945-46 - has resulted in his involvement in eight books to date. Oldham Athletic have been his favourite team since schooldays, and his first visit to Meadow Lane was in December 1963 when the Latics were the visitors. Of more recent times, Garth has been a regular at Meadow Lane, being a season ticket holder and member of the Notts County Supporters' Trust. A number of football caricatures drawn by the author appear on the cover and within the pages of this book. This aspect of his work has featured in five of his previous titles, as well as in football programmes, national magazines and in several sets of trade cards produced by David Rowland of Bury.

BY THE SAME AUTHOR

Oldham Athletic - A Complete Record, 1899 – 1988

(Breedon Books, 1988)

Exeter City - A Complete Record, 1904 – 1990, with Alex Wilson and Maurice Golesworthy

(Breedon Books, 1990)

New Brighton - A Complete Record of the Rakers in the Football League, 1922 – 1951

(Breedon Books, 1990)

Accrington Stanley – A Complete Record, 1894 – 1962, with Mike Jackman

(Breedon Books, 1991)

The United Alphabet – A Complete Who's Who of Manchester United F.C.

(ACL & Polar Publishing (UK) Ltd, 1994)

All The Lads – A Complete Who's Who of Sunderland A.F.C., with Doug Lamming   (Polar Publishing, 1999)

Latics Lads – The Official Who's Who of Oldham Athletic A.F.C., 1907 – 2002

(Yore Publications, 2002)

ACKNOWLEDGEMENTS

In the three years it has taken to research and write this book, I am as ever grateful for the help, encouragement and advice of many friends and fellow statisticians. My particular thanks go, however, to my dear partner Ann for her unfailing love, encouragement and support.

Five gentlemen especially receive my thanks. They include Douglas Lamming, a friend of twenty years, with whom I had hoped to share this book. Sadly, ill health has prevented the most successful and prolific football writer of recent years from taking a full part in this work. It would surely have been fitting if the task of chronicling the players of the Football League's oldest club could have been undertaken by the Football Writers' Association veterans, with a combined age of 162 years. Jim Creasy deserves particular thanks for his immeasurable assistance, not only in the matter of players' birth and death details, but in all areas of football history. His continuing researches at the Family Records Centre, Football Association and elsewhere have enriched this and many other works of football history. Three noted Notts County historians, Tony Brown, Keith Warsop and Paul Wain, have all been generous with their time and knowledge. All have published excellent earlier histories of the club which have proved to be extremely useful. Additionally, a selection from Paul Wain's extensive collection of photographs have greatly enriched the pages of this book.

The author also wishes to thank the most helpful, friendly and courteous staff of the Local Studies Department of Nottingham City Library. Thanks also to Peter Holme, Research Officer of the National Football Museum at Preston, for his kind and valued assistance. Many friends, club and general football statisticians, authors and Magpies' supporters have supplied valuable details. My sincere thanks to: Stuart Basson, Michael Braham, Bill Cook, Mike Davage, Mark Durkin, Ian Gill, Matt Hill, Barry J. Hugman, Mike Jackman, Neilson N Kaufman, John Litster (editor of the Scottish Football Historian), Tom Loakes, Ian Moat, Donald Montgomery, Ian Nannestad, Mike Peterson, Robert W. Reid, Dave Smith, David Sullivan (Millwall F.C. Museum,) Roger J Triggs and Terry Woolhouse.

Finally, my thanks to friend and good neighbour Rajesh "Raj" Jobanputra, whose computing expertise has helped me out on numerous occasions.

AUTHOR'S PREFACE

On March 10th, 1934, Notts County kicked off against Bradford Park Avenue at Meadow Lane in bright sunshine. Sixteen minutes later, torrential rain caused the game to be abandoned. A few hours earlier, in blizzard conditions, I was born at Mellor, near Blackburn. In the intervening 71 years both Notts County and the author have experienced a fair share of life's ups and downs. Thankfully, both are still going strong!

It is over forty years since I first saw Notts County in action. The date was 28th December 1963, and in one of their better performances in a relegation season they despatched opponents Oldham Athletic by 4 – 2, with a hat-trick by Jeff Astle the outstanding feature of the match.

Jeff Astle could be ranked amongst the most illustrious of the 1,027 Magpies who have qualified to appear in these pages, despite the fact that his career, along with that of his contemporary, Tony Hateley, came to full potential after leaving Meadow Lane. The fact that such talent was inevitably sold to balance the books has to be a main reason why the Magpies have spent much of their existence outside of the top flight. Nevertheless, the club's propensity for producing notable local players, right from Walter Bull and Billy Flint in the pre Great War period, to Brian Stubbs and Kelvin Wilson of more recent times, gives real hope for a brighter future for the Football League's oldest club.

Considering the time-scale involved, and the wealth of information required, the 'Who's Who' genre presents its own peculiar difficulties. Neither the author, nor anybody else still about, will have seen, for instance, Harry Daft or Alf Shelton in action. Nevertheless, newspapers of the day have left one with the means to convey an appreciation of the player's abilities and style of play. The early press, however, was less helpful in the matter of player's personal details, rarely mentioning forenames, dates and places of birth, and dates of signing. Amplification of information on any of the club's early players will be welcomed, I can be contacted via the publisher.

Garth Dykes,
Leicester,
May 2005

NOTES ON THE TEXT

For each player I have attempted to provide the following information: full names, recognised playing position, height and weight, date and place of birth and, where applicable, date and place of death. (It should be mentioned here that the dates of birth and death of some pre-war players have been culled from registers that only record such events in three month periods. Hence the use – for example - of 'January quarter 1893', which denotes a span of January/February/March of that year). Also included are Notts County debut, full career and biographical details, a breakdown of appearances made and goals scored, and finally a player's peacetime representative and club honours (if any,) which have been listed at the end of his entry. Every player who has appeared for the Magpies at senior competitive level is included. Not included are appearances in the short-lived United Counties League (East Midlands Division) 1893-95 and the barely commenced season 1939-40. Player's statistics are complete to the end of the 2004-05 season, but any incremental information regarding transfers etc have been included up to the print deadline (end May 2005).

Abbreviations used are those generally occurring in a work of this type, viz:

am	amateur	gls	goals
app.	apprentice	KIA	Killed in action
b.	born	nc	non contract
c.	circa	PL	Premier League
cs	close season	pro	professional
d.	died	q.v.	(quode vide) denotes a cross-reference
Div	Division	SL	Scottish League
ECWC	European Cup Winners' Cup	SPL	Scottish Premier League
ESC	European Super Cup	sub	substitute
FA	Football Association	WW1	The First World War (1914-18)
FL	Football League	WW2	The Second World War (1939-45)
FAYC	FA Youth Cup	YTS	Youth Training Scheme

NOMENCLATURE
Clubs have been given titles used at the time when the transfer or other event took place. Leicester Fosse, for instance, became Leicester City after World War One, Birmingham became Birmingham City in July 1945 and Swansea Town became Swansea City in February 1970.

POSITION
Precise labelling using the classic eleven-position, goalkeeper to outside left, has been used where appropriate. Different modern concepts, however, have necessitated broader terms (midfielder, defender, striker etc) for more recent and present day players.

PHOTOGRAPHS
Are courtesy of Notts County F.C., Paul Wain, The Douglas Lamming Collection and the author's own collection.

TRANSFER FEES
Many of the fees quoted are known to be authentic. The remainder have been culled from newspapers and sporting journals and may be taken to be reasonably near to the mark.

FOREWORD

By Colin Slater M.B.E.
of BBC Radio Nottingham
"The Voice of Notts County"

This book is a most welcome addition to other volumes about Notts County, founded in 1862 and the oldest club in the Football League. Unlike earlier publications it is the first to provide a pen portrait of every single player that has appeared for the Magpies over a period fast approaching a century and a half, plus details of all their managers. So it is unique. As such, it will be an indispensable work of reference, will settle many an argument – and will provide an endless source of material for pub quiz nights. It will also conjure up memories of some of the greatest players in the club's history.

Having reported on Notts matches from 1959 to the present time, a total of 46 seasons, it remains a matter of personal regret not to have been around when England's finest centre forward, Tommy Lawton, spearheaded Notts winning of the championship of the old Third Division South in 1950 with 31 goals in 37 matches – what a record! – and formed such an inspiring partnership with another England international, Jackie Sewell. It was an achievement watched by huge crowds, some of over 40,000.

The question I am most frequently asked is who I believe to have been the best of over 250 Notts players I have seen. Don Masson stands head and shoulders above the rest, gifted as some of them were. His achievement in captaining Notts to three promotions, from the old Fourth Division to the old First, in his two spells at the club, will surely never be repeated. It adds to the romance that 'The Don' was bought from Middlesbrough, along with Bob Worthington, for the paltry joint sum of £7,500, an incredible bit of business on the part of the then-manager, Billy Gray. It was under Billy's long-term successor, Jimmy Sirrel, that Notts won those three promotions, climbing from the depths to the heights and making him the most revered manager in the club's post-war history, though Neil Warnock comes very close to rivalling him. Both had squads of really good players and knew how to get the best out of them.

The fact that, through its youth set-up, Meadow Lane has also been a breeding ground for players who have gone on to win honours elsewhere is also a matter for satisfaction. The likes of Dave Watson, who won 65 England caps in an illustrious career, and the late Jeff Astle, who scored West Bromwich Albion's winner in the 1968 FA Cup final against Everton, come readily to mind – and there have been plenty of others who owe their start in the professional game to Notts. Jeff was transferred by Notts to Albion in 1964 for £25,000. What would he cost in today's inflated market?

My own memories have been stirred by being able to read an advance copy of this book. May yours be too. Enjoy it!

1892 - County versus Forest:
How a magazine of the time saw it.

~ CONTENTS ~

ABRAHAMS, James

Outside-right
CAREER: NOTTS Nov 1891/Stockton June 1892/
Middlesbrough later in the same month.
Debut v Sunderland (a) 5.12.1891, lost 0 – 4

Evidently the outside-right berth caused problems for
Notts in 1891-92, no fewer than eight players appearing
there in what would now be considered an undemanding
24 match League tournament. One of them, Abrahams,
had a run of three successive appearances during December
and another in February. They comprise his total
involvement in the first-class game. In December 1891, an
item appeared in the local press, revealing that Abrahams
had been suspended for insobriety. On leaving the Magpies
he initially joined Stockton in June 1892, apparently had
a change of mind – or a better offer - and joined
Middlesbrough one week later.

Appearances: FL: 4 apps 1 gl Total: 4 apps 1 gl

———————o———————

ABTHORPE, John

Centre-forward
b. Mansfield, 19th January 1933
CAREER: Leicestershire & Rutland F.A./Wolverhampton
Wanderers am/NOTTS am Sept 1955
Debut v West Ham United (a) 3.9.55, lost 1 – 6 (scored)

Class amateur whose talents earned representative honours
besides an acquaintance with two League clubs. Despite
the calls of National Services during his time at Meadow
Lane, his League record for the Magpies – three goals in
five outings – would have been reckoned respectable by a
professional, indicating a likely rewarding career in the
paid ranks.

Appearances: FL: 5 apps 3 gls Total: 5 apps 3 gls
Honours: Represented English Universities against
Scotland in 1954-55.

———————o———————

ADAMSON, Henry 'Harry'

Wing-half   5' 10" 12st 0lbs
b. Kelty, Fife, 27th June 1924
d. Dunfermline, 23rd May 1997
CAREER: Jeanfield Swifts/NOTTS Aug 1946/Gainsborough
Trinity 1956/Wisbech Town 1957
Debut v Norwich City (h) 17.4.48, lost 1 – 2

Spent the whole decade of his senior career at Meadow
Lane. He had previously not played for two years prior
to joining Jeanfield Swifts, where he was capped at junior
level as an inside-left. With the Magpies he gradually
worked his way into the first team, the high point being
an ever-present campaign in the 1949-50 Southern Section
championship side. Adamson showed consistency
throughout the years. After moving to wing-half the

constructive side
of his game
flourished, an
ability to perform
on both flanks a
valued factor. He
worked for the
'Nottingham
Evening Post' for
some 24 years
from 1969,
returning to
Scotland on
retirement.
Obviously loved
his football,
playing for the
works team into
his fifties.

Appearances: FL: 233 apps 5 gls FAC: 16 apps 0 gls
Total: 249 apps 5 gls
Honours: Scottish Junior International. (NOTTS) FL Div
3 South champions 1950.

———————o———————

AGANA, Patrick Anthony Olozinka 'Tony'

Forward   6' 0"   12st 2lbs
b. Bromley, 2nd October 1963
CAREER: Welling United/Weymouth Mar 1984, fee £4,500/
Watford Aug 1987, fee £22,000/Sheffield United Feb 1988,
valued at £35,000 in exchange for M. Kuhl and P.
Hetherston/NOTTS Nov 1991, fee £685,000 (Leeds United
loan Feb 1992)/Hereford United Mar 1997
Debut v Aston Villa (a) 16.11.91, lost 0 – 1

An important figure in County's cavalcade in that he is
their costliest player, topping the previous holder's value
(John Chiedozie) by some £85,000. Tony had reached
League football late by modern standards (aged nearly
24). His best spell was with Sheffield United where he
formed a potent spearhead with the redoubtable Brian
Deane. At this time a club historian described him as "An
attacking player with good control and exceptional pace."
Tony scored one of the goals in the Magpies' 2 – 1 victory
against Ascoli in the Anglo-Italian Cup Final at Wembley
in March 1995, but failed to replicate the strike-rate of his
Sheffield United days. He scored his final two League
goals for Hereford United following his deadline transfer
to Edgar Street, but they were insufficient to save his new
team from relegation to the Conference.

Appearances: FL: 114(31) apps 15 gls FAC: 6(2) apps 2
gls FLC: 8(1) apps 2 gls Other: 17(2) apps 4 gls
Total: 145(36) apps 23 gls
Honours: England Semi-Professional International, 1 cap.
(NOTTS) Anglo-Italian Cup winners 1995, finalists 1994.

AGNEW, David Young

Full-back   5' 8"   11st 2lbs
b. Kilwinning, Ayrshire 4th August 1939
CAREER: Saxone F.C./Leicester City pro Aug 1958/
Scunthorpe United June 1961/NOTTS June 1962/Ilkeston
Town player-manager July 1967
Debut v Coventry City (a) 18.8.62, lost 0 – 2

David had made only one senior appearance – during his
Scunthorpe season – prior to joining Notts. A reserve
until the 1963-64 season, he then took advantage of an
unexpected chance, thereafter enjoying a fair measure of
first team exposure. During his extremely varied five-year
stint at Meadow Lane he was handed a free transfer at the
end of the 1964-65 season. On reconsideration, it was
decided to retain him as a player, with the duel
responsibility of a post as staff joiner! In his first season
as player-manager of Ilkeston Town, he piloted them to
the Midland League championship.

Appearances: FL: 85 apps 1 gl FAC: 4 apps 0 gls FLC: 2
apps 0 gls Total: 91 apps 1 gl

ALLAN, John

Winger 5' 6"   10st 4lbs
b. Glasgow circa 1871
CAREER: Glasgow Thistle/Derby County Aug 1893/NOTTS
Dec 1894/Heanor Town Sept 1898
Debut v Walsall (h) 25.12.1894, won 5 – 0

An ever-present in his one full term with Derby County
(1893-94), for the most part in partnership with the great
Steve Bloomer, and this when the Rams had an excellent
season, finishing third in the First Division. John knew
his way to goal, his aggregate figures below constituting
an excellent return for a wing forward. Three years after
leaving Notts, he was working as a railway clerk and
residing in Derby.

Appearances: FL: 79 apps 27 gls FAC: 5 apps 2 gls Other:
8 apps 0 gls Total: 92 apps 29 gls
Honours: (NOTTS) FL Div 2 champions 1897

ALLEN, Herbert

Inside-left   5' 9"   11st 0lbs
b. Shifnal, Shropshire April quarter 1899
CAREER: Wellington St George/NOTTS Dec 1923/
Stourbridge cs 1926/Burton Town cs 1927/Charlton Athletic
June 1928/Wellington Town Aug 1929/Wellington St George
cs 1930/Oswestry Town 1931/Darlaston/Wellington Town
Aug 1934
Debut v Preston North End (h) 19.1.24, drawn 0 – 0

Deputised for Harold Hill for his solitary
senior appearance. Described in a local
handbook as "promising" and " With a good
knowledge of the art of dribbling, and a first
class marksman." Prior to joining Charlton
Athletic, Herbert assisted Burton Town to win the
championship of the Birmingham League.

Appearances: FL: 1 app 0 gls Total: 1 app 0 gls

ALLEN, Herbert Anthony 'Tanner'

Full-back
b. Beeston, Nottingham, 27th October 1924
CAREER: Cottesmore School/Nottingham Schoolboys/17th
Company Beeston Boys' Brigade/Beeston Boys' Club/
Nottingham Forest Jan 1946/NOTTS Aug 1949/Corby Town
1955/Grantham Town Jan 1957
Debut v Coventry City (a) 15.12.51, won 2 – 0

A locally-born Forest reserve (4 League and FA Cup
matches, 1 goal) recruited by Notts after three and a half
years at the City Ground. Made senior appearances at
Meadow Lane in both full-back positions and at right-
half, his thoughtful work marked by unusual coolness. An
industrial draughtsman by calling, he played football as a
part-time professional. 'Tanner' was a most welcome
guest of the club at the Shrewsbury Town match at
Meadow Lane on 6th November 2004. To celebrate his
eightieth birthday he was presented with a home jersey,
squad number 80!

Appearances: FL: 30 apps 0 gls Total: 30 apps 0 gls

ALLEN, Robert Howard Allen

Full-back
b. Shepton Mallet, 5th December 1916
CAREER: NOTTS Feb 1945/Bristol City Nov 1946 to 1947
Debut v Watford (a) 21.9.46, drawn 2 – 2

Signed late in the War, making four appearances in the
final season and 15 in the transitional 1945-46. Engaged
for the first peacetime campaign, he had only one outing
before a brief liaison with Bristol City (One FL and one
FA Cup appearance). For the record, the FA Cup
encounter, against Hayes Athletic in November 1946,
resulted in a 9 – 3 win for City. His Magpies' debut came
in unusual circumstances, as deputy for George Robinson
when the latter missed the match due to having to attend
a presentation at his works in Melton Mowbray.

Appearances: FL: 1 app 0 gls Total: 1 app 0 gls

ALLIN, Thomas

Centre-forward
CAREER: Accrington F.C./NOTTS cs 1888 to 1889
Debut v Blackburn Rovers (h) 6.10.1888, drawn 3 – 3

Given a run out leading the Notts attack during the first League season, a term when no player emerged as the undisputed centre-forward. Allin scored twice at West Bromwich Albion in a 2 – 4 defeat on 20th October 1888, but failed to score in a further five outings. In the following season the signing of the Scottish international James Osborne from Third Lanark proved to be an unqualified success, as the luxuriantly moustachioed attack leader topped the scoring lists in his first three seasons with the club.

Appearances: FL: 6 apps 2 gls Total: 6 apps 2 gls

ALLSEBROOK, Richard

Left-half   5' 10 ½" 10st 12lbs
b. Newstead, Notts. 25th July 1892
d. Linby, Notts. 15th June 1961
CAREER: Newstead Amateurs/NOTTS Apr 1912/Ebbw Vale June 1920/Hucknall Byron Sept 1922
Debut v Chelsea (h) 21.12.12, drawn 0 – 0

Capped by Nottinghamshire Amateurs against Leicestershire, and when signed by the Magpies the local correspondent considered him to be: " One of the most promising youngsters Notts have had for some time." He took the eye when assisting County's reserve team during the 1911-12 season. Drafted into the League side in an emergency halfway through his first professional season, Allsebrook did so well he made the left-half position his own. Notable for ball control and good, accurate passing. During the Great War he served three and a half years in the Yorks. And Lancs. Regiment.

Appearances: FL: 97 apps 2 gls FAC: 3 apps 0 gls
Total: 100 apps 2 gls
Honours: (NOTTS) FL Div 2 champions 1914

ALLSOPP, Daniel 'Danny'

Forward   6' 1" 12st 0lbs
b. Melbourne, Australia, 10th August 1978
CAREER: South Melbourne (Australia)/Carlton (Australia)/ Port Melbourne Sharks (Australia)/Manchester City Aug 1998, fee £10,000 (NOTTS loan Nov 1999) (Wrexham loan Feb 2000) (Bristol Rovers loan Oct 2000)/NOTTS Nov 2000, fee £300,000/Hull City May 2003, fee 'nominal' Debut v Gillingham (h) 6.11.99, drawn 1 – 1 (scored)

A former Golden Boot winner, awarded for finishing as leading scorer in the World Under-17 championships, Danny struggled to establish himself with Manchester City. Following his initial loan to the Magpies he was on the point of being transferred to Gillingham but decided to stay put and fight for a first team place at Maine Road. He never did re-establish himself, but eventually realised his potential in the Magpies' colours. Tall, strong-running and direct in approach, he had a magnificent season in 2001-02, scoring goals in four different competitions to total 28 in 49(1) matches. Danny was similarly successful following his transfer to Hull City, who won promotion to the re-named Football League Championship 1 in 2003-04.

Appearances: FL: 97(8) apps 42 gls FAC: 8 apps 4 gls FLC: 3 apps 4 gls Other: 2(2) apps 3 gls
Total: 110(10) apps 53 gls
Honours: Australian Youth, U-20 and U-23 International

ALLSOPP, Elijah

Forward, later wing-half
b. Wymeswold, Leics. July quarter 1877
d. Loughborough, Leics. 3rd January 1958
CAREER: Bury/NOTTS season 1893-94 to cs 1897
Debut v Ardwick (h) 15.3.1894, won 5 – 0 (scored one)

Made seven appearances (one goal) in Bury's Lancashire League side in 1893-94 when the Shakers finished runners-up in that strong competition. In the following season, playing against his former team mates, he became the first Notts player to successfully convert a penalty kick in a Football League match. A versatile individual, able to occupy several front line positions and either flank in the middle line. (He had 10 games at right-half in Notts' 1897 championship side.) Tall and slimly built, he left Notts immediately after the 1897 triumph, and was later reported to be working as a railway goods porter.

Appearances: FL: 59 apps 20 gls FAC: 3 apps 2 gls Other: 2 apps 1 gl Total: 64 apps 23 gls
Honours: (NOTTS) FL Div 2 champions 1897

ANDERSON, John

Wing-half   5' 8" 10st 8lbs
CAREER: Vale of Clyde/Port Glasgow Athletic cs 1903/
NOTTS June 1904 to 1905/Port Glasgow Athletic until cs
1906/Hamilton Academical cs 1908 to 1909.
Debut v Everton (h) 3.9.04, lost 1 – 2

Said by the local press to have cost "A stiffish fee",
Anderson played in the first seven League fixtures of 1904-
05 at right-half, but only in two later (on the other flank).
He was replaced by another recruit from the 1904 close
season, Fred Emberton, who went on to become a Notts
stalwart for the ensuing decade. So at any rate Anderson
lost his place to an exceptionally worthy successor.

Appearances: FL: 9 apps 0 gls Total: 9 apps 0 gls

ANDREWS, Harold

Inside-forward 5' 9½" 10st 10lbs
b. Lincoln, 13th August 1903
d. Nottingham, August 1988
CAREER: St Botolph's O.B. (Lincoln)/Lincoln City am
season 1924-25, pro Aug 1925/NOTTS Mar 1928, fee £550/
Barnsley July 1932, in exchange for J.W. Smith/Luton Town
May 1935/Accrington Stanley May 1936 to June 1938/
Players F.C. (Nottingham) cs 1938-40
Debut v Barnsley (a) 31.3.28, drawn 0 – 0

Lincoln City's
local discovery
of the 'Twenties,
an effective
centre or inside-
forward notable
for his fine
headwork and
strong left-foot
shot. An un-
selfish player
whose unob-
trusive work
was not always
fully appreci-
ated. Andrews
gave Notts four
years excellent
service that
included the 1931 promotion season. Latterly played left-
half and finished with FL aggregate figures of 385
appearances, 141 goals. A fitter by trade, after leaving
professional football he worked for Players, the tobacco
firm, assisting the works team. An all round sportsman,
his hobbies included cricket, golf and lawn tennis.

Appearances: FL: 134 apps 55 gls FAC: 6 apps 3 gls
Total: 140 apps 58 gls
Honours: (NOTTS) FL Div 3 South champions 1931.
(Barnsley) FL Div 3 North champions 1934.

ANGELL, Brett Ashley Mark

Forward   6' 2" 13st 11 lbs
b. Marlborough, Wiltshire 20th August 1968
CAREER: Portsmouth trainee, signing pro Aug 1986/
Cheltenham Town/Derby County Feb 1988, fee £40,000/
Stockport County Oct 1988, fee £33,000/Southend United
Aug 1990, fee £100,000/Everton Jan 1994, fee £500,000/
Sunderland Mar 1995, fee £600,000 (Sheffield United loan
Jan 1996) (West Bromwich Albion loan Mar 1996)/
Stockport County Aug 1996, fee £120,000 (NOTTS loan
Dec 1999) (Preston North End loan Feb 2000)/Walsall July
2000/Rushden & Diamonds Feb 2002/Port Vale Aug 2002/
Queens Park Rangers Nov 2002, retired July 2003.
Debut v AFC Bournemouth (h) 8.1.2000, won 5 – 1 (scored
a hat-trick)

A vastly experienced, forceful attack leader who spent an
eventful loan spell at Meadow Lane, Brett scored within
a minute of the kick-off in his debut against AFC
Bournemouth. Notts were three goals ahead within eight
minutes, Angell completing a hat-trick to round off the
Magpies' best win of the season. His month's loan
concluded with a double strike in the 2 – 0 win against
Burnley on 3rd January 2000. In a career spanning the
Conference, Third, Second and First Divisions, and the
Premier League he appeared on all but a handful of the 92
League and Premiership grounds, scoring a career total of
148 League goals in 386 appearances.

Appearances: FL: 6 apps 5 gls Total: 6 apps 5 gls
Honours: (Preston North End) FL Div 2 champions 2000

ANTOINE-CURIER, Mickael

Forward   6' 0" 12st 4lbs
b. Orsay, France 5th March 1983
CAREER: Nancy F.C. (France)/Preston North End Nov
2000/Nottingham Forest June 2001 (Brentford loan Mar
2003)/Burnley nc July - Aug 2003/Oldham Athletic Aug
2003/Kidderminster Harriers nc 19th Sept 2003/Rochdale nc
23rd Sept - Oct 2003/Sheffield Wednesday Nov 2003/
Lillestroem, Norway, trial Jan 2004/NOTTS Feb 2004/
Grimsby Town Mar 2004
Debut v Stockport County (h) 21.2.2004, won 4 – 1

Associated with ten different League clubs, including a
staggering six in season 2003-04, the speedy French front-
runner began brightly at Meadow Lane. His debut, in which
he started in tandem with Paul Heffernan, gave Gary Mills'
team their first victory of 2004, and featured a four-goal
blast from Irish striker Heffernan. A further two
consecutive victories followed, the Frenchman scoring his
first goal in the 3 – 1 midweek win against Grimsby Town.
His ability was not in doubt, but his decision to celebrate
his 21st birthday on the eve of the Plymouth Argyle match
on 6th March was cited as the reason for his hurried exit
from Meadow Lane, manager Mills justifiably affronted
by the player's lack of dedication to the cause.

Appearances: FL: 4 apps 1 gl Total: 4 apps 1 gl

ARKINS, Vincent 'Vinny'

Forward   6' 2" 11st 10lbs
b. Dublin, 18th September 1970
CAREER: Home Farm/Dundee United Dec 1987/Home Farm
Oct 1989/St Johnstone Nov 1991/Shelbourne Oct 1993/
NOTTS Sept 1995, fee £100,000/Portadown Feb 1997
Debut as sub v Shrewsbury Town (a) 16.9.95, won 1 – 0

Fair-haired Irish striker, capped at every level but senior
by Northern Ireland. Initially in the shadow of Devon
White at Meadow Lane, he then enjoyed a lengthy spell
of first team action in mid season before being crowded
out by a welter of new forward signings including Gary
Martindale, Gary Jones and Tony Battersby. He left in
February of the following relegation season after scoring
just once in 13(2) League matches. Vinny subsequently
enjoyed much success, particularly in 2002, when he was
voted ' Player of the Year' by the Football Writers'
Association of Northern Ireland. He also won the 'Sunday
Life Leading Scorers Award' for his 35 goals for Portadown
in the Irish League Premier Division.

Appearances: FL: 30(8) apps 8 gls FAC: 4(1) apps 1 gl
FLC: 2(2) apps 0 gls Other: 4 apps 0 gls
Total: 40(11) apps 9 gls
Honours: Republic of Ireland 'B' International, 1 app. U-
21 International, 8 apps. Youth International, 2 apps.
Schoolboy International, 2 apps. (Portadown) Irish League
Premier Division champions 2002

ARMSTRONG, Kenneth Charles

Central defender   6' 2" 13st 7lbs
b. Bridgnorth, 31st January 1959
CAREER: Beith Juniors/Kilmarnock June 1977/Southampton
June 1983, fee £25,000 (NOTTS loan Mar 1984)/
Birmingham City Aug 1984, fee £100,000/Walsall Feb 1986,
fee £125,000, retired due to injury cs 1987
Debut v Coventry City (h) 17.3.84, won 2 – 1

A Scot in everything but birthplace, this qualification lost
by reason of his father's employment in England. Not the
most elegant of players, Ken had a commanding presence,
was strong defensively and liked to make the occasional
attacking sortie. His career ended after breaking an ankle
while at Walsall. A graduate, Ken later took employment
as a social worker.

Appearances: FL: 10 apps 0 gls Total: 10 apps 0 gls

ARNOTT, Walter 'Watty'

Right-back   5'9"   12st 6lbs
b. Pollockshields, Glasgow 12th May 1861
d. Clarkston, Renfrewshire 18th May 1931
CAREER: Matilda F.C./Pollockshields Athletic/Queen's Park
May 1882/Pollockshields Athletic cs to Dec 1884/Queen's
Park/Also assisted Corinthians 1885-88/Linfield Athletic
1892/NOTTS Feb-Mar 1895 and also guested for Newcastle
West End
Debut v Sheffield Wednesday, FAC 1 (a) 2.2.1895, lost 1 – 5

By some margin the most distinguished of County's 'few
appearance' contingent. For Watty Arnott, besides winning
14 caps (in an era when countries had only three
engagements per season), played for Queen's Park when
the club dominated the Scottish scene. Ideally built,
resourceful, not wanting for speed and reckoned the best
full-back of his time. One correspondent noting: "Tall and
finely built, he is unsurpassed for ease of motion and
grace of carriage." Useful at other sports too: tennis, bowls
and yachting, a diverse trio!

Appearances: FL: 1 app 0 gls FAC: 1 app 0 gls
Total: 2 apps 0 gls
Honours: Scotland International, 14 caps 1883-93.
(Queen's Park) Scottish Cup winners 1884, 1886, 1890;
FA Cup finalists 1884, 1885. Made 11 apps for Glasgow
in inter-city matches.

ARPHEXHAD, Pegguy Michel

Goalkeeper   6' 2"   13st 5lbs
b. Abymes, Guadeloupe, 18th May 1973
CAREER: Brest-Armorique, (France) 1987/RC Lens,
(France) 1991/ (Lille OSC, France, loan Aug 1996)/
Motherwell trial July 1997/Leicester City Aug 1997/
Liverpool July 2000 to June 2003 (Stockport County loan
Sept 2001)/Coventry City Aug 2003 (NOTTS loan Mar
2004)/Marseille (France) Sept 2004.
Debut v Wycombe Wanderers (a) 13.3.2004, drawn 1 – 1

A loan signing from manager Mills previous club, Coventry
City, when injury had sidelined goalkeeper Stuart Garden.
The ideally proportioned deputy's brief spell at Meadow
Lane was not distinguished, as an unfortunate handling
error presented Wycombe Wanderers with an equaliser on
his debut, and a moment's fatal hesitation in his final match
against Chesterfield again proving costly. A knee injury
brought his unhappy sojourn at Meadow Lane to a close.
Earlier in his career Pegguy won seven Under-21 caps for
France, and joined Leicester City as cover for Kasey Keller.
He made 24(5) appearances before joining Liverpool, again
in a covering role, sampling several Cup successes from
his position on the substitute's bench.

Appearances: FL: 3 apps 0 gls Total: 3 apps 0 gls
Honours: France U-21 International, 7 apps.

ASHCROFT, Lee

Winger   5' 10" 11st 2lbs
b. Preston, 7th September 1972
CAREER: Preston North End trainee Jan 1987, pro July 1991/West Bromwich Albion Aug 1993, fee £250,000 (NOTTS loan Mar 1996)/Preston North End Sept 1996, fee £150,000/Grimsby Town Aug 1998, fee £500,000/Wigan Athletic Aug 2000, fee £250,000 (Port Vale loan Oct 2002) (Huddersfield Town loan Dec 2002)/Southport player-coach Feb 2003 (Chorley loan Feb 2004)/Kendall Town June 2004.
Debut v Carlisle United (h) 30.3.96, won 3 – 1

A speedy and accomplished winger able to play on either flank, who commanded some sizeable fees in a career spanning 341(64) League and Cup appearances and 84 goals. He was out of the first team picture at West Bromwich Albion at the time of his loan to the Magpies, but his next permanent move returned him to more first team involvement with his hometown club, Preston North End. Once described as "A scorer of great goals, rather than a great goalscorer," he failed to hit the mark during his spell at Meadow Lane, but proved a capable deputy to Tony Agana in the run-in to a place in the promotion Play-offs in May 1996.

Appearances: FL: 4(2) apps 0 gls Total: 4(2) apps 0 gls
Honours: England U-21 International, 1 app 1992

ASHER, Thomas

Inside-forward   5' 5" 10st 6lbs
b. Hatfield, Yorkshire 21st December 1936
CAREER: Doncaster Schoolboys/Wolverhampton Wanderers am/Wath Athletic/NOTTS am, signing pro July 1954/Peterborough United Aug 1959/Ilkeston Town Aug 1960/Ransome & Marles.
Debut v Swansea Town (h) 12.9.57, lost 2 – 4

Stocky inside-forward. Spent three years as a Notts reserve following an outstanding career in schoolboy football and service as an amateur with the Wolves' nursery side, Wath Wanderers. Regarded as highly promising and, on making his senior debut, impressed with intelligent approach play but had a modest scoring tally. A feeling persists that Tom drifted into non-League football at far too early an age.

Appearances: FL: 31 apps 4 gls Total: 31 apps 4 gls
Honours: England Schoolboy International, 3 caps 1952

ASHTON, Jonathan James 'Jon'

Defender   6' 2" 13st 7lbs
b. Nuneaton, 4th October 1982
CAREER: Leicester City trainee, signing pro Jan 2001 (NOTTS loan Nov-Dec 2002)/Chesterfield trial July 2003/Oxford United Sept 2003
Debut v Mansfield Town (h) 9.11.2002, drawn 2 – 2

A well built young central defender with good pace, whose height and weight made him a useful asset. Jon's spell on loan to the Magpies in the final weeks of Gary Brazil's brief term as manager did not improve performances, two draws and two defeats ensuing. Released by Leicester City, Jon had trials with Chesterfield and Oxford United, the latter being sufficiently impressive to earn him a permanent contract at The Kassam Stadium.

Appearances: FL: 4 apps 0 gls Total: 4 apps 0 gls

ASHURST, William

Right-back   5' 9½" 12st 4lbs
b. Willington, County Durham 4th May 1894
d. Nottingham, 26th January 1947
CAREER: Willington Schoolboys/Durham City/Leeds City May 1919/Lincoln City Oct 1919, fee £500/NOTTS June 1920, fee £1,000/West Bromwich Albion Nov 1926, fee £3,100, appointed coach to junior players Mar 1928/Newark Town trial Aug 1928, pro Oct 1928, retired cs 1929/Bestwood Colliery am Dec 1932.
Debut v Bristol City (a) 28.8.20, won 1 – 0

At the famous – or should it be infamous? – auction of Leeds City players in October 1919, Notts paid out the highest fee (£1,250 for Billy McLeod) and acquired another (Billy Ashurst), via Lincoln City, eight months later. The fee here (£1,000) was double that paid by Lincoln at auction. But Notts were enriched threefold when Ashurst moved to West Bromwich Albion after six years of tremendous service. By 1924-25 he had become the best right-back in England. He possessed all the full-back virtues: bravery, speed, the ability to make measured clearances with either foot, a strong tackle and the capacity to work in small spaces. And he was scrupulously fair. Older brother of Eli Ashurst (Birmingham 1922-26) who also played at right-back.

Appearances: FL: 200 apps 0 gls FAC: 22 apps 0 gls
Total: 222 apps 0 gls
Honours: England International, 5 caps 1923-25. FL Representative, 1 app. FA Representative, 4 apps. (NOTTS) FL Div 2 champions 1923

ASTLE, Jeffrey

Centre-forward 5' 11" 11st 6lbs
b. Eastwood, Notts. 13th May 1942
d. Burton-on-Trent, Staffs. 19th January 2002
CAREER: West Notts. Schoolboys/Holy Trinity Y.C.
(Kimberley)/NOTTS am 1958 then assisted John Player
F.C. until turning pro Oct 1959/West Bromwich Albion Sept
1964, fee £25,000/Dunstable Town July 1974/Weymouth
July 1975, fee £5,000/Atherstone Town late in 1976
(Hillingdon Borough loan Feb 1977), retired later in 1977
Debut v Reading (a) 23.9.61, lost 2 – 4

An outstanding local discovery, recommended to Notts by his headmaster, and taken onto the ground staff at sixteen. Jeff was destined to win high representative and Cup honours after leaving Meadow Lane. He made great strides in season 1962-63, playing inside-right to centre-forward Tony Hateley, the pair forming a potent scoring partnership. After Hateley left for Aston Villa Jeff struggled to adjust to life alongside new centre-forward Terry Bly, and made a transfer request in October 1963. A move did not transpire for almost a year but, when it did, it proved a good one for the player. A splendid header of the ball and deadly around the penalty box, he scored 137 League goals in 290(2) League matches for West Bromwich Albion. He memorably scored the only goal of the 1968 FA Cup Final, a stunning left-foot volley in extra time against Everton, and topped the First Division scoring lists with 35 goals, a feat he repeated in 1969-70 with 25, plus five in FL Cup matches.

Appearances: FL: 103 apps 31 gls FAC: 5 apps 1 gl FLC: 8 apps 9 gls Total: 116 apps 41 gls
Honours: England International, 5 caps 1969-70. FL Representative, 2 apps.
(West Bromwich Albion) FA Cup winners 1968. FL Cup winners 1966, finalists 1967, 1970.

ASTLEY, Joseph Emanuel

Full-back 5' 10" 12st 3lbs
b. Dudley, April quarter 1899
d. Manchester, October quarter 1967
CAREER: Cradley Heath cs 1923/Manchester United Aug
1924/NOTTS June 1928, fee £400/Nantwich Town Aug
1929/Hyde United May 1930
Debut v Port Vale (a) 5.1.29, lost 0 – 3

A reserve during four years at Old Trafford (two League outings only) and similarly graded in his Notts year. In mitigation it can be mentioned that Astley's time with Manchester United coincided with Jack Silcock's tremendous 15-year spell. And at Meadow Lane, Charlie Bisby's career was at its classy peak.

Appearances: FL: 4 apps 0 gls Total: 4 apps 0 gls

AVRAMOVIC, Radojko 'Raddy'

Goalkeeper 6' 0" 12st 0lbs
b. Yugoslavia, 29th November 1949
CAREER: Borac (Yugoslavia)/N.K.Rijeka (Yugoslavia)/
NOTTS Aug 1979, fee £200,000/Inter Montreal (Canada)
May 1983/Coventry City Sept 1983, fee £40,000, retired
1984/Singapore national coach.
Debut v Cardiff City (h) 18.8.79, won 4 – 1

A number of players from Eastern Europe came to Britain in the 1970s. Notts engaged one in Raddy Avramovic. He was a Yugoslavian Cup winner in successive seasons, and cost a tidy sum by goalkeepers' fee standards. He gave Notts four years excellent service before a departure that was dictated by financial considerations. Following a brief interlude in Canada, Raddy joined Coventry City for a fifth of the amount paid by Notts. Things went well until costly errors caused an enraged manager to berate and dismiss the player publicly. Not long afterwards, Raddy returned to his native Yugoslavia and, a man of intellectual ability, he qualified as a lawyer.

Appearances: FL: 149 apps 0 gls FAC: 3 apps 0 gls FLC: 15 apps 0 gls Other: 15 apps 0 gls Total: 182 apps 0 gls
Honours: Yugoslavia International, 4 caps

BAGNALL, Reginald

Centre-half 6' 1" 12st 0lbs
b. Brinsworth, 22nd November 1926
CAREER: Rotherham United am/NOTTS June 1945/
Ransome and Marles Aug 1948
Debut v Norwich City (h) 14.9.46, won 3 – 0

Reg Bagnall's blushes were spared on his debut when his only mistake in an otherwise assured display presented Norwich forward Taylor with a 'goal on a plate.' Magpies' goalkeeper Harry Brown thankfully retrieved the situation with a brilliant save. The towering defender made five of his League outings in 1946-47 and four the following season, when he also made one FA Cup appearance. The first three matches in 1946-47 were at right-back (his other position) but he was better employed as a pivot, where his height could be more usefully employed.

Appearances: FL: 9 apps 0 gls FAC: 1 app 0 gls
Total: 10 apps 0 gls

BAGSHAW, John James

Half-back   5' 9½" 11st 10lbs
b. Derby, 25th December 1885
d. Nottingham, 25th August 1966
CAREER: Graham Street Primitives (Derby)/Fletcher's
Athletic/Derby County Aug 1906 (WW1 guest NOTTS)/
NOTTS Feb 1920, fee £500/Watford July 1921, fee £200/
Ilkeston United Aug 1922/Grantham July 1924/Nottingham
Forest trainer during WW2, subsequently scouted for NOTTS,
Coventry City and Nottingham Forest
Debut v Bradford P.A. (a) 14.2.20, won 1 – 0

A centre or wing-half of all round ability: perceptive, hard
working, quick moving, sound in distribution and tackling.
By the time Jim reached Notts he was in his mid-thirties
and Derby County's longest-serving player. He worked
as Nottingham Forest's trainer during WW2 and scouted
for that club and Coventry City. A lace threader by trade, he
also worked for Raleigh Industries, the local engineering firm.

Appearances: FL: 24 apps 0 gls Total: 24 apps 0 gls
Honours: England International, 1 cap 1920. England
Victory International, 1 app 1919. (Derby County) FL
Division 2 champions 1912, 1915.

BAILEY, L. F.

Centre-forward
CAREER: NOTTS season 1888-89
Debut v Derby County (h) 16.3.1889, lost 3 – 5 (scored
one)

Not many one-appearance players can or could look back
at their game with such pleasure. For a start it was an
exciting home FA Cup-tie with lots of goals, one of which
Bailey scored. A disappointing result though: Notts losing
to local rivals Derby County, 3 goals to 5.

Appearances: FL: 1 app 0 gls Total: 1 app 0 gls

BAKEWELL, George

Outside-right
b. Derby, April quarter 1864
CAREER: Derby Midland/Derby County 1884/NOTTS July
1891/In Mar 1892 press speculation linked him with a
possible transfer to Derby Junction for season 1892-93.
Debut v Preston North End (h) 5.9.1891, won 2 – 0

Brilliant outside-right secured by Notts after he had netted
12 goals for Derby County in 64 League and Cup matches,
two of them in Derby's very first League game (a handsome
6 – 3 away win at Bolton Wanderers). Actually, he was
the second player to join Derby on their formation in
1884. He served on that club's committee later, then
administered things prior to their becoming a limited
liability company. Outside of football, Bakewell worked
originally as a railway clerk but later, in the 1901 Census,
was described as a retired baker.

Which fact irresistibly evokes the comment that
he was most appropriately surnamed!

Appearances: FL: 5 apps 1 gl FAC: 1 app 0 gls
Total: 6 apps 1 gl

BALDRY, Simon Jonathan

Winger/Midfield   5' 10" 11st 6lbs
b. Huddersfield, 12th February 1976
CAREER: Deighton High School (Huddersfield)/Huddersfield
Town associate schoolboy Nov 1990, trainee Aug 1992, pro
July 1994 (Bury loan Sept 1998)/NOTTS Aug 2003 to cs
2004.
Debut v Wrexham (h) 16.8.2003, lost 0 – 1

A local discovery by Huddersfield Town, Simon appeared
at Wembley at just 18 years of age in the Terriers' Autoglass
Trophy Final defeat by Swansea City in April 1994. He
was directly opposed to full-back Steve Jenkins, later to
be capped by Wales, and subsequently a playing colleague
at Meadow Lane in season 2003-04. Simon was one of
Huddersfield's longest-serving players, but in nine seasons
as a professional never managed to hold down a regular
first team place. He was a regular at Meadow Lane until
an injury, and the departure of manager Billy Dearden,
saw him out of the side for most of the months of January
and February. A touch line dribbler of the traditional type
and a fine crosser of the ball from the right flank, he regained
his place under new manager Gary Mills, but was released
at the close of the season. Subsequent trials with Boston
United and Blackpool failed to earn him a permanent
contract.

Appearances: FL: 32(3) apps 1 gl FAC: 3 apps 0 gls FLC:
2 apps 1 gl Other: 1 app 0 gls Total: 1 app 0 gls
Total: 38(3) apps 2 gls
Honours: (Huddersfield Town) Autoglass Trophy finalists
1994

BALL, Geoffrey Hudson

Full-back   5' 9" 10st 11lbs
b. Nottingham, 2nd November 1944
CAREER: Ericson's Athletic (Nottingham)/Nottingham
Forest Feb 1963/NOTTS Nov 1967 to cs 1972, fee £5,000/
Ilkeston Town/Grantham Town Mar 1975 to Aug 1976
Debut v Newport County (h) 4.11.67, won 3 – 1

Mostly at right-back although he could play on the left
side too. Well thought of at Forest, performing
competently when called upon to deputise in the First
Division side – a stout, determined defender. Enjoyed an
amount of first team action on crossing to Meadow Lane,
until replaced by Bill Brindley in season 1970-71

Appearances: FL: 112 apps 0 gls FAC: 5 apps 0 gls FLC:
2(1) apps 0 gls Total: 119(1) apps 0 gls

BALL, William Henry

Wing-half 5' 8" 11st 8lbs
b. West Derby, Liverpool April quarter 1876
d. Colombo, Ceylon February 1929
CAREER: Florence Institute/Liverpool South End/Rock
Ferry F.C. May 1896/Blackburn Rovers May 1897/Everton
May 1898/NOTTS May 1899/Blackburn Rovers May 1901/
Manchester United Oct 1902 to cs 1903/Tranmere Rovers
Oct 1904
Debut v Derby County (a) 2.9.1899, won 1 – 0

By pre-Great War standards, something of a wanderer
although, apart from Nottingham, his itinerary was
confined to the Lancashire/Cheshire area. Notts provided
the bulk of his senior football, however, for he played
only 34 games elsewhere. A regular in the Magpies' 1900-
01 side, which finished third in the First Division, the
club's highest-ever placing. Billy's four League outings
for Manchester United took in all three half-back
positions; with Notts he played mostly at right-half. An
enthusiastic and strong swimmer, he won a number of
prizes in swimming handicaps in Lancashire. By trade a
plumber.

Appearances: FL: 65 apps 2 gls FAC: 5 apps 0 gls
Total: 70 apps 2 gls

BARACLOUGH, Ian Robert

Left-back 6' 1" 12st 2lbs
b. Leicester, 4th December 1970
CAREER: Leicester City trainee July 1987, pro Dec 1988
(Wigan Athletic loan Mar 1990) (Grimsby Town loan Dec
1990)/Grimsby Town Aug 1991/Lincoln City Aug 1992/
Mansfield Town June 1994/NOTTS Oct 1995, fee £150,000/
Queens Park Rangers Mar 1998, fee £50,000/NOTTS July
2001/Scunthorpe United Aug 2004.
Debut v Rotherham United (h) 14.10.95, won 2 – 1

Vastly exper-
ienced and stylish
left-sided defender
or midfielder with
a career figure in
excess of 500
League and Cup
appearances at the
time of his transfer
to Scunthorpe
United in August
2004. Ian's first
spell with the
Magpies ended in
March of the
1997-98 prom-
otion season. One
of a number of
players whose

contracts were due to expire at the end of the season, he
rejected an offer from Sheffield United in favour of a move
to Queens Park Rangers. After a successful three years at
Loftus Road he was welcomed back to Meadow Lane,
and either at left-back or in midfield he continued to be an
entirely reliable and professional member of the first team
squad. In early days Ian played as a striker in Leicester
City's youth team and was converted into an attacking
left-back during his Lincoln City days. In the season prior
to his move to Meadow Lane he helped Mansfield Town
reach the Play-off semi-finals.

Appearances: FL: 200(12) apps 15 gls FAC: 14(1) apps 0
gls FLC: 10(1) apps 1 gl Other: 5(1) apps 0 gls
Total: 229(15) apps 16 gls
Honours: England Youth International. (NOTTS) FL Div
3 champions 1998

BARBER, Michael Phillip

Outside-left 5' 9½" 10st 8lbs
b. Plympton, Devon 24th August 1941
CAREER: Arsenal am/Queens Park Rangers am, signing pro
Dec 1959/NOTTS July 1963, fee £11,500; retired due to
knee injury cs 1965 and joined the Notts. County staff/
Bulwell Forest Villa am Jan 1966.
Debut v Brentford (a) 24.8.63, lost 1 – 4

Unlucky player forced into retirement through knee injury
aged only 24. He had joined Queens Park Rangers on
amateur forms from Arsenal's ground staff, quitting his
job as a ledger clerk at Harrods to turn professional shortly
afterwards. He made his senior debut in September 1960
and had netted 13 goals in 69 League and Cup matches
when Notts signed him. Mike did not settle initially and
wished to return to London. But he persevered, felt more
at home, and proved a real crowd pleaser with his
exceptional speed. The knee injury that terminated his
League career occurred in February 1964. Almost two
years later he made a 'comeback' in the less demanding
ranks of Bulwell Forest Villa.

Appearances: FL: 33 apps 3 gls FAC: 2 apps 0 gls FLC:
4 apps 0 gls Total: 39 apps 3 gls

BARKER, Richard Joseph 'Richie'

Forward 5' 11½" 12st 8lbs
b. Loughborough, 23rd November 1939
CAREER: Morris Sports/Burton Albion Oct 1960/
Loughborough United May 1962/Matlock Town July 1963/
Burton Albion Nov 1963/Primo Hamilton, Canada, loan
Apr 1965)/Derby County Oct 1967, fee £2,000/NOTTS
Dec 1968, fee £10,000/Peterborough United Sept 1971/
Enderby Town coach Aug 1973/Shrewsbury Town coach Feb
1974, manager Feb 1978/Wolverhampton Wanderers

assistant-manager Nov 1978/Stoke City manager June 1981 to Dec 1983/NOTTS manager Nov 1984 to Apr 1985/ Ethnikos, Greece, manager 1985/Zamalek, Egypt manager 1986/Luton Town coach Aug 1988/Sheffield Wednesday assistant-manager Feb 1989; development director 1995 to May 1996/West Bromwich Albion scout Sept 1997; caretaker-manager Dec 1997/Halifax Town assistant-manager Oct 2000 to Aug 2001.
Debut v Exeter City (h) 21.12.68, won 3 – 1

A Magpies supporter in the Tommy Lawton era, Richie was a late arrival to League football. Almost 28 and a part-time professional, he soon gave up his job as a draughtsman to go full-time. He was not overawed by the greater demands, and was able to score his quota of goals from all three inside-forward positions. Broke a leg during a reserve game while at Peterborough, which brought about retirement. Subsequently had a nomadic and variable managerial career, both at home and abroad. The highs included a part in Shrewsbury Town's rise from Division 4 to Division 2, the lows his very brief 1984-85 managerial stint of Notts. Terminated in the wake of five successive defeats that led to the club's relegation to Division 3.

Appearances: FL: 99(13) apps 37 gls FAC: 5 apps 0 gls FLC: 2(2) apps 1 gl Total: 106(15) apps 38 gls
Honours: (NOTTS) FL Div 4 champions 1971

BARLEY, Henry Frank 'Harry'
Outside-right   5' 7½" 11st 2lbs
b. Grimsby, February 1905
d. Scunthorpe, July quarter 1958
CAREER: Humber United (Grimsby)/Grimsby Town July 1929/Hull City May 1931/New Brighton Aug 1932/NOTTS Jan 1934, fee £750/Scunthorpe United Aug 1934/Bristol Rovers May 1935/Barrow May 1936/Kidderminster Harriers July 1937/Frickley Colliery July 1938
Debut v Bradford City (h) 3.2.34, won 3 – 0

Short though sturdily built wingman, whose eleven stones-plus weight facilitated strong shooting. A fact well illustrated on New Brighton's behalf in November 1933 when he burst the net. Other qualities included an ability to provide pinpoint centres. He survived a career threatening injury when he broke his right leg in two places in Grimsby Town's match against Leicester City on Christmas Day 1929. Harry served several clubs, including his native Humberside ones, rather unusually making his best League return with the last (At Barrow, 40 appearances out of a possible 42, scoring 8 goals.)

Appearances: FL: 11 apps 1 gl Total: 11 apps 1 gl

BARNES, Paul Lance
Forward   5' 10" 10st 2lbs
b. Leicester, 16th November 1967
CAREER: Leicester Schoolboys/Leicester City trial/NOTTS app Aug 1984, pro Nov 1985/Stoke City Mar 1990, fee £30,000 (Chesterfield loan Nov 1990)/York City July 1992, fee £50,000/Birmingham City Mar 1996, fee £350,000/ Burnley Sept 1996, fee £300,000/Huddersfield Town Jan 1998/Bury Mar 1999, fee £40,000 (Nuneaton Borough loan Mar 2001)/Doncaster Rovers cs 2001, registered for FL matches July 2003/Tamworth Dec 2003/Hinckley United July 2004.
Debut as sub v Wigan Athletic (h) 4.2.86, drawn 1 – 1

To Notts from school, developing into a prized performer attracting substantial fees. These included a then club record one from York City. It proved an excellent investment for the Minstermen for he scored consistently, once netting four against Scunthorpe United in March 1993. And he was sold for five times the purchase price four years later. Paul excelled in combination, besides having that invaluable opportunist eye. Recovered from a career threatening injury while with Stoke City. He was leading goalscorer in the Nationwide Conference in season 2002-03, with 28 goals in league and cup matches for Doncaster Rovers.

Appearances: FL: 36(17) apps 14 gls FAC: 0(1) apps 0 gls Other: 7(6) apps 5 gls Total: 43(24) apps 19 gls
Honours: (NOTTS) Anglo-Italian Cup finalists 1990

BARRASS, Anthony 'Tony'
Central defender   6' 0"   13st 0lbs
b. Stockton-on-Tees, 29th March 1971
CAREER: St Michael's School (Billingham)/Stockton Town/ Hartlepool United trainee July 1989/Stockport County July 1990 (Rotherham United loan Feb 1994)/York City July 1994, fee £25,000/Reading Mar 1999, fee £20,000/Walsall July 1999, fee £20,000 (Plymouth Argyle loan Nov 2002)/ NOTTS Aug 2003/Macclesfield Town July 2004.
Debut v Bristol City (a) 9.8.2004, lost 0 – 5

A central defender of ripe experience, Tony reached the milestone of 400 League appearances during his season at Meadow Lane. A rugged defender with few frills in his play, he was dangerous in set-piece situations and in open play. Certainly a contender for 'goal of the season' with his 30 yard thunderbolt against Luton Town at Meadow Lane, he also scored an equalising goal against Chelsea in the Carling Cup third round tie at Stamford Bridge, although Claudio Ranieri's star-studded side ran out winners 4 – 2.

Appearances: FL: 38(2) apps 2 gls FAC: 2 apps 1 gl FLC: 3 apps 1 gl Other: 0(1) app 0 gls Total: 43(3) apps 4 gls
Honours: (Stockport County) Autoglass Trophy finalists 1992

BARRY, Leonard James

Outside-left   5' 6½" 9st 12lbs
b. Sneinton, Notts. 27th October 1901
d. Mapperley, Notts. 17th April 1970
CAREER: Sneinton Boys' School/Mundella Grammar School/
RAF Cranwell/NOTTS am May 1920, pro 1923/Leicester
City Sept 1927, fee £3,500/Nottingham Forest Aug 1933;
retired 1934.
Debut v Wolverhampton Wanderers (h) 26.3.21, won 2 – 1

A major Notts County development from the inter-war period. Learned the game during the 1914-18 War to such good effect that Notts signed him on amateur forms and he became an amateur international. Turned professional as soon as his RAF engagement ended. Len played, as one observer wrote, in the Corinthian style: a tricky dribbler able to middle the ball at speed and a scorer of spectacular goals. Gave Leicester City excellent service too (214 League and Cup games, eight goals).

Appearances: FL: 146 apps 10 gls FAC: 7 apps 1 gl
Total: 153 apps 11 gls
Honours: England International, 5 caps 1928-29.England
Amateur International, 1 cap 1923-24.

BARTLETT, Kevin Francis

Forward   5' 9"   10st 12lbs
b. Portsmouth, 12th October 1962
CAREER: Portsmouth app July 1978, pro Oct 1980/Fareham
Town Apr 1982/Cardiff City Sept 1986/West Bromwich
Albion Feb 1989, fee £100,000/NOTTS Mar 1990 (Port
Vale loan Sept 1992)/Cambridge United Mar 1993 to Jan
1995.
Debut v Walsall (h) 17.3.90, won 2 – 0 (scored one)

Had the disappointment of not making the grade at his first (and hometown) club, after turning professional. So the subject of a free transfer at the age of 20. However, the non-League spell with Fareham Town obviously proved beneficial, for a return to the League scene brought much first team football. Kevin's FL figures are 179 appearances plus 54 substitutions, 70 goals.

The possessor of a fine turn of speed, he was runner-up in the Professional Footballer's Sprint Challenge, held prior to the FL Cup final at Wembley in April 1992.

Appearances: FL: 86(13) apps 33 gls FAC: 6 apps 1 gl
FLC: 7 apps 3 gls Other: 6(2) apps 3 gls
Total: 105(15) apps 40 gls
Honours: (Cardiff City) Welsh Cup winners 1988

BASSETT, Edward John "Teddy"

Outside-right   5' 6½" 10st 4lbs
b. Deptford, London 1st January 1889
d. Watford, 25th November 1970
CAREER: Woolwich Arsenal/Deptford Invicta/Dartford Jan
1909/Croydon Common trial Sept 1909/Metrogas Sept 1909/
Charlton Athletic 1910/Millwall Athletic Nov 1911/Newark
Stanley Works 1912/Dartford cs 1912/NOTTS Sept 1913
to 1915 (WW1 guest Fulham and Tottenham Hotspur)/
Watford June 1919/Luton Town June 1921, fee £200/
Dartford Aug 1922/Fordsons, Cork/Finchley Nov 1930
Debut v Bristol City (a) 20.9.13, drawn 1 – 1 (scored)

Sampled nine clubs of varied standing before reaching Meadow Lane as a trialist at the beginning of the promotion season 1913-14. As remarked afterwards, "A surprise packet", seizing an unexpected chance in the first team and becoming the regular outside-right. Only slightly built but plucky and fast and, although wanting in ball control occasionally, could centre accurately. He was, however, apt to spurn shooting opportunities. Resumed his travels after the Great War, his season at Luton marked by a brush with the Football League, for an alleged demand for a share of his transfer fee. Ultimately settled at Watford, where he ran a snooker club for a time. On 22nd February 1964 he was guest of honour at the Watford v Notts County clash.

Appearances: FL: 44 apps 5 gls FAC: 1 app 0 gls
Total: 45 apps 5 gls
Honours: (NOTTS) FL Div 2 champions 1914

BATES, Anthony Norman

Centre-forward
b. Blidworth, 6th April 1938
CAREER: Blidworth Colliery/NOTTS am season 1958-59,
pro July 1959 to June 1960/Sutton Town cs 1960
Debut v Colchester United (h) 25.4.59, lost 0 – 1

His solitary senior appearance occurred in the penultimate (and final home match) of a disastrous relegation season. In that final month of April, six fixtures were fulfilled, resulting in five defeats and one draw.

Appearances: FL: 1 app 0 gls Total: 1 app 0 gls

BATES, Brian Frederick

Winger   5' 8"   10st 4lbs
b. Beeston, Notts. 4th December 1944
CAREER: Loughborough College/NOTTS am July 1963, pro July 1966/Mansfield Town July 1969/Boston United cs 1970/ NOTTS youth team coach Aug 1976/Boston United 1977/ FA Technical Director of Coaching Jan 1985/NOTTS Centre of Excellence Director.
Debut v Bristol Rovers (a) 18.4.64, lost 0 – 4

Joined an amateur forms while studying to become a schoolteacher, turning professional after qualification. Deemed promising from the outset, Brian could play outside-right and outside-left with a penchant for goal scoring (he topped County's list for 1965-66). He did not in season 1966-67 show the form of earlier years, eventually moving to neighbouring Mansfield Town on a free transfer. At Field Mill he appeared mostly at outside-left (17 out of 20 League appearances.) At the time of his appointment as County Technical Director of Coaching by the FA, he was head of department at South Notts. College, West Bridgford.

Appearances: FL: 125(3) apps 24 gls FAC: 2 apps 0 gls FLC: 7 apps 1 gl Total: 134(3) apps 25 gls

---

BATTERSBY, Anthony

Forward   6' 0"   12st 7lbs
b. Doncaster, 30th August 1975
CAREER: Sheffield United trainee Aug 1991, pro July 1993 (Southend United loan Mar 1995)/NOTTS Jan 1996, fee £200,000/Bury Mar 1997, fee £125,000/Lincoln City Aug 1998, fee £75,000 (Northampton Town loan Sept 1999)/ Boston United Oct 2002/Hucknall Town Jan 2003/Rushden & Diamonds Feb 2003/Stevenage Borough Mar 2003/ Gravesend & Northfleet Feb 2004/Cambridge City Apr 2004.
Debut v York City, Auto Windscreens Shield, Northern Section quarter final (a) 9.1.96, lost 0 – 1

Tony Battersby had little first team experience at the time of his £200,000 signing in mid season 1995-96. His first League goal for the Magpies came in his third outing against Peterborough United and he went on to score seven in 14(7) matches, a valuable contribution in a season when the leading scorer was Devon White with eight goals. The Magpies finished fourth in Division Two; narrowly defeated Crewe Alexandra over two legs in the Play-off semi-final, but went down 0 – 2 at Wembley against Bradford City. In the relegation season that followed, Tony was transferred to Bury shortly after the appointment of Sam Allardyce as manager. A striker with the ability to hold the ball up whilst awaiting support, he was a better target man than an out and out marksman on his own account. His modest scoring record at the close of season 2003-04 being 45 League and Cup goals in 185(92) matches.

Appearances: FL: 20(19) apps 8 gls FAC: 0(2) apps 0 gls FLC: 1 app 0 gls Other: 1 app 0 gls Total: 22(21) apps 8 gls

BAUDET, Julien

Defender/Midfield   6' 3"   14st 2lbs
b. Grenoble, France, 13th January 1979
CAREER: Grenoble on schoolboy forms/Toulouse, France/ Boston United trial Feb 2001/Oldham Athletic nc Oct, pro Nov 2001/Rotherham United Aug 2003/NOTTS July 2004.
Debut v Chester City (h) 7.8.04, drawn 1 – 1, (scored from a penalty)

Julien first tasted League football with Oldham Athletic, who signed him on a free transfer after his club Toulouse were relegated and then further demoted due to financial irregularities. After two excellent years at Boundary Park, he fared less well during his season with Rotherham United, but his move to Meadow Lane has seen his form and confidence restored. A combination of strength, athleticism and aerial ability, well abetted by natural physical attributes, have served the Magpies well in a difficult season. His return of six goals, thanks mainly to his cool conversion of penalty awards, has been an added bonus in a low scoring season.

Appearances: FL: 38(1) apps 5 gls FAC: 2 apps 1 gls FLC: 1 app 0 gls Other: 1 app 0 gls Total: 42(1) apps 6 gls

---

BAUSOR, Thomas James

Centre-forward
b. Southwell, Notts., October quarter 1862
d. Mansfield, 28th February 1933
CAREER: NOTTS 1881-82
Debut v Wednesbury Strollers FAC 2 (h) 24.11.1881, won 5 – 3

In addition to his three goals in five FA Cup matches, Bausor played in 14 of the friendly engagements of season 1881-82. He had a prolific spell of goal scoring in mid season, his nine goals in five matches including a hat-trick against Old Carthusians, and two 'doubles' against Forest and Sheffield. He played in the first four matches of the following season, adding a further two goals. Press coverage of the day often omitted to mention who had scored, so it is highly likely that Bausor would have scored many more than his recorded total of 19 goals.

His first appearance for the club was on 10th November 1881 in a 13 – 0 demolition of Grantham. As centre-forward he was likely to have shared in the goal spree, but contemporary press reports of the match failed to record any of the goal scorers.

Appearances: FAC: 5 apps 3 gls Total: 5 apps 3 gls

---------------o---------------

BAXTER, William Amelius
Half-back   5' 8"   12st 0lbs
b. Nottingham, 6th September 1917
d. Nottingham, 21st February 1992
CAREER: Berridge Road School/Nottingham Schoolboys/ Willson's F.C./Vernon Athletic/Berridge Road Institute/ Nottingham Forest am July 1936, pro Dec 1936 (WW2 guest NOTTS, Derby County, Leicester City and Mansfield Town)/NOTTS Oct 1946/Grantham Town July 1954 to Mar 1955.
Debut v Brighton & Hove Albion (a) 12.10.46, lost 2 – 3

Notts knew all about Bill Baxter long before his eventual signing in the first post war season. For he had been with Forest since 1936 and, more pertinently, played for Notts as a wartime guest. Deemed highly promising early on, this promise was blighted by injury. A slight build made for loss of possession to lesser, though more physical, opponents. This did not apply at Meadow Lane: Bill's weight had increased to twelve stones, and he took the pivotal position as well as the flank berth. Latterly captained the Magpies' reserves while still, as a splendid clubman, displaying his deft touches when deputising in the first team.

Appearances: FL: 140 apps 0 gls FAC: 13 apps 0 gls
Total: 153 apps 0 gls
Honours: (NOTTS) FL Div 3 South champions 1950

---------------o---------------

BEADLE, Peter Clifford William James
Forward   6' 1"   13st 7lbs
b. Camberwell, 13th May 1972
CAREER: Lordswood Boys/Gillingham associate schoolboy Dec 1986, trainee July 1988, pro May 1990 (Margate loan Mar 1990)/Tottenham Hotspur June 1992, fee £350,000 (AFC Bournemouth loan Mar 1993) (Southend United loan Mar 1994)/Watford Sept 1994, fee £5,000/Bristol Rovers Nov 1995, fee £40,000/Port Vale Aug 1998, fee £300,000/ NOTTS Feb 1999, fee £250,000/Bristol City Oct 1999, fee £200,000/Brentford Aug 2003/Barnet Sept 2003/Team Bath player-coach Dec 2003/Clevedon Town player-commercial manager June 2004.
Debut v Fulham (a) 20.2.99, lost 1 – 2

The reason for Notts lack of success in 1998-99 was not difficult to pinpoint. After scoring 82 League goals in winning the title of Division Three in 1997-98, they found goal scoring a great deal more difficult on their return to Division Two. Leading scorers for the campaign were Ian Richardson with seven goals and Ian Hendon with six, five of which coming from the penalty spot. As the side seemed doomed to relegation, a late flurry in the transfer market brought a number of new forward recruits. Although Peter Beadle proved to be a short-term buy, his three goals in March, scored against Millwall, York City and Stoke City all contributed to priceless victories. A willing worker, his height and strength and footballing know-how contributed greatly to the team's cause.

Appearances: FL: 14(8) apps 3 gls FLC: 1(3) apps 0 gls
Total: 15(11) apps 3 gls.

---------------o---------------

BEAVER, David
Midfield
b. Kirkby-in-Ashfield, 4th April 1966
CAREER: NOTTS app, signing pro Apr 1984 to June 1985
Debut v Charlton Athletic, FLC 2 (a) 25.9.84, won 1 – 0

In addition to the above debut, David appeared - four days later - in a 4 – 2 League defeat against Shrewsbury Town. He wore the number 11 jersey in both matches and, one notes, that he was only 18 at the time. He was one of three young players who were granted free transfers in February 1985, the others were Mark Jones and Simeon Hodson. Of the three, only Hodson remained in League football.

Appearances: FL: 1 app 0 gls FLC: 1 app 0 gls
Total: 2 apps 0 gls

---------------o---------------

BEAVON, David George
Defender   5' 9"   10st 9lbs
b. Nottingham, 8th December 1961
CAREER: Nottingham Schoolboys/NOTTS app June 1978, pro Dec 1979/Lincoln City Nov 1981/Tsuen Wan (Hong Kong) Nov 1982/Northampton Town Mar 1983/Kettering Town cs 1983/Buxton/Shepshed Charterhouse Oct 1984/ Boston United/Kings Lynn Oct 1985/Boston United July 1986
Debut v Preston North End (a) 27.12.80, drawn 2 – 2

A reserve at both Notts and Lincoln City, where he appeared both as a winger and a full-back. His first team appearances for the Imps numbered seven, plus one substitution. His final involvement at senior level came in two late-season appearances in Division Four with Northampton Town.

Appearances: FL: 5 apps 0 gls FAC: 1 app 0 gls
Total: 6 apps 0 gls

BEAVON, Michael Stuart

Midfield   5' 7"   10st 8lbs
b. Wolverhampton, 30th November 1958
CAREER: Oxford Schoolboys/Tottenham Hotspur app Mar 1975, pro July 1976 (NOTTS loan Dec 1979 to Jan 1980)/ Reading July 1980, fee £35,000/Northampton Town Aug 1990, appointed assistant-manager Apr 1992/Newbury Town cs 1993/Chesham United Sept 1995/Kintbury/Reading Town Jan 1998
Debut v Birmingham City (h) 8.12.79, drawn 1 – 1

Son of a former Wolves and Oxford United full-back. Stuart's chances at his first club, Tottenham, were very limited. However, he grossed 102 outings for their powerful reserve side (42 goals) and Notts certainly liked him during his month's loan, offering a turned-down £50,000 for a permanent move. And he certainly shone at Elm Park, in a full decade there totalling 484 senior appearances, 20 substitutions, and scoring 58 goals. Such figures are a testimony to the player's consistency, fitness, and freedom from injury. All in all, an excellent midfielder.

Appearances: FL: 6 apps 0 gls Total: 6 apps 0 gls
Honours: (Reading) FL Div 3 champions 1986. Simod Cup winners 1988

BEEBY, Oliver

Full-back   5' 9"   11st 6lbs
b. Whetstone, Leics. 2nd October 1934
CAREER: Cosby United/Enderby Town Aug 1952/Whitwick Colliery Mar 1953/Wolverhampton Wanderers trial/ Leicester City May 1953/NOTTS June 1959/Oxford United cs 1960/Burton Albion cs 1962
Debut v Hartlepool United (h) 1.10.59, won 4 – 0

A solitary senior appearance before joining Notts. (and that a 6 – 2 drubbing of Leicester City at Doncaster). But Oliver could point to six years solid work for the reserves at Filbert Street and a taste of representative football. Besides his youth international cap he had assisted the Army's Service Command while on national service. His season at Meadow Lane ended with promotion to Division Three.

Appearances: FL: 13 apps 0 gls FAC: 2 apps 0 gls
Total: 15 apps 0 gls
Honours: England Youth International, 1 app v Scotland season 1952-53

BEECH, Albert

Left-half   5' 9½"   10st 0lbs
b. Fenton, Staffs. 24th September 1912
d. Stoke-on-Trent, Staffs. June 1985

CAREER: Stoke St Peter's/Leek Alexandra/Port Vale am Nov 1930, pro Sept 1931/Altrincham May 1933/ Huddersfied Town May 1934/NOTTS June 1937, fee £1,100/ Northwich Victoria July 1938
Debut v Swindon Town (h) 28.8.37, won 3 – 0

Sampled First Division football while at Huddersfield (aggregate 22 appearances), his best seasonal return 1935-36 (16 games, 4 goals) when the Tykes finished in a lofty third placing. Considered a Notts capture on his 1937 signing, occupying the left-half position for the first eight League fixtures, eventually drifting into the non-League scene after one season.

Appearances: FL: 13 apps 0 gls Other: 1 app 0 gls
Total: 14 apps 0 gls

BELFORD, Dale

Goalkeeper   5' 11"   11st 10lbs
b. Burton-on-Trent, 11th July 1967
CAREER: Aston Villa app, signing pro July 1985/Sutton Coldfield Town/NOTTS Mar 1987 to cs 1998/V.S.Rugby/ Nuneaton Borough/Tamworth/Sutton Coldfield Town/ Tamworth/Nuneaton Borough/Tamworth/Hinckley United/ Atherstone United/Sutton Coldfield Town/Atherstone United/ Gresley Rovers Sept 2003.
Debut v York City (a) 22.8.87, won 5 – 3

Nicely built goalkeeper, a League professional for over a decade, making a single first-class appearance in all that time. Still he had the likes of Steve Cherry to content with, and his single appearance did produce a useful and high scoring away win.

Appearances: FL: 1 app 0 gls Total: 1 app 0 gls

BELL, Ernest

Inside-forward
CAREER: NOTTS Nov 1890
Debut v Accrington (a) 21.11.1891, lost 0 – 2

An unsuccessful season, 1891-92, with Notts finishing mid-table and well beaten by Sunderland in the FA Cup 1st round. Bell played in all three inside-forward positions for his senior outings: one each at centre and inside-right, four at inside-left.

Appearances: FL: 5 apps 0 gls FAC: 1 app 0 gls
Total: 6 apps 0 gls

BEMMENT, Frederick Charles

Half-back   5' 10" 11st 8lbs
b. Lowestoft, 12th October 1884
d. Bolsover, 25th March 1957
CAREER: Lowestoft I.O.G.T./Kirkley 1902/Norwich City
June 1905/NOTTS May 1907/Chesterfield Town Apr 1908/
Hardwick Colliery cs 1909
Debut v Sheffield Wednesday (a) 21.9.07, lost 0 – 2

Scored 31 goals as a centre-forward in one season with
junior Kirkley F.C., but played half-back for his three
professional clubs. Actually one of Norwich City's first
professional signings, for whom he made 67 Southern
League appearances. In his Chesterfield season he played
in 29 FL matches. After leaving football Bemment worked
as a shunter at a colliery.

Appearances: FL: 9 apps 0 gls Total: 9 apps 0 gls

BENJAMIN, Tristan

Defender   6' 0" 11st 2lbs
b. St. Kitts, West Indies 1st April 1957
CAREER: NOTTS app June 1973, pro Mar 1975/
Chesterfield June 1987/Shepshed Charterhouse cs 1988/Corby
Town Oct 1988/Sutton Town/Corby Town
Feb 1997
Debut v West Bromwich
Albion (a) 2.4.75, lost 1 – 4

Made his League debut
at eighteen as a central
defender and while
still a teenager won a
regular first team place
at right-back. Quick and
skilful, Tristan had two
good feet and was effective
in the air. A valuable
member of the first
team squad for over
a decade, his
ability to perform
well in a variety of
positions was an
added bonus. In the promotion season of 1980-81 he
missed only one first team match, and had an identical
record on the side's return to Division One. A season with
Chesterfield rounded off his League career and took his
career figures over the 400 mark.

Appearances: FL: 296(15) apps 4 gls FAC: 17 apps 0 gls
FLC: 29(1) apps 0 gls Other: 25(3) apps 1 gl
Total: 367(19) apps 5 gls
Honours: (NOTTS) Anglo Scottish Cup finalists 1981

BENSKIN, Dennis Walter

Outside-left
b. Ruddington, Notts., 28th May 1947
CAREER: NOTTS am May 1965/Lockheed Leamington/
Bourne Town July 1967/Long Eaton United Feb 1968/
Stamford to cs 1969/Grantham Town Aug 1969 to Sept
1979/Shepshed Charterhouse/Arnold Town/Grantham Town
reserve team joint manager/Ruddington/Emigrated to
Australia.
Debut v Chester (a) 26.2.66, drawn 1 – 1 (scored)

Dennis was one of five different outside-lefts fielded in
1965-66, the season in which Frank Kirkup dominated
the position with 29 League appearances. Despite a scoring
debut at Chester Dennis spent much of the season in
reserve and stepped down into non-League football whilst
still a teenager. He eventually joined up with Terry Bly
(q.v.) at Grantham, scored on his debut against Boston
United, and in the mid point of a ten-year stay was awarded
a joint testimonial. He left London Road for the first time
having scored 115 goals in 464 matches, later returning as
joint manager to the Gingerbreads Reserve team.

Appearances: FL: 4 apps 1 gl Total: 4 apps 1 gl

BERESFORD, John William

Inside-forward   5' 7" 11st 2lbs
b. Sheffield, 25th January 1946
d. Chesterfield, 24th August 2003.
CAREER: Sheffield Schoolboys/Sheffield United trial/
Chesterfield app, signing pro Jan 1963/NOTTS May 1965,
fee £3,750/Matlock Town July 1967/Gainsborough Trinity/
Alfreton Town July 1970/Burton Albion cs 1972/Alfreton
Town July 1975
Debut v Darlington (h) 21.8.65, drawn 0 – 0

A Sheffield native who represented the city schoolboys at
inside-left and also won city schoolboy recognition as a
batsman. His ambitions to play for Sheffield United were
not fulfilled when an expected contract offer failed to
materialise, following a period of training at Bramall Lane.
Nearby Chesterfield introduced him to League football,
his senior debut being made before his 17th birthday.
Mainly from left-half he scored 10 goals in 52 League
appearances for the Spireites, and was still a teenager
when Notts invested a sizeable sum to secure his services.
Operating mainly from the inside-left berth in his first
season at Meadow Lane he scored 11 goals in 29 Division
Four matches. He was less successful in the following
term, failing to maintain a regular berth in a side that
finished 20th in Division Four. His son John won a Division
One championship medal with Newcastle United in 1993
and represented England at Schools, Youth and 'B'
International levels.

Appearances: FL: 50 apps 13 gls FAC: 1 app 0 gls FLC:
2 apps 1 gl Total: 53 apps 14 gls

BERESFORD, Reginald John

Forward   6' 0"   12st 7lbs
b. Lower Pilsley, Derbyshire, 29th June 1925
CAREER: Hardwick Colliery/NOTTS Sept 1945/South Normanton Aug 1949/Hednesford Town Dec 1949/ Parkhouse Colliery Apr 1950
Debut v Bradford City, FAC 1 (h) 17.11.45, drawn 2 – 2

In the transitional season 1945-46 Reg Beresford scored a total of ten goals in 28 matches. Only Aubrey Southwell (35 matches) and Jesse Pye (30 matches) were more regularly employed in a season that saw no fewer than 69 players fielded. The Hardwick Colliery recruit was the first player to occupy the outside-right berth when normal League football resumed in 1946-47, but he was quickly deposed by Horace Cumner. Despite a lengthy association with the Magpies he did not appear at senior level again after playing twice at centre-forward in May 1947. Just prior to his release his activities had been confined to the Midland League side, operating mostly in the full-back position.

Appearances: FL: 9 apps 1 gl FAC: 4 apps 0 gls
Total: 13 apps 1 gl

BETTISON, Frederick Harold

Right-back
b. Hucknall Torkard, Notts. January quarter 1891
CAREER: Mapperley/Netherfield Rangers/NOTTS Oct 1910 to 1911/Grantham Town, and re-signed by them after WW1 in Oct 1919
Debut v Oldham Athletic (a) 5.11.10, lost 1 – 2

Described in the 'Football Post' as "The Mapperley lad", Bettison was introduced as deputy for the injured Arthur Griffiths for his Division One debut at Oldham's Boundary Park. It proved to be his only senior outing, the local correspondent noting that "Bettison was useful at times, at others he was quite lost and over weighted by a sense of his responsibilities. It was asking altogether too much of a lad who has only just come out of junior football."

Appearances: FL: 1 app 0 gls Total: 1 app 0 gls

BEWERS, Jonathan

Defender/Midfield   5' 8"   10st 2lbs
b. Kettering, 10th September 1982
CAREER: Aston Villa trainee, signing pro Sept 1999/ Macclesfield Town trial/AFC Bournemouth trial/NOTTS Mar 2004/Walsall nc Sept to Nov 2004
Debut as sub v Blackpool (h) 3.4.2004, won 4 – 1

Released by Aston Villa after failing to establish himself beyond reserve team level, Jonathan joined the Magpies as manager Gary Mills sought to reduce the average age of the squad for a final effort to avoid relegation. Although his debut from the bench coincided with the team's first win in six games, it was not until the final two fixtures that he reappeared at first team level. He was one of several players seeking new clubs in the summer.

Appearances: FL: 0(3) apps 0 gls Total: 0(3) apps 0 gls
Honours: England Schoolboy and Youth International

BILLINGTON, Brian Keith

Inside-forward
b. Leicester, 28th April 1951
CAREER: Leicester City am/NOTTS Oct 1969/Enderby Town
Debut v Wrexham (a) 8.11.69, lost 0 – 2

A well proportioned inside man who filled a variety of positions in both first team and reserve. The former Leicester City amateur proved a useful auxiliary, also appearing at wing-half and at outside-left in the League team.

Appearances: FL: 4(3) apps 0 gls Total: 4(3) apps 0 gls

BILLY, Christopher Anthony

Midfield   5' 11"   11st 8lbs
b. Huddersfield, 2nd January 1973
CAREER: Huddersfield Town trainee July 1989, pro July 1991/Plymouth Argyle Aug 1995/NOTTS July 1998/Bury Sept 1998/Carlisle United Aug 2003.
Debut as sub v Oldham Athletic (a) 8.8.98, won 3 – 1

Despite being manager Allardyce's first signing in the 1998 close season Chris Billy was allowed to leave within a matter of weeks. He was quickly snapped up by Bury, whose manager Neil Warnock was well aware of the player's strengths, having recruited him earlier when in charge at Plymouth Argyle. A forceful competitor, able to occupy a variety of positions, his League record at the close of season 2003-04, (when his team, Carlisle United, were relegated to the Conference) was 429(49) matches and 27 goals.

Appearances: FL: 3(3) apps 0 gls FLC: 2 apps 0 gls
Total: 5(3) apps 0 gls

BIRCHENALL, Alan John

Midfield   6' 0"   12st 8lbs
b. East Ham, 22nd August 1945
CAREER: Thornewood Thistle/Sheffield United June 1963/
Chelsea Nov 1967, fee £100,000/Crystal Palace June 1970,
fee £100,000/Leicester City Sept 1971 (NOTTS loan Mar
1976) (San Jose Earthquakes USA loan Apr 1977)/NOTTS
Sept 1977/Memphis Rogues USA Apr 1978/Blackburn Rovers
Sept 1978/Luton Town Mar 1979/Hereford United Oct 1979/
Trowbridge player-manager cs 1980
Debut v Oxford United (a) 13.3.76, lost 1 – 2

Extrovert, all action striker and a major character in the
Sixties and early Seventies, his mane of blond hair usually
to be found where the action was at its thickest. Alan
began as a striker, 31 League goals in 106(1) matches for
Sheffield United winning him international recognition at
Under-23 level. His value was underlined by the six-figure
transfer fees paid by Chelsea, Crystal Palace and Leicester
City. During his lengthy association with the Foxes he
was successfully switched into an attacking midfielder, a
position he retained for the remainder of his career. Alan
served eight League clubs and two in the USA, his career
aggregate figures totalling 447(11) League matches and 74
goals. Alan has served Leicester City for many years as
part-time PR man, in addition to running the Griffin Inn
at Swithland.

Appearances: FL: 33 apps 0 gls FAC: 3 apps 0 gls Other:
2 apps 0 gls Total: 38 apps 0 gls
Honours: England U-23 international, 4 apps

BIRCUMSHAW, Peter Brian

Outside-left   5' 8"   11st 3lbs
b. Mansfield, 29th August 1938
CAREER: Mansfield Schoolboys/NOTTS initially on am
forms, signing pro July 1956/Bradford City June 1962, fee
£4,000/Stockport County June 1963 to 1964
Debut v Middlesbrough (a) 19.1.57, drawn 0 – 0

In season 1958-59, a term when Notts suffered a second,
consecutive relegation, National Service soldier Peter
Bircumshaw scored in excess of 120 goals in Army football.
Returning to civilian life during 1959-60 he assisted Notts
to promotion, as runners-up to Walsall, in their inaugural
Division Four campaign. An aggressive wingman with an
eye for goal, he exploded onto the scene with a remarkable
return of 20 League and Cup goals in just 23 appearances.
Despite maintaining an excellent scoring ratio over the
next two seasons, he had strong competition from Alan
Withers for the outside-left position. Altghough he was
Bradford City's joint leading scorer (11 goals in 32
matches) he left Valley Parade after a season in which
they had to apply for re-election to Division Four. Elder
brother of Tony Bircumshaw (q.v.).

Appearances: FL: 72 apps 40 gls FAC: 6 apps 7 gls FLC:
1 app 1 gl Total: 79 apps 48 gls

BIRCUMSHAW, Tony

Full-back   5' 10"   12st 8lbs
b. Mansfield, 8th February 1945
CAREER: Mansfield Schoolboys/Nottinghamshire
Schoolboys/Mansfield St. John's/NOTTS am Apr 1960, app
Mar 1961, pro Feb 1962/Hartlepool United July 1966 to cs
1971/Nuneaton Borough
Debut v Brentford (a) 3.4.61, lost 0 – 3

Tony captained Mansfield Schoolboys and represented
Nottinghamshire in matches against Leicestershire and
Northamptonshire. The younger brother of Peter Brian
(above), he became the youngest player to represent the

Magpies at League
level when he
made his debut on
Easter Monday
1961 at the age of
16 years and 54
days. For the
match at
Brentford, Notts
fielded their
youngest-ever
full-back pairing,
the combined ages
of Tony and Dick
Edwards
amounting to just
34 years. Tony
tackled hard and
used the ball with
a great degree of
accuracy. After leaving Meadow Lane he gave excellent
service to Hartlepool United, appearing in 194 League
and Cup matches.

Appearances: FL: 152 apps 1 gl FAC: 6 apps 0 gls FLC:
11 apps 0 gls Total: 169 apps 1 gl

BIRD, Walter Smith

Inside-forward   5' 11"   11st 8lbs
b. Hugglescote, Leics. July quarter 1891
d. Coalville, Leics. 2nd March 1965
CAREER: Coalville Swifts/NOTTS am Apr 1911 (WW1
guest Leicester Fosse)/Grimsby Town Feb 1920/Bristol Rovers
May 1920/Dundee June 1921/Heart of Midlothian Jan 1924,
fee £600/Kilmarnock June 1924; retired Apr 1925
Debut v Chelsea (a) 26.4.13, lost 2 – 5

Nicely built inside-forward with skilful ball control, Walter
Bird's impressive debut in the last match of season 1912-
13 ensured his re-engagement. The Great War halted his
development but he returned to his old perch in September
1919, when he lined up with the Magpies' Reserves
following demobilisation.

Without appearing at first team level in post war football he moved on to Grimsby Town (seven appearances, two goals) and then to Bristol City (21 appearances, five goals.) Despite approaching the veteran stage he then enjoyed a good run in top flight Scottish football in the 1920s.

Appearances: FL: 10 apps 2 gls Total: 10 apps 2 gls

BIRTLES, Garry

Forward   5' 11" 11st 8lbs
b. Nottingham, 27th July 1956
CAREER: Long Eaton Rovers/Long Eaton United/ Nottingham Forest Dec 1976, fee £2,000/Manchester United Oct 1980, fee £1.25m/Nottingham Forest Sept 1982, fee £250,000/NOTTS June 1987/Grimsby Town Aug 1989 to May 1992/Gresley Rovers joint-manager with Paul Futcher Nov 1995
Debut v Wigan Athletic (h) 15.8.87, drawn 4 – 4 (scored two)

Renowned for his bustling style and piercing runs on goal, Gary was deceptively quick and deft in control. In his first spell with the Forest he scored 51 goals in 131 matches, and his £1.25 million transfer to Manchester United was expected to write a further chapter of success. It was not to be. In 25 League appearances for United in 1980-81 he failed to score a goal. With confidence punctured he rejoined Forest for a cut-price £250,000 and despite injury problems he took his overall scoring record for the Forest to 96 goals before being surprisingly released on a free transfer. Joining Notts, he made an immediate impact, scoring twice on his debut and assisting fully in the run through to the Play-off semi-finals, occupying both attacking and defensive roles during the campaign. His League career ended with Grimsby Town, where he was successfully switched into a central defensive role. Garry is a 'Nottingham Evening Post' columnist and a local radio presenter.

Appearances: FL: 62(1) apps 9 gls FAC: 4 apps 1 gl FLC: 6 apps 1 gl Other: 9 apps 1 gl Total; 81(1) apps 12 gls
Honours: England international, 3 caps 1980-81. England 'B' international. England U-21 international, 2 apps. (Nottingham Forest) European Cup winners 1979 and 1980. FL Cup winners 1979, finalists 1980.

BISBY, Clarence Charles 'Charlie'

Left-back   5' 9½" 12st 0lbs
b. Mexborough, 10th September 1904
d. Nottingham, June 1977
CAREER: Denaby United 1923/NOTTS June 1926/Coventry City June 1932/Mansfield Town Dec 1935/Peterborough & Fletton United Aug 1936/Coventry City scout Sept 1946
Debut v Reading (a) 16.10.26, lost 1 – 7

Cool, calculating and polished, and possessed of a particularly graceful style, Charlie Bisby proved to be a worthy successor to Horace Cope in the left-back position. Despite a hectic debut (above) he held a first team place for the best part of six seasons, reaching the milestone of 200 FL appearances just prior to his benefit match against Bury in March 1932. Two months later he was placed on the transfer list and made an immediate impact with his next club, Coventry City, helping them gain promotion in his first season. He went on to complete exactly 100 League appearances before winding up his League career with Mansfield Town. In February 1940 he joined the R.A.O.C. and was posted missing in Crete in August 1941. He was to spend more than four years as a prisoner-of-war in Germany. After the war he returned to Nottingham and for some years worked as a stock-controller for the Corona soft drinks firm. In 1971 he became a hero when he drove 14 vans to safety after fire in an adjacent warehouse threatened to engulf Corona's depot in Cooper Street.

Appearances: FL: 206 apps 1 gl FAC: 9 apps 0 gls Total: 215 apps 1 gl
Honours: (NOTTS) FL Div 3 South champions 1931. (Coventry City) FL Div 3 South champions 1936

BLOCKLEY, Jeffrey Paul 'Jeff'

Centre-half   6' 1" 12st 0lbs
b. Leicester, 12th September 1949
CAREER: Leicester and Blaby Schoolboys/Blaby Boys' Club/ Midland Athletic/Coventry City app, signing pro June 1967/ Arsenal Oct 1972, fee £200,000/Leicester City Jan 1975, fee £100,000 (Derby County loan Jan 1978)/NOTTS June 1978/Enderby Town player-coach July 1980/Gloucester City June 1981/Leicester United manager July 1983/Shepshed Charterhouse manager May 1984/Hinckley Athletic manager Apr-May 1989.
Debut v Scunthorpe United, FLC 1 (a) 12.8.78, won 1 – 0

Jeff Blockley graduated from Blaby Boys' Club, a noted Sixties nursery side that also groomed future Magpies Ian Bolton and David Needham, and England's goalkeeper, Peter Shilton.

Jeff graduated through the ranks at Highfield Road, winning six of his U-23 caps prior to his £200,000 move to Arsenal. He added a further four U-23 caps and won his full cap against Yugoslavia within a week of joining Arsenal, but his stay at Highbury was not a particularly rewarding one, injuries combined with stiff competition restricting him to just 52 League games. His career took an upturn with Leicester City, his signing in January 1975 helping the Foxes avoid what had seemed to be the certainty of relegation from the top flight. Injuries restricted his appearances for Notts in his final two seasons of League football, but he passed the milestone of 300 League appearances in the Magpies' colours.

Appearances: FL: 57(2) apps 5 gls FAC: 3 apps 0 gls FLC: 6 apps 0 gls Other: 6 apps 1 gl
Total: 72(2) apps 6 gls
Honours: England International, 1 cap 1972. England U-23 International, 10 apps. FL representative, 1 app.

BLOOD, John Foster 'Jack'

Left-back   6' 2"   12st 5lbs
b. Bingham, Notts. 2nd October 1914
d. Kingsteignton, 4th February 1992
CAREER: Johnson & Barnes F.C./NOTTS am July 1936, pro June 1938/Exeter City May 1939 (WW2 guest Rochdale; NOTTS; Southport and Liverpool)/Peterborough United player-manager Apr 1948, manager cs 1949 to May 1950
Debut v Torquay United (a) 31.12.38, won 2 – 0

A lengthy spell on amateur forms preceded Jack Blood's professional engagement at Meadow Lane, as he repeatedly declined the opportunity to join the paid ranks. He had just had a taste of first team football, and had been transferred to Exeter City, when the outbreak of war suspended League football for the duration. Among his wartime guest appearances was a memorable match between Liverpool and Southport on 31st December 1944. Although he had assisted Southport during wartime, on this occasion he was at centre-half for Liverpool who won 12 – 1, six goals coming between the 15th and 27th minutes of the match. In post war football he made 44 League and Cup appearances for the Grecians before joining Peterborough United, at that time operating in the Midland League, as player-manager. During his time with Exeter City, Jack Blood played for South Devon Cricket Club as an opening batsman.

Appearances: FL: 8 apps 0 gls FAC: 3 apps 0 gls
Total: 11 apps 0 gls

BLY, Terrence Geoffrey

Centre-forward 6' 0"   12st 0lbs
b. Fincham, Norfolk 22nd October 1935
CAREER: Norwich City from school/Bury St Edmonds/Norwich City pro Aug 1956/Peterborough United June 1960, fee £5,000/Coventry City July 1962/NOTTS Aug 1963, fee £13,000/Grantham Town player-manager Oct 1964 to 1978, fee £1,250.
Debut v Brentford (a) 24.8.63, lost 1 – 4 (scored)

Just two weeks prior to the opening of season 1963-64, and after a fortnight of negotiations, Magpies' manager Eddie Lowe splashed out £13,000 for proven goal scorer Terry Bly. Along with Vic Povey and Mike Barber, he was one of three big-money signings, none of whom enhanced their reputations in Notts' colours. With a record of a century of League goals in the previous four seasons, Terry Bly failed completely to maintain anything like his normal form. Despite a scoring debut, and three goals in his first eleven matches, he registered just one more League goal as the Magpies disappeared through the relegation trapdoor, finishing at the foot of Division Three. After leaving Meadow Lane for a bargain fee of £1,250 his form and goal scoring prowess returned in Grantham's colours. In a highly successful and lengthy association with the Gingerbreads as player-manager, highlights included two successive Midland League champions between 1972-74. Earlier in his career he scored seven hat-tricks and 52 goals in 46 League appearances for Peterborough United, who won the Division Four title in their first season as a League club.

Appearances: FL: 27 apps 4 gls FAC: 2 apps 1 gl FLC: 2 apps 0 gls Total: 31 apps 5 gls
Honours: (Peterborough United) FL Div 4 champions 1961

BLYTH, George

Goalkeeper   6' 0"   13st 8lbs
b. Motherwell 18th October 1906
d. Nottingham, 30th August 1984
CAREER: Newburgh West End/Hibernian Oct 1929/Perth Rosalea/Perth Y.M.C.A./Hibernian Aug 1933/NOTTS May 1935/Grantham Oct 1938
Debut v Bristol Rovers (a) 31.8.35, drawn 0 – 0

In the two seasons spanned by the years 1936-38 George Blyth was widely acknowledged to be one of the most talented goalkeepers operating in the Southern Section of Division Three. Agile, safe and sure, and with a lengthy goal kick, he dominated his penalty area and was not averse to tackling forwards outside his area when necessary. The latter move, however, came in for a degree of criticism from the 'Football Post' correspondent, who urged Blyth to subdue a tendency to leave his goal, warning of the danger "when the goalkeeper goes so far from home."

Appearances: FL: 99 apps 0 gls FAC: 3 apps 0 gls Other: 4 apps 0 gls Total: 106 apps 0 gls

BOERTIEN, Paul

Defender/Midfield   5' 10" 11st 2lbs
b. Haltwhistle, 21st January 1979
CAREER: Carlisle United trainee, signing pro May 1997/
Derby County Mar 1999, fee £250,000 (Crewe Alexandra
loan Feb 2000) (NOTTS loan Jan - Feb 2004)
Debut v Swindon Town (h) 24.1.04, lost 1 – 2

Paul Boertien's loan spell with the Magpies ended on a
high note. In the unaccustomed role of right full-back he
combined superbly with midfielder David Pipe in the 4 –
1 victory against Stockport County that featured a four –
goal blast from Paul Heffernan. Mainly operating on the
left flank during his spell at Meadow Lane, he would have
made an excellent permanent signing, but was recalled to
Derby to cover for injuries. Sadly, he was injured himself
shortly after his return, damaging cruciate knee ligaments,
but was able to resume full training in November 2004. In
February 2005 he signed a new two-year contract with
the Rams.

Appearances: FL: 5 apps 0 gls Total: 5 apps 0 gls

BOLLAND, Paul Graham

Midfield   5' 11" 11st 0lbs
b. Bradford, 23rd December 1979
CAREER: Bradford City trainee July 1996, pro Mar 1998/
NOTTS Jan 1999, fee £75,000/Grimsby Town June 2005
Debut v AFC Bournemouth (a) 16.1.99, lost 0 – 2

Paul clocked up almost 200 senior appearances for the
Magpies in a seven-year stint, with over half of the total
coming in the last three seasons. A fair indication of his
increasing value to the cause, hampered in earlier days by
injuries and a spell out of favour during the Meadow Lane
managerial merry go round. In earlier days Paul would
have been described as a defensive wing-half, capable also
of occupying the full-back berths. In either role his game
features boundless enthusiasm, a lung-bursting work rate
and strength in the tackle. His surprise decision to join
Grimsby Town has brought about a degree of acrimony
between the player and the Notts club - a sad ending to
his Meadow Lane Career.

Appearances: FL: 153(19) apps 6 gls FAC: 7(1) apps 0
gls FLC: 3(6) apps 0 gls Other: 2(3) apps 1 gl
Total: 165(29) apps 7 gls

BOLTON, Ian Robert

Central defender   6' 0" 11st 9lbs
b. Leicester, 13th July 1953
CAREER: Blaby Boys' Club/Birmingham City app Sept 1968/
NOTTS Mar 1972 (Lincoln City loan Aug 1976)/Watford
July 1977, fee £12,000/Brentford Dec 1983, fee £5,000/
Barnet Mar 1984/Kettering Town Oct 1984/Chalfont St
Peter July 1985/Kingsbury Town 1986-87/Hayes cs 1987
Debut as sub v Chesterfield (h) 18.3.72, lost 1 – 4

Known as 'Bernie' to his colleagues, he began as a striker
or midfielder but settled into a back four position in 1973-
74, establishing himself in the first team with an eight-
match run at the end of the season. A regular for lengthy
spells in the following two seasons, he began 1976-77 on
loan to Lincoln City and featured in only five of the
Magpies' League matches prior to his transfer to Watford.
Under manager Graham Taylor he was a key member in
the Hornets' rise from Division Four to the top flight, in
six years at Vicarage road totalling 280(2) League and Cup
appearances and 35 goals. After a brief spell with
Brentford, he joined non-League Barnet as a part-time
professional, combining football with a job in car sales.

Appearances: FL: 61(9) apps 4 gls FAC: 3 apps 0 gls
FLC: 4(1) apps 0 gls Total: 68(10) apps 4 gls
Honours: (Watford) FL Div 4 champions 1978

BOREHAM, Reginald Walter

Inside-forward   5' 7" 10st 11lbs
b. High Wycombe, 27th May 1896
d. Chilton, Bucks, 3rd February 1976
CAREER: Wycombe Wanderers am/NOTTS am June 1920/
Wycombe Wanderers am July 1924/Arsenal am July 1921/
Wycombe Wanderers am Jan 1924, subsequently appointed
honorary-secretary 1937 to May 1950
Debut v Bristol City (h) 4.9.20, drawn 2 – 2

Reg Boreham assisted Wycombe Wanderers to the
championship of the Spartan League in season 1919-20,
scoring 33 goals in the concluding five months of the
season. He had played a lot of football in India during
WW1 in a team captained by Dickie Downs the England
international. A teetotaller and non-smoker who won the
highest honours available in the amateur game, he also
figured regularly with Arsenal for two seasons, playing in
53 League and Cup matches and scoring 18 goals.

Appearances: FL: 3 apps 0 gls Total: 3 apps 0 gls
Honours: England Amateur International, 2 caps. FA
representative, 2 apps

BOUCHER, Thomas Alfred

Forward   5' 6" 11st 0lbs
b. Pershore, Worcs. January quarter 1879
d. Sodbury, Avon, 17th July 1960
CAREER: Stourbridge/NOTTS May 1896/Bedminster May
1899/Bristol Rovers May 1900/Bristol City Aug 1901/New
Brompton cs 1903/Maidstone United Oct 1905 to 1906
Debut v Loughborough (h) 5.9.1896, won 3 – 1

Described in 1896 as: "A good leader and a goal getter,"
Boucher was a fearless centre-forward who, despite his
modest stature, rushed the burliest of burly defenders

with relish, and quickly had a large collection of goals to his credit. He first came to prominence in Staffordshire League football, and quickly established himself in Division Two, scoring 24 goals in his first season as the Magpies regained their position in the top flight. He remained for a further two seasons as the team consolidated their position in Division One before embarking on a tour of Southern League clubs, initially joining Bedminster, along with goalkeeper George Toone.

Appearances: FL: 79 apps 32 gls FAC: 4 apps 1 gl Other: 4 apps 1 gl Total: 87 apps 34 gls
Honours: (NOTTS) FL Div 2 champions 1897

--------○--------

BOWERS, John Anslow

Outside-left   5' 9"   10st 7lbs
b. Leicester, 14th November 1939
CAREER: Derby Corinthians/Derby County Feb 1957/ NOTTS May 1966
Debut v Bradford P.A. (a) 20.8.66, lost 1 – 4

John Bowers made his League debut for Derby County on his twentieth birthday, deputising at outside-left for Dave Cargill in a 2 – 2 draw at Huddersfield Town. It was some time before he established a regular first team place, his best season being 1964-65 when he scored nine goals in 22 League matches, this despite a lengthy spell on the sidelines after injuring an ankle. Considering his fair amount of Division Two experience, his lack of success with the Magpies was disappointing. John's father, J.W.A.Bowers, was a famous name in Derby County's history. Capped three times by England he scored 183 goals in 220 League and Cup appearances for the Rams and 56 in 84 matches for Leicester City.

Appearances: FL: 5 apps 0 gls Total: 5 apps 0 gls

--------○--------

BOYES, Walter Edward 'Wally'

Outside-left   5' 5"   10st 8lbs
b. Killamarsh, Derbyshire, 5th January 1913
d. Sheffield, 16th September 1960
CAREER: Netherhope Council School/Sheffield Schoolboys/ Woodhouse Mills United/West Bromwich Albion am Feb 1931, pro Mar 1931/Everton Feb 1938, fee £6,000 (WW2 guest Aldershot, Brentford, Clapton Orient, Leeds United, Linfield, Manchester United, Middlesbrough, Millwall, New Brighton, Newcastle United, Preston North End, Sunderland and Wrexham)/NOTTS player-coach Aug 1949/Scunthorpe United Aug 1950 to Apr 1951/Retford Town player-manager 1952/Hyde United manager Apr 1958/Swansea Town trainer 1959; retired due to ill health June 1960
Debut v Exeter City (h) 8.9.49, drawn 3 – 3

Blond-haired and diminutive, Wally Boyes was a fleet-footed wingman with dazzling ball skills and the gift of accurate centering. He began with West Bromwich Albion and was a scorer in the 1935 FA Cup Final against Sheffield Wednesday. After 151 League outings and 35 goals he departed the Hawthorns to join Everton, where he won a League championship medal in the final peacetime season. Joining the Magpies as player-coach in the summer of 1949 at the age of 36 he appeared in only three League matches in the Division Three South championship side. He left after one season to join Scunthorpe United for their debut in the Football League. Wally played at outside-left in their first fixture in the Third Division North, a goal less draw against Shrewsbury Town at the Old Show Ground and made 13 appearances during the season, scoring twice. From 1952 to 1957 he was sports master at the Oakwood Collegiate School, Sheffield.

Appearances: FL: 3 apps 1 gl Total: 3 apps 1 gl
Honours: England International, 3 caps 1935-39. FL Representative, 2 apps. (West Bromwich Albion) FA Cup finalists 1935. (Everton) FL Div 1 champions 1939

--------○--------

BRADD, Leslie John

Centre-forward 6' 0"   12st 12lbs
b. Buxton, 5th November 1947
CAREER: Kent's Bank School (Buxton)/ Earl Sterndale F.C./ Rotherham United Mar 1966/NOTTS Oct 1967, fee £1,000/ Stockport County Aug 1978/Wigan Athletic July 1981 to May 1983(Bristol Rovers loan Dec 1982)/Kettering Town cs 1983/ NOTTS July 1983 as representative for Lottery Division; Promotions Manager Dec 1988/Nottingham Forest Assistant Commercial Manager Nov 1994, Corporate Sales Manager 1998
Debut v Crewe Alexandra (h) 4.10.67, won 1 – 0

Les Bradd began as a free scoring right winger with Earl Sterndale F.C., winners of the Second Division championship of the Fairfield and District League. He also spent some time training with Buxton, but never played for them, eventually taking the giant step from Earl Sterndale to Rotherham United.

Les had appeared in only four first team matches for Rotherham, but in one of them – the first round FL Cup tie at Meadow Lane in August 1967 – he scored the only goal of the game to knock Notts out of the competition. A little over a month later he made his Magpies debut in an eventful Division Four match against Crewe Alexandra. Goalkeeper Mick Rose was injured during the game and Alex Gibson took over. Notts won 1 – 0 with Dave Watson scoring. Les scored his first goal for the Magpies against Rochdale at Meadow Lane on 21st October 1967 and his ten League goals for the season placed him at the head of the scoring list. He remained at Meadow Lane for eleven seasons, took part in two promotions, and in 1976-77 became the club's record League scorer in total aggregate, surpassing Tony Hateley's total of 109. His best individual season, however, was 1971-72. It was the first season back in Division Three and Les scored 25 goals in 53 League and Cup matches and was voted 'Player of the Year.' He continued to find the net on a regular basis after leaving Meadow Lane, adding a further 57 League goals to his career total, his final aggregate figures being 553(23) League matches and 182 goals.

Appearances: FL: 379(16) apps 125 gls FAC: 22 apps 4 gls FLC: 17 apps 7 gls Other: 7(1) apps 1 gl Total: 425(17) apps 137 gls
Honours: (NOTTS) FL Div 4 champions 1971

BRADLEY, Gordon

Goalkeeper   5' 11"   11st 10lbs
b. Scunthorpe, 20th May 1925
CAREER: Scunthorpe United am/Leicester City Nov 1942 (WW2 guest Grimsby Town, Lincoln City, Sheffield United and NOTTS)/NOTTS Feb 1950/Cambridge City Aug 1958/ Glentoran 1959
Debut v Grimsby Town (a) 9.9.50, won 4 – 1

Said to possess a bigger hand span than that of Frank Swift's 11 1/2", Gordon Bradley was one of a select band who played sport all the year round. When the football season closed he turned to tennis and professional coaching engagements. His football career began with Scunthorpe United, where an

early team-mate was Allen Wade (q.v.). During National Service he represented the R.A.F. in matches against the Irish League and played in many other inter-services tournaments prior to his demobilisation in November 1947. In 1949 he took the place of the injured Leicester City goalkeeper Ian McGraw, and appeared in the FA Cup final. For two seasons (1953-54 and 1954-55) he did not miss a League or FA Cup match for Notts., but at either side of his lengthy run of 101 consecutive matches, he found stiff competition from Roy Smith, Jimmy Linton and George Smith.

Appearances: FL: 192 apps 1 gl FAC: 11 apps 1 gl
Total: 203 apps 1 gl
Honours: (Leicester City) FA Cup finalists 1949

BRADLEY, Herbert

Outside-left   5' 8"   11st 12lbs
b. Padiham, Lancs. April quarter 1887
CAREER: Colne F.C./Bury May 1906/NOTTS May 1910/ Preston North End Nov 1911 to cs 1912, fee £35.
Debut v Blackburn Rovers (a) 1.9.10, drawn 1 – 1

A cotton loom weaver at the age of 13 who, some five years later, assisted Colne to win the championship of the Lancashire Combination Division Two in 1905-06. He was 'spotted' by Notts when he had an outstanding game in Nottingham for Bury against Forest in November 1909, and he subsequently became the Magpies first new signing for season 1910-11. He failed to fill what was considered a problem position, and even worse, a Board Minute from October 1910 revealed that a certificate from the club doctor stated that Bradley was "suffering from a certain disease" and that he was to be suspended sine die. In the following month Preston North End paid £35 for him but he appeared only twice in First Division matches and was one of eight players offloaded at the end of the season that ended in relegation.

Appearances: FL: 3 apps 0 gls Total: 3 apps 0 gls

BRAILSFORD, James Roberts

Right-half
b. Lincoln, April quarter 1877
d. Lincoln, 10th April 1946
CAREER: Casuals F.C./Newark Town Feb 1894/Lincoln City May 1895/NOTTS May 1897 to 1898/Lincoln City Sept 1906
Debut v Sheffield Wednesday (a) 2.10.1897, lost 1 – 3

Signed by Lincoln City at eighteen years of age, Brailsford had appeared in 20 Division Two matches for the Imps at the time of his transfer to the Magpies, who had won the championship of Division Two in 1896-97.

In the following season they struggled on their return to the top flight. Aside from his solitary first team outing, Brailsford remained in reserve in a season when the relegation battle ended in remarkable fashion. No fewer than five clubs (Notts included) ended the season with 24 points from 30 matches. In the event all survived, as it was not until the following season that the League was extended to 18 clubs and automatic promotion and relegation was introduced, rather than the previous system of 'Test Matches'.

Appearances: FL: 1 app 0 gls Total: 1 app 0 gls

———————————o———————————

BRAMHAM, Arnold
Centre-forward 5' 8½" 11st 8lbs
b. Rotherham, 16th January 1912
b. Nottingham, September 1989
CAREER: West Melton/Silverwood Colliery/NOTTS am June 1934, pro Feb 1935/Rotherham United July 1937 (WW2 guest Barnsley)/Peterborough United Aug 1946/Sutton Town Aug 1949
Debut v Nottingham Forest (a) 9.2.35, won 3 – 2 (scored two)

Arnold Bramham showed early promise of developing into a capable leader of the attack, his scoring record in limited appearances marking him as a fine prospect. His debut was quite stunning. Without a win on their travels all season, Notts crossed the Trent and proceeded to upset the form book, two goals from their new centre-forward clinching an unexpected victory against the Forest. Subsequently with Rotherham United, he scored 22 goals in 39 League matches in 1937-38, and did even better in 1938-39 with 31 in 42 matches. Arnold scored almost half of Rotherham's total of 64 League goals that season, and was the second highest scorer in the Third Division North. In post war football he scored 32 goals in 58 matches for Peterborough United.

Appearances: FL: 18 apps 10 gls Other: 1 app 1 gl
Total: 19 apps 11 gls

———————————o———————————

BRAMLEY, Charles
Right-half 5' 7" 11st 7lbs
b. Nottingham, 1870
d. Nottingham, Sept 1916, age 46
CAREER: Notts. Jardine's/Notts. St John's/Notts. Rangers/NOTTS June 1891 to season 1897-98
Debut v Stoke (h) 26.9.1891, drawn 1 – 1

Charlie Bramley's fine career ended in tragic circumstances. In a collision with Aston Villa's goalkeeper in a second round FA Cup tie in February 1897 he broke his right leg "With a crack that could be heard half way across the ground," according to the 'Evening News.' Although he managed to play one more game in the following season he was never again able to attain concert pitch and decided to retire.

A locally produced player, he was with St John's when they won the Church Association Cup in season 1888-89. A member of Notts FA Cup winning side of 1894, the gold medal that he won was in the news as recently as 1995. A local company, contracted to frame sporting memorabilia to fill a chain of Labatt's theme pubs, mounted Charlie Bramley's medal. Perhaps unfittingly this was to be displayed at The Pitch, a licensed premises sited at the old Trent End of Forest's City Ground!

Appearances: FL: 126 apps 8 gls FAC: 13 apps 0 gls
Other: 12 apps 0 gls Total: 151 apps 8 gls
Honours: (NOTTS) FA Cup winners 1894. FL Div 2 champions 1897

———————————o———————————

BRANNAN, Michael H.
Goalkeeper 5' 10" 11st 5lbs
b. Wath-on-Dearne, January quarter 1911
CAREER: Yorkshire Schoolboys/Dearne Valley Old Boys/Rotherham Road F.C./Wombwell trial Aug 1928, pro Oct 1928/Denaby United circa 1929/Arsenal am Mar 1932, pro Dec 1932/Hull City Aug 1933/Barnsley Aug 1934/NOTTS June 1937/Grantham Town cs 1945/Peterborough United cs 1947 to 1948
Debut v Reading (h) 29.1.38, won 2 – 1

Despite his association with four League clubs, Mike Brannan's role remained that of reserve 'keeper throughout. His League debut was made during a three-year spell with Barnsley, and in a promising start he remained undefeated in a 1 – 0 win at Norwich City on 9th March 1935. Nevertheless, he played in only another four matches before moving to Meadow Lane. With the very consistent George Blyth firmly established as number one custodian, Brannan was restricted to his familiar role of standby.

Appearances: FL: 3 apps 0 gls Other: 1 app 0 gls
Total: 4 apps 0 gls

———————————o———————————

BREALEY, Harry
Outside-left
b. Nottingham, April quarter 1874
CAREER: NOTTS season 1894-95/Hucknall St John's Feb 1896.
Debut v Lincoln City (a) 12.4.1895, won 3 – 1

With the outstanding career of England international outside-left Harry Daft drawing to a close, Harry Brealey was given a run on the left wing in the penultimate fixture of 1894-95. He also scored three goals in just seven Division Two fixtures in the following season, but efforts to balance the attack finally settled on a formation with Walter Bull on the left wing, and his 15 goals in 30 matches ensured that he retained the position. The 1901 Census lists Harry Brealey as a fruit salesman.

Appearances: FL: 8 apps 3 gls Total: 8 apps 3 gls

BREARLEY, John
Forward or half-back   5' 9"   11st 0lbs
b. West Derby, Liverpool, October quarter 1875
d. Southend, October 1944, age 68
CAREER: Liverpool South End Aug 1896/NOTTS Feb 1897/ Kettering Town Dec 1897/Chatham June 1898/Millwall Athletic May 1899/NOTTS May 1900/Middlesbrough Apr 1901/Everton May 1902, fee £750/Tottenham Hotspur May 1903/Crystal Palace May 1907/Millwall Athletic player-coach cs 1909/Victoria F.C. (Berlin) coach; was interned during WW1
Debut v Burnley, Test Match, (a) 26.4.1897, won 1 – 0 (scored)

As an untried reserve, John Brearley was drafted into the Notts team to oppose Burnley in place of the injured Walter Bull. The match was to decide the 1896-97 promotion issue, and the reserve wingman became an instant hero when he scored the goal that effected the Magpies return to Division One. His second spell with Notts was welcomed by the 'Football News' who considered "Brearley is one of the most gentlemanly footballers in the game." Sadly, his season was blighted by injuries, restricting him to just eight matches.

Appearances: FL: 9 apps 0 gls Other: 1 app 1 gl
Total: 10 apps 1 gl

BRINDLEY, John Charles 'Bill'
Right-back   5' 9"   10st 11lbs
b. Nottingham, 29th January 1947
CAREER: Nottingham People's College/Nottingham Schoolboys/North Midlands Schoolboys/Nottingham Forest from school, pro Feb 1964/NOTTS May 1970, fee £5,000/ Gillingham July 1976/Grantham Town July 1977/Burton Albion 1979-80/Boston F.C. manager/Heanor Town manager/Ilkeston Town manager 1995/Arnold Town assistant-manger June 1996/Arnold Town manager during season 2003-04, resigned May 2005.
Debut v York City (a) 15.8.70, drawn 0 – 0

Won England Schoolboy caps against Wales and Scotland in 1961, and joined the ground staff at Nottingham Forest on leaving school. In April 1965 he appeared in the final of the International Youth Tournament, dubbed 'The Little World Cup,' in West Germany.

He was also a finalist with the Forest Youth team in two International Youth Tournaments in France and Holland in the 1965-66 season. Despite his undoubted pedigree, Bill had to cross the Trent in search of regular first team football. He was immediately successful at Meadow Lane, two promotions in his first three seasons lifting the Magpies into Division Two. Aside from absences through injury, he was a fixture at right-back for five consecutive seasons, and a tremendous stumbling to any "Fancy Dan" (his own words) wingman who crossed his path!

Appearances: FL: 221(2) apps 0 gls FAC: 12 apps 0 gls FLC: 13(1) apps 0 gls Other: 1 app 0 gls
Total: 247(3) apps 0 gls
Honours: England Schoolboy International, 2 caps 1961-62. England Youth International, 1 app v Ireland 1963-64 & 5 apps in the International Youth Tournament, held in West Germany April 1965. (England reached the final but lost 2 – 3 to East Germany). (NOTTS) FL Div 4 champions 1971

BROADBENT, Albert Henry
Outside-left   5' 10"   12st 4lbs
b. Dudley, Worcs. 20th August 1934
CAREER: Dudley Town/NOTTS Mar 1952/Sheffield Wednesday July 1955, fee about £6,000/Rotherham United Dec 1957, player exchange/Doncaster Rovers June 1959, fee £2,000/Lincoln City Nov 1961/Doncaster Rovers Jan 1963, player exchange/Bradford P.A. Oct 1965, fee £4,500/ Hartlepool United Feb 1967, fee £3,000/Rotherham United player and assistant-trainer Mar 1968/Scarborough 1968-69
Debut v Doncaster Rovers (h) 29.8.53, lost 1 – 5

Albert Broadbent was the subject of a rather usual transfer deal when he left Meadow Lane to join Sheffield Wednesday. With both sides unable to agree on a fee, County's manager George Poyser eventually agreed to a fixed sum plus a further £50 for every goal scored by Broadbent in the following season. A fair-haired wingman of many clubs, Albert took over the left wing spot from schoolteacher Bob Crookes in 1954-55 and finished the season as second highest scorer with 11 League goals in 30 matches. He maintained an excellent strike rate throughout his career, scoring just one short of a century of League goals in 485 matches.

Appearances: FL: 31 apps 11 gls FAC: 5 apps 2 gls
Total: 36 apps 13 gls
Honours: (Sheffield Wednesday) FL Div 2 champions 1956

BRODIE, George Woollvend

Inside-right 6' 0" 11st 0lbs
b. Castle Douglas, Kirkcudbrightshire, 17th December 1898
CAREER: Castle Douglas/Preston North End trial/Fleetwood Nov 1920/Wigan Borough Feb 1921/Castle Douglas Aug 1922/NOTTS Sept 1922/Castle Douglas circa 1923/Queen of the South Aug 1924.
Debut v Hull City (h) 9.9.22, lost 0 – 1

After unsuccessful trials with Preston North End, George Brodie joined Fleetwood where his form in Lancashire Combination fixtures led to his joining Wigan Borough, just prior to their first season in the newly formed Third Division North. He appeared in 11 matches and scored two goals in 1921-22 but was not retained and returned to Scotland. Offered a second opportunity at League level by the Magpies, he failed to break into a side destined to win the championship of Division Two.

Appearances: FL: 1 app 0 gls Total: 1 app 0 gls

───────o───────

BROOK, Gary

Forward 5' 10" 12st 4lbs
b. Dewsbury, 9th May 1964
CAREER: Huddersfield Town nc/Frickley Athletic/Newport County Dec 1987, fee £6,500/Scarborough Mar 1988, fee £10,000/Blackpool Nov 1989, fee £80,000 (NOTTS loan Sept 1990) (Scarborough loan Oct 1990)
Debut as sub v Middlesbrough (a) 8.9.90, lost 0 – 1

Former sheet metal worker Gary Brook made his League debut with Newport County, and earned them a quick profit when they transferred him to Scarborough three months later. Season 1988-89 was his first full season, and Scarborough's second as a Football League club. They reached the Play-offs but lost to Leyton Orient at the semi-final stage, Gary's 17 goals in League and Cup being a major contribution. Joining Blackpool in November 1989 he found less success in what proved to be a relegation season. In the Division Four campaign that followed he played in only 3(1) League matches for the Seasiders. His two loan spells during the season included his single substitute appearance for the Magpies, and a brief reunion with his former Scarborough manager, Neil Warnock.

Appearances: FL: 0(1) apps 0 gls Total: 0(1) apps 0 gls

───────o───────

BROOME, Frank Henry

Forward 5' 7½" 10st 11lbs
b. Berkhamsted, Herts 11th June 1915
d. Exeter, 5th September 1994
CAREER: Berkhamsted Victoria C of E School/Boxmoor United/Berkhamsted Town/Aston Villa Nov 1934 (WW2 guest Wolverhampton Wanderers, Birmingham,

Northampton Town, Chesterfield, Nottingham Forest, NOTTS, Watford, Aldershot, Charlton Athletic and Worcester City)/Derby County Sept 1946/NOTTS Oct 1949, in exchange for Harry Brown/Brentford July 1953/Crewe Alexandra Oct 1953/Shelbourne Feb 1955/NOTTS assistant-trainer June 1955, caretaker-manager Jan to May 1957, then assistant-manager to Dec 1957/Exeter City manager-coach Jan 1958/Southend United manager May to Dec 1960/Bankstown, New South Wales, manager-coach July 1961/Corinthians, Sydney, manager-coach Oct 1962/Melita Eagles, Sydney, part-time coach early 1967/Exeter City manager Apr 1967 to Feb 1969, then briefly coached in the Middle East.
Debut v Walsall (h) 29.10.49, drawn 1 – 1

In early days Frank Broome was noted as regular goalscorer from either centre or wing forward positions. Possessed of an amazing burst of acceleration, he appeared to be at full speed within a couple of strides, leaving even the best defenders standing. This, together with his alacrity in seizing a goal scoring opportunity, made him one of the most dangerous forwards of his day. By the time he reached Meadow Lane, at 34 years of age, the winged feet were no more but he had ripened into a wonderfully evergreen performer. Possessing perfect ball control, a deceptive body swerve, and the ability to manoeuvre defenders out of position, he was able to open up the game and create scoring opportunities for his colleagues. For England he appeared in four of the five forward positions, and despite being turned down as 'too small' by both Spurs and Arsenal, he graced the League scene well into his 40th year.

Appearances: FL: 105 apps 35 gls FAC: 9 apps 6 gls Total: 114 apps 41 gls
Honours: England International, 7 caps 1938-39. England Wartime International, 1 app. (Aston Villa) FL Div 2 champions 1938. (NOTTS) FL Div 3 South champions 1950.

───────o───────

BROUGH, Michael

Midfield 6' 0" 11st 7lbs
b. Nottingham, 1st August 1981
CAREER: NOTTS associate-schoolboy Aug 1996, pro July 1999/Macclesfield Town trial Jan 2004/Lincoln City trial Feb 2004/Stafford Rangers/Stevenage Borough Mar 2004.
Debut v Gillingham (a) 7.3.2000, won 1 – 0

After graduating through the youth ranks at Meadow Lane, Michael made steady progress at League level, with the high point his 26(5) League appearances in season 2002-03. By complete contrast, he was dropped after the opening day 0 – 5 defeat at Bristol City in August 2003 and made infrequent first team appearances thereafter. When Gary Mills took over as manager in mid season, Michael was one of several players moved out to accommodate new signings.

Appearances: FL: 67(22) apps 2 gls FAC: 4(5) apps 0 gls FLC: 1 app 0 gls Other: 4 apps 0 gls Total: 76(27) apps 2 gls
Honours: Wales Youth and U-21 International.

BROUGHTON, Matthew

Outside-right
b. Grantham, Lincs. 8th October 1880
d. Grantham, Lincs. 23rd January 1957
CAREER: King's School (Grantham)/Grantham F.C./ Nottingham Forest am Nov, pro Dec 1901/Grantham F.C. Mar 1903/NOTTS am Oct 1904/Watford am Nov 1904/ Grantham F.C.
Debut v Sheffield Wednesday (h) 3.12.04, drawn 2 – 2 (scored one)

In season 1901-02 Matt Broughton played in a little under half of Forest's First Division matches, after taking over on the right wing from Fred Foreman in mid term. A well-known Grantham sportsman – he represented the town in both football and cricket – he additionally worked as a clerk in an iron foundry, and played most of his football as an amateur. In addition to representing, and scoring for, both Nottingham clubs in First Division football, he had a two-and-a-half -year association with Watford, but made only occasional appearances in Southern League matches.

Appearances: FL: 2 apps 1 gl Total: 2 apps 1 gl

BROWN, Alan Winston

Centre-half   5' 11"   11st 6lbs
b. Consett, 26th August 1914
d. Bideford, 8th March 1996
CAREER: Corbridge United Aug 1930/Spen Black & White Nov 1932/Huddersfield Town Mar 1933/Huddersfield Borough Police F.C. May 1936 (WW2 guest Blackburn Rovers, Halifax Town, Liverpool, Nottingham Forest, West Ham United, Barnsley, NOTTS and Fulham)/Burnley Feb 1946/NOTTS Oct 1948, fee £12,000/Sheffield Wednesday trainer-coach Jan 1951/Burnley manager Aug 1954 to July 1957/Sunderland manager July 1957/Sheffield Wednesday manager July 1964 to Feb 1968/Sunderland manager Feb 1968 to Nov 1972/Subsequently held coaching appointments in Norway and with Plymouth Argyle.
Debut v Norwich City (a) 9.10.48, lost 0 – 3

There can be few, if any, central defenders in today's game who could be accurately described as: "Quiet and gentlemanly, a clean player, who relies on pure skill to checkmate opposing forwards." This, however, was an early post war verdict on Alan Brown, penned at a time when he marshalled a superb Burnley defence in their epic bid for the 'double' of promotion and the FA Cup in season 1946-47. As a youngster, a career in either soccer or rugby beckoned. The fact that he had a cousin, Austin Campbell, making his living as a professional footballer, tipped the scales. Campbell put Huddersfield Town onto his track and the tall, eighteen-year-old joined the Leeds Road club in 1933. Despairing of a break through when understudying Alf Young, he gave up football and joined the Police. Later he returned to the game, served during the war in the RAF and was transferred to Burnley in February 1946.

He had actually played for Notts as a guest player during wartime, and the Magpies could have signed him from Huddersfield Town at a fraction of the sizeable £12,000 fee, paid to Burnley in October 1948. Sadly, within six months of his arrival at Meadow Lane, he asked to be placed on the transfer list, having failed to adapt his game to the hurly-burly of Third Division football.

Appearances: FL: 13 apps 0 gls FAC: 2 apps 0 gls
Total: 15 apps 0 gls
Honours: FL Representative, 1 app 1948. (Burnley) FA Cup finalists 1947

BROWN, Cyril

Inside-forward   5' 9"   11st 0lbs
b. Ashington, 25th May 1918
d. Dover, 15th April 1990
CAREER: Felixstowe/Brentford Jan 1939/Sunderland Apr 1945/NOTTS Aug 1946/Boston United 1947/Rochdale Aug 1948/Peterborough United cs 1951
Debut v Bournemouth & Boscombe Athletic (h) 31.8.46, won 1 – 0 (scored)

A goal from Cyril Brown was sufficient to give the Magpies maximum points from their opening fixture in 1946-47. Despite his promising debut, two months later, the 'Football Post' commented; "Brown does not yet appear to have struck his best form. Though he works extremely hard he lacks finish." When the retained list was published at the end of April 1947, some surprise was apparent when his name was omitted. Listed with a fee of £2,000 on his head he dropped into non-League football with Boston United where his form attracted the interest of several League clubs, Rochdale signing him in August 1948. In three seasons at Spotland he was a Lancashire Senior Cup winner in 1949, and completed 61 League appearances and 11 goals before joining Peterborough United. He made his debut at London Road against the Magpies Reserves, who began their Midland League campaign with 4 – 2 victory.

Appearances: FL: 13 apps 5 gls FAC: 1 app 0 gls
Total: 14 apps 5 gls

BROWN, David Carre

Centre-forward 5' 8½" 10st 9lbs
b. Broughty Ferry, Dundee, 26th November 1892
CAREER: Dundee St Joseph's/Dundee Mar 1911/Morton later in 1911/Dundee Feb 1913/Peebles Rovers Aug 1913 (WW1 guest Port Vale; Glasgow Rangers; Nottingham Forest and Birmingham)/Stoke Oct 1919, fee £1,200/NOTTS Aug 1921, fee £950/Kilmarnock Aug 1922/Darlington Aug 1923, fee £80/Crewe Alexandra June 1926/Barrow June 1927 to Mar 1928/Darlington reserve team manager cs 1933.
Debut v Bristol City (h) 27.8.21, lost 0 – 2

Once described as: "A capital shot, good dribbler and very speedy." In League football his full potential as a goal scorer was realised in the Third Division North with Darlington. In the season that the Quakers won the championship, he scored a record 39 League goals, a figure that remains a club record eighty years on. His aggregate record in League football was better than a goal every other game, 132 strikes coming in just 243 matches.

Appearances: FL: 14 apps 7 gls Total: 14 apps 7 gls
Honours: (Darlington) FL Div 3 North champions 1925

BROWN, Gilbert Noel
Forward
b. Nottingham, 10th May 1867
d. Ruddington, Notts. 1st February 1949
CAREER: NOTTS 1887-88
Debut v Beeston St John's FAC 2Q (h) 27.10.1888, won 4 – 2

An occasional member of the 1887-88 side, Noel Brown appeared twice at inside-right and twice on the right wing in four friendly matches. In a season when plenty of goals were scored, both for and against, Brown's four outings were typical of the season: Preston North End (a) lost 2 – 5. Notts Rangers (h) lost 0 – 8. Church F.C. (h) won 6 – 0. Halliwell F.C. (h) lost 1 – 4. According to the 1901 Census, he was employed as a wine merchant.

Appearances: FAC: 1 app 0 gls Total: 1 app 0 gls

BROWN, George H
Right-half
CAREER: Nottingham Forest/NOTTS cs 1888/Nottingham Forest
Debut v Everton (a) 15.9.1888, lost 1 – 2

A regular during the Magpies first season in the Football League – a tournament of just 22 matches at inception – George Brown stayed for only one season before returning to Forest, at that time operating in the Football Alliance. He missed playing in three of the FA Cup matches during 1888-89, but two of his absences were explained by the fact that the first two qualifying rounds were played by the reserve team, before a League match on the same day.

Appearances: FL: 19 apps 1 gl FAC: 3 apps 0 gls
Total: 22 apps 1 gl

BROWN, Harold Thomas
Goalkeeper   6' 0"   11st 4lbs
b. Kingsbury, 9th April 1924
d. Abingdon, Oxfordshire June 1982

CAREER: Queens Park Rangers Apr 1941(WW2 guest Arsenal)/NOTTS Apr 1946, in exchange for Cyril Hatton/Derby County Oct 1949, in exchange for Frank Broome/Queens Park Rangers Aug 1951/Plymouth Argyle Aug 1956/Exeter City Sept 1958.
Debut v Bournemouth & Boscombe Athletic (h) 31.8.46, won 1 – 0

Tall and lithe, Harry Brown made such outstanding progress that within twelve months of joining Q.P.R. he was selected to represent the FA against a Civil Defence side, and the R.A.F. As a guest player he turned out for Arsenal against Moscow Dynamos on the foggy, murky day that went down in football history as one of the biggest ever fiascos. Harry recalled the day as "The Moscow bombardment, I didn't know whether I was coming or going." In November 1948 it was stated that Harry had played in 500 club and Army games without a break, not having missed a Saturday game since April 1942. Rested by the Magpies and replaced by John Mowl for three matches, manager Stollery then signed Roy Smith from Sheffield Wednesday who immediately embarked on a run of 75 consecutive League and Cup matches.

Appearances: FL: 93 apps 0 gls FAC: 9 apps 0 gls
Total: 102 apps 0 gls

BROWN, Henry Harold
Outside-left
b. Nottingham, 2nd July 1864
CAREER: NOTTS 1887-88
Debut v Eckington, FAC 1Q (h) 6.10.1888, won 4 – 1

In addition to his debut (above), Harold Brown scored two goals in the second qualifying round of the FA Cup, a 4 – 2 success against Beeston St Mary's. He first appeared in the Magpies' colours in the opening friendly fixture of season 1887-88 at Walsall, but as understudy to Harry Daft he played in only five matches during the season. It is not known whether Harold was related to the other three Browns (Gilbert Noel, George H. and John H.) who were associated with the club at the same time.

Appearances: FAC: 2 apps 2 gls Total: 2 apps 2 gls

BROWN, John Alfred
Outside-left
b. Nottingham, 20th March 1866
CAREER: NOTTS Mar 1884 to1889
Debut v Walsall Town Swifts, FAC 4 (a) 24.1.1885, won 4 –1 (scored one)

Associated with County for five years prior to their FL entry, John Brown had been a regular until mid season 1887-88.

In this campaign his record of 10 goals in 14 friendly matches included two separate instances of four goals in a match against Leek and Aston Villa, both in October 1887. He was rather less successful when he made his sole appearance in a Football League match. This was against Aston Villa at Perry Bar on 29th September 1888. Reported to have made "An even worse exhibition than usual," the Magpies were four goals in arrears at half time. They pulled one back – through an own goal – but then "never had another look in" as Villa added a further five. The 1 – 9 score line still remains on the record books as Notts' record FL defeat. On two subsequent occasions they went under by the same margin, against Blackburn Rovers in 1889 and against Portsmouth in 1927.

Appearances: FL: 1 app 0 gls FAC: 3 apps 1 gl
Total: 4 app 1 gl

BROWN, Keith

Centre-forward
b. Hucknall, 1st January 1942
CAREER: South Notts. Schoolboys/West Ham United ground staff 1958/NOTTS pro Jan 1959/Rotherham United July 1959/Boston United Aug 1960
Debut v Halifax Town (h) 3.1.59, drawn 4 – 4 (scored one)

Keith Brown was a ground staff boy at West Ham United at sixteen years of age, having earlier won an England Schools cap against Ireland in 1956. Despite a scoring debut with Notts, just two days beyond his seventeenth birthday, and a very respectable return of four goals in eight League matches, Keith was released on a free transfer after just four months as a professional. Signed by Rotherham United in the close season, he failed to graduate beyond reserve level and joined Boston United after a season at Millmoor. It is a fact of footballing life that schoolboy stars often enjoy only moderate success subsequently.

Appearances: FL: 8 apps 4 gls Total: 8 apps 4 gls
Honours: England Schoolboy International, 1 cap 1956

BROWN, Ralph

Inside-forward 5' 10" 10st 12lbs
b. Ilkeston, 26th February 1944
CAREER: Ilkeston Schoolboys/Aston Villa app Mar 1959, pro Mar 1961/NOTTS May 1962/Nuneaton Borough.
Debut v Coventry City (a) 18.8.62, lost 0 – 2

When Notts signed Ralph Brown in May 1962, the eighteen-year-old centre-forward considered that he had been passed over at Aston Villa while other young players had been given first team opportunities. Strangely, his only senior appearance for the Villa was in a Cup Final, as

he appeared in the first leg of the 1960-61 FL Cup Final at Rotherham United. Villa lost 2 – 0 at Millmoor and Brown was dropped for the second leg which Villa won 3 – 0 to become the first holders of the trophy. All of Ralph Brown's appearances for the Magpies were made in season 1962-63 when he made a big initial impact but later lost his place. He did not appear at senior level after the appointment of Eddie Lowe as manager in July 1963.

Appearances: FL: 18 apps 3 gls FAC: 1 app 1 gl
Total: 19 apps 4 gls
Honours: (Aston Villa) FL Cup winners 1961

BROWN, Raymond Moscrop

Outside-left 5' 5" 10st 7lbs
b. Carlisle, 11th February 1928
CAREER: Queen's Park F.C. Aug 1948/NOTTS Aug 1951
Debut v Barnsley (a) 12.9.51, lost 1 – 2

Ray Brown began with Queen's Park, making his debut for the famed Glasgow amateur combination in the Scottish 'B' Division against Raith Rovers on 14th August 1948. In all matches prior to joining the Magpies he scored 21 goals in 79 matches for the Spiders, and was second highest scorer – from outside-left – in 1949-50 with 10 goals in 29 'B' Division fixtures. A clever little player with astute ball control and a strong shot in either foot, he nevertheless failed to dislodge Bob Crookes, the Magpies popular schoolteacher outside-left. Ray Brown was capped by Scotland at amateur level prior to joining Notts. The son of a Scottish father and an English mother, he was born at Carlisle and was really eligible for England. At the time he thought that his father's nationality entitled him to a Scottish claim, and didn't think that his birthplace mattered. Strictly speaking it did matter, rather different to today's somewhat elastic rulings involving great-grandmothers and the like!

Appearances: FL: 7 apps 0 gls Total: 7 apps 0 gls
Honours: Scotland Amateur International, season 1950-51.

BROWN, Roy Eric

Goalkeeper 6' 1" 12st 10lbs
b. Hove, Sussex 5th October 1945
CAREER: Sussex Schoolboys/Tottenham Hotspur app, signing pro Oct 1962/Reading July 1968, fee £5,000 (Dartford loan Mar 1970)/NOTTS July 1970, fee £2,000/ Mansfield Town nc Nov 1975
Debut v York City (h) 17.10.70, won 2 – 1

With his prospects of advancement at Tottenham Hotspur firmly barred by the outstanding Irish international goalkeeper, Pat Jennings, Roy Brown departed White Hart Lane to join Reading.

At Elm Park he enjoyed regular League football for the first time, his first 70 appearances for the Biscuitmen being made consecutively. Initially in reserve at Meadow Lane – he played in only three matches in the 1970-71 season – he then dislodged Barry Watling and missed only three matches himself in 1971-72. In his second season as first choice, Roy's part in the club's promotion to Division Two was rewarded by the supporters' award as 'Player of the Year.' The bearded, athletic shot-stopper conceded only 125 goals in his 133 matches for the Magpies, and was undefeated in 41of them, figures that place him alongside the very best to have represented the club throughout its long history.

Appearances: FL: 113 apps 0 gls FAC: 9 apps 0 gls FLC: 10 apps 0 gls Other: 1 app 0 gls Total: 133 apps 0 gls

––––––––––––––––––––○––––––––––––––––––––

BROWN, William

Goalkeeper
b. Nottingham
CAREER: Notts. Rangers/Nottingham Forest Aug 1890(NOTTS loan Nov 1894)
Debut v Crewe Alexandra (h) 10.11.1894, won 5 – 1

Played both for and against the Magpies in season 1894-95. Borrowed from Forest for a mid-week fixture against Crewe Alexandra, he was back in Forest's goal for the United Counties League fixture in April of the same season. Brown was Forest's first goalkeeper in the Football League, having earlier helped them to the championship of the Football Alliance in season 1891-92. In November 1921 the 'Football Post' reported the sad news that the old goalkeeper was lying dangerously ill, suffering from neuritis and heart trouble. The lack of further bulletins in subsequent issues, however, hopefully indicated that he had made a recovery.

Appearances: FL: 1 app 0 gls Total: 1 app 0 gls

––––––––––––––––––––○––––––––––––––––––––

BRUCE, Daniel

Forward   5' 8"   11st 2lbs
b. Bonhill, Dunbartonshire 20th October 1868
d. Bonhill, Dunbartonshire, 6th February 1931
CAREER: Vale of Leven/Rangers circa 1891/NOTTS Oct 1892/Small Heath Nov 1895, fee £100/Vale of Leven Feb 1897/St Mirren Nov 1897/Vale of Leven Sept 1898
Debut v Bolton Wanderers (h) 6.10.1892, drawn 2 – 2

The 'Evening Post' gave a graphic insight into Dan Bruce's relaxed style in March 1894: "Whilst he does not always over-exert himself, he can be depended upon to make the best of all his opportunities, passing most judiciously and shooting splendidly at goal."

Six months later, at the start of a new season, he had obviously reported back over weight: "Bruce was the best forward, despite his aldermanic proportions, but this did not interfere with his play, except that he perspired profusely." In 1894-95 he underlined his versatility by appearing in successive matches as outside-left, right full-back and centre-forward. He responded to the latter change by scoring five goals against Burslem Port Vale in a 10 – 0 victory on 26th February 1895. A brother, Walter, played for St Mirren.

Appearances: FL: 89 apps 47 gls FAC: 9 apps 3 gls Other: 11 apps 2 gls Total: 109 apps 52 gls
Honours: Scotland International, 1 cap 1890. (Vale of Leven) Scottish Cup finalists 1890. (NOTTS) FA Cup winners 1894.

––––––––––––––––––––○––––––––––––––––––––

BRUNT, Geoffrey Reginald

Half-back or forward   5' 10" 11st 7lbs
b. Nottingham, 24th November 1926
d. Huntingdon, June 2000
CAREER: NOTTS pro Sept 1949 to June 1957/Heanor Town.
Debut v Crystal Palace (h) 14.1.50, lost 0 – 1.

A strong and forceful wing-half, good in both defence and attack, Geoff Brunt actually began as a centre-forward and made his League debut as attack leader in the 1949-50 season. His unenviable task was to deputise for the injured Tommy Lawton, and the 'Football Post' commented: "Brunt showed some nice touches, but his display brought to light the great margin there is between Midland League and Third Division football." His thirty senior appearances spanned five seasons, 1951-52 being his best with eleven Division Two appearances and one FA Cup match. A part-time professional, Geoff was a policeman who worked in the forensic department of the Nottingham City force.

Appearances: 29 apps 1 gl FAC: 1 app 0 gl
Total: 30 apps 1 gl

––––––––––––––––––––○––––––––––––––––––––

BULCH, Robert Stephen 'Bob'

Right-half   5' 11"   11st 6lbs
b. Washington, 1st January 1933
CAREER: Washington/NOTTS am Oct 1952, pro Mar 1953/Darlington June 1958, fee £650/Hartlepools United circa 1960 (But did not play at FL level)
Debut v Port Vale (h) 10.9.55, drawn 0 – 0

Although nominally a wing half-back, Bob Bulch gained useful experience as attack leader in the Midland League and Central Alliance sides. In January 1956 he became the fifth player tried at centre-forward that season, and despite scoring at Port Vale in a 1 – 3 defeat he was not persevered with. His best run of senior action coming in the following term, when he was at right-half for 17 consecutive matches in the second half of the season. In the relegation campaign that followed he lost his place after just four early season matches. He was transferred to Darlington, who were making their debut as a Division Four side following their 20th place finish in the final Division Three North season. In two seasons at the Feethams he played in 51 League and Cup matches, scoring one goal.

Appearances: FL: 27 apps 1 gl Total: 27 apps 1 gl

BULL, Walter

Outside-left, later half-back   5' 7"   12st 8lbs
b. Nottingham, 19th December 1874
d. Nottingham, 28th July 1952
CAREER: Nuncargate/Newstead Byron/St Andrew's, Nottingham/NOTTS April 1894/Tottenham Hotspur May 1904, fee £300/Heanor United June 1910/Esquima, Buenos Aires, Argentina, coach Apr 1911/Northampton Town manager July 1912 to 1913.
Debut v Woolwich Arsenal (a) 3.11.1894, lost 1 – 2

Walter Bull super-seded David Calderhead as the Magpies captain. A deservedly popular player, gifted with great staying capacity and a remarkable talent that saw him equally successful in all parts of the field. Although beginning as an outside-left he subsequently filled every outfield position with great credit. Powerful of build and fearless in action, he was particularly successful in scoring with his head from corner kicks. In May 1904, along with Alex Glen, he was transferred to Tottenham Hotspur. Protracted wrangling over his transfer fee was finally ended by the Football Association, who ordered Spurs to pay £300. After totalling 183 appearances and 15 goals in all competitions for the Spurs he had a brief non-League spell with Heanor Town before accepting a coaching appointment in Buenos Aires.

Appearances: FL: 282 apps 53 gls FAC: 18 apps 5 gls
Other: 6 apps 0 gls Total; 306 apps 58 gls
Honours: FL Representative, 1 app. (NOTTS) FL Div 2 champions 1897

BURDITT, Frederick Charles Kendall 'Ken'

Inside-forward 5' 10½"   11st 3lbs
b. Ibstock, Leics. 12th November 1906
d. Ibstock, Leics. 27th October 1977
CAREER: Ibstock Penistone Rovers/Gresley Rovers trial 1928-29/Bloxwich Strollers 1929-30/Gresley Rovers Aug 1930/Norwich City Nov 1930/Millwall Aug 1936, fee £1,500/NOTTS Jan 1938, fee £1,575/Colchester United May 1939 (WW2 guest Norwich City, Leicester City & Tottenham Hotspur)/Ibstock Penistone Rovers player-manager post war until 1959
Debut v Reading (h) 29.1.38, won 2 – 1

The Magpies invested a sizeable fee to secure the services of Ken Burditt, who had scored 24 League and Cup goals for Millwall in season 1936-37 when the Lions run in the FA Cup took them to a semi-final clash with Sunderland, the eventual winners of the trophy. He had scored six goals in 13 matches at the time of his transfer to Meadow Lane, but he did not live up to expectations, the 'Football Post' ruefully pointing out: "He has not scored a single goal since he arrived." All of which was in direct contrast to his earlier experiences with Norwich City (61 goals in 173 matches) and Millwall (34 goals in 69 matches.) Ken's younger brother, George, scored 10 goals in 20 matches for Forest between 1934-36.

Appearances: FL: 20 apps 0 gls Other: 1 app 0 gls
Total: 21 apps 0 gls
Honours: (Norwich City) FL Div 3 South champions 1934.
(Millwall) FL Division Three South champions 1938.

BURGON, Frederick Archie

Winger 5' 10½"   11st 4lbs
b. Nottingham, 28th March 1912
d. Nocton, Lincs. 20th September 1994
CAREER: West Bridgford Secondary School/Colwick F.C./Burton Joyce F.C./Grantham (trials with NOTTS and Nottingham Forest)/Newark Town Nov 1931/NOTTS June 1932/Grantham Town Aug 1934/Tottenham Hotspur Jan 1935, fee £700/Wrexham Oct 1935/Carlisle United July 1939, fee £150
Debut v Bury (h) 6.10.32, drawn 2 – 2

Five months after his debut at outside-left Archie Burgon was tried at centre-forward against Charlton Athletic. He scored in the 51st and 57th minutes of the match and was unfortunate to miss a hat-trick, having a goal disallowed a few minutes from time. The 'Football Post' commented: "He is not an ideal leader, but he showed no fear and was a constant worry to the opposing defenders." He ended his first season at Meadow Lane with figures of four League matches and three goals. He did not get another run as centre-forward, his 22 League appearances in 1933-34 being split between the extreme wing positions, 15 at outside-left and seven at outside-right.

Tottenham Hotspur paid £700 for him in January 1935 but he played in only four matches before joining Wrexham on a free transfer. In four seasons at the Racecourse he played in 147 League and Cup matches and scored 39 goals. A final move to Carlisle United was abruptly curtailed by the outbreak of war. He served as a fitter in the RAF and entered the licensed trade after the war. During his Meadow Lane spell, his elder brother Hector was an outside-right in the Magpies' Reserve team.

Appearances: FL: 26 apps 7 gls FAC: 1 app 0 gls
Total: 27 apps 7 gls

BURKE, James

Inside-left   5' 6½" 11st 6lbs
b. Scotland circa 1870
CAREER: Cowlairs/Third Lanark/NOTTS June 1892/ Grantham Rovers Aug 1893/Lincoln City May 1894/ Grantham Rovers Jan 1897/Ilkeston Town June 1897 to 1901.
Debut v West Bromwich Albion (a) 29.10.1892, lost 2 – 4 (scored one)

Jimmy Burke, a small but strongly built wingman, played in exactly half of the Magpies Division One matches in 1892-93. After an initial run of three matches – in which he scored two goals – he was rather surprisingly out of favour for several weeks. Returning on New Year's Eve 1892 he then retained his place until the end of the season. In the wake of the Magpies first relegation he was released, but returned to League action with Lincoln City after a season with Grantham Rovers. With the Imps he appeared in 52 matches and scored seven goals, acquitting himself equally well as either inside-forward or half-back.

Appearances: FL: 15 apps 4 gls FAC: 2 apps 1 gl Other: 1 app 0 gls Total: 18 apps 5 gls

---

BURKE, Steven James

Winger 5' 10" 10st 6lbs
b. Nottingham, 29th September 1960
CAREER: Nottingham Forest app, signing pro Mar 1978/ Queens Park Rangers Sept 1979, fee £125,000 (Millwall loan Oct 1983) (NOTTS loan Oct 1984) (Lincoln City loan Aug 1985) (Brentford loan Mar 1986)/Doncaster Rovers Aug 1986 (Stockport County loan Sept - Oct 1987)/Shepshed Charterhouse Aug 1988/Grantham Town Nov - Dec 1988.
Debut v Oldham Athletic (a) 27.10.84, lost 2 – 3

A speedy, locally born wingman who made his Forest debut in an Anglo Scottish Cup semi-final against Ayr United on 20th October 1976. He was just turned sixteen, and still at school. He left Nottingham, unable to dislodge John Robertson at outside-left, and it was from his next club, Q.P.R., that Notts took him on loan. He was the first signing by Jimmy Sirrel – acting at the time as caretaker following the resignation of Larry Lloyd – after Sirrel had seen him help Q.P.R. to a 6 – 2 victory over Partizan Belgrade. Considering the then sizeable fee paid for Steve, who had played only once for Forest, he failed to fulfil the rich potential of his teenage years, appearing in just 67 FL matches during his seven years at Loftus Road.

Appearances: FL: 4(1) apps 0 gls FLC: 2 apps 0 gls
Total: 6(1) apps 0 gls
Honours: England Youth International 1978-79

BURNS, James 'Henry'

Inside-right   5' 9"   11st 4lbs
b. Liverpool, 20th June 1865
d. Hampstead, London 11th September 1957
CAREER: Liverpool & District Schoolboys/Lancashire Schoolboys/Essex Schoolboys/London Caledonians/West Bromwich Albion am Dec 1889, pro Oct 1890/NOTTS Nov 1891/South Weald.
Debut v Aston Villa (a) 7.11.1891, lost 1 – 5

According to the 1901 Census Henry Burns was living in Marylebone and his occupation was stated to be a professional cricketer. He had first played in non-first-class matches for Lancashire between 1884-86, before joining up with Essex in 1887. His first-class debut was for the MCC in 1890, and his final first-class match was for the same club in 1901. A right-handed opening bat, he had a highest score of 114, and as a slow left-arm bowler his best performance was 6 for 41. He was rather less successful as a footballer, scoring five goals in 17 appearances for West Bromwich Albion in addition to his solitary outing with the Magpies.

Appearances: FL: 1 app 0 gls Total: 1 app 0 gls

BURNS, Kenneth

Central defender   5' 10½"   11st 0lbs
b. Glasgow, 23rd September 1953
CAREER: Glasgow Rangers on schoolboy forms/Birmingham City app June 1970, pro July 1971/Nottingham Forest July 1977, fee £150,000/Leeds United Oct 1981, fee £400,000 (Derby County loan Mar 1983 and again Feb 1984)/Derby County Mar 1984 (NOTTS loan Feb 1985)/Barnsley nc Aug 1985/I.F. Elfsborg, Sweden, Mar 1986/Sutton Town Aug 1986, player-manager Mar 1987/Stafford Rangers July 1987/ Grantham Town Oct 1988/Gainsborough Trinity 1989/ Ilkeston Town player-coach July 1989/Oakham United/ Telford United assistant-manager July 1993.
Debut v Grimsby Town (a) 23.2.85, lost 0 – 2

In six years as a Birmingham City professional, fair-haired Kenny Burns proved himself an accomplished striker, scoring 53 League and Cup goals. He had scored 20 in 39 matches in 1976-77 when Forest's manager Brian Clough paid £150,000 for him. Eyebrows were raised when he was surprisingly fielded in a central defensive role alongside Larry Lloyd. Justification, in full measure, came in the shape of the 'Footballer of the Year' award, after a magnificent season for the player and the team who scooped the League championship and the FL Cup. Consecutive European Cup winners' medals and a Super Cup trophy followed, while twelve of his Scotland caps were awarded during his spell at the City Ground. Kenny's appearances in League matches for Birmingham and Forest totalled exactly 300 plus seven as substitute, but only two of his aggregate career total of 411(13) League appearances were made in the Magpies colours. He might have increased the figure by one, had he not missed what should have been his debut v Middlesbrough. Heavy overnight snow blocked him into his Derbyshire home and he was unable to link up with the team coach!

Appearances: FL: 2 apps 0 gls Total: 2 apps 0 gls
Honours: Scotland International, 20 caps 1974-81. Scotland U-23 International, 2 apps. Scotland Youth International. (Nottingham Forest) European Cup winners 1979, 1980. FL Div 1 champions 1978.FL Cup winners 1978, finalists 1980.

BURROWS, William

Goalkeeper
CAREER: NOTTS 1893-94/Notts Olympic Sept 1895 to cs 1896
Debut v Middlesbrough Ironopolis (a) 16.12.1893, drawn 0 – 0

Reserve goalkeeper in the season notable for the Magpies FA Cup final victory against Bolton Wanderers. A third place finish in Division Two in the same season qualified them for the end-of-season Test match but this ended in disappointment, Preston North End winning 4 – 0 to retain their top flight status. Senior custodian George Toone played in all League and Cup matches bar one during the season, missing the trip to Middlesbrough Ironopolis. It was an unfamiliar Magpies line-up that travelled north to oppose the 'Iron.' In addition to Burrows, two other reserve team players, King and F. Wilkinson, were last-minute selections. Although ineffective in attack, a solid defensive performance earned a share of the points and a 'clean sheet' for the debutant goalkeeper.

Appearances: FL: 1 app 0 gls Total: 1 app 0 gls

BURTON, Frank Ernest

Inside-right
b. Nottingham, 18th March 1865
d. Bingham, Notts., 10th February 1948
CAREER: Nottingham High School/NOTTS Oct 1886-Oct 1887/Nottingham Forest Nov 1887-Nov 1891
Debut v Basford Rovers FAC1 (h) 30.10.1886, won 13 – 0 (scored five)

It is extremely doubtful that any Notts player, before or since, can have enjoyed a more successful senior debut than Frank Burton whose first FA Cup match for the Magpies featured five goals each for himself and Harry Daft in the 13 – 0 demolition of Basford Rovers. Surprisingly enough the 13 – 0 score line had been exceeded in the previous season when Rotherham Town were the hapless victims in round one of the FA Cup. The 15 – 0 result remains Notts record win in the FA Cup competition. Frank Burton was capped by England in the 1889 match against Ireland when a Forest player. Outside of the game he was managing director and later chairman of Joseph Burton & Sons Ltd, the grocery chain founded by his father.

Appearances: FAC: 3 apps 7 gls Total: 3 apps 7 gls
Honours: England International, 1 cap 1889

BUSBY, Martyn George

Midfield   6' 2"   12st 3lbs
b. Slough, 24th March 1953
CAREER: Queens Park Rangers app, signing pro July 1970 (Portsmouth loan Feb 1976)/NOTTS Oct 1976, fee £35,000/Queens Park Rangers Sept 1977 (Burnley loan Feb-Mar 1980), retired 1981/Beaconsfield manager.
Debut v Hereford United (a) 23.10.76, won 4 – 1 (scored one)

An International Tournament winner with England Youth in Czechoslovakia in May 1971, he went on to win promotion to Division One with Q.P.R. in 1972-73 and in two separate spells with the Loftus Road club totalled 128(17) League apps and scored 17 goals. He spent slightly less than a year at Meadow Lane, scoring on his debut and lifting the side after a faltering start to the campaign, memorable for the 2 – 1 victory against Forest at the City Ground in March 1977. Incidentally, the return fixture at Meadow Lane attracted a crowd of 32,518 to witness the 1 – 1 draw, the combined attendance figure for the two fixtures amounting to 63,522. Within a month of the start of the new season, Martyn returned homewards for his second spell with Q.P.R. In the following season they were relegated from the top flight, despite his finishing a joint leading scorer for the season with six goals in 29(6) League matches.

Appearances: FL: 37 apps 4 gls FAC: 1 app 0 gls FLC: 1 app 0 gls Other: 5 apps 0 gls Total: 44 apps 4 gls
Honours: England Youth International, 6 apps 1970-71

BUTLER, John Herbert

Right-back   6' 1"   12st 3lbs
b. Birmingham, 10th March 1937
CAREER: Bestwood Colliery/NOTTS Oct 1957/Chester
May 1962 to 1968
Debut v Norwich City (a) 22.11.58, drawn 3 – 3

Elder brother of Peter Leslie Butler (q.v.), John Butler began as an amateur centre-half with Bestwood Colliery and was often selected to represent Notts. F.A. He was offered terms by Torquay United in September 1957 but declined, joining the Magpies a few weeks later. A cool and polished defender who kicked accurately and tackled well, he made an impressive debut in League football at centre-half, later taking over at right-back following John Kilford's transfer to Leeds United. An injury sustained at Easter brought to an end his first season with 15 senior matches to his name. Along with goalkeeper George Smith, he was the only ever-present in the following season when promotion from Division Four was secured. Having recorded in excess of 100 League outings for the Magpies, he joined Chester where he completed 220(2) League matches in a six-year stay.

Appearances: FL: 109 apps 0 gls FAC: 3 apps 0 gls FLC: 3 apps 0 gls Total: 115 apps 0 gls

———————O———————

BUTLER, Peter James F

Role: Midfield   5' 9"   11st 2lbs
b. Halifax, 27th August 1966
CAREER: Huddersfield Town app July 1982, pro Aug 1984 (Cambridge United loan Jan 1986)/Bury July 1986/Cambridge United Dec 1986/Southend United Feb 1988 (Huddersfield Town loan Mar 1992)/West Ham United Aug 1992/NOTTS Oct 1994, fee £350,000 (Grimsby Town loan Jan 1996) (West Bromwich Albion loan Mar 1996/West Bromwich Albion Aug 1996, fee £175,000/Halifax Town player & assistant-manager Aug 1998 to Apr 2001/Sorrento, Western Australia, player-coach/Sabhar Rhinos, Malaysia, head coach May 2003.
Debut v Watford (a) 15.10.94, lost 1 – 3

A midfield anchor man with good tackling and distribution whose progress at Meadow Lane suffered a severe set back when he was stretchered off the field with a leg injury in the semi-final of the Anglo-Italian Cup against Stoke City. Although he recovered in time to resume in three matches during April, he did not feature again, loan spells to Grimsby Town and West Bromwich Albion being his only involvement in 1995-96. Peter assisted eight different League clubs, serving two separate spells with Huddersfield Town and Cambridge United. He totalled 365(22) League appearances and scored 22 goals.

Appearances: FL: 20 apps 0 gls FAC: 2 apps 0 gls FLC: 2 apps 0 gls Other: 3 apps 0 gls Total: 27 apps 0 gls

BUTLER, Peter Leslie

Goalkeeper   5' 11"   12st 2lbs
b. Nottingham, 3rd October 1942
CAREER: South Notts. Schoolboys/Bestwood Youth Club/ NOTTS Nov 1960/Bradford City Aug 1966, retired cs 1967.
Debut v Port Vale (a) 25.9.61, lost 0 – 1

Peter Butler was first noted in the Bestwood area and invited to Meadow Lane for a trial. He quickly established himself as second choice to the long serving and consistent George Smith. He proved a loyal and capable deputy for the best part of six years of which 1961-62 (15 matches) and 1963-64 (22 matches) were his best in terms of senior action. Before hanging up his gloves, Peter played in 17 matches for Bradford City in season 1966-67. Hailing from a footballing family, Peter's father Herbert 'Dick' Butler was a centre-half who played for Birmingham between 1933-39. Peter's elder brother, John Herbert (q.v.) was the Magpies' popular right-back between 1957-62. A cousin Terry Butler, played for Kimberley Town and Bulwell Forest Villa in the 1960s.

Appearances: FL: 44 apps 0 gls FAC: 1 app 0 gls FLC: 3 apps 0 gls Total: 48 apps 0 gls

———————O———————

BUTLIN, Barry Desmond

Forward   5' 11½"   11st 7lbs
b. Rosliston, Derbyshire 9th November 1949
CAREER: Derby County pro Jan 1967 (NOTTS loan Jan to Oct 1969)/Luton Town Nov 1972, fee £50,000/Nottingham Forest Oct 1974, fee £122,000 (Brighton & Hove Albion loan Sept 1975) (Reading loan Jan 1977)/Peterborough United Aug 1977, fee £20,000/Sheffield United Aug 1979
Debut v Peterborough United (h) 25.1.69, won 2 – 1 (scored one)

Although Barry Butlin began with Derby County, much of his early experience of League football came during an extended loan spell at Meadow Lane. There was the possibility of an extension, but when the Magpies were given first option to take him on a permanent basis they were unable to match the £50,000 fee offered by Luton Town. In season 1973-74 he topped the Hatters scoring charts with 17 when they finished as runners-up in Division Two. His record with Forest, 17 League goals in 71(3) matches, included 3 goals in 10(3) matches in his last season at the City Ground when promotion from Division Two was secured. In a career spanning eight different League clubs his aggregate figures were 284(8) League appearances and 81 goals.

Appearances: FL: 29(1) apps 13 gls FLC: 1 app 0 gls Total: 30(1) apps 13 gls

———————O———————

BUXTON, Ian Raymond

Inside-forward 5' 10" 12st 7lbs
b. Cromford, Derbyshire 17th April 1938
CAREER: Cromford Junior School/Anthony Gells Grammar School, Wirksworth/Matlock Town Jan 1958/Derby County Mar 1959/Luton Town Sept 1967/NOTTS July 1969/Port Vale Dec 1969, fee £500/Ilkeston Town July 1970.
Debut as sub v Exeter City (h) 20.9.69, won 4 – 0

A man of many talents, both on and off the field, Ian Buxton reached top level in both cricket and football and held a responsible post in the mechanical engineering industry. Additionally, he was an advanced M.C.C. cricket coach and held the F.A. coaching badge. His football career spanned 210(5) League appearances and 62 goals and in County cricket for Derbyshire he scored 11,803 runs and took 483 wickets, captaining the county from 1970-72. In a brief stay at Meadow Lane he failed to disturb the regular inside trio of Barker, Bradd and Masson. A mid season transfer to Port Vale proved more rewarding as he appeared in most matches until the end of the season, assisting the Valiants to promotion from Division Four.

Appearances: FL: 4(1) apps 1 gl FAC: 0(1) apps 0 gls
Total: 4(2) apps 1 gl
Honours: (Luton Town) FL Div 4 champions 1968

CALDERHEAD, David

Centre-half 5' 10" 11st 8lbs
b. Glasgow, 19th June 1864
d. Fulham, 9th January 1938
CAREER: Wishaw Swifts/Wishaw Thistle/Queen of the South Wanderers, Dumfries 1881/NOTTS Aug 1889/Lincoln City secretary-manager Nov 1900 to May 1907/Chelsea secretary-manager May 1907 to May 1933
Debut v Aston Villa (a) 14.9.1889, drawn 1 – 1

A commanding half-back whose coolness under pressure was coupled with an ability to get through his work with less exertion than the majority of defenders. As one old international commented in 1897: "He plays with his head." At the heart of all of the Magpies early successes, he marshalled his defence superbly.

He also took most of the teams' free kicks, which he was able to place with great accuracy. He qualified for two benefit matches, against Sheffield Wednesday in December 1895 and Tottenham Hotspur in September 1900. He was elected to the Players' Union Management Committee in December 1898 and took his first step into management with Lincoln City two years later. He retired at the age of 69 having managed Chelsea for 26 years, during which time he was responsible for the signing of such stars as Hughie Gallacher and Alex Jackson. Amongst all his distinctions as a player and later manager, his award of the Football League's Long Service medal in May 1922 was unique, as he was the first ex-professional footballer to be so honoured.

Appearances: FL: 278 apps 12 gls FAC: 28 apps 0 gls
Other: 15 apps 0 gls Total: 321 apps 12 gls
Honours: Scotland International, 1 cap 1889. FL Representative, 1 app (This was the first-ever FL fixture versus the Football Alliance at Olive Grove, Sheffield, on 20th April 1891.) (NOTTS) FL Div 2 champions 1897, FA Cup winners 1894, finalists 1891.

CALDERWOOD, Colin

Full-back 6' 0" 12st 12lbs
b. Glasgow, 20th January 1965
CAREER: Inverness Caledonian Thistle/Mansfield Town app 1981, pro Mar 1982/Swindon Town July 1985, fee £30,000/Tottenham Hotspur July 1993, fee £1.25m/Aston Villa Mar 1999, fee £225,000/Nottingham Forest Mar 2000 (NOTTS loan Mar 2001)/Retired May 2001/Northampton Town manager Oct 2003.
Debut v Bury (a) 17.3.2001, drawn 1 – 1

An outstanding career that eventually amounted to a figure in excess of 600 League matches began in the humble enough surroundings of Field Mill, Mansfield. Colin Calderwood joined the Stags at 16, and had appeared in exactly 100 League matches when transferred to Swindon Town. Eight years, and 330 League matches later, he was transferred to the Spurs and a 'sell-on' clause in his earlier transfer to Swindon Town netted the Stags a record incoming fee of £655,000. During his spell at White Hart Lane Colin won the first of his Scotland caps, his international debut against Russia in Moscow being made at the relatively advanced age of 30. The final five of his 612(2) League appearances were made in the Magpies' colours, after he had lost his place with Forest after suffering a broken leg in late season 1999-2000.

Appearances: FL: 5 apps 0 gls Total: 5 apps 0 gls
Honours: Scotland International, 36 caps 1995-99. (Swindon Town) FL Div 4 champions 1986

CALE, Fred

Inside-left
b. Hucknall Torkard, Notts. October quarter 1875
d. Nottingham, 6th July 1950
CAREER: Hucknall St John's Apr 1895/NOTTS May 1895/
Red Hill United Feb 1897
Debut v Newton Heath (h) 23.11.1895, lost 0 – 2

Fred Cale, a local hosiery trimmer, was called upon for first team duty just once. His debut came in the wake of Scottish international Dan Bruce's transfer to Small Heath, and in the home fixture against Newton Heath, County sustained their third consecutive defeat at Trent Bridge. The subsequent introduction of another local, J.F.Kiddier, proved more successful, although the tenth place finish in Division Two constituted Notts worst season since FL entry in season 1888-89.

Appearances: FL: 1 app 0 gls Total: 1 app 0 gls

———————o———————

CALLADINE, Charles Frederick

Outside-right
b. Wessington, Derbyshire, April quarter 1888
CAREER: Notts. Olympic/NOTTS am Nov 1907, pro May 1908.
Debut v Bolton Wanderers (h) 28.12.07, lost 0 – 1

Although awarded a professional contract at the close of his first season, Charlie Calladine's stint with the Magpies was largely spent as an understudy. His son, also Charles Frederick, appeared in inter-war football with Birmingham (115 League matches) and Blackburn Rovers (48 League matches).

Appearances: FL: 3 apps 0 gls Total: 3 apps 0 gls

———————o———————

CAMPBELL, David Anthony

Midfield   5' 9"   10st 9lbs
b. Eglinton, Northern Ireland, 2nd June 1965
CAREER: Oxford Boys' Club (Northern Ireland)/Nottingham Forest app, signing pro June 1983 (NOTTS loan Feb to May 1987)/Charlton Athletic Oct 1987, fee £75,000 (Plymouth Argyle loan Mar 1989)/Bradford City Mar 1989, fee £75,000 (Derry City loan Dec 1990) (Shamrock Rovers loan Jan 1991)/Shamrock Rovers Aug 1991/Rotherham United nc Nov 1992/West Bromwich Albion nc Feb 1993/Burnley Mar 1993 (Lincoln City loan Feb 1994) (Portadown loan Mar 1994)/Wigan Athletic nc Aug 1994/Cambridge United nc Jan 1995
Debut v Fulham (a) 14.2.87, lost 1 – 3

David Campbell won his first international cap at the close of 1985-86, the season in which he had made his debut in Division One. This was swiftly followed by a second cap, during the World Cup in Mexico, playing against Brazil in Guadalajara.

He won seven caps during his time at the City Ground, but had lost his first team place to Gary Mills at the time of his loan move to County. He missed only two of the final 20 League matches in his extended loan period at Meadow Lane in a season when the side narrowly missed a place in the Division Three Play-offs. David won a further three caps during his spell with Charlton Athletic, but his subsequent career was blighted by injuries and was finally terminated when he suffered a broken leg in his very first outing with Cambridge United.

Appearances: FL: 18 apps 2 gls Total: 18 apps 2 gls
Honours: N Ireland International, 10 caps 1986-88

———————o———————

CANTRELL, James

Centre-forward 5' 9½" 11st 8lbs
b. Sheepsbridge, near Chesterfield, 7th May 1882
d. Basford, Notts., 31st July 1960
CAREER: Chesterfield Schoolboys/Bulwell Red Rose/Bulwell White Star/Hucknall Constitutional/Aston Villa July 1904/NOTTS Mar 1908/Tottenham Hotspur Oct 1912, fee £1,500 (WW1 guest Leicester Fosse & NOTTS)/Sutton Town Oct 1923 to retirement in 1925
Debut v Sheffield United (h) 21.3.08, lost 0 – 3

A most dangerous centre-forward in front of goal, Jimmy Cantrell was the Magpies' leading goal scorer in three consecutive seasons between 1908-11. Fast on the ball and a clever dribbler, his deceptive body swerve enabled him to score many brilliant, individualistic goals. Probably as good as any centre-forward in the country in 1909-10, an untimely injury robbing him of his chance at international level. On October 12th 1912, he scored twice against Tottenham Hotspur at White Hart Lane when fog descended after 82 minutes with the Magpies leading 3 – 1. Later in the same week, the Spurs paid £1,500 for his transfer. He starred for the Spurs at either side of the Great War, in all matches scoring 95 goals in 194 matches. He became the oldest player to appear for the club in a Football League match, making his final appearance in April 1923 when a matter of weeks away from his 41st birthday. A sporting all-rounder and the champion golfer amongst footballers, Jimmy learned the art of the game on Bulwell Forest.

In later years a licensee at The Corner Pin in Nottingham, and from November 1935 steward to the Chilwell Manor Golf Club.

Appearances: FL: 131 apps 64 gls FAC: 5 apps 1 gl
Total: 136 apps 65 gls
Honours: (Tottenham Hotspur) FL Div 2 champions 1920. FA Cup winners 1921

――――――○――――――

CARGILL, James Gordon

Goalkeeper   5' 9"   11st 0lbs
b. Alyth, Dundee, 22nd September 1945
CAREER: Dundee Schoolboys/Nottingham Forest ground staff Oct 1961, pro Sept 1962/NOTTS July 1966 to Apr 1967.
Debut v Barrow (h) 10.9.66, drawn 2 – 2

Jimmy Cargill joined Forest from Scottish schools football. He was capped by Scotland Schools in 1961 and in 1963 represented Scotland in the International Youth Tournament at Wembley. He made his FL debut in October 1964 as deputy for Peter Grummitt and kept a good goal in the 3 – 0 win at Arsenal. A more than useful reserve, he was nevertheless unable to break Grummitt's monopoly of the position. At Meadow Lane for a season in Division Four he shared first team duties with George Smith and Mike Rose. He was released from his contract in April 1967, having taken up employment, outside of the game, in Nottingham.

Appearances: FL: 10 apps 0 gls Total: 10 apps 0 gls
Honours: Scotland Schoolboy International, 4 caps 1961. Scotland Youth International, 1app.

――――――○――――――

CARLIN, William 'Willie'

Midfield   5' 6"   9st 7lbs
b. Liverpool South, 6th October 1940
CAREER: Liverpool Schoolboys/Liverpool am, signing pro May 1958/Halifax Town Aug 1962, fee £1,500/Carlisle United Oct 1964, fee £10,000/Sheffield United Nov 1967, fee £40,000/Derby County Aug 1968, fee £63,000/Leicester City Oct 1970, fee £35,000/NOTTS Sept 1971, fee £18,000/Cardiff City Nov 1973, retired May 1974
Debut v Shrewsbury Town (h) 11.9.71, won 1 – 0

The sort of player for whom the well-worn cliché "midfield dynamo" might well have been invented. Aside from Liverpool, whose management considered him too small, he was a regular with all of his subsequent clubs, collecting three championship medals and commanding some hefty fees. Effective in both attack and defence, Willie's career figures were 423(4) League appearances and 75 goals. He enjoyed two good seasons with the Magpies, culminating in promotion from Division Three in his final season. On retiring he ran a newsagent's shop in Derby and later owned a bar in Majorca.

Appearances: FL: 56(3) apps 2 gls FAC: 6 apps 1 gl FLC: 2 apps 0 gls Total: 64(3) apps 3 gls
Honours: England Schoolboy International, 5 caps 1956.England Youth International, 3 apps 1957-59. (Carlisle United) FL Div 3 champions 1965.(Derby County) FL Div 2 champions 1969.(Leicester City) FL Div 2 champions 1971.

――――――○――――――

CARTER, Alfred Burton

Inside-forward
b. Basford, Notts. October quarter 1877
d. Worksop, Notts. 17th April 1951
CAREER: Newstead Byron/NOTTS Feb 1897/Kettering Town May 1899/Newstead Byron Feb 1901
Debut v Gainsborough Trinity (a) 6.3.1897, lost 2 – 3

Signed as cover for the inside-forward berths at the tail end of the Division Two promotion season 1896-97, and immediately drafted into the first team after scoring twice on his reserve team debut. Although described as "Very young and very light and fragile," he successfully took the step up into Division One with 18 appearances in 1897-98. A consistent little player who knew how and when to pass the ball, he was a maker of opportunities rather than a scorer himself. Unfortunate to be injured in a reserve team match in the early part of season 1898-99, he was subsequently restricted to just a single first team outing. He left for Kettering Town shortly after appearing for a 'Rest of the League Xl' versus Forest Reserves (champions of the Notts. League) at Sutton on 15th April 1898.

Appearances: FL: 20 apps 5 gls FAC: 1 app 0 gls
Total: 21 apps 5 gls

――――――○――――――

CARTER, Stephen Charles

Winger   5' 8"   10st 10lbs
b. Great Yarmouth, 23rd April 1953
CAREER: Norfolk Schoolboys/Manchester City app July 1968, pro Aug 1970/NOTTS Feb 1972, fee £18,000/Derby County Aug 1978, in exchange for Don Masson/NOTTS nc Sept 1981/AFC Bournemouth Mar 1982/Torquay United June 1984
Debut v Oldham Athletic (a) 12.2.72, won 1 – 0

In the month of his eighteenth birthday, Steve Carter made his debut for Manchester City at Newcastle, and scored his first League goal against Liverpool at Maine Road. He joined the Magpies in the late stages of the following season, and the small but skilful wingman quickly became a favourite with the Meadow Lane faithful. Notts won promotion in his first full season and consolidated their Division Two status with a period in the mid-1970s when they were genuine contenders for a further upward move.

It was not until Steve reached Bournemouth, however, that he featured in another promotion campaign, his 16 late-season appearances in 1981-82 assisting the Cherries to a fourth place finish and promotion from Division Four. His final career figures were 266(23) League appearances and 26 goals.

At the age of 17 Gerry Carver was playing in the Birmingham League with Boldmere St. Michael's and had received approaches from Aston Villa and Bolton Wanderers in addition to the Magpies' overtures. Happily, he decided to accept Notts' offer, and ten years later had the honour of captaining the Magpies when they opposed the FA XI in May 1962, in a match arranged to celebrate Notts' centenary. A fierce tackler and excellent ball player, he began with Notts in Division Two, missing the Lawton years and the team's run of success. Nevertheless, his time was not without highlights, one particular memory being the fifth-round FA Cup game against Chelsea in 1954-55 when a terrific finish by Albert Broadbent clinched a 1 – 0 victory. In true Magpies style, however, they lost to York City in the next round when considered favourites to reach the semi-final. Gerry hung up his boots after thirteen seasons and three matches short of 300 appearances. He ran a hairdressing business in Radford, and also worked in a young offender's institution. In many respects his career mirrored that of Bert Loxley, both players joining in 1952 and, ten years later, being the longest-serving players with the club.

Appearances: FL: 172(16) apps 21 gls FAC: 9(1) apps 0 gls FLC: 10(3) apps 3 gls Other: 9(3) apps 2 gls Total: 200(23) apps 26 gls

Appearances: FL: 279(1) apps 10 gls FAC: 12 apps 0 gls FLC: 5 apps 0 gls Total: 296(1) apps 10 gls

---

CARTWRIGHT, Michael
Right-back   5' 7½" 9st 10lbs
b. Birmingham, 9th October 1946
CAREER: Coventry City pro Aug 1965/NOTTS June 1967 (Bradford City loan Nov 1967)/Rochdale – date unknown, did not app at FL level/Dover July 1969
Debut v Chester (h) 19.8.67, lost 1 – 2

Part of a dual signing from Coventry City, as Magpies team manager Billy Gray moved to strengthen his side for the upcoming season. Cartwright and Dennis Oakes came hard on the heels of Brian Rushton, signed two days earlier, from Birmingham City. Cartwright played in the opening fixture of 1967-68, but the remainder of his first team appearances commenced in March of the same season, Len Chalmers and Geoff Ball having shared the right-back position between them in the intervening period.

Appearances: FL: 15(1) apps 0 gls FLC: 1 app 0 gls Total: 16(1) apps 0 gls

---

CAS, Marcel
Winger/Midfield   6' 1"   12st 8lbs
b. Breda, Holland, 30th April 1972
CAREER: RBC Roosendaal (Holland)/NOTTS July 2001/Sheffield United Feb 2003/Grimsby Town July 2003/RBC Roosendaal (Holland) Jan 2004.
Debut v Port Vale (a) 11.8.2001, lost 2 – 4 (scored one)

Quickly dubbed 'The Flying Dutchman' on arrival at Meadow Lane, Marcel's speed off the mark and willingness to run at defenders made him a dangerous customer on the Magpies' right flank. In addition to his role as main supply line to the strikers, he had an eye for goal himself, being the first player on the score sheet in League matches in both 2001-02 and 2002-03. His stunning, long - range

CARVER, Gerald Francis 'Gerry'
Wing-half   5' 7"   10st 9lbs
b. Worcester, 27th June 1935
CAREER: Aston Boys/Boldmere St Michael's/NOTTS Aug 1952 to 1966
Debut v Oldham Athletic (a) 1.9.53, won 3 – 1

drive against Brighton at the Withdean Stadium in March 2002 was voted 'Goal of the Season' by supporters. Financial considerations had much to do with his departure from Meadow Lane, but he failed to settle subsequently. His sojourn with Sheffield United was followed by an acrimonious departure from Grimsby Town, just six months into a two-year contract.

Appearances: FL: 49(9) apps 8 gls FAC: 3 apps 0 gls FLC: 3 apps 0 gls Other: 3 apps 0 gls Total: 58(9) apps 8 gls

————————o————————

CASHMORE, Arthur
Forward   5' 9"   11st 9lbs
b. Birmingham, 30th October 1893
d. West Bromwich, January quarter 1969
CAREER: Sparkhill Avondale/Bromsgrove Rovers/ Stourbridge/Manchester United May 1913/Oldham Athletic May 1914, fee £50/Darlaston Sept 1919/Cardiff City Dec 1919/NOTTS Nov 1921, fee £1,500/Darlaston July 1922/ Nuneaton Town Apr 1923/Shrewsbury Town Nov 1923/ Darlaston trial Aug-Sept 1925.
Debut v Nottingham Forest (h) 5.11.21, drawn 1 – 1

In sharing memories of yesteryear in an issue of the 'Football Post' from November 1960, a Mr. Wright of Southwell recalled the signing of Arthur Cashmore from Cardiff City and how he took the field with bandages on both knees and some sticky plaster on his head! No doubt the 26,000 crowd must have had feelings of apprehension as the newcomer made his bow in the local 'derby' match against the Forest. In the event, Cashmore proved himself a dashing and persevering centre-forward with a hard shot in either foot. Earlier in his career he scored eight goals in 16 League appearances for Oldham Athletic, assisting them to finish as runners-up for the First Division championship in 1914-15. With Cardiff City after WW1 he played in their first-ever Football League match and in the same season (1920-21) scored 12 goals in 26 matches when runners-up position in Division Two was secured.

Appearances: FL: 14 apps 6 gls FAC: 4 apps 0 gls Total: 18 apps 6 gls

————————o————————

CASKEY, Darren Mark
Midfield   5' 8"   11st 9lbs
b. Basildon, Essex, 21st August 1974
CAREER: Tottenham Hotspur from the age of eleven; FA School of Excellence; Spurs associate schoolboy Dec 1988, trainee Aug 1990, pro Mar 1992 (Watford loan Oct 1995)/ Reading Feb 1996, fee £700,000/NOTTS July 2001/Bristol City nc Mar-June 2004/Peterborough United trial/ Hornchurch F.C. Aug 2004/Peterborough United nc Nov 2004; contract Dec 2004/ Bath City/American football
Debut v Port Vale (a) 11.8.2001, lost 2 – 4

An outstanding junior, Darren Caskey attended the FA School of Excellence, captained England U-18 to the European title alongside future full internationals including Sol Campbell, Nicky Butt, Gary Neville, Robbie Fowler and Paul Scholes. An assured first touch, vision and a wide range of passing skills from the right side of midfield earned him a Spurs debut, one week before his nineteenth birthday, against Arsenal in August 1993. Appearing in 16(9) Premier League matches and scoring four goals in his first season, he seemed assured of a glittering future at White Hart Lane. The fact that this did not transpire could in some part be attributed to the unsettling effect of Spurs managerial changes, but after a brief loan period at Watford he became Reading's record buy in February 1996. He enjoyed one outstanding season with the Royals, scoring 23 goals from midfield in 1999-2000. Darren's three years at Meadow Lane began quietly, but his skill on the ball, vision and range of passing soon became apparent. Although lacking pace and no great goal scorer, on his day his ability to make defence splitting passes effectively kept the Magpies' attack on the move.

Appearances: FL: 101(13) apps 10 gls FAC: 7 apps 0 gls FLC: 5 apps 0 gls Other: 2(2) apps 1 gl
Total: 115(15) apps 11 gls
Honours: England Schoolboy International. England Youth International.

————————o————————

CATLIN, Robert
Goalkeeper   6' 2"   14st 0lbs
b. Wembley, 22nd June 1965
CAREER: Marconi, Australia/Chelsea, three months trial 1988/NOTTS Aug 1992; released on free transfer May 1994 (Birmingham City loan Mar 1993)
Debut v Peterborough United (a) 29.8.92, won 3 – 1

Born at Wembley, Bob Catlin emigrated to Australia with his family at the age of four. His father was capped by England at schoolboy level and later played in a high standard of amateur soccer for Hendon. Bob won two championship medals with Marconi and played once for Australia in a friendly match. He was recommended to Meadow Lane officials by former Notts goalkeeper Graham Smith who, at that time, was in the Sports Management business. Afforded only a fleeting acquaintance with League action at Meadow Lane he found more opportunity during a loan spell with Birmingham City – 8 League appearances that included four "clean sheets."

Appearances: FL: 3 apps 0 gls FLC: 1 app 0 gls Other: 1 app 0 gls Total: 5 apps 0 gls

————————o————————

CHADBURN, John

Outside-right   5' 8"   11st 7lbs
b. Mansfield, February 1873
d. Mansfield, 31st December 1923
CAREER: Leicester Fosse Reserves/Mansfield Unitarians/
Mansfield Greenhalgh's Mar 1892/Lincoln City cs 1893/
NOTTS Aug 1894/Wolverhampton Wanderers Mar 1897/
West Bromwich Albion Jan 1900/Liverpool May 1903/
Plymouth Argyle Mar 1904 (Mansfield Mechanics Dec
1905)/Swindon Town 1906/Mansfield Town c 1907
Debut v Darwen (h) 15.9.1894, won 2 – 1 (scored one)

A versatile performer with a variety of experience,
Chadburn was equally at home in such diverse roles as
wingman or full-back. In terms of Football League
experience he appeared at senior level with five clubs,
scoring 27 goals in 131 matches. After two seasons as
first choice outside-right at Trent Bridge he lost his place
to Billy Langham in 1896-97, appearing in only four
matches (two goals) in the Second Division championship
season. Aside from football, he was listed as a 'shoe
finisher' in the 1901 Census.

Appearances: FL: 50 apps 15 gls FAC: 2 apps 0 gls
Total: 52 apps 15 gls

CHALMERS, James

Outside-left   5' 9"   12st 0lbs
b. Old Luce, Wigtownshire, 3rd December 1877
CAREER: Beith 1895/Morton July 1896/Sunderland May
1897/Preston North End Oct 1898/NOTTS June 1899/Beith
Sept 1900/Partick Thistle Oct 1900/Watford July 1901/
Tottenham Hotspur May 1902/Swindon Town May 1904/
Norwich City May 1906/Bristol Rovers May 1908/Clyde
Nov 1908/Beith until 1911
Debut v Derby County (a) 2.9.1899, won 1 – 0

Despite his prematurely greying hair, James Chalmers
was only a young man when he joined Notts. He had
already figured with Sunderland and Preston North End
and won a string of junior medals, including one for the
North Ayrshire Cup, won when a teenage member of the
Beith team. Formidably built for a wingman, on his day he
was an extremely difficult opponent to contain, but his
reviews with Notts were mixed. Following his departure,
the 'Football News' commented on reports in the Scottish
press which suggested that Chalmers, then with Partick
Thistle, was showing promise: "His passing is highly
spoken of, and it is predicted that he will prove a decided
acquisition." The 'Football News' correspondent seemed
less than impressed by the news, considering that "He
must have improved wonderfully since he left
Nottingham."

Appearances: FL: 25 apps 2 gls FAC: 3 apps 1 gl
Total: 28 apps 3 gls

CHALMERS, Leonard Austin

Right-back   5' 11½"   12st 7lbs
b. Corby, Northants, 4th September 1936
CAREER: Corby Town/Leicester City Jan 1956/NOTTS June
1966/Dunstable Town manager July 1968/Melita Tigers, New
South Wales, coach.
Debut v Bradford P.A. (a) 20.8.66, lost 1 – 4

Strong-tackling full-back and former military policeman
Len Chalmers appeared in exactly 200 League and Cup
matches for Leicester City. He began as a wing-half, making
his League debut in the final First Division fixture of season
1957-58 at Birmingham City. Leicester needed one point
to avoid relegation and they succeeded in getting two,
winning by the narrow margin of 1 – 0. Late in the following
season he succeeded Willie Cunningham at right-back, and
for the best part of four seasons held the position. He was
famously but unfortunately a victim of the so called
'Wembley hoodoo' in the 1961 FA Cup Final against
Spurs. Leicester were effectively reduced to ten men when
he was injured in a tackle after just 18 minutes play. He
bravely returned to the field for nuisance value at outside-
left, but a depleted side eventually conceded two late goals,
earning Spurs their historic 'double.' Appointed captain
when he joined Notts, he appeared in 35 League matches
in his first season, but in only 16 in 1967-68 after he had
switched to a part-time professional role, in order to
pursue business interests.

Appearances: FL: 51 apps 1 gl FAC: 1 app 0 gls FLC: 2
apps 0 gls Total: 54 apps 1 gl
Honours: (Leicester City) FA Cup finalists 1961. FL Cup
finalists 1965

CHALMERS, Thomas Kennedy

Centre-half   5' 9½"   12st 9lbs
b. Beith, Ayrshire, 1883
CAREER: Beith F.C./NOTTS Dec 1905/Ilkeston United
1909/Shirebrook F.C. 1911
Debut v Bury (a) 24.3.06, drawn 0 – 0

The local 'Football News' correspondent, commenting on
Chalmers' first home appearance against Middlesbrough,
considered him to be "An untiring worker, who gives
promise of still further improvement." On a more
cautionary note he observed that "Speed is not a strong
point." His home debut was in fact a severe examination
as he was directly opposed to an inside-forward trio of
Fred Wilcox, Alf Common (the first £1,000 footballer)
and Steve Bloomer (352 career goals in FL matches).
Chalmers was reported to have "stood the ordeal manfully"
and seemed set fair to succeed club captain Mainman in
the pivotal role. He was, however, overtaken by Arthur
Clamp and made only two senior appearances in his final
two seasons.

In 1911 he captained the newly formed Shirebrook F.C. in their first ever fixture and successfully led them to the championship of the Notts. & Derbyshire League in their first season.

Appearances: FL: 18 apps 1 gl FAC: 1 app 0 gls
Total: 19 apps 1 gl

CHALMERS, William 'Willie'

Inside-forward   5' 9½" 11st 2lbs
b. Bellshill, Lanarkshire, 25th July 1904
CAREER: Bellshill Academy School/Bellshill F.C./ Queen's Park 1922/Glasgow Rangers May 1924/Newcastle United Mar 1928, fee £2,500/Grimsby Town May 1931, fee £1,000/ Bury Apr 1932/NOTTS May 1936/Aldershot June 1938, becoming their trainer & assistant-manager during WW2/ Ebbw Vale manager June 1943/Juventus, Italy, manager 1947/ Bury assistant-trainer & youth coach Sept 1949.
Debut v Exeter City (h) 29.8.36, won 3 –1

Notts narrowly missed elevation from Division Three in 1936-37, finishing second to Luton Town when only the champions earned promotion. Willie Chalmers had an excellent first season, providing the perfect foil to leading scorer, and former Newcastle United colleague, Hughie Gallacher. A typical Scottish inside-forward with perfect ball control, vision and an exemplary work rate, Chalmers was a vocal footballer with an over-enthusiastic tendency to direct operations. A trait nonetheless that proved a distinct advantage in his successful career as coach/manager when his playing days ended.

Appearances: FL: 65 apps 17 gls FAC: 1 app 1 gl Other: 4 apps 0 gls Total: 70 apps 18 gls
Honours: Scotland Amateur International. (Queen's Park) Scottish League Div 2 champions 1923

CHANDLER, Arthur Clarence Hillier

Centre-forward 5' 8"   11st 10lbs
b. Paddington, London, 27th November 1895
d. Leicester, 18th June 1984
CAREER: West London Schoolboys/Handley Page/ Hampstead Town/Queens Park Rangers Sept 1920/Leicester City June 1923, fee £500/NOTTS June 1935/Leicester City training staff Nov 1936 Colts manager 1938-39 and employed in backroom staff until Sept 1969.
Debut v Bristol Rovers (a) 31.8.35, drawn 0 – 0

In the 1930s, Notts recruited a number of celebrated centre-forwards who were reaching the end of their respective careers. Arthur Chandler led the way for the later recruitment of Hughie Gallacher and Dixie Dean. Although billed as a 33 year-old "with much football still in him," he was in fact just five months short of his fortieth birthday when he joined the Magpies. Perhaps not surprisingly he hung up his boots during his spell at Meadow Lane, but

not before he had maintained his reputation as an ace marksman with eight goals in just 13 matches. Strangely enough, when he made his debut for Notts, he was opposed to two former Leicester City team mates, Adcock and Young, in the Bristol Rovers side. Arthur Chandler was the son of a former cycling champion, and was a player with a sunny disposition and a sturdy physique who broke all records during twelve playing seasons with Leicester City, racking up a total of 273 League and Cup goals in 429 matches. He famously scored six goals against Portsmouth in the Foxes' record 10 – 0 League victory on 20th October 1928. With such a record it was surprising that he failed to reach international level, despite appearing once for the North v the South and twice for The Rest v England. He also scored 33 goals in 16 games on the 1929 FA Tour of South Africa. Leicester City awarded him a testimonial match in 1961-62 that attracted a gate of over 13,000. A brother, Sidney Ellis Chandler, was a half-back with Aston Villa, Preston North End and Reading.

Appearances: FL: 10 apps 6 gls FAC: 2 apps 1 gl Other: 1 app 1 gl Total: 13 apps 8 gls
Honours: FL Representative, 1 app 1927. FA Xl Tour to South Africa 1929. (Leicester City) FL Div 2 champions 1925.

CHAPMAN, Gary Anthony

Midfield   5' 10" 12st 0lbs
b. Bradford, 1st May 1964
CAREER: Frickley Athletic/Bradford City Aug 1988 (NOTTS loan Sept-Oct 1989)/NOTTS Feb 1990, fee £15,000 (Mansfield Town loan Oct 1990)/Exeter City Sept 1991, fee £10,000/Torquay United Feb 1993/Darlington Aug 1993/Emley F.C. 1995.
Debut v Chester City (a) 15.9.89, drawn 3 – 3 (scored one)

Gary Chapman had played in only 2(3) League matches for Bradford City at the time of his initial loan to the Magpies. He promptly scored his first ever League goal on his debut at Chester City, and followed by scoring both of Notts' goals in the following week's 2 – 0 victory against Rotherham United. A third, vital goal, clinched a 1 – 0 victory over Tranmere Rovers in the final month of his loan spell. Signed on a permanent basis in the late stages of the same season, Gary was unable to reproduce the fireworks of his first spell, playing in only 3(6) matches as the side pushed on to the Play-offs and promotion at the expense of Tranmere Rovers in the Wembley Final. His final aggregate figures in League football amounted to 104(38) matches and 18 goals. More than half of which were made in the colours of his last League club, Darlington, his two-season record being 57(17) matches and nine goals.

Appearances: FL: 13(12) apps 4 gls Other: 2(1) apps 0 gls Total: 15(13) apps 4 gls

CHAPMAN, H.

Left-half
CAREER: NOTTS debut Feb1880 to final app Mar 1886
Debut v Derbyshire FAC 1 (h) 4.11.1880, drawn 4 – 4

An early group photograph from the 1883-84 season depicts Chapman as a young man, his hair worn with a centre parting, and the obligatory moustache, Harry Dixon being the only clean shaven member of the group. A stalwart member of the side in pre-League days, Chapman did not reach the same dizzy heights as the Cursham brothers, William Gunn and John Dixon, all of whom were capped by England. He did, however, spend five seasons as a regular and valued member of a team ranked amongst the best in the country, who twice reached the semi-final stage of the FA Cup competition in consecutive seasons, 1882-83 and 1883-84.

Appearances: FAC: 25 apps 1 gl Total: 25 apps 1 gl

CHAPMAN, Harry

Right-half   5' 8"   10st 10lbs
b. Liverpool, 4th March 1921
d. Nottingham, 28th August 1990
CAREER: Ellesmere Port Town/Aston Villa Feb 1947, fee £500/Notts Mar 1949/Gorleston F.C. cs 1951/Cambridge United/Blechley Town player coach Oct 1958
Debut v Millwall (h) 19.3.49, lost 1 – 3

Harry Chapman was wounded and taken prisoner of war at Arnhem while serving with the Airborne Division. A sporting all-rounder, he was a useful boxer, representing his regiment during Army service. On demobilisation he returned to his occupation as a plumber and applied for a trial with Ellesmere Port Town and was quickly signed on. Following a strong recommendation from their former England international, 'Pongo' Waring, Aston Villa invited Harry for trials and paid £250 for him in February 1947. They were so satisfied that in July 1948 they sent Ellesmere Port Town a further £250. Signed by the Magpies as Eddie Gannon's replacement, he immediately settled into his new surroundings. Skilful, thoughtful and constructive, he missed only three matches in the 1949-50 Third Division South championship season, but lost his place to Peter Robinson after starting in the first four matches of 1950-51. On leaving Meadow Lane he initially joined Gorleston, who were managed by a former Aston Villa team-mate 'Sailor' Brown.

Appearances: FL: 53 apps 1 gl FAC: 3 apps 0 gls
Total: 56 apps 1 gl
Honours: (NOTTS) FL Div 3 South champions 1950

CHAPMAN, Herbert

Inside-forward 5' 7"   12st 2lbs
b. Kiveton Park, Sheffield, 19th January 1878
d. Hendon, 6th January 1934
CAREER: Kiveton Park School/Kiveton Park F.C. May 1896/Ashton North End Aug 1896/Stalybridge Rovers July 1897/Rochdale Oct 1897/Grimsby Town May 1898/Swindon Town May 1899/Sheppey United Nov 1899/Worksop Oct 1900/Northampton Town July 1901/Sheffield United May 1902/NOTTS May 1903/Northampton Town May 1904/ Tottenham Hotspur Mar 1905, fee £70/Northampton Town player-manager Apr 1907/Leeds City manager May 1912/ Huddersfield Town secretary Sept 1920, assistant-manager Feb 1921, manager Mar 1921/Arsenal manager May 1925 to his death.
Debut v Liverpool (h) 1.10.03, won 4 – 2 (scored one)

Elder brother of Henry Chapman, the celebrated Sheffield Wednesday forward, who was considered the best uncapped inside-forward of his day and scorer of 102 League and Cup goals in 298 matches for the Wednesday. Herbert, by comparison, achieved little as a player but was recognised as one of the most successful managers of his era, steering Huddersfield Town and Arsenal to League Championship and FA Cup success. The brothers shared a great resemblance in appearance and build, Herbert's playing style was described in 1903 as being: "Characterised by great dash, aiming to get to goal by the shortest route and in the least possible time." Despite his many and varied football travels Herbert found the time and energy to study coal mining, and held a colliery manager's certificate under the Board of Trade.

Appearances: FL: 7 apps 1 gl Total: 7 apps 1 gl

CHAPMAN, Robert Dennis 'Sammy'

Central defender   5' 10"   11st 8lbs
b. Walsall, 18th August 1946
CAREER: Staffordshire junior football/Nottingham Forest am Mar 1962, pro Aug 1963/NOTTS Aug 1977, fee £7,500/ Shrewsbury Town July 1978/Tulsa Roughnecks USA Mar to Aug 1979/Burton Albion until Apr 1981/Keyworth United (there Jan 1985)/Selective Travel (there May 1985, when he helped them win the Notts. FA Thursday League Cup.)
Debut v Hull, ASC, (h) 6.8.77, won 1 – 0

Spotted by a Forest scout when playing in Staffordshire Youth football and, after trials at the City Ground, signed professional forms on his 17th birthday. He became the youngest forward ever to appear for the club at senior level when he made his debut against Stoke City in January 1964. He also captained Forest's Youth team in the European International Youth Tournaments in France and Holland in the summer of 1965. Sammy eventually succeeded Frank Wignall as attack leader in 1967-68, but it was not until his conversion to a defender that he found a regular place in the side.

Having helped Forest to promotion from Division Two in 1977, he was allowed to move across the Trent to the Magpies, following the signing of his replacement, Kenny Burns. Despite appearing in all but one of the season's League and Cup matches during his time at Meadow Lane, he moved on to Shrewsbury Town in the close season. He played in 24(1) League matches and scored four goals in a successful season for the Shrews who won the championship of Division Three, they also reached Round Six of the FA Cup before losing to Wolverhampton Wanderers after a replay.

Appearances: FL: 42 apps 0 gls FAC: 3 apps 1 gl FLC: 2 apps 0 gls Other: 7 apps 1 gl Total: 54 apps 2 gls
Honours: (Shrewsbury Town) FL Division 3 champions 1979

CHARLESWORTH, George
Right-back   5'11"   12st 6lbs
b. Bolsover, Derbyshire, July quarter 1893
d. Nottingham, October quarter 1964
CAREER: Sutton Junction 1910/NOTTS Nov 1916/Sutton Town cs 1921
Debut v Burnley (h) 30.8.19, won 2 – 0

A full-back of the robust type, George Charlesworth had five year's experience with Sutton Junction in the Central Alliance when he joined Notts in wartime season 1916-17. He did not appear at senior level until normal League football resumed after WW1, and in the first peacetime season he appeared in 30 of the 42 League fixtures. His four goals all came from the penalty spot in a season that commenced with reasonable success, but ended in relegation from the top flight after the dismal record of just four wins in the New Year. Six years later, a letter to the Editor of the 'Football Post' contained a supporter's recollections of George Charlesworth: "He had a good name for ramming home penalty kicks and a bad one for booting the ball over the stand and into the canal!" The old defender was working in a Nottingham engineering works at that time.

Appearances: FL: 30 apps 4 gls Total: 30 apps 4 gls

CHATHAM, Raymond Harold
Half-back, later full-back   5' 10"   12st 4lbs
b. Wolverhampton, 20th July 1924
d. Sunderland, 1st June 1999
CAREER: Oxby F.C. (Staffordshire)/Wolverhampton Wanderers during wartime season 1940-41, signing pro June 1945/NOTTS Jan 1954, fee £4,000/Margate circa Aug 1958, Fee £260
Debut v Derby County (a) 23.1.54, drawn 0 – 0

Ray Chatham was the Wolves' leading goal scorer in the transitional season 1945-46 with 16 goals, but by the time he had established himself in Division One in the early 1950s he was operating in the middle line. After completing 86 League and Cup appearances for the Wolves he became the first signing made by the Magpies new manager, George Poyser. Strong and effective in either defence or attack, he brought considerable strength to the Notts half-back line. Apart from a lengthy spell of injury in 1954-55, when he was sidelined for a period of five months, he was rarely absent from the first team picture. His utility value underlined by his record of successfully occupying both full-back berths and all three half-back positions. In February 1964 he was reported to be living in London and helping out at Crystal Palace, looking after one of their junior sides.

Appearances: FL: 127 apps 4 gls FAC: 3 apps 0 gls
Total: 130 apps 4 gls

CHERRY, Steven Reginald
Goalkeeper   6' 1"   13st 0lbs
b. Nottingham, 5th August 1960
CAREER: Derby County associate schoolboy Nov 1975, app Aug 1976, pro Mar 1978 (Port Vale loan Nov 1980)/Walsall Aug 1984, fee £25,000/Plymouth Argyle Nov 1986, fee £17,000 (Chesterfield loan Dec 1988)/NOTTS Feb 1989, fee £70,000/Watford July 1995 (Plymouth Argyle loan Feb 1996)/Plymouth Argyle May 1996/Rotherham United Aug 1996/Kettering Town Feb 1997/Rushden & Diamonds Mar 1997/Stalybridge Celtic Jan 1998/NOTTS Mar 1998/Mansfield Town nc Aug 1998/Oldham Athletic nc Mar 1999/Lincoln City goalkeeping coach (there Jan 2001)/Lincoln United/Kidsgrove Athletic Dec 2003/Belper Town Oct 2004.
Debut v Chester City (a) 18.2.89, lost 0 – 1

On arrival at Meadow Lane, Steve Cherry had already won 'Player of the Year' awards with Derby County, Walsall and Plymouth Argyle. The fact that he added a fourth with the Magpies was not un-expected, but the fact that it came at the close on the 1991-92 relegation season spoke volumes for his efforts to keep the Magpies in the top flight.

Brilliant on his day and wonderfully consistent, Steve had few equals in holding the ball tight with his seemingly adhesive hands. In his final season, despite lengthy spells out of the first team, he was selected ahead of Paul Reece for the Anglo-Italian Cup Final against Ascoli, completing an outstanding record of four Wembley appearances in six years. His career aggregate figures, spanning nine clubs, amounted to 542 League matches. His son John, also a goalkeeper, was on Kidsgrove Athletic's books at the same time as his father when he signed from Arnold Town as a 19 year-old in December 2003.

Appearances: FL: 266 apps 0 gls FAC: 14 apps 0 gls FLC: 17 apps 0 gls Other: 31 apps 0 gls
Total: 328 apps 0 gls
Honours: England Youth International, 2 apps 1978-79. (NOTTS) Anglo Italian Cup winners 1995, finalists 1994.

CHIEDOZIE, John Okay

Winger   5' 7"   10st 10lbs
b. Owerri, Nigeria, 18th April 1960
CAREER: St. Bonaventure School/Newham Schoolboys/ London Schoolboys/Leyton Orient app July 1976, pro Apr 1977/NOTTS Aug 1881, fee £450,000/Tottenham Hotspur Aug 1984, fee £425,000/Derby County July 1988/NOTTS nc Jan 1990/Chesterfield nc Mar 1990/Swindon Town trial/ Bashley trial Oct 1991/Barking Dec 1991/Bashley cs 1992
Debut v Aston Villa (a) 29.8.81, won 1 – 0

A refugee from war-torn Biafra at the age of twelve, John Chiedozie joined Leyton Orient at sixteen and made his League debut at the same age. Dubbed the 'Orient Express' by the Brisbane Road faithful, he cost the Magpies their record fee – by a very wide margin – when signed for their long-awaited return to the top flight. The speedy and accomplished wingman took a little time to adjust to life in Division One, but once established gave defenders a great deal of trouble with his pace, direct approach and ability to cross the ball on the run. Despite his best efforts, and twelve goals in League and Cup, the Magpies were relegated in 1983-84 and their star wingman was transferred to the Spurs. Sadly, a catalogue of injuries marred his time at White Hart Lane and he returned to the Midlands, Derby County signing him on a free transfer.

This marked the beginning of a frustrating spell, when injuries restricted his appearances to just two for the Rams, followed by one substitute appearance in an unsuccessful return to Meadow Lane, and 5(2) Division Four matches for Chesterfield. At least he was destined to bow out of senior football on a worthy stage, his last match for Chesterfield being the Division Four Play-off Final at Wembley on 16th May 1990. Sadly, however, the Spireites were beaten 1 – 0 by Cambridge United. When injury finally enforced his retirement from the game, John set up a bouncy castle hire business in Hampshire.

Appearances: FL: 109(3) apps 16 gls FAC: 8 apps 2 gls FLC: 11 apps 2 gls Total: 128 (3) apps 20 gls
Honours: Nigeria International, 12 caps.

CHILDS, Harold

Full-back   5' 8½"   11st 10lbs
b. Acomb, York, 7th November 1908
d. Shildon, 4th July 1977
CAREER: Ferryhill Athletic/Darlington am cs 1927/West Stanley Nov 1927/NOTTS May 1928/Halifax Town Aug 1929 to cs 1930
Debut v Stoke City (a) 27.4.29, lost 0 – 5

Harold Childs was employed at the L.N.E.R. works at Darlington and was playing football locally when given the opportunity to join up with the Magpies. Despite being able to occupy either full-back flank he did not get a run out with the first team until the last match of the season at Stoke City. He was partnered by local product, Fred Wright, who was also making his debut in League football. The 5 – 0 defeat was the heaviest of the season, and probably influenced the decision to allow both players to leave in the summer. Harold joined Halifax Town and appeared in 16 Third Division North matches during his season at The Shay. A younger brother, John Arthur, commonly known as Arthur, was a half-back with Darlington, Hull City, Exeter City and Darlington in the 1920s and 1930s.

Appearances: FL: 1 app 0 gls Total: 1 app 0 gls

CHILVERS, Liam Christopher

Defender   6' 1"   13st 5lbs
b. Chelmsford, Essex, 6th November 1981
CAREER: Arsenal trainee, signing pro July 2000 (Northampton Town loan Dec 2000) (NOTTS loan Nov 2001 to Jan 2002) (Beveren, Belgium, loan to Jan 2003) (Colchester United loan Jan 2003)/Colchester United Aug 2004.
Debut v Queens Park Rangers (h) 3.11.2001, lost 0 – 2

Despite being a Youth Cup winner with Arsenal, the immensely promising young defender failed to reach League level with the Gunners, a series of loan spells finally leading to a permanent move to Colchester United, following his season's loan to the U's in 2003-04. Liam scored his first League goal for the Magpies and was generally impressive during his loan at Meadow Lane, despite his spell being interrupted by injury.

Appearances: FL: 9 apps 1 gl FAC: 2 apps 0 gls
Total: 11 apps 1 gl
Honours: (Arsenal) FA Youth Cup winners 2000

CHIPPERFIELD, John James
Outside-left   5' 8½"   11st 4lbs
b. Bethnal Green, London, 4th March 1894
d. Wandsworth, London, 6th September 1966
CAREER: Commercial Cars F.C./Luton Clarence/Luton Town am, signing pro June 1914 (WW1 guest Arsenal)/Tottenham Hotspur June 1919, fee £1,000/NOTTS Dec 1921, fee £1,500/Northfleet cs 1922/Charlton Athletic May 1923/Chatham Town Aug 1924
Debut v Hull City (h) 24.12.21, won 2 – 0

Signed to replace Billy Death, who one week earlier had entered hospital for a cartilage operation. Chipperfield was not on the Spurs open to transfer list, and they were reluctant to release him, as he was the star of their reserve attack. Misfortune had lost him his first team place, following injury in a match against Forest in November 1919. This gave Dimmock his chance, and he achieved such pronounced success that Chipperfield was unable to reclaim his place in the first team. Sturdily built and tricky, and a strong finisher, he was particularly prominent in the Magpies' FA Cup run. His two goals earned a 2 – 2 draw with Aston Villa in round four, and he was again on the score sheet in the replay at Villa Park, where a famous 4 – 3 victory took Notts into the semi-final. Sadly the adventure ended at Turf Moor, Huddersfield Town, the eventual winners of the trophy, winning by 3 – 1.

Appearances: FL: 18 apps 2 gls FAC: 6 apps 3 gls
Total: 24 apps 5 gls

CHRISTIE, Trevor John
Forward   6' 2"   12st 0lbs
b. Cresswell, Northumberland, 28th February 1959
CAREER: Leicester City app Sept 1975, pro Dec 1976/NOTTS June 1979, fee £80,000/Nottingham Forest July 1984, fee £165,000/Derby County Feb 1985, fee £100,000/Manchester City Aug 1986, in part-exchange for Mark Lillis/Walsall Oct 1986, fee £30,000/Mansfield Town Mar 1989, fee £30,000/Kettering Town July 1991/VS Rugby Mar 1992/Hucknall Town player-coach Nov 1992/Arnold Town Mar 1995.
Debut v Cardiff City (h) 18.8.79, won 4 – 1

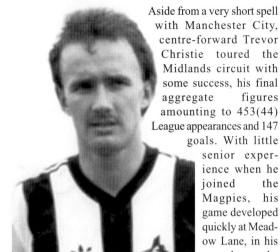

Aside from a very short spell with Manchester City, centre-forward Trevor Christie toured the Midlands circuit with some success, his final aggregate figures amounting to 453(44) League appearances and 147 goals. With little senior experience when he joined the Magpies, his game developed quickly at Meadow Lane, in his second season he topped County's goal charts with 21 in League and Cup. A timely burst of goals in April and May clinching promotion into the top flight after a 55-year exile. Trevor scored the 100th goal of his career for Derby County, assisting them to promotion from Division Three in 1985-86. He was similarly successful in 1987-88, winning promotion from Division Three with Walsall, via the Play-offs.

Appearances: FL: 158(29) apps 63 gls FAC: 8(2) apps 3 gls FLC: 20(1) apps 10 gls Other: 10 apps 3 gls
Total: 196(32) apps 79 gls

CLAMP, Arthur
Centre-half   5' 8"   11st 8lbs
b. Sneinton, Notts., 1st May 1884
d. Stoke-on-Trent, 19th September 1918, age 34
CAREER: Sneinton/NOTTS Oct 1906 to 1915
Debut v Bolton Wanderers (a) 29.12.06, drawn 0 – 0

A sturdy centre-half, ranked amongst the best defenders of his day. Possessed of remarkable stamina, no game seeming too long for him, and no opposition too hard to tackle. A bricklayer by trade, he joined the Magpies from Sneinton, jumping straight from junior to senior football.

He joined the armed forces in April 1918, and was drafted overseas in autumn of the same year. He had been in the front-line trenches for only three days when he received severe wounds, from which he subsequently died in a Stoke-on-Trent hospital, aged 34.

Appearances: FL: 275 apps 3 gls FAC: 14 apps 0 gls
Total: 289 apps 3 gls

CLARE, William Edwin

Right-back   6' 0"   12st 6lbs
b. Newstead, Notts. October quarter 1883
d. Edmonton, 22nd September 1944
CAREER: Kirkby Rovers/Bentinck Colliery/Mansfield Woodhouse/NOTTS Apr 1904/Brighton & Hove Albion May 1905 to May 1906/Mansfield Wesley Aug 1906.
Debut v Small Heath (a) 23.4.04, lost 0 – 2

Edwin Clare played in one League match and three friendly fixtures at the end of season 1903-04, showing sufficient style and ability to win a contract for season 1904-05. A local player who worked as a miner, his early amateur football was played in the colliery district. Standing six feet tall and with weight in proportion, he was ideally built for his position at right-back. Injury to Tom Prescott appeared to have opened the way for the youthful Clare to partner John Montgomery, but he failed to hold down his place. He left to joined Brighton & Hove Albion where he spent a season, appearing in 15 Southern League matches, but returned homewards after one season and joined Mansfield Wesley, a Nottingham & District League side who were the forerunners of Mansfield Town. A cricketer of above average ability, Edwin was a member of the ground staff of Nottinghamshire C.C.C. in 1903.

Appearances: FL: 6 apps 0 gls Total: 6 apps 0 gls

CLARKE, David Alan

Defender/Midfield   5' 10"   11st 0lbs
b. Nottingham, 3rd December 1964
CAREER: Margaret Glen Bott School/NOTTS app Apr 1981, pro Dec 1982/Lincoln City Aug 1987, fee £5,000/ Doncaster Rovers Jan 1994/Gainsborough Trinity Aug 1994
Debut as sub v Aston Villa, FLC 1, (a) 6.10.82, won 2 – 1 (scored one)

Capped by England Youth against Israel in February 1983, Dave Clarke had made his Magpies debut some four months earlier as a seventeen year-old. Introduced as a substitute, he sensationally scored the winner in the FL Cup tie against Aston Villa. Originally considered a midfield player, he made a successful switch to the left full-back position, following Nigel Worthington's transfer to Sheffield Wednesday.

Recruited by Lincoln City for their first season in the GM Vauxhall Conference, following relegation from Division Four in 1986-87, he scored five goals in 26(4) appearances as the Imps won the championship at the first time of asking. He remained at Sincil Bank to complete 141(6) League appearances, scoring nine goals. A brief spell with Doncaster Rovers netted a further 15(1) League outings before he moved into non-League circles with Gainsborough Trinity.

Appearances: FL: 113(10) apps 8 gls FAC: 13 apps 1 gl FLC: 8(2) apps 2 gls Other: 3 apps 0 gls
Total: 137(12) apps 11 gls
Honours: England Youth International 1983. (Lincoln City) GM Vauxhall Conference champions 1988

CLARKE, David Arthur

Outside-left   5' 7"   10st 4lbs
b. Derby, 26th September 1946
CAREER: Derby Schoolboys/Manchester United associate schoolboy Feb 1962/Nottingham Forest trial, pro May 1964/NOTTS July 1966
Debut v Port Vale (h) 27.8.66, drawn 0 – 0

A product of Derby Schools football who was taken onto Manchester United's ground staff but then recommended to Forest manager Johnny Carey by United's manager, Matt Busby. Signed by Forest after a trial, he failed to graduate to senior level during two seasons at the City Ground and joined the Magpies on a free transfer. He made a promising start, holding the left wing spot for 24 consecutive matches. He then lost out to Tony Flower, who in turn competed with John Beresford until the season's end.

Appearances: FL: 23(1) apps 0 gls FAC: 1 app 0 gls FLC: 2 apps 0 gls Total: 26(1) apps 0 gls

---

CLARKE, William George

Half-back   5' 9"   11st 7lbs
Birth and death details unknown
CAREER: Wednesbury/Shrewsbury Town July 1927/Dudley Town/West Bromwich Albion am Aug 1930, pro Sept 1930/ NOTTS May 1933/Dudley Town Sept 1936/Oakengates Town Sept 1937/Brierley Hill Alliance July 1938
Debut v Bradford City (h) 3.2.34, won 3 – 0

The dangers of the hurriedly 'phoned-in match report were never more graphically exposed than in the case of 'Little John's' report for the 'Football Post' on the match at Swindon Town on 23rd November 1935. His message read: "Clarke, **working** up, passed to Notley, who, evading Duckworth, ran on to score a fine goal after five minutes."

By some mischance, the word "**working**" appeared in the 'Football Post' as "**waking**." In apologising to Clarke for the telephonic error he wrote: "If Clarke is anything he is energetic and enthusiastic, and the mere suggestion that he was dozy in play could never be placed at his door."

Appearances: FL: 37 apps 1 gl FAC: 2 apps 0 gls Other: 1 app 0 gls Total: 40 apps 1 gl

———————o———————

CLAYTON, Stanley

Inside-forward 5' 8½" 11st 2lbs
b. Castleford, 21st November 1912
d. Castleford, 2nd July 2002
CAREER: Castleford Town/Bradford P.A. am Jan 1932/Leeds United am Aug 1932/ Castleford (Rugby League Club)/Upton Colliery/NOTTS May 1937 to 1939 (WW2 guest Aldershot, Middlesbrough, Reading and Tottenham Hotspur)
Debut v Millwall (h) 11.9.37, drawn 1 – 1

Said to have been wanted by no fewer than eleven League clubs, no doubt attracted by the fact that he had scored 33 goals for Upton Colliery in 1936-37. Stan Clayton had spent time as an amateur with both Bradford P.A. and Leeds United, and even sampled the handling code with Castleford before starring in the Yorkshire League with Upton Colliery. Befitting a player who was also a schoolteacher, he was often spoken of as "the brains of the attack." Sadly, his goal touch deserted him in League football but in his role as the schemer of the forward line he was an accomplished initiator, adept at keeping his line on the move.

Appearances: FL: 31 apps 3 gls FAC: 5 apps 1 gl
Total: 36 apps 4 gls

———————o———————

CLEMENTS, John Ernest

Full-back
b. East Markham, Notts. October quarter 1867
CAREER: St Savior's (Nottingham)/NOTTS Oct 1888/ Newton Heath June 1892/Rotherham Town Aug 1894/ Newcastle United May 1895
Debut v Burnley (h) 27.10.1888, won 6 – 1

John Clements' career with the Magpies opened in memorable fashion, a 6 – 1 win against Burnley featuring five goals from outside-left Bobby Jardine. The bulk of Clements' appearances were made in his first season, and he was largely unemployed subsequently. This was probably the reason for his run-out with Notts Rangers on 7th December 1889, under the name of A. N. Other – not very subtle, and he incurred the displeasure of the authorities for it.

A move to Newton Heath, for their debut as a Football League club, provided regular first team football, although he lost his place in the side in most unfortunate circumstances. Along with two other players he was suspended for 14 days following alleged misconduct in a match against Derby County in October 1893. His replacement Fred Erentz, promptly seized the opportunity to establish himself in the first team. At a subsequent meeting of the FA Council, the referee in the Derby County match was suspended for the remainder of the season, suggesting that his 'booking' of the Newton Heath trio had been unwarranted. Clements moved on to Rotherham Town, at that time a Second Division club, and played in 27 matches and scored two goals in 1894-95. His final season, with Newcastle United, was marred by injuries. Returning after several weeks out through injury, he sustained knee ligament damage in a 'come back' match with the "A" Team.

Appearances: FL: 14 apps 0 gls FAC: 4 apps 0 gls
Total: 18 apps 0 gls

———————o———————

CLIFF, Edward

Left-back 5' 10" 11st 6lbs
b. Liverpool South, 30th September 1951
CAREER: Liverpool Schoolboys/Burnley app 1967, signing pro Oct 1968/NOTTS July 1973, fee £5,000 (Lincoln City loan Oct 1974)/Chicago Sting, USA, Mar 1975/Tranmere Rovers Sept 1976/Rochdale Sept 1979 to May 1981
Debut v Sunderland (a) 1.1.74, won 2 – 1

Eddie Cliff joined Burnley as a sixteen year-old apprentice, won a FA Youth Cup medal in May 1968, and turned professional in October of the same year. His only extended run of League action with the Clarets (14 matches) was in 1971-72. He was one of two players signed by Notts from Burnley in the close season of 1973. Eric Probert, who cost a £30,000 fee, not surprisingly created a bigger impression at Meadow Lane. With full-backs of the calibre of Brindley, Worthington and later O'Brien to contend with, Eddie Cliff had few opportunities. Released in March 1975 he journeyed to the U.S.A., joined Chicago Sting, and had the cruellest misfortune in breaking his leg on his first appearance against Vancouver. He enjoyed better fortune in subsequent spells with Tranmere Rovers (50 appearances and four goals) and Rochdale (26 appearances).

Appearances: FL: 5 apps 0 gls Total: 5 apps 0 gls
Honours: (Burnley) FA Youth Cup winners 1968

———————o———————

CLINCH, Thomas H.

Right-back   5' 10" 12st 7lbs
b. Bolton, 1875
CAREER: Halliwell Rovers May 1897/Sheffield United June 1899/Reading May 1900/NOTTS May 1904
Debut v Manchester City (h) 17.9.04, drawn 1 – 1

Tom Clinch made his first appearance in League football for Sheffield United in a 2 – 1 win at West Bromwich Albion on 6th November 1899. The Blades had won the FA Cup in the previous season and finished runners-up for the League championship in Clinch's season at Bramall Lane, but the Lancastrian full-back had not featured regularly (nine matches) and, at the opening of the twentieth century, he joined Reading. He spent three successful seasons at Elm Park, totalling 71 Southern League appearances, including 24 (in the 30-match tournament) when Reading finished runners-up to Southampton for the championship. When Tom Prescott's fine career with the Magpies terminated in the early weeks of season 1904-05 there was a vacancy to be filled. Tom Clinch was tried and found wanting, as was the youngster, W.E. Clare. A successful switch from left-half by Arthur Griffiths eventually solved the problem of a regular partner for the long-serving left full-back, John Montgomery.

Appearances: FL: 6 apps 0 gls Total: 6 apps 0 gls

COATES, David Plews

Wing-half   5' 10" 11st 8lbs
b. Shiney Row, County Durham, 11th April 1935
CAREER: Fairfield Juniors/Shiney Row/Hull City Oct 1952/ Mansfield Town Mar 1960, fee £1,000/NOTTS July 1964, fee £2,250, appointed youth coach in 1967/Aston Villa assistant coach Dec 1968/Luton Town coach Jan 1978/Also held coaching appointments with Mansfield Town, Leicester City and Oxford United. Was reported to be scouting for Sunderland in Oct 1994 and for Portsmouth in 2001.
Debut v York City (h) 3.10.64, won 3 – 1

In a most unfortunate start to his career at Meadow Lane David Coates was injured a few days before the start of the season, shortly after his £2,250 transfer from Mansfield Town. As a consequence, he missed the first eleven matches of the season and took some time to fully recover. Nevertheless, the 34 League appearances that he made in his first season proved to be his best return, as he figured little during 1965-66, but then signed off with a run of 24 consecutive matches in the second half of season 1966-67. Although fielded as a wing half-back during his spell with the Magpies, David began as an inside-forward with Hull City (13 goals in 62 League matches) and later with Mansfield Town (17 goals in 159 League matches). He featured in promotion campaigns with both of his early clubs, assisting Hull City to the runners-up position in Division Three in 1959, and Mansfield Town, fourth

place and promotion from Division Four in 1963. His son, Steven, helped Hinckley United to reach the second round of the FA Cup in season 2001-02.

Appearances:
FL: 66 apps 1 gl FAC: 2 apps 0 gls FLC: 3 apps 0 gls
Total: 71 apps 1 gl

COCK, Donald James

Centre-forward 5' 8"   11st 6lbs
b. Phillack, Hayle, Cornwall 8th July 1896
d. Bradmore, Notts., 31st August 1974
CAREER: Palace Road School (Fulham)/Camborne Boys' Brigade/Gwynne's Foundry F.C. (Hammersmith)/ Army football with the Middlesex Regiment from Aug 1914/(WW1 guest Brentford Nov 1917)/Fulham June 1919/NOTTS Oct 1922, fee £1,750/Arsenal Mar 1925, fee £4,000/Clapton Orient Oct 1925, fee £1,500/Wolverhampton Wanderers July 1927/Newport County Sept 1927
Debut v Barnsley (a) 7.10.22, lost 0 – 1

A centre-forward who played with the enthusiasm of an amateur. Strong, bustling and virile he infused much needed dash into the County attack. Not a stylist, but a fine two-footed player who knew how to distribute the ball, and was seldom out of position to meet a centre from the wing. A native of Cornwall, he did well in Army football during WW1, after which he joined Fulham where he was leading scorer in consecutive seasons 1919-20 and 1920-21. Arsenal paid Notts a record fee of £4,000 for him in March 1925, but in only his second match, and against his former colleagues at Meadow Lane, he suffered a broken leg. He played in only one more League match for the Gunners before a cut-price deal took him to Clapton Orient. Happily, at Homerton he returned to fitness and form, leading their scoring charts in both 1925-26 and 1926-27. In 1928, tragedy struck when he suffered grievous injuries in a motorcycle accident at Wolverhampton. Four years later it was reported that he had had to refuse a continental coaching appointment because of his inability to do demonstrations with the ball.

The accident had in fact left him incapable of active work of any kind. His brother Jack, also a centre-forward, was capped twice by England and scored a career total of 234 goals in 391 FL matches.

Appearances: FL: 85 apps 32 gls FAC: 7 apps 2 gls
Total: 92 apps 34 gls
Honours: (NOTTS) FL Div 2 champions 1923. FA representative, 1 app.

COGLIN, Stephen

Inside-left   5' 7"   10st 2lbs
b. Willenhall, Staffs, 14th October 1903
CAREER: Moxley White Star/Darlaston Feb 1921/Lichfield City/Wednesbury Old Athletic/Willenhall cs 1923/Sunderland May 1924/Grimsby Town Feb 1927/NOTTS May 1931, fee £250/Worcester City Aug 1932/Hereford United May 1935/ Cannock Town Dec 1935/Bromsgrove Rovers/Archdales F.C. re-instated am Sept 1936/Worcester City coach Aug 1938; coach to Colts Xl Aug 1952; resigned his post as reserve team trainer July 1956
Debut v Oldham Athletic (h) 23.9.31, won 1 – 0

Both before and after his eight-year spell in League soccer Steve Coglin assisted a remarkable number of non-League clubs in the West Midlands area. A small but clever and purposeful inside-forward, he scored 10 goals in 21 League matches for Sunderland, and 39 in 118 appearances for Grimsby Town, assisting the Mariners to promotion to the top flight in 1929. After a disappointing season at Meadow Lane, when he failed to maintain a first team place, he departed to Worcester City where he enjoyed three excellent seasons, scoring 42 goals in 123 matches. He was later appointed to that club's coaching staff, a position he held until the pressure of business enforced his resignation in July 1956.

Appearances: FL: 13 apps 3 gls FAC: 1 app 0 gls
Total: 14 apps 3 gls

COLES, Frederick Gordon

Wing-half   5' 9"   12st 2lbs
b. Sherwood, Nottingham, October quarter 1875
d. Nottingham, 22nd April 1947, age 71
CAREER: Nottingham Post Office/NOTTS May 1895/ Nottingham Forest Mar 1900/Woolwich Arsenal Aug 1900/ Grimsby Town June 1904/Haessche Voetbal Vereeniging, Holland, trainer-coach Aug 1908/Denmark player-coaching appointment until Jan 1916.
Debut v Burton Swifts (h) 22.2.1896, won 5 – 0

Fred Coles had to leave his native city in order to make his mark in the football world. Never more than a reserve with both Nottingham clubs, he was quickly established as a first team regular with Woolwich Arsenal, appearing in 86 League and Cup matches before losing his place in 1903-04.

Some consolation being gained during his spell in the reserve team, who lifted both the South-Eastern League championship and the London League Reserve championship. Moving on to Grimsby Town, he added a further 44 League matches to his record before becoming one of the pioneer British coaches in Europe. Appointments in Holland and Denmark concluding when he enlisted into the Army and was drafted to Egypt with the Royal Army Medical Corps.

Appearances: FL: 1 app 0 gls Total: 1 app 0 gls

COLLIER, Geoffrey Heywood

Forward   6' 3"   14st 0lbs
b. Blackpool, 25th July 1950
CAREER: Macclesfield Town/NOTTS July 1973 to Oct 1974, fee £4,000/Macclesfield Town
Debut as sub v Fulham (h) 13.10.73, won 2 – 1

Powerfully built centre-forward who attracted the Magpies' attention following his excellent season with Macclesfield Town in 1972-73. Eighteen goals in Northern Premier League matches earned him an opportunity at League level, but he failed to make the grade in Division Two. This despite his record of 24 goals for the reserves in North Midlands League matches in 1973-74. He left Meadow Lane in October 1974 in order to accept an offer of work outside the game in his native Blackpool.

Appearances: FL: 0(3) apps 0 gls Total: 0(3) apps 0 gls

CONNELL, Archibald

Inside-right   5' 9"   12st 0lbs
b. Darvel, Ayrshire, 22nd April 1900
CAREER: Darvel/Motherwell June 1926/Queen of the South Wanderers/NOTTS Oct 1927 to cs 1928, fee £400.
Debut v Port Vale (h) 22.10.27, lost 2 – 4 (scored one)

Archie Connell had scored five goals in as many appearances for the Dumfries club, Queen of the South Wanderers, when the Magpies paid £400 for his signature. He arrived in Nottingham with the reputation of being one of the cleverest young forwards over the border, and within 15 minutes of the kick-off in his debut against Port Vale he scored with a flashing header from a right wing corner. Although showing some clever touches, the local correspondent reckoned that "He still has a good deal to learn." Two months in the reserves followed, but his return to first team action was abruptly curtailed when he was incapacitated by a knee injury after just 15 minutes play against West Bromwich Albion on 27th December. Without further senior involvement he was released at the end of the season.

Appearances: FL: 4 apps 1 gl Total: 4 apps 1 gl

CONNOR, John Henry "Jack"

Right-back   5' 7"   11st 0lbs
b. Staincross near Barnsley, October quarter 1875
CAREER: Newstead National School/Newstead Rovers/
Newstead Byron 1890/Newark cs 1894/NOTTS May 1895/
Newark May 1897
Debut v Lincoln City (h) 19.10.1895, won 2 – 0

In the summer of 1896, following his first season with
Notts, Jack Connor was laid up with the dire disease of
typhoid, and it was not until Christmas that he was once
again able to don the black & white jersey. His appearances,
however, were confined to the Reserve side. The possessor
of six gold medals for football, Connor was also a useful
fast bowler with Newstead Colliery and later with
Mumby's C.C. In 1901 he was employed as a carder in a
glassworks.

Appearances: FL: 17 apps 0 gls FAC: 2 apps 0 gls
Total: 19 apps 0 gls

COOK, John 'Jack'

Inside-forward   5' 7"   11st 2lbs
b. Sunderland, 22nd July 1887
d. Nottingham, 21st April 1952
CAREER: South Bank/Middlesbrough Aug 1911/NOTTS June
1919, fee £350/Northampton Town June 1924/Sneinton
Thursday Nov 1928
Debut v Burnley (h) 30.8.19, won 2 – 0

A paragraph from the 'Football Post' of New Year's Eve
1921 neatly summed up the playing style of Jack Cook:
"He enhanced his reputation as an exponent of the
dribbling art during the Yuletide matches. Sparkling
displays of artistic footwork provided the openings for
three of the goals scored at Meadow Lane. If Cook could
only shoot, what a star he would be." Certainly his scoring
ratio was poor for a forward, nevertheless his goals were
generally of the spectacular type, the odd serpentine
dribble resulting in a stunning, individualistic, solo strike.

Appearances: FL: 98 apps 13 gls FAC: 19 apps 5 gls
Total: 117 apps 18 gls
Honours: (NOTTS) FL Division 2 champions 1923

COOKE, Reuben James

Outside-right   5' 6"   11st 0lbs
b. Ilkeston, October quarter 1893
CAREER: Ilkeston United/Mansfield Mechanics/NOTTS
May 1919/Ilkeston United Nov 1920
Debut v Sheffield United (a) 1.9.19, lost 0 –3

After active service with the Tank Corps and in motor
machine guns, Cooke was given a trial in the late stages of
the final wartime season, 1918-19. In seven outings on the
right wing he impressed with his speed, dribbling abilities
and marksmanship, scoring goals against Grimsby Town,
Leicester Fosse and Forest. Sadly, when the serious
business of Division One football recommenced, he lost
his scoring touch and made only spasmodic first team
appearances.

Appearances: FL: 12 apps 0 gls Total: 12 apps 0 gls

COOKE, Thomas

Outside-right
CAREER: Notts Rangers/NOTTS 1888-89
Debut v Aston Villa (h) 8.12.1888, lost 2 – 4

The Magpies fielded no fewer than six new men for the
visit of Aston Villa to the Trent Bridge ground in December
1888. Among the newcomers were Cooke and Shaw,
normally to be found as the right wing pairing in the ranks
of Notts Rangers. Kicking towards the Gamston Lane
goal, Cooke was instantly noticeable for a fast run and
centre as Notts started off at great pace. In a game played
in pouring rain throughout, Villa lasted the pace better and
ran out 4 – 2 winners, Cooke having little opportunity to
shine in direct opposition to Burton, Villa's hard tackling
defender.

Appearances: FL: 1 app 0 gls Total: 1 app 0 gls

COOKSON, Alfred Ernest

Wing-half
b. Nottingham, April quarter 1873
CAREER: NOTTS 1896/Newark May 1897/Nottingham
Forest Jan 1905
Debut v Newcastle United (a) 12.12.1896, drawn 2 – 2

A reserve wing-half during the Division Two promotion
season. In addition to his debut, Cookson appeared in
two other home matches, a 3 – 0 victory against Newton
Heath and a 5 – 0 drubbing of Burton Wanderers. The
Wanderers, incidentally, failed to gain re-election to the
League at the end of the season, and subsequently
disbanded. Along with a reserve team colleague,
J.H.Connor, Alfred Cookson joined Newark in May 1897.
He later moved to Forest, but did not appear at senior
level. The 1901 Census listed him as a 28 year-old lace
warehouseman.

Appearances: FL: 3 apps 0 gls Total: 3 apps 0 gls

COOLE, William

Outside-right   5' 7½"   11st 2lbs
b. Manchester, 27th January 1925
d. Salford, 12th April 2001
CAREER: Royal Navy football/Mansfield Town Jan 1948/
NOTTS Oct 1953, fee £5,000/Barrow July 1956/Wigan
Rovers cs 1959
Debut v Lincoln City (a) 3.10.53, lost 0 – 3

Signed by Mansfield Town after four years of service in
the Royal Navy, Billy Coole became a warm favourite at
Field Mill. Speed, ball control and the ability to swerve
past an opponent made him a very dangerous customer,
and he was not slow to accept a scoring opportunity,
instanced by his return of 16 goals in 44 League matches
in 1950-51. He missed only two matches in his first season
at Meadow Lane, but then lost his place to Gordon Wills
and never regained it. One of eight Notts professionals
placed on the open to transfer list in May 1956, in the
wake of a 20th place finish in Division Two, he ended his
League career with Barrow, for whom he scored four goals
in 59 League and Cup matches.

Appearances: FL: 42 apps 5 gls FAC: 1 app 0 gls
Total: 43 apps 5 gls

COOPER, Edward

Outside-right   5' 7"   11st 0lbs
b. Walsall, October quarter 1891
CAREER: Stafford Rangers/Glossop May 1912/Newcastle
United Mar 1913, fee £1,300/NOTTS June 1920, fee £500/
Stafford Rangers Nov 1921
Debut v Bristol City (h) 4.9.20, drawn 2 – 2

In a career interrupted by Army service in France with the
West Yorkshire Regiment, Edward Cooper began with
Glossop, scoring five goals in 25 Second Division matches.
He had not completed one season before Newcastle United
paid what was then a very significant sum for his transfer.
At either side of the war he played in 45 League matches
and scored two goals before his transfer from the Tyneside
'Magpies' to the Nottingham ones. After appearing in
four of the first six fixtures of 1920-21, Cooper did not
appear again in the League side, Alf Dolphin and Joe Daly
being the main contenders for the right wing position.
Appearances: FL: 4 apps 0 gls Total: 4 apps 0 gls

COOPER, Joseph

Inside-right   5' 11½"   11st 12lbs
b. Newbold, Derbyshire, July quarter 1899
d. Cleethorpes, Lincs, 22nd January 1959
CAREER: Dronfield Grammar School/Army football/
Sheepbridge Works/Saltney College (Birmingham)/West
Bromwich Albion am trial/Sheffield Wednesday Apr 1921/
Chesterfield June 1921/NOTTS Mar 1923, fee £1,075/
Grimsby Town Sept 1924, fee £500/Lincoln City July 1932
to cs 1933
Debut v Clapton Orient (h) 17.3.23, won 3 – 1 (scored one)

A member of the scholastic profession, and as one scribe
observed: "Brought his brains with him onto the field."
Joe was transfer listed by Notts in May 1924 when he
refused to move his residence to Nottingham. This
presumably did not hamper his progress with Grimsby
Town, although in December 1925 he was appointed
assistant teacher to the Welhome Junior Boy's School,
Grimsby. He remained with the Mariners for almost eight
years, scoring 47 goals in 154 League matches. His final
career figures totalled 70 goals and 272 appearances.

Appearances: FL: 31 apps 4 gls FAC: 2 apps 0 gls
Total: 33 apps 4 gls
Honours: (Grimsby Town) FL Div 3 North champions
1926

COOPER, Sedley

Forward   5' 8½"   10st 7lbs
b. Garforth, Leeds, 17th August 1911
d. Garforth, Leeds, 23rd February 1981
CAREER: Carlton Athletic/Halifax Town Nov 1928/Sheffield
Wednesday June 1931, fee £1,200/Huddersfield Town June
1936/NOTTS Mar 1937 (WW2 guest Lincoln City &
Torquay United)
Debut v Swindon Town (h) 13.3.37, won 3 – 2 (scored two)

After scoring twice on his debut, Sedley Cooper injured a
knee in his second outing and missed the next four matches.
He was more seriously in the wars in 1937-38 when he
injured his other knee and had to undergo surgery. After
five months he returned to League action, but it was not
until 1938-39 that he finally appeared to have put aside
the nervousness evident in his 'come back.' In the early
weeks of that season the 'Football Post' noted: "His speed
was always noticeable, and how pleasant it was to see his
confidence restored. I now predict a bright future for him
with the County." Sadly, the outbreak of war halted his
progress after an excellent season when he scored 12 League
and Cup goals in 36 matches.

Appearances: FL: 56 apps 14 gls FAC: 3 apps 2 gls
Total: 59 apps 16 gls

COOPER, Terry

Defender/Midfield   5' 9"   11st 0lbs
b. Croesyceiliog, Carmarthen, 11th March 1950
CAREER: Newport County ground staff, signing pro July
1968/NOTTS July 1970 (Lincoln City loan Dec 1971 and
July 1972)/Lincoln City Aug 1972, fee £5,000 (Scunthorpe
United loan Nov 1977)/Bradford City June 1979, fee
£10,000/Rochdale Aug 1981, retired cs 1982
Debut v Leyton Orient, FLC 1, (a) 17.8.71, drawn 1 – 1

Associated with the Magpies during an extremely successful period featuring two promotions in three seasons. Terry Cooper showed great promise during infrequent senior outings. Two separate loan spells with Lincoln City preceded his move to Sincil Bank on a permanent basis in the early weeks of season 1972-73. In the best spell of his career, Terry completed 268(2) League appearances for the Imps, scoring 12 goals. He was voted supporters' Player of the Year in 1975 and 1979, and appeared in 45 League matches in 1975-76 when Graham Taylor's side took the Division Four title, scoring a massive 111 goals and conceding just 39 in the 46 match tournament. A former captain of Wales Youth, Terry served six League clubs, his career figures totalling: 421(13) League matches and 17 goals.

Appearances: FL: 3(6) apps 0 gls FLC: 1 app 0 gls Other: 1 app 0 gls Total: 5(6) apps 0 gls
Honours: Wales Youth International. (Lincoln City) FL Div 4 champions 1976

COPE, Horace Walter
Left-back   5' 8½" 12st 10lbs
b. Treeton, near Sheffield, 24th May 1899
d. Nottingham, 4th October 1961
CAREER: Treeton Council School/Treeton Reading Rooms/ Treeton United/NOTTS Dec 1919/Arsenal Dec 1926, fee £3,125/Bristol Rovers July 1933, fee £1,500/Norwich City assistant trainer June 1934/Southampton trainer Feb 1937/ Blackburn Rovers trainer early in 1946 to May 1949
Debut v Birmingham (h) 16.2.21, drawn 0 – 0

A former miner who began in football as a centre-forward with Treeton United but subsequently found his best position as a full-back. Described as "Robust, a resolute tackler and a sure kick," he came within a whisker of international recognition. Damage to his knee ligaments obliged him to drop out after he had been selected to oppose Ireland in 1925. Sadly, he was never given another opportunity. At one time the Magpies spot kick ace, he lost the job after missing two in one match against Newcastle United in April 1925. Fortunately, the misses did not cost Notts the points as they won 2 – 0. A nephew, Harold Cope, played for the Magpies Reserves as an amateur in season 1930-31. He later signed as a professional with Folkestone in July 1931, then Tottenham Hotspur in October 1932 and Heanor Town in August 1932. On retirement from the game Horace Cope managed a Yorkshire social club and was later licensee of the Lord Alcester in Pym street, Nottingham.

Appearances: FL: 125 apps 6 gls FAC: 5 apps 0 gls Total: 130 apps 6 gls
Honours: (NOTTS) FL Div 2 champions 1923

CORKHILL, William Grant
Wing-half   5' 10" 11st 0lbs
b. Belfast, 23rd April 1910
d. Nottingham, 9th August 1978
CAREER: Northern Nomads/Marine F.C./Liverpool am Jan 1931/NOTTS May 1931/Cardiff City May 1938 (WW2 guest Chester, Lincoln City, Derby County, Mansfield Town, NOTTS & Nottingham Forest)/NOTTS Nov 1945, player-coach 1948/Scunthorpe United trainer-coach Feb 1951, becoming manager in the following season/Bradford P.A. manager May 1956 to Nov 1957/Hastings United manager.
Debut v Barnsley (a) 6.2.32, drawn 1 – 1

In addition to the appearance figures given below, Bill Corkhill was a regular player during the Second World War period, appearing in 81 regional matches. A strong, bandy-legged player with ginger hair and an infectious toothy grin, Bill gave yeoman service in a career spanning twenty years. A fine attacking right half-back, he played for an FA X1 against Combined Universities in season 1930-31 and joined the Magpies in the close season. Apart from a season as captain of Cardiff City, and various guest appearances during wartime football, plus a two-year spell in the Police War Reserve, he remained at Meadow Lane long enough to qualify as the club's oldest player in peacetime League matches. He was 41years old when he turned out for the last time at right full-back against Barnsley on 12th September 1951. With an eye to the future, he took his coaching certificates at Birmingham University, and was appointed as senior coach to the Notts. FA. In later years he was mine host at The Earl of Chesterfield, Carlton Road, Nottingham.

Appearances: FL: 264 apps 9 gls FAC: 20 apps 2 gls Other: 4 apps 0 gls Total: 288 apps 11 gls

---

CORNWELL, Ralph Leslie
Left-back   5' 10" 11st 2lbs
b. Nottingham, 7th September 1901
d. Hoveringham, Notts., 6th March 1988
CAREER: Sneiton Institute/NOTTS am Sept 1921, pro Nov 1921/Norwich City July 1926, but retired injured after just 2 FL apps/Mansfield Town cs 1928/Sneiton Church Institute am Jan 1930
Debut v Middlesbrough (a) 29.8.23, won 3 – 2

Locally born, prematurely balding full-back who enjoyed a fair amount of top flight action after first being introduced as deputy for Horace Cope in season 1923-24. Said to be of a retiring disposition and a popular squad member, he was also described as: "A player who has distinguished himself in the senior ranks on numerous occasions. Has plenty of pluck, a powerful kick, and is improving as a tackler." Transfer listed at the end of the relegation season 1925-26, Ralph was quickly snapped up by Norwich City. One of seven new players in the Norwich line up for their opening match (lost 6 – 1 against Millwall) he played only one more League game before he retired from senior soccer with a knee injury. During the Second World War he worked in a Royal Ordnance factory and was later a master grocer in Nottingham.

Appearances: FL: 42 apps 0 gls FAC: 4 apps 0 gls
Total: 46 apps 0 gls

COTTERILL, William Henry
Wing-half
b. Ripley, April quarter 1864
CAREER: NOTTS debut Jan 1885 to 1889
Debut v Notts. Rangers, FAC 2, (h) 13.11.1886, drawn 3 – 3

According to Census records, W.H. Cotterill was a 17 year-old student living in Derbyshire in 1881. By 1901 he had graduated to become a schoolmaster. Between times he had assisted the Magpies in one FA Cup tie in season 1886-87, and another in 1888-89. At the time of the second outing, a 4 – 2 win against Beeston St. John's in the second qualifying round, he was a member of the Magpies' Reserve team. The FA Cup match kicked off in the morning of 27th October 1888 and featured a Reserve team line-up. In the afternoon, the League side entertained Burnley and won 6 – 1, outside-left Bobby Jardine netting five of the goals.

Appearances: FAC: 2 apps 0 gls Total: 2 apps 0 gls

COULBY, George Arthur
Goalkeeper
b. Sherwood, Nottingham, July quarter 1866
d. Sherwood, Nottingham, 4th December 1933
CAREER: Charterhouse School 1883/Cambridge University 1884/NOTTS debut Nov 1884 to 1887/London Amateurs 1888/Captained St. Batholomew's Hospital cricket and football clubs 1888-90
Debut v Queen's Park, FAC 6, (h) 21.2.1885, drawn 2 – 2

Although mainly appearing as a goalkeeper, George Coulby made his debut at centre-forward against Sheffield Wednesday on 1st November 1884. Evidence of his versatility was never more apparent than in season 1885-86 when he played once each at outside-right, centre-half and left-half, and seven times as goalkeeper.

A son of Richard Coulby, a Nottingham lace manufacturer; during school days at Charterhouse George was winner of the Charterhouse Challenge Cup for cricket in consecutive years 1883, '84 and '85. In the latter year he headed the batting averages with a record score of 144 not out, and played for Nottinghamshire Colts v Yorkshire Colts in 1885 and '86. In June 1892 he passed final medical examinations at Cambridge University and subsequently became a member of the Nottingham Medico-Chirurgical Society.

Appearances: FAC: 2 apps 0 gls Total: 2 apps 0 gls

COULSTON, Walter
Outside-right   5' 7½" 10st 10lbs
b. Wombwell, 31st January 1912
d. Barnsley, June 1990
CAREER: Hemsworth West End/Barnsley trial Oct 1928/South Kirkby Colliery Aug 1929/Manchester City Aug 1933/Crystal Palace June 1936/Exeter City June 1937/Barnsley June1938/NOTTS May 1939 (WW2 guest Barnsley, Bradford City and Doncaster Rovers)
Debut v Bristol City (h) 6.5.39, drawn 0 – 0

Walter Coulston joined Notts in the last week of season 1938-39, and played in the final match against Bristol City. Reputed to be one of the fastest wingers in League football, Meadow Lane spectators were given little time in which to appreciate his talents as the outbreak of WW2 suspended League football in September 1939. Coulston's two appearances in the ill-fated 1939-40 season being expunged, along with County's promising record of played 2, won 2; goals for 6, against 3.

Appearances: FL: 1 app 0 gls Total: 1 app 0 gls

COX, Paul Richard
Central defender   5' 11" 11st 2lbs
b. Nottingham, 6th January 1972
CAREER: Nottinghamshire Schoolboys/NOTTS trainee, signing pro Aug 1989 (Hull City loan Dec 1994 to Jan 1995)/Kettering Town Aug 1995/Ilkeston Town Aug 2000/Gresley Rovers/Hucknall Town June 2001/Leek Town player-assistant manager May 2002/Eastwood Town assistant-manager/academy director May 2003.
Debut as sub v Manchester City (a) 25.4.92, lost 0 – 2

Handed an unexpected opportunity by manager Mick Walker when defensive resources were laid bare by injuries in mid season 1992-93. Paul certainly seized the chance, his solid displays ensuring that he retained a first team place for the remainder of the season. He also opened his goal scoring account, scoring one of the goals in the 4 – 0 victory against Southend United in March 1993.

His progress was subsequently disrupted by injuries, a loan spell with Hull City being his final involvement in League football.

Appearances: FL: 39(5) apps 1 gl FAC: 1(1) apps 0 gls
FLC: 3 apps 1 gl Other: 1(2) apps 0 gls
Total: 44(8) apps 2 gls
Honours: FA Xl v Combined Services, 1 app

COZENS, John William
Forward   6' 0"   12st 0lbs
b. Hammersmith, London, 14th May 1946
CAREER: Tonbridge/Hayes (Middlesex Wanderers)/ Hillingdon Borough Aug 1968/NOTTS Aug 1970, fee £10,000/Peterborough United Nov 1972, fee £8,000/ Cambridge United Dec 1977, fee £2,000, retired from playing in 1980, but remained as coach, and later assistant manger until 1985/Ramsey Town/Bourne Town manager/King's Lynn manager/Stamford manager.
Debut v Southend United (h) 5.9.70, won 2 – 1

John Cozens was leading goal scorer in the Southern League in season 1968-69 when his team, Hillingdon Borough, finished runners-up in the Premier Division of the Southern League. His form earned him a move into League football with the Magpies, but his first season at Meadow Lane was spent mainly in the North Midlands League side. He came into his own in 1971-72 with 13 League and four Cup goals, but was not appearing regularly when Peterborough United signed him in November 1972. He helped steer the Posh clear of relegation in his first season, and captained them to the Division Four title in 1973-74, scoring 25 goals in League and Cup during the season. Before injury enforced his retirement he enjoyed a successful promotion campaign with Cambridge United in 1977-78. Runners-up position in Division Three taking them into Division Two, just eight years on from their election into the Football League.

Appearances: FL: 41(3) apps 13 gls FAC: 4 apps 4 gls
FLC: 3 apps 3 gls Total: 48(3) apps 20 gls
Honours: (Peterborough United) FL Division 4 champions 1974

CRAMB, Colin
Forward   6' 0"   12st 6lbs
b. Lanark, 23rd June 1974
CAREER: Hamilton Accies B.C./Hamilton Academical trainee July 1990, pro May 1991/Southampton June 1993, fee £75,000/Falkirk Aug 1994, fee £45,000/Heart of Midlothian Mar 1995, fee £50,000/Doncaster Rovers Dec 1995, fee £25,000/Bristol City July 1997, fee £250,000

(Walsall loan Feb 1999)/Crewe Alexandra Aug 1999, fee £200,000 (NOTTS loan Sept 2000) (Bury loan Feb 2001)/ Fortuna Sittard, Holland, July 2001/Bury Jan 2003/ Shrewsbury Town Aug 2003 and re-registered Aug 2004 to Sept 2004/Grimsby Town trial/Hamilton Academical Jan 2005.
Debut v Swansea City (h) 12.9.2000, lost 0 – 1

One of soccer's wanderers having - to date - assisted fourteen clubs in a nomadic career spanning Scotland, England and Holland. In 2003-04 Colin assisted Shrewsbury Town to win promotion from the Nationwide Conference, returning to League football after a season's absence. In the final against Aldershot Town at the Britannia Stadium, won on penalties after a 1 – 1 draw, Colin made a substitute appearance, replacing another ex-Magpie in Duane Darby. With Doncaster Rovers in 1996-97 he enjoyed much success, scoring 18 League goals and two in Cup matches. At the commencement of the 2003-04 season, his record in Scottish and English League football totalled 68 goals in 241(27) matches.

Appearances: FL: 2(1) apps 0 gls Total: 2(1) apps 0 gls
Honours: (Hamilton Academical) B & Q Cup winners 1992-93

CRANK, Joseph
Right-back   5' 10"   11st 9lbs
b. Leigh, Lancs. July quarter 1876
d. Bolton, 16th August 1946
CAREER: Manchester Fairfield May 1895/NOTTS Mar 1897, fee £15 plus a benefit match/Glossop North End June 1897/Manchester Fairfield Sept 1897/Oldham County October 1897/Berry's F.C., Manchester, later in the same month, until 1899
Debut v Small Heath (a) 10.4.1897, lost 1 – 3

Credited with being the best back in the Lancashire League, on his reserve team debut he was described as "Nicely built and fast." The Evening News correspondent adding: "He can hop it, and no mistake!" Signed as cover for the full-back berths with the prospects of involvement in the end-of-season Test matches, he did not manage to disturb the usual pairing of Prescott and Gibson and departed in the close season. Later in the same year he had the briefest involvement with Oldham County, who were served with a winding-up order in the month that he joined them. He had rather better luck with Berry's, the Manchester boot and shoe polish manufacturers, whose work's team he assisted until 1899.

Appearances: FL: 1 app 0 gls Total: 1 app 0 gls

CRAPPER, Joseph

Outside-right   5' 7"   11st 0lbs
b. Wortley, Sheffield, 3rd March 1899
d. Sheffield, 4th February 1989
CAREER: Swallownest F.C./NOTTS am Apr 1922/
Huddersfield Town am Nov 1922/Swansea Town July 1923
to May 1924.
Debut v Coventry City (a) 22.4.22, lost 2 – 4

Two appearances in late season 1921-22, when he was
tried at outside-right in place of Robert Platts, was the
extent of Joe's first team involvement at Meadow Lane.
Signed by Swansea Town, after a spell in reserve with
Huddersfield Town, he did a little better. Three consecutive
appearances on the left wing, spanning March and April
1924 being his brief taste of League action with the Swans.

Appearances: FL: 2 apps 0 gls Total: 2 apps 0 gls

CRAYTHORNE, Reuben 'Ben'

Left-half   5' 7"   10st 12lbs
b. Aston, Birmingham, 21st January 1882
d. Birmingham, 21st October 1953
CAREER: Small Heath Athletic/Kidderminster Harriers/
Coventry City Mar 1903/Walsall during season 1903-04/
NOTTS Apr 1904 to 1914/Darlington
Debut v Small Heath (a) 10.9.04, won 2 – 1 (scored one)

For the best part
of ten seasons an
indispensable
factor in the
Magpies success.
He began as an
inside-left and
scored the winning
goal on his debut,
but before the end
of his first season
was appearing at
left-half,   a
position he was to
dominate for a
decade. A brainy
half-back,   he
adorned   the
position   with
skill, judgement and scrupulously fair methods, despite
confessing that he really preferred a role in the forward
line. An injury sustained early in season 1912-13 restricted
him to just 13 matches and the Magpies were relegated
from Division One. In the promotion season that followed,
the outstanding form of Richard Allsebrook restricted Ben
to just four League matches. In January 1919 he was a
welcome visitor to the Magpies' dressing room at
Birmingham. He was employed in the munitions industry
in the City at that time. Off the field he was a noted
pigeon fancier and breeder of canaries.

Appearances: FL: 282 apps 12 gls FAC: 14 apps 0 gls
Total: 296 apps 12 gls
Honours: Football League representative, 1 app 1906-07

CREANEY, Gerard Thomas 'Gerry'

Forward   5' 11"   13st 6lbs
b. Coatbridge, 13th April 1970
CAREER: Nottingham Forest Boys' Club/Celtic Boys' Club
1984/Celtic May 1987/Everton trial 16th Jan 1994/
Portsmouth 26th Jan 1994, fee £600,000/Manchester City
Sept 1995, fee £1.1million plus Paul Walsh (Oldham Athletic
loan Mar-May 1996) (Ipswich Town loan Oct 1996) (Burnley
loan Sept 1997) (Chesterfield loan Jan 1998)/West
Bromwich Albion trial July 1998/St Mirren Oct 1998/NOTTS
Feb-May 1999/Queen of the South trial Nov 2000
Debut v Fulham (a) 20.2.99, lost 1 – 2

Gerry Creaney began with Celtic but fell out of favour
during Lou Macari's brief spell in charge at Parkhead. A
move to Portsmouth lifted his game and resulted in his
inclusion in the Scotland squad and a place on the bench
for the Hampden Park fixture against the Faroe Islands.
His scoring record of 36 in 69 matches brought about a £2
million rated transfer to Manchester City, but he quickly
found himself surplus to requirements at Maine Road.
Gerry scored his 100th career goal when on loan at Oldham
Athletic in a spell that helped the Latics retain their
Division One status. His final spell in League football
was with the Magpies, who signed him on a week-to-
week contract. Despite appearing in all but two of the
season's final eighteen matches, he was not offered a
permanent contract.

Appearances: FL: 13(3) apps 3 gls Total: 13(3) apps 3 gls
Honours: Scotland 'B' International, 1 app. Scotland U-
21 International, 11 apps

CRESSWELL, Frank

Inside-left   5' 7"   10st 6lbs
b. South Shields, 5th September 1908
d. Jesmond, Newcastle-upon-Tyne, 2nd December 1979
CAREER: Stanhope Road School/Westoe Central Schools/
South Shields Schoolboys/Durham Schoolboys/Tyne Dock/
Sunderland Nov 1925/West Bromwich Albion June 1929,
fee £975/Chester July 1930/NOTTS Jan 1934/Chester June
1934, retired due to injury 1938/Northampton Town
assistant-manager
Debut v Southampton (h) 20.1.34, drawn 2 – 2 (scored one)

Frank Cresswell captained England Schoolboys on four
occasions – twice each against Scotland and Wales. He
joined his celebrated elder brother, England international
full-back Warney Cresswell, at Sunderland, but failed to
win a regular place.

He then scored six goals in 30 League appearances for West Bromwich Albion in 1929-30 before moving on to Chester, at that time a non-League club. They won election to the League a year later, and Cresswell became one of their key players, totalling 168 Northern Section appearances, scoring 57 goals. In a brief interlude at Meadow Lane he was praised for his clever footwork, constructive ideas and goal awareness. On leaving football, he worked for the Victoria Insurance Company until 1973.

Appearances: FL: 16 apps 4 gls Total: 16 apps 4 gls
Honours: England Schoolboys, 4 caps 1921-22. (Chester) Welsh Cup winners 1933, finalists 1935

CRICHTON, Paul Andrew
Goalkeeper   6' 1"   12st 2lbs
b. Pontefract, 3rd October 1968
CAREER: Nottingham Forest pro May 1986 (NOTTS loan Sept 1986) (Darlington loan Jan 1987) (Peterborough United loan Mar 1987) (Darlington loan Sept 1987) (Swindon Town loan Dec 1987) (Rotherham United loan Mar 1988) (Torquay United loan Aug 1988) (Peterborough United Nov 1988/ Doncaster Rovers Aug 1990/Grimsby Town July 1993/West Bromwich Albion Sept 1996, fee £250,000 (Aston Villa loan Aug 1997) (Burnley loan Aug 1998)/Burnley Nov 1998, fee £100,000/Norwich City June 2001, fee £150,000
Debut v Middlesbrough (h) 21.10.86, won 1 – 0

Although a Forest development from junior football, Paul Crichton made his League debut in the Magpies' goal when on loan as cover for the injured Mick Leonard. It was the first of seven separate loans for the young Yorkshire man, who finally found a permanent billet with Peterborough United. 133 League appearances for Grimsby Town and a 'Player of the Year' award in 1993-94, led to a big money transfer to West Bromwich Albion, where he took over from the veteran Nigel Spink. An early season loan to Burnley was made permanent, Paul completing 82(1) League appearances for the Clarets. A final move in League circles found the vastly experienced goalkeeper restricted at Norwich City by the emerging talents of Robert Green.

Appearances: FL: 5 apps 0 gls Total: 5 apps 0 gls

CRICKMORE, Charles Alfred
Outside-left   5' 9"   10st 9lbs
b. Hull, 11th February 1942
CAREER: Hull Schoolboys/Hull City am Aug 1957, pro Feb1959/Bournemouth & Boscombe Athletic June 1962, fee £2,000/Gillingham June 1966, player exchange/ Rotherham United Nov 1967, fee £17,500/Norwich City Jan 1968, fee £15,000/NOTTS Mar 1970 to 1972, fee £7,500
Debut v Scunthorpe United (a) 14.3.70, won 3 – 2

An exceptionally speedy and elusive wingman, and frequent goal scorer, Charlie was a regular with all of his clubs, his 350th League outing coming in the Magpies' Division Four championship season. An early signing by manager Sirrel, he was ever-present during the successful 1970-71 campaign, scoring ten League goals and two in the FA Cup. Charlie retired in 1972 with career figures of 354(3) League appearances and 64 goals. He returned to live in Hull and joined the Fire Service. He qualified as a class one referee, played rugby league football with West Hull, and at the age of 61 won the fifth Arthur Mann Memorial Golf Day at Beeston Fields in August 2003.

Appearances: FL: 59 apps 11 gls FAC: 4 apps 2 gls FLC: 1 app 0 gls Total: 64 apps 13 gls
Honours: (NOTTS) FL Div 4 champions 1971

CRISPIN, Timothy
Left-back   5' 8½"   10st 8lbs
b. Blaby, Leicester 7th June 1948
CAREER: Leicestershire County Youth/NOTTS July 1966/ Lincoln City 1968
Debut v Newport County (h) 22.4.67, won 2 – 1

Tim Crispin was a member of the highly successful Leicestershire Youth team, County Cup winners in 1965-66. Originally a wing-half, he came to the fore with Notts as a left back, appearing in the final six fixtures of season 1966-67. Despite any number of full-back pairings during the course of the following season – seven players appearing in the number 3 jersey – Crispin appeared in only two Division Four matches. He did not figure in first team football with Lincoln City.

Appearances: FL: 8 apps 0 gls Total: 8 apps 0 gls

CRONE, Robert
Defender   5' 11½"   12st 5lbs
b. Belfast, circa 1865
CAREER: Belfast Schoolboys/Distillery/Middlesbrough 1892/ West Bromwich Albion Mar 1893/Burton Swifts Aug 1895/ Millwall Athletic Apr 1895/NOTTS May 1896/Bedminster May 1898/Bristol City trainer cs 1901-03/Brentford trainer 1903-08/West Bromwich Albion trainer-coach 1908-09/ Workington trainer 1909-10
Debut v Burton Swifts (a) 2.1.1897, won 4 – 1

Two appearances in the Irish Cup final and four international caps paved the way for Bob Crone's entry into English football. Originally a full-back, he played most of his games for the Magpies in the middle line, appearing in eleven League matches and four Test matches in 1896-97 when Notts secured promotion to Division One.

After one season in the top flight he departed to Bedminster and in March 1899 was named in the Ireland squad to oppose Scotland at Celtic Park, Glasgow. In the event, he did not feature in the match, and was probably fortunate not to do so, as Scotland won 9 – 1!

Appearances: FL: 32 apps 0 gls FAC: 3 apps 0 gls Other: 4 apps 0 gls Total: 39 apps 0 gls
Honours: Ireland International, 4 caps 1889-90. (Distillery) Irish Cup winners 1889, finalists 1888. (NOTTS) FL Div 2 champions 1897

CROOKES, Robert Eastland 'Bob'

Forward   5' 11" 11st 6lbs
b. Retford, Notts., 27th February 1924
CAREER: Retford Grammar School/North Leverton F.C./ Retford Town/NOTTS June 1949 to 1956/Worksop Town/ Grantham/Retford Town Nov 1961
Debut v Exeter City (h) 8.9.49, drawn 3 – 3

One of eight footballing brothers, Bobby Crookes was first recommended to the Magpies in 1946 by someone who had seen him play for the Signals Regiment in India. Wishing to concentrate on a teaching career, he declined Notts' offer and on demobilisation joined the staff of the Sir Frederick Milner School, Retford. Magpies' officials made a second offer, following his appearance for Retford Town in the final of the Notts. Senior Cup at Meadow Lane, and he was persuaded to sign as a part-time professional. A fast raider with a good shot, at either inside or outside-left he was a dangerous forward. Introduced during the Division Three South championship season, his career reached its peak in 1951-52, when he was club leading goalscorer in Division Two matches with 15 goals in 38 matches.

Appearances: FL: 177 apps 45 gls FAC: 8 apps 1 gl
Total: 185 apps 46 gls

CROSS, David Barron

Midfield   5' 10" 10st 7lbs
b. Bromley, 7th September 1982
CAREER: NOTTS scholar July 1999
Debut as sub v Chesterfield (a) 29.4.2000, lost 1 – 2

Youthful midfielder who was introduced for his League debut as a late substitute in the final away fixture of season 1999-2000. The Magpies season had petered out in disappointing fashion; without a win in their final eight matches, chances of a place in the Play-offs had vanished. Against already relegated Chesterfield, an early goal from Paul Bolland proved insufficient, former Magpie David Reeves securing the points for Chesterfield with two second - half goals.

Appearances: FL: 0(1) apps 0 gls Total: 0(1) apps 0 gls

CRUICKSHANK, Frank James

Full-back   5' 11" 11st 6lbs
b. Polmont, Stirlingshire, 20th November 1931
CAREER: Nuneaton Borough/NOTTS Jan 1950/Cheltenham Town/Cambridge City season 1961-62, appointed caretaker-manager Mar 1962, manager cs 1962
Debut v Swansea Town (a) 20.3.54, drawn 2 – 2

Frank Cruickshank was serving in the R.A.F. when signed by the Magpies, and did not obtain his release until the end of season 1950-51. He had some time to wait for a senior opportunity, Southwell and Deans being the well-established pairing at full-back. He first played regularly in season 1955-56, commencing at left–back, he then switched flanks and made 31 consecutive appearances, scoring three goals, two from penalty kicks. A popular player with a quiet disposition, he served the Magpies with admirable enthusiasm at a difficult period in their history, consecutive relegations being suffered in 1957-58 and 1958-59. He was the only ever-present in the latter campaign, regaining his position as captain in the closing weeks of the season. His final season, 1959-60, was blighted by a knee injury.

Appearances: FL: 151 apps 5 gls FAC: 4 apps 0 gls
Total: 155 apps 5 gls

CUMNER, Reginald Horace

Forward   5' 8½" 10st 10lbs
b. Cwmaman, Glamorgan, 31st March 1918
b. Poole, Dorset, January 1999
CAREER: Aberaman Athletic/Swansea Town youth team/ Arsenal May 1936 (Margate loan July 1936 to Jan 1938) (Hull City loan Jan 1938) (WW2 guest Aberaman Athletic, Cardiff City, Clapton Orient, Fulham, Liverpool, Morton, Plymouth Argyle, Portsmouth, Port Vale & Swansea Town)/ NOTTS July 1946, part exchange transfer/Watford July 1948, fee 2,200/Scunthorpe & Lindsey United Sept 1950/Bradford City Aug 1953/Poole Town July 1954/Bridport
Debut v Bournemouth & Bos. Ath. (h) 31.8.46, won 1 – 0

Horace Cumner made his League debut in Arsenal's colours, as deputy for the Gunners' celebrated outside-left Cliff Bastin. In a dream debut, he scored the only goal of the game at Wolverhampton Wanderers on 17th September 1938. His progress was rapid in the extreme, being rewarded by international recognition in his debut season. He served in the Royal Marines during World War Two, suffering serious burns whilst on active service. A full recovery enabled him to appear in ten Wartime Internationals, in one of which he scored both goals in Wales' 2 – 1 victory against England at Wolverhampton.

Appearances: FL: 66 apps 11 gls FAC: 8 apps 2 gls Total: 74 apps 13 gls
Honours: Wales International, 3 caps 1939 (Also 10 war-time international apps.) Wales Schoolboy International.

CUNNINGTON, Shaun Gary

Midfield   5' 10" 11st 12lbs
b. Bourne, Lincs., 4th January 1966
CAREER: Bourne Town/Wrexham app 1982, pro Jan 1984/Grimsby Town Feb 1988, fee £50,000/Sunderland July 1992, fee £650,000/West Bromwich Albion Aug 1995, fee £220,000/NOTTS Mar 1997, fee £25,000/Kidderminster Harriers Aug 1998, subsequently appointed youth team manager, caretaker manager Nov 2004
Debut as sub v Rotherham United (a) 15.3.97, drawn 2 – 2

Shaun was playing for Bourne Town Reserves at 15 years of age. He made his League debut for Wrexham when he was 16, and when he left the Racecourse at 22, had appeared in over 250 matches. In two seasons with Grimsby Town he captained the Mariners to successive promotions from Division Four to Division Two. His seven League goals in his first season with Sunderland was a valuable contribution in a campaign that ended with the Black Cats just one point above the Division One relegation places. A catalogue of injuries and illness followed, and he was restricted to a handful of appearances for both West Bromwich Albion and for the Magpies. Shaun did not qualify for a championship medal in the club's runaway success in 1997-98, being restricted to just 3(6) appearances in the season's Division Three matches.

Appearances: FL: 9(8) apps 0 gls FLC: 1(1) apps 0 gls Other: 1 app 0 gls Total: 11(9) apps 0 gls
Honours: (Wrexham) Welsh Cup winners 1986, finalists 1982 & 1983

CURRIE, James Blair

Inside-forward 5' 6½" 10st 9lbs
b. Galston, Ayrshire, 14th February 1896
CAREER: Prestwick F.C./Glenleven Rovers (Kilmarnock)/NOTTS June1919 to cs 1920
Debut v Burnley (a) 6.9.19, lost 1 – 2

Blair Currie, a lightweight inside-forward with clever ball control, played in eight First Division matches but picked up just one winning bonus, and this against fellow strugglers Sheffield Wednesday who accompanied Notts through the relegation trapdoor at the close of the season. Currie's form in Scottish junior football was outstanding and several English League clubs were said to be in contention for his signature, but his lightweight physique hindered his progress in First Division football. During his period of service in the Great War he rose through the ranks to become an Army Lieutenant

Appearances: FL: 8 apps 1 gl Total: 8 apps 1 gl

CURSHAM, Arthur William

Outside-right
b. Wilford, Notts., 14th March 1853
d. Florida, USA, 24th December 1884
CAREER: Oakham School/Nottingham Law Club/NOTTS 1871-84/Sheffield Club
Debut v Nottingham Forest, FAC 1, (h) 16.11.1878, lost 1 – 3

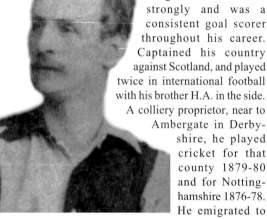

A fast-moving and incisive wingman who dribbled strongly and was a consistent goal scorer throughout his career. Captained his country against Scotland, and played twice in international football with his brother H.A. in the side. A colliery proprietor, near to Ambergate in Derbyshire, he played cricket for that county 1879-80 and for Nottinghamshire 1876-78. He emigrated to Florida in 1884, but died of yellow fever within a year of arrival.

Appearances: FAC: 22 apps 15 gls Total: 22 apps 15 gls
Honours: England International, 6 caps 1876-83

CURSHAM, Charles Lambert

Forward
b. Wilford, Notts., 29th October 1858
d. Minocqua, Wisconsin, USA, 12th April 1923
CAREER: NOTTS 1876-82
Debut v Sheffield, FAC 1, (h) 3.11.1877, drawn 1 – 1

Although tending to be overshadowed by his brothers Arthur and Harry, Charles Cursham was a regular member of the Notts X1 for several seasons. Commencing in December 1876, he made his debut in a 4 – 1 win against Newark. His form in the late stages of 1877-78, when he scored five goals in three matches, earned him a regular berth in the side, a position he retained for the next four seasons.

Appearances: FAC: 10 apps 2 gls Total: 10 apps 2 gls

CURSHAM, Henry Alfred 'Harry'

Left wing forward
b. Wilford, Notts., 27th November 1859
d. Holme Pierrepoint, Notts., 6th August 1941
CAREER: Repton School/NOTTS 1877/Corinthians 1882-86/Grantham/Thursday Wanderers, Sheffield
Debut v Nottingham Forest, FAC 1, (h) 16.11.1878, lost 1 – 3

Began with Notts shortly after leaving Repton aged 18, and appeared regularly afterwards with his brother, A.W., (q.v.). An advocate, and arch exponent of the dribbling game, when interviewed in 1904 by the 'Football Post', he considered that "Individual play was being too greatly sacrificed to the cry of combination." Within his outstanding goal-a-game aggregate, highlights included six goals against Wednesbury Strollers in a replayed FA Cup tie in November 1881, and four against Rotherham Town in Notts' all-time record FA Cup victory in October 1885. In the handling code, he was good enough to represent Nottinghamshire against Bedfordshire in February 1892. Business commitments as an insurance broker precluded a career in county cricket that totalled two matches for Notts. – separated by a 24-year margin!

Appearances: FL: 9 apps 2 gls FAC: 44 apps 51 gls
Total: 53 apps 53 gls
Honours: England International, 8 caps 1880-84

DAFT, Harry Butler

D

Outside-left   5' 9½" 11st 0lbs
b. Radcliffe-on-Trent, Notts, 5th April 1866
d. High Cross, Herts, 12th January 1945
CAREER: Trent College/NOTTS am Mar 1885, pro 1890/Nottingham Forest Jan 1893/NOTTS Aug 1893/Newark Town am Jan 1895 (Also assisted Corinthians 1887-90 and Nottinghamshire in representative matches)
Debut v Rotherham Town, FAC 1, (h) 24.10.1885, won 15 – 0 (scored two)

The youngest son of Richard Daft (Nottinghamshire C.C.C. 1858-91), brother of Richard Parr Daft (Nottinghamshire C.C.C. 1886), nephew of Charles Frederick Daft (Nottinghamshire C.C.C. 1862-64) and cousin to H.C. Daft, the champion hurdle racer. For genuine all-round sporting ability, however, the star of this remarkable family was Harry Butler Daft. In addition to his England football caps, he played in 190 matches for Nottinghamshire C.C.C. and represented the Gentlemen against the Players. Additionally, he was no mean exponent of the game of lacrosse, having represented the North against the South, and was reserve for England when twenty years of age. As a footballer he was noted for his great speed, clever centres and ability as a goalscorer. An invaluable servant to the Notts club who, in 1893, was said to be the one remaining link connecting the present "Notts Incorporated" with the old Notts Club. In January 1893 he was sensationally dismissed after he had declined to travel to Scotland for the New Year tour on account of a foot injury. He was quickly snapped up by Forest, but donned the scarlet jersey on only four occasions, one of his appearances being against the Magpies on 25th February 1893, at the Town Ground, Forest winning 3 – 1. Much to the relief of the Trent Bridge faithful, the rift was healed in the close season and he returned to the Magpies.

Appearances: FL: 137 apps 58 gls FAC: 36 apps 20 gls
Other: 6 apps 3 gls Total: 179 apps 81 gls
Honours: England International, 5 caps 1889-92. FL Representative, 2 apps 1891-92. (NOTTS) FA Cup winners 1894, finalists 1891

DAINTY, Herbert Charles

Half-back   5' 8"   12st 0lbs
b. Geddington, Northants, 6th February 1879
d. Kettering, Northants, 10th September 1957
CAREER: Kettering Town Apr 1897/Leicester Fosse June 1899/New Brighton Tower May 1900, fee £200/Leicester Fosse Aug 1901/Northampton Town May 1902, fee £200/NOTTS May 1903/Southampton May 1904/Dundee May 1905/Bradford P.A. May 1911/Ayr United Oct 1913, appointed player-manager May 1914/Dundee Hibernian player-manager Apr 1915/Montreal, Canada, coach Dec 1923/Guayquil, South America, coach, Apr 1925/Kettering Town manager Aug 1931/Ipswich Town trainer 1932/Northants FA coach circa 1934
Debut v Derby County (a) 19.9.03, won 1 – 0

Commenting on his debut for the Magpies, the 'Football Post' correspondent was obviously impressed: "Brisk and dashing in defence with useful heading powers. He fed his forwards with neat, short passes, delivered with great accuracy." A seasoned campaigner with Football League and Southern League experience when he joined Notts, he later added Scottish football to his c.v. His Scottish Cup medal with Dundee in 1910 was hard earned as it took three attempts to overcome Hibernian in the semi-final, and a further three to see off Clyde, beaten 2 – 1 in the second replay. In October of the same year he represented the Scottish League against the Southern League at The Den, New Cross, London. Outside of football, he was a coach builder by profession.

Appearances: FL: 20 apps 0 gls FAC: 1 app 0 gls
Total: 21 apps 0 gls
Honours: Scottish League representative, 1 app 1910. (Dundee) Scottish Cup winners 1910

DALE, George Henry

Inside-right   5' 6"   10st 4lbs
b. Nottingham, 2nd May 1883
d. Logged at Basford, Notts, April 1957
CAREER: Newark Athletic/Stanley Works (Newark)/Newark Town/NOTTS Feb 1914 (WW1 guest Queens Park Rangers)/Chelsea June 1919 to 1924, fee £500/Weymouth by 1926/Vicker's Crayford (Dartford) Sept 1927
Debut v Liverpool (a) 5.9.14, drawn 1 – 1

George Dale was a former team-mate of Edward Bassett (q.v.) at the Newark Stanley Works. He joined the Magpies from Newark Town where, despite lacking in physique for the position, he was often found at centre-half. Inside-forward was his preferred position, however, and in this role he enjoyed an extended run of First Division football from mid season 1914-15. A skilful dribbler who parted with the ball most effectively and, according to the 'Nottingham Post', was lacking only in the "shooting boots" department. Moving to Chelsea for the first season of League football after the Great War, he was a regular in 1919-20 but subsequently in reserve.

His record of 52 appearances and one goal confirming that his performance in front of goal had not improved.

Appearances: FL: 18 apps 5 gls FAC: 1 app 0 gls
Total: 19 apps 5 gls

DALLMAN, William

Centre-half
b. Mansfield, 8th August 1918
d. Mansfield, December 1988
CAREER: Rufford Colliery/NOTTS Oct 1938/Mansfield Town
Debut v Mansfield Town, Div 3 South Cup round 1 (a) 12.10.38, lost 0 – 3

First tried by Notts in a reserve team match against Forest in October 1938, Dallman made his single senior appearance later in the same month. The Southern Section Cup tie proved a uphill battle for Notts after Alf Feebury received a gash over his left eye which needed hospital treatment. With only ten men for more than half of the match Notts went under by 3 – 0. It was Mansfield Town's first ever victory against the Magpies. The match was poorly attended - 1,616 spectators paying £62 at the gate.

Appearances: Other: 1 app 0 gls Total: 1 app 0 gls

DALTON, Richard Timothy 'Tim'

Goalkeeper   5' 11"   11st 8lbs
b. Paddington, 14th October 1965
CAREER: Coventry City app, signing pro Sept 1983/NOTTS July 1984/Boston United cs 1986/Bradford City Sept 1986 (Tranmere Rovers loan Dec 1986)
Debut v York City (a) 22.4.86, drawn 2 – 2

Despite association with four senior clubs Tim Dalton appeared in only two FL matches. In addition to his solitary outing for the Magpies he played once for Tranmere Rovers, in a 0 – 1 defeat at Exeter City in a Division Four match on 13th December 1986.

Appearances: FL: 1 app 0 gls Total: 1 app 0 gls

DALY, Joseph

Outside-right   5' 8"   10st 10lbs
b. Lancaster, 28th December 1897
d. Logged at Basford, Nottingham, October quarter 1941, age 43
CAREER: Stonehurst College (near Blackburn)/Cliftonville/NOTTS Mar 1921/Northampton Town May 1927/Luton Town May 1928/Gillingham Sept 1930/Notts Corinthians Aug 1932
Debut v Hull City (a) 12.3.21, drawn 1 – 1

The son of a retired army officer, Joe Daly was educated at Stonehurst College and in Belfast. While training for a commission he won several sprint races including the Ulster Amateur Sprint Championship. Recruited by Notts from Cliftonville, he proved an excellent signing. Plucky, clever and elusive he was recognised as one of the fastest outside-rights in the country. After leaving Meadow Lane he spent a season with Northampton Town (33 apps, 4 gls) and two seasons with Luton Town (70 apps, 4 gls). He did not appear at senior level with Gillingham.

Appearances: FL: 139 apps 12 gls FAC: 15 apps 0 gls
Total: 154 apps 12 gls
Honours: (NOTTS) FL Div 2 champions 1923

--------------------o--------------------

DANIEL, Raymond Christopher
Defender   5' 10"   11st 10lbs
b. Luton, 10th December 1964
CAREER: Luton Town app 1980, pro Sept 1982 (Gillingham loan Sept 1983)/Hull City June 1986/Cardiff City Aug 1989, fee £40,000/Portsmouth Nov 1990, fee £80,000 (NOTTS loan Oct-Nov 1994)/Walsall Aug 1995/Gainsborough Trinity Aug 1997
Debut v Burnley (a) 29.10.94, lost 1 – 2

A left-sided full-back or utility defender who spent a month at Meadow Lane, when on Portsmouth's transfer list. Ray Daniel's five appearances included wins against Sunderland and West Bromwich Albion in a season when only nine League wins were secured, Notts being relegated, finishing at the bottom of Division One. He had earlier enjoyed a considerable amount of first team football, most notably with Portsmouth (exactly 100 League matches.) His career aggregate figures totalled 296(27) League and Cup matches and 12 goals.

Appearances: FL: 5 apps 0 gls Other: 1 app 0 gls
Total: 6 apps 0 gls

--------------------o--------------------

DARBY, Duane Anthony
Forward   5' 11"   12st 6lbs
b. Birmingham, 17th October 1973
CAREER: Torquay United trainee, signing pro July 1992/Doncaster Rovers July 1995, fee £60,000/Hull City Mar 1996/NOTTS July 1998 (Hull City loan Mar 1999)/Rushden & Diamonds June 2000/Shrewsbury Town 2003, reregistered Aug 2004.
Debut as sub v Luton Town (h) 7.8.99, drawn 0 – 0

In a most unfortunate start to his career with the Magpies, Duane suffered an Achilles injury in pre-season training. After eight months on the sidelines he was loaned back to his previous club, Hull City, who eased him back into action with eight appearances that included four from the bench.

A bright start to the following season was in no small part due to an immediate understanding forged between Duane and Mark Stallard. Sadly, this proved relatively short lived as the unfortunate target man sustained a groin injury that kept him out of action for two months. On leaving Meadow Lane he enjoyed great success with Rushden & Diamonds, finishing the season as Conference leading scorer with 24 in 38 matches and collecting the 'Player of the Year' award. Later with Shrewsbury Town he scored in the Nationwide Conference Final v Aldershot Town in May 2004 at the Britannia Stadium. Shrewsbury won the final on penalties and returned to the Football League after one season's absence.

Appearances: FL: 22(6) apps 5 gls FLC: 3(1) apps 1 gl
Total: 25(7) apps 6 gls
Honours: (Rushden & Diamonds) Nationwide Conference champions 2001

--------------------o--------------------

DAVIES, John Gerwyn
Goalkeeper   6' 3"   13st 12lbs
b. Llandysul, 18th November 1959
CAREER: Cardiff City app, signing pro Nov 1977/Hull City Feb 1980, fee £12,000 (NOTTS loan Mar-May 1986)/Bridlington Town July 1990/Hull City Football in the Community Officer
Debut v Brentford (h) 29.3.86, lost 0 – 4

Welsh-speaking John Davies had all the physical attributes for his position, but his role was confined to that of a reliable deputy at both Cardiff City (seven League appearances) and Hull City (24 League appearances.) In a late season loan to the Magpies in March 1986, he rounded off his run of ten Division Three matches with three 'clean sheets,' but then tragically suffered a knee injury in the County Cup Final against Forest that ended his first class career.

Appearances: FL: 10 apps 0 gls Total: 10 apps 0 gls

--------------------o--------------------

DAVIES, William 'Willie'
Outside-right   5' 7½"   10st 10lbs
b. Troedyrhiwfach, Glamorgan, 16th February 1900
d. Llandeilo, Carmarthenshire, 6th August 1953
CAREER: Troedyrhiwfach/Rhymney/Swansea Amateurs/Swansea Town May 1921, for a variously reported donation, put at somewhere between 10s./6d and £25!/Cardiff City June 1924, fee £2,700/NOTTS Mar 1928/Tottenham Hotspur Feb 1930, fee £3,000/Bargoed/Swansea Town Sept 1933/Llanelli player-coach April 1936 to 1938
Debut v Leeds United (a) 17.3.28, lost 0 – 6

Despite the fact that his Magpies debut ended in a 6 – 0 defeat, Willie Davies' display found favour with the 'Football Post' correspondent: "I was particularly impressed by the display of Willie Davis, who has a rare turn of speed, splendid ball control, and is a skilful dribbler."

The Wales international forward, who won six of his caps while on the Magpies' books, was a remarkably elusive wingman, able to beat opponents in little space and centre accurately. He netted a sizeable fee when transferred to Tottenham Hotspur in February 1930 but, shorn of their star wingman, the

Magpies crashed out of Division Two, finishing bottom of the League after picking up just one point from their final seven League engagements.

Appearances: FL: 71 apps 9 gls FAC: 2 apps 0 gls
Total: 73 apps 9 gls
Honours: Wales International, 17 caps 1924-30. (Cardiff City) FA Cup finalists 1925. Welsh League representative, 1 app 1928

---○---

DAVIS, Arthur George

Inside-left   5' 10½"   12st 0lbs
b. Birmingham January quarter 1898
CAREER: Birmingham St George's/Evesham Town (WW1 guest Leicester Fosse & Coventry City)/Aston Villa July 1919/Queens Park Rangers May 1922/NOTTS Feb 1924, fee £1,650/Crystal Palace May 1928/Kidderminster Harriers cs 1929
Debut v Chelsea (a) 9.2.24, won 6 – 0 (scored two)

In season 1923-24 the Magpies knocked Queens Park Rangers out of the FA Cup in round one. In the following month they signed the Rangers inside-forward, Arthur Davis. In his first game – a sensational 6 – 0 against Chelsea at Stamford Bridge – he opened his scoring account with two well taken goals. In three of his four full seasons at Meadow Lane Arthur was one of the best marksmen in the attack. He was leading scorer in 1924-25 and 1925-26, and joint leading scorer with Neil Harris in 1926-27. In addition to his prowess as a marksman he was a skilful dribbler and a master of strategy who did plenty of foraging. Included in his final total of 51 League goals was a four goal haul at Barnsley in October 1926, and hat-tricks against Tottenham Hotspur and Huddersfield Town in 1925-26. His career aggregate figures were 212 League matches and 75 goals.

Appearances: FL: 140 apps 51 gls FAC: 6 apps 3 gls
Total: 146 apps 54 gls
Honours: FA representative, 1 app.

DAVIS, Darren John

Defender   6' 0"   11st 0lbs
b. Sutton-in-Ashfield, Notts, 5th February 1967
CAREER: NOTTS from school, signing pro Feb 1985/ Lincoln City Aug 1988/Maidstone United Mar 1991, fee £27,500/Boston United Nov 1992/Eynesbury Rovers Jan 1993/Frickley Athletic Feb 1993/Scarborough Aug 1993/ Grantham Town Aug 1995/Lincoln City nc Sept 1995/ Grantham Town Oct 1995/Leicester United/FB, Malaysia/ Woodland Wellington, Singapore/VS Rugby/Hucknall Town/ Arnold Town/Gedling Town manager 2002/NOTTS Academy coach.
Debut v Sunderland (a) 7.5.84, drawn 0 – 0

Capped by England Youth against Austria and Yugoslavia, blond-haired Darren made his League debut while still on apprentice forms. The satisfaction of an excellent debut at Sunderland was tempered by the breaking news that Notts had lost their place in the First Division. By the time he had established a regular first team place the Magpies had descended into Division Three. Subsequently captain of Lincoln City, until a transfer deadline signing by Maidstone United, he spent a season in non-League circles following Maidstone's resignation from the League in August 1992. Two seasons with Scarborough wound up his League career with aggregate figures of 300(10) League and Cup matches and 13 goals.

Appearances: FL: 90(2) apps 1 gl FAC: 6 apps 1 gl FLC: 6 apps 0 gls Other: 7 apps 0 gls Total: 109(2) apps 2 gls
Honours: England Youth International, 2 apps 1984

---○---

DAVIS, Stephen Mark

Central defender   6' 2"   12st 8lbs
b. Hexham, Northumberland, 30th October 1968
CAREER: Ponteland High School/Northumberland Schoolboys/Montague Boys' Club/Southampton trainee Aug 1986, pro July 1987 (Burnley loan Nov 1989) (NOTTS loan Mar 1991)/Burnley Aug 1991, fee £60,000/Luton Town July 1995, fee £750,000/Burnley Dec 1998, fee £800,000/ Blackpool July 2003 to June 2004/York City cs 2004 to May 2005.
Debut as sub v Barnsley (a) 9.4.91, lost 0 – 1

In two separate spells with Burnley, Steve Davis appeared in a little over 300 League matches and scored 42 goals. In his first full season at Turf Moor he won the 'Player of the Year' award and was nominated for the PFA's Fourth Division 'Team of the Season.' Two years on, he starred in another promotion campaign, this time via a Play-off Final victory against Stockport County. A dominating central defender who scored more than a fair share of goals, mainly due to his power in the air in set piece situations. Between his lengthy spell with Burnley, he gave excellent service to Luton Town (163 matches and 26 goals.)

In his final League season, injury robbed him of a place in Blackpool's LDV Vans Trophy final victory against Southend United at the Millennium Stadium in March 2004. His career aggregate figures totalled 559(18) League and Cup matches and 74 goals.

Appearances: FL: 0(2) apps 0 gls Total: 0(2) apps 0 gls
Honours: (Burnley) FL Div 4 champions 1992

DAVISON, Aidan John
Goalkeeper   6' 1"   13st 2lbs
b. Sedgefield, Co Durham, 11th May 1968
CAREER: Spennymoor United (Newcastle United Youth Team) (Sunderland trial)/Billingham Synthonia 1987-88/NOTTS Mar 1988 (Leyton Orient loan Sept 1989)/Bury Oct 1989, fee £6,000 (Chester City loan Mar 1990) (Blackpool loan Mar 1991)/Millwall Aug 1991/Bolton Wanderers July 1993, fee £25,000 (Ipswich Town loan Oct 1996) (Hull City loan Nov 1996)/Bradford City Mar 1997/Grimsby Town July 1997/Sheffield United Aug 1999 (Bradford City loan Dec 1999)/Bradford City Mar 2000 to June 2003/Grimsby Town Aug 2003
Debut v Preston North End (a) 15.4.89, lost 0 – 3

Aidan Davison was established as first-team goalkeeper with Northern League side Spennymoor United at 17 years of age. He gave up his job as a lorry driver in the North-East to join Notts on transfer deadline day in March 1988. Mick Leonard and Steve Cherry shared first team duties during Davison's time at Meadow Lane but he subsequently appeared in Premier League football with Bolton Wanderers and Bradford City. He won his first Northern Ireland international cap against Sweden in April 1996, after appearing in only two Premier League outings for Bolton. He enjoyed a double success with Grimsby Town in April and May 1998, twice starring in Wembley appearances against Bournemouth in the Auto Windscreens Shield Final and against Northampton Town in the Final of the Division Two play-offs.

Appearances: FL: 1 app 0 gls Total: 1 app 0 gls
Honours: Northern Ireland International, 3 caps 1996-98. Northern Ireland 'B' International, 1 app. (Grimsby Town) Auto Windscreens Shield winners 1998

DAWS, Anthony
Forward   5' 8"   11st 10lbs
b. Sheffield, 10th September 1966
CAREER: Sheffield Schoolboys/Manchester United associate schoolboy Oct 1980 to Oct 1981/NOTTS app, signing pro Sept 1984/Sheffield United Aug 1986/Scunthorpe United July 1987/Grimsby Town Mar 1993, fee £50,000/Lincoln City Feb 1994, fee £50,000/Scarborough Aug 1996/Altrincham Dec 1996/Bradford P.A. later in 1996-97
Debut v Birmingham City (a) 9.3.85, lost 1 – 2

England Schools and Youth international who joined the Magpies after a year at Old Trafford on schoolboy forms.

Tony won his Youth cap alongside Darren Davis (q.v.) and was unfortunate to miss out on a second cap when an injury in an 'A' Team game prevented his joining the squad for the Iceland match in October 1984. During early days at Meadow Lane a lack of physical advantage was seen to be a problem but with maturity came power and strength, and the hard working, opportunist striker enjoyed a successful League career, scoring 87 goals in 269(40) League and Cup matches.

Appearances: FL: 6(2) apps 1 gl Total: 6(2) apps 1 gl
Honours: England Schoolboy International, 1 cap 1982. England Youth International, 1 app, season 1984-85

DAYKIN, Reginald Brian
Left-half   5' 11"   12st 8lbs
b. Long Eaton, Derbyshire, 4th August 1937
CAREER: Ericsson Telephones/Long Eaton Town 1954/Derby County Nov 1955/NOTTS July 1962, fee £1,000/Corinthians, Sydney, Australia, May 1963/Adamstown Rosebuds, Newcastle, NSW, player-coach Jan 1964, fee £1,500/Belper Town Jan 1966/Lockheed Leamington May 1966/Bourne Town player-manager June 1967/Long Eaton West Park player-manager/Long Eaton Albion player-manager 1969/Long Eaton United manager Dec 1972/Brighton & Hove Albion assistant-manager Aug 1974
Debut v Watford (h) 23.8.62, lost 1 – 3

A reserve wing-half with Derby County who had almost five years to wait for a first team call. This came on 12th September 1959 at Plymouth Argyle and he marked the occasion by scoring one of Derby's goals in a comprehensive 5 – 0 victory. On joining Notts some three years later he had added little to his League experience, which stood at just four matches and one goal. In a season at Meadow Lane he played in three August matches, but lost out as the middle line settled with Sheridan, Gibson and Loxley the preferred selection. A successful spell in Australia preceded Brian's return to Draycott, near Long Eaton in December 1965. He later linked up with former Derby County assistant manager, Peter Taylor, at Brighton.

Appearances: FL: 3 apps 0 gls Total: 3 apps 0 gls

DEAN, John Thomas "Jerry"
Inside or Outside-right 5' 7½" 11st 9lbs
b. Hadley, near Wellington, Shropshire, 13th February 1881
CAREER: Trench Victoria/Wolverhampton Wanderers May 1901/Ironbridge Sept 1902/Wellington Town Mar 1903/NOTTS May 1904 to cs 1912, when he emigrated to Canada.
Debut v Small Heath (a) 10.9.04, won 2 – 1 (scored one)

In a letter to the 'Football Post' in September 1929 a Mr. C.R. Foster of Vancouver, a former Magpies supporter who left Radcliffe-on-Trent in 1913 and emigrated to Canada, sent news of 'Jerry' Dean. Two press cuttings ac-companied his letter and gave details of Dean's fine batting for Shelley C.C. Although he had not handled a bat for four years, he knocked up 44 runs in his first innings and then 114 in a second match a week later. Although at the wrong side of forty, 'Jerry' was also reported to be still playing football – also for the Shelley club – at full-back. This despite "Having altered a lot since he left Nottingham, with plenty of room to wear a huge gold watch chain," (worn across the corporation in those days.) In a lengthy spell with the Magpies, rewarded by a lucrative benefit in 1909-10, he was a dependable wingman with the priceless gift of accurate centering. He actually commenced as an inside-forward and scored in each of his first three matches. He managed to maintain a very respectable scoring record after moving to the right wing, his total boosted by his reliability from the penalty spot.

Appearances: FL: 254 apps 49 gls FAC: 14 apps 3 gls
Total: 268 apps 52 gls

motorbike crash, he recovered to score 60 goals in 1927-28, which remains the Football League seasonal scoring record. In fourteen seasons with Everton he scored 349 League goals in 399 matches and 28 in 38 FA Cup ties. After wartime military service he became a licensee in Chester, and later worked for a football pools firm. Sadly, he had to have a leg amputated in 1976, and when his end came some four years later, it seemed entirely fitting that it should come at his beloved Goodison Park, following an Everton/Liverpool derby clash, at which he had been a spectator.

Appearances: FL: 9 apps 3 gls Total: 9 apps 3 gls
Honours: England International, 16 caps 1927-33. FL Representative, 6 apps. (Everton) FL Div 1 champions 1928 & 1932. FL Div 2 champions 1931. FA Cup winners 1933. (Sligo Rovers) FA of Ireland Cup finalists 1939

---○---

DEAN, William Ralph 'Dixie'

Centre-forward 5' 10½"   12st 7lbs
b. Birkenhead, 22nd January 1907
d. Goodison Park, Liverpool, 1st March 1980
CAREER: Albert Industrial School/Laird Street School/ Birkenhead Schoolboys/Moreton Bible Class/Wirral Railways/ Heswall/Pensby United/Tranmere Rovers Nov 1923/Everton Mar 1925, fee £2,500/NOTTS Mar 1938, fee £3,000/Sligo Rovers Jan 1939/Hurst July 1939 (WW2 guest York City)
Debut v Queens Park Rangers (a) 12.3.38, lost 1 – 2

Continuing their policy or recruiting former international centre-forwards, Notts secured the services of Dixie Dean in March 1938. He followed Hughie Gallacher to Meadow Lane, but sadly failed to have the impact generated by the former Scotland international. Almost immediately, Dean required surgery on an ankle injury and played in only a handful of matches thereafter. Throughout his distinguished career, Dean had been notable for his headwork, more goals coming to him from that medium than with his feet. Also, his headed flick-ons were always likely to beat the opposing defender and leave open the way to goal. 27 goals in as many games for Tranmere Rovers in 1924-25 brought him a trip across the Mersey to Goodison Park, the scene of his greatest triumphs. Despite a serious road accident in June 1926, when he fractured his skull in a

DEANS, Thomas Sneddon

Full-back   5' 8½" 11st 5lbs
b. Shieldhill, near Falkirk, 7th January 1922
d. Nottingham, 30th October 2000
CAREER: Armadale Thistle/Clyde 1941/NOTTS Oct 1949, fee £6,500/Boston United 1956/Wisbech Town/Grantham Town cs 1959 to April 1960.
Debut v Newport County (a) 8.10.49, drawn 1 – 1

Tommy Deans was the second Scotsman to be signed by the Magpies within three days when he followed Alex Simpson into Meadow Lane. A strong, fair-haired back, he first attracted attention when playing for Armadale Thistle, one of the most noted Scottish

nurseries. He joined Clyde in 1941, and after a spell in the Army, returned to Scottish football. His display against the Rangers, in the Glasgow Cup Final, convinced Magpies' manager Houghton that he was the type of defender that would assist the season's push for promotion. At either right or left full-back he rendered great service as vice-captain and later captain, for seven seasons a stumbling block to the best of wingers.

Appearances: FL: 239 apps 0 gls FAC: 14 apps 0 gls
Total: 253 apps 0 gls
Honours: Scottish FL Representative, 1 app 1948.
(NOTTS) FL Div 3 South champions 1950

DEATH, William George
Outside-left   5' 9½" 11st 5lbs
b. Rotherham, 13th November 1899
d. Rotherham, 3rd July 1984
CAREER: Broome Athletic (WW1 guest Rotherham Town 1918)/Rotherham Town Sept 1920/NOTTS Jan 1921, fee £400/Mansfield Town Sept 1923/Sunderland Mar 1924, fee £500/Exeter City Sept 1928/Gillingham July 1930/Mansfield Town June 1931/Grantham Town cs 1932/Heanor Town/Sutton Town Feb 1933/Heanor Town Sept 1933/Nottingham City Transport F.C. re-instated am Aug 1934
Debut v Birmingham (a) 5.2.21, lost 1 – 2

Two highlights in Billy Death's career with the Magpies were his scoring of a hat-trick against Wolverhampton Wanderers in the 4 – 0 home victory in September 1921. The second was his trip with the Magpies to Spain and two matches against Barcelona in 1922. On the debit side, he dislodged a cartilage in the first minute of a friendly match against Chesterfield in December 1921 and played in little first team football subsequently. On leaving Meadow Lane he enjoyed a successful season with Mansfield Town, winners of the Midland League championship in 1923-24. Sunderland paid what was then a considerable fee for a non-League player, and he played in 53 First Division matches and scored 14 goals for them before journeying south to Exeter City. A season with Gillingham preceded his return to Field Mill to play in the Stags' first season as a Football League club. When he retired from the game he joined Nottingham City Transport as a driver. Billy was wont to present his name as De'ath, which was quite understandable!

Appearances: FL: 21 apps 4 gls FAC: 2 apps 0 gls
Total: 23 apps 4 gls

DEENEY, Saul
Goalkeeper   6' 1"   12st 10lbs
b. Londonderry, Northern Ireland, 12th March 1983
CAREER: Foyle Harps/NOTTS trainee July 1999, pro Sept 2000 (Hull City loan Oct 2002 to Jan 2003) (Wolverhampton Wanderers trial Nov 2003)
Debut v Huddersfield Town (h) 29.3.2003, won 3 – 2

First spotted by Notts' scout Bob Shaw in the ranks of Foyle Harps, Saul has had a lengthy wait to fully establish himself as first choice goalkeeper at Meadow Lane. Experienced 'keepers Stuart Garden and Steve Mildenhall effectively dominated the position for the best part of three seasons, and as third choice the young Irishman sought a move. A series of trials and loans did not result in a permanent transfer, which, in retrospect, was a happy outcome for the Magpies. Following his introduction for the final three matches of the relegation season 2003-04, Saul has fully established himself, despite a strong challenge during 2004-05 from Wayne Henderson. Widely recognised as one of the best young goalkeepers in the lower divisions, it seems only a matter of time before he becomes a target for bigger clubs.

Appearances: FL: 41(1) apps 0 gls FAC: 4 apps 0 gls
FLC: 2 apps 0 gls Total: 47(1) apps 0 gls
HONOURS: Republic of Ireland Youth & U-21 International.

DEIGHTON, Alexander
Outside-left
b. Gateshead, April quarter 1877
CAREER: Liverpool South End Jan 1896/Rock Ferry May 1896/NOTTS May 1897/Rock Ferry Sept 1898/Haydock Feb 1899
Debut v Preston North End (h) 7.10.1897, drawn 1 – 1

The signing of John Fraser, Motherwell's outside-left, in February 1898 ended Alex Deighton's mid season run on the Magpies' left wing. As a man with strong Merseyside connections he would doubtless have enjoyed his recall to the side in March 1898 for the Division One fixture at Liverpool, despite the 2 – 0 score line in favour of the Reds.

Appearances:
FL: 10 apps 1 gl FAC: 1 app 0 gls Total: 11 apps 1 gl

DERRY, Shaun Peter
Midfield/Defender   5' 10" 10st 13lbs
b. Nottingham, 6th December 1977
CAREER: Nottingham City Schoolboys/NOTTS trainee July 1994, pro Apr 1996/Sheffield United Jan 1998, fee £700,000/Portsmouth Mar 2000, fee £300,000/Crystal Palace Aug 2002, fee £400,000 (Nottingham Forest loan Dec 2004)/Leeds United Feb 2005.
Debut v York City (h) 12.3.96, drawn 2 – 2

Shaun Derry had the worst possible start to his Magpies career, damaging cruciate ligaments in his knee within days of signing as a trainee. Happily, an operation cleared up the problem and he was able to make his League debut, in the unfamiliar role of right-back, while still a trainee.

His assured display ensured that he retained the position until the end of the season and was rewarded with a two-year professional contract. In late January 1998, persistent overtures from Sheffield United and a bid that escalated from £500,000 to £700,000 finally prised Shaun out of Meadow Lane. He left the Magpies in a healthy position, setting a hot pace in the race to the Third Division championship. His 27(1) League appearances in the season eventually qualified him for a medal, when the championship was clinched. In more recent times, Shaun helped lift Crystal Palace into the Premier League, appearing in the Division One Play-off Final at the Millennium Stadium, Cardiff, when the Eagles beat West Ham United by 1 – 0 on 29th May 2004.

Appearances: FL: 76(3) apps 4 gls FAC: 6(1) apps 1 gl FLC: 4(1) apps 0 gls Total: 86(5) apps 5 gls
Honours: (NOTTS) FL Div 3 champions 1998

DEVEY, William

Forward
b. Birmingham, January quarter 1869
d. Handsworth, Birmingham, 24th October 1948
CAREER: Clarendon Montrose/Wellington Town/Aston Unity/Mitchell St George's/Small Heath Alliance Aug 1885/Wolverhampton Wanderers Aug 1891/Aston Villa July 1892/Walsall Town Swifts May 1894/Burton Wanderers May 1895/NOTTS Mar 1897/Walsall Dec 1897/Burton Wanderers/Walsall/Small Heath Mar 1899
Debut v Newton Heath (a) 27.3.1897, drawn 1 – 1 (scored)

Commenting on his debut, the 'Evening News' considered that "The Notts club have without doubt obtained a very capable player in Devey of Burton Wanderers. Appearing at outside-right in place of Allan he was in great form, his sprinting and shooting was much admired. He scored the Notts goal and besides this put the ball into the net on three other occasions when the off-side rule was unfortunately introduced into the question." In the course of 14 League appearances for the Magpies he appeared in every forward position. In the colours of seven different League clubs he totalled 121 appearances and scored 43 goals.

Appearances: FL: 14 apps 3 gls Total: 14 apps 3 gls

DEVLIN, Paul John

Winger/Forward   5' 9"   11st 5lbs
b. Birmingham, 14th April 1972
CAREER: Stafford Rangers/NOTTS Feb 1992, fee £40,000/Birmingham City Feb 1996/Sheffield United Mar 1998, fee £200,000 (NOTTS loan Oct 1998)/Birmingham City Feb 2002, fee £200,000/Watford Sept 2003.
Debut v Coventry City (h) 11.4.92, won 1 – 0

A fiery front-man at either right-wing or centre-forward, Paul's assets surrounded speed and ball control, coupled with a never say die attitude. He was leading scorer in 1994-95 with 12 goals in all competitions and in 1995-96 had scored seven goals when Birmingham City signed him, along with Andy Legg. A life-long Blues fan, he had the ultimate satisfaction of helping his favourite club into the Premiership during his second spell at St Andrews in 2002. In September 2003 a Watford fan put up the money to cover an undisclosed transfer fee, plus his wages. Proof that time had not mellowed Paul came when he was sent off in his first appearance for the Hornets!

Appearances: FL: 137(9) apps 25 gls FAC: 8 apps 1 gl FLC: 11(1) apps 1 gl Other: 17(2) apps 5 gls
Total: 173(12) apps 32 gls
Honours: Scotland International, 8 caps 2003. (NOTTS) Anglo-Italian Cup winners 1995, finalists 1994

DEWICK, John Albert

Goalkeeper
b. Rotherham, 28th November 1919
d. Bracknell, Berks, June 1997
CAREER: NOTTS am, signing pro Oct 1946
Debut v Queens Park Rangers (h) 2.11.46, lost 1 – 2

John Dewick's sole League outing occurred in a matter of days after he had signed a professional form. He was pressed into service when regular 'keeper Harry Brown was unable to obtain release from military duties. Commenting on his debut, the 'Football Post' reported that the newcomer "Showed a weakness in goal kicking and made one error when Neary scored for Q.P.R. The ball passing under his body when he appeared to have it well covered."

Appearances: FL: 1 app 0 gls Total: 1 app 0 gls

DICKSON, William

Wing-half   5' 10"   12st 0lbs
b. Lurgan, Northern Ireland, 15th April 1923
CAREER: Glenavon/NOTTS Nov 1945/Chelsea Nov 1947, in part exchange for Tommy Lawton/Arsenal Oct 1953, fee £15,000/Mansfield Town July 1956/Glenavon Jan 1958
Debut v Northampton Town (h) 1.2.47, won 1 – 0

Bill Dickson won high praise for his display when first introduced by Notts at senior level, as stand-in for the injured Eddie Gannon. The 'Football Post' considering that he: "Showed a complete aptitude for the wing half-back berth, tackling with speed and judgement and using the ball well when in possession." Part of the deal that brought Tommy Lawton to Meadow Lane, Dickson was comparatively unknown at the time and considered to be a 'make weight' in the deal but he played himself to international recognition at Stamford Bridge.

Chelsea's only Irishman at that time, he won nine caps as a Pensioner and a further three during his spell with Arsenal.

Appearances: FL: 21 apps 2 gls Total: 21 apps 2 gls
Honours: Northern Ireland International, 12 caps 1951-55

———————o———————

DIJKSTRA, Meindert
Defender   5' 11" 12st 0lbs
b. Eindhoven, Holland, 28th February 1967
CAREER: NAC Breda/Willem 11 Tilburg/NOTTS Aug 1992 to July 1994 when released on a free transfer.
Debut v Leicester City (h) 22.8.92, drawn 1 – 1

Seven years after first visiting Nottingham when he was a member of the NAC Breda squad competing in a Under-18 tournament, Dutch defender Dijk – pronounced Dyke – joined the Magpies. He was signed with a view to filling a vacancy at left-back caused by injury to Alan Paris. Despite his additional ability to operate in midfield or as a central defender, he struggled to establish himself at Meadow Lane. Prior to leaving, however, he had the satisfaction of a Wembley appearance in March 1994, despite the disappointment of defeat by Brescia in the Anglo Italian Cup Final.

Appearances: FL: 27(2) apps 1 gl FAC: 3 apps 0 gls FLC: 1(1) apps 0 gls Other: 8 apps 0 gls Total: 39(3) apps 1 gl
Honours: (NOTTS) Anglo Italian Cup finalists 1994

———————o———————

DINSDALE, Norman
Centre-half   5' 10" 11st 7lbs
b. Hunslet, Yorks, 20th June 1898
d. Nottingham, 6th October 1970
CAREER: Anston Athletic/NOTTS am Mar, pro May 1920/ Coventry City Mar 1928, along with Alfred Widdowson for a combined fee of £500/Bristol Rovers June 1930 to Feb 1932, fee £425/Kidderminster Harriers.
Debut v Stoke (h) 16.10.20, won 3 – 0

Nearing the close of the relegation season 1919-20 the Magpies made three new signings. All were relatively young and inexperienced players, and the trio comprised Norman Dinsdale, Alf Widdowson and Robert Platts. Between them, they were destined to appear in a fraction over 500 matches for the Magpies. Norman Dinsdale was recommended to the club by their former full-back

Bert Morley and he cannot have disappointed his sponsor. A great asset in defence for eight seasons, he never spared himself in the team's cause and was possessed of indomitable pluck and energy. Transferred, along with Alf Widdowson, to Coventry City in March 1928, he scored ten goals in 90 League matches before a final move in League circles took him to Bristol Rovers. At Eastville he added a further 31 League appearances and three goals to finish his League career with an impressive overall record of 388 matches and 22 goals.

Appearances: FL: 267 apps 11 gls FAC: 27 apps 0 gls
Total: 294 apps 11 gls
Honours: (NOTTS) FL Div 2 champions 1923

———————o———————

DIUK, Wayne John
Midfield   5' 11" 11st 0lbs
b. Nottingham, 26th May 1980
CAREER: NOTTS associate schoolboy July 1995, trainee Aug 1996, registration cancelled Dec 1998/Kettering Town
Debut as sub v Chesterfield (a) 3.5.1997, lost 0 – 1

Despite appearing an outstanding prospect in the successful youth team of 1996-97, rewarded by a taste of senior football from the bench whilst still a sixteen year-old, Wayne failed to maintain his progress. Subsequently, however, he has enjoyed a very lengthy association with Kettering Town, a highlight being his appearance in the FA Trophy Final at Wembley in May 2000.

Appearances: FL: 0(2) apps 0 gls FLC: 0(1) apps 0 gls
Other: 0(1) apps 0 gls Total: 0(4) apps 0 gls

———————o———————

DIXON, Harry
Outside-left
b. Kettering, Northants, October Quarter 1870
CAREER: Kettering Town/NOTTS Aug 1893/Kettering Town
Debut v Crewe Alexandra (a) 2.9.1893, won 2 – 0

In a season when Notts finished third in Division Two and won the FA Cup, Harry Dixon appeared in the first three matches of the campaign before English international Harry Daft took over the left wing berth following his sojourn with Nottingham Forest. Dixon returned to Kettering Town and some years later was a member of their team that lost 2 – 0 to Notts in the first round of the FA Cup in season 1898-99. Outside of football he was employed in the footwear industry as a boot laster.

Appearances: FL: 3 apps 0 gls Total: 3 apps 0 gls

———————o———————

DIXON, John Auger
Inside-left
b. Grantham, Lincs, 27th May 1861
d. Nottingham, 8th June 1931

CAREER: Played soccer at his three schools (Grantham Grammar, Nottingham High & Chigwell Grammar)/NOTTS am cs 1883 to 1888, also assisted Corinthians.
Debut v Sheffield Heeley, FAC 1, (h) 10.11.1883, won 3 – 1

John Dixon made the bulk of his appearances in seasons 1883-84 and 1884-85. In addition to the FA Cup ties noted below he appeared in 47 first team matches and scored 13 goals. A fine all-round sportsman, he was captain of Notts. C.C.C. for ten seasons, appearing in 235 matches between 1882-1905. In first class matches he scored 9,527 runs with a highest score of 268* against Sussex in 1897. Additionally he took 184 wickets and held 180 catches. He served as a J.P. and was managing director of Messrs. Dixon & Parker, the Nottingham clothing firm.

Appearances: FAC: 14 apps 2 gls Total: 14 apps 2 gls
Honours: England International, 1 cap 1885

DOBSON, Alfred Thomas Carrick
Right-back
b. Sherwood, Nottingham, 28th March 1859
d. 22nd October 1932
CAREER: Downside College, near Bath/NOTTS am 1877-85/Also assisted Corinthians.
Debut v Sheffield, FAC 1 replay (a) 15.12.1877, lost 0 – 3

Defined in 1882 as "A safe back, fast, a good tackler, his bad sight being his weakest point." His myopia, however, was not an undue hand-icap, as it did not prevent the award of four inter-national caps by England. He was also a very keen cyclist, and won a number of troph-ies, besides taking a keen interest in

the affairs of the Notts. Amateur Cycling club. Along with his father and younger brother Charles (q.v.) he was associated with the firm of W.E. and F. Dobson, Meadows Mill, Queen's-road, lace manufacturers and doublers. Later he became a director of Wrights and Dobson Bros., dyers, bleachers and dressers, Nottingham.

Appearances: FAC: 27 apps 0 gls Total: 27 apps 0 gls
Honours: England International, 4 caps 1882-84

DOBSON, Charles Frederick
Wing-half
b. Basford, Nottingham, 9th September 1862
d. Ealing, London, 18th May 1939
CAREER: Stoneyhurst College, Lancashire/Corinthians/ NOTTS am Mar 1880 to season 1888-89
Debut v Wednesbury Strollers, FAC 2, (h) 24.11.1881, won 5 – 3

A lengthy association with Notts terminated with a single FL appearance against Aston Villa on 8th December 1888. Earlier he was capped by England against Ireland in Belfast on 13th March 1886, and assisted his country to a 6 – 1 victory in this, his only international appearance. He was a director of W.E. and F. Dobson Ltd., Lace manufacturers, and a member of Nottinghamshire County Tennis and Golf Clubs. Younger brother of Alfred (above.)

Appearances: FL: 1 app 0 gls FAC: 35 apps 6 gls
Total: 36 apps 6 gls
Honours: England International, 1 cap 1886

DOCHERTY, Bernard
Inside-left
b. Bellshill, Lanarkshire, 11th August 1941
CAREER: Cowdenbeath/Cambuslang Rangers/NOTTS Aug 1964 to June 1965
Debut v Tranmere Rovers (h) 27.8.64, lost 2 – 4

In May 1964, Notts' manager Eddie Lowe signed outside-right Eddie Kavanagh from Cambuslang Rangers. Three months later he further depleted the Cambuslang ranks when he signed inside-left Bernard Docherty from the same Scottish junior club. Docherty was said to have sampled senior soccer with Cowdenbeath, and in early season he took over the number ten jersey from the former Manchester City and Newcastle United star, George Hannah. In a season of few highlights, the two former Cambuslang colleagues had identical appearance records, but Kavanagh outscored his former team mate by four goals to two.

Appearances: FL: 25 apps 2 gls FAC: 2 apps 0 gls FLC: 3 apps 0 gls Total: 30 apps 2 gls

DOCHERTY, Edward

Inside-forward 5' 9" 11st 0lbs
b. Scotland, circa 1871
CAREER: Jordanhill/Partick Thistle 1891-92/NOTTS Aug 1892, released Jan 1893/Duntocher Harp/Lincoln City June to Oct 1895
Debut v Sheffield Wednesday (h) 3.9.1892, lost 0 – 1

A reserve team player with only two first team outings with Partick Thistle, Docherty did little better with the Magpies. After six League appearances he was released, along with J. Parke, in January of the relegation season 1892-93. He was at inside-right in three of the opening four fixtures of the season and scored in the 3 – 1 win against Preston North End on 1st October. Thereafter, he appeared once at inside-left and once at right-half before his release and return to Scotland. A second sojourn in England proved similarly unrewarding, after two goals in five matches he departed Lincoln City after a stay of just five months. At the outset of his career he assisted Jordanhill to win the Renfrewshire Cup in 1891, and took part in two inter-county contests.

Appearances: FL: 6 apps 1 gl Total: 6 apps 1 gl

DODD, George Francis

Forward 5' 7½" 11st 4lbs
b. Whitchurch, Shropshire, 7th February 1885
d. Croydon, London, 1st January 1960
CAREER: Wallasey United/Rock Ferry/Stockport County Aug 1905/Workington July 1907/NOTTS Dec 1907/Tunbridge Wells Rangers 1911/Chelsea May 1911/Millwall May 1913/Brighton & Hove Albion Dec 1913/Darlington June 1914/West Ham United 1914/Luton Town Oct 1919/Treherbert Aug 1920, appointed player-manager Oct 1920/Charlton Athletic May 1921/Catford South End secretary-manager July 1924 to Apr 1925
Debut v Everton (h) 25.12.07, won 2 – 1

In January 1910 the 'Athletic News' reported that Notts County spies had gone to watch another player but were more impressed by George Dodd. "A strong speedy forward who is inclined to be selfish, but is quite effective." It was also revealed that Dodd rarely headed the ball, having once sustained severe concussion by doing so. Although the transfer fee was not revealed, it was said to be substantial and involved payments to both Stockport County and Workington. His Notts career was a curious mixture of occasional brilliance and disappointment. Always a genuine trier, he occupied every forward position, but was most effective at inside-left. One unwanted record was revealed in the 'Football Post' in January 1909: "Dodd has appeared six times on grounds in Manchester, and has been injured on each occasion."

His career after leaving Notts was certainly varied and long-lived, as he made his final appearance for Charlton Athletic at the age of 36. He worked at Woolwich Arsenal during WW1.

Appearances: FL: 91 apps 20 gls FAC: 1 app 0 gls
Total: 92 apps 20 gls

DOHERTY, James Clarkson

Forward 5' 10" 11st 0lbs
b. Douglas, Lanarkshire, 31st January 1957
CAREER: Ayr United 1973/Cumnock Juniors/Albion Rovers/Cumnock Juniors/NOTTS July 1979 to cs 1982/Motherwell Reserves.
Debut v Queens Park Rangers (a) 12.1.80, won 3 – 1

A Scottish Junior Cup winner with Cumnock in 1979, Jim Doherty spent three years at Meadow Lane. He captained the Magpies Reserves, playing in a variety of positions, without mounting a serious bid for a first team place. Released on a free transfer in the summer of 1982 he returned to Scotland. While employed by an electrical company, supervising their apprentices, he was approached by Motherwell's manager, Jock Wallace, to play for his reserve side. He was seeking a player with some experience to blend with a crop of very talented youngsters.

Appearances: FL: 6(2) apps 0 gls Total: 6(2) apps 0 gls

DOLPHIN, Alfred

Outside-right 5' 6" 10st 10lbs
b. Redditch, Worcs, April quarter 1890
d. Bromsgrove, Worcs, April quarter 1940, age 50
CAREER: Nuneaton Town/Oldham Athletic May 1919, fee £100/NOTTS June 1920, fee £100/Darlington June 1921/Stockport County June 1922/Walsall July 1923/Weymouth cs 1924
Debut v Bristol City (a) 28.8.20, won 1 – 0

A late entrant into League football at 29 years of age, Alf Dolphin assisted five League clubs in as many seasons. He made a promising start with Oldham Athletic until a broken collar-bone halted his progress. A wingman with pace, craft, and the ability to centre on the run, he scored his first League goal in his fourth appearance in Notts' colours, the winner in a 2 – 1 victory against Fulham. In March 1921, after having played in most Division Two matches, he lost his place to the new signing Joe Daly. He departed in the close season and was signed by Darlington, and assisted them to the runners-up position in the Third Division North in 1921-22, scoring three goals in 33 appearances.

Appearances: FL: 24 apps 3 gls Total: 24 apps 3 gls

DONALDSON, Joseph

Goalkeeper
b. Probably in Lanarkshire, Scotland
CAREER: Holytown Thistle, NOTTS Jan to May 1899
Debut v Sunderland (a) 18.3.1899, drawn 1 – 1

Hailed by the 'Football Post' as: "A smart youth, with a big reputation in his county." He made his debut in the Reserves against Newstead Byron shortly after signing, but had little to do in a 4 – 1 victory. This was not the case when he made his League debut at Sunderland. His opportunity came when the Notts directors agreed to release goalkeeper Suter to play in an important Notts Alliance match for his team, Southwell St Mary's, against Boots Athletic. Donaldson's debut display won wide praise, his brilliant display including a penalty save from Sunderland's McLatchie. He retained his place for the following two matches, a 2 – 0 defeat at Preston North End and an identical score line against Wolverhampton Wanderers at Trent Bridge. With three other goalkeepers already on the books (Toone, Suter and Sharman), it was decided not to retain Joe Donaldson at the end of the season.

Appearances: FL: 3 apps 0 gls Total: 3 apps 0 gls

———————————o———————————

DONNELLY, Samuel

Inside-forward   5' 8"   11st 2lbs
b. Annbank, Ayrshire
CAREER: Annbank/NOTTS July 1893-95/Blackpool June 1896
Debut v Crewe Alexandra (a) 2.9.1893, won 2 – 0

The small Ayrshire village of Annbank reared many footballers who subsequently found fame in professional ranks, Sam Donnelly being a typical example. Persevering, tricky and hardworking, he showed a marked improvement during the course of his first season with Notts as he acclimatised to English football. He established a regular berth by mid season and crowned a term of genuine progress by collecting a FA Cup winners' medal for his appearance in the Goodison Park final against Bolton Wanderers. Sadly, his second season ended prematurely when he suffered a broken right leg in a collision with Graham, the Newcastle United defender, in March 1895. Ironically, Graham was born in the same Scottish village as Donnelly. He was out of senior football for over a year before joining Blackpool for whom he scored five goals in 14 Second Division matches.

Appearances: FL: 32 apps 7 gls FAC: 6 apps 2 gls Other: 1 app 0 gls Total: 39 apps 9 gls
Honours: (NOTTS) FA Cup winners 1884

———————————o———————————

DOWALL, William

Full-back   5' 10"   11st 0lbs
b. Thornliebank, Renfrewshire
CAREER: Spiersbridge Church/Kilbirnie Ladeside/Motherwell Sept 1929/St Mirren Dec 1934/Bury July 1935/Lincoln City Aug 1936/Red Star (Paris) July 1937/Ballymena (Ireland)/ NOTTS Oct 1938
Debut v Mansfield Town (a) 12.11.38, lost 0 – 2

First crossed the border to join Bury for their jubilee season, and was charged with the unenviable task of following Wally Amos, Bury's long serving outside-left who appeared in 482 League and Cup games for the Shakers. Before the season ended, seven left wingers had been tried, Dowall's contribution being two goals in 11 League and Cup matches. In his sojourn with Lincoln City he appeared as both winger and full-back but made only five League appearances. Reserve full-back during his brief stay with Notts, he added only six League appearances to his record in English football. His best years were spent with Motherwell where he played in 118 Scottish League matches and scored 43 goals.

Appearances: FL: 6 apps 0 gls Total: 6 apps 0 gls
Honours: (Motherwell) Scottish League champions 1932

———————————o———————————

DOWNING, Keith Gordon

Midfield   5' 8"   11st 0lbs
b. Oldbury, Warwickshire, 23rd July 1965
CAREER: Chelsea app/ Mile Oak Rovers (Tamworth)/ NOTTS May 1984/Wolverhampton Wanderers July 1987/ Birmingham City July 1993/Stoke City Aug 1994/Cardiff City Aug 1995/Hereford United Sept 1995, retired Mar 1997/ Wolverhampton Wanderers Academy coach/Cheltenham Town assistant-manager 2003.
Debut v Leeds United (h) 25.8.84, lost 1 – 2

Keith Downing made his debut in the 1984-85 relegation season, when his twelve appearances were made under three different managers (Larry Lloyd, Ritchie Barker and Jimmy Sirrel.) In the period of relative calm that followed, he was unfortunate to figure little in manager Sirrel's plans, and was released on a free transfer after three years at Meadow Lane. Joining Wolves, his career 'took off,' consecutive promotions taking the once great Wanderers back to respectability in Division Two. Keith's six years at Molineux were undoubtedly the best of his career, featuring in excess of 200 League and Cup matches and 11 goals. Reunited with his former Wolves boss, Graham Turner, at Hereford United, Keith's career ended painfully. A back injury enforcing his retirement in late season 1996-97, the term in which United suffered relegated into the Conference.

Appearances: FL: 23 apps 1 gl Total: 23 apps 1 gl
Honours: (Wolverhampton Wanderers) FL Div 4 champions 1988. FL Div 3 champions 1989. Sherpa Van Trophy winners 1988

DOWSEY, John

Right-half   5' 9"   12st 8lbs
b. Willington, County Durham, 1st May 1905
b. Costock, Notts, 27th October 1942
CAREER: Hunwick Villa/Newcastle United June 1924, for a donation of £10/West Ham United May 1926, fee £250/Carlisle United July 1927/Sunderland Nov 1927/NOTTS Feb 1929, with I.McGorin for a combined fee of £500/Northampton Town Nov 1931/Nuneaton Town Aug 1934
Debut v Middlesbrough (h) 16.2.29, lost 0 – 3

Jack Dowsey began his career as an inside forward and was a frequent goalscorer in Newcastle United's North Eastern League side. Nevertheless, he had seen little first team football when he arrived at Meadow Lane, despite almost five years as a professional. After occupying all three inside forward berths within the space of fourteen Division Two matches he was moved to right-half and retained the position throughout successive relegation and promotion seasons. Having passed the milestone of 100 senior appearances for the Magpies he left in November 1931 to join Northampton Town. In three seasons at the County Ground he appeared in 86 Third Division South matches and scored five goals.

Appearances: FL: 98 apps 4 gls FAC: 5 apps 0 gls
Total: 103 apps 4 gls
Honours: (NOTTS) FL Div 3 South champions 1931

DRAPER, Mark Andrew

Midfield   5' 10"   11st 0lbs
b. Long Eaton, Derbyshire, 11th November 1970
CAREER: Wilsthorpe Comprehensive College/Sandiacre Town/NOTTS trainee, signing pro Dec 1988/Leicester City July 1994, fee £1.25million/Aston Villa July 1995, fee £3.25million (Rayo Vallecano, Spain, loan Jan 2000)/Southampton July 2000, fee £1.5million, retired due to injury Dec 2003.
Debut v Mansfield Town, FLC 2 (a) 6.9.88, lost 0 – 1

A little over a year after leaving Wilsthorpe Comprehensive College Mark made his County debut as a 17 year-old. Originally signed as an outside-right from Sandiacre Town, he quickly developed into an attacking midfielder with creative and goal scoring abilities that earned him England U-21 recognition for the first time in season 1990-91. Two promotions in successive years took the Magpies from Division Three to Division One, Mark's contribution in the second promotion was particularly memorable, his ten senior goals including two within nine minutes at West Ham United. The 2 – 1 victory robbing the Hammers of the championship. A relegation season ensued, but Mark scored 30 goals in the following two seasons. A tribunal set fee of £1.25 million took him to Leicester City, but the Foxes were relegated from the Premier League in his only season at Filbert Street. A reunion with manager Brian

Little took Mark to Aston Villa where he collected a League Cup winners' medal in 1996. A sojourn in the sun with Rayo Vallecano preceded his final move to Southampton where a serious knee injury enforced his retirement. His career figures totalled 423(39) League and Cup matches and 62 goals.

Appearances: FL: 206(16) apps 41 gls FAC: 10 apps 2 gls FLC: 14(1) apps 2 gls Other: 21(2) apps 5 gls
Total: 251 (19) apps 50 gls
Honours: England U-21 International, 3 apps 1991-92. (Aston Villa) FL Cup winners 1996. (NOTTS) Anglo-Italian Cup finalists 1994

DRYDEN, Richard Andrew

Defender   6' 0"   11st 12lbs
b. Shipton Moyne near Stroud, Gloucestershire, 14th June 1969
CAREER: Bristol Rovers trainee, signing pro July 1987 (Exeter City loan Sept 1988)/Exeter City Mar 1989, fee £10,000/NOTTS Aug 1991, fee £250,000 (Plymouth Argyle loan Nov-Dec1992)/Birmingham City Mar 1993, fee £165,000/Bristol City Dec 1994, fee £140,000/Southampton Aug 1996, fee £150,000 (Stoke City loan Nov 1999 and again Mar 2000) (Northampton Town loan Sept 2000) (Swindon Town loan Nov 2000)/Luton Town Feb 2001 to cs 2002 (Scarborough loan Dec 2001)/Worksop Town/Tamworth assistant-manager Nov 2003.
Debut v Chelsea (a) 28.8.91, drawn 2 – 2

Richard Dryden scored seven goals in 30 Division Four matches for Exeter City in season 1989-90, assisting the Grecians to their first ever championship in League football. One year on, he cost the Magpies a quarter of a million pounds, netting Exeter City a handsome profit on their £10,000 outlay some three years earlier. Sadly, his first season at Meadow Lane ended in relegation from the top flight. On a personal level, however, his first goal for the club, scored against local rivals Forest at the City Ground in January 1992, was a highlight. After playing in 28(1) League matches in his first season, a knee injury, plus an early challenge for the left back spot from Meindert Dijkstra got his 1992-93 campaign off to depressing start.

A loan spell at Plymouth Argyle proved some much-needed League action, and three months on he was transferred to Birmingham City. His overall record in League football amounted to 312(14) appearances and 17 goals.

Appearances:
FL: 30(1) apps 1 gl FAC: 2(1) apps 0 gls FLC: 1(1) apps 0 gls Other: 2 apps 0 gls Total: 35(3) apps 1 gl
Honours: Exeter City FL Division 4 champions 1990

DUDLEY, Craig Brian
Forward   5' 10"   11st 2lbs
b. Ollerton, Notts, 12th September 1979
CAREER: NOTTS associate schoolboy Dec 1993, trainee Aug 1996, pro Apr 1997 (Shrewsbury Town loan Jan 1998) (Hull City loan Nov 1989)/Oldham Athletic Mar 1999 (Chesterfield loan Aug 1999) (Scunthorpe United loan Feb 2002)/Burton Albion Aug 2002.
Debut as sub v Rotherham United (a) 15.3.97, drawn 2 – 2

An England Youth international alongside Michael Owen, Craig Dudley failed to realise his early promise. In a stop-start career the pacy striker assisted six League clubs (four in loan spells) totalling 53(55) League appearances and 15 goals. Ironically, his 100th League match and 15th goal were scored for Oldham Athletic against the Magpies in September 2001. A change of manager at Boundary Park, followed by Craig suffering ruptured ankle ligaments, led to his release by the Latics and a move into the Nationwide Conference with Burton Albion at the age of 23.

Appearances: FL: 11(20) apps 3 gls FAC: 1(2) apps 0 gls
FLC: 1(2) apps 1 gl Total: 13(24) apps 4 gls
Honours: England Youth International

DUNN, Mark Anthony
Forward   5' 8"   11st 3lbs
b. Newport, Gwent, 18th September 1982
CAREER: Everton associate schoolboy/NOTTS scholar July 1999 to May 2002
Debut v Port Vale, LDV Vans Trophy, (a) 9.1.2001, lost 0 – 3

The Magpies' line up for the LDV Vans Trophy defeat at Port Vale in January 2001 contained a number of unfamiliar faces. Mark Dunn was one of three players who failed to graduate at Meadow Lane. In addition to Mark, who was replaced by Paul Heffernan during the match, Brian Gellert made his only senior appearance. While Ryan Ford's only previous experience came in an outing from the bench against Bury in the final fixture of season 1999-2000. Mark was winner of the 'Youth Team Player of the Year' award for season 2000-01, and looked an outstanding prospect when partnering Paul Heffernan in attack. Unlike the Irishman, however, Mark failed to maintain his early form and scoring touch.

Appearances: Other: 1 app 0 gls Total: 1 app 0 gls

DYER, Alexander Constantine
Defender/Midfield   6' 0"   12st 0lbs
b. Forest Gate, 14th November 1965
CAREER: Watford app Aug 1982/Blackpool Oct 1983/Hull City Feb 1987, fee £37,000/Crystal Palace Nov 1988, fee £250,000/Charlton Athletic Nov 1990, fee £100,000/Oxford United July 1993/Lincoln City nc Aug 1995/Barnet Sept 1995/FC Maia (Portugal) May 1996/Huddersfield Town Aug 1997/NOTTS Mar 1998/Kingstonian Nov 2000/Hayes Jan 2001/Dulwich Hamlet/Reading coaching staff/West Ham United backroom staff 2003.
Debut v Exeter City (a) 3.3.98, won 5 – 2

Towards the close of a lengthy career in League football Alex won the 'Player of the Year' award at Meadow Lane in season 1999-2000. It was a fitting recognition for the popular utility player who began his career as a striker with pace, ball control and sufficient promise to command a fee of £250,000 when he left Hull City to join Crystal Palace. He subsequently re-emerged as an outstanding utility man with the talents and versatility to enable him to fill a wide variety of roles, as diverse as striker, central defender, wing-back and full-back. His career aggregate figures were 395(70) FL matches and 63 goals.

Appearances: FL: 58(20) apps 6 gls FAC: 5(1) apps 0 gls
FLC: 3(2) apps 0 gls Other: 0(1) apps 0 gls
Total: 66(24) apps 6 gls

DYER, Paul David
Defender/Midfield   5' 9"   10st 11lbs
b. Leicester, 24th January 1953
CAREER: NOTTS Sept 1972/Colchester United July 1975 to June 1980/Chelmsford City June 1982
Debut as sub v Shrewsbury Town (h) 17.2.73, won 1 – 0

Six substitute appearances in the 1972-73 promotion season, and one full appearance in the following term was the extent of Paul's first team involvement with the Magpies. Colchester United suffered relegation in his first season at Layer Road, but they came straight back up again by finishing third in Division Four. They also enjoyed a good run in the FA Cup, taking First Division Derby County to a replay before bowing out in the fourth round. Paul played little first team football in his final season, but his five-year record with The U's totalled 124(20) League appearances and 4 goals.

Appearances: FL: 1(6) apps 0 gls Total: 1(6) apps 0 gls

EARLE, Harry Thomas
Goalkeeper   5' 10½"   12st 7lbs
b. East Grinstead, Sussex, 23rd November 1868
d. Frome, Somerset, 27th September 1951
CAREER: Poplar Trinity/Millwall Athletic Jan 1890/Royal Arsenal cs 1892/Clapton cs 1893/NOTTS July 1904-05
Debut v Everton (h) 3.9.04, lost 1 – 2

Luxuriantly moustachioed Harry Earle, a schoolmaster by profession, spent a season as the Magpies last line of defence, appearing in most Division One matches. A shaky spell in late January, however, led to his being replaced, resulting in opportunities for Pennington, Nugent and the emerging Albert Iremonger to stake their claim. Despite bringing in 'Gunner' Reilly for the new season, it was the giant figure of Iremonger who was to dominate the position for the next twenty years. Harry Earle began in junior football as a forward and played for Millwall Athletic at full-back before finally settling as a goalkeeper. In later years he was trainer to West Ham Schools, where his son Stanley commenced a glittering career in the game. Capped by England at Schools, Amateur and full levels, he was nearly 28 before he took up professionalism with West Ham United, for whom he scored 58 goals in 273 League and Cup matches in eight seasons, commencing from 1924-25.

Appearances: FL: 23 apps 0 gls FAC: 1 app 0 gls
Total: 24 apps 0 gls

EDGE, Declan John
Forward
b. Malacca, Malaysia, 18th September 1965
CAREER: Gisbourne C (New Zealand)/NOTTS Dec 1985/ Gisbourne C/Melville United (New Zealand) assistant-manager.
Debut as sub v Wolverhampton Wanderers (h) 26.12.85, won 4 – 0

Following his first impressive outing from the bench in the emphatic 4 – 0 victory against relegation bound Wolves, Declan scored at Doncaster in his first starting appearance just two days later. In January and February he played in most matches, alongside Mick Waitt in place of Rashid Harkouk, and scored at Chesterfield in a 2 – 2 draw on 8th February. The New Zealand international eventually lost out to the emerging talents of first-year professional Paul Barnes, the scorer of four League goals in 11(3) matches in his debut season.

Appearances: FL: 7(3) apps 2 gls FAC: 3 apps 0 gls
Other: 1(1) apps 0 gls Total: 11(4) apps 2 gls
Honours: New Zealand International

EDWARDS, John 'Jack'
Inside-forward 5' 10" 11st 0lbs
b. Salford, Lancs, 23rd February 1924
d. Nottingham, December 1978
CAREER: Adelphi Lads' Club/Long Eaton United/ Nottingham Forest May 1944/Southampton June 1949, fee £10,000(Kidderminster Harriers loan June 1952)/ NOTTS Nov 1952, in exchange for Alex Simpson/Kings Lynn cs 1954/Great Yarmouth Town player-manager Aug 1955 to Jan 1956
Debut v Lincoln City (h) 29.11.52, drawn 1 – 1

Jack Edwards developed his game with the Adelphi Lads' Club, a noted nursery side who supplied Manchester United with several of their star players in the immediate post war period. While playing for a Navy representative side during the war, he impressed an onlooker who recommended him to Nottingham Forest. When normal League football recommenced Forest were in receipt of a number of offers for him, but held on to their star man until they were relegated from Division Two in 1949. Southampton paid £10,000 to take him to the Dell where he appeared in 85 matches and scored 16 goals in a three-year stay. He was out on loan at Kidderminster Harriers at the commencement of the 1952-53 season when Notts concluded transfer arrangements with Southampton, Alex Simpson moving to the Dell in exchange. After appearing regularly in his first season at Meadow Lane, he did not feature after the appointment of new manager George Poyser on 22nd October 1953.

Appearances: FL: 25 apps 3 gls Total: 25 apps 3 gls

EDWARDS, Michael
Central defender 6' 1" 12st 10lbs
b. North Ferriby, 25th April 1980
CAREER: Hull City trainee July 1996, pro July 1998/ Colchester United Mar 2003/Grimsby Town Aug 2003/ NOTTS July 2004
Debut v Chester City (h) 7.8.2004, drawn 1 – 1

Mike Edwards made his League debut with Hull City as an 18 year-old in a high scoring match at Rotherham United on 28th December 1998, won 5 – 4 by the Millers. When released from his contract in season 2002-03, Mike was the club's longest serving player with exactly 200 League and Cup appearances. A cruciate ligament injury had enforced a lengthy spell on the sidelines prior to his release, and similar problems have unfortunately brought an early end to his first season at Meadow Lane. Prior to his injury Mike had impressed as a watchful, fast moving central defender who patrolled the edge of the penalty area, resolutely guarding the main entrance to goal.

Appearances: FL: 8(1) apps 0 gls FLC: 2 apps 0 gls
Total: 10(1) apps 0 gls

EDWARDS, Richard Thomas

Full-back/Half-back   6' 0"   13st 3lbs
b. Kirkby-in-Ashfield, Notts, 20th November 1942
CAREER: Kingsway School (Sutton-in-Ashfield)/West Notts Schoolboys/East Kirkby Welfare Juniors/Nottingham Forest trial/NOTTS ground staff Feb 1959, pro Nov 1959/Mansfield Town Mar 1967, fee £5,000/Aston Villa Mar 1968, fee £30,000/Torquay United June 1970, fee £8,000/Mansfield Town July 1973/Torquay United May 1974/Bath City 1974-76/Brixham United manager
Debut v Rochdale (h) 26.12.59, won 2 – 1

Dick Edwards was picked up at East Kirby after Forest had rejected him after trials. After ten months as a ground staff boy he signed professional forms on his 17th birthday. His first League outing, one month later, was made at left full-back. For his next appearance, a little over a year later, he was selected to play at Halifax as an inside-forward but the game was called off. A left-half in schools football, he was to occupy every outfield position but outside-left during his eight seasons at Meadow Lane. As a keen gymnast he possessed untiring stamina, and the ability to launch long throws from the touch-line, once directly hitting Manchester City's crossbar in a FL Cup match in December 1963. Later in his career he followed manager Tommy Cummings from Mansfield Town to Aston Villa and ended his League career with aggregate figures of 464(5) League matches and 29 goals. During his time with Torquay United he formed his own country and western group, working in hotels and clubs on the Devon coast. As recently as 2002 he entertained guests in the Don Masson Suite at Meadow Lane.

Appearances: FL: 221 apps 20 gls FAC: 10 apps 0 gls FLC: 14 apps 1 gl Total: 245 apps 21 gls
Honours: England Youth International

ELLEMAN, Allan Richard

Outside-right
b. Birmingham, 3rd November 1862
d. Nottingham, January quarter 1939
CAREER: Stoke St. Peter's/Glentoran 1882-83/Cliftonville 1883-1890/West Bromwich Albion 1890-91/NOTTS Aug 1891/Grimsby Town Mar 1892/Mansfield Town Aug 1892
Debut v West Bromwich Albion (h) 10.10.1891, won 4 – 0 (scored one)

Allan Elleman was the first Englishman to captain Ireland in an international match. This was in 1890, when England won 9 – 1. In those days, seven years residence on Irish soil was qualification for an Irish cap. He actually lived in Ireland for nine years and was honorary secretary and captain of the Cliftonville club. In addition to playing, he also acted as umpire (as referees were first designated) and was an official in the England v Ireland match at Liverpool in March 1889. When he made his debut for the Magpies he scored one of four goals against his previous club, West Bromwich Albion who won the FA Cup that season. In a 1934 interview he recalled a highlight from his youth. When playing for Stoke St Peter's against Bucknall St Mary's in 1886, his team won 44 – 0. A result all the more remarkable because only 35 minutes each way was played!

Appearances: FL: 6 apps 2 gls Total: 6 apps 2 gls
HONOURS: Northern Ireland International, 2 caps 1889-90. (Cliftonville) Irish Cup winners 1888; finalists 1887& 1890

ELLIOT, Robert

Goalkeeper   6' 3"   14st 12lbs
b. Greenwich, London, 30th April 1986
CAREER: Erith Town/Charlton Athletic cs 2002, pro Jan 2005 (Erith & Belverdere loan 2003-04) (Bishop's Stortford loan 2004-05)(NOTTS loan Jan 2005)
Debut as sub v Kidderminster Harriers (h) 18.3.2005, lost 1 – 3

Rob's debut in League football was hardly what he would have wished for. His first touch was to pick the ball out of the net after a successful penalty conversion. He had replaced Saul Deeney, who had been sent off for his challenge on a Kidderminster forward. It was the Harrier's second penalty of the match, reflecting the afternoon's ill-tempered exchanges. Awarded a professional contract by Charlton Athletic immediately prior to his loan to the Magpies, Rob endured a tough baptism in League football, but the ideally proportioned youngster presents a formidable barrier, and at just nineteen years of age he looks an excellent prospect.

Appearances: FL: 3(1) apps 0 gls Total: 3(1) apps 0 gls
HONOURS: Republic of Ireland U-19 International

ELLIOTT, John Walter

Outside-left
b. Warkworth, Northumberland, 23rd December 1946
CAREER: Ashington/NOTTS Aug 1967-69
Debut v Chesterfield (a) 26.8.67, lost 0 – 4

Hailed as 'the find of the season', the young outside-left was elevated to senior level after just three games in the 'A' Team as season 1967-68 got underway.

An extremely tricky customer on the left touch line, he was often the victim of over-robust attentions by opposing full-backs. He nevertheless remained in prime condition throughout his first season of senior football, appearing in 39(1) Division Four matches and scoring five goals. As is often the case with emerging players, he was less successful in his second season, despite having the advantage of Don Masson as an inside partner. Released on a free transfer in May 1969, Press speculation linked him with a possible move into non-League football with King's Lynn.

Appearances: FL: 61(3) apps 7 gls FAC: 2 apps 0 gls FLC: 2 apps 0 gls Total: 65(3) apps 7 gls

――――――――○――――――――

ELLIOTT, Sidney

Inside-forward 5' 10½"   12st 12lbs
b. Sunderland, 14th January 1908
d. Gravesend, Kent, September 1986
CAREER: Arcade Mission (Sunderland)/Margate F.C./ Durham City June 1926/Fulham May 1927/Chelsea May 1928, fee £3,000/Bristol City July 1930/NOTTS Mar 1932, fee £690/Bradford City June 1934/Rochdale Sept 1935, fee £400/FB Minter Sports (London) July 1936
Debut v Chesterfield (h) 19.3.32, drawn 1 – 1 (scored)

Two months prior to his signing, Sid Elliott had done much towards Bristol City's success against the Magpies in the FA Cup third round. The subsequent decision to move for his signature was prompted by the fact that prolific centre-forward Tom Keetley was injured, and the attacking output was suffering as a result. Elliott made a good start, scoring on his debut, and he became a useful member of the first team squad with his ability to fill any of the three inside forward positions. Noted for his powerful shooting and clever headwork, Sid gave good value to each of his seven League clubs, scoring a career total of 93 goals in 227 League matches.

Appearances: FL: 51 apps 16 gls FAC: 2 apps 0 gls Total: 53 apps 16 gls

――――――――○――――――――

EMBERTON, Frederick Percival 'Teddy'

Right-half 5' 10½"   11st 4lbs
b. Titchmarsh, Northants, 23rd June 1884
d. Radcliffe-on-Trent, Notts, 21st December 1957
CAREER: Stafford Wesleyans/Stafford Rangers July 1902/ NOTTS May 1904 to cs 1915
Debut v Preston North End (a) 15.10.04, lost 1 – 3

After graduating with Stafford Rangers for two seasons, Teddy Emberton was given an early run-out at senior level by the Magpies. His skill, speed and resource at right-half quickly made him an indispensable member of

the side. His untiring efforts and sheer consistency seemed well worth representative honours, but the call never came. In his final season he shared with goal-keeper Albert Iremonger the distinction of being the club's senior professional. His goals were in the category of coll-ector's items, his first coming in the FA Cup against Burslem Port Vale in February 1907 and his last (which was also his first League goal) came at Chelsea in November 1914. Outside of the game, Teddy was a fitter in an engineering works.

Appearances: FL: 365 apps 1 gl FAC: 17 apps 1 gl Total: 382 apps 2 gls
Honours: (NOTTS) FL Div 2 champions 1914

――――――――○――――――――

EMENALO, Michael

Left-back 5' 11"   11st 4lbs
b. Aba, Nigeria, 14th July 1965
CAREER: Eintracht Trier (Germany)/RWD Molenbeek (Belgium)/NOTTS trial July, pro Aug 1994/San Jose Earthquakes (USA)/U.E. Lleida (Spain) 1997-98/Maccabi Tel-Aviv (Israel) 1998-2000.
Debut v Wolverhampton Wanderers (h) 21.8.94, drawn 1 – 1

Michael Emenalo arrived at Meadow Lane after a successful World Cup tournament with Nigeria, but he failed to settle in English football. Problems with his work permit meant that he missed pre-season training and a lack of understanding with his colleagues was immediately apparent. Later in the season he was a surprise call-up for the Anglo Italian Cup Final at Wembley, where he appeared as a substitute for the last 16 minutes. Before his unhappy sojourn in Nottingham ended he was tried, without success, as a striker. Currently employed as a FIFA licensed agent.

Appearances: FL: 7 apps 0 gls Other: 3(1) apps 0 gls Total: 10(1) apps 0 gls
Honours: Nigeria International. (NOTTS) Anglo-Italian Cup winners 1995

――――――――○――――――――

EMMITT, Herbert William

Half-back
b. Nottingham, 6th August 1857
d. Nottingham, 21st April 1901
CAREER: NOTTS 1881-89/Nottingham Forest
Debut v Wednesbury Strollers, FAC 2 replay (h) 24.11.1881, won 11 – 1

A versatile sportsman who played twice in County cricket matches for Nottinghamshire in 1888 as a middle order batsman. He also played for Newport, South Wales, and in March 1899 obtained an appointment as coach to Dalkeith Cricket Club in Edinburgh. His Magpies debut featured a double hat-trick by Harry Cursham and was, at that time, the club's record win. The match was a replay, ordered after Wednesbury Strollers had protested about the referee and one of the Notts' players, following a comfortable enough 5 – 3 win by the home side at the Castle Ground. The Strollers must have rued their decision to protest as the replay, held at the Derby Cricket Ground, resulted in a shattering defeat by ten clear goals. Outside of sporting activities, Herbert Emmitt worked as a yeast salesman.

Appearances: FL: 4 apps 0 gls FAC: 31 apps 4 gls
Total: 35 apps 4 gls

EVANS, Frederick John

Forward   5' 9½" 10st 8lbs
b. Petersfield, Hants, 20th May 1923
CAREER: Portsmouth Jan 1945/NOTTS July 1947/Crystal Palace Mar 1951/Rochdale June 1953/Biggleswade Town
Debut v Ipswich Town (a) 23.8.47, lost 0 – 2

Fred Evans joined the Magpies as a centre-forward, but it was not until new manager, Eric Houghton, picked him at outside-right that he enjoyed a lengthy run in the first team. As a former international outside-right himself, Houghton felt that Evans' chief asset – he was considered one of the fastest forwards in the game – would be better utilised along the touch line. The Magpies set a cracking pace from the outset of season 1949-50, Fred Evans scoring the first goal of the season in the opening day 2 – 0 win against Southend United. The Third South championship was eventually secured, with a margin of seven points over Northampton Town, and a record of 95 League goals and a further seven in three FA Cup matches.

Appearances: FL: 39 apps 14 gls Total: 39 apps 14 gls
Honours: (NOTTS) FL Div 3 South champions 1950

EVANS, William Emanuel

Inside-forward 5' 8"   10st 8lbs
b. Aston, Birmingham, 5th September 1921
d. Grimsby, 26th July 1960
CAREER: Linread F.C. (Birmingham)/Aston Villa Sept 1946/NOTTS June 1949/Gillingham July 1953/Grimsby Town June 1955, appointed assistant-trainer July 1958
Debut v Southend United (h) 20.8.49, won 2 – 0

Billy Evans was the first player signed under the new management of Eric Houghton, who returned to his old club to recruit the former Birmingham Works League forward who had scored prolifically for Linread in 1945-46. Despite a scoring debut for the Villa, against Liverpool in 1947, he had played in only seven League matches (three goals) at the time of his move to Meadow Lane. His Magpies debut was eventful, as the team contrived to miss two penalties but still managed to beat Southend United 2 – 0. A wholehearted forward with useful utility value, he was used as an inside-left with a roving commission during his successful first season when he missed only one match in the championship winning line-up of 1949-50. In the following term he had a lengthy run at outside-right, but spent much of his last season in the Reserves. He subsequently gave excellent service to both Gillingham (89 matches and 12 goals in two seasons) and Grimsby Town (102 matches and 27 goals in three seasons.) His contribution to the Mariners' Third Division North championship win in 1956 being 11 goals in 46 matches.

Appearances: FL: 96 apps 14 gls FAC: 7 apps 0 gls
Total: 103 apps 14 gls
Honours: (NOTTS) FL Div 3 South champions 1950.
(Grimsby Town) FL Div 3 North champions 1956

FAIRCLOUGH, Courtney Huw 'Chris'

Central defender   5' 11" 11st 7lbs
b. Nottingham, 12th April 1964
CAREER: Nottingham Forest associate schoolboy Nov 1978, app Jul 1980, pro Oct 1981/Tottenham Hotspur July 1987, fee £387,000/Leeds United Mar 1989, fee £500,000/Bolton Wanderers July 1995, fee £500,000/NOTTS July 1998/York City, initially on loan Mar 1999 to Feb 2001/Nottingham Forest Academy coach.
Debut v Oldham Athletic (a) 8.8.98, won 3 – 1

An outstanding Forest development who was unfortunate to miss full international recognition, suffering a serious pelvic injury at a time when he was being widely tipped for promotion to the full England squad. Elder brother of Wayne (q.v.), Chris commanded some hefty fees, reflecting his value as a defensive lynchpin with keen awareness and the ability to marshal a defence. Joining Notts on a free transfer after an injury-plagued final season with Bolton Wanderers, he was loaned to York City after 19 early season matches. Chris had scored his only Magpies goal at Bootham Crescent in his penultimate outing on 7th November 1998 and he was signed permanently by the Minstermen following his loan period.

Appearances: FL: 16 apps 1 gl FAC: 1 app 0 gls FLC: 2 apps 0 gls Total: 19 apps 1 gl
Honours: England 'B' International, 1 app. England U-21 International, 7 apps. (Leeds United) FL Division 2 champions 1990. FL Division 1 champions 1992. (Bolton Wanderers) FL Division 1 champions 1997

––––––––––––––––––○––––––––––––––––––

FAIRCLOUGH, Wayne Ricks
Midfield/Defender   5' 10" 12st 2lbs
b. Nottingham, 27th April 1968
CAREER: Top Valley School/ NOTTS app Aug 1984, pro Apr 1986/Mansfield Town Mar 1990, fee £80,000/ Chesterfield June 1994 (Scarborough loan Mar 1996)/ Northwich Victoria cs 1996/Grantham Town cs 1998/ Northwich Victoria/Ilkeston Town 1999/Hucknall Town/ Matlock Town Feb 2002.
Debut v Darlington (a) 22.9.85, won 3 – 2

Younger brother of Chris (q.v.), strong-tackling utility defender Wayne occupied a number of roles at Meadow Lane. With the Reserves and 'A' Team he appeared in every outfield position. His versatility tended to work against him, however, as he made the ideal substitute being able to cover for most positions with equal faculty. He enjoyed his first extended run in the League side in 1987-88 when promotion ambitions ended in the Play-off semi-finals against Walsall. He cost Mansfield Town their joint record fee at the time of his move to Field Mill and he completed 131(10) League appearances and 12 goals for the Stags.

Appearances: FL: 39(32) apps 0 gls FAC: 3 apps 0 gls FLC: 1(2) apps 0 gls Other: 11(2) apps 0 gls
Total: 54(36) apps 0 gls

FALLON, William Joseph
Outside-left   5' 9"   11st 7lbs
b. Larne, Republic of Ireland, 14th January 1912
d. Nottingham, March 1989
CAREER: Brideville/Dolphin F.C., Dublin/ NOTTS Feb 1934/Sheffield Wednesday Mar 1938(During the WW2 period assisted Shamrock Rovers, Shelbourne, Dundalk and made one guest app for York City in 1941-42)/NOTTS June 1946/Exeter City June 1947/ Peterborough United cs 1948 to 1950
Debut v Grimsby Town (a) 3.3.34, drawn 2 – 2

Bill Fallon had scored 26 goals for Dolphin F.C. when Notts recruited him, and considering the fact that he joined a struggling side, who were relegated from the Second Division in his first full season, he nevertheless became the Magpies' first Republic of Ireland International. His first spell at Meadow Lane ended when he followed manager Jimmy McMullen to Sheffield Wednesday. In the final season before WW2 Bill scored 10 League goals in 34 matches but Wednesday missed out – by a single point – as rivals Sheffield United took second place in Division Two and were promoted along with Blackburn Rovers. Returning to Meadow Lane for the first season of peacetime football, and by this time a veteran in footballing terms, he appeared in 16 matches and scored four goals. A season with Exeter City followed, and he wound up with two years with Peterborough United, operating mainly at centre half-back. A younger brother, Peter Fallon, played for Exeter City and Queens Park Rangers in early post war football.

Appearances: FL: 135 apps 23 gls FAC: 10 apps 3 gls Other: 3 apps 0 gls Total: 148 apps 26 gls
Honours: Republic of Ireland International, 9 caps 1935-39

––––––––––––––––––○––––––––––––––––––   ––––––––––––––––––○––––––––––––––––––

FARINA, Frank

Forward   5' 9"   11st 0lbs
b. Darwin, Australia, 5th September 1964
CAREER: Sydney City (Australia)/Marconi F.C. (Australia)/ Club Brugge KV (Belgium)/Bari (Italy) (NOTTS loan Mar - Apr 1992)/R.C. Strabourg cs 1992/Australian National coach.
Debut as sub v Crystal Palace (h) 28.3.92, lost 2 – 3

Frank Farina's brief stay at Meadow Lane almost didn't happen. On transfer-deadline day the Australian World Cup striker was still awaiting clearance to allow him to play. With hopes of a settlement seeming unlikely, Frank had gone to the cinema. It took a deputation from Meadow Lane a hair-raising rush around nine cinemas before they located their man, and another mad dash back to Meadow Lane to complete formalities. In two appearances from the bench, and one in the starting line-up (versus Spurs), the Aussie striker showed some inventive touches, but could not halt the Magpies free-fall through the relegation trapdoor.

Appearances: FL: 1(2) apps 0 gls Total: 1(2) apps 0 gls
Honours: Australia International

FARMER, Ronald James

Wing-half   5' 8**2**"   12st 3lbs
b. Guernsey, Channel Islands, 6th March 1936
CAREER: North Athletic Club/Nottingham Forest May 1953/Coventry City Nov 1958, with Arthur Lightening for a combined fee of £6,000/NOTTS Oct 1967, fee £12,000/ Grantham Town July 1969, retired 1970/Coventry City youth-team coach
Debut v Bradford P.A. (h) 7.10.67, drawn 0 – 0

An important element in Coventry City's meteoric elevation from Division Four to Division One, Bill Farmer appeared in over 300 first team matches for the Sky Blues as an attacking wing-half, scoring 52 goals in nine seasons at Highfield Road. When joining the Magpies he was returning to the city where he learned his football, both he and his goalkeeper brother Bill having left Guernsey to join the Forest in 1953. Manager Billy Gray paid out the biggest fee to leave the Meadow Lane coffers for a very long time when signing Farmer, and the vastly-experienced wing-half proved to be an excellent capture, missing only a handful of games in his two seasons at the club.

Appearances: FL: 69 apps 5 gls FAC: 2 apps 0 gls
Total: 71 apps 5 gls
Honours: (Coventry City) FL Division 3 champions 1964. FL Div 2 champions 1967

FARRELL, Sean Paul

Forward   6' 0"   13st 7lbs
b. Watford, 28th February 1969
CAREER: Luton Town app, signing pro Mar 1987 (Colchester United loan Mar 1988) (Northampton Town loan Sept 1991)/Fulham Dec 1991, fee £100,000/ Peterborough United Aug 1994, fee £120,000/NOTTS Oct 1996, fee £80,000/Burton Albion July 2001, retired May 1903
Debut v Chesterfield (h) 15.10.96, drawn 0 – 0

Alongside Gary Jones in the Magpies run away success of the 1997-98 championship, Sean proved himself a match - winning striker. Overcoming early season injury problems the long–haired, hard running centre-forward hit the goal trail from mid season, finishing with 15 in 32(3) Third Division matches. In earlier days Sean forged an excellent partnership at Fulham with Gary Brazil, later to coach and manage at Meadow Lane. He had scored 31 goals in 93(1) League matches at the time of his transfer to Peterborough United, where he scored 20 League goals in 49(17) matches. A most unfortunate player in the way of injuries, Sean was always to be found where the action was, his fearless approach resulting in a catalogue of injuries, directly responsible for his relatively modest appearance record of 99 matches in five seasons.

Appearances: FL: 58(29) apps 22 gls FAC: 6(2) apps 1 gl FLC: 2(1) apps 0 gls Other: 1 app 0 gls
Total: 67(32) apps 23 gls
Honours: (NOTTS) FL Division 3 champions 1998

FASHANU, Justinus Soni 'Justin'

Forward   6' 1"   12st 7lbs
b. Hackney, London, 18th September 1962
d. Shoreditch, London, 2nd May 1998
CAREER: Shropham/Attleborough/Peterborough United/ Norwich City app Sept 1977, pro Dec 1978 (Adelaide City, Australia, loan May to July 1980)/Nottingham Forest Aug 1981, fee £1million (Southampton loan Aug-Oct 1982)/ NOTTS Dec 1982, fee £150,000/Brighton & Hove Albion June 1985/Los Angeles Heat (USA) player-manager/ Edmonton Brickmen (Canada) July 1988/Manchester City trial Oct 1989/West Ham United trial Nov 1989/Ipswich Town trial Feb 1990/Leyton Orient trial Feb 1990/Southall player-coach Mar 1991/Newcastle United trial July 1991/ Leatherhead Nov 1991/Torquay United player-manager Dec 1991, assistant-manager June 1992 to Jan 1993/ Airdrieonians Feb 1993/Trelleborg (Norway) May 1993/ Heart of Midlothian July 1993 to Feb 1994/Toronto Blizzard (Canada) Mar 1994/USA coaching appointment Apr 1994/Miramar Rangers, (New Zealand) Oct 1996/ Atlanta Ruckus (USA) 1997.
Debut v West Ham United (h) 18.12.82, lost 1 – 2

Forty goals in 97(6) matches for Norwich City launched the career of the former Dr. Barnardo's boy, who had reached the final of the British Schoolboy Heavyweight Boxing Championship in 1977. The most memorable of his Norwich City goals was the one scored against League champions Liverpool in a 3 – 5 home defeat on 9th February 1980. His spectacular long range volley, captured by 'Match of the Day' cameras, was named as the BBC Television's 'Goal of the Season.' Despite having cost £1 million, Justin was not a success with Forest, scoring only three League goals during a traumatic eighteen months at the City Ground. A loan spell with Southampton and three goals in nine matches helped restore some confidence, and on moving to Meadow Lane in mid season he scored nine goals in 17 League and Cup matches before injury brought a premature end to his season. Fitness problems marred his time at Meadow Lane, restricting his appearances during the next two seasons, both of which ended in relegation. Justin was one of the first footballers to publicly admit to being 'gay.' Unfortunately, this did nothing to enhance his popularity in the macho world of football. He tragically committed suicide at the age of 35, having fled from the USA when facing a criminal charge. Justin's elder brother, John, scored over 100 League goals for Wimbledon and was capped twice by England.

Appearances: FL: 63(1) apps 20 gls FAC: 2 apps 2 gls FLC: 8 apps 1 gl Total: 73(1) apps 23 gls
Honours: England Youth International, 2 apps 1978-79. England U-21 International, 11 apps 1980-83. England 'B' International, 1 app.

FAWELL, Derek Stuart

Inside-forward
b. Hartlepool, 22nd March 1944
CAREER: Spennymoor United/NOTTS Oct 1964/Lincoln City Sept 1965/Wisbech Town Nov 1965/Ilkeston Town Jan 1967/Redditch United Aug 1968/Lockhead Leamington cs 1969
Debut v Oxford United (a) 27.2.65, lost 0 – 4

Derek Fawell's solitary Division Four outing came when he deputised for fellow North-Eastener Jim Rayner at Oxford United. In a two-month trial period with Lincoln City he appeared in three Division Four matches but failed to earn an extension to his contract.

Appearances: FL: 1 app 0 gls Total: 1 app 0 gls

FEATHERBY, Walter Leonard 'Len'

Inside-forward   5' 9½"   11st 7lbs
b. Kings Lynn, 28th July 1905
d. Kings Lynn, 22nd February 1972
CAREER: Lynn Whitefriars 1921/South Lynn Wednesday 1922/Lynn Town/Norfolk Juniors/Norfolk County 1923-25/Glasgow Rangers trial Jan 1924/Norwich City am May, pro June 1924/Northfleet Sept 1927/Millwall Oct 1927/Peterborough & Fletton United Mar 1928/Merthyr Town Aug 1928/Wolverhampton Wanderers Jan 1929/Reading June 1930/Queens Park Rangers May 1931/Mansfield Town Dec 1931/Crewe Alexandra July 1932/Merthyr Town cs 1933/Plymouth Argyle Mar 1934/NOTTS June 1935 to 1936/Carlisle United trial 1936/Scarborough Sept 1936/Kings Lynn to Apr 1939.
Debut v Bristol Rovers (a) 31.8.35, drawn 0 – 0

As an amateur represented Norfolk County on four occasions, and scored three goals in 26 appearances for Norwich City but gathered no moss subsequently in clocking up a further 103 League appearances and 18 goals in the colours of seven different clubs. At the end of his footballing travels Len won a Norfolk Senior Cup medal with his hometown club, King's Lynn, in 1939. Outside of the game, he was a well-known pigeon fancier, with many notable racing successes. Latterly employed as a groundsman in Norfolk.

Appearances: FL: 3 apps 0 gls Other: 1 app 0 gls Total: 4 apps 0 gls

---

FEEBERY, Alfred

Left-back   5' 9½"   12st 6lbs
b. Hucknall, Notts, 10th September 1909
d. Hucknall, Notts, 23rd December 1989
CAREER: Hucknall Schoolboys/Hucknall Congregationalists/NOTTS Aug 1928 and loaned to Newark Town/NOTTS May 1929/ Bristol Rovers July 1939
Debut v Chelsea (a) 22.2.30, lost 1 – 3

Alf Feebery appeared in ten seasons of League football for the Magpies as a left-back with all the necessary attributes of strength in the tackle, coupled with excellent positional play and a strong kick.

He recovered well from a broken leg that sidelined him for almost all of the 1932-33 season. Afterwards, he was virtually an automatic choice for the next six seasons, apart from 1937-38 when he lost out to the challenge of Irish international Con Moulson, and played in only 19 matches. He was awarded a benefit match in September 1935, Heart of Midlothian providing the opposition. The Inland Revenue subsequently brought a test case to court and established the precedent for taxing footballer's benefits.

Appearances: FL: 221 apps 1 gl FAC: 7 apps 0 gls Other: 4 apps 0 gls Total: 232 apps 1 gl

---

FEENEY, Thomas Wilfred
Inside-forward   5' 8"   11st 11lbs
b. Grangetown, North Yorkshire, 26th August 1910
d. Grangetown, North Yorkshire, 5th March 1973
CAREER: Normanby Magnesite/ Whitby United/Newcastle United Dec 1930, fee £25/NOTTS June 1932, fee £500/ Lincoln City June 1933, in part exchange for Harold Riley/ Stockport County Feb 1934/Halifax Town Aug 1934/ Chester May 1937/Darlington Feb 1938 to cs 1939/Ferryhill Athletic committee Dec 1948
Debut v Chesterfield (a) 17.9.32, drawn 0 – 0

Tom Feeney began in Division One with Newcastle United, playing in four matches (one goal) in 1931-32, the club's FA Cup winning season. He did not establish himself at Meadow Lane, his in-and-out season illustrated by the fact that he never appeared in more than four consecutive matches at a time. He subsequently did the rounds of Third Division North clubs, enjoying his best form with Darlington where he netted 25 goals in 43 League and Cup matches. His career aggregate figures were 128 League matches and 36 goals.

Appearances: FL: 17 apps 2 gls Total: 17 apps 2 gls

FENNER, Thomas
Inside-right   5' 10"   11st 5lbs
b. Uxbridge, 12th May 1904
CAREER: Warrington Juniors/Wigan Borough, initially on am forms, May 1924/NOTTS Feb 1928/Bradford City Nov 1933; retired due to injury Nov 1934.
Debut v Reading (h) 18.2.28, drawn 1 – 1 (scored)

Tom Fenner first wore the distinctive red & blue quartered colours of Wigan Borough in 1924-25 and scored six goals in nine Third Division North matches. At the time of his move to Meadow Lane his League aggregate had risen to 38 goals in 94 matches.
During a lengthy spell with the Magpies he passed the milestone of 100 League goals, his tally including four

goals in one match against Burnley in December 1932. Here it should be said that the awarding of the match ball to the scorers of hat-tricks and above is a comparatively recent practise. Tom Fenner, however, was rewarded due to the kindness of a supporter who had won the match ball in a 'Penny-on-the-Ball' raffle and kindly presented it to the player. Often described as 'the brains of the attack', Fenner was equally at home in any of the three inside-forward berths. He was unfortunate in the matter of injuries, and twice had to undergo knee operations during his spell at Meadow Lane. He played in only seven League matches for Bradford City before being forced to retire due to rheumatoid arthritis in his knee. In April 2004 his 1930-31 championship medal was included in Bonham's auction sale of sporting memorabilia. It realised exactly £1,000.

Appearances: FL: 158 apps 69 gls FAC: 5 apps 1 gl Total: 163 apps 70 gls
Honours: (NOTTS) FL Division 3 South champions 1931

FENTON, Nicholas Leonard 'Nicky'
Defender   5' 10"   10st 4lbs
b. Preston, Lancs, 23rd November 1979
CAREER: Manchester City associate schoolboy and trainee, signing pro Nov 1996 (NOTTS loan Oct 1999) (AFC Bournemouth loan Mar 2000 and again Aug 2000)/NOTTS Sept 2000, fee £150,000/Doncaster Rovers July 2004.
Debut v Bury (a) 9.10.99, won 3 – 1

Nicky was associated with Manchester City from the age of eleven, despite being a Manchester United supporter. He actually made his City debut against the Magpies in a FL Cup match, and had two years left on his City contract when he took the decision to join Notts on a permanent basis, due to restricted opportunities at Maine Road. A scorer on his home debut against Wycombe Wanderers, the classy central defender or right-back had been rarely absent in the Magpies defence for three consecutive seasons prior to his unexpected release, in the wake of relegation to Division Three.

Nicky's twin-brother, who also began with Manchester City, had trials at Meadow Lane in the summer of 2003 but was not offered a contract.

Appearances: FL: 166(2) apps 10 gls FAC: 12 apps 2 gls FLC: 7 apps 0 gls Other: 5 apps 0 gls
Total: 190(2) apps 12 gls
Honours: England Youth International

FENWICK, Robert William 'Bob'
Centre-half   5' 11" 12st 10lbs
b. Walker, Newcastle-on-Tyne, 29th September 1894
d. Newcastle-on-Tyne, July quarter 1973, aged 78
CAREER: Ashington/Lincoln City July 1920/NOTTS Feb 1923/Lincoln City Jan 1925/Shirebrook June 1926/Newark Town cs 1927/Horncastle Town Sept 1928/Shildon Athletic 1928-29
Debut v Manchester United (a) 21.2.23, drawn 1 – 1

A robust, forceful centre-half who assisted Lincoln City to the championship of the Midland League in season 1920-21, having earlier represented the North Eastern League during his Ashington spell. Arriving at Meadow Lane in February 1923 he appeared in three matches during the run in to the Third Division South championship, but thereafter was virtually unemployed at senior level, Norman Dinsdale dominating the pivotal position. A return to Sincil Bank increased his record with the Imps to 114 appearances and five goals, the total including 38 appearances and three goals in the Midland League.

Appearances: FL: 6 apps 0 gls Total: 6 apps 0 gls

FERGUSON, Alex 'Sandy'
Right-half   5' 6" 10st 8lbs
b. Glasgow circa 1867
CAREER: Glasgow Rangers/NOTTS Aug 1889/Newark Town cs 1891
Debut v Wolverhampton Wanderers (a) 7.9.1889, lost 0 – 2

After appearing in all but two matches in his debut season, Sandy Ferguson began 1890-91 in the Reserves, his first team place at right-half taken over by Archie Osborne, the new signing from Vale of Leven. Sandy appeared in a variety of positions for the second string, eventually settling in a full-back role where he seemed best suited, despite his lightweight build and lack of a powerful clearance kick. Having played in just two first team matches all season he was selected for the FA Cup Final team on the strength of his assured display in the final League match of the season. This was against Blackburn Rovers, and the Magpies rounded off their League programme with an emphatic 7 – 1 win. Faced with the same opponents one week later at the Kennington Oval, the Magpies were favourites to win the final, but it was the Rovers who surprisingly lifted the trophy by virtue of a 3 – 1 victory. Sandy departed in the close season to captain Newark Town.

Appearances: FL: 22 apps 0 gls FAC: 7 apps 0 gls
Total: 29 apps 0 gls
Honours: (NOTTS) FA Cup finalists 1891

FERGUSON, Charles
Inside-left   5' 10" 11st 8lbs
b. Dunfermline, 22nd November 1910
d. North Shields, 16th April 1995
CAREER: Yoker Athletic/Glasgow Benburb July 1930/Middlesborough May 1932, fee £150/NOTTS May 1936, fee £250/Luton Town June 1937/Aberdeen Aug 1939 (WW2 guest Middlesbrough 1944-45)/North Shields player-manager 1946/Sunderland chief scout/Corinthians, Newcastle, manager-coach/Gateshead manager April 1960 to Aug 1961/Also scouted for Sheffield United and Burnley
Debut v Exeter City (h) 29.8.36, won 3 – 1 (scored two)

Charlie Ferguson began at outside-right for Notts and scored twice in the opening day fixture against Exeter City. Rather surprisingly dropped after just four outings he was then re-introduced at inside-left in mid October. In the following month the Football Post observed: "Since Ferguson took over the inside-left position he has done remarkably well, and in addition to his hard work is blending more effectively with centre-forward Hughie Gallacher. He has also shown an ability to get amongst the goals." In the close season Ferguson was transferred to Luton Town, the team that had very narrowly overtaken the Magpies for the one promotion spot available from the Third Division South. After his playing career ended he particularly proved his worth as Sunderland's chief scout, being credited with the recruitment of no fewer than nine of their 1973 FA Cup winning side.

Appearances: FL: 22 apps 8 gls FAC: 1 app 0 gls Other: 2 apps 2 gls Total: 25 apps 10 gls
Honours: Scotland Junior International

FERGUSON, James Stirling
Goalkeeper   6' 02" 13st 6lbs
b. Longriggend, near Airdrie, 30th August 1896
d. Caldercruix, Lanarkshire, 21st September 1952
CAREER: Partick Thistle June 1916 to Apr 1918/St Roch's/Brentford June 1926/NOTTS Mar 1928 to 1932
Debut v Leeds United (a) 17.3.28, lost 0 – 6

It is interesting to note that during Jimmy Ferguson's two years with Partick Thistle his basic wage was £1 per week. In comparative terms, the £10 signing-on fee that he received in June 1916 must have constituted a tidy sum! He was a Glasgow Cup finalist with the Jags against the Rangers in

October 1917. He joined the Magpies after two seasons with Brentford during which he appeared in 65 League matches. Ideally built for his position and with a safe pair of hands, he proved a valuable signing, despite the embarrassment of a six-goal reverse on his debut. He missed only one of the next 118 League and Cup matches, starring in both relegation and promotion campaigns along the way. His younger brother Alex, also a goalkeeper, was on the books of eight Football League clubs and appeared in 494 League matches, 280 of them with Swansea Town between 1926-35.

Appearances: FL: 158 apps 0 gls FAC: 6 apps 0 gls
Total: 164 apps 0 gls
Honours: (NOTTS) FL Div 3 South champions 1931

FERRIER, David

Right-back
CAREER: Dundee/NOTTS Mar 1895
Debut v Newcastle United (h) 23.3.1895, won 2 – 1

David Ferrier had first signed a League form with Notts as early as the 1893-94 season, but difficulties arose with Dundee that prevented his coming to England. Early in the 1894-95 season efforts were again made to secure his services, but Dundee refused to part with him. In early March 1895 Notts centre-forward Jimmy Logan returned to Scotland to join Dundee and, through an agent, an exchange deal for Ferrier was suggested. Notts thought that a deal had been struck, but when Ferrier arrived in Nottingham he advised Notts' directors that he had been given permission to stay for only one week. There was no doubt that Notts had been 'done' in this matter, as Dundee obtained Logan's valuable services for nothing, when a transfer fee would otherwise have been involved. Ferrier therefore was restricted to just two appearances.

The kick-off in his debut match was delayed by some 20 minutes after it was discovered that Newcastle United had brought only their usual strip which, then as now, exactly matched Notts colours. In unfamiliar pale blue and white Notts won 2 – 1 despite playing for over an hour of the match with ten men after Sam Donnelly suffered a broken leg in an accidental collision with Graham, the Newcastle captain. Despite having arrived in Nottingham in the early hours of the same morning, Ferrier, after recovering from a nervous start, was reported to have "Played a capital game, tackling with vigour, and kicking with splendid judgement."

Appearances: FL: 2 apps 0 gls Total: 2 apps 0 gls

FINNAN, Stephen John

Midfield   5' 10" 11st 6lbs
b. Limerick, Ireland, 20th April 1976
CAREER: Wimbledon A.S./Welling United July 1993/ Birmingham City June 1995, fee £100,000 (NOTTS loan Mar 1996)/NOTTS Oct 1996, fee £300,000/Fulham Nov 1998, fee £500,000/Liverpool June 2003, fee £3.5million. Debut v Walsall (h) 6.3.96, won 2 – 1

The escalating fees involved in Steve Finnan's transfers accurately reflect his ever-growing reputation as one of the best wing-backs in the game. Despite scoring for Birmingham City at Watford on his League debut in September 1995 he left St. Andrews having failed to secure a regular first team place. Initially on loan to the Magpies, his promise was noted by the Republic of Ireland selectors, his first Under-21 cap being awarded in May 1996. County were relegated in the season of his £300,000 signing from Birmingham City, but they made a swift return in 1997-98. Initially fielded on the right wing, Steve's goal at Cardiff City at the end of August earned a share of the points. Throughout the memorable championship campaign he chipped in with six goals, and many more came as a result of his skill in open play and set piece situations.

Transferred to Fulham in November 1998, Steve added a Division Two championship medal to his collection in his first season at Craven Cottage. Two years on, Fulham reached the Premier League and in their first season he was ever-present, voted supporters' 'Player of the Year,' and won selection to the PFA's Premiership team of 2002. On the international front, he had an outstanding World Cup in South Korea and Japan in 2002. Injuries blighted his first season at Anfield following his £3.5 million transfer in June 2003 , but 2005 has brought European glory in Liverpool's historic Champions League triumph against AC Milan.

Appearances: FL: 85(12) apps 7 gls FAC 7 apps 1 gl FLC: 4 apps 0 gls Other: 4 app 1 gl
Total: 100(12) apps 9 gls
Honours: Republic of Ireland International, 28caps, 2000-04; Republic of Ireland U-21 International, 8 apps; Republic of Ireland 'B' International, 1 app. (NOTTS) FL Div Three champions 1998. (FULHAM) FL Div 2 champions 1999; FL Div 1 champions 2001. (Liverpool) FL Cup finalists 2005. European Cup winners 2005.

FISHER, Frederick

Inside-forward 5' 11" 12st 2lbs
b. Hucknall, Notts, January quarter 1910
CAREER: Hucknall Schoolboys/Hucknall Y.M.C.A./ Staveley Town cs 1928/Newark Town Mar 1929/NOTTS May 1929/Torquay United May 1930/Mansfield Town June 1931/Swindon Town May 1933/Gillingham July 1935/ Clapton Orient May 1936/Dudley Town Sept 1937/ Bestwood Colliery reinstated am Mar 1938/Newport, Isle of Wight, (WW2 guest Derby County, Southampton & Arsenal)
Debut v West Bromwich Albion (a) 23.11.29, lost 2 – 4 (scored one)

Despite a very respectable goal scoring record throughout his career Fred Fisher was generally considered reserve team material at all of his clubs bar Swindon Town. Within an overall career aggregate of 30 goals in 85 League matches spanning six clubs, he appeared in 46 matches for the Wiltshire club and scored 16 goals. A man of diverse hobbies, he was said to enjoy pigeon fancying and oil painting.

Appearances: FL: 3 apps 1 gl Total: 3 apps 1 gl

FLANAGAN, Daniel Christopher

Centre-forward
b. Dublin, Republic of Ireland, 24th November 1924
CAREER: Dundalk/NOTTS am Dec 1946/Shelbourne Jan 1947/Manchester City Feb 1947/Bradford City Dec 1947 to cs 1948
Debut v Bournemouth & Boscombe Athletic (a) 28.12.46, won 2 – 1 (scored one)

Despite netting Notts' winner against Bournemouth on his debut, and following up with a goal against the season's run-away champions of the Third Division South, Cardiff City, Flanagan did not remain at Meadow Lane beyond a matter of a few weeks. Following his debut he admitted that he had found Third Division football "almost three times as fast as Irish football." And this from a young man who held so many sprinting championships in his own country. He was offered maximum terms to sign but declined, preferring to return to Ireland. Within a few weeks he was back in England but did not reach senior level during a brief spell with Manchester City. He scored on his Christmas Day debut for Bradford City and totalled six League goals in 13 appearances for the Bantams in 1947-48.

Appearances: FL: 2 apps 2 gls Total: 2 apps 2 gls

FLEMING, Gary James

Full-back 5' 9" 11st 4lbs
b. Derry, N Ireland, 17th February 1967
CAREER: Nottingham Forest app July 1983, pro Nov 1984/ Manchester City Aug 1989, fee £150,000 (NOTTS loan Mar 1990)/Barnsley Mar 1990, fee £85,000; released during season 1996-97 (injury).
Debut v Bolton Wanderers (a) 10.3.90, lost 0 – 3

Stylish full-back Gary Fleming began with Forest, where he won the first nine of his 31 international caps for Northern Ireland. He made his League debut at Arsenal on 13th April 1985 and completed 78(6) League and Cup games before his transfer to Manchester City, newly promoted to the First Division. A change of manger in mid season, Howard Kendall replacing Mel Machin, almost immediately curtailed Gary's prospects at Maine Road, as the new manager's first signing was full-back Alan Harper from Sheffield Wednesday. Later in the same season Gary appeared on loan at Meadow Lane as cover for Palmer and Platnauer, but in the same month Barnsley, by this time managed by ex-Manchester City boss Mel Machin, recruited Gary again. In a lengthy spell at Oakwell he completed 271 appearances in all competitions before a serious knee injury enforced his retirement.

Appearances: FL: 3 apps 0 gls Other: 1 app 0 gls
Total: 4 apps 0 gls
Honours: Northern Ireland International, 31 caps 1987-95. Northern Ireland U-23 International, 1 app.

FLETCHER, Fred

Forward
b. Ripley, Derbyshire, January quarter 1877
CAREER: Derby County Aug 1892/NOTTS Nov 1894/
Worcester Rovers Oct 1895
Debut v Bury (h) 24.11.1894, won 2 – 1

Fred Fletcher had two years to wait before making his League debut for Derby County. Unfortunately, his big day was to end in disappointment, the Rams being comprehensively defeated 8 – 0 at Sunderland in the opening fixture of season 1894-95. After a further two first team outings he joined Notts and appeared on both wings during the season when second place in Division Two was secured. As this was in the days before automatic promotion and relegation, the Magpies were involved in a Test Match against Derby County, who had finished in 15th place (out of 16 clubs) in Division One. Fred Fletcher faced his former colleagues and scored the Magpies goal in the decider played at Filbert Street, Leicester, but Derby County won 2 – 1 to retain their top-flight status. In November 1945 he was living at St. Mary's-gate and at the age of 68 had fairly recently resigned as captain of Rushcliffe Golf Club. He wrote to the 'Evening News' following a series of articles contributed by old-time supporters of the Magpies. In his letter to the editor, Mr. Fletcher revealed that one of his most treasured possessions was a letter dated 14th June, 1895, when Notts County's headquarters were situated at the Lion Hotel. It read: "Your name was particularly mentioned for helping us in the Test match, and for the splendid game that you played," wrote the hon. Secretary Mr. T.E. Harris, expressing the wish of the directors that Mr. Fletcher would assist the club when business permitted. (He was a member of the local lace firm, Fletcher & Sons.)

Appearances: FL: 9 apps 3 gls Other: 3 apps 1 gl
Total: 12 apps 4 gls

FLETCHER, Henry Handley "Harry"

Inside-left   5' 6"   10st 11lbs
b. Birmingham, 17th June 1873
d. Camberwell, 30th November 1923
CAREER: Albion Swifts (Birmingham)/Grimsby Town Nov 1892/NOTTS Mar 1898/Grimsby Town Sept 1900/Fulham cs 1903/Brentford Nov 1904/Grimsby Town Oct 1905, appointed reserve team manager-coach Aug 1908 to 1910.
Debut v Liverpool (h) 2.4.1898, won 3 – 2

Auburn-haired Harry Fletcher was initially transferred to Notts on a temporary basis, when the Magpies seemed inevitably bound for the ordeal of the Test Matches (to decide relegation issues from Division One.)

Three wins from the last four matches saved the day, with Harry credited as being the man most instrumental in the great escape. In the close season he was signed permanently, and in his first full season imported some much needed sting into the Magpies attack. As the 'Football News' commented: "Not only is Fletcher the possessor of a straight hard shot, but he also works untiringly in midfield." In November 1899 his outstanding form was recognised by the Football League who selected him to play against the Irish League at Grosvenor Park, Belfast. From inside-left he scored one goal in a 5 – 1 victory. Unfortunately, however, he was much upset by the rough channel crossing after the match, and was confined to bed for several days! In three separate spells with Grimsby Town he recorded figures of 272 League appearances and 92 goals, ranking him amongst the most illustrious Mariners of all time.

Appearances: FL: 60 apps 17 gls FAC: 2 apps 1 gl
Total: 62 apps 18 gls
Honours: FL Representative, 1 app 1899. (Grimsby Town) FL Div 2 champions 1901

FLETCHER, Herbert Senior

Right-half
b. Nottingham, 31st May 1860
CAREER: NOTTS (debut) Nov 1881 to (final appearance) Jan 1882/Also said to have played for Nottingham Forest but dates unknown. Around 1885 he was captain of Bank F.C.
Debut v Wednesbury Strollers, FAC 2 (h) 24.11.1881, won 5 – 3

Herbert Fletcher's brief association with the Magpies was not without highlights, his four friendly appearances and four FA Cup ties producing a glut of goals, at both ends of the pitch. At right-half throughout, his debut came on 10th November against Grantham in a friendly fixture at the Castle Cricket Ground, Notts winning by a crushing score line of 13 – 0. Continuing in similar vein two days later, Staveley were despatched 7 – 0. A taste of their own medicine followed with a 1 – 10 defeat at Queen's Park on the 26th November, but pride was restored when Forest were defeated 5 – 0 on December 17th. Fletcher's four FA Cup matches featured three meetings with Aston Villa, two replays being needed to separate the teams in round three, Villa progressing after winning 4 – 1, following two drawn matches that both ended 2 – 2 after extra time. Some twenty years later Fletcher was working as a labourer in a mould shop

Appearances: FAC: 4 apps 0 gls Total: 4 apps 0 gls

FLINT, William Arthur

Inside-forward, later wing-half   5' 6**2**" 11st 6lbs
b. Underwood, Notts, 21st March 1890
d. West Bridgford, Nottingham, 5th February 1955
CAREER: Underwood & Bagthorpe/Eastwood Rangers/
NOTTS am Jan 1909, pro Sept 1909 to cs 1926
Debut v Sunderland (h) 3.4.09, drawn 0 – 0

The 'Football Post' introduced Billy Flint in January 1909 as "The Eastwood youth, who is another addition to the ranks of footballing cricketers." In early days an inside-forward, Billy was given a speedy introduction to Division One, but he did not appear regularly until season 1910-11.

He enjoyed an excellent season in 1913-14 when the Magpies finished top of Division Two. The season's inside-forward trio of Flint, Peart and Richards scoring between them 63 of the team's 77 League goals. When promotion was won again in 1922-23, the team scored only 46 goals, and took the title by beating their nearest rivals, West Ham United, in the season's final fixture. The title was won on the back of an outstanding defensive performance, with Billy, by now operating at right-half, a key member. In a career divided by Army service during World War One he nevertheless appeared in fourteen seasons of League football, proving himself supremely efficient, enthusiastic and versatile, and without doubt a club man par excellence. As a cricketer, he blossomed after the war, playing in 145 matches for Nottinghamshire between 1919-29 as a right-arm medium pace bowler and middle order right-hand batsman (3,345 career runs and 236 wickets.) A younger brother Benjamin also played cricket for Nottinghamshire in 13 matches between 1919-20. A nephew, Derrick Flint, played for Warwickshire between 1948-49 and married the celebrated lady cricketer, Rachel Heyhoe Flint.

Appearances: FL: 376 apps 40 gls FAC: 32 apps 1 gl
Total: 408 apps 41 gls
Honours: (NOTTS) FL Div 2 champions 1914 and 1923

FLOWER, Anthony John

Winger   5' 11" 10st 7lbs
b. Carlton, Nottingham, 2nd February 1945
CAREER: Cavendish School/South Nottinghamshire Schoolboys/NOTTS am Apr 1960, pro Jan 1962/Halifax Town July 1967
Debut v Hull City (a) 10.3.62, lost 1 – 2

One of Tony's teachers at Cavendish School, Barry Blenkinsop, had played for the Magpies at reserve level, and would no doubt have been gratified when his protégé joined the Meadow Lane ground staff at fifteen years of age. His career almost ended in very short order, however, as he was one of seven players transfer listed by manager Frank Hill in December 1960. In the event, he remained with Notts for a further six years as an eager and quick-moving wingman who first benefited from an extended run in the side after Mike Barber was sidelined in the late stages of season 1963-64. After leaving Meadow Lane, Tony notched up his 200th League appearance in Halifax Town's colours, his final aggregate figures amounting to 205(3) League appearances and 23 goals.

Appearances: FL: 127(2) apps 17 gls FAC: 5 apps 0 gls
FLC: 6 apps 0 gls Total: 138(2) apps 17 gls

FLOWER, Thomas

Goalkeeper   5' 11**2**"   12st 0lbs
b. Toxteth Park, Liverpool, October quarter 1916
d. Rhosneigr, Anglesey, 5th February 1962
CAREER: Cadby Hall F.C./Liverpool am Nov 1934, pro Oct 1936/NOTTS June 1938 to Sept 1939, fee £200
Debut v Swindon Town (a) 27.8.38, lost 1 – 4

Described in glowing terms by the 'Football Post' in October 1938: "A goalkeeper of exceptional ability – it is not only what he does, but how he does it. There is no jerkiness of movement. His whole body is the acme of rhythmic action. And what a kick!" Tom was signed from Liverpool, on the recommendation of Matt Busby, for the ludicrously small fee of £200. He was a regular in the Notts goal until injured at Port Vale in April 1939, but resumed again and played in the first two games before the outbreak of war. Tom died at his residence, the Railway Station, Rhosneigr, Anglesey, aged 45.

Appearances: FL: 36 apps 0 gls FAC: 3 apps 0 gls Other:
1 app 0 gls Total: 40 apps 0 gls

FOLEY, Domonic Joseph

Forward   6' 1"   12st 8lbs
b. Cork, Republic of Ireland, 7th July 1976
CAREER: St James' Gate/Wolverhampton Wanderers Aug 1995, fee £35,000 (Watford loan Feb 1998) (NOTTS loan Dec 1998) (Ethnikos, Greece, loan Jan to Mar 1999)/ Watford June 1999 to June 2003 (Queens Park Rangers loan Oct 2001) (Swindon Town loan Jan 2002) (Queens Park Rangers loan Mar 2002) (Southend United loan Feb 2003) (Oxford United loan Mar 2003)/Sporting Braga (Portugal) 2003-04
Debut v Preston North End (h) 12.12.98, lost 2 – 3

Almost fifty percent of Domonic Foley's appearances in English football were made whilst out on loan from the Wolves and later from Watford. Despite winning six full international caps for the Republic of Ireland, the tall, rangy striker was unable to fully establish himself, the bulk of his appearances coming from the substitute's bench, his career aggregate being: 41(56) League and Cup matches and 12 goals.

Appearances: FL: 2 apps 0 gls Total: 2 apps 0 gls
Honours: Republic of Ireland International, 6 caps 2000-01. Republic of Ireland U-21 International, 8 apps.

FORD, Ryan

Midfield   5' 9"   10st 4lbs
b. Worksop, Notts, 3rd September 1978
CAREER: NOTTS juniors/Manchester United trainee July 1995, pro July 1997/NOTTS Feb 2000/Ilkeston Town Mar 2002/Gresley Rovers
Debut as sub v Bury (h) 6.5.2000, drawn 2 – 2

Ryan Ford began with the Magpies at junior level before becoming a trainee with Manchester United. In his first season at Old Trafford he was a Lancashire FA Youth Cup winner, scoring in the final against Blackburn Rovers. In the same season he played in 28 Lancashire League Division Two fixtures for United's 'B' Team and continued to make steady progress, rewarded with a professional contract in July 1997. In search of first team football he returned to Meadow Lane, but his only involvement at senior level came on the final day of season 2000-01, and a second half appearance from the bench against Bury. He was released in March of the following season having added a single LDV Vans Trophy appearance to his record.

Appearances: FL: 0(1) app 0 gls Other: 1 app 0 gls
Total: 1(1) apps 0gls

FORREST, John Robert 'Bobby'

Inside-forward   5' 10"   11st 6lbs
b. Rossington, South Yorkshire, 13th May 1931
CAREER: Rossington Y.C./Rossington Colliery/Retford Town/Leeds United Dec 1952, fee £500/NOTTS Feb 1959, fee £4,500 plus J.D. Kilford/Weymouth July 1962
Debut v Bury (a) 7.2.59, won 1 – 0 (scored)

In Bobby Forrest's first full season at Meadow Lane he scored 19 goals in 44 Division Four matches, Notts winning promotion as runners up to Walsall. It was a season of exciting attacking play with five of the team's forwards registering a double-figure total of goals. In a pulsating final home encounter against Darlington on 30th April – won 5-4 by the Magpies – Bobby scored the 100th League goal of the season. Although failing to maintain his scoring ratio in subsequent seasons, he remained immensely valuable by virtue of his shrewdly intelligent use of the ball. A former miner at Rossington Colliery, his League record with Leeds United (119 matches and 36 goals) was strikingly similar to his record with the Magpies, below.

Appearances: FL: 117 apps 37 gls FAC: 6 apps 0 gls
FLC: 3 apps 1 gl Total: 126 apps 38 gls

FORSYTH, Michael Eric

Left-back   5' 11"   12st 2lbs
b. Liverpool, 20th March 1966
CAREER: Earlswood Juniors/West Bromwich Albion app June 1982, pro Nov 1983 (Northampton Town loan Mar 1986)/Derby County Mar 1986, fee £25,000/NOTTS Feb 1995, fee £200,000 (Hereford United loan Sept 1996)/ Wycombe Wanderers Dec 1996, fee £50,000/Burton Albion Oct 1999 (Gresley Rovers loan Mar 2001)/Wycombe Wanderers reserve-team coach July 2001
Debut v Reading (h) 25.2.95, won 1 – 0

Michael Forsyth won England Youth caps with West Bromwich Albion. He was hurriedly recalled from a loan spell with Northampton Town in March 1986 in order to join Derby County, just before the transfer deadline.

He was to spend eight seasons at the Baseball Ground as a determined, strong tackling left-back. Winner of the Rams' 'Player of the Year' award in 1987-88 he completed 323(1) League appearances and exceeded 400 in all competitions. His move to Meadow Lane was blighted by injury, and following a successful loan spell with Hereford United, he joined Wycombe Wanderers and helped them steer clear of relegation in his first season. Increasingly troubled by injuries, he played only a handful of matches in 1998-99 and was released in the close season.

Appearances: FL: 7 apps 0 gls Total: 7 apps 0 gls
Honours: England 'B' International, 1 app. England U-21 International, 1 app. England Youth International, 8 apps. (Derby County) FL Div 2 champions 1987

FOSTER, Colin John

Central defender   6' 4"   14st 1lb
b. Chislehurst, 16th July 1964
CAREER: Leyton Orient associate schoolboy Sept 1978, app July 1980, pro Feb1982/Nottingham Forest Mar 1987, fee £50,000/West Ham United Sept 1989, fee £750,000 (NOTTS loan Jan - Mar 1994)/Watford Mar 1994, fee £80,000/Cambridge United Mar 1997 to July 1998
Debut v Birmingham City (h) 11.1.94, won 2 – 1

At the time of Colin Foster's loan move from West Ham United to the Magpies, the towering central defender was available for a fee, reported to be £150,000. Unable to agree terms for a permanent move, he returned to West Ham. His first move to Nottingham was to join Forest, after a thorough grounding with Leyton Orient in which he totalled 204(1) League and Cup matches. With all the necessary attributes for his position in central defence, he gave excellent value throughout his career, totalling in excess of 500 League and Cup appearances.

Appearances: FL: 9 apps 0 gls Other: 2 apps 0 gls
Total: 11 apps 0 gls

FOSTER, John Henry

Half-back   5'11 2" 12st 7lbs
b. Wombwell, South Yorkshire, 24th January 1889
d. Loughborough, Leicestershire, January quarter 1972
CAREER: Barnsley 'A' Team/Worksop Town/NOTTS 1914 (WW1 guest Huddersfield Town)/Luton Town June 1921/Hartlepools United July 1924 to 1927
Debut v Burnley (a) 6.9.19, lost 1 – 2

Jack Foster joined Notts in the 1914-15 season but his debut was not made until after the Great War. During the period of hostilities he was able to assist Huddersfield Town, and when normal League football recommenced in

1919-20 he featured regularly for the Magpies, occupying all three half-back positions. A hard-working and capable half defensively, he was said to lack accuracy in distribution, and did not add to his senior appearances in 1920-21, as the trio of Flint, Dinsdale and Pembleton dominated the middle line. Foster found regular employment with his two subsequent clubs – Luton Town (45 matches and three goals) and Hartlepools United (54 matches and two goals).

Appearances: FL: 32 apps 1 gl FAC: 3 apps 0 gls
Total: 35 apps 1 gl

FOUNTAIN, Richard Ernest

Inside-left   5' 9 2" 11st 10lbs
b. Leeds, July quarter 1882
CAREER: Scarborough/NOTTS May 1905/Accrington Stanley Oct 1906
Debut v Stoke (a) 2.9.05, lost 0 – 3

After appearing in the opening fixture of season 1905-06 – an uninspiring 0 – 3 defeat at Stoke – Richard Fountain was immediately deposed by Walter Tarplin who proved to be one of the successes of an otherwise disappointing season. Notts finished 16th in Division One, largely due to defensive deficiencies. A fairly settled attack featured four players with a double-figure tally of goals, Green and Tarplin being joint leading scorers with 13 each.

Appearances: FL: 1 app 0 gls Total: 1 app 0 gls

FRANCIS, Willis David

Midfield   5' 5"   10st 10lbs
b. Nottingham, 26th July 1985
CAREER: NOTTS trainee July 2001, released June 2004/ Grantham Town June 2004.
Debut as sub v Blackpool (a) 30.11.2002, drawn 1 – 1

If lacking something in height, Willis Francis lacked nothing in endeavour. A busy right-side midfielder with good distribution, he appeared to progressing on the right lines when he made the breakthrough into the first team squad in 2002-03. Unable to maintain the form that had marked him as an excellent prospect in the previous term, he made little impact in 2003-04. A loan spell with Grantham Town in the second half of the season eventually led to his signing for the Gingerbreads on a permanent basis when released by the Magpies.

Appearances: FL: 2(11) apps 0 gls Total: 2(11) apps 0 gls

FRASER, John

Outside-left 5' 11" 13st 0lbs
b. Dumbarton, 10th November 1876
d. Stoke Newington, 1st October 1952
CAREER: Dumbarton Oct 1896/Motherwell Aug 1897/
NOTTS Feb 1898, fee £70/Newcastle United June 1899/St
Mirren July 1901/Southampton May 1902/Dundee May
1905, subsequently appointed player-manager/Chelsea scout,
then assistant manager until 1925
Debut v Sunderland (h) 5.2.1898, lost 0 – 1

In September 1898 the 'Football News' correspondent
considered that Fraser's transfer from Motherwell was
one of the best pieces of business ever effected by the
Notts directors. Taller than the average wingman and
strongly built, he was a difficult customer to contain on
account of his speed, scoring ability and appetite for the
big occasion. Transferred to Newcastle United at the close
of the 1898-99 season, in his fifth appearance for his new
club he scored twice against Notts who were soundly
beaten by a margin of 6 - 0 at St. James Park in October
1899.

Appearances: FL: 41 apps 5 gls FAC: 2 apps 0 gls
Total: 43 apps 5 gls
Honours: Scotland International, 1 cap 1907. (Dumbarton)
Scottish Cup finalists 1897.(Southampton) Southern
League champions 1903 and 1904. (Dundee) Scottish Cup
winners 1910

FREEMAN, Anthony

Outside-right 5' 4" 10st 0lbs
b. Melton Mowbray, Leics, 29th August 1928
d. Melton Mowbray, 1st February 2004
CAREER: Melton Town/NOTTS Jan 1946/Boston United
c 1950
Debut v Leyton Orient (h) 26.5.47, lost 1 – 2

Popularly known as 'Tich,' on account of his lack of
inches, the young and elusive right winger made rapid
strides in season 1947-48 when his pin-point centres
were tailor made for the one and only Tommy Lawton,
who scored exactly a goal-a-game in his first 24
appearances for the Magpies. Spoken of as "A second
Sammy Crooks," Freeman nevertheless failed to maintain
the progress of his first season in League football and the
outside-right position was taken over by England
international Eric Houghton in 1948-49. When Houghton
was appointed manager in May 1949, Fred Evans and
later Frank Broome contested the number seven shirt. In
what proved to be his final season at Meadow Lane
Freeman played only twice as the Magpies celebrated
promotion from the Third Division South.

Appearances: FL: 44 apps 2 gls FAC: 6 apps 1 gl
Total: 50 apps 3 gls

FRIARS, Emmet Charles

Defender 6' 2" 12st 4lbs
b. Londonderry, Northern Ireland, 14th September 1985
CAREER: Foyle Harps/ NOTTS scholar Aug 2002
Debut v Wrexham, LDV Vans Trophy 1 (h) 28.9.2004,
lost 2 – 3

One of several young Meadow Lane prospects knocking
on the first team door, who with experience should develop
into a fine player. A lengthy injury list gave Emmet his
first opportunity at senior level when he was last-minute
selection for the LDV Vans Trophy match against
Wrexham at Meadow Lane. The tall, dark-haired teenager
gave a most composed defensive display, and later in the
season he was rewarded with his first League start against
Kidderminster Harriers, paired with Kelvin Wilson in
central defence.

Appearances: FL: 4(4) apps 0 gls Other: 1 app 0 gls
Total: 5(4) apps 0 gls
HONOURS: Northern Ireland U-21 International, 1 app.

FROGGATT, Frank

Centre-half 5' 9½" 11st 7lbs
b. Sheffield, 21st March 1898
d. Sheffield, 6th March 1944
CAREER: Army football/Rose Athletic/Attercliffe F.C./
Denaby United Apr 1921/Worksop Town/Sheffield
Wednesday Oct 1921/NOTTS Nov 1927, fee £1,000/
Chesterfield May 1931, fee £230/Scarborough Aug 1934/
Manchester North End Sept 1935
Debut v Barnsley (h) 19.11.27, won 9 – 0

Frank Froggatt spent his early years with Sheffield
Wednesday as understudy to England's centre-half,
George Wilson. When the international departed to join
Nelson after refusing terms for season 1925-26, Froggatt
was appointed captain and led the Owls to promotion
from Division Two, appearing in all 42 League matches
during the season. He could hardly have wished for a
better start to his career as a Magpie, Barnsley being
routed 9 – 0 on his Meadow Lane debut. He was appointed
captain in the following month, being the third player to
hold the position that season, the others being Syd Plackett
(appointed 17th August) and Chris Staniforth (from 25th
October.) A reliable pivot in both defensive and
constructional roles, he was a regular until his final season,
when he played in only 14 matches in the Third Division
South championship season. His son, Redfern Froggatt,
played for Sheffield Wednesday, and won four England
caps, from the immediate post war period until season
1959-60. He scored 149 League and Cup goals for the
Owls in 458 matches and emulated his father's feat in
captaining Wednesday to the Second Division
championship in season 1958-59.

Appearances: FL: 115 apps 1 gl FAC: 3 apps 0 gls
Total: 118 apps 1 gl
Honours: (Sheffield Wednesday) FL Div 2 champions
1926. (NOTTS) FL Div 3 South champions 1931

---------------○---------------

FROGGATT, John Laurence

Forward   5' 11"   12st 3lbs
b. Sutton-in-Ashfield, Notts, 13th December 1945
CAREER: East Kirkby Colliery/NOTTS am, signing pro
June 1964/Ilkeston Town July 1965/Boston United/
Colchester United July 1974/Port Vale Feb 1978, fee
£10,000/Northampton Town Sept 1978, fee £8,000/Boston
United, subsequently appointed assistant manager
Debut v Bristol Rovers (a) 18.4.64, lost 0 – 4

Tall, teenage forward who spent a season at Meadow
Lane without establishing himself, but who polished his
skills in a lengthy spell in non-League circles, earning
himself a second chance in senior soccer. His 1974 move
to Colchester United reunited him with manager Jim Smith
(ex Boston United), and John scored 29 goals in 155
League matches for the Layer Road club, starring in their
1976-77 promotion campaign from Division Four. Spells
with Port Vale and Northampton Town took his career
aggregate to 213(2) League matches and 44 goals, before
he returned to Boston United as player-assistant manager.

Appearances: FL: 4 apps 0 gls FLC: 1 app 1 gl
Total: 5 apps 1 gl

---------------○---------------

FRY, Keith Frederick

Outside-right   5' 8"   10st 4lbs
b. Cardiff, 11th April 1941
CAREER: Newport County pro Oct 1958/NOTTS Feb 1962/
Merthyr Tydfil cs 1964/Chesterfield trial Jan 1966/Merthyr
Tydfil Feb 1966/Latrobe, Brisbane/Hakoah, Sydney/Merthyr
Tydfil/Bridgend Town
Debut v Portsmouth (a) 24.2.62, drawn 0 – 0

A slightly-built, fair-haired wingman, whose signing was
reported to be Notts' first move into the transfer market
for three years. The former Wales schoolboy international
was expected to provide the high and accurate crosses
from the right wing that centre-forward Tony Hateley
had been lacking. In Keith Fry's first full season, Hateley
missed many matches due to a cartilage operation, but
still managed to score 22 League goals in 32 matches,
leading to his upward move to Aston Villa. Shorn of their
star forward, Notts were relegated in 1963-64, although
Keith enjoyed his best season, scoring eight League and
Cup goals in 39 matches.

Appearances: FL: 73 apps 9 gls FAC: 4 apps 0 gls FLC:
6 apps 3 gls Total: 83 apps 12 gls
Honours: Wales Schoolboy International

GADSBY, Michael David

Goalkeeper   6' 1"   11st 10lbs
b. Oswestry, Shropshire, 1st August 1947
CAREER: Ashbourne/NOTTS am, signing pro
Jan 1968/York City July 1969 (Grimsby Town
loan Sept 1970) (Bradford City loan Dec 1970)/Hartlepool
United July 1971/Dover 1972/Weymouth Apr 1976/
Portesham.
Debut v Chester (a) 16.12.67, won 3 – 1

Mick Gadsby was rather unfortunate at Meadow Lane.
Having ousted Mike Rose, while still an amateur, his run
of eleven consecutive League matches was ended when
he was injured in a third team game and was out for the
remainder of the season. At one stage widely tipped to
win Amateur International honours, he had only just signed
professional forms with the Magpies when the FA named
him in their Amateur Xl to meet the Army. At the time
manager Billy Gray suggested that his young goalkeeper
was likely to win professional honours, if he continued
to improve with experience. In the event, Gadsby's record
in League football was a modest one. A career total of 53
appearances spanned five clubs, his highest seasonal
return coming with Hartlepool United, 21 League matches
in season 1970-71.

Appearances: FL: 11 apps 0 gls Total: 11 apps 0 gls

---------------○---------------

GALBRAITH

Centre-forward
b. CAREER: Dundee/NOTTS Dec1888
Debut v Blackburn Rovers (a) 15.12.1888, lost 2 – 5

Reporting on the Magpies game at Blackburn, in which
Galbraith made his debut, the 'Nottingham Daily Express'
reported that the game had been played under great
difficulties. "The fog was so dense for most of the time
that the two wings could only just discern one another
through the fog, and at hardly any period of the match
was more than half of the length of the field visible." That
stated, the correspondent has seen sufficient of Galbraith
to deliver a withering verdict – "Notts hooked only a
gudgeon (a small fresh water fish) in making a cast as far
as Dundee for a centre forward. Galbraith will probably
not be heard of again." – He wasn't!

Appearances: FL: 1 app 0 gls Total: 1 app 0 gls

---------------○---------------

GALLACHER, Hugh Kilpatrick

Centre-forward 5'5" 10st 5lbs
b. Bellshill, Lanarks, 2nd February 1903
d. Gateshead, 11th June 1957
CAREER: Tannockside Athletic/Hatton Rigg Thistle/
Bellshill Academy/Bellshill
Athletic Mar 1920/Queen
of the South Dec 1920/
Airdrieonians May 1921/
Newcastle United Dec
1925, fee £6,500/Chelsea
May 1930, fee £10,000/
Derby County Nov 1934,
fee £3,000/NOTTS Sept
1936, fee £2,000/Grimsby
Town Jan 1938, fee
£1,000/Gateshead
June 1938, fee
£500, retired Sept
1939
Debut v Torquay
United (h) 26.9.36,
won 2 – 0

Although not too notable in height or weight, Hughie Gallacher was a complete little footballer. In inter-war years he became a household name, and commanded an absolute fortune in transfer fees. Uncanny ball control, positional play, deadly shooting from all angles and an ability to go right through a packed defence, made him a footballing genius. Some idea of his impact on arrival at Meadow Lane can be judged by the fact that the attendance figure for his home debut (16,201) was more than treble the 5,013 who witnessed the previous match at Meadow Lane. Not even the great Tommy Lawton had such an immediate effect on gate receipts. Although past his prime on arrival, he was far too good for most Third Division defenders, and took the Magpies to within a whisker of promotion in his first season. Second place to Luton Town by a narrow margin of two points being insufficient to win promotion in the days when only the team at the top of the table was promoted. In Scottish and English League matches Hughie scored 387 goals. He also scored 23 goals for Scotland in home championship matches, his total including five in one match against Northern Ireland in February 1929. Once described as 'a stormy petrel' he was often in trouble both on the field and off it. Personal problems led him to commit suicide by throwing himself in front of the York to Edinburgh express train.

Appearances: FL: 45 apps 32 gls FAC: 1 app 0 gls Other: 1 app 0 gls Total: 47 apps 32 gls
Honours: Scotland International, 20 caps 1924-35. Scottish League representative, 2 apps. (Airdrieonians) Scottish Cup winners 1924. (Newcastle United) FL Division 1 champions 1927

GALLAGHER, James

Half-back   5' 11" 12st 0lbs
b. Radcliffe, Lancs, 2nd September 1911
d. Southampton, 4th December 1972
CAREER: Manchester Schoolboys/Lancashire Schoolboys/
Army football (Grenadier Guards)/Bury Jan 1936/Lancaster Town July 1936/NOTTS Aug 1937/Exeter City June 1939 (WW2 guest Southport 1944-45; Manchester United 1945-46). Exeter City trainer, during which time he appeared in one match v Norwich City (a) 1.1.49, in an emergency/ Southampton trainer May 1953
Debut v Cardiff City (a) 2.10.37, drawn 2 – 2

Jim Gallagher appeared in exactly half of Notts' 42 Southern Section matches in his season at Meadow Lane. Mainly at centre-half, where he deputised for Hugh McLennahan, and later at centre-forward, following Hughie Gallacher's transfer to Grimsby Town, he displayed forceful qualities and was a capable player in either position. In a lengthy subsequent spell as Exeter City's trainer he qualified for a benefit with the Grecians in May 1950. Some three years on he applied for the vacant post of manager at St James' Park but was unsuccessful, Norman Dodgin being appointed.

Appearances: FL: 23 apps 2 gls FAC: 2 apps 1 gl
Total: 25 apps 3 gls

GALLAGHER, Thomas Duncan

Full-back/Midfield   5' 10" 11st 8lbs
b. Nottingham, 25th August 1974
CAREER: Bramcote Hills Comprehensive School (Nottingham)/Parkview College, Bramcote/NOTTS associate schoolboy Jan 1990, pro June 1992, until Feb 1997
Debut as sub v Derby County, Anglo-Italian Cup, (a) 2.9.92, lost 2 – 4

A successful member of the Magpies Youth team that won the Purity League 'double' in season 1990-91. Tommy turned down a Y.T.S. opportunity at Meadow Lane in order to attend college, but graduated to the professional ranks in 1992 and made his senior debut at the age of eighteen. At either right full-back or right midfield he tackled strongly and exploited his wing in attacking moves without neglecting defensive duties. His best run of first team football was sadly curtailed by a broken leg injury sustained in training in late season 1995-96. Although returning to first team duty in October of the following term, he was destined to make only one League start. In February he was released after failing to agree terms for a new contract.

Appearances: FL: 42(1) apps 2 gls FAC: 3 apps 1 gl
FLC: 1 app 0 gls Other: 9(3) apps 0 gls
Total: 55(4) apps 3 gls
Honours: (NOTTS) Anglo-Italian Cup winners 1995

GALLOWAY, Michael Anthony

Midfield   5' 11"   11st 5lbs
b. Nottingham, 13th October 1974
CAREER: Haywood Comprehensive (Arnold)/Nottingham City & Nottinghamshire Schoolboys/Pheasant Colts (Arsenal trial)/NOTTS associate schoolboy May 1989, trainee July 1991, pro June 1993 (Gillingham loan Mar 1997)/Gillingham Mar 1997, fee £10,000 (Lincoln City loan Sept 1999)/Chesterfield Nov 1999, fee £15,000/Carlisle United Nov 2000 (Gretna loan Mar 2002) (Hereford United loan Nov 2002)/Gretna Jan 2003/Workington Jan 2005
Debut as sub v Luton Town (a) 8.4.95, lost 0 – 2

Named as one of five substitutes for the Anglo-Italian Cup Final against Ascoli in March 1995. Mick did not get on at Wembley, but in the following month made his League debut and held his place for the final seven matches of the Division One relegation season. A busy, left-sided midfielder who virtually disappeared from the first team scene following a welter of new signings during Colin Murphy's spell as manager in 1995-96. A loan spell with Gillingham led to a permanent signing and to a Wembley appearance in the Division Two Play-off Final against Manchester City in May 1999. With two minutes of normal playing time left, Gillingham led 2 – 0. Snatching defeat from the jaws of victory, they conceded two late goals and lost the penalty shoot-out by 1-3.

Appearances: FL: 18(3) apps 0 gls FAC: 0(2) apps 0 gls FLC: 2 apps 0 gls Other: 4 apps 0 gls Total: 24(5) apps 0 gls

———————o———————

GANNON, Edward

Wing-half   5' 9 2"   11st 9lbs
b. Dublin, 3rd January 1921
d. Dublin, 31st July 1989
CAREER: Star Celtic/O'Connell Celtic/Distillery/Shelbourne/NOTTS Aug 1946/Sheffield Wednesday Mar 1949, fee £15,000/Shelbourne player-manager 1955
Debut v Bournemouth & Boscombe Athletic (h) 31.8.46, won 1 – 0

In 1949 Eddie Gannon related that his first transfer in football was between Star Celtic, Dublin, and a Sunday League team. The fee was 5s.6d., equivalent to about 27 pence in today's money. Reports of Gannon's brilliant attacking half-back play with Shelbourne reached Meadow Lane in 1946, and a great stroke of business was done when his transfer was arranged. Eddie made the first team immediately and became a great crowd favourite, his fine form ranking him as one of the best attacking wing-half backs in the country. He won his first international cap against Switzerland in Dublin whilst on County's books, but his form was inevitably attracting the attention of bigger clubs. Offers from Chelsea and Arsenal were refused, but eventually unsettled he asked for a transfer that was reluctantly granted.

Sheffield Wednesday stepped in, and in seven seasons at Hillsborough he appeared in 219 League and Cup matches. Highlights included two promotion campaigns in 1950 and 1952, a run to the FA Cup semi-final in 1954, and the award of a further eleven caps for his country.

Appearances: FL: 107 apps 2 gls FAC: 11 apps 0 gls
Total: 118 apps 2 gls
Honours: Republic of Ireland International, 14 caps 1949-55. (Sheffield Wednesday) FL Div 2 champions 1952

———————o———————

GANNON, James Paul

Central defender/Midfield   6' 2"   13st 0lbs
b. Southwark, London, 7th September 1968
CAREER: Dundalk 1985/Sheffield United Apr 1989, fee £50,000 (Halifax Town loan Feb 1990)/Stockport County Mar 1990, fee £70,000 (NOTTS loan Jan 1994)/Crewe Alexandra Dec 2000/Shelbourne July 2001/Dundalk manager cs 2004.
Debut v Luton Town (h) 15.1.94, lost 1 – 2

Born in London of Irish parents, Jim Gannon was a West Ham United supporter as a youngster. He moved to Dublin with his family at the age of fifteen, returning to England to sign for Sheffield United. Failing to make the breakthrough into the first team at Bramall Lane, a brief loan spell with Halifax Town gave him his first League outing. Within a month he joined Stockport County, and in season 1990-91 assisted them to promotion from Division Four. Progress continued when in 1996-97 promotion to Division One was secured. In a stay of ten years, rewarded by a testimonial match against Manchester City, Jim made a total of 440(40) appearances and scored 64 goals in all competitions. A cruciate ligament injury marred his final months with County, and he ended his League career with a short-term contract with Crewe Alexandra before returning to Ireland.

Appearances: FL: 2 apps 0 gls Total: 2 apps 0 gls
Honours: (Stockport County) Autoglass Trophy finalists 1992 and 1993

GARCIA, Anthony

Midfield   6' 0"   12st 2lbs
b. Pierre Patte, France, 18th March 1972
CAREER: Marseilles/Lille OSC/Sheffield Wednesday trial/
NOTTS Sept 1998 to April 1999/Valaenciennes/AC Ajaccio/
Saint-Etienne/Laval.
Debut as sub v Millwall (h) 26.9.98, won 3 – 1

Tall midfielder playmaker originally signed on a month-to-month contract, Tony certainly added something extra to the squad with his skill on the ball, although the state of the Meadow Lane surface did not aid his skills as a distributor. Failing to settle in England, he was released at the end of April.

Appearances: FL: 10(9) apps 2 gls FAC: 3(2) apps 0 gls
Other: 1 app 0 gls Total: 14(11) apps 2 gls

GARDEN, Stuart Robertson

Goalkeeper   6' 0"   12st 5lbs
b. Dundee, 10th February 1972
CAREER: Dundee North End/Dundee Mar 1993/Brechin City Jan 1995/Forfar Athletic Aug 1999/NOTTS July 2001/Ross County July 2004.
Debut v York City, LDV Vans Trophy, (h) 16.10.2001, won 2 – 0

In three seasons at Meadow Lane, Stuart proved a most competent goalkeeper, without being in any way showy. Throughout his tenure, he shared first team duties with Steve Mildenhall. Beginning as reserve to the £150,000 signing from Swindon Town, he took over in mid season and appeared in 21 League matches. He began 2002-03 in pole position, but lost out in November following a 3 – 2 home defeat by Colchester United and spent the remainder of the season in reserve. An opening day 5 – 0 defeat at Bristol City saw Stuart immediately deposed, but he returned when Mildenhall suffered a cheekbone injury at the end of January. A five-match unbeaten run in February and March followed, raising hopes of avoiding relegation, but a dismal run-in ended with the dreaded drop and the inevitable clear out. Stuart was among the released, but was quickly fixed up with Ross County. Stuart is the son-in-law of former Notts manager, Jocky Scott.

Appearances: FL: 51(1) apps 0 gls FAC: 1 app 0 gls
FLC: 1 app 0 gls Other: 2 apps 0 gls Total: 55(1) apps 0 gls

GARNER, William David 'Bill'

Forward   6' 0"   12st 0lbs
b. Leicester, 14th December 1947
CAREER: Leicestershire FA Youth Xl/Bedford Town/NOTTS July 1966/Loughborough United Apr 1967/Dunstable Town/Southend United Nov 1969/Chelsea Sept 1972, fee £80,000/Cambridge United Nov 1978/Chelmsford City/Brentford nc Aug 1983/Whytleafe
Debut v Wrexham (h) 7.9.66, drawn 2 – 2

Bill Garner made a faltering start to his career. Signed by Notts manager Jack Burkitt, he was released by new manager Billy Gray after just two senior outings. From Loughborough United he was taken to Dunstable Town by their then manager Len Chalmers (q.v.) At Dunstable his game improved dramatically, leading to a return to League football with Southend United. Three years later he cost Chelsea £80,000 and in a little over five seasons at Stamford Bridge scored 37 League and Cup goals in 105(14) appearances.

Appearances: FL: 2 apps 0 gls Total: 2 apps 0 gls

GARRETT, Frederick Howard

Half-back   5' 9"   11st 4lbs
b. Stanton Hill, Notts, October quarter 1888
d. Stockport, 16th December 1967
CAREER: Stanton Hill Victoria/NOTTS May 1909/Stockport County July 1912 to May 1921
Debut v Middlesbrough (a) 26.3.10, lost 0 – 2

Once described as "A cool and calculating player who could do, perhaps, with a little more dash." Garrett failed to win his spurs in League football with the Magpies. With Stockport County, however, he proved a great success. Appointed captain in his first season at Edgeley Park he remained for nine seasons. Initially at centre-half and later as full-back he recorded 143 League and Cup appearances and scored ten goals. Additionally, he appeared in 73 wartime matches, scoring three goals.

Appearances: FL: 8 apps 0 gls Total: 8 apps 0 gls

GAUGHRAN, Bernard Michael 'Benny'

Centre-forward 5' 8"   11st 10lbs
b. North Dublin, 29th September 1915
d. Dundalk, 20th September 1977
CAREER: Bohemians, Dublin, 1935/Glasgow Celtic Nov 1936/Southampton June 1937/Sunderland Nov 1937, fee £1,000/NOTTS May 1938/Dundalk Aug 1939/Portadown Feb 1940/St James Gate, Dublin, Aug 1941/Distillery May 1942/Brideville Mar 1943
Debut v Swindon Town (a) 27.8.38, lost 1 – 4 (scored)

Dark-haired and handsome, Benny Gaughran made a promising start at Southampton (4 goals in seven matches) following his free transfer signing from Celtic. The Saints made a tidy profit just five months later when Sunderland paid £1,000 for him, but he failed to impress at Roker, playing only twice in the League side. Although he scored on his debut for the Magpies he failed to establish himself, despite the vacancy at centre-forward, as Dixie Dean's injuries failed to respond to treatment.
After leaving Meadow Lane Benny's wartime tour around Irish clubs did not lack variety.

Appearances: FL: 2 apps 1 gl Other: 1 app 0 gls
Total: 3 apps 1 gl.

GEE, Ellis

Outside-left   5' 6**2**" 12st 7lbs
b. Grassmoor, 15th June 1877
d. Chesterfield, 30th December 1948
CAREER: Grassmoor Red Rose/Sheepbridge Works May 1895/Chesterfield Town May 1896/Everton Mar 1898, fee £100/NOTTS May 1900/Reading May 1907/Ilkeston United May 1908
Debut v Sunderland (h) 1.9.00, drawn 2 – 2

"Adipose but agile" was one early verdict on Ellis Gee who joined the Magpies after service with Chesterfield and Everton. He certainly made his most distinct mark with Notts, being an invaluable member of the first team in seven seasons of top-flight football. Small but stocky he possessed a fine touch line sprint and a neat sense of timing in his centres. He had a share in many goals, engineered by his adroit footwork, but his record as a goal scorer was not distinguished. On December 24th, 1905, at Derby County he scored what was his first League goal since September 6th, 1902. In a Lancashire sporting paper there appeared the following: "The reporter rushed into the Editor's den; And his eyes commenced to roll; Oh, sir, I hope your heart's not weak, For it's come at last – Gee's goal."

Appearances: FL: 214 apps 21 gls FAC: 14 apps 2 gls
Total: 228 apps 23 gls

GELLERT, Brian

Midfield   5' 11" 12st 7lbs
b. Kolding, Denmark, 10th May 1977
CAREER: IF Kolding (Denmark)/Brescia (Italy)/Xanthi (Greece)/NOTTS Oct 2000 to July 2001/Akademisk BK (Denmark).
Debut v Port Vale LDV Vans Trophy (a) 9.1.2001, lost 0 – 3

Although the Magpies fielded no fewer than 35 players in Division Two in 2000-01, Brian Gellert was not among them. Despite experience in Denmark, Italy and Greece, the 23 year-old midfielder did not graduate beyond reserve team football at Meadow Lane.

Appearances: Other: 1 app 0 gls Total: 1 app 0 gls

GIBBON, Henry

Outside-right   5' 9"   11st 0lbs
b. Hetton-le-Hole, April quarter 1906
d. Barrow-in-Furness, January quarter 1972
CAREER: Bishop Auckland/Sunderland am May 1926, pro Sept 1926/NOTTS July 1927 /Seaham Harbour Sept 1928
Debut v Southampton (h) 10.9.27, drawn 0 – 0

Three appearances, as deputy for George Taylor on the Magpies' right wing, was the extent of Gibbon's League experience, as he had not reached senior level in his season with Sunderland. As a cricketer he reached Minor Counties level, appearing as an amateur with Durham C.C.C.

Appearances: FL: 3 apps 0 gls Total: 3 apps 0 gls

GIBSON, Alexander Pollock Stitt

Centre-half   5' 11"   11st 10lbs
b. Kirkconnel, Dumfrieshire, 28th November 1939
d. Basford, Nottingham, 22nd November 2003
CAREER: Cumnock Academy/East Ayrshire Schoolboys/ Trials with Dundee and Partick Thistle/Saxone F.C./ Auchinleck Talbot 1956/NOTTS Apr 1959/Boston United July 1969
Debut v Gateshead (a) 7.9.59, drawn 0 – 0

Dominant in the air and a fine tackler, Alex was a fine stopper type of pivot who gave Notts exceptional service  during ten years at Meadow Lane. A former miner and Scotland Schoolboys trialist at the age of 14, he began as a wing-half in season 1959-60, playing in 17 matches during the Division Four promotion campaign. Fifth place in Division Three in the following season proved to be the best that the team achieved during his decade of service. Undoubtedly worthy of a higher grade, he was several times linked with moves to bigger clubs but remained happy in Nottingham. With defensive duties paramount, Alex took over five years to open his goal scoring account. In season 1964-65 his four League goals included three from the penalty spot, but his header from a corner kick against Division Four champions elect, Doncaster Rovers, was the one that remained in the memory.

It set up a 3 – 0 victory at Belle Vue on 6th May 1966 in front of a crowd of 16,389. Alex's son, Simon, also a central defender, appeared in League football with Swindon Town, Preston North End and Rochdale in the 1980s.

Appearances: FL: 344 (3) apps 10 gls FAC: 10 apps 0 gls FLC: 16 apps 0 gls Total: 370(3) apps 10 gls

---

GIBSON, Paul Richard
Goalkeeper   6' 3"   13st 0lbs
b. Sheffield, 1st November 1976
CAREER: Manchester United trainee, signing pro July 1995 (Mansfield Town loan Oct 1997) (Hull City loan Nov 1998)/ NOTTS Mar 1999 (Rochdale loan Feb 2000)/Northwich Victoria July 2001
Debut v Gillingham (h) 8.5.99, lost 0 – 1

Paul Gibson's League debut came in October 1997 during a loan spell at Mansfield Town. He made an excellent start in a 1 – 0 win at Swansea City and completed 13 Division Three matches before returning to Old Trafford. A second loan spell took him to Hull City where he played in four matches before an injury sustained in training cut short his stay at Boothferry Park. Signed by the Magpies on transfer deadline day in 1999, as back up for Darren Ward, it was not until season 2000-01 that he enjoyed anything other than occasional outings in the first team. In the summer he was released and joined Northwich Victoria. In his first season with the Vics he was their only ever-present player with 42 Conference appearances.

Appearances: FL: 11 apps 0 gls FLC: 2 apps 0 gls Other: 1 app 0 gls Total: 14 apps 0 gls

---

GIBSON, Thomas
Full-back 5'10" 12st 4lbs
b. Maxwelltown, Dumfermline 23rd October 1888
CAREER: Maxwelltown Volunteers/Morton/Nottingham Forest June 1907/NOTTS Dec 1919, fee 'over £1,000'/ Southend United June 1923; retired May 1924.
Debut v Bradford City (a) 20.12.19, won 4 – 3

Notts were relegated in Tom Gibson's first season at Meadow Lane, and promoted from Division Two in his final term. By this time, however, he was approaching the veteran stage and made only four appearances in 1922-23, Horace Cope by this time being the first choice at left full-back. Gibson served in the Great War as a R.S.M. in the Footballer's Battalion and joined Notts midway through the relegation campaign 1919-20.

A resolute tackler with effective headwork, he was a reliable man from the penalty spot, converting three spot kicks within the space of one week in early March 1921, two against South Shields and one against Hull City. A lengthy spell with Forest preceded his move to Meadow Lane, his record in the red jersey totalling 192 League and Cup matches and 35 goals.

Appearances: FL: 63 apps 5 gls FAC: 6 apps 1 gl Total: 69 apps 6 gls

---

GIBSON, William
Left-back   5' 9"   14st 4lbs
b. Flemington, Lanarkshire 1868
d. Lincoln, 15th September 1911, age 43
CAREER: Flemington Thistle/Cambuslang 1887/Sunderland Aug 1888/Glasgow Rangers May 1894/Sunderland May 1895/NOTTS May 1896/Bristol City Mar 1898/Lincoln City May 1898, retired 1903
Debut v Loughborough (h) 5.9.1896, won 3 – 1

When Notts regained their top-flight status in 1897, they were required to take part in the long-defunct system of 'Test Matches'. After heading the Division Two table they went through four matches – home and away fixtures were played – against Sunderland and Burnley. The Magpies defence took the chief honours, with 'Big Bill' Gibson and Tom Prescott the full-backs, and the redoubtable George Toone behind them. Only one goal was conceded in the four matches, two wins and two draws clinching the coveted return to Division One. Earlier in his career, six seasons spent with Sunderland saw the Wearsiders twice League champions, and twice runners-up. Turning the scales at over 14 stones, Gibson presented a formidable barrier to opposing forwards, but he also possessed great skill and constructive abilities. For several seasons after leaving Notts he captained Lincoln City before retiring to become a licensee there.

Appearances: FL: 41 apps 0 gls FAC: 3 apps 0 gls Other: 4 apps 0 gls Total: 48 apps 0 gls
Honours: Scottish League representative, 1 app 1895. (Sunderland) FL champions 1892 and 1893. (NOTTS) FL Div 2 champions 1897

GILL, Matthew James
Defender/Midfield   5' 11"   12st 10lbs
b. Cambridge, 8th November 1980
CAREER: Cambridge United Juniors/Peterborough United trainee, pro Mar 1998/NOTTS June 2004.
Debut v Chester City (h) 7.8.04, drawn 1 – 1

Dependable and adaptable, Matthew has successfully negotiated an eventful first season at Meadow Lane. A strong running midfielder with the added bonus of a long throw-in, he began with Cambridge United, but made his

League debut with Peterborough United at seventeen years of age. Matthew reached the semi-finals of the FA Youth Cup and went on to complete in excess of 150 League appearances for the Posh. He very effectively confounded his critics after an uncertain start with the Magpies, which included a spell on the transfer list during the late stages of Gary Mills' spell as manager.

Appearances:FL: 38(5) apps 0 gls FAC: 3(1) apps 0 gls FLC: 2 apps 0 gls Other: 1 app 0 gls
Total: 44(6) apps 0 gls

GILLET, Leonard Francis
Goalkeeper
b. Derby, 21st January 1861
d. Harbertonford, near Totnes, Devon, 23rd November 1915
CAREER: Charterhouse School/Oxford University/Old Carthusians/NOTTS season 1882-83/Derby County Nov 1884
Debut v Sheffield Wednesday, FAC 4, (a) 12.2.1883, won 4 – 1

In 1879 the Charterhouse School Magazine – 'The Carthusian' - described Gillet as "A most sure goalkeeper, very sharp. He has been of infinite service to the Eleven." An Oxford University football blue and FA Cup winner in 1881, two seasons later he assisted Notts to reach the semi-final of the FA Cup, where they lost 1 – 2 against Old Etonians at Kenington Oval. In November 1884 he appeared for Derby County in their first-ever FA Cup tie, a 0 – 7 defeat against Walsall Town. The 1901 Census listed him as a retired mining engineer, residing at Llanarmon in Wales. **Note**: The spelling of this player's forename is shown with two Ts in the Family Records Centre, but he was more generally known as Gillet.

Appearances: FAC: 3 apps 0 gls Total: 3 apps 0 gls
Honours: (Old Carthusians) FA Cup winners 1881

GISSING, John William D
Outside-right   5' 6**2**" 9st 5lbs
b. Stapleford, Notts, 24th November 1938
CAREER: Stapleford Boys' Club/NOTTS am 1955, pro July 1956/Chesterfield July 1961/Alfreton Town June 1962
Debut v Bristol City (a) 26.10.57, lost 1 – 3

The calls of National Service hampered John Gissing's progress after he had broken into League football when still one month short of his nineteenth birthday. The bulk of his 22 appearances came in 1957-58 (10 matches) and 1958-59 (8 matches) two terms when the Magpies fortunes were very much in decline, successive relegations ensuing. In his final season Gissing scored his only League goal at Saltergate, in the 1 – 3 defeat against Chesterfield in March 1961.

In the following month he was placed on the transfer list and joined the Spireites on a free transfer. He made only two league appearances for them before dropping into non-League football with Alfreton Town.

Appearances: FL: 22 apps 1 gl Total: 22 apps 1 gl

GLEN, Alexander
Inside-left   6' 1"   12st 0lbs
b. Kilsyth, Stirlingshire, 11th December 1878
CAREER: Fitzhugh Rovers/Glasgow Parkhead/Clyde/Grimsby Town July 1902/NOTTS May 1903/Tottenham Hotspur May 1904/Southampton May 1906/Portsmouth May 1907/Brentford July 1908
Debut v Sunderland (a) 1.9.03, lost 1 – 4 (scored)

Alex Glen was certainly a contender for the first recorded League goal of season 1903-04, when he slipped the ball past Sunderland's goalkeeper Ned Doig within three minutes of the kick off. Sadly, Notts season began with a 4 – 1 defeat at Roker Park and the tall and willowy Glen was quickly consigned to reserve team football. In late December the 'Football Post' commented "Including Division One, Notts League and friendly matches, Glen has scored 17 goals so far this season. And yet he has disappointed us when playing in the first team." Prior to embarking on a football career Alex Glen had served in the Boer War as a surgical dresser.

Appearances: FL: 20 apps 3 gls FAC: 1 app 0 gls
Total: 21 apps 3 gls

GOATER, Leonard Shaun, M.B.E.
Forward   6' 1"   12st 0lbs
b. Hamilton, Bermuda, 25th February 1970
CAREER: North Village (Bermuda)/Manchester United May 1989/Rotherham United Oct 1989 (NOTTS loan Nov 1993)/Bristol City July 1996, fee £175,000/Manchester City Mar 1998, fee £400,000/ Reading Aug 2003, fee £500,000 (Coventry City loan Mar 2005)
Debut v Charlton Athletic (a) 13.11.93, lost 1 – 5

Bermudan international centre-forward, signed on loan from Rotherham United, with a view to a permanent deal. Within five minutes of his debut the lanky striker created a goal for Tony Agana, but he did not play again. Although selected to accompany the side on their first European trip to oppose Bresica in the Anglo-Italian Cup, problems regarding a work permit caused his late withdrawal and he returned to Rotherham. A proven scorer throughout his career, Shaun was awarded the M.B.E. in the Queen's Birthday Honours List in 2003, for his services to sport and young people in his native Bermuda (the island celebrates Shaun Goater Day on 21st June every year.)

He topped the Division One scoring charts in 1999-2000 and in a five-year stay with Manchester City became a huge favourite with the fans, scoring in excess of 100 League and Cup goals. In terms of League and Premier League goals alone, Shaun passed the 200 mark in season 2003-04.

Appearances: FL: 1 app 0 gls Total: 1 app 0 gls
Honours: Bermuda International, 19 caps. Bermuda Youth International. (Rotherham United) Auto Windscreens Shield winners 1996. (Manchester City) FL Div 1 champions 2002

--------o--------

GOOCH, Percy George
Centre-forward 6' 0"   11st 11lbs
b. Lowestoft, 1st September 1882
d. Lowestoft, 22nd June 1956
CAREER: Leiston Road School/Lowestoft Fearnoughts 1896/Kirkley Juniors/Lowestoft Harriers/Lowestoft I.O.G.T./Lowestoft Town Nov 1901/Norwich City am July 1903, pro Sept 1905 (Norfolk County 1903-05)/Birmingham Mar 1907/NOTTS Mar 1908/Norwich City May 1909, retired 1910/Lowestoft Town trainer
Debut v Sheffield United (h) 21.3.08, lost 0 – 3

Although Percy Gooch's record in League football spanned just seven matches and two goals, the former apprentice painter and decorator was a prolific marksman. A centre-forward of the bustling type and a rear terror to opposing defences, he had scored in excess of a goal a game for Lowestoft Town (85 goals in 81 matches), prior to his first spell with Norwich City. For the Canaries he totalled 36 goals in 65 matches, covering all competitions. He also represented Norfolk County on five occasions, and scored in every match. His trio of matches for the Magpies came consecutively in the late stages of the 1907-08 season. Aside from his debut, he scored against Forest in a 2 – 0 win, and was on the winning side on his final appearance, a 1 – 0 victory at Manchester United.

Appearances: FL: 3 apps 1 gl Total: 3 apps 1 gl

--------o--------

GOODWIN, Mark Adrian
Midfield   5' 10"   10st 9lbs
b. Sheffield, 23rd February 1960
CAREER: Leicester City app July 1976, pro Oct 1977/NOTTS Mar 1981, fee £60,000/Walsall July 1987/Kettering Town cs 1990/Eastwood Town player-coach cs 1991/Arnold Town player-coach 1992/Hucknall Town cs 1994
Debut v Grimsby Town (a) 14.3.81, lost 1 – 2

Fair-haired midfielder Mark succeeded his former Leicester City team mate, Eddie Kelly, in the Magpies midfield in March 1981, appearing in ten matches and scoring two goals in the run-in to promotion to the top flight.

Although only 21 years old when he arrived at Meadow Lane he was an experienced campaigner who had assisted Leicester City to promotion in the previous season. On leaving Meadow Lane Mark joined Walsall who promptly won promotion to the Second Division through the end of season Play-offs. Ironically, he helped the Saddlers overcome the Magpies in the semi-finals by an aggregate score of 4 – 2. His League career ended in disappointing fashion after successive demotions with Walsall. His career aggregate figures totalled: 376(44) League appearances and 33 goals.

Appearances: FL: 226(11) apps 23 gls FAC: 14(1) apps 0 gls FLC: 19(1) apps 3 gls Other: 10 apps 0 gls
Total: 269(13) apps 26 gls
Honours: (Leicester City) FL Div 2 champions 1980. (NOTTS) Anglo Scottish Cup finalists 1981

--------o--------

GORAM, Andrew Lewis
Goalkeeper   5' 11"   12st 6lbs
b. Bury, Lancs, 13th April 1964
CAREER: Tottington High School/Bury & Manchester Schoolboys/West Bromwich Albion app June 1980/Oldham Athletic Aug 1981/Hibernian Oct 1987, fee £325,000/Glasgow Rangers June 1991, fee £1million/NOTTS nc 3rd Sept 1998/Sheffield United nc 7th Sept 1998, pro 14th Sept 1998/Motherwell Jan 1999/Manchester United Mar 2001, fee £100,000/Boreham Wood July 2001/Hamilton Academical trial Aug 2001/Blackpool trial/Coventry City Sept 2001 to Feb 2002/Oldham Athletic Mar 2002/Motherwell goalkeeping coach June 2002/Queen of the South July 2002 to July 2003
Debut v Wigan Athletic (h) 5.9.98, lost 0 – 1

Although born in Lancashire, Andy Goram qualified for Scotland by parentage, his father Lewis, also a goalkeeper, played for Third Lanark and Bury in the 1950s. Andy made his League debut with Oldham Athletic at 18 years of age, and went on to complete 212 League and Cup matches. A multi-talented sportsman, he became a double international when he represented Scotland at cricket in a Nat West Trophy match against Yorkshire.

After leaving Oldham, he played in 138 Scottish League matches (and scored one goal) for Hibernian. Rangers paid one million pounds for him in June 1991, and one year later he was awarded a silver medal to mark the milestone of his 25th Scotland cap. His seven seasons at Ibrox won him an enviable collection of medals, but his international career ended in controversial circumstances. He walked out of the Scotland camp in New Jersey, USA, during warm-up preparations for the World Cup Finals in France, blaming media intrusion into his private life. A number of trials – including his solitary appearance for Notts – followed before a two-year spell with Motherwell saw him regain much of his earlier form. Manchester United signed him in March 2001 but played him only twice, at a time when both of their senior goalkeepers were injured.

Appearances: FL: 1 app 0 gls Total: 1 app 0 gls
Honours: Scotland International, 43 caps 1986-98. Scotland U-21 International, 1 app. (Glasgow Rangers) Scottish Premier Division champions 1992, 1993, 1995, 1996, 1997. Scottish Cup winners 1992, 1993, 1996, finalists 1994. Scottish League Cup winners 1993, 1997.

GORDON, Kenyatta Gavin
Forward   6' 1"   12st 0lbs
b. Manchester, 24th June 1979
CAREER: Hull City trainee, pro July 1996/Lincoln City Nov 1997, fee £30,000/Cardiff City Dec 2000, fee £275,000 (Oxford United loan Sept 2002)/NOTTS July 2004.
Debut v Chester City (h) 7.8.04, drawn 1 – 1

As a Stretford schoolboy, Gavin was associated with both of Manchester's senior clubs, but it was a trial with Hull City that resulted in his being offered a trainee post, and an eventual entry into League football. Within sixteen months of signing a professional form with Hull City he was on the move, and his £30,000 transfer to Lincoln City proved a bargain as the ideally built striker assisted the Imps to promotion from Division Three in his first season. In the best spell of his career to date, his return of 31 League and Cup goals in 98(12) appearances attracted a sizeable fee from Cardiff City. A five-goal blast for the Bluebirds against Rushden & Diamonds in a 7 – 1 LDV Vans Trophy victory in October 2001 proved an isolated high spot in a largely unrewarding spell at Ninian Park. Injuries have hampered his progress at Meadow Lane, where his better displays have come in the season's FA Cup matches. Good in the air and in combination, he has yet to replicate the strike rate that he achieved with Lincoln City.

Appearances: FL: 23(4) apps 5 gls FAC: 4 apps 3 gls Other: 0(1) app 0 gls Total: 27(5) apps 8 gls

GOSS, William
Outside or inside-left
b. Nottingham, January quarter 1879
CAREER: Nottingham St. Peter's/Heanor Town/NOTTS May 1899/Portsmouth June 1900/Newark Town Sept 1901
Debut v Manchester City (a) 23.9.1899, lost 1 – 5

William Goss began with St Peter's in the Nottingham Thursday League and assisted other local clubs before an upward step took him to Heanor Town. In the close season of 1899, along with another local, Alfred Warner (q.v.) he was recruited by the Magpies. His 19 appearances comprised an initial six at outside-left and the remainder at inside-left, in a season when relegation was only narrowly avoided. His season in the south with Portsmouth featured only one Southern League appearance and was followed by a homeward move to Newark Town.

Appearances: FL: 16 apps 1 gl FAC: 3 apps 1 gl Total: 19 apps 2 gls

---

GOUCHER, George Henry
Right-back   5' 9"   11st 9lbs
b. Whaley Thorns, Derbyshire, 18th May 1902
d. Mansfield, January 1987
CAREER: Whaley Thorns School/Hawthorn Exchange/Norwood Rangers/Shirebrook May 1926/NOTTS Nov 1926, fee £200/Nottingham Forest June 1928, fee £100/Torquay United Aug 1929/Shirebrook Aug 1930/Sutton Town 1931/Ilkeston United Aug 1934
Debut v Blackpool (a) 7.5.27, lost 0 – 5

George Goucher cost the Magpies £200 from Shirebrook but it was not until the final match of the season that he turned out for the first team, recording his solitary League appearance in a 0 – 5 defeat at Blackpool. He fared little better after crossing the Trent, at half the fee originally paid for him. His record with Forest was one League appearance against Barnsley at the City ground, the visitors winning 3 – 1. A season in the south with Torquay featured six first team matches. In the last of these he finally collected a winning bonus, Torquay rounding off their season with a 2 – 1 win against their next-door neighbours, Exeter City.

Appearances: FL: 1 app 0 gls Total: 1 app 0 gls

GOULD, Geoffrey
Outside-left   5' 8½"   9st 4lbs
b. Blackburn, 7th January 1945
CAREER: Bradford P.A. am 1960, pro Jan 1962 (Lincoln City loan Feb 1968)/NOTTS July 1969
Debut v Oldham Athletic (h) 9.8.69, drawn 0 – 0

A lightweight, curly-haired wingman, Geoff Gould became a professional with Bradford P.A. at seventeen years of age. He made his FL debut before his eighteenth birthday and went on to total 143(2) League and Cup appearances and 18 goals for the Park Avenue club. Highlight was the 1965-66 season when he was a regular in an attack that scored 102 goals in Division Four – and yet could finish no higher than 11th in the table. In the late Sixties the rot set in at Park Avenue with a vengeance, Gould departing after three consecutive re-election applications had found favour at the AGM of the Football League. (A fourth application, at the end of season 1969-70, unsurprisingly failed and their place in Division Four was taken by Cambridge United.) Signed for a two-month trial, Gould played only once for the Magpies, in the opening fixture of season 1969-70. In weather more suited to cricket than football he had a quiet game, directly opposed to Oldham Athletic's newly-signed left full-back, Ray Wilson, who was a World Cup winner with England in 1966.

Appearances: FL: 1 app 0 gls Total: 1 app 0 gls

———————o———————

GRANT, Kimberley Tyrone 'Kim'

Forward   5' 10"   11st 6lbs
b. Sekondi-Takarad, Ghana, 25th September 1972
CAREER: Buckingham Road School/King's Manor School/ Brighton Schoolboys/Charlton Athletic trainee, signing pro Mar 1991/Luton Town Mar 1996, fee £250,000/Millwall Aug 1997, fee £185,000 (NOTTS loan Dec 1998 to Feb 1999)/KFC Lommel SK (Belgium) Aug 1999, fee £65,000/ F.C. Marco (Portugal)/Scunthorpe United trial July 2001/ Yeovil Town Oct 2001
Debut v Northampton Town (h) 26.12.98, won 3 – 1 (scored one)

A mid term loan signing from Millwall, where he was out of the first team picture, Kim Grant scored in the first minute of his debut for the Magpies but in his five other matches both he and the team failed to find the net. Injury cut short his loan period at Meadow Lane where a late-season upturn consolidated the team's newly won status in Division Two. A quick, hard working striker the Ghanaian international commanded some substantial transfer fees both at home and abroad but his overall goal scoring record in League football was an extremely modest one, 36 in 136(89) appearances.

Appearances: FL: 6 apps 1 gl Total: 6 apps 1 gl
Honours: Ghana International

———————o———————

GRAY, Andrew Mullen

Forward   5' 11"   11st 10lbs
b. Glasgow, 30th November 1955
CAREER: Clydebank Strollers/Dundee United from school Dec 1972, signing pro May 1973/Aston Villa Sept 1975, fee £110,000/Wolverhampton Wanderers Sept 1979, fee £1.46million/Everton Nov 1983, fee £200,000/Aston Villa July 1985, fee £150,000 (NOTTS loan Aug 1987)/West Bromwich Albion Sept 1987/Glasgow Rangers Sept 1988 to July 1989, fee £25,000
Debut v Wigan Athletic (h) 15.8.87, drawn 4 – 4

A total of 44 goals in just 76 matches for Dundee United paved the way for Andy Gray's £110,000 transfer to Aston Villa. Four years later, his £1.46 million transfer to the Wolves created a new British record. Although in monetary terms his value had declined dramatically when he joined Everton, his impact at Goodison Park was nothing short of sensational. A hat-trick of successes in League, FA Cup and European Cup Winners' Cup, earned him a recall to the Scotland side for his 20th international cap. In a final spell with Rangers, who signed him as cover for the injured Ally McCoist, he rounded off his career by helping the Light Blues to win the Scottish League championship. Notts' fans were afforded the briefest glimpse of Andy Gray in the black and white stripes, during the only loan spell of his career. At his peak, his fine heading ability and extreme courage in opposition penalty areas ranked him as one of the great strikers of his era. He left the game to take up a career in television and currently works as an analyst with Sky TV.

Appearances: FL: 3(1) apps 0 gls FLC: 2 apps 1 gl
Total: 5(1) apps 1 gl
Honours: Scotland International, 20 caps 1975-85. Scotland U-23 International, 4 apps. Scotland Youth and Schoolboy International. (Dundee United) Scottish Cup finalists 1974. (Aston Villa) FL Cup finalists 1977. (Wolverhampton Wanderers) FL Cup winners 1980. (Everton) European Cup Winners' Cup winners 1985; FL Div 1 champions 1985; FA Cup winners 1984, finalists 1985. (Glasgow Rangers) Scottish League champions 1989.

———————o———————

GRAYSON, Simon Nicholas

Defender   6' 0"   13st 7lbs
b. Ripon, 16th December 1969
CAREER: Leeds United trainee, signing pro June 1988/ Leicester City Mar 1992, fee £50,000/Aston Villa July 1997, fee £1.35million/Blackburn Rovers July 1999, fee £750,000 (Sheffield Wednesday loan Aug 2000) (Stockport County loan Jan 2001) (NOTTS loan Sept to Nov 2001) (Bradford City loan Feb 2002)/Blackpool Aug 2002
Debut v Wrexham (h) 8.9.2002, drawn 2 – 2

Simon Grayson was twice voted 'Player of the Year' by Leicester City supporters. In either central defence, midfield or at full-back his grit, enthusiasm and immense capacity for work made him a key member during six eventful seasons at Filbert Street.

Four Play-off Finals (two won, two lost,) one relegation, two seasons at Premiership level and a FL Cup Final victory were all contained in his 213(16) appearances and 10 goals for the Foxes. Simon's career was never to reach the same heights again, although a victory in the 2004 LDV Vans Trophy Final at the Millennium Stadium with Blackpool was a bonus. Simon's brief association with the Magpies was just one of a series of loans from Blackburn Rovers where, apart from his first season, he featured little at senior level following the appointment of Graeme Souness as manager. Simon's brother Paul has appeared in county cricket with Yorkshire and Essex.

Appearances: FL: 10 apps 1 gl FLC: 1 app 0 gls Other: 2 apps 0 gls Total: 13 apps 1 gl
Honours: (Leicester City) FL Cup winners 1997. (Blackpool) LDV Vans Trophy winners 2004

GREATOREX, Lawrence
Forward   5' 10"   11st 9lbs
b. Unstone, Derbyshire, January quarter 1901
d. Unstone, Derbyshire, April quarter 1960
CAREER: Sutton Junction/Lincoln City 1922/Dronfield F.C./NOTTS am Jan 1924, pro June 1924/Southend United Aug 1926/Mansfield Town cs 1928
Debut v Leeds United (a) 10.9.24, drawn 1 – 1

Laurie Greatorex had scored 25 goals in eleven matches as centre-forward for Dronfield in the Derbyshire Senior League, and was acquired by Notts on the strength of this performance. A well-built, bustling attacker, he nevertheless lacked the pace and craft necessary for success in the First Division.

Appearances: FL: 4 apps 0 gls Total: 4 apps 0 gls

GREEN, Arthur William
Centre-forward 5' 10**2**"   12st 4lbs
b. Aberystwyth, 5th December 1881
b. Nottingham, 24th September 1966
CAREER: Aberystwyth Town 1897/Swindon Town 1899/Aston Villa Aug 1900/Ebbw Vale/Walsall Sept 1901/NOTTS May 1902/Nottingham Forest Jan 1907, fee £350/Stockport County May 1909/Brierley Hill Alliance 1911-12
Debut v Stoke (a) 15.9.02, won 2 – 0 (scored one)

In November 1903 the 'Football Post' gave a graphic description of the Magpies' Welsh International centre-forward: "Broad, strong and tall, a capable dribbler and a sticker when he gets on the ball. He is a very accurate shooter, and something of a man of moods, at times apt to slow down a bit, but at his best, one of the best."

In season 1903-04 he successfully converted seven penalty kicks, a record he held until 1972-73 when Kevin Randall scored from ten such awards. Arthur was one of the first footballers to be transferred between Notts and the Forest. Aside from football he rep-resented Nottinghamshire County at tennis and was an eight - handicap golfer. For many years, up to his retirement in 1949, he was a representative for Critall's, the window manufacturers. A qualified draughtsman, he was a prominent member of the Nottingham Mechanics Institution.

Appearances: FL: 134 apps 56 gls FAC: 8 apps 3 gls Total: 142 apps 59 gls
Honours: Wales International, 8 caps 1901-08. (Nottingham Forest) FL Div 2 champions 1907. (Aberystwyth Town) Welsh Cup winners 1900

GREEN, Richard 'Rick'
Forward   6' 1"   12st 12lbs
b. Scunthorpe, 23rd November 1952
CAREER: Appleby Frodingham/Lincoln City/Scunthorpe United Sept 1975/Chesterfield Feb 1977, fee £20,000/ NOTTS June 1978, fee £40,000/Scunthorpe United Aug 1979/Brigg Town 1981/Barton Town cs 1982/Brigg Town
Debut v Mansfield Town, Anglo Scottish Cup, (a) 31.7.78, lost 0 – 1

Notts lacked fire power in 1978-79(48 League goals in 42 matches) and newly-signed Rick Green had a unhappy season, failing to find the net in any of his 7(4) first team matches. Earlier, a promising start to his League career with Scunthorpe United attracted a record transfer fee from Chesterfield. At Saltergate he scored 13 goals in 45(3) matches, but failed to reproduce such form at Meadow Lane. His League career wound up with a return to Scunthorpe United and, by coincidence, his record of 19 goals in 66(5) matches was virtually identical to that recorded in his first spell with The Iron – 19 goals in 66 matches – no substitute appearances.

Appearances: FL: 6(3) apps 0 gls Other: 1(1) apps 0 gls Total: 7(4) apps 0 gls

GREEN, Ronald Clarence George

Inside or Outside-left   5' 9"   11st 0lbs
b. Frampton Cotterell, Gloucs, 12th March 1912
d. Coalpit Heath, 16th October 1979
CAREER: Coalpit Heath/Bath City 1930-31/Bristol Rovers
June 1932/Arsenal July 1933/NOTTS Feb 1935, fee £1,500/
Charlton Athletic July 1936, fee £500/Swansea Town May
1937/Coalpit Heath 1938, becoming a committee member
June 1946.
Debut v Sheffield United (h) 23.2.35, lost 0 – 1

Ron Green joined a struggling side when he was pitched
into the desperate relegation battle of 1934-35. Despite
his best efforts, the speedy wingman was unable to turn
the tide as the chocolate and blue clad County dropped
like a stone into Division Three South. They fared
somewhat better in the Southern Section, with Green
operating mainly at inside-left. His best performance came
in late December 1935 when he had the satisfaction of
scoring twice in a 6 – 0 win against one of his former
clubs, Bristol Rovers. He played little first team football
after leaving Meadow Lane, although he usually found
the net when selected. For Charlton Athletic he scored
twice in three matches, and for Swansea Town four goals
in eight matches.

Appearances: FL: 36 apps 5 gls FAC: 4 apps 1 gl Other:
1 app 1 gl Total: 41 apps 7 gls

GREENHALGH, Ernest Harwood

Full-back
b. Mansfield, March 1849
d. Nottingham, 11th July 1922
CAREER: NOTTS Feb 1869 to Nov 1883, afterwards was
secretary of Greenhalgh's F.C. (Mansfield)
Debut v Sheffield, FAC 1 (h) 3.11.1877, drawn 1 – 1

Strong and full of energy, Ernest Greenhalgh was the first
Notts County player to win an international cap. He was
a member of the England team in the first - ever
international match against Scotland, played at the West
of Scotland Cricket Ground, Partick, on 30th November
1872. He also played in the second such fixture at the
Kennington Oval Cricket Ground on 8th March 1873. At
the time of his international debut 'Alcock's Annual'
described him as "Very effective in the charge and of
great service to his club." He was proprietor of the Field
Mill at Mansfield and in business as a cotton doubler,
dyer and bleacher. The firm's team played at the rear of
the mill and the ground, still bearing the name 'Field Mill'
has been the home of the Mansfield Town club since
1905.

Appearances: FAC: 18 apps 1 gl Total: 18 apps 1gl
Honours: England International, 2 caps 1873

GREENHALGH, Harold

Goalkeeper
b. Mansfield, October quarter 1852
CAREER: NOTTS Jan 1873 to Feb 1881
Debut v Sheffield, FAC 1 (h) 3.11.1877, drawn 1 – 1

Brother to Ernest (above) and Richard (below), Harold
had a lengthy stint under the Magpies' woodwork in pre-
League football. Described in the 1879 issue of 'Alcock's
Annual' as: "A good goalkeeper, cool and very quick." At
the time of the 1901 Census he was aged 48 and working
as a cotton yarn agent.

Appearances:FAC: 7 apps 0 gls Total: 7 apps 0 gls

GREENHALGH, Richard James

Inside forward/Half-back
b. Mansfield October quarter 1856
d. Wallasey, 18th May 1936
CAREER: NOTTS Nov 1875 to Jan 1881
Debut v Sheffield, FAC 1 (h) 3.11.1877, drawn 1 – 1

The youngest of the Greenhalgh brothers, Richard first
played alongside his two siblings in a match against
Cambridge University on 24th February 1876. There were
also three Cursham brothers playing at the same time,
who between them scored most of the Magpies goals,
but Richard Greenhalgh took the scoring honours on 19th
October 1878 with a hat-trick against the Sheffield club,
in a famous 8 – 0 victory. Richard was also in the textile
business, as a manufacturer of blouses.

Appearances: FAC: 3 apps 0 gls Total: 3 apps 0 gls

GRICE, Frank

Half-back   5' 9"   11st 7lbs
b. Derby, 13th November 1908
d. Dundee, 29th April 1988
CAREER: Army football with the King's Own Scottish
Borderers/Linby Colliery/Linfield Mar 1930/NOTTS am
June 1931, pro Aug 1931/Tottenham Hotspur Mar 1936 to
cs 1939/Glentoran player-manager by Mar 1940,
subsequently appointed manager, and then secretary July
1946 (During WW2 period also guested for Dundalk and
represented the British Army)/Cambridge City manager
Debut v Oldham Athletic (h) 23.9.31, won 1 – 0

Although recruited as an amateur inside-left, with a record
of 20 goals in 40 matches for Linfield in 1929-30, Frank
Grice developed into excellent centre-half at Meadow
Lane. Despite his earlier experience as a forward, he was
initially better in defence than attack in his new role. He
improved the constructive side of his game considerably
during the course of his first season, his ground passing
initiating many fruitful attacks.

After three years with Tottenham Hotspur (55 matches, one goal) he returned to Ireland during the war and in March 1940 represented the Irish League against the League of Ireland at Dalymount Park, Dublin
.

Appearances: FL: 102 apps 4 gls FAC: 5 apps 1 gl Other: 2 apps 0 gls Total: 109 apps 5 gls
Honours: Irish League representative, 1 app 1940

———————————o———————————

GRICE, Reuben

Outside-left   5' 6**2**" 10st 4lbs
b. Ruddington, Notts, January quarter 1886
d. West Bridgford, Nottingham, 19th May 1967
CAREER: Grove Celtic/NOTTS Mar 1911/Rotherham County 1912/Burnley May 1914
Debut v Bradford City (a) 17.4.11, won 1 – 0

With Ike Waterall firmly established on the Magpies' left wing, there were few opportunities for Reuben Grice, a fair-haired reserve outside-left who combined football with a labouring job in a brickyard. A move to Midland League football with Rotherham County certainly improved his chances, in two seasons he scored 40 league goals, never missed a match, and collected six gold medals. His form brought an upward move to Burnley but he failed to hold a first team place after appearing in the first two matches of season 1914-15.

Appearances: FL: 4 apps 0 gls Total: 4 apps 0 gls

———————————o———————————

GRIFFITHS, Arthur

Full-back   5' 9"   11st 6lbs
b. Birmingham, 16th March 1879
CAREER: Park Mills F.C./Lozells/Aston Villa am 1897/ Bristol Rovers May 1899/NOTTS May 1903, retired cs 1912
Debut v Sheffield United (a) 10.10.03, lost 1 – 3

An early copy of 'The Glance Football Guide' had warm praise for Arthur Griffiths: "He is a thorough athlete both in reality and appearance, beautifully proportioned, lithe and active, relying more on cleverness than bashing tactics, and should materially strengthen the Notts defence." Hailing from the Aston district, as a youngster he took every opportunity of watching Villa, the great early exponents of the game. He had actually signed an amateur form with the Villa in 1897 but preferred to start his career in Bristol. When the Villa became aware of his intended move to Nottingham, they offered him professional terms which he refused. Signed as a full-back, he was fielded in the half-back line with some success, but was really seen to advantage in his original position. Later in his career he became a general utility man, able to occupy any defensive position while acting as guide and coach to the club's younger players.

Arthur settled in Nottingham and established a tobacconist business, close to Meadow Lane. On February 12th, 1949 the 'Football News' reported the happy news that Mr and Mrs Griffiths were " t o d a y celebrating their golden wedding anniversary."

Appearances: FL: 163 apps 1 gl FAC: 11 apps 0 gls Total: 174 apps 1 gl

———————————o———————————

GROOME, Patrick Bernard

Left-back   5' 11" 11st 11lbs
b. Nottingham, 16th March 1934
CAREER: Bonsall/NOTTS Nov 1951 to June 1958/Skegness Town/Sutton Town Aug 1960/Arnold St Mary's Aug 1961/ Spalding United Aug 1963
Debut v Fulham (h) 11.9.52, drawn 1 – 1

Well built and capable of occupying either flank, Pat Groome spent a lengthy spell in reserve at Meadow Lane. After a single appearance in season 1952-53, he enjoyed his best spell of senior football in 1955-56 appearing in 21 League matches and one FA Cup tie. His greatly improved form was not sustained, however, as the 'Post Annual' for 1957-58 commented " He faded out after a promising start." The annual also recorded the player's height and weight as 5'5 1/2" and 10 stones, but it is unlikely that he had faded out to such a drastic degree!

Appearances: FL: 40 apps 0 gls FAC: 1 app 0 gls Total: 41 apps 0 gls

———————————o———————————

GUNN, William

Winger 6'4**2**" 12st 12lbs
b. Nottingham, 4th December 1858
d. Nottingham, 29th January 1921
CAREER: Nottingham Forest (1 app 1881)/NOTTS Feb 1882; was re-instated as an am in Sept 1890 and played junior football in the Nottingham area. NOTTS director, from Aug 1890, President from July 1920 to his demise.
Debut v Sheffield, FAC 1, (h) 4.11.1882, won 6 – 1

In a series of reader's letters appearing in the 'Football Post' in 1920, a Mr. W. Dawson of Sutton-in-Ashfield, shared his reminiscences of William Gunn: "The finest outside-right who ever played football. How he used to delight the Trent Bridge spectators with his delightful runs along the wing. He seemed to go from one end of the field to the other in about three strides." The latter observation obviously associated with his great height and resultant long stride. Gunn was also renowned – before the law changed – for massive one-armed throws from the touchline. He was also a great cricketer who played in 363 matches for Notts. C.C.C. between 1880-1904 and in eleven Tests for England. A right-handed bat, his highest score was 273 for Notts v Derbyshire in 1901. He was co-founder of Gunn & Moore, the well-known sports goods firm.

Appearances: FL: 3 apps 1 gl FAC: 25 apps 13 gls
Total: 28 apps 14 gls
Honours: England International, 2 caps 1884

GUTTRIDGE, Frank
Full-back
b. Nottingham, 24th April 1866
d. Nottingham, 13th June 1918
CAREER: Heanor Town/NOTTS Mar 1888/Nottingham Forest 1889/NOTTS 1894/Nelson 1895.
Debut v Everton (a) 15.9.1888, lost 1 – 2

Frank Guttridge was a footballer of some ability but was rather better know as a cricketer, having appeared in 58 matches for Nottinghamshire and in 49 for Sussex. A useful fast bowler, when playing for Notts in 1896 he bowled John Rawlin of Middlesex, sending one of the bails flying 42 yards. As a batsman he had a highest score of 114 v Oxford University. After retiring from active participation in the game he was appointed to the list of first class umpires and officiated for some years. His obituary was erroneously published in a cricket journal in 1906.

Appearances: FL: 18 apps 0 gls FAC: 1 app 0 gls
Total: 19 apps 0 gls

HACKWORTH, Anthony
Forward   6' 1"   13st 7lbs
b. Durham, 19th May 1980
CAREER: Leeds United trainee, signing pro May 1997/ NOTTS July 2001, fee £150,000 (Scarborough loan Mar 2004)/Scarborough July 2004.
Debut as sub v Wrexham (h) 8.9.2001, drawn 2 – 2

In season 1996-97 Tony Hackworth was a leading light in Leeds United's Youth Team. They swept all before them, winning the Northern Intermediate Championship and the FA Youth Cup, Tony scoring 15 goals in 20(2) matches.

Also included in the all-conquering team were future stars Paul Robinson, Harry Kewell, Jonathan Woodgate, Stephen McPhail and Matt Jones. Tony continued to progress at Elland Road, being leading scorer in the Premier Reserve League in the season prior to his joining the Magpies. With such a pedigree, his lack of success at Meadow Lane was difficult to understand, but he made only spasmodic first team appearances in his final two seasons, and left with a year still to run on his contract. Tony scored three goals in eleven matches for Scarborough in a late season loan in 2003-04, and joined the Conference side on a permanent basis in the summer.

Appearances: FL: 17(37) apps 1 gl FAC: 2(1) apps 0 gls FLC: 0(3) apps 0 gls Other: 4 apps 1 gl
Total: 23(41) apps 2 gls
Honours: England Youth International. (Leeds United) FA Youth Cup winners 1997

HADEN, Samson
Outside-left   5' 72" 10st 8lbs
b. Royston, Yorks, 17th January 1902
d. Peterborough, February 1974
CAREER: Carlton St John's Sunday School/Castleford Town/ Arsenal am Mar 1922, pro Apr 1922/NOTTS Oct 1927, player-coach from Aug 1935/Peterborough United player-manager June 1938, resigned Apr 1948/A.F.A. Coach Nottinghamshire.
Debut v Chelsea (h) 6.10.27, lost 0 – 1

A very worthy successor to Len Barry on the Magpies left wing. At the age of twenty Sam went to Arsenal on trial and was almost immediately signed up. Some stiff competition, and a broken leg in February 1926, restricted his League appearances to 88 in the Gunners' colours. Although slightly built he was remarkably fit and injury free and hardly missed a match in his first six seasons at Meadow Lane. A footballer in every sense of the word, Sam could occupy either wing position, left-half, and even full-back in emergencies.

Appointed player-coach at the start of season 1935-36, his final five League outings in the same season took him past the milestone of 300 senior appearances.

Appearances: FL: 289 apps 36 gls FAC: 11 apps 2 gls
Other: 1 app 0 gls Total: 301 apps 38 gls
Honours: (NOTTS) FL Div 3 South champions 1931

———————o———————

HADLEY, Arthur
Outside-right   5' 9"   9st 10lbs
b. Reading, 5th May 1876
CAREER: Reading Abbey F.C./Reading Apr 1896/NOTTS May 1898/Leicester Fosse June 1902/NOTTS Nov 1906
Debut v Newcastle United (a) 17.9.1898, won 2 – 1 (scored one)

Arthur Hadley was apprenticed to the printing trade at the office of the 'Reading Standard,' and first played in serious football for Reading Abbey at the age of 17. While he was with them they won the championship of the local Junior League and the Tyler Cup. He was selected to represent the League, but received a late call up by Reading F.C., initially to appear in a friendly match against the Scots Guards. After two years of Southern League football he joined Notts, was given an early trial in Division One, and became a regular first-teamer at outside-right. Exceptional speed combined with an assortment of tricks often took him into goal scoring positions, ten goals in 28 First Division matches in 1899-1900 being his best seasonal return. His second signing by Notts in November 1906 was in response to the player's stated desire to "Have an occasional game." He did not feature in the League side during this second spell.

Appearances: FL: 76 apps 22 gls FAC: 6 apps 0 gls
Total: 82 apps 22 gls

———————o———————

HAIG, Paul
Outside-left
b. Nottingham
CAREER: Mapperley/Eastwood Rangers cs 1907/Leicester Fosse Feb 1911, fee £25/Mansfield Mechanics cs 1911/Stanton Hill Victoria Jan 1912/Eastwood Rangers cs 1912/NOTTS Aug 1913/Mansfield Town Nov 1913/Loughborough Corinthians cs 1914/Grantham Town Oct 1919.
Debut v Bristol City (a) 20.9.13, drawn 1 – 1

With Horace Henshall unfit to take his accustomed place at outside-left for the commencement of season 1913-14, candidates in the running for the role of his deputy were Paul Haig and the ex-Glossop utility forward David Williams. In the pre-season practice match played on 16th August the 'Football Post' reported that "Haig has something to learn in the art of centering", and it was Williams who started the season on the left wing.

By the end of September Henshall was fit to resume and was quickly back into his stride, scoring a stunning individual and winning goal in the 2 – 1 victory against Lincoln City on Goose Fair Thursday.

Note: Although generally referred to as 'Haig' in contemporary reports, and said to be a local man, no trace of his birth has been found, despite searches through the likely variations of Haigh and Hague.

Appearances: FL: 1 app 0 gls Total: 1 app 0 gls

———————o———————

HALL, George William ' Willie'
Inside-forward   5' 8"   11st 0lbs
b. Newark, Notts, 12th March 1912
d. Newark, Notts, 22nd May 1967
CAREER: Lover's Lane Primary School (Newark)/Nottinghamshire Schoolboys/Ransome & Marles/NOTTS Nov 1930/Tottenham Hotspur Dec 1932, fee £2,500 (WW2 guest West Ham United), retired Feb 1944/Clapton Orient coach Aug 1945, manager Sept-Nov 1945/Chelmsford City manager/Chingford Town manager Aug 1949
Debut v Thames (a) 2.5.31, drawn 0 – 0

The works side, Ransome & Marles, launched the careers of several excellent footballers, but none better than Willie Hall who joined the Magpies at the age of 18. Taking over the inside-left berth from Harry Andrews in his second season, the fair-haired youngster made real head-way and quickly earned himself an upward move to Tottenham Hotspur. He was selected to play for England against France in 1934, but did not get another opportunity until 1937-38, when he appeared in all of the internationals in that season. At international level he forged a brilliant partnership with Stanley Matthews, and in the England v Ireland match of 1938 scored five goals that commenced with a hat-trick in **3½** minutes, a feat unlikely to be bettered. Rejected for Army service on health grounds, he served with the police war reserve force in London. He became seriously ill with thrombosis in the mid-1940s and had to have both of his legs amputated.

He subsequently had a sports outfitting shop in Ilford, which he opened with his great friend Vic Buckingham (Spurs centre-half,) and later was landlord of the Archers public house in Whitechapel, London. In February 1959 he was honoured by the BBC, being the subject of the 'This is your Life' television programme. He died after suffering a heart attack at his sister's house in Newark. He was 55 years old.

Appearances: FL: 34 apps 7 gls FAC: 1 app 1 gl
Total: 35 apps 8 gls
Honours: England International, 10 caps 1934-39. England Wartime International. FL representative, 3 apps.

─────────────○─────────────

HALL, William Henry
Right-back
CAREER: NOTTS season 1894-95
Debut v Burslem Port Vale (h) 26.2.1895, won 10 – 0

As Notts spread their net in search of a successor to their FA Cup winning right-back, 'Fay' Harper, four candidates received League baptisms. Hall's introduction for two consecutive matches spanned the sublime and the ridiculous, as immediately following the 10 – 0 trouncing inflicted on Burslem Port Vale, Notts themselves were put to the sword by Manchester City, 7 – 1 victors at Hyde Road.

Appearances: FL: 2 apps 0 gls Total: 2 apps 0 gls

─────────────○─────────────

HALTON, Reginald Lloyd
Outside-right   5' 11**2**"   11st 4lbs
b. Buxton, Derbyshire, 11th July 1916
d. Leek, Staffs 17th March 1988
CAREER: Cheddington Mental Hospital/Stafford Rangers/ Buxton Aug 1934/Manchester United Oct 1936/NOTTS June 1937/Bury Nov 1937 (WW2 guest Aldershot, Millwall, Southampton, York City, Rochdale, Fulham, Portsmouth and Arsenal)/Chesterfield Dec 1948, fee £3,000/Leicester City Sept 1950, in exchange for J. Marsh/Scarborough player-manager Feb 1953/Goole Town Jan 1954/ Symington's May 1954/Brush Sports Oct 1954
Debut v Swindon Town (h) 28.8.37, won 3 – 0

Reg Halton spent less than a season with Manchester United and only five months at Meadow Lane but his move to Bury – who developed him into a fine, constructive wing-half – proved an excellent one all round. At either side of WW2 he recorded career figures of 249 League appearances and 33 goals (114 appearances and 19 goals in Bury's colours). A talented all-round sportsman, he played in Minor Counties cricket for Staffordshire, and also played golf, snooker and billiards with above average ability.

Appearances: FL: 6 apps 0 gls FAC: 1 app 0 gls Other: 1 app 0 gls Total: 8 apps 0 gls

HAMILTON, Ian Richard
Midfield   5'9"   11st 3lbs
b. Stevenage, Herts, 14th December 1967
CAREER: Southampton app, signing pro Dec 1985/ Cambridge United Mar 1988/Scunthorpe United Dec 1988/ West Bromwich Albion June 1992, fee £160,000/Sheffield United Mar 1998 (Grimsby Town loan Nov 1999)/NOTTS Aug 2000/Lincoln City Nov 2001/Woking Oct 2002 to 2003.
Debut as sub v Millwall (h) 19.8.2000, lost 3 – 4

Ball winning midfielder who showed his mettle at Cambridge United and Scunthorpe before proceeding to render excellent service to West Bromwich Albion, his career figures with the Albion were 229(11) League matches and 23 goals. In season 1992-93 he was a key member of the promotion winning side, via a Wembley Play-off Final, appearing in all 46 League matches and scoring seven goals. Signed by Jocky Scott on a two-year deal, Ian's experience and composure in central midfield was most evident in the first half of the season, at which point his first team place was seriously challenged by Michael Brough and extended loan signing Adam Newton. Ian was released in the following season, shortly after Gary Brazil was appointed manager. He subsequently reached the milestone of 500 League appearances in Lincoln City's colours.

Appearances:
FL: 29(5) apps 0 gls FAC: 3(1) apps 0 gls FLC: 3(2) apps 0 gls Other: 2(1) apps 0 gls Total: 37(9) apps 0 gls

─────────────○─────────────

HAMILTON, William 'Billy'
Outside-right   5' 6"   11st 5lbs
b. Musselburgh, 24th October 1904
d. Springburn, Glasgow, 19th July 1984
CAREER: Tollcross YMCA/Vale of Clyde/Shettleston/ Belshill Athletic/Bradford City Aug 1925/Southport July 1927/Barrow July 1928/Accrington Stanley June 1929/ NOTTS June 1930/Alloa Athletic cs 1931 to Sept 1933/ Shettlestone 1942 to 1982 as trainer, groundsman, secretary, vice-chairman and chairman.
Debut v Gillingham (a) 28.2.31, won 5 – 0

Billy Hamilton made his first appearance in League football for Bradford City against Nottingham Forest, at the City Ground in February 1926, and his final outing for them was against the Magpies at Valley Parade in April of the following year. Prior to his arrival at Meadow Lane he assisted a trio of Third Division North clubs, and gave excellent service to each. In terms of League outings, his figures were as follows: Southport (31 matches eight goals), Barrow (41 matches, 11 goals) and Accrington Stanley (41 matches and 14 goals.) With such a record it was surprising that he failed to make an impact at Meadow Lane, with only two first team outings in the Division Three South championship side.

On returning to Scotland he resumed his trade as an electrician, and in 1942 commenced upon a remarkable spell of forty years in the service of Shettlestone F.C.

Appearances: FL: 2 apps 0 gls Total: 2 apps 0 gls

HAMMOND, Leonard

Goalkeeper   6' 0"   12st 6lbs
b. Rugby, 12th September 1901
d. Rugby, 24th June 1983
CAREER: Rugby Town/Northampton Town May 1923/ NOTTS May 1933/Rugby Town July 1934
Debut v Hull City (a) 26.8.33, won 1 – 0

Considered to be one of the best goalkeepers in the Third Division South – and certainly one of the most experienced – Len Hammond appeared in 301 League matches for Northampton Town during his ten-year stay at the County Ground. At Meadow Lane he lost his first team place, after 27 consecutive appearances, to the newly signed Tommy Knox, the former Hartlepools United goalkeeper, whose brilliant form did much to steer the side clear of relegation.

Appearances: FL: 26 apps 0 gls FAC: 1 app 0 gls Total: 27 apps 0 gls

---

HAMPSON, Thomas

Goalkeeper   6' 0"   12st 7lbs
b. Bury, 2nd May 1898
CAREER: South Shields/Walker Celtic (WW1 guest Accrington Stanley, Leeds City, South Shields and Rochdale)/ West Ham United May 1920/Blackburn Rovers Oct 1925/ Annfield Plain Dec 1925/Burnley later in Dec 1925/ Darlington Oct 1926/West Stanley Nov 1926/Cardiff City Jan 1927/NOTTS May 1929/Notts Co-op Dairy am Sept 1930
Debut v Wolverhampton Wanderers (h) 15.2.30, lost 0 – 3

Tommy Hampson gained valuable First Division experience during two seasons when he successfully deputised for the Hammers international goalkeeper, Ted Hufton. Rather surprisingly, he added little to his total of 70 League and nine FA Cup appearances after leaving the Boleyn Ground. Meadow Lane proved to be his last port of call in senior football, and he played only once, as deputy for James Ferguson, in a season when Notts were relegated from Division Two.

Appearances: 1 app 0 gls Total: 1 app 0 gls

HAMPTON, Ivan Keith

Full-back   5' 10"   10st 12lbs
b. Kimberley, Notts, 15th October 1942
CAREER: Nuthall Boys (Notts. Youth League)/Rotherham United am/NOTTS am Oct 1960, pro Mar 1961/Halifax Town July 1967/Peterborough United July 1969 to cs 1970.
Debut v Chesterfield (a) 25.3.61, lost 1 – 3

Ivan Hampton began as an amateur wing-half with Rotherham United before joining Notts as a part-time professional. He signed full-time after completing an engineering apprenticeship at Stanton Ironworks. After a somewhat indifferent start at Meadow Lane he developed into a very promising full-back, first appearing regularly at senior level in season 1962-3. After leaving Meadow Lane, two seasons with Halifax Town brought his total of FL appearances to exactly 200, but he featured little during a season with Peterborough United.

Appearances: FL: 139(2) apps 1 gl FAC: 3 apps 0 gls FLC: 12 apps 0 gls Total: 154(2) apps 1 gl

---

HANDLEY, George

Inside-right
b. Burton-on-the-Wolds, Leicestershire, October quarter 1868
CAREER: Loughborough/NOTTS Dec 1895/Coalville Town Sept 1897/Derby County Dec 1897/Northampton Town Aug 1899/Newark Town
Debut v Darwen (a) 1.1.1896, lost 0 – 2

Farmer's son George Handley did not progress beyond a single New Year's Day appearance for the Magpies, but he did rather better with Derby County. Showing a useful versatility he appeared in seven FL matches as centre-half or left-half in 1897-98, and at outside-right for seven matches in the following season. Derby County reached the final of the FA Cup in both seasons, but Handley did not appear in any of the ties.

Appearances: FL: 1 app 0 gls Total: 1 app 0 gls

HANNAH, George

Inside-forward 5' 8"   9st 12lbs
b. Liverpool, 11th December 1928
d. Manchester, 5th May 1990
CAREER: Liverpool City Schoolboys/Everton am/Linfield/ Newcastle United Sept 1949, fee £23,000, including Alf McMichael/Lincoln City Sept 1957, fee £4,500/Manchester City Sept 1958, fee £10,000 plus John McClelland/NOTTS July 1964, fee £2,000/Bradford City Oct 1965, retired May 1966, fee £1,000
Debut v Wrexham (a) 22.8.64, lost 0 – 4

George Hannah captained Liverpool City Boys but was then rejected by Everton, who considered him too frail. National Service took him to Northern Ireland, where his professional career commenced with Linfield. Shortly after representing the Irish League against the Scottish League at Ibrox Park on 7th September 1949, Newcastle United paid £23,000 to bring both Hannah and Alf McMichael to St. James' Park. With no physical advantages, Hannah relied entirely on skill to achieve his ends, and whilst his classic ball skills and vision flourished in the top flight, it proved unsuited to life at the wrong end of Division Four. Not helped by a series of niggling injuries, he did not live up to expectations at Meadow Lane where he struggled to overcome the unceremonious attentions of brawny opponents. Earlier in his career, the undoubted highlight was his appearance at Wembley in the 1955 FA Cup Final for Newcastle United against Manchester City. George Hannah scored Newcastle's third goal in their 3 – 1 victory.

Appearances: FL: 25 apps 1 gl FLC: 1 app 0 gls
Total: 26 apps 1 gl
Honours: FA Xl Tour 1957, 1961 and 1964. Irish League representative, 1 app 1949. (Newcastle United) FA Cup winners 1955

--------------------------------o--------------------------------

HANNIGAN, Richard

Outside-right
CAREER: Greenock Morton/NOTTS July 1898, in exchange for R.Hendry plus a transfer fee/Woolwich Arsenal May 1899/Burnley Dec 1899/Ilkeston Town Nov 1900/ Newton Rovers July 1904/Somercotes United July 1905 to 1907
Debut v Burnley (a) 3.9.1898, drawn 1 – 1

One of two outside-rights signed by Notts for season 1898-99 (Hadley was the earlier recruit), Hannigan was said to have cost a substantial fee in addition to player-exchange element that took centre-forward Robert Hendry to Greenock Morton. He began as first choice but did not hold the position. An early season match report indicated that while he was happy enough in open play and knew how to centre, he was not anxious to come to close quarters with robust full-backs and had a decided objection to being tackled. On leaving Notts he played only once for Woolwich Arsenal in a brief stay. Moving to Burnley in mid season he had the satisfaction of scoring twice against his former team-mates when Burnley beat Notts 3 – 0 at Turf Moor in March 1900.

Appearances: FL: 15 apps 2 gls FAC: 1 app 0 gls
Total: 16 apps 2 gls

--------------------------------o--------------------------------

HARBOTTLE, Mark Stuart

Forward   5'10"   10st 4lbs
b. Nottingham, 26th September 1968
CAREER: Nottingham Forest associate schoolboy/NOTTS app, signing pro Sept 1986 to cs 1988 (Doncaster Rovers loan Jan-Feb 1988)/Scarborough 1988/Oakham United Aug 1988/Shepshed Charterhouse 1988-89/Burton Albion 1990/ Barwell F.C./Shepshed Dynamo/Hucknall Town Sept 2001/ Grantham Town/King's Lynn/Hinckley United/Stamford Town/Leicester United/Scarborough/Doncaster Rovers/ Dunkirk 2003-04
Debut as sub v York City (h) 17.9.85, won 3 – 1

Mark's Midlands apprenticeship appeared to have fitted him for a senior career, as he made his debut in Division Three before signing a professional form. He scored at Darlington one week later, but a further three appearances from the bench, concluding against the Wolves on Boxing Day, wrapped up his involvement at senior level. A mid season loan to Doncaster Rovers in 1987-88 added four Division Three outings, but he did not feature again in League football. Released by Scarborough in August 1988, Mark initially teamed up alongside his brother, David, at Oakham United. His subsequent tour around the non-League circuit has not been designed to make life easy for the football researcher!

Appearances: FL: 1(3) apps 1 gl FLC: 0(1) app 0 gls
Total: 1(4) apps 1 gl
Honours: England Youth International

--------------------------------o--------------------------------

HARDING, Paul John

Midfield   5' 10"   12st 5lbs
b. Mitcham, 6th March 1964
CAREER: West Ham Schoolboys/Sutton United/Whyteleafe F.C./Epsom & Ewell/Carshalton Athletic/Dulwich Hamlet/ Enfield F.C./Barnet Feb 1990/NOTTS Sept 1990, fee £60,000 (Southend United loan Aug 1993) (Watford loan Nov 1993)/Birmingham City Dec 1993, fee £50,000/ Cardiff City Aug 1995/Worcester City 1996/Halesowen Town 1998, fee £5,000
Debut v Plymouth Argyle (a) 23.10.90, drawn 0 – 0

A latecomer into League football who joined the Magpies at 26 years of age in the joint transfer deal that also brought Dave Regis to Meadow Lane. A hard tackling and energetic midfielder whose service was marred by a catalogue of injuries, most seriously by an Achilles tendon problem that required surgery.

Appearances: FL: 45(9) apps 1 gl FAC: 6 apps 0 gls
FLC: 1 app 0 gls Other: 7(1) apps 1 gl
Total: 59(10) apps 2 gls
Honours: (Enfield) FA Trophy winners 1988

--------------------------------o--------------------------------

HARKER, Edward

Forward/Wing-half
b. Plumtree, Notts. October quarter 1862
CAREER: NOTTS Nov 1882 to Nov 1889
Debut v Notts Olympic, FAC 1, (h) 8.11.1884, won 2 – 0

A seven-year association with the Magpies concluded in 1888-89, and although Harker appeared in Notts' first ever Football League fixture at Everton, he played in only one other League match, the 3 – 3 draw against Accrington in November 1888. His first recorded appearance for the club was made against the crack Scottish amateurs, Queen's Park, in November 1882, but it was not until 1886-87 that he featured on a regular basis. 25 matches and six goals in that season being his best return, within overall figures of 66 matches and 11 goals. Variously employed outside of the game as a warehouseman and later a maltster's clerk.

Appearances: FL: 2 apps 0 gls FAC: 12 apps 2 gls
Total: 14 apps 2 gls

———————o———————

HARKIN, John Terence 'Terry'

Centre-forward 6' 0"   11st 8lbs
b. Londonderry, Northern Ireland, 14th September 1941
CAREER: Derry City/Wolverhampton Wanderers am Mar 1960/Derry City/Coleraine 1960/Port Vale Sept 1962, fee £2,000/Crewe Alexandra June 1964, fee £3,000/Cardiff City Aug 1965, fee £12,000/NOTTS Sept 1966, fee "about £5,000"/Southport Aug 1967, fee £2,300/Shrewsbury Town Mar 1969, fee £10,000/Finn Harps 1971-79/Toronto Metros, Canada/Dundalk
Debut v Lincoln City (h) 24.9.66, won 2 – 1

Joined the Magpies after a disappointing spell with Cardiff City where he scored on debut and notched seven goals in eight matches but failed to maintain his form. The tall and willowy Irishman had a similar experience at Meadow Lane, where he faded after a bright start. Notts lost heavily when he joined Southport at less than half the fee invested eleven months earlier. Having earlier prospered with Crewe Alexandra (35 goals in 42 League matches), he enjoyed an excellent spell with Southport (31 goals in 63 + 1 matches). He caught the eye of the international selectors during his Haig Avenue spell, becoming the first Southport player to be capped since Patrick McConnell in October 1931. A dangerous marksman throughout his League career, Terry's aggregate figures, spanning six League clubs, amounted to 126 goals in 257(4) matches.

Appearances: FL: 27(1) apps 10 gls FAC: 1 app 0 gls
Total: 28(1) apps 10 gls
Honours: Northern Ireland International, 5 caps 1968-71. Northern Ireland U-23 International, 1 app.

———————o———————

HARKOUK, Rachid Peter

Forward/Midfield   6' 02"12st 5lbs
b. Chelsea, 19th May 1956
CAREER: Lyced School, London/Feltham F.C.(Trials with Chelsea and Fulham)/Crystal Palace June 1976, fee £2,000/Queens Park Rangers June 1978, fee £100,000/NOTTS June 1980 to cs 1986, fee £50,000
Debut v Bristol City (a) 20.9.80, won 1 – 0

Leading scorer and a key figure in Crystal Palace's Division Two promotion campaign of 1976-77, Rachid attracted much interest and eventually a hefty fee when he moved from Selhurst Park to join Q.P.R. in June 1978. He was severely restricted by injuries during two years at Loftus Road, and his problems continued at Meadow Lane although he played in 15(10) League matches in his first season when promotion to Division One was achieved. Highlights during his six years with the Magpies included his six-minute hat-trick against Bolton Wanderers in the third round of the FL Cup. Notts were six goals up at half time, with five goals coming within a seven-minute spell. The final result was 6 – 1. His first cap for his adopted country Algeria, versus East Germany in March 1985, was cause for much celebration, but he played the match in borrowed boots. Having forgotten his own footwear, he played in a pair borrowed from Mark Goodwin! Successive relegations, from Division One in 1983-84, and from Division Two in 1984-85, saw him selected for the 1986 Mexico World Cup Finals as a Third Division player. Two appearances, against Northern Ireland and Spain, sadly proved to be his last. An injury sustained in the latter match enforcing his retirement.

Appearances: FL: 124(20) apps 39 gls FAC: 9(2) apps 5 gls FLC: 13 apps 5 gls Other: 6(1) apps 3 gls
Total: 152(23) apps 52 gls
Honours: Algeria International. (NOTTS) Anglo-Scottish Cup finalists 1981

———————o———————

HARPER, Rowland Richard G

Outside-right
b. Lichfield
CAREER: Walsall Wood/Birmingham July 1904/Burton United May 1907/Aston Villa Aug 1907/NOTTS Mar 1908/Mansfield Invicta Aug 1910
Debut v Sheffield United (h) 21.3.08, lost 0 – 3

One of three new recruits enlisted by the Magpies in March 1908. All from the Birmingham area, they comprised Harper and Cantrell from Aston Villa, and Gooch from Birmingham F.C. Despite being haunted by suspense in the final month of season 1907-08, the new signings were successful in their efforts to keep Notts in the First Division.

Needing to win their final fixture of the season, away at Chelsea, a goal from Harper and a penalty by Dodd, converted five minutes from full time, kept them up. Of the trio of newcomers, Jimmy Cantrell was the only one to enhance his reputation, scoring 65 League and Cup goals in 136 matches before joining the Spurs in October 1912.

Appearances: FL: 10 apps 1 gl Total: 10 apps 1 gl

HARPER, Theophilus 'Fay'

Right-back
b. Brierley Hill, July quarter 1866
CAREER: Mansfield Town/Notts Rovers 1892/NOTTS (debut) Jan 1893/ Mansfield Town July 1895 to Nov 1899 when he announced his retirement.
Debut v Everton (a) 7.1.1893, lost 0 – 6

At the time of the Magpies FA Cup Final appearance in 1894, right-back Fay Harper was working as a collier and living at Annesley Woodhouse. He came into prominence with Mansfield Town as a strong tackling defender, and joined Notts Rovers in 1892. Here it should be mentioned that 'Notts Rovers' was the name under which Notts County's Reserve team operated in the early 1890s. Despite a traumatic debut in League football, Harper generally acquitted himself most creditably when called upon for the first eleven. A tall, broad shouldered back who cleared his lines promptly, he appeared in all but four of the season's League matches in 1893-94, and in all six FA Cup games, including the Final against Bolton Wanderers at Goodison Park. He returned to Mansfield Town, captaining them for several years before announcing his retirement. The 1901 Census confirmed his Brierley Hill birth, and gave his occupation as a coal miner stallman. In 2004 his FA Cup winner's medal realised £8,000 at auction.

Appearances: FL: 46 apps 0 gls FAC: 6 apps 0 gls Other: 5 apps 0 gls Total: 57 apps 0 gls
Honours: (NOTTS) FA Cup winners 1894

HARRAD, Shaun Nicholas

Forward   5' 10"   12st 4lbs
b. Nottingham, 11th December 1984
CAREER: West Bridgford Colts/Nottingham Forest juniors 1996/NOTTS juniors 1998,trainee July 2001, pro Apr 2004(Gresley Rovers loan Sept 2003) (Tamworth loan Sept 2004)
Debut as sub v Tranmere Rovers (a) 21.12.2002, drawn 2 – 2

A youthful central defender turned striker, Shaun notched his first senior goal at Shrewsbury Town in April 2005, from the unaccustomed position of right-side midfield. In earlier loan spells with non-League clubs, his scoring record was excellent. Loaned to Tamworth for a month at the start of season 2004-5, Shaun scored on his debut at Exeter City, and scored a-goal-a-game in his first three matches. Associated with the Magpies since the age of thirteen, he was voted 'Reserve Player of the Year 2002-3' and has subsequently continued to improve his speed and strength on the ball. After a season of real progress in 2004-05, quite how the decision to resign from the Pontins League in 2005-06 will affect the progress of the club's young players has yet to be revealed. Never a better time to establish a first team place would seem to be the answer.

Appearances: FL: 4(24) apps 1 gl FAC: 1(2) apps 0 gls Total: 5(26) apps 1 gl

---

HARRIS, George Thomas

Wing-half   5' 9"   11st 4lbs
b. High Wycombe, Bucks, 14th June 1904
d. Watford, Herts, 6th January 1986
CAREER: Wycombe Wanderers/NOTTS am July, pro Sept 1922/Queens Park Rangers May 1924/Fulham May 1926/Margate 1928/Watford Wednesday Oct 1930/Wycombe Wanderers trainer coach to beyond 1935
Debut v Rotherham County (h) 10.3.23, won 2 – 0

Described in the 'Nottingham Post Annual' for 1923-24 as "An improving half-back with plenty of energy, and a resolute tackler." Despite his undoubted promise, the youthful Wycombe Wanderers recruit added only one First Division appearance to his debut in the 1922-23 Second Division championship season. He was more regularly employed at senior level during two seasons with Queens Park Rangers (43 League and Cup matches,) but he returned to reserve team level in two seasons with Fulham (eight League matches and one goal.)

Appearances: FL: 2 apps 0 gls Total: 2 apps 0 gls

HARRIS, Thomas Kevin

Right-half
b. Dublin, 20th February 1918
d. 1984
CAREER: NOTTS Sept 1945/Brentford Aug 1948
Debut v Bradford City, FAC 1, (h) 17.11.45, drawn 2 – 2

In addition to his four FA Cup appearances, Kevin Harris played in 14 matches in the Third Division South (Northern Section) and a further four matches in the Cup Qualifying Competition. His first outing was at left-half in a 2 – 2 draw against Norwich City on 22nd September 1945, but he was more regularly fielded at right-half, a position he occupied for the best part of three months from October 1945. At the time of his signing, the Army guardsman was said to have been associated with both Tottenham Hotspur and Carlisle United in wartime football. He re-appeared in League football with Brentford in 1948, but played in only four Second Division matches during his spell at Griffin Park.

Appearances: FAC: 4 apps 0 gls Total: 4 apps 0 gls

―――――――――○―――――――――

HARRIS, Neil
Centre-forward 5' 7 2" 10st 4lbs
b. Shettleston, Lanarkshire 30th October 1894
d. Swindon, 3rd December 1941
CAREER: Vale of Clyde/Partick Thistle June 1913 (WW2 guest Belfast Distillery, Kilmarnock & Fulham)/Newcastle United May 1920, fee £3,300/NOTTS Nov 1925, fee £3,000/Dublin Shelbourne May 1927/Oldham Athletic July 1927, fee £400/Third Lanark Mar 1929, fee £400/Burton Town player-manager July 1929/Belfast Distillery manager May 1932/Swansea Town manager July 1934/Swindon Town manager May 1939 to his death.
Debut v Everton (h) 14.11.25, lost 0 – 3

Neil Harris' debut match for the Magpies was marred by an injury to Jimmy Sullivan after just ten minutes play. Left with ten men for the remainder of the match, Harris had a difficult afternoon but impressed the 'Football Post' correspondent who reported: "Harris has the subtlety and finesse of the Scotsmen, and can hustle into the bargain. He gave glimpses of those electric dashes for goal which have made him famous." A mater of weeks later, on Boxing Day 1925, he scored all of Notts' goals in the 4 – 0 victory against Arsenal. Earlier in his career Neil won his Scotland cap against England at Wembley in 1924. In the same year he scored one of Newcastle United's goals in their 2 – 0 win against Aston Villa in the FA Cup Final. His son, John Harris, was a wing-half with Chelsea between 1946-56 and later managed Chester and Sheffield United.

Appearances: FL: 49 apps 23 gls FAC: 3 apps 2 gls Total: 52 apps 25 gls
Honours: Scotland International, 1 cap 1924. Scotland Junior International. (Newcastle United) FA Cup winners 1924

―――――――――○―――――――――

HARRISON, Albert W
Outside-right
CAREER: Ruddington/NOTTS Sept 1905
Debut v Everton (a) 14.10.05, lost 2 – 6

Prior to the visit to Everton in October 1905 the Magpies had three regulars on the injured list. The opportunity was taken to give Harrison a run on the right wing. The 'Evening News' correspondent noted that Harrison had been the only forward to show any form in the reserve forward line in the midweek Midland League match against Rotherham County. Although County's weakened side were heavily defeated at Goodison Park the newcomer was praised for his efforts. "Harrison had a capital idea of the game and if he thickens out a bit should prove a useful forward. He always did something good on the few occasions that Green slung the ball out to him, and he was not intimidated by the weighty and clever half-back, Abbott, opposed to him."

Appearances: FL: 3 apps 0 gls Total: 3 apps 0 gls

―――――――――○―――――――――

HARRISSON, Alfred Everson
Goalkeeper
b. Holbeach, Lincs, January quarter 1872
d. Rugby, 23rd August 1947
CAREER: Nottingham Forest 1893/NOTTS Nov 1894
Debut v Bury (h) 24.11.1894, won 2 – 1

Another of the cricketing-footballer brigade, Harrisson played the summer game for Lincolnshire in addition to his association with both of the Nottingham football clubs. He appeared just once for the Magpies as deputy for their long serving England international, George Toone. Two goals from Elijah Alsopp, one a penalty, secured the points against Bury on his debut. The 1901 Census listed Harrisson as a medical practitioner.

Appearances: FL: 1 app 0 gls Total: 1 app 0 gls

―――――――――○―――――――――

HART, Paul Anthony
Central defender 6' 2" 12st 8lbs
b. Golborne, Lancs, 4th May 1953
CAREER: Manchester Schoolboys/Whalley Range/Stockport County Sept 1970/Blackpool June 1973, fee £25,000/Leeds United Mar 1978, fee £300,000/Nottingham Forest May 1983, fee £80,000/Sheffield Wednesday June 1985/Birmingham City Dec 1986/NOTTS player-coach June 1987/Chesterfield player-manager Nov 1988 to Jan 1991/Grantham Town cs 1991/Nottingham Forest youth coach June 1991/Leeds United director of youth coaching cs 1992/Nottingham Forest director of youth coaching June 1997, manager July 2001 to Feb 2004/Barnsley manager Mar 2004 to Mar 2005/Leeds United Youth Academy coach June 2005.
Debut v Fulham (a) 1.9.87, drawn 0 – 0

Nearing the end of a distinguished playing career when he arrived at Meadow Lane, Paul Hart lost his first team place in mid season but then made a valuable contribution in guiding a youthful Reserve team along the right lines.

Although reluctant to loose his services, the club did not stand in his way when he was offered the player-manager post at Chesterfield. A commanding central defender, fearless in the tackle and quick in decision, Paul gave excellent value throughout a playing career totalling 567 League appearances and 41 goals. As Nottingham Forest's manager he guided them to the Division One Play-offs in season 2002-03, but lost his job in February of the following season after Forest had gone for fourteen games without a win. Paul's father Johnny Hart was an inside-forward with Manchester City from 1994 to 1963 when he became coach, and briefly manager from May to November 1973.

Appearances: FL: 23 apps 0 gls FAC: 2 apps 0 gls Other: 4 apps 0 gls Total: 29 apps 0 gls

―――――――――○―――――――――

HATELEY, Tony
Centre-forward 6'1" 12st 7lbs
b. Derby, 13th June 1941
CAREER: Normanton Sports Club/Derby County associate schoolboy Apr 1955/NOTTS am May 1956, pro June 1958/ Aston Villa Aug 1963, fee £25,000/Chelsea Oct 1966, fee £100,000/Liverpool July 1967, fee £100,000/Coventry City Sept 1968, fee £80,000/Birmingham City Aug 1969, fee £72,000/NOTTS Nov 1970, fee £20,000/Oldham Athletic July 1972, fee £5,000/Bromsgrove Rovers May 1974/Prescot Town July 1975/Keyworth United Dec 1978
Debut v Stockport County (a) 8.11.58, drawn 1 – 1 (scored)

Originally a promising centre-half, Tony Hateley developed into a highly successful centre-forward. Never a stylist, but most dang-erous when near to goal and with headwork rem-iniscent of the great Tommy Lawton, his consistent scoring quickly attracted the attention of several Division One clubs. His initial breakthrough with Notts came in 1959-60 when he was thrust into the first team whose promotion push was being threatened by an indifferent spell of form. His response was eight goals in ten matches and promotion was clinched from Division Four. In September 1960 he achieved the unusual feat of scoring a hat-trick of headed goals in the 5 – 1 win against Barnsley.

The first of his big money moves took him to Aston Villa and four years on his three transfers had involved some £200,000, at that time the most ever paid for a player who did not become an international. He made a triumphant return to Meadow Lane in November 1970, spearheading the Division Four championship side with 22 goals in 29 matches. His career spanned seven League clubs and an impressive return of 210 goals from 429 matches. His son, Mark, who inherited his father's heading ability, won 32 England caps between 1984-92.

Appearances: FL: 188 apps 109 gls FAC: 13 apps 4 gls FLC: 6 apps 1 gl Total: 207 apps 114 gls
Honours: (Chelsea) FA Cup finalists 1967. (NOTTS) FL Div 4 champions 1971

―――――――――○―――――――――

HATTON, Cyril
Inside-forward 5' 8"   10st 7lbs
b. Bulwell, Nottingham, 14th September 1918
d. Grantham, Lincs, 3rd July 1987
CAREER: Nottingham Corinthians/Grantham Co-op/ NOTTS am 1935-36, pro July 1936 (WW2 guest Queens Park Rangers)/Queens Park Rangers Apr 1946, in exchange for Harry Brown/Chesterfield June 1953/Grantham Town player-manager May 1954 to 1957.
Debut v Northampton Town (a) 20.2.37, drawn 1 – 1 (scored)

Fair-haired Cyril Hatton had every reason to remember his debut in League football, as he scored the Magpies' equaliser at Northampton, and played alongside the legendary Scottish centre-forward, Hughie Gallacher. He was later to play in the same forward line as another celebrated attack leader, 'Dixie' Dean. Had he stayed a little longer at Meadow Lane Tommy Lawton would have completed a fabulous treble. After war service he returned to Meadow Lane, having made guest appearances for Q.P.R. He did in fact score twice for Q.P.R. against Southend United on 1st September 1945, when on leave from Hamburg; in mid week he turned out for Notts Reserves. Later in the same season he moved to Loftus Road on a permanent basis, where he sampled a higher grade of football after scoring 25 League and Cup goals in the Rangers 1947-48 promotion season. After a term with Chesterfield Cyril returned to Grantham as player-manager at London Road, combining his duties with the running of a newsagent's business. Two years prior to his death in 1987 he was working part-time in the motor trade.

Appearances: FL: 62 apps 15 gls FAC: 3 apps 0 gls Other: 2 apps 1 gl Total: 67 apps 16 gls
Honours: (Queens Park Rangers) FL Div 3 South champions 1948

―――――――――○―――――――――

HEATHCOTE, James

Inside-left   5' 8½" 11st 4lbs
b. Bolton, 17th January 1894
CAREER: Bolton Wanderers during WW1 period/Blackpool May 1918/NOTTS June 1922, fee £1,000/Pontypridd cs 1923/Lincoln City June 1924/Mansfield Town May 1925/ Coventry City July 1926, fee £400/Accrington Stanley Jan to Mar 1929
Debut v Coventry City (a) 26.8.22, won 2 – 1

Notts were indebted to their miserly defence when they won the championship of Division Two in 1922-23. Despite two untypical aberrations in the shape of home defeats by Manchester United (1 – 6) and Crystal Palace (0 – 4), they ended the season having conceded only 34 goals from their 42 match League programme. On the credit side, over half of the 46 goals scored were credited to Donald Cock (13) and Harold Hill (12). Forward changes were the order of the day, and Jimmy Heathcote with only one goal in the first ten matches of the season was deposed in October and was recalled only twice thereafter. Aside from his indifferent spell at Meadow Lane, Heathcote had a deserved reputation as a clever inside-forward and an opportunist of the first order, instanced by his career aggregate figures of 197 League matches and 88 goals.

Appearances: FL: 12 apps 1 gl Total: 12 apps 1 gl
Honours: (NOTTS) FL Div 2 champions 1923

HEFFERNAN, Paul

Forward   5' 10" 10st 7lbs
b. Dublin, 29th December 1981
CAREER: Newtown (County Wicklow)/NOTTS Oct 1999/ Bristol City July 2004, fee £125,000 (with a provision for another performance related £25,000)/Doncaster Rovers June 2005, fee £125,000
Debut as sub v Oldham Athletic (h) 24.4.2000, lost 0 – 1

Selected 'Young Player of the Year' by Notts in 2002-03, a season in which he scored 10 League goals in 25(11) matches. The talented Irish striker doubled his tally of League goals in 2003-04, a performance made all the more creditable as it was achieved in a struggling side. Despite beginning the season on the bench, when Mark Stallard and Clive Platt were manager Dearden's initial front

line pairing, Paul hit the goal trail from November onwards. Highlights being his Boxing Day hat-trick against Queens Park Rangers, and a four-goal salvo against Stockport County on 21st February. Out of contract at the end of the season, he expressed his intention to leave and was not selected for the final two matches of the campaign. He signed off, in typical style, by scoring twice for the Reserves in a 3 – 2 victory at Darlington.

Appearances: FL: 74(26) apps 36 gls FAC: 2(2) apps 1 gl FLC: 2(3) apps 1 gl Other: 2(3) apps 0 gls
Total: 80(34) apps 38 gls
Honours: Republic of Ireland U-21 International, 3 apps.

HENDERSON, Wayne

Goalkeeper   5' 11" 12st 2lbs
b. Dublin, 16th September 1983
CAREER: Bohemians/Cherry Orchard F.C./Aston Villa trainee 1998, pro Sept 2000 (Tamworth loan Mar 2004) (Wycombe Wanderers loan Apr 2004) (NOTTS loan Aug to Oct 2004 and again Dec 2004)
Debut v Kidderminster Harriers (a) 10.8.04, drawn 0 – 0

Aston Villa's FA Youth Cup winning goalkeeper, Wayne was third choice at Villa Park at the time of his first loan spell with the Magpies. A clean sheet on his debut was not effected without some degree of good fortune. Cheltenham forwards being denied twice by the woodwork, and once by a timely goal line clearance from Ian Richardson. A second consecutive clean sheet at Northampton featured many excellent saves. Doubtless a young goalkeeper with a big future, Wayne hails from a family of shot-stoppers, his father played for Shamrock Rovers and an elder brother for Bohemians. A second loan spell found Wayne in the shadow of the emerging Saul Deeney, quite deservedly first choice under new manager Ian Richardson.

Appearances: FL: 11 apps 0 gls Other: 1 app 0 gls
Total: 12 apps 0 gls
Honours: Republic of Ireland U-21 International. Republic of Ireland Youth International. (Aston Villa) FA Youth Cup winners 2002.

HENDON, Ian Michael

Defender   6' 0" 12st 10lbs
b. Ilford, 5th December 1971
CAREER: Havering Schoolboys/Tottenham Hotspur trainee, signing pro Dec 1989 (Portsmouth loan Jan 1992) (Leyton Orient loan Mar 1992) (Barnsley loan Mar 1993)/ Leyton Orient Aug 1993, fee £50,000 (Birmingham City loan Mar 1995)/NOTTS Feb 1997, fee £50,000/ Northampton Town Mar 1999, fee £30,000/Sheffield Wednesday Oct 2000, fee £40,000/Peterborough United nc Jan 2003/Barnet player-coach May 2003.
Debut v Millwall (a) 25.2.97, lost 0 – 1

Magpies' popular skipper in the record breaking 1997-98 Division Three championship season. Ian began with the Spurs but forged his reputation with Leyton Orient for whom he made just short of 150 appearances and was awarded their 'Player of the Year' trophy in 1995-96. It was against the Orient that Ian captained the Magpies to promotion on 28th March 1998, the teams' elevation being confirmed following the 1 – 0 victory before a crowd of 8,383 at Meadow Lane. It was the first time that a promotion issue had been clinched as early as March, and the Magpies went on to win the championship with a points total of 88 – a club record. Ian was selected in the PFA Division Three squad in 1997, and again in 1998, when four of Notts' players were honoured.

Appearances: FL: 82 apps 6 gls FAC: 8(1) apps 0 gls FLC: 5 apps 1 gl Total: 95(1) apps 7 gls
Honours: England U-21 International, 7 apps. England Youth International. (NOTTS) FL Div 3 champions 1998 (Barnet) Conference National champions 2005.

———————o———————

HENDRY, John "Jack"

Left-back   5'10**2**"13st 0lbs
b. Scotland, circa 1869
CAREER: Uddingstone F.C./ Glasgow Rangers/NOTTS July 1890/Heanor Town 1896/Sheppey United June 1897/Rushden Town July 1898/Northampton Town May 1899
Debut v Bolton Wanderers (a) 6.9.1890, lost 2 – 4

Jack Hendry first came into notice with the Uddingstone club and added to his reputation in representative matches for Lanarkshire against Forfarshire and for Glasgow against Edinburgh. He joined Notts from Glasgow Rangers, and was immediately effective and consistent, appearing in every League and cup match in his first three seasons. He first missed a match in February 1894, thus ending a run of 116 consecutive League and Cup appearances. At the time of the 1894 FA Cup Final he was the heaviest man in the team at thirteen stones, a weight that was thrown usefully into the fray.

Described as "A player of the robust type who has little difficulty in withstanding the charges of opposing forwards and clearing his lines." In June 1894 he was married in Nottingham, and just prior to the outbreak of World War One was still resident in the city.

Appearances: FL: 163 apps 1 gl FAC: 19 apps 0 gls Other: 1 app 0 gls Total: 183 apps 1 gl
Honours: (NOTTS) FA Cup winners 1894; finalists 1891

———————o———————

HENDRY, Robert

Centre-forward
b. Dumbarton, circa 1876
CAREER: Dumbarton June 1896/Everton May 1897/NOTTS Oct 1897/Greenock Morton July 1898, in part exchange for R.Hannigan/Dumbarton Sept 1898/Renton Aug 1899
Debut v Wolverhampton Wanderers (a) 30.10.1897, lost 1 – 3

According to contemporary press reports Robert Hendry was "Tried and found wanting by Everton." He did little better after joining the Magpies, an initial five-match run at centre-forward brought little success, two draws and three defeats ensuing, the new centre-forward finding life in the English First Division less rewarding than in the Second Division in Scotland.

Appearances: FL: 7 apps 0 gls Total: 7 apps 0 gls
Honours: (Dumbarton) Scottish Cup finalists 1897

———————o———————

HENFREY, Arthur George

Inside-forward
b. Wellingborough, January quarter 1868
d. Wellingborough, 17th October 1929
CAREER: Wellingborough Grammar School/Cambridge University (Blue 1890-91)/Finedon F.C./Corinthians 1890-93/NOTTS Jan 1894/Also represented Northamptonshire
Debut v Burnley, FAC 1, (h) 27.1.1894, won 1 – 0

In the season that Notts won the FA Cup, the Corinthian and England international Henfrey played in the first round tie against Burnley at Trent Bridge, before an attendance of 8,000 spectators. Logan scored what proved to be the winning goal after seven minutes play, and later Dan Bruce failed to add to the lead when his penalty kick hit the crossbar. In subsequent heated exchanges Calderhead (Notts) and Espic (Burnley) were ordered off for kicking each other. A talented all-rounder, Henfrey played cricket for Cambridge University and Northamptonshire 1886-99.

Appearances: FAC: 1 app 0 gls Total: 1 app 0 gls
Honours: England International, 5 caps 1891-96

HENRYS, Arthur

Left-half
b. Nottingham, 1867
d. 30th June 1922
b. CAREER: Newton Heath cs 1891/NOTTS Jardines cs 1892/Newton Heath Oct 1892/Leicester Fosse Mar 1893/ NOTTS June 1896 to cs 1897
Debut v Loughborough (h) 5.9.1896, won 3 – 1

Arthur Henrys joined Newton Heath for what proved to be their last season of Alliance football. He missed only two matches, assisting the Heathens to finish as runners-up to Nottingham Forest for the championship. His move to Notts Jardines for the 1892-93 season resulted in a FA inquiry. Henrys was suspended until 31st October 1892 and the Notts Jardines' secretary was banned from management. Henrys played in only three League matches for Newton Heath and moved on to Leicester Fosse, then a Midland League side. They were elected to Division Two in the following season and Arthur was at centre half-back in their first League fixture. After 51 League and Cup games he joined the Magpies who won the Second Division championship and were undefeated in the season's Test Matches. He failed to hold down the left-half spot, however, after appearing in the first seven matches of the season.

Appearances: FL: 7 apps 0 gls Total: 7 apps 0 gls

HENSHALL, Horace Vincent

Outside-left   5' 9"   11st 10lbs
b. Hednesford, 14th June 1889
d. Nottingham, 7th December 1951
CAREER: Queen Mary's School (Walsall)/ Bridgetown Amateurs/Crewe Alexandra/Aston Villa May 1906/NOTTS Nov 1912 (WW1 guest West Ham United Nov 1916)/ Sheffield Wednesday player-coach June 1922/Chesterfield June 1923/Lincoln City secretary-manager May 1924/ NOTTS secretary-manager May 1927, resigned as manager in May 1934, but stayed on as secretary to Apr 1935.
Debut v Aston Villa (h)
9.11.12, drawn 1 – 1

Said to have cost a record fee when signed from Aston Villa, Horace Hen-shall certainly just-ified the outlay. An ideal wingman with the right temp-erament, his spec-ialities included spectacular goal-scoring and accurate centering. An attack of appendicitis side-lined him for part of

his first season, but he recovered to play a full part in the promotion season of 1913-14. Horace served in the R.N.A.S. during WW1, and was awarded a benefit by Notts in season 1920-21. He retired from playing in 1924 with an overall record of 259 League appearances and 39 goals, and returned to Meadow Lane in May 1927 as secretary-manager. He entered the licensed trade after leaving County, moving a short distance up the road to take over The Navigation Inn, near to Meadow Lane.

Appearances: FL: 164 apps 27 gls FAC: 16 apps 2 gls
Total: 180 apps 29 gls

HENSHAW, Terence Robert

Defender   5' 10"   11st 0lbs
b. Nottingham, 29th February 1980
CAREER: NOTTS trainee Aug 1996/Burton Albion June 1999
Debut as sub v Burnley, Auto Windscreens Shield, (a) 27.1.98, lost 0 – 2

One appearance from the bench in the Auto Windscreen Shield match at Burnley was Terry's only involvement at senior level. Failing to establish himself beyond reserve team football at Meadow Lane, he has since enjoyed a lengthy association with Burton Albion. Unibond League Premier Division champions in 2002-02, Terry has remained a fixture in the Eton Park club's defence in subsequent Conference seasons.

Appearances: Other: 0(1) apps 0 gls Total: 0(1) apps 0 gls

HESFORD, Iain

Goalkeeper   6' 2"   14st 0lbs
b. Noola, Kenya, 4th March 1960
CAREER: Blackpool app, signing pro Aug 1977/Sheffield Wednesday Aug 1983 (Fulham loan Jan 1985) (NOTTS loan Nov 1985 to Feb 1986) (Sunderland loan Aug 1986)/ Sunderland Sept 1986, fee £80,000/Hull City Dec 1988/ Maidstone United Aug 1991/Eastern, Hong Kong, Nov 1992/Golden, Hong Kong, May 1993 to 1997
Debut v Swansea City (h) 30.11.85, won 3 – 0

Iain Hesford won England Youth and Under-21 honours with Blackpool before Sheffield Wednesday signed him. He stayed for three years at Hillsborough without making a League appearance as Martin Hodge clocked up 126 consecutive matches. His loan spell with the Magpies came in a season when five different goalkeepers were fielded in Third Division matches, after Mick Leonard had held the position for the first 19 fixtures. Transferred to Sunderland, he had a roller-coaster spell involving relegation in his first season and immediate promotion in the next.

After exactly 100 League and Cup appearances for Hull City, Iain spent his final season with Maidstone United who resigned from the League in August 1992, having won only eight matches in 1991-92. One of the wins, a 3 – 2 home victory against Hereford United came courtesy of a winning goal from their goalkeeper whose huge punt found the net at the opposite end of the field. Iain's father, Bob Hesford was also a goalkeeper with Huddersfield Town, whose 220 appearances included the 1938 FA Cup Final, won in the last minute of extra time by Preston North End.

Appearances: FL: 10 apps 0 gls Other: 1 app 0 gls
Total: 11 apps 0 gls
Honours: England U-21 International, 7 apps 1982-83. England Youth International, 1 app 1978. (Sunderland) FL Div 3 champions 1988

HIBBERT, C
Centre-half
CAREER: Heanor Town/NOTTS Nov 1889
Debut v Sheffield Wednesday, FAC 3, 2nd replay, (Played at Derby County) 3.3.1890, lost 1 – 2

Two earlier meetings between Notts and Sheffield Wednesday in the FA Cup had been subject to protest and declared void by the Football Association. A neutral venue –Derbyshire cricket ground – staged the third meeting, where gate receipts of £342 were taken from an attendance estimated at 10,000. Unfortunately, Notts had to contest the tie without three of their principal professionals, and Calderhead's absence from the half-back line was "A loss impossible to counter–balance" according to the 'Nottingham Daily Express.' In the matter of Hibbert, they went on to say that form in second team matches was deceptive and that "The difference between a crack second team man and a first-rater was never more apparent." Wednesday were said to be "Unscientific, though dashing and impetuous", and won 2 – 1. Notts apparently considered lodging a third protest, based on the question of a player's qualification, but decided to let the matter drop and concentrate on improving their League position. Sheffield Wednesday went on to reach the final of the FA Cup where they were soundly beaten 6 – 1 by Blackburn Rovers.

Appearances: FAC: 1 app 0 gls Total: 1 app 0 gls

HIGGINS, Andrew Kincade
Inside-right   5' 8"   11st 0lbs
b. Gartsherrie, near Coatbridge, 29th April 1909
d. Newport, Gwent, 9th November 1966

CAREER: Gartsherrie Athletic/Stoneburn Juniors/Dunblane Rovers/Cowdenbeath July 1929/West Bromwich Albion Dec 1930/Millwall July 1931/Exeter City May 1932/Newport County June 1933/NOTTS Sept 1934/Olympique Lillios, France, June 1935/Racing Club d'Arras player-coach June 1936/Newport County juniors coach Nov 1938 to Jan 1940
Debut v Nottingham Forest (h) 29.9.34, lost 3 – 5 (scored one)

In the relegation season of 1934-35, Notts' new manager Charlie Jones moved into the transfer market after the team scored just five goals in their first seven fixtures. Andrew Higgins was felt to be the type of thrustful forward who would introduce some power to the front line. The fact that he scored on his debut was overshadowed by the fact that Notts failed to stem the tide at the other end of the pitch and were beaten 5 – 3 by local rivals Forest. Earlier failings had been attributed to too much concentration on defence, the 'third back' policy of the manager failing to work as the players available to him were not good enough to make the system a success. Higgins' ten League outings were made consecutively and featured one win, one draw and eight defeats. In mid season manager Jones was sacked, and Higgins did not appear again in the first team. In two spells with Newport County he scored 13 goals in 42 matches, but played only twice when they won the championship of the Third Division South in 1938-39. He returned to his trade as an electrician in January 1940 and remained in that occupation until his untimely death in the Newport works of Messrs. Stewart and Lloyds.

Appearances: FL: 10 apps 2 gls Total: 10 apps 2 gls

HILL, Harold
Inside-forward   5' 5**2**"   10st 8lbs
b. Blackwell, Derbyshire, 24th August 1898
d. Blackwell, Derbyshire, 14th February 1969
CAREER: Birdholme Rovers/New Hucknall Colliery/NOTTS pro Oct 1919/Sheffield Wednesday Oct 1924, fee £1,700/Scarborough June 1929/Chesterfield reserve team player-coach May 1932/Mansfield Town Sept 1933/Sutton Town Aug 1934.
Debut v Manchester City (a) 27.9.19, lost 1 – 4

A diminutive but dangerous forward signed from New Hucknall Colliery after scoring 15 goals in the opening weeks of season 1919-20. He was quickly a hero at Meadow Lane, being carried shoulder high off the field by spectators after scoring both goals as Notts beat West Bromwich Albion 2 – 0 in his fifth first team appearance. The Albion, incidentally, finished the season as First Division champions and had thrashed Notts 8 – 0 the week before. In five seasons at Meadow Lane Hill proved to be a match-winning forward, at times too individualistic

but a source of continual anxiety to opposing defenders. He was a key member of the Magpies 1922-23 championship side, and made a similar contribution in Sheffield Wednesday's successful 1925-26 season when they won the Division Two championship.

Appearances: FL: 151 apps 50 gls FAC: 19 apps 6 gls
Total: 170 apps 56 gls
Honours: (NOTTS) FL Div 2 champions 1923. (Sheffield Wednesday) FL Div 2 champions 1926

HILLHOUSE, John

Right-half   5' 10"   11st 7lbs
b. Hurlford, 14th January 1898
CAREER: Hurlford/Middlesbrough June 1921/Sanquahar/Nithsdale Wanderers/Workington June 1924/Rochdale June 1925/NOTTS Feb 1927/Bury Apr 1928/Arthurlie Oct 1928
Debut v Middlesbrough (h) 23.2.27, drawn 2 – 2

John Hillhouse enjoyed two excellent seasons with Rochdale, after joining them from non-League Workington. His arrival at Spotland coincided with the introduction of the new off-side law, the Dale immediately cashing in with a 6 – 0 opening day victory against Hartlepools United. Throughout the 1925-26 season, and the one that followed, attractive, attacking football took the side within a whisker of promotion on each occasion – third in 1925-26 and second in 1926-27, when only the champions were promoted. Sadly, his move to Nottingham was not a success and he requested a transfer within six months of his arrival. In August 1927 the 'Football Post' revealed that: "Hillhouse has never been well since he came to Nottingham, and his prospective departure from the city is prompted by this reason." A brother, Hugh, played for Clyde and had trials with Liverpool.

Appearances: FL: 4 apps 0 gls Total: 4 apps 0 gls

HILLS, Walter John

Utility   5' 8"   11st 4lbs
b. Ferozepore, India, 18th July 1898
d. Portsmouth, 10th May 1985
CAREER: Army football/Meadow Thursday/NOTTS am May, pro Aug 1924/Grantham Nov 1927/Radford Thursday Aug 1928/Notts Corinthians Sept 1930
Debut v Liverpool (a) 26.12.24, lost 0 – 1

The 'Notts. Post Annual' for season 1925-26 revealed that Walter Hills was: "A versatile player who attracted attention whilst with Meadow Thursday, and figured as full-back, half-back and inside-forward in the reserve team last winter." He carried his versatility into the first team, his four senior appearances being made as inside-right (once); right-back (once) and left-half (twice.)

Appearances: FL: 3 apps 0 gls FAC: 1 app 0 gls
Total: 4 apps 0 gls

HILTON, Fred

Half-back   5' 11"   11st 10lbs
b. Sheffield, 8th July 1903
CAREER: Sunday Schools football/Sheffield works football/Grimsby Town Sept 1922/NOTTS Feb 1925/Scunthorpe United June 1930/Gainsborough Trinity Sept 1931/Lincoln Wednesday Aug 1934
Debut v Everton (a) 18.3.25, lost 0 – 1

In two and a half seasons with Grimsby Town Fred earned a reputation as the best centre-half in the Third Division. A fearless tackler who realised the value of accurate ground passes to his forwards, he completed over a century of First and Second Division matches for the Magpies. Just as efficient at left-half, a position that he took up following the signing of Frank Froggatt in November 1927. Fred was also effective from the penalty spot, with three successful conversions in 1927-28.

Appearances: FL: 109 apps 3 gls FAC: 5 apps 0 gls
Total: 114 apps 3 gls

HINDMARSH, John Smith

Wing-half   5' 8²"   10st 9lbs
b. Ashington, 29th January 1913
d. Ashington, June 1990
CAREER: Ashington Welfare/Ashington June 1931/Sheffield Wednesday May 1934/Burnley June 1935/NOTTS May 1937/Ashington Aug 1939
Debut v Watford, semi-final of Div 3 South Cup, (a) 13.9.37, lost 3 – 8

After a season in reserve with Sheffield Wednesday, John Hindmarsh made his debut in League football with Burnley at Bradford City on 28th September 1935.

He scored his first League goal in the Christmas Day 3 – 2 win against Blackpool at Turf Moor. Later in the season he lined up behind sixteen year-old Tommy Lawton when the future England international centre-forward began his senior career in a 1 – 1 draw against Doncaster Rovers at Turf Moor on 28th March 1936. After appearing in 41 League and Cup matches for the Clarets, and representing the Central League versus the London Combination, he was recruited by the Magpies in May 1937. A quick and forceful tackler, better in defence than attack, he missed only three of the seasons' League and Cup matches in his final season before returning to Ashington on the eve of World War Two.

Appearances: FL: 57 apps 0 gls FAC: 5 apps 0 gls Other: 3 apps 0 gls Total: 65 apps 0 gls

————————o————————

HOBSON, John
Winger   5' 6 2"9st 9lbs
b. Barnsley, 1st June 1946
CAREER: Barnsley Schoolboys/Blackpool Sept 1963/ Barnsley July 1965/NOTTS May 1969 to 1971
Debut v Mansfield Town, FLC 1, (a) 13.8.69, lost 1 – 3

John Hobson joined Blackpool from Barnsley Schoolboys but failed to reach senior level. He returned to his hometown club where his League career commenced, in Division Four, on 20th October 1965 at Torquay United in a 0 – 3 defeat. Before leaving Oakwell, he assisted his team to win promotion from Division Four in 1967-68, when they ended the season as runners-up to the champions, Luton Town. At Meadow Lane he missed only one League or Cup match in his first season, but in the promotion season that followed he made only 1(3) League appearances. Crickmore and Nixon becoming established as regular wingmen during the campaign that featured an unbeaten home record and a nine point margin at the head of Division Four.

Appearances: FL: 46(3) apps 6 gls FAC: 1 app 0 gls FLC: 2 apps 0 gls Total: 49(3) apps 6 gls

————————o————————

HODDER, William
Outside-right
b. Stroud, Gloucestershire, October 1865.
d. 1897
CAREER: Notts Rangers/NOTTS cs 1888/Nottingham Forest Sept 1889/Sheffield United/Sheffield Wednesday Jan 1891/Lincoln City/Mansfield Town 1893
Debut v Everton (a) 15.9.1888, lost 1 – 2

William Hodder's season with the Magpies coincided with their debut in the Football League, and he was at outside-right in the historic opening fixture.

He missed only two of the season's League matches, finding his 'shooting boots' in mid-term with goals against Blackburn Rovers and Derby County in December, and against West Bromwich Albion in January. The Magpies fielded a total of 33 different players in League engagements, and this in an undemanding programme of only 22 matches. Their eleventh place finish, in a league of twelve clubs, ensured sweeping changes in personnel during the close season, Hodder being among the casualties.

Appearances: FL: 20 apps 3 gls FAC: 2 apps 0 gls
Total: 22 apps 3 gls

————————o————————

HODSON, Simeon Paul
Full-back   5' 10" 11st 2lbs
b. Lincoln, 5th March 1966
CAREER: Lincoln Schoolboys/Swinderby F.C./ NOTTS app 1982, pro Mar 1984/Charlton Athletic Mar 1985/Lincoln United Dec 1985/Lincoln City Jan 1986/Newport County Aug 1987/West Bromwich Albion Mar 1988, fee £5,000/ Doncaster Rovers nc Sept 1992/Kidderminster Harriers nc Jan 1993/Mansfield Town Feb 1993/Shrewsbury Town trial Aug 1993/Kidderminster Harriers Sept 1993/Rushden & Diamonds Sept 1996
Debut v Norwich City (a) 13.3.84, won 1 – 0

Injuries to Tristan Benjamin and Aki Lahtinen resulted in an unexpected senior opportunity in Division One for Simeon Hodson, just eight days beyond his eighteenth birthday. His introduction resulted in a rare away win after Notts had failed to win in their previous twelve League games. He held his place for the remainder of the season, and began 1984-85 as a first team player. Before the end of the following season, a term that ended in a second, consecutive, relegation, he departed to Charlton Athletic on a free transfer. After a nine-month stay at the Valley he was released, returned to live in Lincoln and after a very brief stay with Lincoln United joined up with Lincoln City. The Imps became the first League club to be automatically relegated to the GM Vauxhall Conference in 1987, and he must have thought himself jinxed when his next club, Newport County, suffered a similar fate in the following season. A more stable period with West Bromwich Albion preceded a period of some success with Kidderminster Harriers, 'giant killers' of season 1993-94 when they reached round five of the FA Cup as well as lifting the championship of the GM Vauxhall Conference.

Appearances: FL: 26 apps 0 gls FLC: 3 apps 0 gls
Total: 30 apps 0 gls
Honours: England Semi-professional international 1994. (Kidderminster Harriers) GM Vauxhall Conference champions 1994

————————o————————

HOGG, Graeme James

Central defender   6' 1"   12st 4lbs
b. Aberdeen, 17th June 1964
CAREER: Aberdeen & District Schoolboys/Manchester
United app July 1980, pro June 1982 (West Bromwich Albion
loan Nov – Dec 1987)/Portsmouth Aug 1988, fee £150,000/
Heart of Midlothian Aug 1991, fee £200,000/NOTTS Jan
1995, fee £75,000/Brentford Jan 1998, fee £5,000; retired
June 1998.
Debut v Tranmere Rovers (a) 4.2.95, lost 2 – 3

An effective stopper who won most of the aerial battles,
Graeme spent eight years with Manchester United,
initially as understudy to Gordon McQueen, thereafter
the emerging talents of Paul McGrath and Kevin Moran
limited his opportunities. He nevertheless completed
107(2) first team matches, and was desperately unlucky
to miss the FA Cup Final victory against Everton in 1985,
sustaining an injury after having played in five of the
earlier rounds. He arrived at Meadow Lane after spells
with Portsmouth (100 League games, three as substitute),
and Heart of Midlothian, managed by ex-United striker
Joe Jordan. Graeme arrived at Meadow Lane in the
Division One relegation season, and his tenure was not
lacking in drama. The team qualified for the Second
Division Play-offs in 1996, suffered a second relegation
in 1997-98, and Graeme left midway through the
promotion season that followed. An Achilles tendon
injury severely restricted him in season 1995-96, but he
proved a tower of strength in the following season,
appearing in 39 League and Cup matches. A brief period
with Brentford (17 matches, two goals) preceded his
retirement and a return to his native Scotland.

Appearances: FL: 66 apps 0 gls FAC: 4 apps 1 gl FLC:
4(1) apps 0 gls Other: 4 apps 0 gls Total: 78(1) apps 1 gl
Honours: Scotland U-21 International, 4 apps 1984-85.
Scotland Youth International

————————o————————

HOLD, Oscar

Inside-left   5' 9"   11st 0lbs
b. Carlton, Barnsley, 19th October 1918
CAREER: Regent Street Congregationals/Denaby United/
Manchester United 'A' Team/Barnsley Aug 1937/Aldershot
Town Apr 1939/Norwich City Mar 1946/NOTTS Oct 1948,
fee £6,000/Chelmsford City Aug 1949/Everton Feb 1950/
Queens Park Rangers Feb 1952/March Town player-
manager July 1953/Gainsborough Trinity manager/Wisbech
Town player-manager Feb 1957 to Feb 1960/FA Coach in
Nigeria June to Oct 1960/Cambridge City Mar 1961 to Mar
1962/Doncaster Rovers manager Feb 1964/Fenerbache,
Turkey, Jan 1965/Ankara, Turkey, Jan 1966/National
Sporting Club, Saudi Arabia 1968/Apollon, Cyprus, 1972 to
1974/Coaching in Kuwait to 1982/Apollon, Cyprus.
Debut v Exeter City (h) 16.10.48, won 9 – 0 (scored one)

Three days after penetrating the Notts rearguard when
spearheading the Norwich City attack, the dark-haired,
quick moving Oscar Hold was signed by Magpies'
manager, Arthur Stollery. He had been under review since
the beginning of the 1948-49 season, but at that time the
inside-left berth was satisfactorily filled by Jack Marsh.
When Marsh was transferred to Coventry City in
September 1948, Hold was signed as his replacement.
His dream debut was witnessed by 36,615 spectators
and featured four goals each for Tommy Lawton and
Jackie Sewell. A goal scorer in his first and last appearances
for the Magpies, Oscar found stiff competition during
his stay from Fred Evans, who scored seven goals in just
ten matches in the same season. Apart from his spell with
Everton, he operated in the lower divisions as a player,
his aggregate figures being 36 goals in 104 League matches.
His coaching and managerial skills took him to many parts
of the world, including a seven-year stint in Kuwait and a
final return to live in Cyprus.

Appearances: FL: 19 apps 9 gls FAC: 4 apps 0 gls
Total: 23 apps 9 gls

————————o————————

HOLDER, David James

Centre-half   6' 1"   12st 8lbs
b. Cheltenham, 15th December 1943
d. Cheltenham, 26th April 2002
CAREER: Cardiff City am/NOTTS Oct 1962/Barrow July
1964 to cs 1965
Debut v Walsall (h) 24.10.63, lost 0 – 1

Fair-haired David Holder was recommended to County
following trials with Cardiff City. Considered an
outstanding prospect with total command in the air, it
was not until his second season at Meadow Lane that he
was given a League outing, the consistent form of Alex
Gibson blocking his prospects of advancement. Released
on a free transfer in April 1964 he joined Barrow, at that
time a Division Four club. At either centre-half or right-
back he played in 29 League matches and three FA Cup
ties in his single season at Holker Street.

Appearances: FL: 8 apps 0 gls FAC: 1 app 0 gls FLC: 2
apps 0 gls Total: 11 apps 0 gls

————————o————————

HOLDER, Stephen William

Outside-right   5' 3"   9st 6lbs
b. Nottingham, 21st April 1952
CAREER: Nottingham Schoolboys/NOTTS app Aug 1967,
pro Apr 1970
Debut as sub v Northampton Town (h) 24.4.70, won 2 – 0

Notts were not alone in their appreciation of Steve Holder, the much sought after right-winger of Nottingham Boys 1966-67 side. Secured on apprentice forms he turned professional at 18 years of age and made his League debut in the same month. The fact that he appeared only once at senior level could have surrounded his lack of physical advantage. At just five feet and three inches tall, he is thought to be the shortest player ever to have represented Notts in a League match.

Appearances: FL: 0(1) apps 0 gls Total: 0(1) apps 0 gls

───────○───────

HOLLAND, John Henry
Goalkeeper
b. Bulwell, Nottingham, July quarter 1861
CAREER: NOTTS (debut) Oct 1886/Nottingham Forest June 1889
Debut v Basford Rovers, FAC 1, (h) 30.10.1886, won 13 – 0

A Bulwell tramcar conductor who began with Notts two seasons prior to their entry into the Football League. In both seasons he was virtually an automatic choice in goal, this despite a shaky start that included consecutive defeats of 14 – 0 against Preston North End and 8 - 0 against Accrington. He played in nine Football League matches in 1888-89, his total including a final outing as inside-left at Wolverhampton Wanderers in February 1889.

Appearances: FL: 9 apps 0 gls FAC: 9 apps 0 gls
Total: 18 apps 0 gls

───────○───────

HOLMES, Harry
Outside-right
b. Ambergate, Derbys, 18th August 1908
d. Ambergate, Derbys, April quarter 1976
CAREER: Milford Ivanhoe/Heanor Town/Coventry City am Nov 1931/Heanor Town Nov 1933/NOTTS am Dec 1933/Heanor Town/Birmingham am Oct 1934/Heanor Town Aug 1935
Debut v Hull City (h) 30.12.33, drawn 0 – 0

Amateur wingman Harry Holmes received warm praise for his debut against Hull City. The 'Nottingham Guardian' reporting that "Holmes possesses a good knowledge of the game and although he tired near the end, the honours in the forward line went to him." Earlier, he had starred with Coventry City in limited appearances (22 matches and 12 gls, including two hat-tricks). He was said to have left Coventry because of difficulties in getting away from business, and this proved to be the case with both Notts and Birmingham. Work as an engineering draughtsman seriously restricting his opportunities in senior football.

Appearances: 2 apps 0 gls Total: 2 apps 0 gls

HOLMES, Richard
Right-back   5' 10"   10st 7lbs
b. Grantham, 7th November 1980
CAREER: Bottesford/NOTTS associate schoolboy Mar 1996, pro Mar 1999 (Hereford United loan Mar 2002)/ Harrowby United Sept 2003.
Debut as sub v York City (h) 13.3.99, won 4 – 2

After making his first League appearance in the late stages of season 1998-99, Richard made outstanding progress in the following term, holding down the first team right-back role in all but a handful of the season's fixtures. The appointment of Jocky Scott as manager brought new faces and systems, and Richard returned to reserve football where he remained until his release at the close of the 2002-03 season. At the age of 22 he stepped down into the United Counties League, linking again with Harrowby United's manager Graham Drury, who had been in charge of Bottesford, where Richard first made his mark as a schoolboy.

Appearances: FL: 47(12) apps 0 gls FAC: 2(2) apps 0 gls FLC: 3(1) apps 0 gls Other: 2(1) apps 0 gls
Total: 54(16) apps 0 gls

───────○───────

HOOKS, Paul
Midfield/Forward   5' 8"   10st 11lbs
b. Wallsend, 30th May 1959
CAREER: NOTTS app Jan 1976, pro July 1977/Derby County Mar 1983, fee £60,000/Mansfield Town nc trial Aug 1985/Boston United Aug 1985/Cotgrave Miner's Welfare 1987
Debut v Charlton Athletic (h) 14.5.77, lost 0 – 1

Despite the offer of an apprenticeship by Aston Villa, Paul joined the Magpies in order to remain near to his home at Ollerton, near Mansfield. He was introduced to League football as a 17 year-old apprentice in the final match of season 1976-77 and made steady progress, claiming a regular first team place in 1978-79 when he scored 13 goals in 43(2) League and Cup matches. Unspectacular but versatile and accomplished, Paul spent lengthy spells in midfield although regarded mainly as a striker. A key member of the side that won promotion to the First Division in 1980-81, Paul dropped down a Division when joining Derby County in March 1983. Despite a bright start at the Baseball Ground when he scored two goals within the space of his first three appearances, he lost his place in the following season as the Rams were relegated to Division Three.

Appearances: FL: 144(29) apps 30 gls FAC: 6(3) apps 1 gl FLC: 15(1) apps 6 gls Other: 16(3) apps 4 gls
Total: 181(36) apps 41 gls
Honours: (NOTTS) Anglo-Scottish Cup finalists 1981

HOOLEY, A.

Outside-right
CAREER: Stapleford F.C./NOTTS Feb 1892. In Aug 1893 applied for reinstatement as an amateur, and in the following month indicated that he would play again for Stapleford, once reinstatement was granted.
Debut v Burnley (h) 1.3.1892, won 5 – 1 (scored one)

One of seven different outside-rights fielded by the Magpies in season 1891-92, Hooley was the sixth to be tried in the Shrove Tuesday match against Burnley at Trent Bridge. Despite scoring on his debut he was deposed after a further two outings by Albert Widdowson. As the 'Football News' commented: "It does seem strange that it is impossible to find a partner for McInnes who will suit for longer than a couple of matches." Rather more strongly they concluded: "The outside right wing position cannot have cost less than £300 already, and yet for that large expenditure there is not a man for the position that any other Football League club would look at." In the close season Notts' directors moved to solve the problem position when they re-registered Andrew McGregor, who had reached the FA Cup final with the Magpies in 1890-91, scoring 13 League and Cup goals from 28 appearances at outside-right.

Appearances: FL: 3 apps 1 gl Total: 3 apps 1 gl

HOOPER, William George

Outside-right   5' 5"   10st 6lbs
b. Lewisham, 20th February 1884
d. Southport, 3rd September 1952
CAREER: Catford Southend/Army football (RASC)/Grimsby Town Aug 1905/Nottingham Forest Feb 1907/NOTTS Sept 1912/Barrow June 1913/Gillingham May 1914 (Southport Vulcan guest Dec 1916) /Southport 1919-20/Lancaster Town 1920-21.
Debut v Middlesbrough (h) 19.10.12, lost 1 – 3

Small and dashing wingman who began with Grimsby Town in Division Two, making his debut at Barnsley in a 0 – 2 defeat on 30th September 1905. His record of seven goals in 35 League and Cup appearances for the Mariners included a goal against Nottingham Forest in a 3 – 0 victory at the City Ground in December 1906. Obviously impressed, Forest moved to sign him in February of the same season, and in his five years with the Reds he scored 24 League and Cup goals in 153 matches. He made a sensational start to his Forest career. Playing in the final thirteen matches of season 1906-07, he scored against Hull City and Glossop as the Division Two title was secured, with a record of eleven wins and two draws in the final thirteen fixtures. The Magpies were without a victory in the opening nine Division One fixtures in 1912-13 and scored only 28 League goals in the season.

Not surprisingly they were relegated, Billy Hooper's solitary goal for the season coming in the final fixture of a depressing season, a 2 – 5 defeat against Chelsea at Stamford Bridge. After Army service in WW1 he spent the first peacetime season with Southport, and his goal from the penalty spot earned a 1 – 0 victory in the final of the Lancashire Junior Cup against Lancaster Town. A prominent local cricketer, he captained Southport & District representative teams. At the time of his death he was steward of the Churchtown Conservative Club.

Appearances: FL: 16 apps 1 gl FAC: 1 app 0 gls
Total: 17 apps 1 gl
Honours: (Nottingham Forest) FL Div 2 champions 1907. (Southport) Lancashire Junior Cup winners 1920

HOPKINS, George Henry

Goalkeeper   5' 10"   11st 10lbs
b. Sheffield, 11th May 1901
d. Sheffield, July quarter 1974
CAREER: Normanton Springs/Wombwell cs 1923/ Rotherham County May 1924/Normanton Springs 1925/ Newark Town June 1926/NOTTS Jan 1927, fee £200/ Scarborough Aug 1928
Debut v South Shields (h) 15.1.27, won 4 – 1

George Hopkins was recruited immediately after County's crushing 8 – 1 defeat in the FA Cup third round tie against the season's FL champions Newcastle United at St James' Park on 8th January 1927. Six goals down at half time, shell-shocked goalkeeper George Streets was replaced by Hopkins, and the two contested the first team jersey until the arrival of James Ferguson from Brentford in March 1928.

Appearances: FL: 28 apps 0 gls Total: 28 apps 0 gls

HOROBIN, Roy

Inside-forward   5' 7"   10st 10lbs
b. Brownhills, 10th March 1935
CAREER: Erdington Albion/Walsall Wood/West Bromwich Albion am June 1950, pro Oct 1952/NOTTS Nov 1958, fee £4,000/Peterborough United June 1962, fee £3,500/ Crystal Palace July 1964/Weymouth Oct 1965/West Bromwich Albion youth coach Oct 1972; youth development officer 1973-86/Chelsea scout 1987.
Debut v Norwich City (a) 22.11.58, drawn 3 – 3

Roy Horobin was the first signing made by Magpies' manager Frank Hill. The sale of Ron Wylie to Aston Villa in the same month helping to finance a recruiting campaign that subsequently saw Alan Withers (Lincoln City) and Bob Forrest (Leeds United) arriving to strengthen the Meadow Lane ranks.

Despite the new signings, Notts were relegated from Division Three in Horobin's first season, but they made an immediate return as runners-up in Division Four. At inside-forward or as a utility wingman, Roy was brilliantly constructive, and an outstanding ball player by Third Division standards. He scored a hat-trick at Bournemouth in a 3 – 1 win in season 1960-61, this being the only treble in his career. After leaving Meadow Lane he scored 20 goals in 80 League matches for Peterborough United, and wound up his senior career with four appearances for Crystal Palace. His aggregate career figures totalled: 261 League matches and 63 goals.

Appearances: 123 apps 37 gls FAC: 7 apps 0 gls FLC: 2 apps 2 gls Total: 132 apps 39 gls

---o---

HOTEN, Ralph Vincent

Inside-left   5' 8**2**" 11st 2lbs
b. Pinxton, 27th December 1896
d. Wellingborough, 1st February 1978
CAREER: Lady Bay F.C./RAF football/Pinxton Colliery/ NOTTS am Feb 1920/Portsmouth June 1921/Luton Town Mar 1923/Northampton Town Dec 1924/Queens Park Rangers May 1930/Wellingborough coaching appointment.
Debut v Bradford P.A. (a) 14.2.20, won 1 – 0

Said to have acquired much of his skill as a footballer during military service, Ralph Hoten showed excellent form with Notts Reserves but lacked opportunity at senior level. He scored on his final first team appearance for the Magpies, against West Ham United in March 1921, and departed three months later. He was to become a familiar figure in the Southern Section of Division Three for the next ten years, accumulating an exemplary career record of 102 goals in 308 League matches which included 75 goals in 197 matches for Northampton Town. Subsequently, and rather diversely, employed in business as a coffin maker and a coal merchant in Wellingborough.

Appearances: FL: 4 apps 1 gls Total: 4 apps 1 gl
Honours: Southern League representative v Welsh League at Portsmouth 4th October 1922.

---o---

HOUGHTON, Roy

Outside-right   5' 8**2**" 11st 7lbs
b. Billingborough, Lincs. March 1921
CAREER: NOTTS am June 1937, pro Mar 1938 (WW2 guest Wolverhampton Wanderers and Walsall)/Boston United May 1946
Debut v Bournemouth & Boscombe Athletic (a) 26.2.38, drawn 1 – 1

A cousin of W.E. Houghton (right), Roy made rapid progress with the Reserves as an amateur wingman and was signed as a professional on his 17th birthday.

At the commencement of season 1938-39 the wing positions were causing the greatest concern, but in two early season outings, when given an opportunity to challenge for a first team place, Houghton was said to be "Unaccountably slow off the mark." Commencing after the war with Boston United there was speculation, towards the end of his first season, linking him with a possible return to Meadow Lane. This did not materialise, however, and in May 1947 he re-signed for another season with the Stumpites.

Appearances: FL: 8 apps 0 gls Other: 2 apps 0 gls
Total: 10 apps 0 gls

---o---

HOUGHTON, William Eric

Winger   5'8"   12st 7lbs
b. Billingborough, Lincs. 29th June 1910
d. Sutton Coldfield, 1st May 1996
CAREER: Donington Grammar School/Billingborough F.C./ Bourne Town/Boston United/Aston Villa am Aug 1927, pro Aug 1928 (WW2 guest Leicester City, Nottingham Forest, Brentford, NOTTS and Coventry City)/NOTTS Dec 1946; retired May 1949/NOTTS manager May 1949 to Aug 1953/ Aston Villa manager Sept 1953 to Nov 1958/Nottingham Forest head scout July 1959 to Nov 1960/Rugby Town manager Feb 1961 to Mar 1964/Walsall scout 1965, joining that club's board Jan 1966/Aston Villa director Dec 1979/ Walsall general secretary in the early 1980s
Debut v Norwich City (a) 18.1.47, drawn 2 – 2

Eric Houghton joined Aston Villa on the recommendation of his uncle, Cecil Harrison, who had been a full-back with the club. Partnered by Billy Walker, who later went on to manage Forest, his game developed to such an extent that he became known as the hardest dead ball kicker of his time.

In season 1930-31 he hammered home 30 goals from the wing in 41 League matches, as part of a potent attack that scored 128 League goals. Before leaving Villa Park to join the Notts he recorded 170 League and Cup goals in 392 matches. He was 38 years old when he commenced his final season as a player with the Magpies but completed 35 League and Cup matches and scored six goals before hanging up his boots.

In his first season as manager, he guided the team to a season of great success and astronomical attendance figures at Meadow Lane, culminating in promotion as champions of the Third Division South.

Appearances: FL: 55 apps 10 gls FAC: 5 apps 0 gls
Total: 60 apps 10 gls
HONOURS: England International, 7 caps 1931-33. FL Representative, 4 apps. (Aston Villa) FL Div 2 champions 1938

HOULT, Alfred Aubrey
Outside-right   5' 9"   10st 7lbs
b. Whitwick, Leics, 17th July 1915
d. Leicester, 3rd December 1998
CAREER: Oaks Parish Church/NOTTS am Jan 1934, pro May 1934/Northampton Town June 1936/Millwall June 1938
Debut v Bury (h) 27.4.35, lost 1 – 2

Described in the local press as "A young wing forward who promises well", Aubrey Hoult was given his first run in the seniors in the penultimate fixture of relegation season 1934-35. As Notts failed to mount a promotion challenge in the following term, Ernie Steele, a wingman of wider experience, was generally the first choice, with Hoult and the veteran player-coach Sam Haden as back up. A move to Northampton Town featured a very similar appearance record – One Southern Section appearance in his first season and nine in 1937-38. He did not appear at senior level with Millwall.

Appearances: FL: 8 apps 0 gls Other: 1 app 0 gls
Total: 9 apps 0 gls

HOWE, Herbert Alexander 'Bert'
Left-back   5' 10 **2** "   12st 4lbs
b. Rugby, 1st April 1916
d. Rugby, 14th June 1972
CAREER: Braunston/Rugby Town/Leicester City trial Aug 1935/Market Harborough Town Aug 1935/Leicester Nomads Sept 1935/Leicester City Feb 1937 (WW2 guest Northampton Town)/NOTTS July 1947/Rugby Town player-coach 1949/Hinckley Athletic Aug 1953, player-manager Sept 1954
Debut v Ipswich Town (a) 23.8.47, lost 0 – 2

Bert Howe's experience was invaluable to the Magpies youthful League side in 1947-48 when his many sterling performances bolstered a suspect defence. The strong tackling full-back was particularly outstanding on heavy grounds in a season when the Magpies captured the attention of the footballing world by splashing out a club record fee to obtain the signature of England's centre-forward, Tommy Lawton.

In the following term, just prior to Christmas, a defensive re-shuffle saw Purvis, the former Plymouth Argyle defender, introduced at left-back in place of Howe and he held the position for the remainder of the season. Not having worn the senior's colours for the best part of four months, Bert had the cruel misfortune to break his left leg in what proved to be his final League outing, at Swindon Town on 23rd April 1949.

Appearances: FL: 52 apps 0 gls FAC: 7 apps 0 gls
Total: 59 apps 0 gls

HOWELL, Dean George
Midfield/Defender   6' 1"   12st 5lbs
b. Burton-on-Trent, 29th November 1980
CAREER: Stoke City on academy forms/ NOTTS trainee Sept 1997, pro July 1999/Crewe Alexandra July 2000 (Rochdale loan Mar 2001)/Southport June 2001/Morecambe June 2003/Halifax Town during season 2003-04.
Debut as sub v Blackpool (a) 4.3.2000, lost 1 – 2

As a fast raiding, overlapping left full-back or midfielder, Dean failed to establish himself at senior level, his League experience with a trio of clubs amounting to just two starts and three substitute outings. He has, however, enjoyed more regular first team football in subsequent spells with Southport and Morecambe.

Appearances: FL: 0(1) app 0 gls Total: 0(1) app 0 gls

HOYLE, Colin Roy
Defender   5' 11"   12st 3lbs
b. Wirksworth, 15th January 1972
CAREER: Derbyshire Schoolboys/Arsenal trainee, pro Jan 1990 (Chesterfield loan Feb 1990)/Barnsley July 1990/ Bradford City Oct 1992, fee £25,000/NOTTS Aug 1994 (Mansfield Town loan Oct 1994)/Kings Lynn cs 1996/Burton Albion (Nuneaton Borough loan during 2003-04)
Debut v Portsmouth (a) 13.8.94, lost 1 – 2

A free-scoring striker in Derbyshire Schools football, Colin Hoyle was the target for several clubs, including the Magpies. Arsenal was his preferred destination, but he had not progressed beyond reserve level at the time of his free transfer to Barnsley. Similarly, he had not played at League level during his time at Oakwell, but Bradford City paid £25,000 for him in October 1992 and he played in 33 Division Two matches in his first season at Valley Parade. An early season injury, and a change of manager, halted his progress, and he was allowed to leave on a free transfer. In part due to a strong recommendation from his previous manager, Frank Stapleton, he was offered a contract by the Magpies.

Deposed after appearing in the first three matches of 1994-95, he was retained for a further season of reserve team football before being released on a free transfer.

Appearances: FL: 5 apps 0 gls Other: 1 app 0 gls
Total: 6 apps 0 gls

HUBBARD, John

Wing-half   5' 9"   11st 8lbs
b. Wath-on-Dearne, 24th March 1925
d. Rotherham, June 2002
CAREER: NOTTS Feb 1945 to Apr 1948/Scarborough Aug 1949/Scunthorpe United Aug 1950 to 1960
Debut v Bradford City, FAC 1, (h) 17.11.45, drawn 2 – 2 (scored one)

Best remembered for his decade of service to Scunthorpe United, during which time he clocked up 390 appearances and 14 goals. His debut for the Magpies, in the month that he returned home from military service in Germany, was at centre-forward, and his display earned praise from the 'Evening Post' who commented: "Hubbard is the best choice of attack leader so far this season. He possesses the energy the will, and certainly plays well up to the opposing defence. Whole-hearted in the extreme, he is a fine club member, for wherever he is called upon to play, he can be relied upon for 100% effort." Considering his early promise, and subsequent sterling efforts on behalf of Scunthorpe, it was unfortunate that he was allowed to leave Meadow Lane with his potential still unrealised.

Appearances: FL: 13 apps 2 gls FAC: 5 apps 1 gl
Total: 18 apps 3 gls
Honours: (Scunthorpe United) FL Division 3 North champions 1958

HUGHES, Andrew John

Midfield   5' 11"   12st 2lbs
b. Manchester, 2nd January 1978
CAREER: Stockport Schoolboys/Oldham Athletic associate schoolboy Feb 1992, trainee July 1994, pro Jan 1996/NOTTS Jan 1998, fee £150,000/Reading July 2001, fee (set by tribunal) £250,000 plus a further £50,000, based on appearances.
Debut as sub v Mansfield Town (a) 31.1.98, won 2 – 0

Associated with Oldham Athletic for a lengthy spell, Andy was first noted by the Latics in Stockport Boys Under-11s, and was invited to their Centre of Excellence. A member of the Youth Team that reached the quarter-finals of the FA Youth Cup in 1995-96, he made his League debut as a seventeen year-old, but left Boundary Park having played little first team football in 1997-98 under manager Neil Warnock.

A hard-tackling right-sided midfielder with plenty of pace and confidence, Andy was an immediate hit at Meadow Lane, almost instantaneous success coming as the Magpies swept to the Division Three championship. With his contract up at Meadow Lane Andy moved to Reading, but he returned to haunt his former colleagues, scoring within four minutes of the kick-off for The Royals when they visited Meadow Lane on 20th October 2001. Despite winning only once during March and April Reading won promotion to Division One as runners-up to Brighton & Hove Albion. They came close to a further success in 2002-03, finishing in fourth place in Division One, only to lose to the Wolves in the Play-off semi-finals.

Appearances: FL: 85(25) apps 17 gls FAC: 10 apps 2 gls
FLC: 6(1) apps 1 gl Other: 2 apps 0 gls
Total: 103(26) apps 20 gls
Honours: (NOTTS) FL Division 3 champions 1998

HULME, John

Centre-half   6' 0**2**"12st 1lb
b. Mobberley, 6th February 1945
CAREER: Stockport Schoolboys/Cheshire County Schoolboys/Bolton Wanderers app, signing pro Feb 1962 (NOTTS loan Mar 1972)/Reading July 1972, player-coach Mar 1974, fee £7,000/Bury July 1974, fee £6,500/Chaux-de-Fonds, Switzerland, player-manager 1976.
Debut v Plymouth Argyle (a) 11.3.72, drawn 1 – 1

John Hulme made his Bolton Wanderers debut, at seventeen years of age, in the First Division on 27th October 1962 when Bolton beat Forest by 1 – 0 at Burden Park. Some ten years later he arrived at Meadow Lane on loan. With over 200 League and Cup matches under his belt, he was available for a permanent move at a fee of £12,000. The Magpies were without David Needham and Bill Brindley for the entire Easter programme and Hulme's loan spell proved invaluable, but personal terms could not be agreed to keep him at Meadow Lane. He eventually joined Reading, then managed by former Bolton teammate Charlie Hurley, and concluded his League career with two seasons as Bury's captain. John married a French girl and was bilingual, which doubtless proved an asset in his role of player-manager at Chaux-de-Fonds.

Appearances: FL: 8 apps 0 gls Total: 8 apps 0 gls

HUMPHREYS, Percy

Inside-right   5' 7"   12st 4lbs
b. Cambridge, 3rd December 1880
d. Stepney, 13th April 1959
CAREER: Cambridge St Mary's/Queens Park Rangers May 1900/NOTTS May 1901/Leicester Fosse June 1907, fee £600/Chelsea Feb 1908, fee £350/Tottenham Hotspur Dec 1909/Leicester Fosse Oct 1911, fee £500/Hartlepools United player-manager circa 1912/Norwich City Nov 1914
Debut v Sheffield Wednesday (h) 14.9.01, won 6 – 1 (scored one)

Percy Humphreys was an extremely versatile footballer. During his lengthy spell with the Magpies he played in all forward positions apart from outside-left and was successfully fielded at centre-half for lengthy spells in 1904-05. A tricky, well-built forward, he was a fine dribbler who scored his fair share of goals. His outstanding season of 1902-03 (16 goals in 37 League and Cup matches) won him the ultimate honour of representing England against Scotland at Sheffield on 4th April 1903. In his first spell with Leicester Fosse he scored 19 goals in 26 Division Two matches, setting the Fossils up for their first promotion, before moving to Chelsea in February of the same season. Ironically, in season 1909-10, and following his transfer to Tottenham Hotspur, he was instrumental in condemning his former team to relegation. In the season's final game Chelsea were the visitors to White Hart Lane and to be safe from relegation Spurs had to win. Goals from Minter and Humphreys gave Spurs the points in a 2 – 1 win that effectively relegated Chelsea from Division One.

Appearances: FL: 189 apps 66 gls FAC: 13 apps 7 gls
Total: 202 apps 73 gls
Honours: England International, 1 cap 1903. FL Representative, 1 app.

———————○———————

HUNT, David

Midfield   5' 11"   11st 0lbs
b. Leicester, 17th April 1959
CAREER: Derby County app 1975, pro May 1977/NOTTS Mar 1978, fee £40,000/Aston Villa July 1987/Mansfield Town June 1989/Burton Albion Aug 1991/Leicester United Sept 1991
Debut v Charlton Athletic (a) 17.3.78, drawn 0 – 0

Among the very best of Jimmy Sirrel's signings, David Hunt was still a teenager and had played only five times for Derby County when the Magpies' boss invested £40,000 to bring him to Meadow Lane. He proved to be excellent value, completing a little over 400 matches, including an ever-present record in the 1980-81 promotion season.

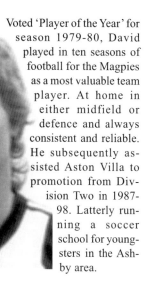

Voted 'Player of the Year' for season 1979-80, David played in ten seasons of football for the Magpies as a most valuable team player. At home in either midfield or defence and always consistent and reliable. He subsequently assisted Aston Villa to promotion from Division Two in 1987-98. Latterly running a soccer school for youngsters in the Ashby area.

Appearances: FL: 331(5) apps 28 gls FAC: 21(1) apps 2 gls FLC: 28(1) apps 5 gls Other: 21 apps 2 gls
Total: 401(7) apps 37 gls
Honours: (NOTTS) Anglo Scottish Cup finalists 1981

———————○———————

HUNT, James Malcolm

Midfield   5' 8"   10st 3lbs
b. Derby, 17th December 1976
CAREER: NOTTS associate schoolboy May 1992, trainee July 1993, pro July 1994/Northampton Town Aug 1997/Oxford United July 2002
Debut as sub v Chesterfield, Auto Windscreens Shield, (a) 17.10.95, lost 1 – 2

Fair-haired midfielder James Hunt made a dream start in League football when he volleyed a stunning goal on his debut against Bournemouth at Dean Court on 27th February 1996. It appeared that the skilful youngster had finally made a break through when he enjoyed a nine game consecutive run as the Magpies pushed on to a Play-off place. Earlier in the season he had struggled to find a place in the reserve team, due to the number of midfield players on the club's books. As the Magpies promotion push ended in disappointment at Wembley against Bradford City, so did James Hunt's, as he failed to build on his promising start and was released on a free transfer in the summer of 1997. After five years with Northampton Town, for whom he made 150(22) League appearances and eight goals, he joined Oxford United, reuniting with former Cobblers' manager, Ian Atkins.

Appearances: FL: 15(4) apps 1 gl FAC: 0(1) app 0gls Other: 2(2) apps 1 gl Total: 17(7) apps 2 gls

———————○———————

HURST, Glynn

Forward 5'10" 11st 10lbs
b. Barnsley, 17th January 1976
CAREER: Tottenham Hotspur trainee/Barnsley July 1994
(Swansea City loan Dec 1995) (Mansfield Town loan Nov
1996)/Emley F.C./Ayr United Mar 1989, fee £150,000/
Stockport County Feb 2001, fee £150,000/Chesterfield Dec
2001/NOTTS July 2004
Debut v Chester City (h) 7.8.04, drawn 1 – 1

Initially spotted
by Tottenham
Hotspur in South
Africa, where he
had starred as
leading scorer in a
national U-16
competition,
Glynn was in-
vited for trials
and secured an
apprenticeship at
White Hart Lane.
His League debut,
however, came
with his home
town team Barns-
ley, and his first
senior goal was
scored for Swansea City against Burnley in December
1995. His career gathered momentum following his move
to Scotland, his 51 Scottish League and Cup goals for Ayr
United coming in just 84 matches. He had scored 17
goals in 19 games in 2001-02 (including five in one match
at Morton in January,) when he returned to the English
First Division with Stockport County. He subsequently
dropped down a division when he joined Notts from
Chesterfield, and despite ending his first season at
Meadow Lane as leading scorer, the hard working striker
has at times struggled to convert chances into goals.
Notable exceptions during the campaign being his hat-
trick at Rochdale, contained within an early season
productive run of eight goals in as many matches.

Appearances: FL: 36(4) apps 14 gls FAC: 2(1) apps 0 gls
FLC: 2 apps 0 gls Other: 1 app 1gl Total: 41(5) apps 15 gls

INNES, Robert

Right-half   5' 9½" 11st 12lbs
b. Lanark, 23rd July 1878
d. Swindon, 3rd March 1959
CAREER: Royal Ordnance Factories Oct 1895/Gravesend
United May 1896/New Brompton May 1898/NOTTS May
1901/Nottingham Forest Sept 1903/Brighton & Hove
Albion May 1905/Swindon Town June 1906; retired 1909
Debut v Derby County (a) 7.9.01, lost 0 – 2

Having crossed the border to find work, Bob Innes
commenced his football career in the Royal Ordnance
Factories Southern League side. In the same competition
he also assisted Gravesend United and New Brompton
before stepping up to Division One as a professional
with the Magpies. After appearing regularly for two
seasons as a hard working wing half with typical Scottish
style and craft in his play, he crossed the Trent to join
Forest, departing after just 23 League outings in two
seasons. His career ended back in Southern League
football, his final three appearances coming in season
1908-09 when Swindon Town were runners-up to
Northampton Town for the championship.

Appearances: FL: 48 apps 0 gls FAC: 3 apps 0 gls
Total: 51 apps 0 gls
Honours: Southern League representative, 1 app 1899

IRELAND, Craig

Central defender   6' 3"   13st 9lbs
b. Dundee, 29th November 1975
CAREER: Aberdeen pro Oct 1994/Dunfermline Athletic
Feb 1996/Dundee Oct 1999 /Airdrieonians, initially on loan
Oct 2000, fee £50,000 (NOTTS loan Feb 2001)/NOTTS July
2001, fee £50,000/Barnsley Aug 2003/Peterborough United
Aug 2004 (Bristol City loan Jan 2005)/Falkirk June 2005
Debut v Oldham Athletic (h) 3.2.2001, won 1 – 0

Injuries to Mark Warren and Ian Richardson led to the
recruitment of Craig Ireland, a tall central defender who
was also capable of filling the left-back role. A dogged and
relentless tackler with a good left foot and very effective
in the air, Craig had played previously under Magpies
manager Jocky Scott, when they were together at Dundee.
His initial loan spell was impressive enough to win him a
permanent move, and he formed an effective partnership
with Nick Fenton in the centre of Notts defence.

Appearances: FL: 77(3) apps 2 gls FAC: 1 app 0 gls
FLC: 2 apps 0 gls Total: 80(3) apps 2 gls

IREMONGER, Albert

Goalkeeper   6' 5½" 13st 6lbs
b. Wilford, Notts, 15th June 1884
d. Nottingham, 9th March 1958
CAREER: Notts Jardines/Nottingham Forest trial Mar 1903/
NOTTS am Apr 1904, pro Feb 1905 (WW1 guest
Nottingham Forest, Hull City and Leeds City)/Lincoln City
May 1926; retired cs 1927/Appointed NOTTS chief scout
in Nov 1946.
Debut v Sheffield Wednesday (a) 1.4.05, lost 0 – 1

The Magpies record appearance holder by many a mile,
who at one stage of his remarkable career recorded a total
of 222 consecutive League and Cup games, only ended
by suspension in October 1912.

In the days when six footers were a rarity, Albert at 6' 51/2" in his socks was a veritable giant in both height and playing ability. Thanks to his exceptional reach he made the most difficult saves look simple, and in clearing his lines he could throw the ball further than most men could kick it. Said to be a quiet,

unassuming fellow off the field, he was anything but when on it. His total commitment to the cause often landing him in hot water with referees and his own board of directors. A board minute from 1923 instructing: "Secretary to inform Iremonger not to leave his goal to argue with referee or linesman." An earlier story was that he once chased Hampton, Aston Villa's centre-forward, half the length of the field, aimed a terrific kick at his backside, then turned and raced away. Albert played in county cricket for Nottinghamshire, as did his brother James, who also played football for Forest. Albert served in the Footballer's Battalion in the Great War, and outside of the game was employed as a lace machine builder. Once described as "A goalkeeper in a thousand," there was never a more popular Magpie, despite his fabled shortcomings, and his name is immortalised in Nottingham with Iremonger road, adjacent to County's ground at Meadow Lane.

Appearances: FL: 564 apps 0 gls FAC: 37 apps 0 gls
Total: 601 apps 0 gls
Honours: FL Representative, 2 apps 1911-12. (NOTTS)
FL Div 2 champions 1914 and 1923

———————o———————

JACKSON, Craig
Central defender   6' 0"   12st 1lb
b. Renishaw, Derbys, 17th January 1969
CAREER: NOTTS trainee, signing pro Aug 1986, released Oct 1988
Debut as sub v Darlington (h) 6.5.86, won 5 – 0

Aside from his debut match above, three starting appearances and one as substitute during season 1986-87 was Craig Jackson's first real taste of senior football, but increasing competition denied him any further opportunities at League level.

Although the management thought his decision to retire from professional football at the age of nineteen was premature, Craig was released from his contract and took up a new career as a policeman.

Appearances: FL: 3(2) apps 0 gls FLC: 0(1) apps 0 gls
Total: 3(3) apps 0 gls

———————o———————

JACKSON, Harry
Centre-forward
b. Nottingham, 23rd April 1864
CAREER: Sneinton Wanderers/NOTTS debut Mar 1884/ Nottingham Forest debut Mar 1890
Debut v Notts Olympic, FAC 1, (h) 8.11.1884, won 2 – 0

A prolific goal scorer in Notts non-League years, with just six short of 100 goals in 123 recorded appearances, Harry Jackson was rightly dubbed "A goal scoring wizard." In FA Cup matches alone his total of 19 exceeded by some margin Tommy Lawton's 13 in the same competition, but when Notts became a Football League club in 1888-89 his star was on the wane. He was one of several locally born players who were allowed to move on as the Magpies strengthened their ranks with an influx of top-class Scottish players. Jackson was one of a number of the discarded men who joined up with the Forest, but he played only once for the Reds, and this in a 0 – 9 defeat at Darwen.

Appearances: FL 5 apps 3 gls FAC 21 apps 19 gls
Total: 26 apps 22 gls

———————o———————

JACKSON, James
Inside-forward 5' 82" 11st 7lbs
b. Glasgow, 26th March 1931
CAREER: Trent Bridge School/Robin Hood F.C./Mapperley Celtic/NOTTS am 1944, signing pro Mar 1949/Canadian football (Toronto)/NOTTS again Dec 1954/Headington United July 1958/Sutton Town/Arnold St Mary's Aug 1960.
Debut v Bristol City (h) 16.4.49, won 2 – 1

A Scot who moved to Nottingham at five years of age, Jimmy Jackson was only 13 when he first interested Notts' then manager, Major Buckley. In his first senior appearance in a Third Division South match he was injured after just two minutes, and was unable to continue. Despite the unfortunate start, military service with the R.A.F. continued his football education, and in his third FL match he scored four goals against Everton in a 5 – 1 victory at Goodison Park in October 1951. (Incidentally, the last Notts forward to score four in an away game was Arthur Davis, against Barnsley in a 4 – 4 draw at Oakwell in October 1926.)

Returning to Meadow Lane after a spell in Canada midway through season 1954-55 he scored 17 League goals in just 20 matches, his haul including four against West Ham United on New Years' Day 1955.

Appearances: FL: 113 apps 47 gls FAC: 10 apps 3 gls
Total: 123 apps 50 gls

JACKSON, Justin Jonathan
Forward   6' 0"   11st 6lbs
b. Nottingham, 10th December 1974
CAREER: Everton (trial)/Bolton Wanderers trainee/ Lancaster City/Ayr United July 1994/Penrith cs 1995/ Ilkeston Town Oct 1995/Morecambe Feb 1996/ Woking Jan 1997, fee £30,000/NOTTS Sept 1997, fee £30,000 (Morecambe loan Oct 1998) (Rotherham United loan Jan 1999)/Halifax Town Feb 1999, fee £30,000/Morecambe Aug 1999/Rushden & Diamonds June 2000, fee £180,000/ Doncaster Rovers Sept 2001, fee £120,000/Accrington Stanley Oct to Dec 2003
Debut as sub v Darlington (h) 4.10.97, drawn 1 – 1

A proven goal scorer in non-League and Scottish football, Justin took some time to adjust to the requirements of League football after joining the Magpies. He appeared to have bridged the gap during the run in to the Third Division championship, appearing in the final nine matches, three in the starting line up. A striker whose main asset was his blistering turn of pace, he nevertheless failed to maintain his improved form in 1998-99, two loan spells preceding a return to non-League football. Subsequent highlights included his contribution of 18 goals in Rushton & Diamonds Conference championship in 2000-01, and Doncaster Rovers promotion from the Conference in 2002-03.

Appearances: FL: 7(18) apps 1 gl FAC: 3(2) apps 0 gls
Other: 2 apps 0 gls Total: 12(20) apps 1 gl
Honours: England semi-professional International, 2 caps. (Woking) FA Trophy winners 1997. (NOTTS) FL Division Three champions 1998. (Rushden & Diamonds) Nationwide Conference champions 2001

JACOBSEN, Anders
Central defender   6' 3"   13st 7lbs
b. Norway, 18th April 1968
CAREER: IK Start (Norway)/Sheffield United Dec 1998/ Stoke City Aug 1999/NOTTS Sept 2000/Skeid Oslo (Norway) July 2001
Debut as sub v Walsall (a) 30.9.2000, lost 1 – 5

A late comer to English League football, the former captain of IK Start actually made his debut for Sheffield United against the Magpies, as a late substitute in the FA Cup third round in 1999.

His contract up at the end of the season he joined Stoke City where an injury curtailed his season, although he appeared in 33(4) League and Cup matches and scored two goals. He was an unused substitute at Wembley when the Potters won the Auto Windscreens Shield in April 2000. Aside from a spell on the sidelines in March and early April, Anders was a fixture in the heart of the Magpies' defence in a season when they reached eighth place in Division Two. Released in the summer he returned to Norway.

Appearances: FL: 27(2) apps 2 gls FAC: 5 apps 0 gls
Total: 32(2) apps 2 gls

JAKEMAN, George William
Half-back   5' 9"   11st 10lbs
b. Small Heath, Birmingham, 19th May 1903
d. Birmingham, 19th May 1973
CAREER: Yardley Road School, Birmingham/Small Heath Boys' Club/Wolseley Motor Works/Metropolitan Carriage Works/Aston Villa am, signing pro May 1922/NOTTS Aug 1929, fee £1,350/Kidderminster Harriers Aug 1933/Cradley Heath Aug 1935/Rugby School assistant coach
Debut v Bristol City (a) 31.8.29, won 3 – 1

Came into prominence in the football world as a schoolboy international, representing England against Scotland in 1917. He joined Villa as a centre-forward but subsequently occupied most outfield positions. His Magpies career began at right full-back and started exceptionally well, but in October a cartilage injury kept him out of the side for the remainder of the season. The term ended in relegation from Division Two, but in the promotion season that immediately followed George appeared in all three half-positions during the course of his 12 League outings. He was more regularly seen during 1931-32, the majority of his 30 League outings being made at right-half. In what proved to be his final season, he lost his place to Joe Smith, the former Barnsley player. A talented cricketer, he played for Warwickshire Second X1.

Appearances: FL: 70 apps 0 gls FAC: 1 app 0 gls
Total: 71 apps 0 gls
Honours: England Schoolboy International, 1 cap 1917

JAMES, Lancelot
Full-back   5' 8"   11st 4lbs
b. Nottingham, 11th January 1890
d. Loughborough, July quarter 1983
CAREER: NOTTS Sept 1909 to 1914
Debut v Bradford City (a) 17.4.11, won 1 – 0

A full-back pairing of Morley and West was very much the norm during Lance James' four seasons at Meadow Lane. In the run-in to promotion from Division Two in season 1913-14 he played in three out of the last four matches, two wins and a draw ensuring a return to the top flight. Lance hailed from a sporting family and played cricket for Nottinghamshire Club & Ground. His elder brother, Charles Cecil, played in County cricket for Nottinghamshire (20 matches between 1906-21).

Appearances: FL: 6 apps 0 gls Total: 6 apps 0 gls

JAMES, Wilfred Bernard
Inside-forward   5' 7"   11st 2lbs
b. Cross Keys, Monmouthshire, June 1904
d. Cross Keys, Monmouthshire, November 1996, age 92
CAREER: Cross Keys School/Abercarn Welfare/Ynysddu Crusaders/Newport County Oct 1925/Thorne Colliery cs 1927/Owston Park Rangers 1927/NOTTS Oct 1928, fee £50/West Ham United May 1930, fee £250/Charlton Athletic Feb 1932, fee £600/Workington Nov 1933/Carlisle United Sept 1935 to April 1937
Debut v Wolverhampton Wanderers (h) 1.4.29, won 3 – 0 (scored one)

Wilf had to wait until towards the end of the season before being given an opportunity in the first team. He immediately made a name for himself, scoring three goals in six matches. Despite the promising start, he spent much of the following season as understudy to Harry Andrews. His move to West Ham United proved beneficial, as his excellent distributive work caught the eye of the Wales selectors, who awarded him two caps – both against Ireland – in April and December 1931. Two seasons with Charlton Athletic preceded a move north, his League career winding up with Carlisle United. Wilf's career aggregate figures were 142 League matches and 23 goals.

Appearances: FL: 16 apps 5 gls Total: 16 apps 5 gls
Honours: Wales International, 2 caps 1931-32

JARDINE, Robert J "Bobby"
Forward
b. Glasgow
d. Nottingham, 30th July 1941
CAREER: Halliwell F.C./NOTTS cs 1888/Heanor Town June 1889/Derby County Oct 1889/Nottingham Forest 1889/Heanor Town/Sheffield United/Mellors United
Debut v Everton (a) 15.9.1888, lost 1 – 2

From the unlikely position of outside-left Bobby Jardine scored five of the Magpies goals in the 6 – 1 win against Burnley on 27th October 1888. Sadly, his goals dried up

afterwards although his season's total of nine from 18 matches was sufficient to make him leading scorer in Notts first season as a Football League club. On 11th December 1937 the 'Football Post' recalled his feat when reporting that he had been a spectator at Meadow Lane for the match against Northampton Town. The first Scottish player to be engaged as a professional by a Nottingham club, he enjoyed a lengthy association with the Forest. When his days of activity in the red jersey ended he was employed at the ground as a steward over a very long period.

Appearances: FL: 18 apps 9 gls Total: 18 apps 9 gls

JARVIS, Harry
Wing-half   5' 8½"   11st 7lbs
b. Maltby, 8th October 1928
CAREER: Worksop Town/NOTTS May 1951/Nottingham Forest circa 1955 (no FL apps)
Debut v Rotherham United (a) 1.9.52, won 3 – 2

Described as: "A wholehearted player, showing plenty of promise," Harry spent a season in reserve before making his first League appearance at Rotherham. As understudy to Tommy Johnston, who had first moved back into the middle line in season 1952-53, he was restricted to five League outings. In the following season he had an extended run in the seniors until the signing of Ray Chatham from Wolves; the first signing by new team manager, Mr George Poyser. Harry Jarvis linked up with Forest after leaving Meadow Lane, but did not appear at senior level with the Reds.

Appearances: FL: 29 apps 0 gls FAC: 1 app 0 gls
Total: 30 apps 0 gls

JAYES, Alfred Gordon
Forward   5' 9"   11st 7lbs
b. Leicester, 26th September 1923
d. Leicester, 26th March 1997
CAREER: Leicester Schoolboys/ Leicester City am June 1938/Landsdowne Institute/Nuneaton Borough/NOTTS am Oct 1946 to Apr 1948/Nuneaton Borough/Hinckley Athletic Jan 1951/Barwell 1952
Debut v Brighton & Hove Albion (a) 12.10.46, lost 2 – 3

Gordon Jayes represented England Schoolboys against Northern Ireland in consecutive seasons and made his Leicester City debut at the age of 16 years and 46 days during wartime season 1939-40. He subsequently served as an Army P.T.I. before joining Notts on amateur forms in the early stages of season 1946-47. The 'Football Post', reporting on his debut, stated:

"Jayes is the best centre-forward Notts have had on view all season. He knows how to keep the attack together, and with accurate ball control possesses all the essentials for a successful leader."

Appearances: FL: 27 apps 7 gls FAC: 3 apps 1 gl
Total: 30 apps 8 gls
Honours: England Schoolboy International, 2 caps 1937-38

JEMSON, Nigel Bradley

Forward   5' 10"   12st 0lbs
b. Hutton, Lancs, 10th August 1969
CAREER: Preston North End trainee, signing pro July 1987/ Nottingham Forest Mar 1988, fee £150,000 (Bolton Wanderers loan Dec 1988) (Preston North End loan Mar 1989)/Sheffield Wednesday Sept 1991, fee £800,000 (Grimsby Town loan Sept 1993)/NOTTS Sept 1994, fee £300,000 (Watford loan Jan 1995) (Rotherham United loan Feb 1996)/Oxford United July 1996, fee £60,000/Bury Feb 1998, fee £100,000/Ayr United July 1999/Oxford United Jan 2000/Shrewsbury Town July 2000/Lincoln City trial July 2003/Bristol Rovers trial Sept 2003/Ballymena Oct 2003/Ilkeston Town Aug 2004.
Debut v Bristol City (a) 10.9.94, lost 1 – 2 (scored)

Appearances for eleven different English League clubs, plus one each in Scotland and Ireland, places Nigel very firmly amongst the ranks of football's happy wanderers. At the ripe old footballing age of 35 he continues to enjoy his football with Ilkeston United, bringing experience and quality to Phil Stant's side. Highlights of his long career include his Wembley winner for Forest against Oldham Athletic in the FL Cup Final of 1990, and both of Rotherham United's goals in their 2 – 1 victory in the Auto Windscreens Shield Final at Wembley in April 1996. More recently, his two goals for Shrewsbury Town knocked Everton out of the FA Cup in January 2003. Ironically, despite scoring 17 goals in all competitions for relegated Shrewsbury Town in the same season, he was unable to secure another engagement at League level.

Appearances: FL: 7(7) apps 1 gl FLC: 2(2) apps 1 gl
Other: 1 app 0 gls Total: 10(9) apps 2 gls
Honours: England U-21 International, 1 app 1991. (Nottingham Forest) FL Cup winners 1990. (Rotherham United) Auto Windscreens Shield winners 1996

JENKINS, Stephen Robert 'Steve'

Defender   5' 11"   12st 3lbs
b. Merthyr Tydfil, 16th July 1972
CAREER: Swansea City trainee June 1998, pro July 1990/ Huddersfield Town Nov 1995, fee £275,000 (Birmingham City loan Dec 2000)/Cardiff City Feb 2003/NOTTS Aug 2003/Peterborough United Jan 2004 (Swindon Town loan Oct 2004)/Swindon Town Dec 2004.
Debut v Bristol City (a) 9.8.2003, lost 0 – 5

A vastly experienced international full-back who was installed as captain on arrival at Meadow Lane. An early victim of the team's dreadful start to the season, he had re-established himself at the time of a rather abrupt departure in mid season. His move to Peterborough United was followed within a week by Clive Platt's transfer to the Posh, both players having been on monthly deals at Meadow Lane due to the club being in administration. Despite Steve Jenkins' brief stay, he passed the milestone of 500 League and Cup appearances during his spell with County.

Appearances: FL: 17 apps 0 gls FAC: 2 apps 0 gls FLC: 3 apps 0 gls Other: 1 app 0 gls Total: 23 apps 0 gls
Honours: Wales International, 16 caps 1996-2002. Wales U-21 International, 2 apps 1993. Wales Schoolboy and Youth International. (Swansea City) Autoglass Trophy winners 1994

JENNINGS, William 'Bill'

Centre-half   6' 0"   12st 0lbs
b. Cinderhill, Nottingham, 25th February 1891
d. Luton, 2nd March 1953
CAREER: Rigby Athletic/Arnold St Mary's/NOTTS Jan 1913/Army football (RGA)/NOTTS May 1918/Norwich City May 1919/Merthyr Town June 1920/Luton Town June 1922/Northampton Town Oct 1926/Peterborough & Fletton United Dec 1926/Hearts of Winnipeg Feb 1929.
Debut v Clapton Orient (a) 4.10.13, lost 0 – 1

Two serious injuries to Arthur Clamp in season 1913-14 provided the opening for Bill Jennings who understudied most effectively in 20 matches, collecting a Division Two championship medal in his debut season. Described as: "Young, vigorous, of splendid stamina, and with a good knowledge of the game," he shared the centre-half berth with Clamp in the Division One season that followed. The outbreak of hostilities suspended League football in 1915 and, after four years of army service, Bill joined his elder brother Sam for a season with Norwich City. He went on to complete a career total of 227 League and Southern League matches and scored seven goals. His son, Henry William, later played for Northampton Town, Ipswich Town and Rochdale.

Appearances: FL: 42 apps 0 gls FAC: 1 app 0 gls
Total: 43 apps 0 gls
Honours: (NOTTS) FL Div 2 champions 1914

JESSOP, E

Winger
CAREER: NOTTS Dec 1877 to Feb 1884
Debut v Sheffield, FAC 1 replay, (a) 1.12.1877, lost 0 – 3

Aside from season 1879-80 when he was the only player to feature in all friendly and cup matches, E. Jessop was an infrequent member of the side, despite his lengthy association with the club. The 1901 Census lists one E. Jessop, age 40 and a dentist born at Cheltenham. Traced in birth records as Ernest Charles Hall Jessop, born in the July quarter of 1860. At the time of writing, it has not been possible to positively confirm that the dentist was also the footballer!

Appearances: FAC: 2 apps 0 gls Total: 2 apps 0 gls

JESSOP, Henry John

Left-back or Goalkeeper
b. Exeter, October quarter 1858
d. Margate, 24th May 1914
CAREER: NOTTS Jan 1875 to Feb 1884
Debut v Sheffield, FAC 1, (h) 3.11.1877, drawn 1 – 1

In a nine-year association with the Magpies, versatile Henry Jessop appeared mainly on the left side of defence, but in season 1881-82 he succeeded Harold Greenhalgh and was the team's regular custodian until the advent of Mordecai Sherwin in 1883-84. At one time a director of a brewery, he was mine host at the White Hart Hotel in Margate at the time of his death.

Appearances: FAC: 11 apps 0 gls Total: 11 apps 0 gls

JOHNSON, Frank

Right-back
CAREER: NOTTS Jan 1885
Debut v Walsall Town Swifts, FAC 4 (a) 24.1.1885, won 4 – 1

The Magpies made good progress in the FA Cup competition of 1884-85, accounting for Notts Olympic, Staveley, Sheffield and Walsall Town Swifts. They enjoyed a bye in round five before being drawn against the crack Scottish amateurs, Queen's Park. The game attracted a crowd of around 17,000 to the Trent Bridge ground, which was the largest ever gathering of spectators to witness a Notts match at that time. The game ended in a 2 – 2 draw, and the replay, staged one week later at the Derby Cricket Ground, ended in defeat by 2 – 1. Queen's Park went on to defeat Forest in the semi-final, but were beaten 2 – 0 by Blackburn Rovers in the final. Frank Johnson made his solitary appearance for the Magpies in the fourth round match at Walsall, as deputy for regular right-back, Alfred Dobson.

Appearances: FAC: 1 app 0 gls Total: 1 app 0 gls

JOHNSON, Joseph

Full-back   5' 9"   12st 4lbs
b. Stamford
CAREER: Stamford Town/Mansfield Mechanics (WW1 guest Nottingham Forest and NOTTS)/NOTTS Aug 1919/ Watford May 1920/Luton Town June 1924, fee £75; retired due to injury 1925
Debut v Burnley (h) 30.8.19, won 2 – 0

Joe Johnson was first associated with the Magpies during wartime season 1915-16, his first outing coming on Christmas Day 1915 in a 1 – 2 home defeat against Leicester Fosse. When normal League football resumed in August 1919 he was first choice left-back in the opening three fixtures but then was replaced by Frank Marriott. Thereafter a useful reserve, Joe was called upon to fill in at right-back and inside-left before the end of the season. He enjoyed a more settled and productive spell with Watford (94 League matches and one goal), but shortly after moving to Luton Town he received a leg injury in a reserve-team match. He was unable to play again, and received £300 compensation. His birth and death details have proved elusive, but it is known that he had died prior to July 1948, as his widow received Benevolent Fund monies from the FA at this time.

Appearances: FL: 10 apps 0 gls Total: 10 apps 0 gls

JOHNSON, Michael Owen

Central defender   5' 11"   11st 12lbs
b. Clifton, Nottingham, 4th July 1973
CAREER: Clifton All Whites/Nottingham Schoolboys/ NOTTS trainee July 1989, pro July 1991/Birmingham City Sept 1995, fee £225,000/Derby County Aug 2003
Debut v Sheffield United, Zenith Data Systems Cup round 2 (a) 22.10.91, drawn 3 – 3 and won a.e.t. on penalties by 2 – 1

A catalogue of injuries in 1990-91, as the Magpies attempted to come to terms with life in the top flight, had something of a silver lining. The selection crisis providing the opportunity for 18 year-old Michael Johnson – Youth Team 'Player of the Year' in season 1990-91 - to stake his initial claim for a place at senior level. After winning high praise for his classy display in the ZDS Cup against Sheffield United, four days later he was facing Ian Wright at Highbury. Despite injury to Dean Yates during the match, the makeshift pairing of Michael and Gary Lund did exceptionally well, although Arsenal won the match 2 – 0. Despite his increasingly assured defensive displays, the Magpies suffered two relegations during his time at Meadow Lane. By contrast, his eight-year stay at St. Andrews saw Birmingham City runners-up for the FL Cup and Division One promotion winners, via a Wembley Play-off Final, in 2002.

Appearances: FL: 102(5) apps 0 gls FAC: 4 apps 0 gls FLC: 9 apps 0 gls Other: 15(1) apps 0 gls
Total: 130(6) apps 0 gls
HONOURS: Jamaica International, 14 caps. (NOTTS) Anglo-Italian Cup winners 1995, finalists 1994. (Birmingham City) FL Cup finalists 2001

JOHNSON, Thomas

Forward 5' 10" 10st 0lbs
b. Newcastle-upon-Tyne, 15th January 1971
CAREER: NOTTS associate schoolboy July 1986, trainee July 1987, pro Jan 1989/Derby County loan and permanent Mar 1992, fee £1.3million/Aston Villa Jan 1995, fee £1.45million/Celtic Mar 1997, fee £2.4million (Everton loan Sept 1999)/Sheffield Wednesday Sept 2001/Kilmarnock Dec 2001/Gillingham Aug 2002 to Jan 2005.
Debut as sub v Preston North End (h) 24.9.88, drawn 0 – 0

Despite his youth and relative inexperience, flame-haired Tommy Johnson scored 41 goals in his first two full seasons. His contribution to two successive promotions, when he was a scorer in both Wembley Play-off Finals, can hardly be over-stated. Raw pace and a desire to shoot from any angle when given a sight of goal marked him as an outstanding prospect, despite his lightweight frame and initial lack of stamina. Given his ratio of goals against appearances, early speculation surrounded the possibility of his mounting a challenge for the title of all-time club leading scorer. Sadly, the economics of the situation precluded any possibility of his remaining at Meadow Lane long enough to overhaul Les Bradd's record, a £1.3 million bid from Derby County being the first of a series of transfers involving astronomical fees. With over 140 League and Cup goals in English and Scottish football, Tommy, at 33 years of age, was linked with a possible return to Meadow Lane from Gillingham in January 2004. No deal was struck, however, despite the feeling that he might have provided the goals to turn around the relegation season.

Appearances: FL: 100(18) apps 47 gls FAC: 3(2) apps 1 gl FLC: 7(2) apps 5 gls Other: 15(2) apps 4 gls
Total: 125(24) apps 57 gls
Honours: England U-21 International, 7 apps. (Aston Villa) FL Cup winners 1996. (Celtic) SPL winners 2001; SL Cup winners 2000; SC winners 2001, finalists 1999

JOHNSTON, Thomas Deans

Outside-left/Left-half 5' 9" 11st 4lbs
b. Berwick-on-Tweed, 30th December 1918
d. Nottingham, 27th November 1994
CAREER: Berwickshire High School, Duns/ Peterborough United 1939/Nottingham Forest May 1944/NOTTS Aug 1948, fee £8,500/Birmingham City coach Sept 1957/ Heanor Town player-manager July 1958/Rotherham United manager Nov 1958/Grimsby Town manager July 1962/ Huddersfield Town manager Oct 1964 to May 1968/York City manager Oct 1968/Huddersfield Town general manager and manager Jan 1975 to Aug 1978
Debut v Torquay United (a) 21.8.48, lost 1 – 3

A speedy and opportunist wingman who, although a Scot, played all of his football with English clubs. He was playing for Berwickshire High School when Peterborough United's manager Sam Haden (q.v.) moved in swiftly to

sign him. The war broke out soon afterwards but Tom remained in the Midlands. He crossed the Trent from Forest in August 1948 and had an outstanding first season, scoring 26 League and Cup goals – all from outside-left – in 45 matches. His total including successive hat-tricks against Crystal Palace and Watford in February 1949. He scored a further 17 goals in the championship season that followed, displaying the form that had earlier brought him the honour of being Scotland's reserve in international matches. In later seasons he developed as a fine left half-back, but it was in his favoured number eleven jersey that he made his final appearance against Grimsby Town at Meadow Lane on 22nd December 1956, just eight days away from his 38th birthday. Tom scored 26 goals in 69 matches for Forest, and had the distinction of recording 100 goals in post - war football during season 1953-54. A qualified FA coach who spent several of his summers working in Finland, he joined the coaching staff at Birmingham City on leaving Meadow Lane.

Appearances: FL: 267 apps 88 gls FAC: 19 apps 4 gls
Total: 286 apps 92 gls
Honours: (NOTTS) FL Div 3 South champions 1950

JONES, Aaron
Inside-forward   5' 8"   11st 0lbs
b. Walsall, circa 1882
CAREER: Newstead Byron/Barnsley cs 1903/Birmingham May 1905/NOTTS Dec 1906, retired due to injury 1907.
Debut v Bristol City (h) 22.12.06, lost 2 – 3

Although not a locally born man, Aaron Jones began with Newstead Byron, very much a name of the past, but at one time the best team in the Notts. League. He scored on his debut for Barnsley against Glossop in October 1903, and in two seasons scored 17 League and Cup goals in 35 matches. His spell with Birmingham (later Birmingham City, and, at the time of his signing just two months on from their change of name from Small Heath), was not distinguished covering just five first team outings. He was immediately popular on joining the Magpies, as he scored within three minutes of the kick off on his debut. An artistic performer at inside-left, despite his preference for the centre-forward position, his career was cut short by injury, just six matches into season 1907-08. Earlier, the 1901 Census had listed him as a nineteen year-old colliery worker (underground) living in Royston in Yorkshire, and born at Walsall.

Appearances: FL: 22 apps 6 gls FAC: 4 apps 2 gls
Total: 26 apps 8 gls

JONES, Albert Thomas
Right-back   5' 10"   12st 4lbs
b. Talgarth, 6th February 1883
d. Belper, 28th July 1963
CAREER: Builth Juniors/Builth Town/Talgarth/Harbone Lynwood/Aston Villa trial/Swindon Town Nov 1902/ Nottingham Forest Aug 1903/NOTTS Dec 1905/Norwich City May 1907/Wellington Town Sept 1908/Swansea Town am 1913
Debut v Newcastle United (a) 9.12.05, lost 1 – 3

The son of a Builth chemist, both Albert and his younger brother Gordon each won two Wales caps. Albert's awards, both against England, were separated by a year, one whilst on Forest's books and one when with Notts. Brother Gordon was a Wrexham player when he was capped against Ireland and Scotland in 1907. Sadly, an injury when playing against England halted Albert's progress, but when fit he was described as: "A dashing tackler with a beautiful kick in either foot." Much later he made a surprise return to the game as a reinstated amateur, and was still a potent force, being capped by Wales at that level. Following in father's footsteps, he qualified as a Pharmacist in 1931 and worked for Boots in Treorchy. Later he set up in business on his own account in Llantwit Vardre, Pontypridd.

Appearances: FL: 30 apps 0 gls FAC: 1 app 0 gls
Total: 31 apps 0 gls
Honours: Wales International, 2 caps 1905-06. Wales Amateur International

JONES, Barrie
Centre-forward 5' 11" 11st 0lbs
b. Barnsley, 31st October 1938
CAREER: Army football/NOTTS Sept 1961/King's Lynn 1964
Debut v Shrewsbury Town (a) 28.3.62, lost 0 – 3

Quick off the mark and with a fierce shot, Barrie Jones was credited with the club record for the quickest goal scored – 6 seconds after the kick-off – in his first League appearance at Meadow Lane against Torquay United on 31st March 1962. Bought out of the forces – a move costing Notts about £150 – his best season was 1962-63 when as deputy for Tony Hateley at centre-forward, he scored 12 goals in 26 League and Cup matches.

Appearances: FL: 42 apps 15 gls FAC: 2 apps 0 gls FLC: 6 apps 2 gls Total: 50 apps 17 gls

---

JONES, Fred
Centre-forward 5' 10" 10st 12lbs
b. Pontypool, 26th August 1909
d. Chelmsford, August 1994
CAREER: Began in Rugby football/Pontnewedd F.C./ Aberaman Athletic 1931/Swansea Town July 1932/NOTTS July 1934/Millwall Dec 1934/Folkestone Town Aug 1936/ Ipswich Town Feb 1938, fee £150 plus £100 depending on appearances (WW2 guest Watford and Fulham); retired 1945/Marconi F.C. manager.
Debut v Bolton Wanderers (h) 15.9.34, lost 0 – 2

The outbreak of the Second World War terminated Fred Jones' career just as he was enjoying his best spell in senior football. Having done little of note with Swansea, Notts and Millwall, he was immediately successful with Ipswich Town. The scorer of their first goal in League football, he added another in their 4 – 2 win against Southend United on 27th August 1938, ending the season with 10 League and Cup goals in 23 matches.

Appearances: FL: 1 app 0 gls Total: 1 app 0 gls

JONES, Frederick
Inside-left   5' 10 2"   11st 6lbs
b. Bestwood, Notts, 25th December 1888
CAREER: Annesley/Sutton Town Feb 1907/NOTTS May 1907/Coventry City cs 1911/NOTTS May 1912/Coventry City June 1913/Southampton Apr 1914/Coventry City cs 1919/Pembroke Dock 1920-21.
Debut v Bury (h) 3.10.07, won 2 – 1

In two separate spells with Notts, and three with Coventry City, Fred Jones proved a dangerous marksman. His best season with the Magpies was 1909-10, when he scored 19 League and Cup goals in 37 matches, forming an effective forward partnership with Jimmy Cantrell (22 goals in 30 matches). His first season with Coventry City saw him lead the club's scoring charts with 22 Southern League and one FA Cup goal in 39 matches. In a season with Southampton his record was a similarly impressive 14 goals in 35 Southern League and FA Cup matches. A favourite description of him in the sporting press was "A burly, bustling inside-left," tactics that earned him career figures of 73 goals in 186 matches.

Appearances: FL: 86 apps 27 gls FAC: 5 apps 4 gls
Total: 91 apps 31 gls

───────────o───────────

JONES, Gary

Forward   6' 1"   12st 9lbs
b. Huddersfield, 6th April 1969
CAREER: Rossington Main/Doncaster Rovers Jan 1989/ Grantham Nov 1989, fee £8,500/Kettering Town Jan 1990, fee £17,500/Boston United Aug 1991, fee £3,000/Southend United June 1993, fee £25,000 (Lincoln City loan Sept 1993)/NOTTS Mar 1996, fee £140,000 (Scunthorpe United loan Feb 1997)/Hartlepool United Mar 1999, fee £75,000/ Halifax Town Mar 2000/Nuneaton Borough/Hucknall Town/ Gainsborough Trinity/Armthorpe Welfare.
Debut v Hull City (h) 2.3.96, won 1 – 0

In season 1997-98, when the Magpies were assured of promotion as early as March, Gary Jones was in unstoppable form from mid season and finished as Division Three leading scorer with 28 goals. Only Kevin Phillips (Sunderland) and Pierre Van Hooijdonk (Forest,) each with 29 in Division One, did any better. It was quite a turn round for the lively and mobile centre-forward who had been allowed to join Scunthorpe United on loan in the latter stages of the previous season. Gary averaged exactly a goal-a-game in the second half of the promotion season and was a popular choice as supporters' 'Player of the Year.'

Appearances: FL: 103(14) apps 38 gls FAC: 9(1) apps 7 gl FLC: 5(1) apps 1 gl Other: 1 app 0 gls
Total: 118(16) apps 46 gls
Honours: (NOTTS) FL Div 3 champions 1998

JONES, James Willie

Outside-left   5' 8"'   10st 7lbs
b. Chesterfield, October quarter 1896
CAREER: Welbeck Colliery 1914/NOTTS Mar1920/ Mansfield Town trial May 1921/Alfreton Town Sept 1921/ Brighton & Hove Albion June 1922/Mansfield Town Mar 1924/Crystal Palace trial Aug 1924/Worksop Town June 1927/Welbeck Colliery/Shirebrook June 1930
Debut v Chelsea (a) 17.3.20, lost 0 – 2

Welbeck Colliery lost two of their best players to Football League clubs in March 1920. Fred Halstead joining Blackpool a fortnight after Jimmy Jones had joined Notts. Described at the time of his Magpies debut by the 'Football Post' as "A well-built youth with plenty of speed and pluck," Jones made ten late-season appearances in 1919-20 as the Magpies descended through the relegation trapdoor. Despite starring in Central Alliance football he failed to establish himself in senior football, appearing in 19 matches in a little under two seasons with Brighton, and later in just four matches for Crystal Palace in their Division Two relegation season, 1924-25.

Appearances: FL: 11 apps 0 gls Total: 11 apps 0 gls

───────────o───────────

JONES, Mark Richard

Central defender   5' 10"   11st 12lbs
b. Mansfield, 21st December 1965
CAREER: NOTTS app, signing pro Dec 1983 to Feb 1985
Debut as sub v Everton (a) 4.2.84, lost 1 – 4

After making two substitute appearances in 1983-84 relegation season, Mark Jones began the Division Two campaign that followed with four first team outings. As the losing sequence spilled over into the new campaign he was deposed after the side sustained defeat in the opening four matches. In a season destined to end in a second, successive, relegation, Mark did not appear again at senior level and was given a free transfer in February 1985.

Appearances: FL: 4(2) apps 0 gls Total: 4(2) apps 0 gls

───────────o───────────

JONES, Michael

Central defender   5' 11"   10st 11lbs
b. Sunderland, 24th March 1947
CAREER: Derby County app, signing pro Nov 1964/NOTTS July 1969, fee £4,000/Peterborough United Aug 1973, fee £6,000/Kettering Town player-manager 1976-79/Mansfield Town manager Aug 1979 to May 1981/Bradford City coach 1981 to Nov 1982/Derby County coach Nov 1982 to Jan 1984/Nottingham Forest assistant coach early season 1984-85/Halifax Town manager Nov 1984 to Dec 1986/ Peterborough United assistant manager, then manager July 1988 to Aug 1989/Blackpool scout 1989/NOTTS coach, then assistant manager July 1990 to Jan 1993 (Subsequently Plymouth assistant, most probably under Warnock)/Brunci national manager 1998-2001/Telford manager until Apr 2004.
Debut v Oldham Athletic (h) 9.8.69, drawn 0 – 0

Mick Jones left Derby County at the age of 22, having failed to progress beyond reserve-team football at the Baseball Ground. He actually interrupted his honeymoon to sign for Notts, where he was reunited with former Derby team-mates, Richie Barker and Barry Butlin. It was not until his second season at Meadow Lane that the tough, uncompromising, central defender broke through into regular League football. Having achieved his aim, he then helped steer the Magpies to two promotions within the space of three seasons. Moving on to Peterborough United he added a second Division Four championship medal to his collection, missing only one match during the successful 1973-74 campaign. A career in coaching and management followed which included three spells as assistant to Neil Warnock. Undoubted highlight, however, was his spell as Brunei's national manager. After guiding the side to victory in the Malaysian Cup he was personally awarded a medal by the Sultan of Brunei for services to his country.

Appearances: FL: 82(18) apps 1 gl FAC: 7 apps 0 gls FLC: 6 apps 0 gls Other: 1 app 0 gls
Total: 96(18) apps 1 gl
Honours: (NOTTS) FL Div 4 champions 1971. (Peterborough United) FL Div 4 champions 1974

JORGENSEN, Henrik

Central defender   6' 2"   14st 0lbs
b. Denmark, 12th January 1979
CAREER: Odense BK (Denmark)/B 1909 (Denmark)/ NOTTS Oct 2000/B1909 (Denmark) Apr 2002
Debut v Port Vale, LDV Vans Trophy round 1, (a) 9.1.2001, lost 0 – 3

Ideally built central defender who joined the Magpies at the close of the Scandinavian season 1999-2000. After an initial outing in the LDV Vans Trophy, he made his first League appearance as a substitute in the 1 – 0 away win at Swansea City on 20th February 2001. In the late stages of the campaign he did enough in three starting appearances, and another from the bench, to win a contract for 2001-02. Sadly, his only starting appearance in the new term was in the LDV Vans Trophy and in April he agreed a termination of his contract to enable him to rejoin B1909 in time for the start of their domestic season.

Appearances: FL: 3(4) apps 0 gls FAC: 0(2) apps 0 gls FLC: 0(1) apps 0 gls Other: 2 apps 0 gls
Total: 5(7) apps 0 gls

JOSEPH, David

Forward   5' 10"   12st 7lbs
b. Guadeloupe, 22nd November 1976
CAREER: Montpellier, France (NOTTS loan Aug 2000 – July 2001)/Montpellier.
Debut v Luton Town (a) 12.8.2000, won 1 – 0

Shaven-headed and speedy, David joined the Magpies on a season's loan from Montpellier, with an option to purchase him at the end of the term. Despite the language barrier he settled in well, but the arrival of Danny Allsopp from Manchester City in December effectively marked the end of David's involvement, the Australian striker immediately forming an excellent front line partnership with Mark Stallard. Five late season appearances saw David on the mark in victories over Swindon Town and Oxford United, but he returned to France in the close season without an offer being made for his continued services.

Appearances: FL: 13(14) apps 4 gls FAC: 0(1) apps 0 gls FLC: 3(1) apps 0 gls Other: 1 app 0 gls
Total: 17(16) apps 4 gls

JOYCE, Christopher

Inside-forward   5' 8"   10st 9lbs
b. Dumbarton, 19th April 1933
d. Nuneaton, 20th December 2002
CAREER: Vale of Leven/Nottingham Forest Sept 1956/ NOTTS July 1959/Nuneaton Borough July 1962
Debut v Chester (h) 22.8.59, won 2 – 1

In three years at the City Ground Chris Joyce disappeared from the League side after making ten First Division appearances in his first season. One of a large contingent of Scottish players on Forest's books, he had played in 29 Football Combination matches and scored six goals in 1958-59 when he joined the Magpies on a free transfer. He proved a valuable acquisition, scoring ten goals in 22 matches in his first season, assisting his new team to promotion from Division Four. In the Third Division campaign that followed Chris lost his place at inside-right in mid season but later returned to first team status on the wing.

Appearances: FL: 62 apps 18 gls FAC: 1 app 0 gls FLC: 1 app 0 gls Total: 64 apps 18 gls

---

JOYNES, Richard Albert "Dickie"

Outside-right   5' 9"   12st 0lbs
b. Grantham, Lincs, July quarter 1877
d. Bingham, Notts., April quarter 1949, age 71
CAREER: Newark Avenue F.C./Newark June 1900/NOTTS Dec 1901 to May 1903/Newark Aug 1903/Brighton & Hove Albion May 1905/Leeds City May 1908 to 1910
Debut v Small Heath (h) 26.12.01, won 6 – 1

Signed by Notts after three seasons with Newark, where he began as a centre-forward before successfully converting to outside-right. A boilermaker by trade, Dickie was a fast and elusive forward who was introduced at senior level after four previous right wingers had been tried and found wanting. After an excellent debut in the 6 – 1 win against Small Heath, he scored his first League goals in the following week's 3 – 2 win against Derby County. Thereafter, aside from a short spell on the injured list, he remained first choice outside-right until his release in May 1903. After two seasons in Midland League football he moved south to Brighton and in a three-year spell appeared in 78 Southern League and FA Cup matches, scoring 12 goals. His career concluded with 22 appearances for Leeds City.

Appearances: FL: 46 apps 3 gls FAC: 1 app 0 gls
Total: 47 apps 3 gls

JULIAN, Walter

Right-back   5' 10**2**"   11st 0lbs
b. Hucknall, Notts, 24th December 1914
d. Logged at Basford, January quarter 1972
CAREER: West Bridgford/NOTTS am Dec 1933, pro Oct 1934/Crewe Alexandra June 1938/Scunthorpe & Lindsey United June 1939
Debut v Sheffield United (a) 13.10.34, lost 0 – 3

According to the 'Football Post' correspondent, Walter Julian's lack of true positional play caused him to be involved in a lot of chasing. This might explain his modest return of 17 senior outings in a comparatively lengthy stay of four and a half years at Meadow Lane. His best seasonal return came in the 1936-37 season when he appeared in eight Third Division South matches and three Southern League Cup ties.

Appearances: FL: 14 apps 0 gls Other: 3 apps 0 gls
Total: 17 apps 0 gls

JUPP, Duncan Alan

Full-back/Midfield   6' 0"   12st 12lbs
b. Guildford, 25th January 1975
CAREER: Shere Tigers (Guildford)/ Fulham trainee 1992, pro July 1993/Wimbledon June 1996, fee £125,000/NOTTS nc Nov 2002 to Feb 2003/Luton Town Feb 2003/Southend United July 2003.
Debut v Colchester United (h) 23.11.2002, lost 2 – 3

Duncan made his League debut with Fulham at eighteen years of age and won nine Scotland U-21 caps during his spell at Craven Cottage. He was still only 21, but had played in over 100 League matches when he took a giant stride upwards, joining Premier League Wimbledon. Despite a lengthy stay, his first team appearances with the Dons were infrequent, at the time of his free transfer to the Magpies he had appeared in only 34(11) League and Cup matches in six years.

He played little first team football at Meadow Lane, or in a brief spell with Luton Town, but an excellent season with Southend United in 2003-04 was rewarded with a new contract.

Appearances: FL: 6(2) apps 0 gls FAC: 0(1) apps 0 gls
Total: 6(3) apps 0 gls
Honours: Scotland U-21 International, 9 apps 1995-97

KAVANAGH, Edward Mark

Outside-right
b. Milton, Glasgow, 20th July 1941
CAREER: Cambuslang Rangers/NOTTS May 1964, fee £1,900/Boston United 1965/Spalding United July 1966
Debut v Wrexham (a) 22.8.64, lost 0 – 4

A desire to complete an engineering apprenticeship with a Glasgow-based company caused Eddie to turn down the opportunity to join Wrexham in 1962. When signing for Notts some two years later he was 23 years old and without senior experience. He had starred as a part-timer with Cambuslang, who won the Scottish Junior Cup, the Glasgow Cup, and the West of Scotland Tournament in 1963-64. The transition from minor soccer to the FL proved more difficult than expected, and in a single season at Meadow Lane he vied with David Coates for the first-team spot at outside-right.

Appearances: FL: 25 apps 4 gls FAC: 2 apps 1 gl FLC: 3 apps 0 gls Total: 30 apps 5 gls

---

KAVANAGH, Terrence

Left-half   5' 9"   11st 10lbs
b. Dublin, circa 1913
CAREER: Drumcondra circa 1931/Wigan Athletic July 1933/Everton Feb 1934/NOTTS June 1936/Exeter City Aug 1937, released May 1938
Debut v Crystal Palace (h) 7.9.36, lost 0 – 1

Kavanagh was without League experience when he joined Notts after two and a half years with Everton. He spent a single season at Meadow Lane, appearing only twice – within the space of five days – in mid September when consecutive home matches were lost to Crystal Palace and Queens Park Rangers. Transferred to Exeter City in late August 1937 he again failed to establish himself, appearing in six Third Division South matches before being released on a free transfer in May 1938.

Appearances: FL: 2 apps 0 gls Other: 1 app 0 gls
Total: 3 apps 0 gls

KEARTON, Jason Brett

Goalkeeper   6' 1"   11st 10lbs
b. Ipswich, Australia, 9th July 1969
CAREER: Brisbane Lions (Australia)/Everton Oct 1988
(Stoke City loan Aug 1991) (Blackpool loan Jan 1992)
(NOTTS loan Jan 1995)/Crewe Alexandra Oct 1996/
Brisbane Strikers (Australia) Aug 2001
Debut v Sunderland (a) 21.1.95, won 2 – 1

Unfortunate to be with Everton at the same time as the
celebrated Wales international goalkeeper Neville Southall,
the bulk of Jason Kearton's early experience of first team
football came from three loan spells. A consolation prize
from his time at Goodison was a FA Cup winners' medal
for his role as unused substitute in the final against
Manchester United in 1995. He enjoyed his best spell in
League football with Crewe Alexandra, appearing in over
200 League and Cup matches spanning five seasons. The
Railwaymen won promotion from Division Two in his
first season, beating Brentford 1 – 0 in the Wembley Play
off final.

Appearances: FL: 10 apps 0 gls Other: 2 apps 0 gls
Total: 12 apps 0 gls

KEEBLE, Walter Frederick T

Inside-forward   5' 8**2**"   11st 10lbs
b. Coventry, 30th August 1919
d. Nuneaton, May 1987
CAREER: North Warwickshire League football/Coventry
City am 1935/Services football/Albion Rovers pro late 1943/
Grimsby Town Sept 1946/NOTTS July 1947 to 1948
Debut v Queens Park Rangers (a) 18.9.47, lost 1 – 4 (scored)

Walter Keeble appeared at inside-left in seven First
Division matches for Grimsby Town in season 1946-47
when the first team number ten jersey was usually worn
by the durable veteran, Billy Cairns. Despite his top-
flight experience, Keeble's time at Meadow Lane was
spent mainly in reserve with Sewell, Lawton and Marsh
the regular, and potent, inside-forward trio.

Appearances FL: 4 apps 1 gl Total: 4 apps 1 gl

KEELING, Percy

Outside-right   5' 6"   9st 8lbs
b. Logged at Basford, Notts, January quarter 1903
d. Mansfield, April quarter 1939
CAREER: New Hucknall Colliery/Alfreton Town/NOTTS
Dec 1923 to May 1926, fee £200/Ilkeston Town
Debut v Liverpool (a) 26.12.24, lost 0 – 1

Described by the 'Nottingham Post Annual'
for 1925-26 as: "Small but good. An outside-
right with speed and grit, and a regular box of
tricks." His lack of first-team football probably
surrounded his extremely lightweight build, as
he was scarcely strong enough physically on heavy
grounds. A younger brother, Harry, was also on Notts'
books without reaching senior level. He did, however,
appear in League football as an inside-forward with
Torquay United, Swindon Town, Norwich City and
Mansfield Town in the late Twenties and early Thirties.

Appearances: FL: 6 apps 0 gls Total: 6 apps 0 gls

KEELY, Erasmus Middleton

Forward
b. Woodthorpe, Nottingham.
CAREER: NOTTS Nov 1875 (first app) to Jan 1878 (final
app)
Debut v Sheffield F.C. FAC 1 (h) 3.11.1877, drawn 1 – 1

Notts first ever appearance in the FA Cup came in season
1877-78. Their opponents, the Sheffield club, were a well-
known combination, formed in 1857, and regular
adversaries in Notts' schedule of friendly fixtures since
as far back as season 1864-65. Erasmus Keely played in
the meeting at Trent Bridge and the subsequent replay at
Bramhall Lane. From an opening worked by Keely, Harry
Cursham opened the scoring in the first match. Sheffield
equalised through Arthur Cursham, and the same player
scored twice in the replay, won 3 – 0 by Sheffield. Quite
why Arthur Cursham, a leading member of the Notts club
and an England International, decided to temporarily
transfer his services to the Yorkshire club was never
explained. Thankfully, his defection was short-lived, and
back in the Magpies ranks, presumably with all forgiven,
he scored twice against Sheffield in a 7 – 0 victory in
February of the same season.

Appearances: FAC: 2 apps 0 gls Total: 2 apps 0 gls

KEELY, St. John Wyer

Defender
b. Woodthorpe, Nottingham, October quarter 1848
d. Dunstable, 15th March 1908, age 59
CAREER: NOTTS Dec 1876 (first app) to Jan 1878 (final
app)
Debut v Sheffield F.C. FAC 1 replay (a) 1.12.1877, lost 0 – 3

Described in the 1881 Census as: "A gentleman" and "A
man of means." All suggesting that the public school
background continued to dominate the Notts eleven, with
professionalism still some four years away from
ratification by the Football Association.

In addition to E.M. Keeley (above), a third member of the Keeley clan, Edwin R.P. Keely (Shrewsbury public school and Cambridge University) also assisted the club, but did not play in any FA Cup matches.

Appearances: FAC: 1 app 0 gls Total: 1 app 0 gls

KEETLEY, Thomas Edward
Centre-forward 5' 8 **2**" 11st 10 lbs
b. Derby, 16th November 1898
d. Derby, 19th August 1958
CAREER: Victoria Ironworks (Derby)/Derby County am/ Bradford P.A. Feb 1920/Doncaster Rovers July 1923/NOTTS July 1929, fee £750/Lincoln City June 1933/Gresley Rovers Aug 1934/Heanor Town Jan 1935
Debut v Bristol City (h) 31.8.29, won 3 – 1 (scored a hat-trick)

Ace sharp-shooter Tom Keetley's record of 39 League goals for the Magpies in 1930-31 remains the highest number ever scored for the club in a single season. Perhaps more remarkable was the fact that the goals came in just 34 matches and, for good measure, he scored a further two in four FA Cup matches. His marksmanship took the Magpies to promotion as champions of the Third Division South. The hat-trick that marked his debut was just the first of ten, five of which were scored in away matches. Three of them being netted in successive matches in 1931-32, at Plymouth Argyle, Manchester United and Chesterfield. Illness kept him out for a lengthy spell in his first season – he played in only 20 League matches and scored 12 goals – and his absence was cited as the main reason for Notts relegation from Division Two. Despite being in the wars with a dislocated shoulder in 1931-32 he scored 30 goals in 31 League and Cup matches. Certainly one of the best centre-forwards of his day, Keetley scored 284 League goals – Five for Bradford P.A., 180 for Doncaster Rovers, 94 for Notts and five for Lincoln City. Tom Keetley had eight brothers and one sister. Four of his brothers – Charlie, Frank, Harold and Joe - played in League football, all were forwards and all knew where the goals were.

Charlie was the most successful marksman, scoring 108 League goals for Leeds United in 160 matches between 1927-34.

Appearances: FL: 103 apps 94 gls FAC: 7 apps 4 gls Total: 110 apps 98 gls
Honours: (NOTTS) FL Division 3 South champions 1931

KELLY, Edward Patrick
Midfield 5' 9 **2**" 12st 4lbs
b. Possilpark, Glasgow, 7th February 1951
CAREER: Possilpark Y.M.C.A./Arsenal app July 1966, pro Feb 1968/Queens Park Rangers Sept 1976, fee £80,000/ Leicester City July 1977, fee £50,000/NOTTS July 1980/ Bournemouth & Boscombe Athletic Aug 1981/Leicester City Dec 1981/Kettering Town Mar 1983/Melton Town 1984/ Torquay United Oct 1984, appointed first team coach Aug 1985/Saltash United 1986/Barnstaple manager 1995
Debut v Leyton Orient, ASC, (h) 2.8.80, drawn 2 – 2

Eddie Kelly's season at Meadow Lane saw the Magpies promoted to the top flight after a 55-year exile. The highly experienced midfield anchor man played in most matches until mid March, at which time he made way for former Leicester City colleague, Mark Goodwin. At the outset of his career, Kelly made his debut for Arsenal in September 1969. He was a scorer in the second leg of the Inter Cities Fairs Cup Final against Anderlecht, and played in 26(4) League and Cup matches in the 1970-71 double winning season. He became the first substitute to score in a FA Cup Final when he netted Arsenal's first goal against Liverpool in the Gunners' 2 – 1 victory. Eddie played in 168(7) League matches for Arsenal, and in 119, in two separate spells, for Leicester City. Despite relatively short spells with his other clubs, he nevertheless had a career aggregate of just three short of 400 League matches.

Appearances: FL: 26(1) apps 1 gl FAC: 1 app 0 gls FLC: 5 apps 2 gls Other: 7 apps 0 gls Total: 39(1) apps 3 gls
Honours: Scotland Youth International, 5 apps 1969. Scotland U-23 International, 3 apps 1971-74. (Arsenal) FL Division 1 champions 1971. FA Cup winners 1971. European Fairs Cup winners 1970. (Leicester City) FL Division 2 champions 1980. (NOTTS) Anglo-Scottish Cup finalists 1981

KELLY, Peter 'Ginger'
Inside-right 5' 7" 11st 7lbs
b. Tyldesley, 20th March 1901
CAREER: Tyldesley Celtic (Bolton Wanderers WW1 guest 1917-19)/Chorley Nov 1921/New Brighton Aug 1924/ NOTTS Feb 1926, fee £1,500/New Brighton Oct 1929/ Chorley July 1930/Hindsford F.C. (Manchester) am Dec 1933
Debut v Bury (a) 27.2.26, Lost 1 – 3 (scored)

In December 1924 the 'Topical Times' described Peter Kelly as "A Tyldesley lad, with auburn hair and a sturdy frame." The former collier first appeared in League football with New Brighton where his all-action style realised the Rakers a useful fee when he was transferred to Notts, shortly after the FA Cup meeting between the two sides. 'Ginger' Kelly, as he was popularly known, scored 20 League goals in 63 matches for New Brighton, and his record with the Magpies was not dissimilar when a knee injury curtailed his career. He returned to New Brighton but played in only eight League matches before leaving on a free transfer to rejoin the club where he first made his name, Chorley of the Lancashire Combination. Peter Kelly had another, rather unusual, sporting pastime. He was a champion all-in wrestler.

Appearances: FL: 69 apps 19 gls FAC: 1 app 0 gls
Total: 70 apps 19 gls

---○---

KELLY, William

Half-back   5' 8**2**" 12st 2lbs
b. Kirkintilloch, Dunbartonshire, 27th March 1880
CAREER: Cadzow Oak/Hamilton Academical Aug 1898/ West Ham United (debut) Nov 1900/NOTTS May 1903/ Brighton & Hove Albion May 1904/Bathgate July 1905/ Maxwelltown Volunteers Sept 1906
Debut v Newcastle United (h) 17.10.03, won 3 – 2

'The Glance Football Annual' for 1903-04 described Kelly as "A brawny Scot" and an "Indefatigable centre-half, said to be able to play all day without feeling any the worse for it." A Junior Inter-County cap for Dunbartonshire, a Glasgow League cap against Ireland and two Junior International caps suggested a worthy pedigree, but his spell in English football was not distinguished. "Did not give complete satisfaction on his debut" was the opinion of the 'Football Post' in October 1903, and aside from a late-season outing against Sheffield Wednesday, his season was spent at reserve team level.

Appearances: FL: 2 apps 0 gls Total: 2 apps 0 gls
Honours: Scotland Junior International

---○---

KEMP, Haydn

Wing-half   5' 7**2**" 10st 11lbs
b. Mosborough, near Bolsover South Yorkshire, 17th January 1897
d. Nottingham, 15th April 1982
CAREER: New Bolsover Wesleyans/Staveley West End/ Auston United/Bolsover Colliery/Bolsover Town/ NOTTS am season 1918-19/Chesterfield Municipal cs 1919/NOTTS May 1920/Thames F.C. Aug 1931, fee £250/Grantham Town cs 1932/Heanor Town Dec 1933.
Debut v Barnsley (a) 6.9.20, drawn 2 – 2

A former collier, Haydn Kemp was quick off the mark and skilful alike in both defence and attack. He began as an inside-forward, Notts signing him after he had scored a hat-trick against their Reserve team, when playing for Chesterfield Municipal. He was a prominent schoolboy footballer at Bolsover, where he helped his school win the Phillips Shield and medals. He played for Bolsover Colliery for several seasons, winning along the way two cups, a shield and four sets of gold medals. In 1918-19 he scored 30 goals. Thence to Chesterfield as inside-right where he was leading scorer with 21 in 1919-20 when the Midland League championship was won. Haydn played for Notts in eleven seasons and became fully established in 1922-23 when the Second Division championship was secured. He figured in a second championship in his final season at Meadow Lane, before joining the ill-fated Thames F.C. who did not seek re-election to the League after finishing at the foot of the Division Three South table in season 1931-32.

Appearances: FL: 286 apps 6 gls FAC: 26 apps 0 gls
Total: 312 apps 6 gls
Honours: (NOTTS) FL Division 2 champions 1923. FL Division 3 South champions 1931

---○---

KENNEDY, Peter Henry James

Winger   5' 11" 11st 11lbs
b. Lurgan, N. Ireland, 10th September 1973
CAREER: Glentoran/Glenavon July 1992/Portadown 1995/ NOTTS Aug 1996, fee £100,000/Watford July 1997, fee £130,000/Wigan Athletic July 2001, fee £300,000(Derby County loan Oct 2003)/Peterborough United Aug 2004.
Debut as sub v York City (h) 31.8.96, lost 0 –1

One of a pair of signings as season 1996-97 got underway. Phil Robinson returned to Meadow Lane for a second spell from Chesterfield and Peter Kennedy arrived from Portadown. The Irish wingman had been voted 'Footballer of the Year' in Northern Ireland in 1995-96, but he struggled to impress in a poor County side who, with half of the season's fixtures completed, had managed just five League wins. When the inevitable change in management occurred – Sam Allardyce taking over in January – Peter Kennedy did not feature again at senior level. His fortunes certainly improved after leaving Meadow Lane, with Division Two championship medals accruing from his spells with Watford and Wigan Athletic.

Appearances: FL: 20(2) apps 0 gls FAC: 2 apps 1 gl FLC: 1 app 0 gls Other: 0(1) apps 0 gls
Total: 23(3) apps 1 gl
Honours: Northern Ireland International, 20 caps. Northern Ireland 'B' International, 1 app. (Watford) FL Division 2 champions 1998. (Wigan Athletic) FL Division 2 champions 2003

KERR, George
Inside-forward
CAREER: Kilmarnock/NOTTS Aug 1893 to cs 1894
Debut v Crewe Alexandra (a) 2.9.1893, drawn 2 – 2

George Kerr's single season with the Magpies ended on a disappointing note. After missing only one League match until mid January a dip in form saw him out of the side. He missed playing in all but one of the season's FA Cup ties and didn't feature in the final against Bolton Wanderers. Notts became the first side from Division Two to win the FA Cup, but their attempt at a 'double' was unsuccessful, Preston North End winning the Test Match at Olive Grove, Sheffield, by the comfortable margin of 4 – 0

Appearances: FL: 23 apps 6 gls FAC: 1 app 0 gls
Total: 24 apps 6 gls

KEVAN, David John
Midfield   5' 8"   9st 10lbs
b. Wigtown, Scotland, 31st August 1968
CAREER: NOTTS from school, app Aug 1984, pro Aug 1986 (Cardiff City loan Sept 1989)/Stoke City (initial loan) Jan 1990, fee £75,000 (Maidstone United loan Feb 1991)/ AFC Bournemouth Mar to cs 1994/Stoke City Juniors coach.
Debut as sub v Gillingham (a) 1.2.86, lost 0 – 4

As a member of the Magpies' Midland Intermediate League championship side of 1986, David was handed his League debut in that season as a 17 year-old substitute at Gillingham.

In the following season he appeared in 33 League matches and scored his first senior goal in the 5 – 2 win against Newport County on 3rd March 1987. Despite a season of rapid personal progress, it all ended in disappointment as a place in the Play-offs was squandered, one point from the final four matches of the season ending the Magpies' hopes. A call-up by Scotland U-21 resulted in a place on the bench against Yugoslavia, but he did not get on to the pitch. His fortunes at Meadow Lane, in terms of first team action, declined following the appointment of Neil Warnock as manager. Signed by Stoke City's manager Alan Ball, it was not until the appointment of Lou Macari, and a switch to right full-back, that he prospered at the Victoria Ground. The undoubted highlight being his winners' medal from the 1992 Wembley Autoglass Trophy Final.

Appearances: FL: 82(7) apps 3 gls FAC: 6 apps 1 gl FLC: 4 apps 0 gls Other: 9 apps 0 gls
Total: 101(7) apps 4 gls
Honours: Scotland Schoolboy International. (Stoke City) Autoglass Trophy winners 1992

KIDDIER, James Frederick
Centre-forward
b. Nottingham, July quarter 1874
d. West Bridgford, 21st April 1935
CAREER: NOTTS 1895/Bulwell United July 1896/Sutton Town June 1898 to 1899
Debut v Rotherham Town (h) 30.11.1895, drawn 0 – 0

The departure of Scottish international centre-forward Dan Bruce – transferred to Small Heath for £100 – opened the way for local product James Kiddier. In his second appearance, in December 1895, he scored once in the 7 – 2 demolition of Burslem Port Vale at Trent Bridge. Thereafter he found goals difficult to come by but retained his place in the side until the end of the season, at which point he departed to Bulwell United. The 1901 Census listed his occupation as a machine fitter.

Appearances: FL: 15 apps 4 gls Total: 15 apps 4 gls

KILCLINE, Brian
Central defender   6' 2"   12st 10lbs
b. Nottingham, 7th May 1962
CAREER: Christ the King School (Arnold)/Nottingham and South Notts. Schoolboys/NOTTS associate schoolboy, app May 1978, pro May 1980/Coventry City June 1984, fee £60,000/Oldham Athletic Aug 1991, fee £400,000 (Newcastle United loan Feb 1992)/Newcastle United Mar 1992, fee £250,000/Swindon Town Jan 1994, fee £90,000/ Mansfield Town Dec 1995/Halifax Town 1997/Atrincham player-coach cs 1998 to Oct 1998
Debut v Torquay United, FLC 2, (a) 5.9.79, won 1 – 0

Originally a free-scoring centre-forward in schools football, Brian Kilcline was destined to follow a famous line of youthful Magpies central defenders of the calibre of David Needham and Brian Stubbs. He had, in fact, Brian Stubbs and Jeff Blockley as competition in his earliest days, but the towering,  moustachioed Kilcline made rapid strides, developing into a tremendously popular, hard defender, of the never-say-die type. In the Second Division promotion season, 1980-81, he appeared in all 42 League matches and was ever-present in a further 17 Cup ties. After leaving Meadow Lane he famously lifted the FA Cup in Coventry City's first-ever Cup Final appearance. Five years on he captained Newcastle United to the First Division championship, and finally, at the age of 36, he steered Halifax Town to the championship of the Conference, by a margin of nine points over runners-up, Cheltenham Town.

Appearances: FL: 156(2) apps 9 gls FAC: 10 apps 2 gls
FLC: 18 apps 1 gl Other: 9 apps 1 gl
Total: 193(2) apps 13 gls
Honours: England U-21 International, 2 apps 1983.
(Coventry City) FA Cup winners 1987. (Newcastle United) FL Division 1 champions 1993. (NOTTS) Anglo-Scottish Cup finalists 1981. (Halifax Town) Football Conference champions 1998

KILFORD, John Douglas
Right-back   5' 10"   12st 1lb
b. Derby, 8th November 1938
CAREER: Stainsby House School (Smalley)/Derby Corinthians/NOTTS am, signing pro July 1957/Leeds United Feb 1959, in part exchange for Bobby Forrest/Tonbridge F.C. 1962
Debut v Wrexham (a) 27.8.58, lost 2 – 3

John Kilford played in 34 matches for Notts Reserves in 1957-58. The powerfully-build back won a first-team place in the following season and earned an upward move to Leeds United after just 26 matches. At Elland Road he made his debut in Division One against Portsmouth on 28th February 1959, appeared in First and Second Division

matches, but the bulk of his appearances came in his role as captain of the Reserves. Later with Tonbridge he was a Kent Senior Cup winner in 1965. In 1973 he studied for the ministry at Oak Hill Theology College and in the late 1980s his parish was in South London, adjacent to Crystal Palace's ground at Selhurst Park.

Appearances: FL: 26 apps 0 gls FAC: 1 app 0 gls
Total: 27 apps 0 gls

KING, Colin W
Goalkeeper 6'0" 11st 2lbs
b. Edinburgh, 1958
CAREER: Blackpool July 1973/Clydebank 1977-78/NOTTS June 1978 (Rotherham United loan Oct 1979 to cs 1980)/Mansfield Town Aug 1980, registration cancelled Oct 1981/Shepshed Charterhouse
Debut v Grimsby Town, FLC, round 3, (a) 25.9.79, lost 1 – 3

Colin King did not reach senior level with Blackpool, George Wood and John Burridge dominating the position during his four years at Bloomfield Road. A second spell in English football with the Magpies followed his season with Clydebank, but he suffered cruel misfortune in breaking his leg at Meadow Lane, and had similar misfortune when he moved on to Mansfield Town. In late 1981 Colin was reported to be carving a new career outside of the game, running a sports training and recreation scheme for the unemployed people of Leicester.

Appearances: FLC: 1 app 0 gls Total: 1 app 0 gls

KING, Jeffrey
Midfield   5' 8"   11st 0lbs
b. Fauldhouse, 9th November 1953
CAREER: Fauldhouse United/Albion Rovers Dec 1972/ Derby County Apr 1974, fee £7,000 (NOTTS loan Jan 1976) (Portsmouth loan Mar 1976)/Walsall Nov 1977/ Sheffield Wednesday Aug 1979, fee £30,000/Sheffield United Jan 1982/Chesterfield trial Oct 1983/Stafford Rangers Nov 1983/Altrincham Feb 1984/Burton Albion Aug 1984/ Kettering Town 1984/Jubilee Sports/ Wadsley Bridge
Debut v York City (h) 10.1.76, won 4 – 0

Jeff King's career peaked during four years in Sheffield. He assisted Wednesday to win promotion from Division Three in 1979-80, and followed by helping United to win Division Four in 1981-82. In earlier days, he had played little senior football until he followed his former Derby County manager, Dave Mackay, to Walsall. Over half a century of League appearances for the Saddlers effectively launched his senior career that concluded with aggregate figures: 159(8) League matches and 14 goals.

Appearances: FL: 3 apps 0 gls Total: 3 apps 0 gls
Honours: (Sheffield United) FL Division 4 champions 1982

KING, Louis Henry

Outside-right
b. Nottingham, April quarter 1873
d. Ruddington, 22nd August 1952
CAREER: Mansfield Greenhalgh's/Notts County Rovers/
NOTTS Jan 1893 to cs 1894
Debut v Everton (a) 7.1.1893, lost 0 – 6

Louis King's stint with the Magpies was spent largely as an understudy. Sadly, his introduction - along with another reserve team player, Frank Wilkinson - failed to have the desired effect. The visit to Everton resulting in the heaviest defeat of the season, the term ending with relegation from Division One. If not quite in the top rank as a soccer player, Louis King was an outstanding sportsman in other areas. He was a member of one of the most successful rowing crews in the history of the Nottingham Rowing Club, who won many trophies all over the Midlands. He was also a great gymnast and a member of the Nottingham Amateur Gymnastic Club. He also raced, on a penny-farthing cycle, at Nottingham Forest's sports, an important spring meeting held on the Trent Bridge cricket ground. In later years he took up golf and became very fond of bowls. Louis King was a well-known Nottingham businessman, for over fifty years the proprietor of King's Restaurant on Beastmarket Hill.

Appearances: FL: 3 apps 0 gls Total: 3 apps 0 gls

KING, Philip Geoffrey

Left-back   5' 10**2**"   12st 7lbs
b. Bristol, 28th December 1967
CAREER: Exeter City app, signing pro Jan 1985/Torquay United July 1986, fee £3,000/Swindon Town Feb 1987, fee £155,000/Sheffield Wednesday Nov 1989, fee £400,000 (NOTTS loan Oct 1993)/Aston Villa Aug 1994, fee £250,000 (West Bromwich Albion loan Oct 1995)/Swindon Town Mar 1997 (Blackpool loan Oct 1997)/Brighton & Hove Albion Mar - Apr 1999/Kidderminster Harriers May 1999 to 2000.
Debut v Portsmouth (h) 23.10.93, drawn 1 – 1

Phil King joined the Magpies on a one-month loan from Sheffield Wednesday in October 1993 and had a busy time. He appeared in six Division One fixtures and two Anglo-Italian Cup ties, the last of which was an away match against Brescia for the Magpies first-ever competitive fixture against European opposition. His form suggested that he could have solved the problem left-back position on a permanent basis, but his next permanent move took him to Aston Villa where a cruciate ligament injury marked a change in his fortunes. At the time of his move to Villa Park he had clocked up in excess of 300 League appearances, but he played little first team football subsequently, finishing with career figures of: 321(15) League matches and nine goals.

Appearances: FL: 6 apps 0 gls Other: 2 apps 0 gls
Total: 8 apps 0 gls
Honours: England 'B' International, 1 app. (Sheffield Wednesday) FL Cup winners 1991. (Kidderminster Harriers) Conference champions 2000

KING, Thomas Parkinson

Right-back   5' 8**2**" 10st 6lbs
b. Woolsthorpe-by-Belvoir, 29th June 1909
d. Scarborough, 7th June 1993
CAREER: Woolsthorpe-by-Bevoir F.C./NOTTS am Aug 1930/Sneinton/NOTTS am Aug, pro Nov 1934/ Bournemouth & Boscombe Athletic Aug 1935/Luton Town Feb 1937; retired due to knee injury during WW2/Luton Town groundsman July 1954 to 1964
Debut v Bradford P.A. (h) 16.3.35, drawn 1 – 1

A former gardener's boy on the estate of the Duke of Rutland, Tom King found little opportunity of first-team football at Meadow Lane. He soon found his place in League football after being allowed to join Bournemouth, where he made 66 League appearances in a little short of two seasons at Dean Court. Moving to Luton Town in February 1937 he was able to assist them to promotion, making 11 appearances during the run-in to the championship of the Third Division South. He had played in 58 League matches for the Hatters before the outbreak of WW2. Subsequently employed in the engineering trade, he returned to Kenilworth Road in 1954 as groundsman.

Appearances: FL: 2 apps 0 gls Total: 2 apps 0 gls
Honours: (Luton Town) FL Division 3 South champions 1937

KINSEY, George

Left-half
b. Burton-on-Trent, October quarter 1866
d. Aston, Birmingham, January quarter 1911
CAREER: Burton Crusaders 1883/Burton Swifts 1885/ Mitchell St George's 1888/Wolverhampton Wanderers Aug 1891/Aston Villa June 1894/Derby County May 1895/ NOTTS Mar 1897/Eastville Rovers May 1897/Burton Swifts Sept 1900/Gresley Rovers Aug 1901/Burton Early Closing Sept 1902
Debut v Newton Heath (a) 27.3.1897, drawn 1 – 1

The Magpies made several late-season signings in 1896-97, the possibility of their appearing in the Test Matches obviously in mind. In the event, the tried and trusted members of the team that took them to the top of Division Two contested the four-match Test series.

The notable exception being John Brearley (q.v.) whose goal clinched promotion and a return to the top flight. George Kinsey, at the end of his 1890s tour around the Midlands' circuit, played in the final five Second Division matches but Bob Crone took the right-half spot in the four-match Test series. Earlier in his career Kinsey was capped by England on four occasions, twice when a Wolves player and twice at Derby County. He was a FA Cup winner with the Wolves, who beat Everton 1 – 0 on the ground of the Manchester Athletic Club, Fallowfield, Manchester in 1893. It was the first cup final, apart from re-plays, to be played outside of London. The money taken at the gate amounted to £2,559, the highest total for a football match anywhere, either in Scotland or England. The Wolves, who sported jerseys of black and yellow diagonal halves, were generally popular winners, if only for the fact that their eleven was composed entirely of Englishmen, and most of the players born, or resident, within the immediate neighbourhood of Wolverhampton.

Appearances: FL: 4 apps 0 gls Total: 4 apps 0 gls
Honours: England International, 4 caps 1892-96.
(Wolverhampton Wanderers) FA Cup winners 1893

KIRK, James John
Left-half
b. Southwell, Notts., January quarter 1879
d. Southwell, Notts., April quarter 1953
CAREER: Southwell St Mary's/NOTTS am Nov 1902/ Newark Town cs 1903/Lincoln City May 1909/Worksop Town cs 1911
Debut v Grimsby Town (h) 28.2.03, lost 0 – 1

A puncher in a lace factory, recruited on amateur forms from Southwell St Mary's. He deputised once at left-half for Ted McDonald in a side showing four team changes from the eleven who had lost at home to Liverpool, earlier in the month. The home defeat by Grimsby Town did nothing to alleviate the Magpies' relegation worries, but they eventually rallied to finish in 15th place. Kirk departed in the close season to Newark Town where he joined two other former Notts men, Dickie Joynes and Bob Suter. Six years on he joined Lincoln City, but in two seasons at Sincil Bank he operated as a reserve right-back, appearing in just five League matches before returning to non-League circles with Worksop Town.

Appearances: FL: 1 app 0 gls Total: 1 app 0 gls

KIRKHAM, Royce
Full-back   5' 11"   12st 0lbs
b. Ollerton, 17th October 1937
CAREER: Ollerton Colliery/Notts am 1954-55, pro May 1955 to June 1959/Workington.
Debut v Doncaster Rovers (a) 29.12.56, lost 2 – 4

Impressive displays as an amateur in the Magpies' Reserve team earned Royce Kirkham a professional contract at the close of 1954-55. A strong and resourceful back, he had a lengthy wait for a senior outing, despite which he was only nineteen when he made what proved to be a solitary League outing at right-back against Doncaster Rovers. The Belle Vue encounter rounding off a thoroughly miserable Christmas holiday period for the Magpies who lost four matches within the space of seven days. They did, however, begin the New Year with the season's best victory, 5 – 0 against Stoke City, and for the second season in succession avoided relegation from Division Two, finishing in 20th position in the table.

Appearances: FL: 1 app 0 gls Total: 1 app 0 gls

KIRKUP, Frank William
Outside-left   5' 9**2**"   11st 6lbs
b. Spennymoor, 12th January 1939
CAREER: Spennymoor United/Blackburn Rovers Feb 1957/ Workington June 1959/Carlisle United Dec 1962/NOTTS June 1965/Workington Nov 1966
Debut v Darlington (h) 21.8.65, drawn 0 – 0

A professional with Blackburn Rovers for a little over two seasons, Frank had not reached senior level at the time of his transfer to Workington in June 1959. His sprightly displays on the Reds left wing (31 goals in 140 League matches) earned him an upward move to Carlisle United in December 1962. Although unable to prevent the Cumbrians relegation at the end of his first season at Brunton Park, Frank was able to assist them to a speedy return to Division Three, as runners-up to Gillingham in 1963-64. His contribution being six goals in 37 League appearances, as an integral part of the most potent attack in the English Football League that season with 113 goals in 46 matches. His season with the Magpies unfortunately contained a lengthy mid-season spell on the sidelines, and his senior career ended after just eight matches in his second spell with Workington. His aggregate career figures were 253 League appearances and 49 goals.

Appearances: FL: 29 apps 3 gls FAC: 1 app 0 gls FLC: 2 apps 0 gls Total: 32 apps 3 gls

---

KIWOMYA, Andrew Derek

Winger   5' 10"   10st 10lbs
b. Huddersfield, 1st October 1967
CAREER: Barnsley app, signing pro July 1985/Sheffield Wednesday Oct 1986, fee £5,000/Dundee Sept 1992/ Rotherham United Oct 1993/Halifax Town cs 1994/ Scunthorpe United Mar 1995/Bradford City July 1995 (Luton Town loan Mar 1997) (Burnley loan Sept 1997)/NOTTS Dec 1997/Halifax Town Feb 1998
Debut as sub v Doncaster Rovers (h) 13.12.97, won 5 – 2

Elder brother of Chris, the Ipswich Town and Arsenal forward, Andy won England Youth honours but had less success in his League career. This spanned seven English clubs and totalled 47(23) League matches and seven goals, Bradford City providing his only spell of regular first team involvement with 27(16) League appearances and three goals. Notts proved to be his final port of call in senior football, when a mere glimpse of his speedy wing play was afforded during the Magpies run-away championship success in season 1997-98.

Appearances: FL: 0(2) apps 0 gls Other: 1 app 0 gls Total: 1(2) apps 0 gls
Honours: England Youth International

KNOX, Thomas

Goalkeeper   6' 0"   12st 0lbs
b. Ushaw Moor, Durham, April quarter 1906
CAREER: Ushaw Moor Labour Party F.C./Bearpark F.C./ Darlington F.C. 'A' Team/Chilton Colliery/Bolton Wanderers am and then pro Nov 1928/West Stanley July 1929/Norwich City trial 1930/Bradford City trial Aug 1930/Leeds United trial Sept 1930/Durham City trial Nov 1930/Crook Town Feb 1931/Darlington cs 1931/Hartlepools United Aug 1933/ NOTTS Jan 1934, fee £350/Crystal Palace May 1936/ Norwich City Dec 1936/Carlisle United June 1937 and again as a WW2 guest in season 1939-40
Debut v Bradford City (h) 3.2.34, won 3 – 0

Tommy Knox, the son of a former Ushaw Moor and Crook Town player, had trials with a number of clubs before making his League debut with Darlington in September 1931.His first outing was against Hartlepools United, the team destined to become his second port of call, after he had completed 52 League and Cup matches for the Quakers. After 29 League and Cup outings during his spell at the Victoria Ground he joined the Meadow Lane staff. He immediately displaced Len Hammond as the Magpies' last line of defence and his confidence and coolness under pressure helped steer the side clear of relegation in his first season. Sadly, despite appearing in most matches during the following term, he was unable to save an extremely poor County team from relegation. In the Third Division South season that followed he shared the first team jersey with George Blyth.

After leaving Meadow Lane he completed a career total of 200 League appearances before the outbreak of World War Two. Tommy qualified as a masseur during his time with the Magpies, and in August 1951 was appointed club scout in the Stockton area.

Appearances: FL: 72 apps 0 gls FAC: 5 apps 0 gls Other: 1 app 0 gls Total: 78 apps 0 gls

---

KUDUZOVIC, Fahrudin

Midfield
b. Bosnia, circa 1985
CAREER: Derby County scholar and app/Port Vale trial/ NOTTS nc Sept 2004 (Northwich Victoria nc late Sept 2004)/Released by Notts Jan 2005/Sligo Rovers (Ireland)
Debut as sub v Cheltenham Town (h) 4.9.2004, drawn 0 – 0

A refugee from war-torn Bosnia in 1993 who joined Derby County at the age of twelve and who had completed a three-year apprenticeship with the Rams prior to being released in the 2004 close season. He had a five-week trial with Port Vale before joining the Magpies on a non-contract basis in September 2004. Fahrudin received an early, if brief, opportunity when appearing as a substitute for the injured Kelvin Wilson against Cheltenham Town, and didn't look out of his depth. A brief loan spell with Northwich Victoria followed, but he remained at Meadow Lane to feature regularly at reserve level until his non-contract deal was terminated in January 2005.

Appearances: FL: 0(3) app 0 gls Total: 0(3) app 0 gls

KUHL, Martin

Midfield   5' 11"   11st 3lbs
b. Frimley, Surrey, 10th January 1965
CAREER: Chelsea associate schoolboy May 1979/ Birmingham City app June 1981, pro Jan 1983/Sheffield United Mar 1987/Watford Feb 1988, in exchange for two players plus £40,000/Portsmouth Sept 1988, fee £125,000/ Derby County Sept 1992, fee £650,000 (NOTTS loan Sept 1994)/Bristol City Dec 1994 to cs 1997, fee £330,000/ Farnborough Town/Weymouth Aug 2002/Aldershot Town coach
Debut v Bristol City (a) 10.9.94, lost 1 – 2

Certainly lived up to his reputation as an aggressive midfielder during the briefest of stays at Meadow Lane. Signed on a month's loan from Derby County, in the early stages of the 1994-95 relegation season, he was allowed back to the Baseball Ground less than a week after his arrival, having been sent off in his second appearance at Barnsley. Martin assisted seven different League clubs during his career, appearing in a total of 446(28) FL matches, scoring 44 goals.

Appearances: FL: 2 apps 0 gls Total: 2 apps 0 gls

LADD, Ian Martin

Central defender   6' 0"   11st 2lbs
b. Peterborough, 22nd November 1958
CAREER: NOTTS pro Sept 1977/Cambridge United 1978-79/Bourne Town/Stamford/Corby Town/Boston United Aug 1984
Debut v Luton Town (a) 1.10.77, lost 0 – 2

Ian made his solitary League appearance at Luton Town in the eighth fixture of season 1977-78, and the Magpies winless streak continued. The sequence was to prove the undoing of manager Ronnie Fenton, who was dismissed five days later, Jimmy Sirrel taking over for his second spell in charge. The team line-up was by necessity subject to a variety of permutations, but Ian Ladd was not called upon again. He left in the close season to join Cambridge United, but did not feature in their first team.

Appearances: FL: 1 app 0 gls Total: 1 app 0 gls

LAHTINEN, Aki Arimo

Central defender   5' 11"   11st 3lbs
b. Finland, 31st October 1958
CAREER: O.P.S. Oulo (Finland)/NOTTS Sept 1981 to May 1985
Debut as sub v Swansea City (a) 12.9.81, lost 2 – 3

With a figure in excess of 25 international appearances for Finland, and consecutive championships with O.P.S. Oulo before joining Notts, Aki Lahtinen nevertheless struggled to establish himself at Meadow Lane. The six-figure signing made only five starts and three substitute appearances in his first season, and a fractured cheekbone curtailed his progress in 1982-83. After appearing at right back in the first five matches of 1983-84, a severe hamstring injury then sidelined him for six months. Certainly one of the most unfortunate players in regard to injuries, he was released at the close of the 1984-85 relegation season.

Appearances: FL: 37(8) apps 2 gls FAC: 3 apps 0 gls FLC: 4(1) apps 0 gls Total: 44(9) apps 2 gls
Honours: Finland International

LAIRD, Alexander

Outside-right
b. Newmains, 2nd June 1926
d. West Lothian, 2004
CAREER: Stirling Albion/Chelsea Nov 1951, fee £8,000/Corby Town 1952-53/NOTTS July 1953, fee £2,500/Cheltenham Town Jan 1954
Debut v Leeds United (a) 19.8.53, lost 0 – 6

Notts made the worst possible start to season 1953-54, sustaining a 6 – 0 drubbing at Leeds United.

Celebrated Welsh international John Charles scoring four of Leeds' goals in the season in which he broke the club's individual scoring record with 42 League goals in 39 appearances. Alex Laird's County debut also proved to be his final appearance and in mid term he joined Cheltenham Town, at that time a Southern League outfit. Despite commanding what were respectable fees in the early 1950s, Laird – who did not appear at senior level for Chelsea – failed to fulfil expectations in English football.

Appearances: FL: 1 app 0 gls Total: 1 app 0 gls

LAMB, John A "Jack"

Inside-forward   5' 6"   11st 0lbs
b. Birmingham, circa 1893
CAREER: Long Eaton/Tramways F.C. (Birmingham)/Worcester City Mar 1910/Brierley Hill Alliance June 1912/Worcester City July 1913/NOTTS Mar 1914, fee £150/Worcester City Sept 1919 to cs 1920
Debut v Wolverhampton Wanderers (a) 21.3.14, lost 1 – 4

A short but sturdily built inside-forward, Jack Lamb was a late season recruit from Worcester City. As Notts rounded off a successful season – winning back their First Division place at the first attempt – the newcomer was given his first taste of League football in consecutive fixtures against Wolves and Hull City. Despite scoring in both of County's opening matches of the new season, against Aston Villa and Liverpool, he did not secure a regular berth, although his return of three goals in six matches seemed imminently respectable in a season when only 41 goals were scored in 38 matches. Jack, and his brother Walter, were notable figures in Worcester City's early history. Jack scored 69 goals in 137 matches. Outside-left Walter scored 41 goals in 127 games.

Appearances: FL: 8 apps 3 gls Total: 8 apps 3 gls

LANE, Frank

Goalkeeper   6' 1"   12st 10lbs
b. Wallasey, 20th July 1948
CAREER: Stanley Arms F.C. (Wallasey)/Tranmere Rovers Aug 1968/Liverpool Sept 1971, fee £15,000/NOTTS July 1975/Kettering Town 1977
Debut v Oxford United (a) 3.3.76, lost 1 – 2

After three seasons and 76 League appearances for Tranmere Rovers, Frank Lane made an upward move to First Division neighbours Liverpool. As understudy to Ray Clemence at Anfield, he was called into senior action just once in a stay approaching four years. He fared little better at Meadow Lane where Eric McManus was firmly established as first choice.

Appearances: FL: 2 apps 0 gls Total: 2 apps 0 gls

LANE, John George 'Jackie'

Forward   6' 0"   13st 5lbs
b. Selly Oak, Birmingham, 10th November 1931
CAREER: Selly Oak Old Blacks/Boldmere St Michael's/
Birmingham City am, signing pro Sept 1949/NOTTS July
1956, fee £7,500/Hinckley Athletic Aug 1959/
Kidderminster Harriers/Evesham United June 1961/Belper
Town Oct 1961
Debut v Bury (h) 18.8.56, drawn 2 – 2.

Lack of a top-class centre-forward was considered the
main reason for Notts poor showing in season 1955-56
when they narrowly avoided relegation from Division
Two. After a lengthy search – which included unsuccessful
approaches for Cardiff City's Trevor Ford and
Sunderland's Ted Purdon – Jackie Lane of Birmingham
City was the man expected to fit the bill. He had assisted
Birmingham City to promotion in 1954-55 and to a
Wembley FA Cup final in 1956, but his role at St Andrews
in 1955-56 was that of understudy to the mercurial Eddie
Brown. Powerfully built and with a tremendous shot, he
was nevertheless unable to lift the Magpies' fortunes,
relegation from Divisions Two and Three, in consecutive
seasons, ensuing.

Appearances: FL: 57 apps 19 gls FAC: 3 apps 0 gls
Total: 60 apps 19 gls
Honours: (Birmingham City) FL Div 2 champions 1955

LANGFORD, John William

Outside-left   5' 9"   10st 8lbs
b. Kirkby-in-Ashfield, 4th August 1937
CAREER: Leicester City am/Nottingham Forest am, signing
pro Aug 1955/NOTTS Aug 1958, fee £600/Bourne Town/
Long Eaton Jan 1961/Spalding United cs 1962/Ilkeston
Town Dec 1962
Debut v Accrington Stanley (h) 23.8.58, drawn 1 – 1

In his first season as a part-time professional (he worked
as an underground electrician in a local colliery) John
Langford scored 17 goals in 37 Midland League
appearances for Forest Reserves. Additionally, he had a
run of four matches in the first team. He was unable to
capitalise on his bright start, however, Stuart Imlach very
successfully dominating the outside-left position. After
appearing for Notts in the first 14 Division Three fixtures
of 1958-59 – only one of which was won – he lost his
place, the mid-term signing of Alan Withers ending
Langford's involvement at senior level.

Appearances: FL: 16 apps 0 gls Total: 16 apps 0 gls

LANGHAM, William 'Billy'

Outside-right   5' 8**2**" 11st 7lbs
b. Lenton, Notts, circa 1876
CAREER: Notts County Rovers/Stapleford Aug 1893/
Leicester Fosse trial Mar 1894/Hucknall Portland/South
Shore 1894/NOTTS May 1896/Bristol City May 1898/
Leicester Fosse Dec 1900/Doncaster Rovers Aug 1901/
Gainsborough Trinity May 1903/Doncaster Rovers Aug
1906/Irish football/Lincoln City Mar 1907
Debut v Newcastle United (h) 19.9.1896, won 3 – 1 (scored
one)

Billy Langham was born at Lenton and learned his football
in the city, but neither of the local FL clubs noted his
worth until after he joined Blackpool South Shore in 1894.
Notts 'spotted' him and induced him to return to his
native parts. The possessor of an almost phenomenal
turn of speed, on receipt of a forward pass he accelerated
into top speed within a few strides, leaving the opposing
defender in his wake. His centres were not always
accurate, but he was very successful as a goal-getter. In
the Division Two championship season, 1896-97, he
scored ten goals in 25 matches from outside-right, and
vitally, the only goal of the game in the first Test Match
fixture against Sunderland. In the summer of 1889 he was
professional with the Sefton Park Cricket Club.

Appearances: FL: 47 apps 15 gls FAC: 3 apps 0 gls
Other: 4 apps 1 gl Total: 54 apps 16 gls
Honours: (NOTTS) FL Division 2 champions 1897

LAW, Nicholas

Central defender   6' 0"   13st 5lbs
b. Greenwich, 8th September 1961
CAREER: Blackheath S.F.A./Arsenal app, signing pro July
1979/Barnsley Aug 1981/Blackpool Aug 1985, fee £12,000/
Plymouth Argyle Mar 1987, fee £40,000/NOTTS June
1988, fee £70,000 (Scarborough loan Nov 1989)/Rotherham
United Aug 1990, fee £35,000/Chesterfield Oct 1993, in
exchange for Tony Brien/Hereford United Oct 1996/
Ilkeston Town Mar 1997/Chesterfield Community Officer
cs 1998/Bradford City manager Jan 2002 to Nov 2003/
Grimsby Town manager Mar to May 2004/Buxton F.C.
manager Jan 2005.
Debut v Bristol City (h) 27.8.88, drawn 0 – 0

Blond-haired Nicky Law had an excellent first season at
Meadow Lane, missing only three matches during the
campaign. A commanding central defender, he also chipped
in with four League goals, and an added bonus was his
ability to reach the near post with throw-ins. He was a
star in schools football, winning eight England caps that
included three against Scotland and an appearance in the
prestigious Queen's Silver Jubilee Match. Nicky left
Arsenal in search of first team football and made significant
contributions, and in excess of 100 League appearances,
for Barnsley, Rotherham United and Chesterfield.

His final aggregate figures were an impressive 575(12) League and Cup matches and 27 goals.

Appearances: FL: 44(3) apps 4 gls FAC: 1 app 0 gls
FLC: 4 apps 0 gls Other: 4 apps 0 gls
Total: 53(3) apps 4 gls
Honours: England Schoolboy International, 8 caps 1977

LAWLESS, Patrick Joseph Henry

Centre-half
CAREER: Calthorpe F.C./NOTTS Nov 1929/Loughborough Corinthians Aug 1930/Boston Town Aug 1931/Distillery July 1932/Coleraine Aug 1933/Distillery Jan 1934
Debut v Chelsea (a) 22.2.30, lost 1 – 3

Lawless joined Notts in the season when they secured only one point from their final seven Division Two matches and were relegated. Signed as understudy to Frank Froggatt, he was called upon only twice. In addition to his debut (above), he retained the centre-half berth for the following week's home match with Bury, which also resulted in a 3 – 1 defeat.

Appearances: FL: 2 apps 0 gls Total: 2 apps 0 gls

LAWRENCE, Edward

Wing-half   5' 8"   10st 12lbs
b. Cefn Mawr, near Wrexham, 24th August 1907
d. Nottingham, 20th July 1989
CAREER: Druids F.C./Wrexham am Feb 1926, pro Feb 1927/ Clapton Orient Aug 1928/NOTTS June 1931, fee £350/ Bournemouth & Boscombe Athletic Aug 1936/Clapton Orient May 1937/Players Athletic, Nottingham cs 1938/ NOTTS 1939/Grantham Town Aug 1946 to Dec 1948
Debut v Bradford City (a) 5.9.31, won 2 – 0

Eddie Lawrence began as a nineteen year-old amateur with Wrexham, and was still actively involved in the game in his fortieth year, when retained by Grantham Town for a second season in August 1947. Despite modest beginnings – he was allowed to leave the Racecourse after just 21

League matches – he improved steadily with Clapton Orient. Selected for the Welsh FA's tour of Canada in 1929, he gained his first full cap in 1930 and joined the newly promoted Magpies in June 1931. He was to enjoy a regular berth at left-half for four of his five seasons at Meadow Lane, his constructive approach coupled with outstanding headwork winning him a second cap against Scotland in 1932. After spells with Bournemouth and a second term with Clapton Orient, Eddie returned to Nottingham. He was working for John Player, the cigarette manufacturer, when recalled to Meadow Lane in 1939, but the outbreak of war saw him join the RAF, his tour of duty including three years spent in South Africa. He scouted for Notts for many years after the Second World War.

Appearances: FL: 138 apps 2 gls FAC: 4 apps 0 gls
Other: 1 app 0 gls Total: 143 apps 2 gls
Honours: Wales International, 2 caps 1930-32. Wales Junior International, 1 cap. Welsh FA Tour to Canada 1929

LAWTON, Thomas

Centre-forward 5' 11" 12st 0lbs
b. Bolton, 6th October 1919
d. Nottingham, 6th November 1996
CAREER: Lancashire Schoolboys/Hayes Athletic/ Rossendale United/Bolton Wanderers am 1934/Sheffield Wednesday am 1934/Burnley am May 1935, pro Oct 1936/ Everton Jan 1937, fee £6,500 (WW2 guest Aldershot; Morton & Tranmere Rovers)/Chelsea Nov 1945, fee £11,500/NOTTS Nov 1947, fee £20,000 plus another player/Brentford Mar 1952, fee £12,000, being player-manager from Jan 1953/Arsenal Sept 1953, fee £10,000 plus another player/Kettering Town Player-manager Feb 1956 to Apr 1957, fee £1,000/NOTTS manager May 1957 to July 1958/Kettering Town manager Nov 1963 to Apr 1964 when appointed a club director/NOTTS coach and chief scout Oct 1968 to Apr 1970
Debut v Northampton Town (a) 15.11.47, won 2 – 1 (scored one)

One of England's finest centre-forwards, Tommy Lawton scored an incredible 570 goals in three seasons of schoolboy football and was promptly snapped up by Burnley. His immense promise as a junior was fully realised in first-class football. Superlative in the air and equally brilliant on the ground, when at the height of his powers he was almost impossible to contain. He made his debut in League football at the age of sixteen and in his second game scored two goals at Swansea's Vetch Field in a 3 – 1 win. Five goals in his first seven matches proved to be a major contribution towards saving Burnley from relegation to the Third Division. A £6,500 transfer took him to Everton, initially as understudy to the great Dixie Dean.

After appearing alongside Dean in 1936-37 he took over as attack leader in 1937-38, and when World War Two suspended League football he had scored 70 League and Cup goals in only 95 matches. His international career commenced in season 1938-39 and spanned 23 full caps (22 goals). In wartime internationals he appeared in 23 matches, scoring 24 goals. A big money signing by Chelsea in November 1945, he was destined to stay for only one full League season (1946-47) but scored 35 League and Cup goals in 53 matches before his sensational transfer to Notts in November 1947.

Despite overtures from several First Division clubs, Tommy stunned the soccer world when he elected to join the Magpies, at that time standing in nineteenth place in the Third Division South. In his first season he lifted the side to sixth in the table; an incredible total of 76,566 spectators witnessing his first two home matches against Bristol Rovers and Swansea Town. Season 1948-49 saw stunning victories of 9 – 0 against Exeter City and 11 – 1 against Newport County, and a total of 102 goals, the only three-figure total in the Football League. 1949-50 saw the team run away winners of the Third Division South, with gates in excess of 40,000 turning up for Meadow Lane fixtures against Walsall, Ipswich Town, Torquay United and Forest. With gates the envy of most First Division teams, it was obvious that what was initially considered a prodigious outlay, Tommy's transfer fee of £20,000 had quickly been recouped by the vastly increased home gate receipts. Back in Division Two, the team struggled to adjust. Despite the outlay of a new club record transfer fee of £25,000 to recruit centre-half Leon Leuty from Bradford P.A., the departure of Jackie Sewell to Sheffield Wednesday – club leading scorer at the time – proved hugely disappointing.

What had been fondly dubbed 'The Lawton Era' ended in March of the following season when Tommy was transferred to Second Division Brentford. Despite taking over as player-manager in January 1953, he left Griffin Park in a surprise transfer to Arsenal and a return to Division One at 34 years of age. He spent two years at Highbury, scoring 13 goals in 35 League matches before joining Kettering Town as player-manager. In 1956-57 he led the Poppies to the championship of the Southern League with an eight points margin over Bedford Town, Tommy scoring 17 goals in 26 appearances. Goalkeeper during the successful campaign was Jack Wheeler who left with Lawton at the end of the season, when he was appointed manager at Meadow Lane in succession to caretaker Frank Broome. Without a win in his first seven matches in charge, a season of struggle ended in relegation from Division Two. In July 1958 Notts Board Minutes revealed that it was: 'Decided unanimously to dispense with the services of manager Mr. Tom Lawton.'

Despite approaching his 39th birthday he initially expressed a wish to resume his playing career but then changed his mind and decided to retire. His assistant, Jack Wheeler, remained at Meadow Lane completing 26 years as trainer, a stay that included 1,000 consecutive matches. He was rewarded with a benefit match against Forest in 1971.

————o————

Appearances: FL: 151 apps 90 gls FAC: 15 apps 13 gls
Total: 166 apps 103 gls
Honours: England International, 23 caps 1939-49. England Wartime International, 15 apps. FL Representative, 3 apps. (Everton) FL Division 1 champions 1939. (NOTTS) FL Division 3 South champions 1950

LEE, Garnet Morley

Right-back   5' 8"   12st 0lbs
b. Calverton, Nottingham, 7th June 1887
d. Calverton, Nottingham, 29th February 1976
CAREER: NOTTS Jan 1909 to 1911
Debut v Manchester United (a) 12.11.10, drawn 0 – 0

Garnet Lee was much better known as a county cricketer with Nottinghamshire (140 matches between 1910-22) and Derbyshire (229 matches, 1925-33). He also toured Jamaica with Tennison in 1927-28. An opening or middle order right-hand batsman and leg break and googly bowler he scored 14,858 runs, took 397 wickets and held 156 catches. His highest score was 200* for Notts v Leicestershire at Trent Bridge in 1913. As a soccer player he first appeared for Notts Reserves in season 1909-10, and deputised at right-back for Arthur Griffiths in four consecutive First Division matches spanning November/ December 1910. At the time he was the Reserve team's outside-right, but he made a good impression in his unfamiliar position. Directly opposed to George Wall the England international outside-left, the 'Football Post' reported that "His turn of speed considerably surprised George Wall, and the power of his returns astonished his own friends."

Appearances: FL: 4 apps 0 gls Total: 4 apps 0 gls

LEGG, Andrew

Left wing/Midfield   5' 8"   10st 7lbs
b. Neath, 28th July 1966
CAREER: Britton Ferry/Swansea City Aug 1988/NOTTS July 1993, fee £275,000/Birmingham City Feb 1996 (Ipswich Town loan Nov 1997)/Reading Feb 1998, fee £75,000 (Peterborough United loan Oct 1998)/Cardiff City Dec 1998/Peterborough United player-coach July 2003. Retired due to ill-health Apr 2005.
Debut v Middlesbrough (h) 14.8.93, lost 2 – 3

Andy's lengthy career began with Swansea City, where he had gained the experience of 200 plus matches and 38 goals at the time of his transfer to the Magpies. Renowned as a long-throw expert, he also had a sweet left foot, a great work ethic and the ability to out jump much taller opponents in aerial encounters. During his spell at Meadow Lane he was also found to be a valuable utility man, successfully filling the role of left-back in emergencies. He won full international recognition following his move to Birmingham City and later captained Cardiff City to promotion from Division Three in season 2000-01.

Appearances: FL: 85(4) apps 9 gls FAC: 7(1) apps 2 gls
FLC: 11 apps 0 gls Other: 13(2) apps 3 gls
Total: 116(7) apps 14 gls
Honours: Wales International, 6 caps. (Swansea City) Welsh Cup winners 1989 and 1991. (NOTTS) Anglo Italian Cup winners 1995, finalists 1994

LEONARD, John

Outside-right
CAREER: St Mirren/Derby County May 1897/NOTTS Mar 1898/Bedminster June 1898/Bristol Eastville Rovers May 1899
Debut v Liverpool (h) 2.4.1898, won 3 – 2 (scored one)

John Leonard played in only one First Division match for Derby County, scoring in a 1 – 2 defeat against Sheffield Wednesday. One week earlier he had made his first senior appearance for the Rams and scored the only goal of the game in a second round FA Cup win against Wolverhampton Wanderers. Derby reached the final at Crystal Palace, but Leonard had departed one month earlier, reported to be on trial with Notts. Despite a scoring debut against Liverpool he was not offered a longer engagement and departed in the close season to Bedminster. New to both professionalism and the Southern League, Bedminster was a brand new team and their recruits for the season also included two other former Notts players, Crone and Stewart.

Appearances: FL: 1 app 1 gl Total: 1 app 1 gl

LEONARD, Michael Christopher

Goalkeeper   5' 11"   11st 0lbs
b. Carshalton, 9th May 1959
CAREER: London Schoolboys/Epsom & Ewell/Halifax Town July 1976/NOTTS Sept 1979, fee £32,500/ Chesterfield Mar 1989, fee £20,000 (Halifax Town loan Nov 1990)/Instant Dict, Hong Kong 1994/South China, Hong Kong 1998/Nottingham Forest Academy coach 2001/ New Zealand national goalkeeping coach.
Debut v Luton Town (h) 15.9.79, drawn 0 – 0

Surrey born Mick Leonard supported West Ham United as a youngster, but his League career commenced with 68 appearances for Halifax Town. Initially in reserve to County's first six-figure signing, Raddy Avramovic, he eventually replaced Jim McDonagh in mid season 1983-84 and remained very much the man in possession thereafter. Having sampled League action in Divisions One, Two and Three during his Meadow Lane career, he unsurprisingly considered his most memorable match to be his first appearance in Division One when the Magpies won 1 – 0 against Manchester City at Maine Road on 19th February 1983.

Appearances: FL: 204 apps 0 gls FAC: 20 apps 0 gls FLC: 15 apps 0 gls Other: 15 apps 0 gls
Total: 254 apps 0 gls

---o---

LEUTY, Leon Harry

Centre-half 5' 11½" 12st 3lbs
b. Meole Brace, near Shrewsbury, 23rd October 1920
d. Nottingham, 19th December 1955
CAREER: St. James' Church School/Derby Schoolboys/ Derby County am 1936 (WW2 guest NOTTS)/Derby Corinthians/Rolls Royce/Derby County am Aug 1943, pro May 1944/Bradford P.A. Mar 1950, fee £20,000/NOTTS Sept 1950 to his death, fee £25,000.
Debut v Preston North End (h) 23.9.50, lost 1 – 3

Tall and dark and with a film star profile, Leon Leuty first appeared in Derby County's Central League side at the age of 17. When the Rams closed down during the war he appeared as a guest player for the Magpies but returned to Derby as a professional and was a member of their FA Cup winning team in 1946. A stylish and constructive centre-half with outstanding headwork, he combined football with his work as an engineer at the Rolls-Royce works. Considered to be one of the best uncapped centre-half backs in the country, he cost a record fee when signed from Bradford P.A. and was captain and king-pin of the Magpies defence until his untimely death from leukaemia at the age of 35.

Appearances: FL: 188 apps 3 gls FAC: 13 apps 1 gl
Total: 201 apps 4 gls
Honours: England 'B' International, 3 apps 1948-49. FL Representative, 2 apps 1947-48. (Derby County) FA Cup winners 1946

---o---

LEVERTON, Roland 'Tot'

Inside-forward 5' 8" 11st 2lbs
b. Whitwell, Derbyshire, 8th May 1926
d. Bulwell, Nottingham, 19th August 2003
CAREER: Whitwell School/Calverton Colliery/Clowne Town/Nottingham Forest Oct 1943/NOTTS Oct 1953/ Walsall July 1956 to 1957/Wisbech Town/Arnold St Mary's/ Calverton Colliery Aug 1962
Debut v Lincoln City (a) 3.10.53, lost 0 – 3

'Tot' Leverton was given his nickname during schooldays, when the tiny left winger showed up well against boys twice his size. After working for a time as a collier he realised his ambition to become a professional footballer. Beginning with Forest during wartime, he was signed after just one trial game. Enthusiastic and speedy, he overcame a double fracture of his left leg in October 1949 and went on to record 105 League and Cup appearances, scoring 36 goals. Strong and energetic, he was a regular first team player with the Magpies until a double fracture of a facial bone, sustained at Eastville in February 1954, halted a successful run of 20 matches. Outside of the game he worked at Calverton Colliery until 1982.

Appearances: FL: 45 apps 5 gls FAC: 6 apps 0 gls
Total: 51 apps 5 gls
Honours: (Nottingham Forest) FL Division Three South champions 1951

---o---

LEWIS, George

Full-back 5' 7½" 12st 8lbs
b. Chasetown, Staffs, January quarter 1875
CAREER: Walsall Town Swifts Nov 1894/Wellinborough Town July 1897/NOTTS Dec 1897/Bristol City July 1902/ Stourbridge/Leicester Fosse Oct 1903/Stourbridge 1904
Debut v Sheffield United (h) 1.1.1898, lost 1 – 3

Notts were very greatly in need of good left-back when they obtained George Lewis from Wellinborough Town at the mid point of season 1897-98. For several weeks before joining the Magpies he had not played, but a few weeks of training with his new colleagues returned him to concert pitch. By no means a graceful performer, but a stumbling block to the best, he proved to be a mainstay of the team that seemed unable to break a cycle of promotion challenges and relegation battles at twelve monthly intervals.

Appearances: FL: 129 apps 1 gl FAC: 8 apps 1 gl
Total: 137 apps 2 gls

---o---

LEWIS, Harold Howells 'Harry'

Inside-left   5' 8"   11st 0lbs
b. Abergavenny, Wales, 25th October 1910
CAREER: Dowlais United/Rochdale am July, pro Aug 1928/
Arsenal Mar 1931/Southend United May 1932/NOTTS June
1933/West Ham United June 1935/Swansea Town Mar
1937/Queen of the South June 1939/Watford Oct 1940
(WW2 guest Reading and Southend United)
Debut v Fulham (h) 2.9.33, won 4 – 1

Harry Lewis had a splendid debut with the Magpies, the
'Football Post' enthusing: " He showed excellent ball
control, and his passes to the wings were never off the
mark." A fair-haired Welsh schoolboy international, he
joined Rochdale as a youngster. Plucked from the foot of
Division Three North by the mighty Arsenal, he spent a
season as Alex James' understudy before returning to the
more modest theatre of Division Three South with
Southend United. After starting his first campaign at
Meadow Lane in such bright fashion, he made less
headway in his second term. He was one of many casualties
in the inevitable clear-out that followed the teams'
relegation from the Second Division. Joining West Ham
United, he was given an early first team debut, having
scored five goals in one London Combination fixture just
days before. Despite his goal-a-game aggregate, he was
restricted to just four first team matches for the Hammers.
He rounded off his League career with Swansea Town,
taking his career figures to 46 goals in 161 League matches.
Outside of the game he was an optician in Watford.

Appearances: FL: 32 apps 7 gls FAC: 1 app 0 gls
Total: 33 apps 7 gls
Honours: Wales Schoolboy International

LIBURD, Richard John

Utility 5' 10"   11st 1lb
b. Nottingham, 26th September 1973
CAREER: Nottingham Schoolboys/Clifton All Whites/
Eastwood Town Dec 1992/Middlesbrough Mar 1993, fee
£20,000/Bradford City July 1994, fee £200,000/Carlisle
United Feb 1998/NOTTS Aug 1998/Lincoln City Aug 2003/
Eastwood Town July 2004.
Debut as sub v Oldham Athletic (a) 8.8.98, won 3 – 1

Richard hit the local soccer headlines at an early age when
he helped Nottingham Schools Under-11s to win the
Evening Post Trophy, scoring the winner against
Birmingham Schools in April 1985. Four months later he
was voted 'Junior Player of the Year' by Clifton All
Whites. A cousin of Jermaine Jenas, the England
international, Richard also had early connections with
Forest but had slipped into non-League football with
Eastwood Town. A fee of £20,000 took him to
Middlesbrough where he played in 41 Division One
matches in 1993-94.

He followed his old manager, Lennie Lawrence, to
Bradford City moving on, very briefly, to Carlisle United
before returning homeward to Meadow Lane. In either
full-back role or midfield he remained a familiar and
popular figure in the Magpies line up, a competent
professional with great utility value and occasional flashes
of outstanding constructive brilliance.

Appearances: FL: 127(27) apps 9 gls FAC: 8(4) apps 2
gls FLC: 5(2) apps 0 gls Other: 1(1) apps 0 gls
Total: 141(34) apps 11 gls

LINDLEY, James Edward

Goalkeeper   6' 2"   13st 0lbs
b. Sutton-in-Ashfield, 23rd July 1981
CAREER: NOTTS trainee May 1996, pro July 1999
(Lincoln City loan Aug 2000) (Mansfield Town loan Dec
2000) (Gresley Rovers loan Feb 2001)/Gresley Rovers July
2001/Hucknall Town/Tamworth Aug 2003 (Hucknall Town
loan Feb 2004)/Stafford Rangers Mar 2004/Hucknall Town
June 2004/Stafford Rangers Aug 2004.
Debut as sub v Cardiff City (a) 18.9.99, lost 1 – 2

Nicely built for his position, Jim progressed through the
Magpies youth system to become a professional at
eighteen years of age. Nevertheless, his time at Meadow
Lane was spent as understudy to Darren Ward, with added
competition in the shape of Paul Gibson. His two
appearances in the starting line-up came consecutively in
season 2000-01 and both ended in comprehensive defeat
at Walsall (1 – 5) and Wycombe Wanderers (1 – 3). After
three separate loan spells in the same season he was
released in the summer, and was quickly snapped up by
Gresley Rovers.

Appearances: FL: 2(1) apps 0 gls FLC: 0(1) apps 0 gls
Total: 2(2) apps 0 gls

LINDLEY, Dr. Tinsley O.B.E.

Centre-forward 5' 9"   10st 9lbs
b. Nottingham, 27th October 1865
d. Nottingham, 31st March 1940
CAREER: Nottingham High School/The Leys, Cambridge/
Cambridge University (Blue 1885-6-6-8, captain '88)/
Nottingham Forest 1883-94/Corinthians 1885-94/ He also
played occasionally for the Casuals, London Swifts and
Crusaders, played three times for NOTTS between Nov
1889 and Mar 1890, and once for Preston North End in
Feb 1892.
Debut v Aston Villa (h) 9.11.1889, drawn 1 – 1

In the days when an England cap against Scotland was
the game's highest honour, Tinsley Lindley was capped
in the showpiece event for four consecutive years.

Once described as "the ideal centre-forward in an ideal international team," he was a true sporting all rounder, appearing as a right-hand batsman and slow bowler for Cambridge University in 1885 and for Nottinghamshire C.C.C. in 1888. In the latter year he took his B.A. Degree and was called to the bar in 1889. He had a long career practising in common law on the Midland Circuit, and graduated as a Doctor of Laws at Cambridge in 1900. The 1901 Census showed him to be a barrister at law with a wife, six children and three servants. His debut for the Magpies, which came about when James Oswald was suspended, leaving a vacancy at centre-forward, caused Aston Villa to protest that he was not registered. The Football League upheld the accusation and Notts were fined £5 and had one point deducted, Lindley appealed against the judgement personally, asking the League to reconsider their decision. He must have wished that he hadn't bothered, as the League increased the fine to £30, plus the original £5, and two points deducted! During the First World War he did a tremendous amount of work in connection with the special constable movement. He became an O.B.E. in January 1918 and was awarded the King's Jubilee Medal in 1935.

Appearances: FL: 2 apps 0 gls FAC: 1 app 0 gls
Total: 3 apps 0 gls
Honours: England International, 13 caps 1886-91

———————o———————

LINTON, James A

Goalkeeper   6' 0"   12st 6lbs
b. Tollcross, Glasgow, 2nd December 1930
CAREER: Beith Juniors/Vale of Clyde am July 1948/ Kirkintilloch Rob Roy am/NOTTS am, signing pro July 1951/Watford June 1959, fee £877-10s./Poole Town July 1963/Ramsgate Athletic/Dunstable Town/Hatfield Town
Debut v Huddersfield Town (a) 8.11.52, lost 0 – 1

First pressed into League service when Gordon Bradley was injured, goalkeeper Jimmy Linton made his debut against Huddersfield Town at Leeds Road in November 1952. The goalkeeper at the other end of the field was Jack Wheeler, who subsequently became Notts' trainer for 26 years and well in excess of 1,000 consecutive matches prior to his retirement. Linton completed his period of National Service in March 1953, but it was not until season 1955-56 that he enjoyed an extended run in the first XI. It was a depressing period for the Meadow Lane faithful, who saw their team suffer consecutive relegations from Division Two in 1957-58 and Division Three a year later. When Linton returned to Meadow Lane in February 1960 – as Watford's captain for the day – he was unable to prevent the Magpies from recording their 14th consecutive home League win, but both teams won promotion that season, Notts as runners-up to Walsall with Watford in fourth place.

Appearances: FL: 114 apps 0 gls FAC: 6 apps 0 gls
Total: 120 apps 0 gls

LISTER, Eric

Outside-left   5' 7"   10st 8lbs
b. Willenhall, 13th August 1933
CAREER: Wolverhampton Wanderers am/NOTTS Sept 1951 to 1957/Boston United
Debut v Doncaster Rovers (h) 11.4.55, won 4 – 0

Signed as a promising eighteen year-old wingman in 1951, Eric Lister had some considerable time to wait for a senior outing. This came late in season 1954-55, the 4 – 0 victory against Doncaster Rovers featuring a hat-trick from Jimmy Jackson. Oddly enough, Doncaster Rovers provided the opposition in his final League outing, a 2 – 4 defeat at Belle Vue on 29th December 1956. In season 1961-62 Eric was a member of the Boston United team that won the championship of the Central Alliance.

Appearances: FL: 8 apps 0 gls Total: 8 apps 0 gls

———————o———————

LIVESEY, Daniel 'Danny'

Central defender   6' 2"   13st 0lbs
b. Salford, 31st December 1984
CAREER: Bolton Wanderers trainee, signing pro Aug 2002 (NOTTS loan Sept to Dec 2003) (Rochdale loan Feb to May 2004) (Blackpool loan Aug 2004) (Carlisle United loan Dec 2004)/Carlisle United Jan 2005.
Debut v Luton Town (h) 6.9.2003, drawn 1 – 1

One of manager Billy Dearden's best loan signings, the young Bolton Wanderer made an immediate impact when drafted in to a struggling side, (and a club struggling to raise £250,000 to save themselves from unthinkable extinction.) Notts secured their future, and in Livesey's second appearance claimed their first win of the season to lift themselves off the foot of Division Two. A hamstring injury necessitated his return to Bolton, and the Magpies were unable to complete the signing of the 19 year-old defender ahead of the year-end deadline for the arrangement of long-term loan deals.

Appearances: FL: 9(2) apps 0 gls Other: 1 app 0 gls
Total: 10(2) apps 0 gls

———————o———————

LOCKER, William 'Billy'

Inside-left   5' 6 2"   10st 4lbs
b. Long Eaton, 16th February 1866
d. Derby, 15th August 1952
CAREER: Long Eaton Rangers/Stoke 1889/Long Eaton Rangers/Derby County/NOTTS June 1890/Loughborough Mar 1892
Debut v Bolton Wanderes (a) 6.9.1890, lost 2 – 4

A biography in the 'Nottingham Daily Express' in 1891 ran as follows: "Locker is a very good player of a game peculiarly his own. He is fast, a good shot on goal, and most energetic in the field."

Another correspondent had a slightly different view: "Locker is seldom brilliant, but has a knack of scoring goals, and I fancy that this is the most useful quality a player can possess." Apart from McInnes he was the lightest member of the team that reached the FA Cup Final in 1891, but despite his slight physique he was strong and a good finisher. He came close to international recognition, appearing for the North against the South at Sunderland in 1889, and was chosen as a reserve for the international against Ireland. Outside of the game the 1901 Census gave his occupation as a Lace threader. In the years immediately preceding the Great War he was a described as 'An important personage in Long Eaton and a local councillor.'

Appearances: FL: 21 apps 12 gls FAC: 6 apps 2 gls
Total: 27 apps 14 gls
Honours: (NOTTS) FA Cup finalists 1891

———————o———————

LOCKIE, Alexander James
Centre-half   5' 10"   11st 13lbs
b. South Shields, 11th April 1915
CAREER: Stanhope Road School/South Shields Schoolboys/ Y.M.C.A. Juniors/South Shields St. Andrew's Juniors/ Reyrolle's F.C. (where he worked as a draughtsman)/ Sunderland Aug 1935/North Shields Oct 1939 (WW2 guest Newcastle United)/NOTTS Sept 1946
Debut v Norwich City (h) 14.9.46, won 3 – 0

Alex Lockie was making very satisfactory progress with Sunderland (29 appearances in 1938-39) when the outbreak of War halted his progress. He was still on the books at Roker Park when post-war football resumed, but the reason given for his release was – if true – highly unusual. Employed as an electrical engineer's draughtsman, he was said to find difficulty in getting off work to play in away matches! This did not appear to hamper his availability at Meadow Lane, although the fact that he continued to reside in Sunderland involved him in some marathon train journeys. It was estimated that he had travelled something approaching 1,000 miles over the Christmas period of 1946. Although he did not feature during season 1947-48, in December 1947 he was still on the books, but on the open to transfer list.

Appearances: FL: 23 apps 0 gls FAC: 3 apps 0 gls
Total: 26 apps 0 gls

———————o———————

LOGAN, James
Centre-forward 5' 8"   11st 12lbs
b. Troon, Ayrshire 24th June 1870
d. Loughborough, 25th May 1896, age 25
CAREER: Ayr F.C./Sunderland Aug 1891/Ayr F.C. Nov 1891/ Aston Villa July 1892/NOTTS Oct 1893, fee £15/Dundee Mar 1895/Ayr United Apr 1895/Dundee May 1895/ Newcastle United June 1895/Loughborough Jan to Mar 1896
Debut v Grimsby Town (h) 5.10.1893, won 3 – 0 (scored two)

One of only three players to score a hat-trick in a FA Cup Final, Jimmy Logan was described in 1894 as: "A capital centre-forward who keeps his wings well together. He passes very accurately and shoots most effectively at goal." Only two years after his moment of national glory, his untimely death was brought about by a chill that developed into pneumonia. This occurred when the Loughborough teams' kit failed to arrive in Manchester for the game against Newton Heath. In typical Lancashire weather - torrential rain – the Loughborough team had to play in their own clothes. The train return journey, in sodden clothes, was to end in tragedy for the 25 year-old Scot whose brief association with the Loughborough club had inspired them to seven late season wins, and an unlikely escape from relegation.

Appearances: FL: 40 apps 31 gls FAC: 7 apps 6 gls
Other: 7 apps 0 gls Total: 54 apps 37 gls
Honours: Scotland International, 1 cap 1891. (NOTTS) FA Cup winners 1894

———————o———————

LOGAN, Peter "Paddy"
Centre-forward 5' 9"   11st 9lbs
b. Glasgow, circa 1877
CAREER: Motherwell Dec 1896/NOTTS May 1898/ Woolwich Arsenal May 1899/Reading May 1900/Woolwich Arsenal July 1901/Brentford Nov 1901
Debut v Blackburn Rovers (h) 5.11.1898, won 5 – 3 (scored two)

For a free transfer signing Paddy Logan proved to be a thoroughly competent leader of the attack who successfully challenged Boucher for the first team jersey. 5'9" in height and sturdily built, he believed in keeping the ball on the ground and shooting hard and often. In two subsequent and separate spells with Woolwich Arsenal he recorded, in all competitions, 21 goals in 53 matches.

Appearances: FL: 16 apps 6 gls FAC: 1 app 0 gls Total: 17 apps 6 gls

———————o———————

LORMOR, Anthony

Forward   6' 0"   13st 6lbs
b. Ashington, 29th October 1970
CAREER: Newcastle United trainee, signing pro Feb 1988
(Norwich City loan Nov 1988)/Lincoln City Jan 1990, fee
£25,000 (Halifax Town loan Feb 1994)/Peterborough
United July 1994/Chesterfield Dec 1994/Preston North End
Nov 1997, fee £130,000 plus David Reeves (NOTTS loan
Feb - Mar 1998)/Mansfield Town July 1998, Fee £20,000/
Hartlepool United Aug 2000, fee £30,000 (Shrewsbury Town
loan Feb 2002)/Telford United 2002; retired Jan 2003/
Sutton Town coach Dec 2003.
Debut v Scarborough (h) 21.2.98, won 1 – 0

Lack of first team opportunities with Newcastle United,
where he had scored three goals in six starts and two
substitute appearances, saw Tony Lormor drop down
two divisions when he joined Lincoln City. For the Imps
he recorded 30 League goals in 90(10) appearances, this
despite a serious knee injury that sidelined him for the
whole of season 1992-93. Five months with Peterborough
United preceded his move to Chesterfield, where he scored
10 goals in 23 League matches in his first season. He was
also a scorer in both the semi-final and Wembley final in
the end of season play-offs that took Chesterfield into
Division Two. After 35 goals in 97(16) matches, a brief
spell with Preston North End was followed by his loan
spell with the Magpies, a move that briefly reunited him
with former Chesterfield colleague, Phil Robinson. Tony
passed the milestone of a century of League goals with
Hartlepool United, appeared briefly with Telford United
before announcing his retirement in January 2003 with
the intention of concentrating on a refereeing career.

Appearances: FL: 2(5) apps 0 gls Total: 2(5) apps 0 gls

———————o———————

LOVATT, Harold Albert

Centre-forward 5' 9"   12st 4lbs
b. Audley, Staffs, 18th August 1905
d. Stafford, October quarter 1971
CAREER: Wood Lane United/Red Street St Chad's/Audley
1923/Sunderland trial/Stoke trial/Port Vale Mar 1924/
Preston North End July 1924/Crewe Alexandra June 1925/
Bradford City Mar 1926, fee £500/Wrexham Nov 1926,
fee £300/Scarborough Aug 1927/Leicester City May 1928/
NOTTS Dec 1930/Northampton Town Oct 1931/
Macclesfield Town July 1932/Stafford Rangers Nov 1934/
Winsford United July 1936
Debut v Coventry City (h) 27.12.30, won 4 – 1 (scored
one)

Harry Lovatt made his League debut with Crewe Alexandra
in August 1925. After eight matches at outside-left,
without a goal, he was switched to centre-forward and
responded with 15 goals in 29 matches. He left to join
Bradford City in March of the same season and scored
against the Wolves on his debut, but was never again able
to reproduce the form of his first season of League football.

Despite an excellent scoring ratio throughout his career
(41 League goals in 84 matches for six different clubs,) he
failed to establish a regular first team berth anywhere. At
Meadow Lane he appeared in seven matches in the run in
to promotion from Division Three South, and scored twice
in his final outing, against Barnsley, in September of the
following season.

Appearances: FL: 9 apps 3 gls FAC: 2 apps 0 gls
Total: 11 apps 3 gls

———————o———————

LOVELL, Frederick W

Inside-forward
b. Crewe, 18th June 1929
CAREER: Loughborough College/RAF football/NOTTS am
Apr 1953 to 1954
Debut v Hull City (h) 25.4.53, won 2 – 0

Fred Lovell was invited to sign amateur forms after playing
an outstanding game for the RAF against the Magpies
Reserve team. A Flying Officer stationed at RAF Spitalgate
at Grantham, he showed great promise as an enthusiastic
inside forward with a fearless, determined approach and
a fine shot. Services commitments limited his availability,
but in six early-season matches in 1953-54 he found the
net in matches against Bury and Bristol Rovers.

Appearances: FL: 7 apps 2 gls Total: 7 apps 2 gls

———————o———————

LOWE, Edward

Wing-half   5' 11"   11st 10lbs
b. Halesowen, Worcs, 11th July 1925
CAREER: Halesowen & Stourbridge Schoolboys/Napier
Aircraft Company/Millwall am/Finchley/Kynoch's Works
(Birmingham)/Aston Villa Sept 1945/Fulham May 1950,
fee £10,000/NOTTS manager June 1963, player-manager
Sept 1963 to Apr 1965/Plymouth Argyle scout Sept 1965
Debut v Oldham Athletic (a) 26.12.63, lost 0 – 2

Hard working and stylish, Eddie Lowe's well-judged
passes and positional play earned him three England caps
during his Aston Villa days. On the summer tour of 1947
he played in the remarkable 10 – 0 victory against Portugal
in Lisbon. He was transferred to Fulham, along with his
brother Reg, and stayed for thirteen seasons, accumulating
in excess of 500 League and Cup appearances, a record
later surpassed by Johnny Haynes. On June 1st 1963 he
was appointed player-manager of Notts, taking over the
seat vacated by Tim Coleman. For a lengthy spell he
resisted the playing urge, but in the hope that his
experienced leadership would lead the club away from
the foot of the table, he made his debut at Oldham Athletic
on Boxing Day 1963.

Unfortunately he succumbed to injuries, and relegation from Division Three ensued. He made a final playing appearance in the first home match of the following season at the age of 39. He was dismissed in April 1965, following a depressing run of results in February and March - one win in ten Division Four matches.

Appearances: FL: 9 apps 0 gls Total: 9 apps 0 gls
Honours: England International, 3 caps 1947

LOXLEY, Herbert

Wing-half   5' 11"   11st 4lbs
b. Bonsall, Derbyshire, 3rd February 1934
CAREER: Bonsall School/Bonsall F.C./Derbyshire County Amateurs (Trials with Derby County, York City and Coventry City)/NOTTS pro Mar 1952/Mansfield Town July 1964/Lockheed Leamington Sept 1965/Lincoln City trainer-coach July 1966 to cs 1987 (including a spell as manager July 1970 to Mar 1971)
Debut v Ipswich Town (h) 30.4.55, won 2 – 1

Bert Loxley won a County cap with Derbyshire Amateurs, helping them to victory against Lancashire at Boundary Park, Oldham. He had a number of unsuccessful trials with League clubs before a scout invited him to Meadow Lane. Just one outing with the Reserves against Mansfield Town was sufficient for him to be signed on professional forms. A versatile, whole-hearted defender and loyal club man, Bert played mostly at left and centre-half, with occasional outings in the attack. He appeared in Divisions Two, Three and Four during his twelve years at Meadow Lane, sampling two relegations and one promotion along the way. During a lengthy association with Lincoln City, where he was a member of the training staff, he was obliged to make a playing "come back" in an injury crisis, playing in seven first team matches. Bert left Lincoln City following their relegation to the Conference and opened his own sports physiotherapy business. His son Tony was also on Lincoln City's books in the 1970s.

Appearances: FL: 245 apps 9 gls FAC: 13 apps 1 gl FLC: 8 apps 1 gl Total: 266 apps 11 gls

LUDLAM, Craig

Full-back   5' 11"   11st 5lbs
b. Sheffield, 8th November 1976
CAREER: Sheffield Wednesday trainee, signing pro May 1995 to cs 1997 (NOTTS loan Oct 1996)
Debut v Burnley (a) 19.10.96, lost 0 – 1

Craig Ludlam's solitary League appearance at Burnley was cut short by injury, terminating his loan spell to the Magpies in the relegation season 1996-97. A reserve full-back with Sheffield Wednesday, he was released in the summer without having made a senior appearance for the Owls.

Appearances: FL: 1 app 0 gls Total: 1 app 0 gls

LUND, Gary James

Forward   5' 11"   11st 0lbs
b. Grimsby, 13th September 1964
CAREER: Humberside Schoolboys/Grimsby Town app, signing pro July 1983/Lincoln City Aug 1986, in exchange for Philip Turner/NOTTS June 1987, fee £27,000 (Hull City loan Aug 1992 and again Jan 1993 and Mar 1995)/Chesterfield Dec 1995 to cs 1997/Gedling Town/Ilkeston Town manager.
Debut v Wigan Athletic (h) 15.8.87, drawn 4 – 4

Originally a midfield player, Gary was quickly switched into a forward role by Grimsby Town and in three seasons scored 24 League goals in 47(13) matches. He arrived at Meadow Lane from Lincoln City who, despite Gary's 13 goals in 41(3) matches in 1986-87, suffered relegation from the Football League for the fourth time in their 95-year history. During his eight seasons at Meadow Lane Gary experienced fluctuating fortunes with two promotion campaigns and two demotions. In terms of goal scoring, his best campaigns were his first, 1987-88, when he netted 21 in all competitions; and 1993-94 when he scored 18. The great Tommy Lawton's verdict on Gary, shortly after his arrival at County was: "Good in the air, not too bad on the ground, and he scores goals."

His League career ended at Chesterfield, with aggregate figures of 106 League goals in 345(46) matches.

Appearances: FL: 223(25) apps 62 gls FAC: 13(3) apps 4 gls FLC: 15(3) apps 5 gls Other: 28(6) apps 8 gls
Total: 279(37) apps 79 gls
Honours: England Schools U-18 International, 3 caps 1983. England U-21 International, 3 apps 1985-86. (NOTTS) Anglo Italian Cup finalists 1994

LUNN, Henry "Harry"

Outside-right   5' 6"   10st 10lbs
b. Lurgan, N Ireland, 2nd March 1925
d. Swindon, 2nd February 1980
CAREER: Glenavon/NOTTS July 1946/Portsmouth July 1947/Swindon Town May 1948 to 1953
Debut v Brighton & Hove Albion (a) 12.10.46, lost 2 – 3 (scored one)

One of five Irishmen on the Magpies' books in 1946, Harry Lunn did not begin the season as first choice, but a scoring debut at Brighton was followed by a 23-match run in the seniors. He played in only one First Division game during his season with Portsmouth, but prospered in the Third Division South with Swindon Town, appearing in 195 League matches and scoring 30 goals in an excellent five years at the County Ground.

Appearances: FL: 24 apps 5 gls FAC: 3 apps 0 gls
Total: 27 apps 5 gls

LYLE, David

Inside-left
CAREER: NOTTS Nov 1890
Debut v Sunderland (a) 24.1.1891, lost 0 – 4

Deputised twice at inside-left for Billy Locker in the late stages of season 1890-91. After losing 4 – 0 in his debut match, the Magpies completed a 'double' when they beat Burnley 4 – 0 a fortnight later. Locker returned for the season's final League fixture, and scored one of the goals in a 7 – 1 hammering of Blackburn Rovers. One week later, the teams met again in the FA Cup Final at Kennington Oval. Despite starting as strong favourites, the Magpies were three goals behind at half time and were disappointingly beaten 3 – 1, the Rovers lifting the trophy for the fifth time.

Appearances: FL: 2 apps 0 gls Total: 2 apps 0 gls

LYMAN, Colin Charles

Forward   5' 10 2"   11st 6lbs
b. Northampton, 9th March 1914
d. Cambridge, 9th May 1986
CAREER: East End Rangers/Semilong United/Northampton Town 'A' Team/Rushden Town (West Bromwich Albion trial)/Southend United am Mar 1934/Northampton Town am Mar, pro Nov 1934/Tottenham Hotspur June 1937 (WW2 guest Aldershot, Chesterfield, Coventry City, Derby County, Leicester City, Northampton Town, Nottingham Forest, NOTTS and Port Vale)/Port Vale May 1946/Nottingham Forest Oct 1946/Ransome & Marles player-manager June 1947/NOTTS Aug 1947/Nuneaton Borough player-coach June 1948, and by early 1950 player-manager, resigned Jan 1951/Long Eaton Town player-manger Jan 1951/British Timken F.C.
Debut v Ipswich Town (a) 23.8.46, lost 0 – 2

Prior to the outbreak of WW2, Colin Lyman had enjoyed productive spells with Northampton Town (31 goals in 85 League matches) and with the Spurs (10 goals in 46 League matches.) During the period of hostilities he assisted no fewer than nine different clubs, and three of them were sufficiently impressed to sign him in the immediate post war years. Notts brought him back for a final season of senior football after he had left Forest to become player manager of Ransome and Marles. In the month of his 34th birthday he netted the winner against Crystal Palace and played in his final League match, a 0 – 1 defeat at Aldershot. His career aggregate figures were 56 goals in 187 League matches.

Appearances: FL: 21 apps 5 gls Total: 21 apps 5 gls

MACARTNEY, Charles William

Centre-forward 5'9"   11st 7lbs
b. Stamford, Lincs, 4th February 1910
d. Peterborough, January quarter 1982
CAREER: St Martin's School (Stamford)/Stamford Town/NOTTS June 1932/Wrexham June 1935/Carlisle United July 1937/York City Nov 1937/Darlington Mar 1938/Peterborough United Aug 1938/Grantham Town 1946, subsequently becoming manager.
Debut v Bradford City (h) 24.9.32, won 2 – 0

Charlie Macartney began, alongside his elder brother Ernest, with his local club Stamford Town. An excellent 1931-32 season, when he scored 26 goals in as many matches, attracted the attention of a number of League clubs, the Magpies winning the race for his signature. Initially as understudy to the free scoring Tom Keetley he was limited to eight first team appearances in his first season at Meadow Lane. He had shown sufficient promise, however, to allow the Magpies to transfer Keetley to Lincoln City in June 1933, feeling that they had a ready made replacement already to hand. Their faith was justified in 1933-34 when Macartney finished the season as leading scorer, by a wide margin, with 15 goals in 34 matches.

Along with team, relegated from Division Two in 1934-35, he had a season to forget, losing his place in early season after a disastrous start that featured just one win in the first 17 matches. His goal scoring touch returned following his transfer to Wrexham, with 24 League goals in 36 matches in 1935-36. In the final season prior to the outbreak of the Second World War, 1938-39, he signed off with 29 Midland League goals plus nine in the FA Cup.

Appearances: FL: 52 apps 19 gls FAC: 1 app 0 gls
Total: 53 apps 19 gls

———————o———————

McCAIRNS, Thomas
Centre-forward   5'9"   11st10lbs
b. Dinsdale, Co Durham, 22nd December 1873
d. Willesden, Middlesex, July quarter 1932
CAREER: Middlesbrough Ironopolis/Whitby 1891/Grimsby Town May 1893/Bristol Rovers May 1898/NOTTS May 1899/Lincoln City Nov 1899/Barnsley June 1901/Wellingborough May 1902/Queens Park Rangers May 1903/Brighton & Hove Albion Dec1903/Southern United Sept 1904/Kettering Town
Debut v Sheffield United (a) 30.9.1899, lost 1 – 2

Two pieces of soccer history were made when the Magpies opened the Spurs new ground at White Hart Lane with a friendly match against the Magpies. Tom McCairns became the first player to score a goal on the new ground. In the same match, Notts' goalkeeper Suter was injured and Walter Bull went into goal, thus completing a remarkable record of having appeared in every position on the field for Notts. For the record, Spurs won by 4 – 1. A cricket professional with Caistor, near Lincoln, McCairns teamed up with Harry Fletcher a former Grimsby Town colleague, when he moved to Trent Bridge. Sadly, he was unable to reproduce his Mariners' form (86 goals in 137 appearances,) quickly moving on to Lincoln City, where he reached the milestone of 100 League goals.

Appearances: FL: 4 apps 0 gls Total: 4 apps 0 gls
Honours: FL Representative, 1 app 1895

———————o———————

McCALL, John
Outside-right   5' 7"   11st 7lbs
b. Muirkirk, Ayrshire, 1877
CAREER: Muirkirk Athletic/Glasgow Strathclyde/Kilmarnock Dean Park/Hibernian Aug 1901/Bristol Rovers June 1902/NOTTS May 1903 to 1904
Debut v Sunderland (a) 1.9.03, lost 1 – 4

A Scot of varied experience, John McCall was the first outside-right fielded by Notts in season 1903-4.

Deposed after appearing in the first three fixtures, he was not called upon again. Notts' directors must have regretted the release of Richard Joynes – who played in all but three League matches in 1902-03 – as they fielded no less than seven players on the right wing in 1903-04. McCall's best season was spent with Hibernian, who in addition to their success in collecting the Scottish Cup also won the Glasgow Charity Cup, the East of Scotland League championship and the Rosebury Charity Bowl in season 1901-02.

Appearances: FL: 3 apps 0 gls Total: 3 apps 0 gls
Honours: Scotland Junior International. (Hibernian) Scottish Cup winners, 1902

———————o———————

McCALLUM, Cornelius J. 'Neil'
Inside-right
b. Bonhill, Dunbartonshire, 3rd July 1868
d. Glasgow, 5th November 1920
CAREER: Renton Athletic 1884/2nd Renton 1885/Renton 1886 (Glasgow Rangers loan Feb 1888)/Celtic May 1888/Blackburn Rovers Feb 1890/Celtic Jan 1891/Nottingham Forest Aug 1892/Loughborough 1894/Newark Town 1894/NOTTS June 1895/Heanor Town Sept 1896/Middleton Sept 1897/Folkestone Aug 1898/Gravesend Oct 1903/Celtic May 1905
Debut v Darwen (h) 28.9.1895, won 4 – 1

A famous name in Celtic's history, being the scorer of their first goal in their very first fixture, a 5 – 1 win against Shettleston in September 1888. Earlier, he was capped by Scotland as a Renton player, and assisted the Renton club to victory in the Scottish Cup Final in February 1888 with a record score of 6 – 1 against Cambuslang. In English football, he did rather better with Forest than with Notts, scoring 13 goals in 37 matches for the Reds, making his debut in Forest's first Football League fixture, a 2 – 2 draw at Everton on 3rd September 1892. All of his appearances for the Magpies were made at inside-right, whereas his reputation had been made as an extreme wingman, elusive to a degree and fully warranting his nickname 'The Shadow.'

Appearances: FL: 13 apps 3 gls FAC: 2 apps 0 gls
Total: 15 apps 3 gls
Honours: Scotland International, 1 cap 1888. Scottish League representative, 1 app. (Renton) Scottish Cup winners 1888. (Celtic) Scottish Cup winners 1889; finalists 1892

———————o———————

McCANN, Grant Samuel
Defender/Midfield   5'10"   12st 0lbs
b. Belfast, 14th April 1980
CAREER: West Ham United trainee, signing pro July 1998
(Livingston loan Aug 1999) (NOTTS loan Aug 2000)
(Cheltenham Town loan Oct 2000 and again Oct 2002)/
Cheltenham Town Jan 2003, fee £57,000
Debut v Millwall (h) 19.8.2000, lost 3 – 4

Injury cut short Grant McCann's early season loan spell
with the Magpies, and in October he embarked on another
loan to Cheltenham Town. Afforded few opportunities
with West Ham United, the talented left-side midfielder
had a second lengthy loan spell with Cheltenham before
finally becoming their record buy in January 2003. Grant
was in the Robins' team that opposed Notts in the final
fixture of the season, when a 1 – 0 result in favour of the
Magpies condemned them to relegation from Division
Two.

Appearances: FL: 2 apps 0 gls FLC: 1 app 0 gls
Total: 3 apps 0 gls
Honours: Northern Ireland International, 9 caps 2000-
03. Northern Ireland U-21 International, 11 apps.

McCAPPIN, Samuel A
Goalkeeper   5'11 **2**"   13st 0lbs
b. Kilburn, London, July quarter 1875
d. Ilford, Essex, April quarter 1945
CAREER: Barking Excelsior/St. Luke's (Canning Town)/
Barking Woodville/Ilford F.C. 1896 (Played once for The
Vampires in Nov 1896)/ NOTTS Oct 1899
Debut v Burnley (h) 28.10.1899, won 6 – 1

As is the case with many goalkeepers, McCappin began
as a forward with Barking Excelsior, a London suburban
club. Being injured he was placed in goal, and never played
anywhere else subsequently. He was an Essex County
player on 27 occasions, and was first 'spotted' by Notts
when he played for The Vampires against County in a
friendly match on 5th November 1896. Although Notts
won 7 – 3, McCappin received warm praise for his display.
"His clearances were a feature of the game, and better
goalkeeping has not been seen at Trent Bridge for some
time," reported the local correspondent. A dip in form
and confidence by goalkeeper Suter led to McCappin's
introduction, and he was signed on a professional form
immediately following his debut, a 6 – 1 win against
Burnley. In the 1901 Census McCappin's occupation
was given as a gas fitter's labourer.

Appearances: FL: 7 apps 0 gls Total: 7 apps 0 gls

McCARTHY, Patrick 'Paddy'
Defender   6'1"   12st 8lbs
b. Dublin, 31st May 1983
CAREER: Manchester City trainee, signing pro June 2000
(Boston United loan Nov 2002-Feb 2003) (NOTTS loan
Mar-Apr 2003)/Leicester City Mar 2005, fee £100,000
Debut v Huddersfield Town (h) 29.3.2003, won 3 – 2

Tall, slim defender whose League debut was memorable
for the wrong reasons. On loan from Manchester City to
Boston United, he was sent off at Hull City in his first
match for The Pilgrims. Nevertheless, after 11(1) outings
he had impressed sufficiently to warrant the offer of a
contract at York Street. Opting to return to Manchester
City, a second loan spell brought him to Meadow Lane
where he impressed as a strong tackling right-back who
liked to get forward in support of the attack. In March
2005, when still without a senior appearance for
Manchester City, Paddy was transferred to Leicester City,
who had two first team central defenders sidelined due to
injury.

Appearances: FL: 6 apps 0 gls Total: 6 apps 0 gls
Honours: Republic of Ireland Youth International

McCAVANA, William Terence
Centre-half   6'0"   12st 0lbs
b. Belfast, 24th January 1921
CAREER: Coleraine/NOTTS am Aug 1948/Coleraine
Debut v Leyton Orient (h) 2.4.49, won 2 – 1

Terence McCavana, an Irish amateur international centre-
half, was on the books of Coleraine before he was posted
with the RAF to Newton Aerodrome. As he was unable
to continue with the Irish club he asked for his release.
This was granted and he signed an amateur form at
Meadow Lane at the end of August 1948. He had an
unfortunate start, pulling a leg muscle on his debut for
the Reserves against Forest Reserves and then suffered a
broken leg. Happily, he made a fine recovery, his three
first team outings being made as right full-back, as deputy
for Aubrey Southwell, whose long ever-present run was
broken by injury. McCavana rejoined Coleraine on
demobilisation and won three full caps for his country,
deputising at centre-half for the Manchester United pivot,
Jackie Blanchflower, in matches against Scotland (twice)
and England.

Appearances: FL: 3 apps 0 gls Total: 3 apps 0 gls
Honours: Northern Ireland International, 3 caps 1955-
56. Northern Ireland Amateur International. Irish League
representative, 6 apps 1949-55. (Coleraine) Irish Cup
finalists 1948 & 1953

McCLELLAND, John

Central defender   6' 12" 12st 4lbs
b. Belfast, 7th December 1955
CAREER: Portadown/Cardiff City Feb 1974/Bangor City
cs 1975/Mansfield Town May 1978, fee £8,000/Glasgow
Rangers May 1981, fee £90,000/Watford Nov 1984, fee
£225,000/Leeds United June 1989, fee £100,000 (Watford
loan Jan 1990) (NOTTS loan Mar 1992)/St Johnstone
player-coach cs 1992, acting player-manager Dec 1992,
manager Apr to Nov 1993/Carrick Rangers Nov 1993/
Wycombe Wanderers nc Mar 1994/Yeovil Town nc Mar
1994/Doncaster Rovers coach 1995/Farsley Celtic Aug
1995/Bradford City reserve-team manager Mar 1996/
Darlington player-coach Oct 1996
Debut v Wimbledon (a) 7.3.92, lost 0 – 2

Mansfield Town's manager Billy Bingham resurrected
John McClelland's career after he had been released by
Cardiff City and drifted into non-League football. Despite
operating in Divisions Three and Four, his outstanding
displays earned him his first six international caps, and
the Stags a handsome fee when he joined Glasgow
Rangers. An outstanding centre-half and captain, fast
moving and untiring with excellent vision and leadership
qualities, John totalled 53 full caps for Ireland and played
against the Rest of the World X1 in the Football League's
centenary game. In English and Scottish football he totalled
571(11) League and Cup matches and scored 22 goals. At
the age of 40 he had the misfortune to break his leg when
playing for Darlington against Hartlepool United in
October 1996.

Appearances: FL: 6 apps 0 gls Total: 6 apps 0 gls
Honours: Northern Ireland International, 53 caps 1980-
90. FL representative. (Glasgow Rangers) Scottish League
Cup winners 1982 and 1984. (Leeds United) FL Division
1 champions 1992

---o---

McCORMACK, John Cecil

Centre-forward 5'8"   11st 4lbs
b. Chester-le-Street, 15th February 1922
d. Canada, 1995
CAREER: Gateshead Sept 1941(WW2 guest Middlesbrough)/
Middlesbrough Apr 1947, fee £6,500/Chelmsford City Aug
1948/Barnsley July 1950, fee £6,500/NOTTS Nov 1951to
cs 1956, fee £20,000/Emigrated to Canada
Debut v Cardiff City (h) 24.11.51, drawn 1 – 1

A spell in non-League football with Chelmsford City
appeared to have re-charged Cecil McCormack's batteries.
In his first 17 matches for Barnsley the speedy and
enterprising inside-forward scored 24 goals and although
the goals dried up somewhat from mid November he
finished with 33 for the season. This total remains
Barnsley's record for the most League goals scored in a
season. He arrived at Meadow Lane immediately following
an outstanding display at the City Ground when he scored
two of Barnsley's goals in a 3 – 3 draw against Forest.

He was carrying an injury when he arrived at Meadow
Lane and unsurprisingly made an uncertain start. He
became successor to the great Tommy Lawton when he
took over the number nine jersey following the famous
international's transfer to Brentford. Comparisons were
inevitable, if somewhat unfortunate, but the feeling
remains that McCormack did not do himself full justice
at Meadow Lane.

Appearances: FL: 82 apps 35 gls FAC: 3 apps 1 gl
Total: 85 apps 36 gls

---o---

MACRAE, Stuart

Centre-half   5' 102"   14st 0lbs
b. Port Bannatyne, Bute, Scotland circa 1856
d. Marylebone, London, 27th January 1927
CAREER: An amateur player throughout, he assisted
Edinburgh Academicals (rugby team)/Newark F.C. circa
1878/NOTTS (debut) Nov 1879 to (last app) Feb 1887/
Also assisted the Corinthians 1883-90 and played
occasionally for Bolton Association, prior to 1877.
Debut v Nottingham Forest, FAC 1, (a) 8.11.1879, lost 0 – 4

Rather a late convert to the Association code, having
initially starred as a three-quarter back with Edinburgh
Academicals. In the late 1870s his vocation as a maltser
took him to Newark, where he took up soccer. It was in a
match against Notts County that his outstanding display
led to his being invited by Harry Cursham (q.v.) to join
the Notts Club. Some three years later MacRae was
selected to play for England. The embodiment of honest
strength and endeavour, he gave and received hard knocks,
his 'fighting weight' of 14 stones presenting a formidable
barrier to opposing forwards.

Appearances: FAC: 26 apps 2 gls Total: 26 apps 2 gls
Honours: England International, 5 caps 1883-84

---o---

McCULLOCH, John Balfour 'Iain'

Forward   5' 10" 11st 6lbs
b. Kilmarnock, 28th December 1954
CAREER: Ayr Albion/Hurlford United (trials with Ayr
United, and St Mirren)/Kilmarnock pro 1973/NOTTS Apr
1978, fee £80,000/ retired due to injury Apr 1985/Arnold
Town manager/Pelican coach June 2004.
Debut v West Ham United (a) 19.8.78, lost 2 – 5 (scored
two)

The son of William B McCulloch (Kilmarnock, Airdrie,
Ayr United, St Mirren and Morton.) Iain followed in his
father's footsteps, beginning as a youngster in an Under-
18 team, Ayr Albion. When age ruled him out he joined
junior club, Hurlford United. His stay was brief, however,
as he was quickly snapped up by Kilmarnock who played
him as an attacking midfielder.

In April 1978 he became the Magpies record signing and made an impressive start with two goals on his debut in League football. Raw pace, courage, and a fierce competitive spirit made him an extremely dangerous customer, both in the scoring and setting up of opportunities for  his colleagues. In the season that promotion to the First Division was secured, Iain scored 11 goals in 39 matches. Settling well in the top flight he topped the scoring charts with 16 goals in 40 matches in 1981-82, his total including a hat-trick at West Bromwich Albion. He was leading scorer again in the following season with 10 goals, but in his final season his scoring touch had deserted him, when on 14th April 1984 he suffered a broken leg in an accidental collision with Manchester United's goalkeeper, Gary Bailey. Eventually, on specialist's advice, he was forced to retire from senior football, a sad blow for the club and one of their most popular players. Iain subsequently worked in the commercial department at Meadow Lane, and also acted as co-ordinator for the Junior Magpies. As some small consolation, he recovered sufficiently to turn out again for Plessey in the Notts. Alliance. He also had a lengthy spell as manager Arnold Town, working alongside former Magpies full-back, Ray O'Brien.

Appearances: FL: 212(3) apps 51 gls FAC: 10(1) apps 2 gls FLC: 17 apps 1 gl Other: 17 apps 0 gls
Total: 256(4) apps 54 gls
Honours: Scotland U-21 International, 2 apps. (NOTTS) Anglo Scottish Cup finalist 1981

McCULLOCH, John Gordon
Centre-forward 6'0"   12st 0lbs
b. Hinckley, Leics, 3rd March 1888
d. KIA France, 23rd October 1918
CAREER: Ilkeston United/Ripley 1910/Sutton Town/ NOTTS Aug 1911/Sutton Town cs 1912/Lincoln City Apr 1913/Bentley Colliery cs 1914
Debut v Oldham Athletic (h) 6.4.12, drawn 1 – 1

One of two forward signings from junior football in late August 1911; the other, Luther Dexter, did not appear at senior level. Gordon McCulloch, the son of a master milliner, did marginally better, appearing once in late

season as deputy for Jimmy Cantrell. A second opportunity in League football came with Lincoln City where he was mainly employed at reserve level, but made 11 Second Division appearances in 1913-14. As an Army reservist he was called up to serve in the Great War, and was killed in action while serving with the Eighth Battalion, Leicestershire Regiment, on 28th October 1918. His grave is located at Fontaine-au-Bois.

Appearances: FL: 1 app 0 gls Total: 1 app 0 gls

McDERMENT, William Stirling
Wing-half   5' 8"   11st 4lbs
b. Paisley, Renfrewshire, 5th January 1943
CAREER: Johnstone Burgh/Leicester City May 1961/Luton Town July 1967/NOTTS May 1969/Morton Oct 1969/ Lockheed Leamington Feb 1972
Debut v Oldham Athletic (h) 9.8.69, drawn 0 – 0

A lengthy spell with Leicester City, which included his captaincy of the Reserves, netted Billy McDerment only 20(3) League appearances. He almost doubled his total in his first season with Luton Town, playing in 20 Division Four matches in the Hatters' championship season. They came very near to achieving back-to-back promotions, finishing third in Division Three with McDerment appearing in 15 matches, scoring once. A fleeting involvement with the Magpies ended in the month prior to the appointment of Jimmy Sirrel as manager in November 1969.

Appearances: FL: 2(1) apps 0 gls FLC: 1 app 0 gls
Total: 3(1)apps 0 gls
Honours: (Luton Town) FL Division 4 champions 1968

McDERMOTT, Andrew
Defender   5'9"   11st 3lbs
b. Sydney, Australia, 24th March 1977
CAREER: Australian Institute of Sport/Queens Park Rangers Aug 1995/West Bromwich Albion Mar 1997, fee £400,000/ NOTTS Aug 2000/Northern Spirit (NSL) June 2001
Debut v Luton Town (a) 12.8.2000, won 1 – 0

Andy McDermott had played in just six League matches for Q.P.R. when West Bromwich Albion splashed out a sizeable £400,000 fee for his services. His eventual total of 49(3) League matches for the Baggies was a disappointing return from his three and a half years at the Hawthorns. A free transfer signing by the Magpies he began in impressive form before suffering a thigh injury that restricted him to a handful of appearances in the second half of the season. His contract was cancelled in the summer and he returned to Australia.

Appearances: FL: 20(5) apps 0 gls FAC: 1 app 0 gls
FLC: 4 apps 1 gl Total: 25(5) apps 1 gl
Honours: Australia U-23 International

McDONAGH, James Martin 'Seamus'

Goalkeeper   6' 0"   13st 9lbs
b. Rotherham, 6th October 1952
CAREER: Rotherham United app, Nov 1968, pro Oct 1970
(Manchester United loan 1972-73)/Bolton Wanderers Aug
1976, fee £10,000/Everton July 1980, fee £250,000/Bolton
Wanderers Aug 1981, in exchange for M. Walsh plus
£90,000/NOTTS July 1983, fee £50,000 (Birmingham City
loan Sept 1984) (Gillingham loan Mar 1985) (Sunderland
loan Aug 1985)/Wichita Wings, USA, Oct 1985/Scarborough
Nov 1987 (Huddersfield Town loan Jan 1988)/Charlton
Athletic Mar 1988/Galway United, Rep of Ireland, player-
manager/Derry City manager to May 1989/Spalding United
July 1989/Grantham Town cs 1990/Telford United player-
reserve team manager 1990/Grantham Town Aug 1991/
Telford United Mar 1992/Arnold Town/Ilkeston Town Vet./
Subsequently had spells as goalkeeping coach with
Nottingham Forest, Leicester City and Coventry City and
scouted for the Irish FA.
Debut v Leicester City (a) 27.8.83, won 4 – 0

One substitute appearance for England Youth against
Spain in season 1970-71 did not disbar Seamus McDonagh
from eventually reaching full international level with the
Republic of Ireland. The burly shot-stopper assisted nine
clubs at senior level, totalling 471 appearances and even
managed to score a goal for Bolton Wanderers against
Burnley at Burnden Park in January 1983. Between 1976
and 1980 he made a club record 161 consecutive
appearances for the Trotters, totalling 274 League and
Cup matches before joining Everton in July 1980. He
joined the Magpies after a second spell with Bolton
Wanderers. He was first choice goalkeeper as Notts kicked-
off in Division One with a memorable 4 – 0 opening day
victory against Leicester City. By mid season, however,
he had lost out to Mick Leonard as the struggling Magpies
crashed out of the top flight. He featured little in the
following term when the slide continued with a further
relegation from Division Two resulting. When playing
days ended he was employed in the insurance business
before becoming a licensee in Nottingham.

Appearances: FL: 35 apps 0 gls FAC: 4 apps 0 gls FLC:
7 apps 0 gls Total: 46 apps 0 gls
Honours: England Youth International, 1 app 1970-71. .
Republic of Ireland International, 25 caps 1981-86.
(Bolton Wanderers) FL Division 2 champions 1978

---o---

MACDONALD, Edward

Left-half   5' 9½"   12st 0lbs
b. Newcastle-under-Lyme October quarter 1875
d. Birmingham, 12th October 1938
CAREER: Newcastle White Star/Burslem Port Vale June
1894/Stoke Aug 1896/Burslem Port Vale June 1897/NOTTS
Nov 1899/Portsmouth May 1904 to 1909
Debut v Nottingham Forest (h) 11.11.1899, lost 1 – 2

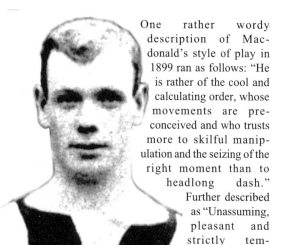

One rather wordy
description of Mac-
donald's style of play in
1899 ran as follows: "He
is rather of the cool and
calculating order, whose
movements are pre-
conceived and who trusts
more to skilful manip-
ulation and the seizing of the
right moment than to
headlong   dash."
Further described
as "Unassuming,
pleasant   and
strictly   tem-
perate," at the time
of his signing he
became the fourth
'Mac' on the Magpies' books – Maconnachie, McMain,
McCappin and Macdonald. Only the first named was a
Scotsman. Macdonald effectively replaced David
Calderhead in the Notts team. The re-arranged half-back
line of Bull, Ball and Macdonald being the first all-English
line fielded for over a decade since the days of Dobson,
Emmitt and Alfred Shelton, who were all Nottingham
born. One of the conditions of Macdonald's transfer was
that Notts would play Port Vale in a friendly match at
Burslem. This took place on 27th November 1899, Port
Vale winning 3 – 2.

Appearances: FL: 139 apps 3 gls FAC: 13 apps 0 gls
Total: 152 apps 3 gls

---o---

MACDONALD, John Sutherland

Left-back
b. Edinburgh, 23rd September 1922
CAREER: Carshalton Athletic/NOTTS Aug 1948/Queens
Park Rangers Mar 1949
Debut v Bristol City (a) 20.11.48, lost 1 – 3

The 'Football Post', commenting on the debut of
Macdonald, were not impressed. A late replacement for
Bert Howe at left-back, he was said to be: "A strong
player, but scarcely ready for the League side. He appears
to lack match fitness and did not have a very happy
match." He did not appear at senior level with Q.P.R.

Appearances: FL: 1 app 0 gls Total: 1 app 0 gls

---o---

McFAUL, Shane

Midfield   6' 1"   11st 10lbs
b. Dublin, 23rd May 1986
CAREER: Cherry Orchard, Ireland/NOTTS trainee May 2002, pro Feb 2004
Debut as sub v Swindon Town (a) 23.8.2003, lost 0 – 4

Shane attracted the attention of scouts from several Premiership sides during his early days with the Cherry Orchard club. Although he began as a central defender, he made his League debut in central midfield under manager Billy Dearden. Season 2004-05 has been one of marked progress for the young Irishman, who was given his first run in the seniors under caretaker boss Ian Richardson. In either a midfield role or at right full-back, Shane tackles well and passes constructively out of defence. In April 2005 his progress was rewarded when he was called up to the Republic of Ireland U-19 squad, to participate in a mini tournament in Serbia and Montenegro.

Appearances: FL: 19(11) apps 0 gls FAC: 2(1) apps 0 gls
Other: 1 app 0 gls Total: 22(12) apps 0 gls
Honours: Republic of Ireland U-19 International

McGOLDRICK, David

Forward   6' 1"   11st 11lbs
b. Nottingham, 29th November 1987
CAREER: NOTTS associate schoolboy/Blackburn Rovers trial July 2004/Everton trial July 2004/Southampton Aug 2004.
Debut as sub v Swindon Town (h) 24.1.04, lost 0 – 1

As a sixteen year-old playing for the Magpies Under-19s, David was an obvious talent with ball skills and awareness well in advance of his tender years. He had not trained with the first team until the appointment of Gary Mills as manager, and it was Mills who handed him his League debut at the age of 16 years and 57 days. His substitute appearance against Swindon Town making David the second-youngest player to represent the Magpies at League level. (The youngest, by the slender margin of three days, was Tony Bircumshaw in April 1961.) Sadly, Notts were unable to hang on to their budding star who declined to sign a contract at the close of season 2003-04, and was signed by Premier League side, Southampton.

Appearances: FL: 2(2) apps 0 gls Total: 2(2) apps 0 gls

McGORIN, Isaac Moor

Wing-half   5' 11"   11st 3lbs
b. Silksworth, Co Durham, 19th October 1901

CAREER: Thornley Albion/New Silksworth Colliery/ Sunderland am Apr 1924, pro Jan 1925/NOTTS Feb 1929, along with John Dowsey for a combined fee of £750/Carlisle United Feb 1930/Shotton Colliery Welfare Aug 1931/ Thurnscoe Victoria circa 1932/Thurnscoe St Hilda's Nov 1933
Debut v Oldham Athletic (a) 23.2.29, lost 2 – 3

Recruited from Sunderland towards the end of season 1928-29, in a joint transfer with John Dowsey, both were effectively reserve team players at Roker Park, although Ike McGorin had rather more first team experience (23 League and Cup matches and one goal.) A constructive wing-half, able to occupy either flank, he was surprisingly unable to establish a place in the Southern Section of Division Three and departed after twelve months to Carlisle United. **Note**: Although details from his birth certificate confirm the spelling of his surname as McGorin, he is named in most records – including those of the Football League – as McGorian.

Appearances: FL: 1 app 0 gls Total: 1 app 0 gls

McGOVERN, Patrick Munro

Inside-forward
b. Edinburgh, 14th May 1948
CAREER: Royston Boys' Club/NOTTS July 1967 to 1968.
Debut as sub v Barnsley (a) 25.11.67, lost 1 – 3

Season 1967-68 was not a memorable one for the Meadow Lane faithful. Seventeenth place in Division Four being only a marginal improvement on the twentieth place finish of the previous term. McGovern's brief association with the first team included a solitary starting appearance in the 0 – 0 draw at Aldershot, and an appearance from the bench in the embarrassing first round exit from the FA Cup at the hands of Cheshire County League side, Runcorn, by 1 – 0.

Appearances: FL: 1(2) apps 0 gls FAC: 0(1) app 0 gls
Total: 1(3) apps 0 gls

McGRATH, James

Outside-right   5' 9"   12st 0lbs
b. Washington, County Durham, 4th March 1907
d. Durham East, October quarter 1950.
CAREER: Ryhope Colliery/Washington Colliery/Cardiff City Dec 1928/Port Vale May 1932/NOTTS June 1934/ Bradford P.A. Dec 1934, appointed to training staff cs 1938.
Debut v Swansea Town (a) 25.8.34, lost 1 – 2 (scored)

Despite his bright start at Meadow Lane, featuring two goals in his first three matches, Jimmy McGrath lost his right wing slot to Ernie Steele and departed in mid-season to Bradford Park Avenue.

His brief spell with the Magpies was in contrast to the rest of his career. Although unable to command a regular place with his first club, Cardiff City, he enjoyed lengthy spells of first team football with both Port Vale and Bradford P.A. Originally a wing half-back, the stockily built Geordie's exceptional speed off the mark was often utilised in a wing forward role, although he reverted to the middle line during his final spell with Bradford P.A.

Appearances: FL: 11 apps 3 gls Total: 11 apps 3 gls

---○---

McGRATH, John

Wing-half   5' 9$\frac{2}{}$" 11st 4lbs
b. Tidworth, 21st May 1932
CAREER: Aldershot am/NOTTS Aug 1953/Darlington May 1958, fee £1,220/Boston United 1959
Debut v Middlesbrough (a) 20.8.55, lost 0 – 3

A strong and speedy wing-half with attacking ideas, Johnny McGrath had a spell as inside-forward during his spell at Meadow Lane, but seemed happier in the middle-line. In the Summer of 1958, in preparation for their first season of Division Four football, Darlington signed him and Bob Bulch from the Magpies. With the Quakers, McGrath was fielded exclusively at inside-forward and scored six goals in 25 League matches and three in four FA Cup ties.

Appearances: FL: 54 apps 5 gls FAC: 3 apps 0 gls Total: 57 apps 5 gls

---○---

McGREGOR, Andrew Clark

Outside-right   5' 5$\frac{2}{}$" 11st 2lbs
b. Wishaw, Lanarkshire, 1867
CAREER: Wishaw Thistle/NOTTS June 1890; re-registered July 1892/Notts Rovers Mar 1893
Debut v Bolton Wanderers (a) 6.9.1890, lost 2 – 4

Quickly marked as a player of exceptional ability on joining the Magpies, Andrew McGregor was a small but stocky speed merchant, and a skilful dribbler. In addition to his ability to centre accurately from anywhere on the wing, he was not afraid to cut in for a shot, his 13 goals in 1890-91 including four in one match against Sheffield United in the first round of the FA Cup. The 9 – 1 score line launched what was to become the Magpies most successful run in the FA Cup at that time. Sadly, the final ended in defeat, and McGregor was allowed to leave in the close season. The decision was obviously an unwise one, as no fewer than nine different outside-rights were tried, and found wanting, in 1891-92. Re engaged for season 1892-93 he was unable to recapture his earlier form, the Magpies suffering their first relegation after finishing in fourteenth place (in a league of sixteen clubs) and losing the resultant Test Match against Darwen at Hyde Road, Manchester, by 2 – 3.

Appearances: FL: 44 apps 11 gls FAC: 7 apps 5 gls
Total: 51 apps 16 gls
Honours: (NOTTS) FA Cup finalists 1891

---○---

McHUGH, Frazer

Midfield   5' 9"   12st 5lbs
b. Nottingham, 14th July 1981
CAREER: Swindon Town trainee, signing pro Aug 1999, released June 2001/Tamworth/Gainsborough Trinity/ Bromsgrove Rovers/Halesowen/Bradford City nc Mar, pro May 2003/NOTTS Jan to May 2004/Hucknall Town Aug 2004.
Debut v Swindon Town (h) 24.1.2004, lost 1 – 2

A Gary Mills signing, locally born midfielder Frazer McHugh had been released by Bradford City some six weeks earlier. Initially signed for one month, he made his debut against his first professional club, Swindon Town. A hard-working display ended in disappointment, the Magpies losing to a late goal, when appearing to be heading for a share of the points. Without establishing a regular berth, McHugh's grafting displays ensured an extension to his initial agreement. He was, however, released at the end of the season and in the summer joined Nationwide North side, Hucknall Town.

Appearances: FL: 9(4) apps 0 gls Total: 9(4) apps 0 gls

---○---

McINNES, Thomas

Inside-right   5' 5"   9st 7lbs
b. Glasgow Central, 29th August 1870
CAREER: Cowlairs/NOTTS 1889/ Rangers June 1892/ Everton Aug 1894/Luton Town May 1896 to 1900/Bedford Queens Engineers
Debut v Wolverhampton Wanderers (a) 14.12.1889, lost 0 – 2

Popularly known as 'Ginger' McInnes, the smallest and lightest member of the team became an immediate favourite with the Trent Bridge crowd. A brilliant little player who dribbled with great skill, he was also an extremely hard

worker, going at a tremendous pace from start to finish. Capped by his country when a Cowlairs player, he scored against Ireland at Ibrox Park on 9th March 1899, Scotland winning 7 – 0. His second appearance for the Football League was in the first-ever fixture against the Scottish League at Pike's Lane, Bolton on 11th April 1892. Another Notts player, Harry Daft, was at outside-left in the match that ended in a 2 – 2 draw. In June of the same year McInnes turned up in Glasgow and played for the Rangers in the Glasgow Cup Final against Celtic, but he resumed with Notts in October for what proved to be his final season. He subsequently gave good service to Everton (42 League matches and 18 goals) and Luton Town (93 matches and 20 goals). The 1901 Census listed him as an iron moulder's labourer (which seemed a heavy job for so small a man) and living in Luton, aged 32.

Appearances: FL: 73 apps 20 gls FAC: 15 apps 7 gls
Other: 1 app 0 gls Total: 89 apps 27 gls
Honours: Scotland International, 1 cap 1889. FL Representative, 2 apps 1891-92. (NOTTS) FA Cup finalists 1891

McINTYRE, James Alfred

Inside-left   5' 10"   11st 4lbs
b. Walsall, Staffs, circa 1881
d. Surrey, March quarter 1954
CAREER: Witton/Darlaston Town/Wednesbury Old Athletic/Walsall July 1901/NOTTS May 1902/Northampton Town 1903/Reading June 1904/Coventry City May 1905/Dudley Aug 1906/Bournbrook Oct 1907/Coventry City assistant trainer 1907, trainer 1908 to 1912/Southampton trainer Apr 1912 to 1915, manager Aug 1919 to Dec 1924/Coventry City manager June 1928 to Feb 1930/Fulham manager Apr 1931 to Feb 1934
Debut v Derby County (a) 13.9.02, lost 1 – 4

A 1902 'Who's Who' publication, commenting on his move to Notts, considered James McIntyre to be one of the most scientific players in the ranks of the professionals. His playing record, however, suggested no more than average ability, as he played in only 44 matches at senior level, scoring 12 goals. As a manager he proved well above average, winning Third Division South championships with Southampton in 1922 and with Fulham ten years later. Between times he had taken a break from football, running a hotel in Scotland for four years after leaving Southampton.

Appearances: FL: 9 apps 3 gls Total: 9 apps 3 gls

MACKEY, James Alfred

Outside-right   5' 8"   11st 7lbs
b. Ryton-on-Tyne, County Durham, 25th November 1897
d. Canterbury, 15th December 1990
CAREER: Newburn Colliery/Coventry City May 1920/Carlisle United cs 1922/NOTTS May 1923/Lincoln City Sept 1923/Luton Town July 1924/Crewe Alexandra July 1925/West Stanley Aug 1926 to January 1927/Torquay United June 1927/Dartford Aug 1929/Sheppey United c Aug 1930/Bexleheath & Welling July 1932/Dargas Sports (Dartford) Oct 1933/V.C.D. Athletic Oct 1935
Debut v Burnley (h) 25.8.23, won 2 – 1

According to reports on the pre-season practice match at Meadow Lane, Mackey was described as being: "Speedy, with plenty of tricks, combined with not a little pluck." Sadly, he did not live up to his promise when the serious action commenced. On his debut in Division One, the 'Football News' commented that he "Sent across some beautiful centres, but was much too slow off the mark." If not quite fitting the bill at the highest level, he saw plenty of League action elsewhere, including 67 in Torquay United's first two seasons as a Football League club.

Appearances: FL: 3 apps 1 gl Total: 3 apps 1 gl

MACLACHLAN, James

Inside-right
CAREER: Vale of Leven/Derby County cs 1890/NOTTS Sept 1893/Derby County Sept 1894/Ilkeston Town May 1895
Debut v Newcastle United (h) 14.10.1893, won 3 – 1

In two separate spells with Derby County the former Vale of Leven inside-forward enjoyed his best run in 1890-91 and 1891-92, seasons that included the bulk of his 66 League and Cup matches and 17 goals. Aside from his Notts debut (above) he appeared in only one more first team match, the 1 – 2 defeat by Lincoln City at Trent Bridge in November 1893.

Appearances: FL: 2 apps 0 gls Total: 2 apps 0 gls

McLEAN, Thomas

Right-back   5' 6"   10st 5lbs
b. Alexandria, August 1866
d. Nottingham, 27th November 1936
CAREER: Vale of Leven/NOTTS cs 1888/Heanor Town June 1889, but returned to NOTTS Aug 1889/Derby County Aug 1892/NOTTS Sept 1893/NOTTS assistant trainer 1908 to 1929
Debut v Everton (a) 15.9.1888, lost 1 – 2

Despite lacking any physical advantage at 5'6" and 10st 5lbs Tom McLean was a strong defender with a magnificent clearing kick.

He joined Notts before the legalising of professionalism, having first come to Nottingham on holiday. In the event, he remained for the rest of his life, marrying a local girl in 1892. The return half of his rail ticket remained a treasured relic. He was desperately unfortunate to miss the 1891 FA Cup Final, suffering a knee injury in the period between the semi-final and the final, lost to Blackburn Rovers. In 1893 continuing knee problems enforced his retirement and he then entered the licensed trade. In 1908 a career change saw him appointed the Magpies' assistant trainer.

Appearances: FL: 66 apps 0 gls FAC: 12 apps 0 gls
Total: 78 apps 0 gls

McLENAHAN, Hugh

Half-back   5' 10"   11st 4lbs
b. West Gorton, Manchester, 23rd March 1909
d. Macclesfield, May 1988
CAREER: St. Francis' School (Gorton)/Manchester Schoolboys/Lancashire Schoolboys/Ambrose F.C./Longsight 'A' Team/Ashton Brothers/Manchester United am May 1926/Stalybridge Celtic 1926-27/Stockport County trial Feb 1927/Blackpool trail Mar 1927/Manchester United May 1927/NOTTS Dec 1936 to 1939
Debut v Luton Town (a) 25.12.36, lost 1 – 2

Hugh McLenahan made his Manchester United debut at Tottenham as an eighteen year-old part-time professional, combining football with his work as an electrician with the Manchester Evening Chronicle newspaper. In nine seasons at Old Trafford as a versatile utility player he made 112 League and Cup appearances and scored 12 goals. Major honours eluded him during his time with United and he was similarly unfortunate in his first season with the Magpies, who finished as runners-up for the Third Division South championship. His period with Notts ended painfully when he sustained a double fracture of his left forearm in the home League match against Reading on 1st October 1938.

Appearances: FL: 54 apps 1 gl FAC: 2 apps 0 gls Other: 2 apps 0 gls Total: 58 apps 1 gl
Honours: England Schoolboy International, 2 caps 1923

McLEOD, William

Centre-forward 5' 9"   11st 10lbs
b. Hebburn-on-Tyne, June 1887
CAREER: Hebburn Argyle/Peebles Rovers/Lincoln City June 1906, fee £25/Leeds City Nov 1906, fee £350 plus proceeds from a match/NOTTS Oct 1919, fee £1,250/Doncaster Rovers cs 1921
Debut v West Bromwich Albion (a) 25.10.19, lost 0 – 8

Billy McLeod made Lincoln City a handsome profit in 1906, his record of eight goals in 13 matches tempting Leeds City to invest a sizeable fee, plus the proceeds from a friendly match. In addition to being a 'scratch' golfer, McLeod was also a very effective centre-forward who fell just short of international recognition, despite an outstanding scoring ratio with Leeds – 177 goals in 301 League and Cup matches. Notts paid a four-figure fee at the Leeds City auction, but in the relegation season that followed, his return of nine League goals in 30 First Division matches was hardly up to expectations. In the close season, another sizeable fee was invested in the Hull City centre-forward, Sam Stevens.

Appearances: FL: 40 apps 10 gls FAC: 3 apps 2 gls
Total: 43 apps 12 gls

McMAIN, Joseph

Centre-forward 5' 6½"   11st 7lbs
b. Preston circa 1873
CAREER: South Shore/Preston North End Reserves/Kettering Town Sept 1895/Wolverhampton Wanderers Nov 1896/NOTTS May 1899/Kettering Town Sept 1900/Wednesbury Old Athletic Dec 1904/Wellingborough Montrose Sept 1905
Debut v Derby County (a) 2.9.1899, won 1 – 0

Wolverhampton Wanderers were said to be reluctant to part with Joe McMain, who sought a move in order to play in his favoured position of centre-forward. He had played mainly at inside-right for the Wolves and scored 19 goals in 46 League matches. He was said to possess a collection of fifteen football medals when he joined Notts in 1899. Five of them were obtained as a junior at Preston; four at Kettering included a Midland League championship and Northamptonshire Cup. Six at Wolverhampton included winners' medals for the Birmingham League (twice), and the Staffordshire Cup. Despite an excellent season with the Magpies when he headed the scoring charts, he returned to Kettering and in April 1900 was granted the license for The Robin Hood Inn in the town.

Appearances: FL: 26 apps 13 gls FAC: 3 apps 2 gls
Total: 29 apps 15 gls

McMANUS, Charles Eric

Goalkeeper   6' 0"   11st 2lbs
b. Limavady, Northern Ireland, 14th November 1950
CAREER: Coleraine 1966/Coventry City Aug 1968, fee
£8,000/NOTTS May 1972/Stoke City Oct 1979, fee
£85,000 (Lincoln City loan Dec 1979)/Bradford City Aug
1982, fee £15,000 (Middlesbrough loan Jan 1986)
(Peterborough United loan Mar 1986)/Tranmere Rovers
Aug 1986/Boston United Sept 1986; retired 1987/Eccleshill
United manager July to Oct 1987
Debut v Bristol Rovers (a) 7.11.72, lost 0 – 1

There was never
much doubt that
Eric McManus
would make good
in League foot-
ball, as, at the age
of 18, he had
already   been
capped   by
Northern Ireland
at Schools, Youth
and   amateur
level, and been
reserve for the
Under-23 squad.
Never-theless,
his baptism with
Coventry City
was a severe one,

as he was only a 17 year-old when selected to face Bayern
Munich in the European Fairs Cup. As a last-minute
deputy for Bill Glazier, he found himself facing seven of
Germany's World Cup squad, and was on the receiving
end of a 6 – 1 defeat. Some four years later he arrived at
Meadow Lane, on a free transfer, initially as cover for
Roy Brown. After a season in reserve, when his skills
were polished by intensive coaching from the Magpies
trainer, Jack Wheeler, himself a former goalkeeper, Eric
claimed the first team jersey. Voted 'Player of the Year' in
1979, he nevertheless failed to agree terms for a new
contract and joined Stoke City for a tribunal set fee of
£85,000. He played in only four First Division matches
for the Potters, failing to dislodge Peter Fox, but was
successful in a four-year spell with Bradford City. His
113 League outings including 40 in the Third Division
championship season 1984-85. His playing career
terminated at Boston United due to a knee injury, but his
involvement in the game continued as Youth Development
Officer at Bradford City, and later in the same role with
Walsall. Eric's son, Steven, a midfield player with Walsall,
followed in his father's footsteps when he appeared in
the Northern Ireland Youth team. A cousin, 'Ally' Doyle
was a Northern Ireland schoolboy and youth international
who appeared in League football as a full-back with
Oldham Athletic from 1965 to 1969.

Appearances: FL: 229 apps 0 gls FAC: 9 apps 0 gls FLC:
13 apps 0 gls Other: 14 apps 0 gls Total: 265 apps 0 gls
Honours: Northern Ireland Schoolboy, Youth and Amateur
International. (Bradford City) FL Division 3 champions 1985

McMILLAN, James

Left-back
CAREER: Queen of the South Wanderers/NOTTS cs 1889
to 1890
Debut v Wolverhampton Wanderers (a) 7.9.1889, lost 0 – 2

Notts second season in the Football League saw a more
settled line-up operating after 32 players had been utilised
in the previous term. The all Scottish full-back pairing of
McLean and McMillan each made maximum League
appearances, as did goalkeeper Toone and inside-left
Oswald. In terms of league placing, however, only a slight
improvement was made – one place higher but still a
disappointing tenth in a league of just twelve clubs.
Despite missing only one first team match during the
course of the season McMillan was not retained. His
successor at left-back, another Scotsman, Jack Hendry
enjoyed much success in a six-year stay which included
two FA Cup final appearances.

Appearances: FL: 22 apps 0 gls FAC: 5 apps 0 gls
Total: 27 apps 0 gls

McMORRAN, James Wilson

Midfield   5' 7"   10st 12lbs
b. Muirkirk, Ayrshire, 29th October 1942
CAREER: Ayrshire East Schoolboys/Aston Villa ground staff
June 1958, pro Oct 1959/Third Lanark Feb 1963/Walsall
Nov 1964/Swansea Town June 1968/Walsall Nov 1968/
NOTTS July 1969/Halifax Town Aug 1970/Worcester City
July 1971/Hednesford/Redditch United Aug 1974; retired
1977
Debut v Brentford (a) 16.8.69, lost 0 – 1

Released by Walsall after two separate spells and a little
over 100 League appearances, the former Scotland
Schoolboy International joined the Magpies, initially on
trial for a month. Although his period was extended,
Jimmy appeared in just six early season matches, and
these proved to be his last at senior level. Earlier in his
career, in his one full season with Third Lanark he scored
nine goals in 29 Scottish League matches.

Appearances: FL: 6 apps 0 gls Total: 6 apps 0 gls
Honours: Scotland Schoolboy International, 2 caps 1958

McNAMARA, Niall Anthony

Forward   5' 11"   11st 12lbs
b. Limerick, Republic of Ireland, 26th January 1982
CAREER: Nottingham Forest trainee, signing pro Feb 1999/
NOTTS July 2001/Belper Town Aug 2002/Alfreton Town
(Eastwood Town loan)
Debut as sub v Northampton Town (h) 29.1.2002, lost 0 – 3

Niall appeared on the fringes of the first team in the second half of season 2001-02 when a productive front pairing was proving elusive. Given his first chance by new manager Billy Dearden, his performances in four outings from the bench proved insufficient to prolong his stay at Meadow Lane. By contrast, fellow countryman Paul Heffernan's senior career was finally taking off. Selection by the Republic of Ireland at Under-21 level, and six League goals during the season announcing his arrival as a striker with massive potential.

Appearances: FL: 0(4) apps 0 gls Total: 0(4) apps 0 gls
Honours: Republic of Ireland Youth International

McNAMEE, Peter

Outside-left   5' 8"   11st 0lbs
b. Glasgow, 20th March 1935
CAREER: Lanark Athletic/Peterborough United May 1955/
Kings Lynn Dec 1966/NOTTS Jan 1966/March Town
(manager during the 1970s)
Debut v Darlington (a) 29.1.66, lost 0 – 1

Managerial changes at Meadow Lane were rife in the 1960s, a decade that began with Frank Hill in charge and ended with Jimmy Sirrel in the hot seat. Peter McNamee was the first player signed during a short period when Andy Beattie and Peter Doherty were acting as 'advisors.' McNamee had ended an eleven-year association with Peterborough United and moved into non-League football with King's Lynn. Sadly, his 'come back' into League football ran to only three matches. Peterborough United historian Matt Hill revealing that McNamee had realised that his time was up when he was asked to 'tackle back,' claiming that he had never made a tackle in his life!

Appearances: FL: 3 apps 0 gls Total: 3 apps 0 gls
Honours: (Peterborough United) FL Division 4 champions 1961

MACONNACHIE, Alexander

Inside-right
CAREER: Glasgow Ashfield/Derby County May 1897NOTTS Apr 1898/Third Lanark June 1901, fee £75/ Ripley Athletic Aug 1902/Newton Rovers 1903/Ilkeston United Sept 1905/Alfreton Town/Tibshelf cs 1908.
Debut v Burnley (a) 3.9.1898, drawn 1 – 1 (scored)

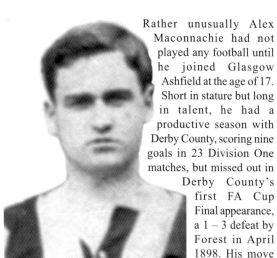

Rather unusually Alex Maconnachie had not played any football until he joined Glasgow Ashfield at the age of 17. Short in stature but long in talent, he had a productive season with Derby County, scoring nine goals in 23 Division One matches, but missed out in Derby County's first FA Cup Final appearance, a 1 – 3 defeat by Forest in April 1898. His move to Notts was said to be "A costly business," although the fee was not revealed in the local press. A wonderful dribbler, often too elusive for opponents, he had some memorable goals to his credit. He was the Magpies' leading goal scorer in his first season with 15 League and Cup goals in 35 matches, and second highest in 1899-1900 with 13 in 36 matches. Sadly, his spell at Trent Bridge ended in acrimony, when he was suspended sine die for leaving Nottingham without permission in February 1901. In August 1901 the 'Scottish Referee,' a Glasgow sports newspaper, welcomed him back to Scotland and Third Lanark with the following comments: "As to Maconnachies' ability there is not the slightest doubt, for in England he frequently captivated the spectators by his smart and tricky manipulation of the ball."

Appearances: FL: 76 apps 26 gls FAC: 5 apps 2 gls
Total: 81 apps 28 gls

McPARLAND, Ian John 'Charlie'

Forward   5' 8"   10st 8lbs
b. Edinburgh, 4th October 1961
CAREER: Sunderland app Aug 1978 to Jan 1979/Ormiston Primrose/NOTTS Dec 1980/Hull City Mar 1989, fee £155,000 (Walsall loan Mar 1991)/Dunfermline Athletic July 1991/Lincoln City nc Aug 1992/Northampton Town Oct 1992/Hong Kong football Mar 1993/Arnold Town Aug 1996
Debut as sub v Preston North End (a) 27.12.80, drawn 2 – 2

Although on the small side, 'Charlie' foraged purposefully, shot hard and was useful in the air. He took some time to establish a regular berth at Meadow Lane, his first senior goal coming in May 1983. In the final Division One match of the season he opened his account in memorable fashion, scoring the winner against Manchester United in a 3 – 2 win at Meadow Lane.

Consecutive relegations quickly followed, but Division Three defences were given a great deal of trouble from 1985-86 onwards when he found his shooting boots with a vengeance. In terms of League goals alone, his seasonal totals were 15, 24 and 21. He was seeking a change in 1988-89, but signed off with goals from the bench against Bury and Fulham. Wanted by both Bristol City and Hull City, he elected to move north and cost the Tigers a club record fee of £155,000, but achieved little at Boothferry Park, scoring seven goals in 31(16) League matches.

Appearances: FL: 193(28) apps 69 gls FAC: 14(3) apps 9 gls FLC: 15(2) apps 5 gls Other: 10(2) apps 7 gls
Total: 232(35) apps 90 gls

McPHERSON, Ian Buchanan. D.F.C.
Outside-right   5' 10"   11st 12lbs
b. Glasgow, 26th July 1920
d. St. Albans, 20th March 1983
CAREER: Glasgow Rangers 1939 (WW2 guest Arsenal & NOTTS)/NOTTS Aug 1945/Arsenal Aug 1946, in part exchange for R.H. Cumner/NOTTS Aug 1951/Brentford July 1953/Bedford Town Oct 1953/Cambridge United 1954-55
Debut v Bradford City, FAC 1, (h) 17.11.45, drawn 2 – 2 (scored one)

A Flying Officer Mosquito pilot during the war who was awarded the D.F.C. and bar. After appearing as a guest player for Notts in war-time games he joined Arsenal and was a Division One championship winner in 1947-48, scoring five goals in 29 League matches, sharing the left wing berth during the campaign with Denis Compton, the famous Middlesex and England cricketer. He returned to Meadow Lane in the close season following Jackie Sewell's transfer to Sheffield Wednesday. Tall, dark and dashing, he enjoyed a good first season at outside-right, scoring six goals in 34 League matches. A knee injury that necessitated an operation curtailed his second season.

Four matches for Brentford wound up his career in senior football, and in 1954 he rejoined the R.A.F. as a physical fitness instructor. Five years later he became sales manager of a St. Albans pharmaceutical company.

Appearances: FL: 50 apps 7 gls FAC: 4 apps 3 gls
Total: 54 apps 10 gls
Honours: (Arsenal) FL Div 1 champions 1948

McPHERSON, Kenneth
Centre-forward 6' 0"   12st 0lbs
b. Hartlepool, 25th March 1927
CAREER: Horden Colliery/NOTTS Aug 1950/ Middlesbrough Aug 1953, fee £15,000/Coventry City Nov 1955, fee £8,000/Newport County June 1958, fee £2,500/ New York Americans June 1961/Swindon Town Aug 1961, fee £2,250; retired cs 1965
Debut v Bury (a) 30.9.50, drawn 0 – 0

Flame-haired former paratrooper Ken McPherson joined the Magpies from a West Hartlepool junior club. A strong, sturdy, bustling player he spent two seasons in reserve, deputising for Tommy Lawton on a handful of occasions. It was not until season 1952-53 that he earned an extended run, when he took over at centre-forward from Cecil McCormack. He seized his chance with alacrity and seven goals in five games, starting with a four-goal blast against Blackburn Rovers. By the end of the season he had scored 14 League and Cup goals in 23 matches. His scoring spree had not gone unnoticed, and in the close season he was prised away from Meadow Lane, a £15,000 fee taking him to First Division Middlesbrough. Ill health and injuries restricted his appearances to 33, from which he scored a very respectable total of 15 goals. He enjoyed better spells with each of his next three League clubs, amassing a total of 383 League appearances and 118 goals. In his final four-year spell with Swindon Town he was switched to centre-half. At the age of 38 he retired from the game and became a grocer.

Appearances: FL: 26 apps 10 gls FAC: 4 apps 4 gls
Total: 30 apps 14 gls

McPHERSON, Lachlan
Inside-right   5' 9 2" 12st 0lbs
b. Dennistoun, Glasgow, 11th July 1900
CAREER: Cambuslang Rangers/NOTTS May 1921/Swansea Town June 1924/Everton Dec 1929, fee £5,000/New Brighton Aug 1933/Hereford United player-coach July 1935
Debut v Bristol City (a) 3.9.21, drawn 2 – 2 (scored one)

Despite his winning a Division Two championship medal with the Magpies in 1922-23, 'Lachy' McPherson's qualities were not fully appreciated. Said to play in a typical Scottish style, he was an artist with the ball who dribbled and passed dexterously.

He crossed the border as an inside-forward, but Notts felt that he was better suited to a place in the middle line. As a wing-half, however, he failed to maintain a place in the League side. His move to Swansea Town was as a direct result of his having been 'spotted' by Swansea officials when the Magpies and the Swans were undertaking a summer tour of Denmark in 1923. One year later, he moved to the Vetch Field and collected a Third Division South championship medal. He cost Everton a sizeable fee in December 1929 but was unable to steer them clear of relegation. The following season, however, they regained their First Division status. New Brighton was his last League club, and although his subtleties were not always fully appreciated, or acted upon by less talented colleagues, he enjoyed an excellent first season at Rake Lane. In his final season, injuries sustained both on and off the field curtailed his season. He sustained injuries to both of his ankles in a most unfortunate accident when an out of control car mounted the pavement and hit him.

Appearances: FL: 32 apps 5 gls Total: 32 apps 5 gls
Honours: (NOTTS) FL Division 2 champions 1923. (Swansea Town) FL Division 3 South champions 1925. Welsh Cup runners-up 1926. (Everton) FL Div 2 champions 1931

McSTAY, William

Defender   5' 11"   11st 7lbs
b. Hamilton, 26th November 1961
CAREER: Holy Cross (Hamilton)/Hamilton Thistle/ Celtic 'S' form Dec 1977/Celtic B.C./Celtic pro Aug 1979/ Huddersfield Town Mar 1987/NOTTS Feb 1988, fee £15,000 (Hartlepool United loan Nov 1989) (Partick Thistle loan Jan-Feb1990)/Kilmarnock July 1990/Sligo Rovers player-manager Oct 1992/Celtic coach July 1994
Debut v Aldershot (a) 23.2.88, won 2 – 0

A star in Scottish Schools football, Willie McStay was not lacking in admirers. He was actually on the points of signing for Forest when Celtic offered him a place at Parkhead, where he complete 90 matches as a speedy full-back or sweeper. Signed by Huddersfield Town shortly before transfer deadline day, he suffered a broken ankle in his first substitute appearance and played in only 4(5) League matches in eleven months at Leeds Road. Notts reached the Play-off semi-finals shortly after his arrival at Meadow Lanc, but were beaten by Walsall over two legs by an aggregate score of 2 – 4. After appearing in most matches in 1988-89, he made only four substitute appearances in the 1989-90 promotion season. Before returning to Celtic in 1994 he had a successful spell in charge of Sligo Rovers, highlights including a First Division championship and an appearance in the FAI Cup Final in May 1994.

Appearances: FL: 33(12) apps 1 gl FLC: 2(2) apps 0 gls Other: 5(2) apps 0 gls Total: 40(16) apps 1 gl
Honours: Scotland Schoolboy International, 5 caps 1977. (Celtic) Scottish Cup winners 1985, finalists 1984; Scottish League Division 1 champions 1986

McSWEGAN, Gary John

Forward   5' 8"   10st 9lbs
b. Glasgow, 24th September 1970
CAREER: Woodside Secondary School (Glasgow)/Rangers Amateur B.C./Rangers June 1986/NOTTS July 1993, fee £400,000/Dundee United Oct 1995, fee £375,000/Heart of Midlothian Oct 1998 (Barnsley loan Dec 2001) (Luton Town loan Feb 2002)/Kilmarnock Mar 2002/Ross County July 2004
Debut v Middlesbrough (h) 14.8.93, lost 2 – 3

With international strikers of the calibre of Mark Hateley and Ally McCoist to contend with, Gary McSwegan found few opportunities with the Rangers, his seven years at Ibrox netting him just 9(9) Scottish League appearances and four goals. For his role as unused substitute, however, he was awarded a Scottish Cup winners' medal in 1993, when Rangers beat Aberdeen 2 – 1 at Celtic Park. Although on the small side, Gary was a bustling, persistent and speedy striker with a strong shot. Hamstring injuries blighted his spell at Meadow Lane, particularly in season 1994-95 when his presence was greatly missed as the side failed to convert chances into goals, leading to relegation from Division One. Notts recouped most of their outlay when Gary returned to Scotland to join Dundee United. Aside from two unrewarding loan spells from Tynecastle, at Barnsley and Luton Town in 2001-02, he has remained north of the border. Gary joined Ross County in July 2004 having scored exactly a century of goals in English and Scottish League football in 195(113) matches.

Appearances: FL: 47(15) apps 21 gls FAC: 4(1) apps 1 gl FLC: 6(1) apps 3 gls Other: 6 apps 0 gls
Total: 63(17) apps 25 gls
Honours: Scotland Schoolboy International, 1985. Scotland Youth International. (NOTTS) Anglo Italian Cup finalists 1994

McVAY, David Reid

Defender/Midfield   6' 1"   11st 11lbs
b. Workington, 5th March 1955
CAREER: Milford Junior School/South Nottingham U-11/ Fairham School (Clifton)/Clifton All Whites/NOTTS pro July 1973 (Torquay United loan Sept 1977)/Peterborough United July 1979, fee £25,000/Lincoln City Aug 1981/ Boston United trial/Grantham Town trial Nov 1981/Boston United Nov 1981; retired Jan 1983
Debut v Crystal Palace (a) 25.8.73, won 4 – 1

David became the first Nottinghamshire player to win an England Under-18 cap, captaining his country in the 2 – 1 win against Scotland and the 0 – 0 draw against Wales. In addition to his two England appearances he had played in three international trials and twelve County games. Other memorable displays in the 1972-73 season helped his Fairham School team to victory in the ESFA Under-19 national trophy in the two-legged final against Cheltenham, won 1 – 0 on aggregate. Rightly considered a tremendous prospect, he made his League debut within weeks of leaving school, appearing in 27 matches in both defence and midfield in his debut season. In his role as a sports journalist with the 'Evening Post' he recalled that his first League goal was scored "At the wrong end of the pitch" against Carlisle United. If this was disappointing, so too was his eventual return of just 130 first team matches in six seasons at Meadow Lane, when his early promise had suggested a more rewarding career. He did, however, return to haunt his former colleagues when a member of the Peterborough United team who produced a giant–killing performance in round four of the FA Cup in season 1980-81. Promotion bound County were surprisingly defeated 1 – 0 at home by their Division Four opponents, who themselves bowed out in round five, beaten 1 – 0 by the eventual finalists, Manchester City. David worked as a sports reporter for the 'Nottingham Evening Post' before joining 'The Times.' In 2003 his hilarious and irreverent book 'Steak Diana Ross; Diary of a Football Nobody' was published to great critical acclaim and is destined to be made into a film, the rights being sold to the team that produced 'Four Weddings and a Funeral,' 'Notting Hill' and 'Love Actually.'

Appearances: FL: 101(12) apps 2 gls FAC: 4 apps 0 gls FLC: 8 apps 1 gl Other: 5 apps 0 gls Total: 118(12) apps 3 gls
Honours: England Schools U-18 International, 2 caps 1973 (both as captain)

MABBOTT, John "Jack"
Inside/Outside-right
CAREER: Nottingham St. John's/NOTTS Aug 1892/Mansfield Town June 1895
Debut v Aston Villa (a) 18.3.1893, lost 1 – 3

Reserve forward whose debut was made at outside-right in the closing stages of the Division One relegation season 1892-93. He made only one further senior appearance in the Division Two campaign that followed, playing at inside-right against the eventual champions, Liverpool, in a 1 – 1 draw at Trent Bridge. In February 1920, in a letter to the 'Football Post', Jack Mabbott mentioned that he was living at Bolton, only a few minutes walk away from where Bolton Wanderers' old Pikes Lane Ground used to be, in the Deane area of the town.

He recalled that, twenty-seven years earlier, he had been in the Magpies squad that opposed Bolton Wanderers at Pikes Lane, on Cup Final day, 25th March 1893. (Incidentally, the Pikes Lane ground was initially offered to the Wanderers at an annual rental of £35, but five years later they were having to pay £175, no doubt leading to the move to Burnden Park – once a refuse tip – first used in August 1895.)

Appearances: FL: 2 apps 0 gls Total: 2 apps 0 gls

MACHIN, Prestwood Udall
Right-back   5' 8"   10st 11lbs
b. Nottingham, 1st July 1892
CAREER: Halifax Place Mission F.C./Nottingham Forest am then pro 1912/NOTTS July 1913 to 1914
Debut v Bristol City (a) 20.9.13, drawn 1 – 1

The Magpies added two young and inexperienced ex-Foresters to their ranks in the close season of 1913. H.W.Lane was a schoolteacher by profession and had been on Forest's books for about a year without making a senior appearance. Similarly, he failed to reach League level with the Magpies. The unusually named Prestwood Machin had played in one Second Division match for the Reds in the final fixture of season 1911-12. He made an early debut for Notts when he deputised for Herbert Morley, but did not get another opportunity to break into a strong and settled side that won promotion back to the top flight after just one season in Division Two.

Appearances: FL: 1 app 0 gls Total: 1 app 0 gls

MADDISON, Frank
Left-back   5' 10"   11st 7lbs
b. Worksop, 6th May 1934
d. Chesterfield, 31st October 1993
CAREER: Worksop junior football/NOTTS am, signing pro Aug 1953 to June 1958
Debut v Middlesbrough (h) 15.9.56, won 2 – 1

During the two seasons that encapsulated Frank Maddison's 15 League appearances, the Magpies fortunes were at an extremely low ebb. A placing of twentieth in Division Two in 1956-57 was followed by relegation in the following term. As in most struggling sides, team changes were the order of the day. Pat Groome was the regular left-back at the start of 1956-57 but was replaced by Maddison, newly 'demobbed' from National Service, for most of October and November's fixtures. Frank Cruickshank and later Roy Pritchard were also contenders for the number three jersey. After again being on the fringes of the senior side Maddison was released on a free transfer at the end of the 1957-58 campaign.

Appearances FL: 15 apps 0 gls Total: 15 apps 0 gls

MAIDMENT, James Henry C.

Goalkeeper   5' 10**2**"   11st 4lbs
b. Monkwearmouth, Sunderland, 28th September 1901
d. Edwalton, Notts, 12th February 1977
CAREER: Robert Thompson's Workers (Wearside League)/
South Shields/Southend United am May, pro Sept 1923/
Newport County Aug 1924/Lincoln City May 1930/NOTTS
May 1931/Accrington Stanley July 1933 to June 1934/
Nottingham Co-op Diary am Oct 1934
Debut v Tottenham Hotspur (h) 17.10.31, won 3 – 1

Signed to understudy James Ferguson, Jim Maidment
proved an excellent deputy when Ferguson was injured,
his form in twelve first team matches earning him a
contract for another season. In 1932-33, the England
amateur international K.C. Tewkesbury provided the main
competition until his transfer back to Aston Villa in mid
season. Jim Maidment appeared in 354 Football League
matches in a varied career. His main spell was with
Newport County (219 appearances). In October 1927 he
earned a rare distinction, for a goalkeeper, when he scored,
from the penalty spot, in two successive matches. His
record might have been more impressive, but on 2nd
February 1929 he took two penalty kicks for Newport
County against Torquay United. He scored from the first
award, but missed from the second. Jim was an elder
brother of Thomas Maidment (Lincoln City, Portsmouth
and Cardiff City) and a nephew of William Charlton
(Tranmere Rovers.)

Appearances: FL: 44 apps 0 gls FAC: 1 app 0 gls
Total: 45 apps 0 gls

―――――――o―――――――

MAINMAN, Henry Layfield

Half-back   5' 7"   11st 4lbs
b. Liverpool, 7th April 1877
d. Reading, 29th January 1953
CAREER: Everton Dec 1896/Liverpool June 1897/Burton
Swifts May 1898/Reading/NOTTS May 1901 to 1906
Debut v Newcastle United (h) 3.10.01, lost 0 – 2

"A sturdy and powerful half-
back, possessing any
amount of energy,"
according to the 'Glance
Annual' for season
1904-05. A strong tackler
with unquenchable
enthusiasm, he captained
the Magpies for the final
three years of his stay at Trent
Bridge. After appearing in all
three half-back positions,
he settled at centre-
half following
Walter Bull's
transfer to

Tottenham Hotspur. A most unlucky player
in respect of injuries, although virtually an
automatic selection when fit. Outside of the
game, he worked as a fitter in an engineering
works.

Appearances: FL: 130 apps 0 gls FAC: 7 apps 0 gls
Total: 137 apps 0 gls

―――――――o―――――――

MAIR, Gordon

Midfield/Winger   5' 11"   10st 6lbs
b. Bothwell, near Glasgow, 18th December 1958
CAREER: Fir Park Boys' Club/NOTTS app Aug 1975, pro
Dec 1976/Lincoln City Aug 1984, fee £25,000/Motherwell
cs 1986/Clydebank Apr 1991/Ayr United May 1992 to May
1994
Debut as sub v Fulham (a) 20.11.76, won 5 – 1

A skilful and speedy Scot, essentially a left-sided player,
Gordon came through apprentice ranks to make a League
debut at seventeen years of age. The slightly-built winger
first established himself in season 1979-80 when he was
the only player ever-present in League matches, but was
then injured and missed all but four matches of the 1980-
81 promotion season. Returning to the side in the following
season, he gave Division One defences a great deal of
trouble, scoring nine goals in 32(2) matches. He left
Meadow Lane at the close of the relegation season 1983-
84, and in two seasons with Lincoln City made 57 League
appearances and scored three goals.

Appearances: FL: 123(8) apps 18 gls FAC: 4 apps 0 gls
FLC: 10(4) apps 2 gls Other: 5(1) apps 1 gl
Total: 142(13) apps 21 gls
Honours: Scotland Schoolboy International

―――――――o―――――――

MALTBY, Charles Langley

Left-half
b. Farndon, Notts, April quarter 1858
d. Southwell, Notts, 16th July 1936
CAREER: NOTTS (debut) Nov 1880 to (final app) Feb
1882
Debut v Derbyshire, FAC 1, (h) 4.11.1880, drawn 4 – 4

Charles Maltby was the third son of Brough Maltby,
Canon of Lincoln and Archdeacon of Nottingham. In
addition to appearing for Notts County, he was for 25
years a prominent member of the Nottinghamshire
Amateur Club. He was educated at Newark Magnus, was
employed as a bank manager, and served as a J.P.

Appearances: FAC: 1 app 0 gls Total: 1 app 0 gls

―――――――o―――――――

MANN, Arthur Fraser

Midfield/Defender   5' 9"   10st 10lbs
b. Falkirk, 23rd January 1948
d. Birmingham, 3rd February 1999
CAREER: Denny High School/Lochore Welfare/Heart of Midlothian 1967/Manchester City Nov 1968, fee £85,000 (Blackpool loan Nov 1971)/NOTTS July 1972, fee £15,000/Shrewsbury Town June 1979, fee £30,000/Mansfield Town Oct 1979, fee £36,000/Boston United July 1982/Kettering Town cs 1983 for three months before returning to Boston United, appointed caretaker player-manager Nov 1983, player-manager June 1984/Grimsby Town assistant-manager June 1989/West Bromwich Albion assistant-manager Oct 1994
Debut v Shrewsbury Town (a) 12.8.72, drawn 0 – 0

Within six months of being offered a trial by Heart of Midlothian, Arthur Mann was established in their first team. At nineteen years of age he was signed by Manchester City for £85,000, becoming the most expensive fullback to come out of Scotland at that time. Despite winning a FL Cup medal during his stay at Maine Road, limited first team opportunities led him to join the Magpies. A drop into Division Three could have been considered a descent too far, but promotion was won in his first season, and there were two other close run promotion campaigns that sadly ended in disappointment. Best remembered in midfield with Ray O'Brien behind and Don Masson in tandem, Arthur's surging runs down the left flank provided the springboard for many successful attacks. He left Meadow Lane after seven years to seek a fresh challenge, but within three months of signing for Shrewsbury Town he was on the move again. His final move in League circles took him to Mansfield Town where he passed the milestone of 400 League appearances. His death was the result of a tragic accident involving a fork lift truck, in the delivery yard of his employers.

Appearances: FL: 243(10) apps 21 gls FAC: 14 apps 1 gl FLC: 16 apps 2 gls Other: 9 apps 1 gl
Total: 282(10) apps 25 gls
Honours: (Heart of Midlothian) Scottish Cup finalists 1968. (Manchester City) FL Cup winners 1970

MANN, Ronald Harold

Left-half   5' 9½"   11st 12lbs
b. Nottingham, 8th October 1932
CAREER: Trent Bridge School/Nottingham Schoolboys/Meadows Boys' Club/Nottingham Forest ground staff/Coventry City am 1948/NOTTS Dec 1950/Aldershot July 1956/Skegness Town 1959/Loughborough United July 1963, later appointed manager.
Debut v West Ham United (a) 14.4.51, lost 2 – 4

Having captained Nottingham Schoolboys for two seasons and been included in two England trials Ronnie was seen as an outstanding prospect. He also achieved international status with appearances against Scotland and Ireland in Boys' Club representative matches during three seasons spent with Meadows Boys' Club. Despite making his FL debut aged 18, he was to spend the remainder of his time at Meadow Lane in the Midland League side. Transfer listed at the end of season 1955-56, he was signed by Aldershot. Their scouts had first spotted his potential during Army service, when he was stationed nearby at Crookham. After one season with the Shots (24 FL apps and 3 gls), he captained Skegness Town for four seasons and subsequently managed Loughborough Town.

Appearances: FL: 1 app 0 gls Total: 1 app 0 gls

MANNS, Paul Henry

Forward   5' 6"   10st 7lbs
b. Great Haywood, Staffs, 15th April 1961
CAREER: Cardiff City app/NOTTS Aug 1979/Chester City Mar 1983 to Dec 1984
Debut v Sheffield United, Anglo Scottish Cup, (h) 7.8.79, lost 0 – 1

Slightly-built striker Paul Manns, a former Cardiff City apprentice, had his first outing in League football when he came off the bench in the Magpies 3 – 2 victory at Bristol Rovers on 6th October 1979. All of his limited senior involvement came in his first two seasons at Meadow Lane, and despite scoring goals in League and FA Cup in the Division Two promotion season, he did not get another opportunity in First Division football. After a bright start with Chester, three goals in his first seven outings, his goals dried up in 1983-84 and after 16 matches without scoring, he was released in mid season.

Appearances: FL: 5(2) apps 1 gl FAC: 1 app 1 gl FLC: 1 app 0 gls Other: 1(3) apps 0 gls Total: 8(5) apps 2 gls

---

MANSLEY, Allan

Outside-left   5' 7"   10st 10lbs
b. Liverpool, 31st August 1946
d. Sefton North, 4th February 2001
CAREER: Sheffield Wednesday am/Crewe Alexandra am/
Guinness Exports/Skelmersdale United Nov 1966/Blackpool
June 1967/Brentford Jan 1968 (Fulham loan Dec 1970)/
NOTTS Mar 1971 to June 1972 (Lincoln City loan Dec
1971)
Debut v Rochdale (h) 14.8.71, won 4 – 0 (scored one)

Recruited by Blackpool two months after appearing in
the FA Amateur Cup Final of 1966-67, Allan Mansley
did not reach League level until his move to Brentford.
His 93(1) League matches and 24 goals for the Bees in
Division Four comprising the major part of his final career
aggregate figures of 108(1) matches and 26 goals. Despite
finishing on the losing side in the FA Amateur Cup Final,
Allan had the once in a lifetime experience of playing at
Wembley (attendance 75,000) and in the replay at Maine
Road (attendance 55,388.)

Appearances: FL: 11 apps 2 gls FLC: 3 apps 0 gls
Total: 14 apps 2 gls
Honours: (Skelmersdale United) FA Amateur Cup finalists
1967

MARDON, Harry James

Inside/Centre-forward   5' 8**2**" 12st 2lbs
b. Cardiff, 8th June 1914
d. Bristol, 5th January 1981
CAREER: Ashton Gate School/Bristol Schoolboys/Victoria
Albion (Bristol & District League)/Hereford United/NOTTS
May 1936/Bournemouth & Boscombe Athletic Dec 1937,
in exchange for Joe Riley/Bristol City Nov 1938
Debut v Queens Park Rangers (h) 12.9.36, lost 1 – 2

A centre-forward with plenty of power and shooting
ability, Harry Mardon made a good understudy to the
famous Scottish international Hughie Gallacher. His form
in the reserve team led to an experiment to play him
alongside Gallacher, and the move was not unsuccessful.
The 'Football Post,' reporting on his first outing at inside-
right against Swindon Town in November 1936,
considered that: "He did not quite fit the bill as a schemer.
He did, however, score one goal, put the ball in the net a
second time, when he was only just offside, and had
wretched luck with another fine shot." In a career cut
short by the outbreak of war, Harry wound up with 14
goals in 25 matches for Bournemouth, and three in 13
matches for Bristol City.

Appearances: FL: 22 apps 8 gls FAC: 1 app 0 gls Other:
4 apps 5 gls Total: 27 apps 13 gls

MARRIOTT, Frank

Left-back   5' 7"   11st 8lbs
b. Sutton-in-Ashfield, 26th October 1893
d. Nottingham, 10th September 1947
CAREER: Sutton Junction/NOTTS during season 1917-18/
Swansea Town Aug 1923/Lincoln City Sept 1924/Grantham
Town Aug 1925
Debut v Sheffield Wednesday (a) 13.9.19, drawn 0 – 0

Frank joined the Magpies after four years of military
service during World War One, serving in the Dardanelles,
Egypt, France and Belgium. Although not very tall he
was a resolute, fearless defender who used the ball with
skill and accuracy. A serious arm injury brought a
premature end to his first season in March 1920, and he
could only watch from the sidelines as the Magpies were
relegated from the top flight. He departed Meadow Lane
after five years, having lost his first team place at left
back to Horace Cope, but played in eleven League matches
in the successful 1922-23 campaign when the Division
Two title was won in the most dramatic circumstances. A
1 – 0 victory at West Ham United clinching the title by a
two-point margin over the defeated Hammers.

Appearances: FL: 96 apps 1 gl FAC: 16 apps 0 gls
Total: 112 apps 1 gl
Honours: (NOTTS) FL Division Two champions 1923

MARSDEN, Christopher

Midfield   5' 11"   10st 12lbs
b. Sheffield, 3rd January 1969
CAREER: Sheffield United app June 1985, pro Jan 1987/
Huddersfield Town July 1988 (Coventry City loan Nov
1993)/Wolverhampton Wanderers Jan 1994, fee £250,000/
NOTTS Nov 1994, fee £250,000/Stockport County Jan
1996, fee £70,000/Birmingham City Oct 1997, fee
£500,000/Southampton Feb 1999, fee £800,000/Pusan
Icons, South Korea Jan 2004/Sheffield Wednesday June 2004.
Debut v Venezia, Anglo Italian Cup, (h) 15.11.94, drawn 3
– 3 (scored one goal)

Balding midfield playmaker who experienced an unhappy
time at Meadow Lane, this despite a scoring debut in the
Anglo-Italian Cup Group "A" match at Meadow Lane,
shortly after his arrival from Wolverhampton Wanderers.
Chris regained form and confidence after joining Stockport
County for a bargain fee of £70,000, assisting them to
promotion from Division Two, and to a place in the semi-
final of the FL Cup in 1996-97. At the age of thirty he
was re-united with his former Stockport manager, Dave
Jones, who took him to Southampton. In a five-year spell
with the Saints Chris reached the milestone of 400 League
appearances.

Appearances: FL: 10 apps 0 gls FAC: 1 app 0 gls Other:
1 app 1 gl Total: 12 apps 1 gl
Honours: (Southampton) FA Cup finalists 2003

MARSH, Isaac William

Half-back   5' 10"   12st 7lbs
b. Burton-on-Trent, Staffs, January 1877
CAREER: Notts Jardines/Clifton Colliery/Hucknall Portland/ Burton Wanderers Jan 1897/Northfleet June 1897/ West Herts. Sept 1897/Gainsborough Trinity Dec 1898/Hucknall Portland Mar 1899/NOTTS Sept 1899/Newark June 1900/ Doncaster Rovers June 1901, fee £10/Somercotes United Mar 1903/Chesterfield Town 1903-04/Worksop Town Sept 1905/Worksop North End Jan 1906/Dinnington Main Colliery Aug 1907/Birchwood Colliery Nov 1908/Denaby United 1908-09/Chesterfield Town 1909-10/Denaby United 1910-11
Debut v Sunderland (a) 2.12.1899, lost 0 – 5

Notts Reserves fielded three new half-backs against Bulwell in late September 1899, one of them was 'Ike' Marsh, who was working as a pit hand at Wollaton Colliery at the time. He was the only one of the trio to reach first team level, but appeared only as cover for the established middle line of Ball, Bull and Macdonald. Earlier in his career Marsh assisted West Herts, who amalgamated with Watford St Mary's to form Watford F.C. in 1898. One of the club's earliest professional players, he scored a hat-trick in their very first game – a friendly – but shortly afterwards moved from centre-forward to wing half-back, a position he retained throughout his career.

Appearances: FL: 3 apps 0 gls Total: 3 apps 0 gls

———————o———————

MARSH, John Kirk

Inside-forward   5' 8²"   11st 7lbs
b. Mansfield, 8th October 1922
d. Mansfield, 5th December 1997
CAREER: Mansfield Boys' Club/NOTTS Aug 1942/ Coventry City Sept 1948, fee £8,000/Leicester City Mar 1950/Chesterfield Sept 1950, in exchange for Reg Halton/ Worksop Town June 1951
Debut v Swindon Town (a) 26.12.46, lost 2 –4

Jack Marsh showed much promise before he joined the Army, and when news was received in September 1946 that he was on his way back from India, his return to Meadow Lane was eagerly awaited. Perhaps unsurprisingly, he took some time to acclimatise, with his first run in the League team commencing in October 1947. Eleven months on Coventry City, struggling in the lower reaches of Division Two, paid a sizeable fee for his signature but he was injured in his very first appearance for them and played in only 20 League matches. Brief spells with both Leicester City and Chesterfield followed, but Jack was unable to recapture the form that had made him such an exciting prospect during his time at Meadow Lane, alongside England's crack centre-forward, Tommy Lawton.

Appearances: FL: 42 apps 18 gls FAC: 5 apps 3 gls Total: 47 apps 21 gls

MARSHALL, Arthur T

Inside-right/Right-back
CAREER: Nottingham Mellors/NOTTS (debut) Nov 1884 to (Final app) Jan 1888
Debut v Staveley, FAC 2, (a) 6.12.1884, won 2 – 0

Arthur Marshall began with Notts as an inside-forward and made a stunning start, recording a hat-trick in his first match against the crack amateur combination the Corinthians in a famous 7 – 1 victory. He scored nine goals in 12 matches in his first season, was missing for most of 1885-86, but returned in the following season to play in 20 Friendly matches and six FA Cup ties, by this time operating as a right full-back.

Appearances: FAC: 8 apps 1 gl Total: 8 apps 1 gl

———————o———————

MARSHALL, J.T

Inside-right
CAREER: NOTTS (debut) Dec 1887 to (final app) Oct 1889
Debut v Eckington, FAC 1 Q, (h) 6.10.1888, won 4 – 1 (scored two)

In the season prior to the formation of the Football League, Marshall played in nine friendly matches and scored one goal. In 1888-89 he was a member of the reserve team who played in the first two of the season's FA Cup qualifying matches. Both matches had a morning kick-off and preceded a League game on the same day. Marshall scored twice on his debut and once against Beeston St John's in the second round, but his exemplary goal scoring ratio did not earn him another run in the seniors.

Appearances: FAC: 2 apps 3 gls Total: 2 apps 3 gls

———————o———————

MARSHALL, Stanley Kenneth

Inside-forward   5' 10"   11st 7lbs
b. Goole, 20th April 1946
CAREER: Grimsby Town Reserves/Goole Town/ Middlesbrough Aug 1963/NOTTS June 1966 to cs 1968
Debut v Bradford Park Avenue (a) 20.8.66, lost 1 – 4

Stan Marshall began in Grimsby Town's Northern Intermediate League team before joining up with his hometown club, Goole Town. He was still a comparative youngster when Middlesbrough signed him, and he had some time to wait for his League debut (October 1965) despite being a prolific scorer in the Northern Intermediate League side.

Lack of first team opportunities led him to seek a move and at Meadow Lane, despite not commanding a regular place, he finished leading goalscorer in his first season with 13 League and Cup goals in 24 starts and two substitute appearances.

Appearances: FL: 43(6) apps 17 gls FAC: 1 app 1 gl FLC: 1(1) apps 0 gls Total: 45(7) apps 18 gls

---○---

MARTIN, David Kirker 'Boy'
Centre-forward
b. Belfast, 1st February 1914
d. Belfast, 10th January 1991
CAREER: Royal Ulster Rifles Boys' Xl/Cliftonville circa 1930/Belfast Celtic Mar 1932, fee £5/Wolverhampton Wanderers Dec 1934, fee £5,750/Nottingham Forest June 1936, fee £3,000/NOTTS Nov 1938, fee 'approximately £3,500'/Royal Ulster Rifles 1940-41/Glentoran Mar 1941 to Apr 1943/Royal Ulster Rifles (WW2 guest Watford, Aldershot and Fulham)/Derry City 1945-46/Ballymoney United Apr 1946/Ballymena United Apr 1947
Debut v Queens Park Rangers (h) 19.11.38, drawn 0 – 0

An orphanage boy who commanded a record fee for an Irish player when he moved to the Wolves in December 1934. Earlier he was bought out of the Army to sign for Belfast Celtic. His nickname 'Boy' was earned from his army days when he served as a drummer boy in the Royal Ulster Rifles. He saw active service during WW2, was wounded at Caen in 1944, but made a full recovery. Martin starred on both sides of the Trent, netting 46 goals in 84 matches for Forest, before heading the Magpies scoring lists in the final peacetime season. He won his first international cap in September 1933 and scored against Scotland in a 1 – 2 defeat. Within a matter of weeks he was snapped up by the Wolves. Clever, quick off the mark and a fine marksman, he lacked quality support during his relatively brief spell with the Magpies.

Appearances: FL: 26 apps 16 gls FAC: 3 apps 0 gls Total: 29 apps 16 gls
Honours: Northern Ireland International, 10 caps 1934-39

---○---

MARTINDALE, Gary
Forward   6' 0"   12st 1lb
b. Liverpool, 24th June 1971
CAREER: Burscough/Bolton Wanderers Mar 1994/Peterborough United July 1995/NOTTS Mar 1996, fee £175,000 (Mansfield Town loan Feb 1997)/Rotherham United Mar 1998 (Telford United loan Mar 2000)/Telford United June 2000/Burscough Aug 2002
Debut v Blackpool (a) 9.3.96, lost 0 – 1

Gary Martindale, had scored 15 League goals in 26(5) appearances for Peterborough United at the time of his £175,000 transfer to Meadow Lane. Thrust straight into the Magpies push for promotion, he scored the goals that took the team to Wembley and the ultimately disappointing 2 – 0 reverse against Bradford City. In the relegation season that followed he was loaned to Mansfield Town in February but still finished as Notts leading scorer, albeit with just six goals, twenty less than he had totalled in the previous term. Gary, a great snapper up of half-chances and a very reliable man from the penalty spot, scored both of Burcough's goals in their 2 – 1 FA Vase Final victory against Tamworth at Villa Park in May 1903.

Appearances: FL: 34(32) apps 13 gls FAC: 3(1) apps 0 gls FLC: 3(1) apps 0 gls Other: 3 apps 1 gl Total: 43(34) apps 14 gls
Honours: (NOTTS) FL Division 3 champions 1998. (Burscough) FA Vase winners 2003

---○---

MASSON, Donald Sandison 'Don'
Inside-forward/Midfield 5' 8"   10st 12lbs
b. Banchory, Kincardineshire, 26th August 1946
CAREER: Marton Road School/Middlesbrough Schoolboys/Middlesbrough app 1963, pro Sept 1963/NOTTS Sept 1968, fee £6,000/Queens Park Rangers Dec 1974, fee £100,000/Derby County Oct 1977, in exchange for Leighton James/NOTTS Aug 1978 (Minnesota Kicks, USA, May 1981)/Bulova, Hong Kong, April 1982/Kettering Town player-manager Apr to Nov 1983/Los Angeles Kickers manager Mar 1987
Debut v Darlington (a) 14.9.68, lost 2 – 3 (scored one)

Don Masson was born in Scotland but raised in Middlesbrough, and joined the Ayresome Park playing staff at the age of seventeen. He made his league debut at eighteen and in 1966-67 played in 19 matches as Boro won promotion from Division Three. He was out of the first team picture at the time of his transfer to Meadow Lane, and he dropped down two Divisions in joining a team struggling at the wrong end of Division Four. A midfield specialist of vision and skill, he made an enormous contribution, captaining the side to two promotions in his first spell, and into the top flight following his return in 1978. Don enjoyed a successful spell with Queens Park Rangers winning fourteen Scotland caps, and a Division One runners-up medal in 1975-76. He did less well in a season with Derby County but continued to represent his country during his spell at the Baseball Ground. Although not nearly as successful as a goal scorer on his return, his influence on the side could not be overstated, his ability to find space and time in midfield and deliver the defence-splitting pass remaining undiminished. Don was a great favourite at Meadow Lane – perhaps the favourite of all time.

DON MASSON

Appearances: FL: 402 apps 92 gls FAC: 17 apps 3 gls
FLC: 23 apps 1 gl Other: 13 apps 1 gl Total: 455 apps 97 gls
Honours: Scotland International, 17 caps, 1976-78.
(NOTTS) FL Division 4 champions 1971. Anglo Scottish
Cup finalists 1981

MATTHEWS, Cecil Henry Wheeler 'Cyril'

Outside-right   5' 9**2**" 10st 7lbs
b. Cowes, Isle of Wight, 1ˢᵗ December 1901
d. Shanklin, Isle of Wight, 14ᵗʰ July 1973
CAREER: Cowes/Walney United/Barrow am Aug 1921, pro
Feb 1922, fee £150/Bury Dec 1923, fee £500/NOTTS Mar
1928, fee £1,000/Stockport County Sept 1930, fee £200/
Chester June1931/Hyde United Aug 1932
Debut v Leeds United (a) 17.3.28, lost 0 – 6

Described as a player of ripe experience and proven ability
at the time of his signing, he nevertheless failed to fulfil
expectations at Meadow Lane. Released by Bury due to
financial considerations, he had scored on his debut for
the Shakers in January 1924 and assisted them to
promotion to the top flight, as runners-up to Leeds
United, in his first season. One of very few professional
footballers to emerge from the Isle of Wight; Matthews –
popularly known as Cyril – reached first team level with
all five of his League clubs, scoring 41 goals in 209
appearances.

Appearances: FL: 15 apps 0 gls Total: 15 apps 0 gls

MATTHEWS, Lee Joseph

Forward   6' 3"   12st 6lbs
b. Middlesbrough, 16ᵗʰ January 1979
CAREER: Leeds United trainee, signing pro Feb 1996
(NOTTS loan Sept 1998) (Gillingham loan Mar 2000)/
Bristol City Mar 2001, fee £100,000 (Darlington Dec 2003)
(Bristol Rovers loan Jan 2004) (Yeovil Town loan Mar
2004)/Port Vale July 2004.
Debut v Millwall (h) 26.9.98, won 3 – 1

In the opening fixture of 2003-04, Notts arrived late at
Bristol City after being held up in a motorway accident.
Their problems continued at Ashton Gate with a 5 – 0
thrashing, two of City's goals coming from substitute
Lee Matthews in the second half. The tall, bustling striker
had spent a month on loan at Meadow Lane during his
Leeds United days. He had failed to graduate at Elland
Road, despite starring alongside the likes of Harry Kewell
and Jonathan Woodgate in the 1997 Youth Cup winning
side. More recently, Lee was released by Bristol City
after three injury plagued years and just 14(29) League
appearances.

Appearances: FL: 4(1) apps 0 gls Total: 4(1) apps 0 gls
Honours: England Youth International. (Leeds United)
FA Youth Cup winners 1997

MATTHEWS, Robert David

Forward   6' 0"   12st 5lbs
b. Slough, Berks, 14th October 1970
CAREER: Loughborough University/Shepshed Charterhouse/NOTTS Mar 1992/Luton Town Mar 1995, fee £80,000/York City Sept 1995, fee £90,000/Bury Jan 1996, fee £100,000/Stockport County Nov 1998, fee £120,000 (Blackpool loan Dec 1999) (Halifax Town loan Feb 2001)/Hull City Mar 2001, fee £30,000/Northwich Victoria Oct 2002/Mossley 2002-03/Altrincham cs 2003/ Mossley Sept 2003.
Debut as sub v Coventry City (h) 11.4.92, won 1 – 0

Rob Matthews was studying geography at Loughborough University at the time of his debut for the Magpies, and he certainly made an early impact in the late stages of the relegation season 1991-92. He scored the only goal of the game in his second substitute outing against Norwich City, and in his first starting appearance scored twice against Luton Town in the 2 – 1 win that condemned the Hatters to relegation. Ironically, it was Luton Town who signed him from the Magpies, but he failed to settle until he reached Bury. At Gigg Lane he won a Division Two championship medal before being sold to Stockport County by new manager Neil Warnock. Rob's tour around the League circuit concluded in his 32nd year, his career aggregate figures being 156(64) League matches and 34 goals.

Appearances: FL: 21(22) apps 10 gls FAC: 3(2) apps 2 gls FLC: 0(2) apps 0 gls Other: 4(3) apps 0 gls
Total: 28(29) apps 12 gls
Honours: Great Britain representative in the World Student Games 1991. (Bury) FL Division 2 champions 1997

MATTHEWS, William

Inside-right   5' 7**2**" 12st 0lbs
b. Derby, October quarter 1882
d. Melbourne, Derbyshire, 1st May 1916
CAREER: Nottingham Forest Sept 1899/Ripley Athletic Oct 1901/Aston Villa Oct 1903/NOTTS Dec 1906/Derby County July 1912/Newport County Aug 1913
Debut v Bristol City (h) 22.12.06, lost 2 – 3

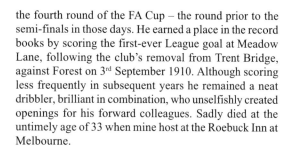

Although the transfer fee involved in Billy Matthews' signing was not made public, it was said to be the highest ever paid by the Magpies at that time. Whatever the amount, he proved a bargain. Joining with the club in dire straits in Division One his eleven goals ensured safety from relegation and carried the side into the fourth round of the FA Cup – the round prior to the semi-finals in those days. He earned a place in the record books by scoring the first-ever League goal at Meadow Lane, following the club's removal from Trent Bridge, against Forest on 3rd September 1910. Although scoring less frequently in subsequent years he remained a neat dribbler, brilliant in combination, who unselfishly created openings for his forward colleagues. Sadly died at the untimely age of 33 when mine host at the Roebuck Inn at Melbourne.

Appearances: FL: 177 apps 37 gls FAC: 11 apps 6 gls
Total: 188 apps 43 gls

MAW, Arthur 'Digger'

Inside-forward 5' 6"   10st 7lbs
b. Frodingham, near Scunthorpe, 29th December 1909
d. Frodingham, 20th April 1964
CAREER: Frodingham United/Brigg Town Sept 1927/ Scunthorpe United Aug 1928/NOTTS Mar 1929, fee £550/ Leicester City July 1932/Scunthorpe United July 1939 (WW2 guest Grimsby Town 1940-41)
Debut v Wolverhampton Wanderers (a) 2.4.29, lost 1 – 3

Once described as: "Small, neat and natty," Maw was a somewhat diminutive inside-forward who made his name in Midland League football with Scunthorpe United. Naturally relying on craft and skill for success he joined Notts as a very promising youngster, but this was not fully realised until his transfer to Leicester City. In League and Cup matches 'Digger' scored 64 goals in 189 matches for City and came close to international recognition in 1933-34 when selected as travelling reserve for England against Ireland at Belfast in October.

Appearances: FL: 35 apps 11 gls FAC: 1 app 0 gls
TOTAL: 36 apps 11 gls

MAY, Edward Henry 'Ted'

Forward
b. Hull, October quarter 1865
d. Nottingham, 6th January 1941
CAREER: Notts Rangers/Burslem Port Vale Sept 1886/ NOTTS Nov 1888/Nottingham Forest debut Oct 1890/ Burton Swifts 1892/Greenhalgh F.C., Mansfield Aug 1893/ Burton Swifts 1895 to 1896
Debut v Blackburn Rovers (a) 15.12.88, lost 2 – 5

Twin brother of William (over), Ted began with Burslem Port Vale and mainly from outside-left played in 65 matches and scored 18 goals. At a time when Notts invariably came out second best in matches against Aston Villa, his hat-trick against them in the 4 - 1 FA Cup second round win in February 1890 was the undoubted highlight of his Notts career.

Appearances: FL: 29 apps 4 gls FAC: 9 apps 5 gls
Total: 38 apps 9 gls

MAY, William Owen

Centre-forward
b. Hull, October quarter 1865
d. Nottingham, 13th October 1936
CAREER: Long Eaton Rangers/NOTTS Nov 1888/Notts Rangers 1889/Greenhalgh F.C. (Mansfield) 1893/Burton Swifts 1895-96.
Debut v Accrington (h) 10.11.1888, drawn 3 – 3

Two of William's appearances for Notts were made alongside his twin Edward. Unlike his brother, however, he did not gain a regular berth in the side. The 1901 Census listed William as a Burton-on-Trent victualler.

Appearances: FL: 4 apps 0 gls Total: 4 apps 0 gls

———————o———————

MAYS, Albert William 'Billy'

Centre-forward 5' 9" 11st 4lbs
b. Ynyshir, near Merthyr, 18th July 1902
d. Derby, 3rd November 1959
CAREER: Ynyshir Swallows/Porth/Wattstown/Bristol City Sept 1923/Plymouth Argyle June 1926/Merthyr Town June 1927/Wrexham Aug 1928/NOTTS Mar 1930, fee £650/Burnley May 1930/Walsall Jan 1931/Halifax Town June 1931/Margate July 1932/Gresley Rovers Sept 1934/Shardlow St James July 1936
Debut v Blackpool (a) 8.3.30, won 2 – 1

Season 1929-30 proved a bitter disappointment to the Meadow Lane faithful. After pressing for promotion for much of the previous season, they dropped like a stone and finished at the foot of Division Two. In late February the directors announced that no new signings would be made; they changed their minds, however, and invested £650 in bringing Albert Mays on board. It was certainly a purchase made in a hurry, and the local correspondent forecast that Notts would probably repent at their leisure, considering that the new signing was: "Too temperamental to make good in this company." There was also the fact that the prematurely balding centre-forward had spent most of his career in the lower divisions. However, he was a proven goal scorer, his Wrexham record, 46 goals in 60 matches, earning him a Wales cap against Ireland in 1928-29. He made a promising start with the Magpies, scoring once on his home debut, a 3 – 0 win against Barnsley, following up with both goals in a 2 – 1 victory against West Bromwich Albion a fortnight later. Seven matches in April rounded off the season and the Magpies disastrously lost six of them and drew the other. After just two months at Meadow Lane Billy Mays was on his way to Burnley for another disappointingly brief stay, covering just two League appearances. His son, also called Albert Mays, played in 281 matches and scored 21 goals for Derby County.

Appearances: FL: 8 apps 4 gls Total: 8 apps 4 gls
Honours: Wales International, 1 cap 1929

MEADS, Thomas

Wing-half 5' 9" 12st 6lbs
b. Grassmoor, Derbyshire, 2nd November 1900
d. Chesterfield, 30th January 1983
CAREER: Grassmoor Ivanhoe/Clay Cross Town/Matlock Town/Stockport County Dec 1923/Huddersfield Town Mar 1927/Reading Oct 1928/Tottenham Hotspur May 1929, fee £2,750/NOTTS June 1935, fee £250/Frickley Colliery player-coach Sept 1936/Dinnington Athletic 1937/Frickley Colliery player-coach Sept 1937/Scarborough trainer-coach May 1939/Chesterfield reserve team coach circa 1945/Middlesex AFA coach.
Debut v Bristol Rovers (a) 31.8.35, drawn 0 – 0

In early days a promising centre-forward, Tom Meads made his debut as attack leader for Stockport County in December 1923, but in April of the same season reappeared in the first team at right-half. He went on to appear in 120 League and Cup matches, scoring 21 goals. He was very unfortunate during his spell with Huddersfield Town, missing out on a FA Cup Final appearance after playing in the semi-final and the first of two replays against Sheffield United in 1927-28. There was also the disappointment of consecutive near misses in the League - runners-up position in successive seasons. A season with Reading preceded his move to the Spurs, where he was a promotion winner from Division Two in season 1932-33, but lost his place in 1934-35 when they were relegated from the top flight. Appointed captain on his arrival at Meadow Lane he faded after a bright start in what proved to be his final season of League football. A younger brother, Jack Meads, appeared in League football with Chesterfield in season 1925-26.

Appearances: FL: 18 apps 2 gls FAC: 2 apps 0 gls Other: 1 app 0 gls Total: 21 apps 2 gls

———————o———————

MELLORS, Mark

Goalkeeper 6' 2" 13st 0lbs
b. Basford, Nottingham, 30th April 1880
d. Otley, 20th March 1961
CAREER: Carrington F.C./Nottingham Forest am/Bulwell United/NOTTS Nov 1902/Brighton & Hove Albion May 1904/Sheffield United May 1906, fee £100/Bradford City April 1909, fee £350; retired 1918
Debut v Sheffield United (a) 10.4.03, lost 0 – 3

A large man hailing from a large family, the 1901 Census revealing that Mark was one of a family of eight children. An amateur with Forest; County was his first professional club, and they held his registration following his move to Brighton, eventually receiving a fee for his services when he moved to Sheffield United. Mark had an unfortunate start with the Magpies, being badly injured in his second League appearance at Wolverhampton Wanderers on 13th April 1903.

He made his 'comeback' in October, replacing Harry Pennington for a run of seven First Division matches. Later in his career he had a lengthy spell with Bradford City, sharing in the club's greatest triumph, the 1911 FA Cup Final victory against red-hot favourites Newcastle United. He defied their attack in both the original game, which finished 0 – 0, and the replay that was won by 1 – 0. Mark was one of two Nottingham-born players in City's final team – right-half George Robinson (ex Forest) being the other. The balance of the side comprised of eight Scotsmen and one Irishman.

Appearances: FL: 9 apps 0 gls Total: 9 apps 0 gls
Honours: (Bradford City) FA Cup winners 1911

MENDEZ, Gabriel

Midfield   5' 9"   11st 10lbs
b. Buenos Aires, Argentina, 12th March 1973
CAREER: Parrametta, Argentina (NOTTS loan Mar 1997)
Debut as sub v Bury (h) 25.3.97, lost 0 – 1

Despite his obvious talents as a creative midfielder with vision and passing skills worthy of a higher stage, Mendez was unable to lift a Magpies side, sliding towards inevitable relegation. In addition to his debut appearance from the bench, his three matches within the space of six days featured two other goal less encounters, and the continuance of a winless run of twenty League matches.

Appearances: FL: 2(1) apps 0 gls Total: 2(1) apps 0 gls

MEREDITH, Robert Garfield

Outside-left
b. Swansea, 3rd September 1917
d. Merton, Surrey May 1994
CAREER: Carlisle United 1943/ NOTTS Nov 1945/Carlisle United Jan 1947/Worcester City trial Mar 1947
Debut v Northampton Town, FAC 2, (a) 8.12.45, lost 1 – 3

Following a guest appearance against Port Vale on 19th September 1945, and another against Mansfield Town on 27th October, Robert Meredith signed a professional form. In the following month he played in both legs of the FA Cup second round against Northampton Town. The Magpies were unable to pull back the 1 – 3 deficit of the first leg, despite the encouragement of a crowd of 18,000 who witnessed the 1 – 0 win at Meadow Lane. During the course of the 1945-46 season, Meredith appeared in 10 regional matches for Notts and in seven for Carlisle United. When normal League football recommenced in 1946-47, he played in only one League match for the Cumbrians.

Appearances: FAC: 2 apps 0 gls Total: 2 apps 0 gls
Honours: Wales Schoolboy International

MERRITT, Richard

Outside-left   5' 8**2**" 11st 5lbs
b. Shiney Row, County Durham, 22nd July 1897
d. Sunderland, January quarter 1978
CAREER: Easington Colliery Welfare/South Shields Nov 1921/Durham City July 1923/Lincoln City May 1925/York City Sept 1926/NOTTS May 1929/Easington Colliery Welfare Sept 1930
Debut v Tottenham Hotspur (h) 30.11.29, lost 0 – 1

Richard Merritt began in League football with South Shields in Division Two, but played only once for them before embarking on his tour of the cathedral cities. He played in 72 Third Division Northern Section matches for Durham City, scoring 11 goals. In a season with Lincoln City he scored three goals in 22 appearances, next moving to York City – at that time a Midland League club – in the summer of 1926. Approaching the veteran stage when recruited by the Magpies, he failed to mount a serious challenge to Sam Haden's monopoly of the left wing berth.

Appearances: FL: 1 app 0 gls Total: 1 app 0 gls

MILDENHALL, Stephen James

Goalkeeper   6' 4"   14st 0lbs
b. Swindon, 13th May 1978
CAREER: Swindon Town trainee, signing pro July 1996/ NOTTS July 2001, fee £150,000/Oldham Athletic Dec 2004/Grimsby Town June 2005
Debut v Port Vale (a) 11.8.2001, lost 2 – 4

Steve immediately endeared himself to Magpies supporters when, just two months after arriving at Meadow Lane, he scored against local rivals Mansfield Town at Field Mill. A free kick, taken from outside his own penalty area, embarrassed the Stags' goalkeeper and was Notts' fourth strike in the 4 – 3 victory. A tall and commanding goalkeeper, Steve was not without serious competition during his spell at Meadow Lane. His first team involvement virtually ended after he sustained a nasty facial injury after colliding with an upright in the 1 – 1 draw against Barnsley in January 2004.

Appearances: FL: 75(1) apps 0 gls FAC: 6 apps 0 gls FLC: 5 apps 1 gl Other: 3 apps 0 gls Total: 89(1) apps 1 gl

---

MILLINGTON, John

Outside-left
b. Leigh, Lancs April quarter 1912
CAREER: Bolton Wanderers am May, pro Aug 1933/Clapton Orient June 1934/NOTTS May 1935/Birmingham May 1937/Swansea Town Dec 1937/Scunthorpe & Lindsey United June 1939
Debut v Bristol Rovers (a) 31.8.35, drawn 0 – 0

Commenting on the deficiencies of the Notts forward line in September 1935, the 'Football Post' stated: "Millington on the left wing is patchy. Occasionally he does brilliant things, and then, to the amazement of everybody, is responsible for the most elementary errors." After appearing in the opening six matches of 1935-36 he was dropped and did not reappear until the final two matches, scoring from outside-right on his comeback against Newport County in a 6 – 2 win. In the following season, when Notts finished as runners-up for the Third Division South championship, Millington appeared in only seven League matches, Fallon and Rickards being the preferred wingmen. Before the outbreak of war halted League football Millington enjoyed his most productive spell with Swansea Town in Division Two (44 League appearances and seven goals.)

Appearances: FL: 15 apps 2 gls Other: 1 app 0 gls
Total: 16 apps 2 gls

———————o———————

MILLS, Bertie Reginald 'Paddy'

Centre-forward 5' 10" 11st 5lbs
b. Multan, India, 23rd February 1900
d. Scunthorpe, 22nd January 1994
CAREER: Barton Town/Hull City Sept 1920/NOTTS Mar 1926, fee £3,750/Birmingham Feb 1929/Hull City Dec 1929/Scunthorpe & Lindsey United player-coach Oct 1933/ Gainsborough Trinity July 1935/Barton Town Nov 1936
Debut v West Bromwich Albion (h) 20.3.26, drawn 0 – 0

An all-action, bustling centre-forward, Paddy Mills was at the top of his goal scoring form at the time of his big money transfer to the Magpies. Within his overall record of 83 goals in 184 matches for the Tigers was a total of 29 in 1924-25 and 17 in 28 matches at the time of his move to Meadow Lane. He was unable to halt the slide that took Notts out of Division One in 1925-26, and injuries curtailed his performances in the following term after he had been switched into the half-back line. A lengthy and uninterrupted run at centre-forward in 1927-28 paid dividends. In early November he scored nine goals in two matches for the Reserves including six of the seven scored against Wombwell. Reinstated to the first team for the visit of Barnsley on 19th November his purple patch continued. In wretched weather with rain descending in torrents he led the line with intelligence and refreshing dash, scoring five of the nine goals netted. The 9 – 0 victory, incidentally, providing a memorable debut for Notts newly-signed centre-half from Sheffield Wednesday, Frank Froggatt.

Appearances: FL: 76 apps 35 gls FAC: 3 apps 1 gl
Total: 79 apps 36 gls
Honours: (Hull City) FL Division 3 North champions 1933

———————o———————

MILLS, Gary Roland

Midfield   5' 9"   11st 10lbs
b. Northampton, 11th November 1961
CAREER: Northamptonshire Schoolboys/Nottingham Forest app June 1977, pro Nov 1978 (Seattle Sounders loan Mar 1982) (Derby County loan Oct 1982) (Seattle Sounders loan Apr 1983)/NOTTS Aug 1987, fee £57,500/Leicester City Mar 1989, part exchange for Phil Turner plus £175,000/ NOTTS Sept 1994, fee £50,000/Grantham Town player-manager Sept 1996 to May 1998/Gresley Rovers Aug 1998/ Kings Lynn Sept 1998, player-manager Oct 1998/Boston United Nov 2000/Tamworth player-manager Jan 2001/ Coventry City first team coach May 2002/NOTTS manager Jan to Nov 2004 /Alfreton Town manager May 2005.
Debut v Wigan Athletic (h) 15.8.87, drawn 4 – 4

The son of a former Northampton Town winger 'Roly' Mills, who scored 30 goals in 305 matches for the Cobblers, Gary inherited his father's talent for the game, winning nine England Schoolboy caps and going on to make his League debut with Forest at sixteen years of age. Falling just short of full international level, he was a midfielder with pace, vision and skill. He joined Notts after appearing in 142(30) matches and 14 goals for Forest, and missed only one League match before joining Leicester City. At Filbert Street he won 'Player of the Year' awards in 1990 and 1992, captained the Foxes at Wembley in the 1993 Play-off Final against Swindon Town, completing exactly 200 League/Premier League appearances prior to his return to Meadow Lane in September 1994. A Wembley appearance in the Anglo Italian Cup Final was the only highlight in a season when the Magpies lost their top flight status. Leaving after two years to embark on his apprenticeship in management, Gary was a widely popular choice as Magpies' manager when he succeeded the unfortunate Billy Dearden in January 2004. Sadly, despite his best efforts to revive the club's fortunes, relegation to the League basement followed. A new-look side opened the 2004-05 season with high hopes of a quick return to the Division renamed 'League One.' The hopes soon proved unrealistic, results and performances proving unacceptable to the board. Although offered another coaching position when relieved of managerial duties, Gary declined.

Appearances: FL: 119(3) apps 8 gls FAC: 9 apps 0 gls
FLC: 11 apps 1 gl Other: 17 apps 0 gls
Total: 156(3) apps 9 gls
Honours: England U-21 International, 2 apps 1980-81. England Youth International, 2 apps 1978-79. England Schoolboy International, 9 apps 1977. (Nottingham Forest) European Cup winners 1980. (Seattle Sounders) NASL Soccer Bowl finalists 1982. (NOTTS) Anglo Italian Cup winners 1995

———————o———————

MILLS, Percy Clifford

Right-back   6' 0½" 12st 7lbs
b. Barton-on-Humber, 10th January 1909
d. Nottingham, October quarter 1967
CAREER: Barton Town/Grimsby Town/Hull City trial/
NOTTS Aug 1927 (WW2 guest Mansfield Town,
Nottingham Forest); retired during WW2 period.
Debut v Barnsley (a) 31.3.28, drawn 0 – 0

Percy Mills began
his football as a
centre-half with
Barton Town in
the Grimsby
League. A
younger brother
of 'Paddy' Mills
(q.v.) he joined
Notts as a
youngster and
remained at
Meadow Lane for
twelve years,
making his 400th
L e a g u e
appearance on
Easter Saturday
1939. A strong
and fearless defender, able to occupy either full-back
position, he was subject to several enquiries from First
Division clubs during his lengthy stay at Meadow Lane,
but was happy to remain a one-club man. The directors
were also happy to keep him, rejecting an offer of £3,500
for him in 1935. Percy was a reliable man from the penalty
spot, most of his goals coming from such awards. After
making local guest appearances during the war for Forest
and Mansfield Town, he applied for a permit to assist
Butchers F.C. in the Notts. Thursday League in
September 1946. Percy was one of six brothers, the two
eldest being killed in WW1. In addition to Paddy (Notts
County,) Arthur played for Luton Town and Gillingham
in the 1930s. Nigel Pearson, recently appointed assistant
manager to Bryan Robson at West Bromwich Albion, is
Percy's grandson.

Appearances: FL: 407 apps 21 gls FAC: 20 apps 0 gls
Other: 7 apps 0 gls Total: 434 apps 21 gls
Honours: (NOTTS) FL Division 3 South champions 1931

MIMMS, Robert Andrew

Goalkeeper   6' 2"   12st 3lbs
b. York, 12th October 1963
CAREER: North Yorkshire Schoolboys (trials in 1979 with
Barnsley, Sheffield Wednesday and Preston North End)/
Halifax Town associate schoolboy Oct 1979,app Apr 1980,
pro Aug 1981/Rotherham United Nov 1981, fee £15,000/
Everton June 1985, fee £150,000 (NOTTS loan Mar 1986)
(Sunderland loan Dec 1986) (Blackburn Rovers loan Jan
1987) (Manchester City loan Sept 1987)/Tottenham
Hotspur Feb 1988, fee £325,000 (Aberdeen loan Feb 1990)/
Blackburn Rovers Dec 1990, fee £250,000/York City trial
cs 1996/Bradford City trial cs 1996/Crystal Palace nc Aug
1996/Preston North End Sept 1996/Rotherham United Aug
1997/York City Aug 1998, appointed player-assistant
manager May 1999/Mansfield Town Mar 2000; retired July
2001/Wolverhampton Wanderers goalkeeping coach.
Debut v Bristol City (a) 15.3.86, lost 0 – 3

Notts fielded no fewer than five different goalkeepers in
Division Three in season 1985-86. Bobby Mimms, on
loan from Everton, took over from Mick Leonard for two
League matches and one Freight Rover Trophy tie against
Mansfield Town. A confident and ideally proportioned
goalkeeper, his League career was launched, as an 18 year-
old, at Rotherham United. He won England Under-21
caps whilst at Millmoor and cost Everton £150,000 in
June 1985. As understudy to Neville Southall at Goodison,
first team opportunities were at a premium, and his brief
association with the Magpies came in the first of four
loan spells that he undertook during his Everton spell.
Terry Venables paid £325,000 to take him to White Hart
Lane, but it was at Blackburn that he enjoyed the best
period of his career, helping Rovers into the Premiership,
following his £250,000 transfer in December 1990.
Bobby's lengthy career spanned eleven different League
clubs and he totalled 530(2) League and Cup appearances.

Appearances: FL: 2 apps 0 gls Other: 1 app 0 gls
Total: 3 apps 0 gls
Honours: England U-21 International, 3 apps. (Everton)
FA Cup finalists 1986; FL Division 1 champions 1987

———————o———————

MITCHELL, Arnold

Outside-right   5' 11" 11st 9lbs
b. Rawmarsh, Yorkshire, 1st December 1929
CAREER: Sheffield & Hallamshire Youths/Sheffield
Wednesday am/Derby County Feb 1948/Nottingham Forest
Mar 1950/NOTTS May 1951/Exeter City July 1952/
Taunton Town 1966; retired in the same year and appointed
assistant trainer to Exeter City.
Debut v Queens Park Rangers (h) 22.9.51, drawn 0 – 0

Despite his association with four different League clubs,
when Arnold Mitchell joined Exeter City in July 1952 he
had appeared in just one Football League match, his
Magpies debut above.

Things changed when he moved south, however, apart from a serious knee injury in his tenth season with the Grecians he was rarely absent. Beginning as an outside-right (he scored 10 goals in 38 matches in his first season), he soon settled into his preferred position of right-half where his ability to read the game was his greatest advantage. He captained the Grecians 1963-64 promotion winning side before retiring in 1966 with a club record 495 League appearances. Taking into account Cup matches, his overall totals were 516 matches and 46 goals. Subsequently persuaded to play a few matches for Taunton Town, a broken leg enforced his retirement.

Appearances: FL: 1 app 0 gls Total: 1 app 0 gls

---○---

MITCHELL, Michael Jeffray

Right-half   5' 8½" 11st 8lbs
b. Milton, Glasgow, 4th October 1903
CAREER: Lanarkshire County/Burnbank Athletic/NOTTS May 1924/New Bedford Whalers Dec 1926/J & P Coates Mar 1927/Brooklyn Wanderers May 1928 to April 1929
Debut v Cardiff City (h) 11.10.24, won 3 – 0

Described in a local handbook as "A strong, determined right half-back, who can still improve. Is not afraid to mix it, and is useful in support." With Billy Flint dominating the first team berth, Mitchell found few opportunities but "mixed it" quite successfully in his first two outings, his debut victory being followed one week later by a 1 – 0 away win at Preston North End. **Note**: The unusual spelling of his second forename is not a misprint.

Appearances: FL: 5 apps 0 gls Total: 5 apps 0 gls

---○---

MITCHELL, Paul Robert

Midfield/Defender   5' 8"   10st 8lbs
b. Nottingham, 8th November 1978
CAREER: NOTTS trainee July 1995, pro July 1997, released June 1998/Hucknall Rolls Royce/Arnold Town/Hucknall Town/Eastwood Town Oct 2003.
Debut v Burnley (h) 26.4.97, drawn 1 – 1

Paul graduated through the Magpies youth system and earned a League debut in the final home game of the relegation season 1996-97. Despite a taste of first team football before becoming a professional, he was unable to build on his promising start, being restricted to a single substitute appearance in the following season's promotion drive, and an Auto Windscreens outing, in the 0 – 2 defeat at Burnley. Released while still a teenager, Paul has since assisted several local non-League sides.

Appearances: FL: 1(1) apps 0 gls Other: 1 app 0 gls
Total: 2(1) apps 0 gls

MOLLOY, Peter 'Paddy'

Half-back   5' 10" 11st 10lbs
b. Haslingden, Lancs., 20th April 1909
d. St. Albans, 16th February 1993
CAREER: Accrington Stanley am July 1930/Fulham am Aug, pro Dec 1931/Bristol Rovers May 1933/Cardiff City Feb 1934/Queens Park Rangers July 1935/Stockport County July 1936/Carlisle United May 1937/Bradford City May 1938/Distillery cs 1943 (WW2 guest Accrington Stanley, Watford, Chelsea, Clapton Orient, Hartlepools United, Rochdale, Ballymena & Dundalk)/Kettering Town player-manager cs 1946/Belfast Distillery 1947/NOTTS Apr 1948/Fulham trainer 1948/Turkey national coach 1949/Watford trainer 1951-91
Debut v Watford (h) 1.5.48, drawn 3 – 3

Paddy Molloy would probably have had a better chance to impress at Meadow Lane had travelling arrangements been more straightforward. Although linked with a move to County in February 1948, his 'Permit to Travel' was held up by the Ministry of Labour, and the season was virtually over before he made his debut against Watford. In the event, his one outing with the Magpies proved to be his last, rounding off a varied playing career, largely at reserve team level, spanning nine different League clubs and 108 matches. A qualified FA coach, his appointments included the management of the Turkish national team in 1949, and a remarkable forty-year stint on Watford's training staff.

Appearances: FL: 1 app 0 gls Total: 1 app 0 gls
Honours: Irish League representative, 1947. (Bradford City) FL Division 3 North Cup winners 1939

---○---

MOLLOY, William

Centre-forward 5' 9½" 10st 12lbs
b. High Spen, 2nd April 1900
CAREER: Benwell Colliery/Spen Black & White/Northampton Town Sept 1924/Spen Black & White/Ashington May 1926/Stockport County July 1927/Dick Kerr's (Preston)/NOTTS Mar 1932/Dick Kerr's cs 1932 to 1936
Debut v Stoke City (h) 2.4.32, won 2 – 1

William Molloy had already scored 49 goals in 37 matches for Dick Kerr's in season 1931-32 (including seven in one match, six in succession, against Horwich R.M.I.) when the Magpies signed him. Their efforts to boost the attack also included the signing of Elliott from Bristol City, all of the transfer activity being undertaken to offset the consequences of the injury that had sidelined their prolific centre-forward, Tom Keetley. Molloy scored at Southampton in his second appearance but in the following month was released on a free transfer. The verdict of the 'Football Post' being: "He is too raw, a hard worker but lacks ball control."

Appearances: FL: 2 apps 1 gl Total: 2 apps 1 gl

MONTGOMERY, John

Left-back   5' 8"   12st 10lbs
b. Chryston, 8th June 1876
d. Edmonton, 6th April 1940
CAREER: Tottenham Hotspur Jan 1896/NOTTS May 1898 to cs 1912
Debut v West Bromwich Albion (h) 9.3.1899, drawn 0 – 0

One of Tottenham Hotspur's earliest professional players, John Montgomery was chosen to represent the Southern League during his two and a half years with the Spurs, during which time he accumulated 132 appearances in all competitions. He had been with the Magpies for less than a season when he was selected to play for the Anglo Scots at Cathkin Park in March 1899. A fearless and sturdy back, who revelled in his work, an extra yard of pace would have placed him in the very top rank. At various times during his marathon spell of service he served as captain and vice-captain, and was rewarded with a benefit match against Oxford University in December 1903. Described in 1912 as "The father of the flock" and about to embark on his fifteenth season, the 'Post Annual' commented: "Much to his regret he did not appear with the League team last season, but was an invaluable mentor for the Reserves. Does loyally all that he is asked to do, and is one of the best servants the club has ever had." His elder brother Archie was a goalkeeper with Glasgow Rangers, Bury and Manchester United in the period 1894 to 1906, and was appointed Bury manager in February 1907. **Note:** After nine years of blameless service John blotted his copybook twice within a matter of weeks in season 1907-08, being sent off the field at Stoke on January 19th, and again against Birmingham at Trent Bridge on February 9th.

Appearances: FL: 316 apps 2 gls FAC: 2 apps 0 gls
Total: 318 apps 2 gls

MOORE, Albert Edward

Inside-right
b. Nottingham, October quarter 1863
CAREER: NOTTS (debut) Feb 1883 to (final app) Feb 1889
Debut v Walsall Swifts, FAC 4, (a) 24.1.1885, won 4 – 1

Forever assured a place in the Magpies long history as the scorer of their first goal in a Football League match. This came on September 15th 1888 when the inaugural fixture took Notts to Everton where a crowd of about 6,000 spectators saw the home side victorious by 2 – 1. Albert Moore's career with the Magpies began some five years earlier when a visit to the Sheffield club on 6th February 1883 resulted in a 8 – 2 win. Harry Cursham scored four, but more remarkably three of Sheffield's players scored own-goals! In addition to the appearances and goals listed below, Moore played in 71 friendly matches and scored 20 goals. His FA Cup goals include a hat-trick scored against Lincoln Ramblers who were beaten 9 – 0 in the first round on 15th October 1887.

Appearances: FL: 10 apps 3 gls FAC: 17 apps 6 gls
Total: 27 apps 9 gls

MOORE, Brian

Outside-right   5' 9½"   12st 2lbs
b. Hemsworth, Yorkshire, 24th December 1938
CAREER: Loughborough College/Mansfield Town am Sept 1960/NOTTS am Aug 1961, pro Dec 1961/Doncaster Rovers July 1963
Debut v Queens Park Rangers (h) 2.12.61, drawn 0 – 0

A powerfully built and speedy outside-right, initially recruited as an amateur in August 1961. Quickly secured on professional terms, the city schoolteacher played on both wings and at centre-forward, the late season signing of Keith Fry restricting his senior appearances in his preferred position on the right wing. In 1962-63, a goal from Brian and one from Tony Hateley helped secure the first victory of the season against Bournemouth, but it was not until late season that he enjoyed a regular taste of first team football.

Appearances: FL: 27 apps 3 gls FAC: 1 app 0 gls FLC: 1 app 1 gl Total: 29 apps 4 gls

---

MOORE, George William

Inside-right   5' 8"   11st 7lbs
b. Newport, Salop, January quarter 1887
CAREER: Stafford Rangers/NOTTS May 1907
Debut v Bolton Wanderers (h) 28.12.07, lost 0 – 1

Recruited from the same club that produced Magpies stalwart Teddy Emberton, George Moore was signed following a satisfactory trial match with the Reserves in the Midland Alliance. His only League appearance came in mid-season when a chronic lack of firepower caused the directorate to make sweeping changes. In addition to the introduction of Moore at inside-right, his wing partner C.F. Calladine was an amateur also making his League debut.

Walter Tarplin continued at centre-forward but the left wing was revamped, George Dodd and Tom Waterall replacing Fred Jones and David Munro. Sadly, the new combination failed to impress, or score, and a more familiar front line was fielded one week later. If nothing else, the wake-up call on the players dropped the week before had the desired effect. Sunderland were beaten 4 – 0 on 4th January to register the season's best victory.

Appearances: FL: 1 app 0 gls Total: 1 app 0 gls

MOORE, Henry 'Harry'

Left-half   5' 8"   11st 2lbs
b. Worksop, 5th August 1896
d. Worksop, July 1984
CAREER: Worksop Congregational/Worksop Town cs 1919/NOTTS Aug 1921, fee £350/Boston Town June 1922/ Worksop Town May 1923/Mansfield Town Aug 1924/ Worksop Town 1928/Manton Colliery Sept 1930
Debut v Blackpool (h) 8.10.21, won 2 – 1

In August 1921 the 'Athletic News,' reviewing prospects for the new season, pointed out: "Notts only weakness would appear to be at half-back, for at the present there are only four players for three positions – Flint, Woodland, Dinsdale and Pembleton, and the three last-named were all signed as centre half-backs." Later in the same month, moves to address the problem were made, 25 year-old Harry Moore being signed from Worksop Town. He made a successful debut in League football and held his place in the side for an eleven-match run. At this point he lost his first team place when a total shake-up – six team changes for the visit of Hull City on Christmas Eve 1921- saw him out of favour until mid April when he was recalled for five of the last six matches. Sweeping changes in the close season saw the release of Moore and eight others, plus the appointment of a new team manager, Captain Charles Bell from Scotland. Harry Moore returned to non-League football and in 1925 won a Midland League championship medal with Mansfield Town.

Appearances: FL: 16 apps 0 gls Total: 16 apps 0 gls

MOORE, Henry Thomas

Left-back
b. Nottingham, 27th June 1861
d. Hendon, 24th September 1939
CAREER: NOTTS (debut) Nov 1881 to (final app) Mar 1888
Debut v Wednesbury Strollers, FAC 2, (h) 24.11.1881, won 5 – 3

Less beefy than most full-backs of his era, but a wholehearted performer, quick of movement, who kicked and tackled well from left full-back. His Notts career terminated in the season prior to FL entry (1888-89), but he was an outstanding performer, particularly in the early 1880s, when Notts reached the semi-final stage of the FA Cup in consecutive seasons.

Appearances: FAC: 28 apps 0 gls Total: 28 apps 0 gls

MOREAU, Fabrice

Midfield   5' 9"   11st 4lbs
b. Paris, France, 7th October 1967
CAREER: La Roche/Paris St Germain/Le Mans UC 72/ Meaux/Racing Paris/Olympique Marseille/AS St Etienne/ SC Toulon/ AD Rayo Vallecano/Talavera/Quan Guoan/SC Numancia/Airdrieonians Aug 2000/NOTTS Mar to May 2001when he returned to France.
Debut as sub v Peterborough United (h) 23.3.2001, drawn 3 – 3

Despite being in his early twenties, Fabrice Moreau had been associated with no fewer than a dozen clubs in his native France and Spain when he arrived in the U.K. to join Airdrieonians. With the assistance of their French playmaker the Diamonds won the Bell's Challenge Cup at Broadwood Stadium in a penalty shoot-out against Livingston after a 2 – 2 draw. Morreau also scored six goals in 21(3) Scottish League matches before crossing the border to take up a short-term contract with the Magpies just prior to the transfer deadline. Deft footwork and excellent ball distribution were apparent in his initial appearances, but he was not offered an extension to his contract, and he returned to France in the close season.

Appearances: FL: 2(3) apps 0 gls Total: 2(3) apps 0 gls
Honours: (Airdieonians) Bell's Challenge Cup winners 2001

MORGAN, John Richard

Right-back
b. Pengwern near Swansea, October quarter 1854
d. Bath, 11th April 1937
CAREER: NOTTS (debut) Nov 1879 to (final app) Mar 1880
Debut v Nottingham Forest FAC 1 (a) 8.11.1879, lost 0 – 4

The 1879 issue of 'Alcock's Annual' described John Morgan as: "A powerful back with a very good kick who never funks a charge. In addition to his bravery, strength in both feet enables him to successfully occupy either of the full-back berths."

Appearances: FAC: 1 app 0 gls Total: 1 app 0 gls

MORLEY, Haydn Arthur

Right-back
b. Derby, 26th November 1860
d. Bakewell, Derbyshire, 15th May 1953
CAREER: Derby Midland/ Derby County cs 1884/NOTTS (first app) Mar 1886 (Nottingham Forest Sept 1888)/Derby County 1889/Sheffield Wednesday 1889 to 1890/ Loughborough Feb 1892
Debut v Notts Rangers, FAC 2, (h) 13.11.1886, drawn 3 – 3

A famous name in the history of Derby County football club. His father, William Morley, being the person credited with the practical moves that brought the club into being during the spring of 1884. In a classic case of nepotism, Mr. Morley's first signing was his son, Haydn Morley! The second signing, incidentally, was George Bakewell (q.v.) another player with Magpie connections. Haydn Morley played in the FA Cup Final of 1890 for Sheffield Wednesday against Blackburn Rovers at the Oval. The powder-blue shirted Wednesday were out-played, being four goals down at half-time, and despite pulling a goal back at the start of the second half, they ultimately lost 6 – 1. It might have been even worse, but as one contemporary match report stated: "Right at the end it looked as if a seventh goal would accrue, but Morley stepped in at the nick of time." A solicitor and a sporting all rounder, he played cricket for Derbyshire in 1891.

Appearances: FL: 2 apps 0 gls FAC: 7 apps 0 gls
Total: 9 apps 0 gls
Honours: (Sheffield Wednesday) FA Cup finalists 1890

MORLEY, Herbert

Right-back   6' 1"   13st 4lbs
b. Kiveton Park, Sheffield, October 1882
d. Skegness, 16th July 1957
CAREER: Kiveton Park F.C./Grimsby Town Sept 1904/ NOTTS Mar 1907; retired during the WW1 period. Scouted for Notts post-war.
Debut v Derby County (h) 29.3.07, won 4 – 0

A 'Letter to the Editor' in the 'Football Post' of September 1960 recalled Bert Morley's debut for Notts at Trent Bridge in 1907. Jack Hendry, a Notts back of earlier vintage, was a spectator in the director's stand. At one point Morley lofted the ball and a cross-wind carried it over the grandstand. Asked his opinion of Morley by one of the directors, Hendry replied in

his native Lowland Scots: "The field's no wide enough for yin feller, it's high enough, but no wide enough." Despite the early put-down, Bert Morley became a great favourite who captained Notts to promotion in 1914. One of the finest defensive backs of his era, and said to have been the innovator of the notorious offside trap that is generally ascribed to Bill McCracken (Newcastle United 1904-23). **Note:** In the same month that Herbert signed for Notts, the FA deleted a rule – that he long been ignored – that players should wear knickers (shorts) reaching to the knees.

Appearances: FL: 258 apps 0 gls FAC: 11 apps 0 gls
Total: 269 apps 0 gls
Honours: England International, 1 cap 1910. (NOTTS) FL Div 2 champions 1914

MORRAD, Frank George

Centre-forward/Full-back   5' 9"   12st 10lbs
b. Brentford, Middlesex, 28th February 1920
CAREER: Brentford am 1936/Southall F.C./NOTTS Aug 1944 (WW2 guest Arsenal, Clapton Orient and Crystal Palace)/Leyton Orient Nov 1946/Fulham Aug 1947/ Brighton & Hove Albion Feb 1948/Brentford Aug 1951/ Bedford Town Aug 1953
Debut v Bristol City (h) 11.9.46, lost 0 – 3

Frank Morrad, briefly on Brentford's books as a sixteen year-old, played for Athenian League side, Southall, until the outbreak of World War Two. He joined the Magpies during the period of hostilities, appearing in 13 matches in season 1944-5 (3 goals) and in seven matches in 1945-46. He played in only one League match in 1946-47 before joining Leyton Orient for whom he scored 11 League goals in 25 matches. He did not reach senior level with Fulham, but after trials was signed as a part-time professional by Brighton & Hove Albion. By this time operating mainly as a full-back he played in 43 League matches and scored three goals. His League career wound up where it had started, some 15 years earlier, at Brentford. He appeared in six League matches and scored two goals before moving into non-League football with Bedford Town.

Appearances: FL: 1 app 0 gls Total: 1 app 0 gls

MORRIS, John James "Jack"

Inside-left   5' 6"   10st 4lbs
b. Liscar, Wallasey, January quarter 1876
d. Liverpool, 16th July 1947
CAREER: Liverpool South End June 1898/Blackpool Mar 1899/NOTTS May 1900/Bristol City cs 1903/New Brompton May 1904/Accrington Stanley June 1905/ Blackpool cs 1906
Debut v Sunderland (h) 1.9.00, drawn 2 – 2

Although light in build, and not too notable in inches, Jack Morris was a quick thinker and alive to every possibility when approaching goal. He had two excellent seasons after joining the Magpies from Blackpool, scoring 19 League and Cup goals in 1900-01 and 12 in 34 matches in 1901-02. In a League career that started and ended with Blackpool, he scored a career total of 49 goals in 128 matches. Jack Morris was a colourful character who married three times and fathered seven children. In the 1920s he was a bookmaker and the proud owner of a Rolls Royce. In 1940 he moved with his family to Solihull, where he worked at the Rover factory.

Appearances: FL: 77 Apps 30 gls FAC: 5 apps 3 gls
Total: 82 apps 33 gls

---○---

MORSE, Harold
Full-back/Forward
b. Birmingham, 4th December 1859
CAREER: NOTTS (first app) Oct 1878 to (final app) Oct 1882
Debut v Nottingham Forest, FAC 1, (h) 16.11.1878, lost 1 – 3

A regular in Notts' back line for two seasons between 1878-80, he was described as "A fast and powerful defender who kicked too strongly at times". A switch to centre-forward in 1880-81 was noted in the season's 'Allcock's Annual' with the comment: "Morse did not show to so much advantage in his new position." This despite a promising start in his new role, a hat-trick against Sheffield F.C. in an 8 – 1 victory.

Appearances: FAC: 5 apps 1 gl Total: 5 apps 1 gl

---○---

MOSLEY, Andrew
Full-back   6' 0"   12st 0lbs
b. Sneinton, Notts, 25th December 1885
d. Coventry, 4th July 1971
CAREER: Sneinton FC/NOTTS Oct 1906 to 1910
Debut v Manchester City (a) 16.3.07, lost 1 – 2

Well-built local full-back whose promising displays for Sneinton F.C. led to his recruitment by the Magpies. In a four-year stay he made steady progress at reserve level without mounting a serious challenge to the established order of Griffiths, Montgomery and Morley, the dominant trio in the full-back department. Outside of the game employed in the building trade, the 1901 Census listing him as a 16 year-old apprentice bricklayer.

Appearances: FL: 11 apps 0 gls Total: 11 apps 0 gls

---○---

MOULDEN, Anthony
Inside-forward 5' 8"   11st 0lbs
b. Farnworth, Lancs, 28th August 1942
CAREER: Blackburn Rovers am/Bury May 1960/Rochdale June 1962/Peterborough United Sept 1962/NOTTS May 1965/Rochdale Sept 1966/Buxton Nov 1966
Debut v Darlington (h) 21.8.65, drawn 0 – 0

Manager Tim Coleman's first close season signing in May 1965, Tony Moulden was said to have cost "a sizeable four-figure sum." Beginning in his native Lancashire, he had made his League debut at inside-right with Bury at the age of eighteen in a 3 – 0 win against Swindon Town at Gigg Lane on 10th September 1960. Restricted to a further three senior matches before joining Rochdale, he had played in just five games for his new team, and scored his first League goal against Doncaster Rovers, when he was on the move again, Peterborough United paying £6,000 for his signature. He scored on his Posh debut, a 3 – 0 win against Bournemouth, and had his best season at London Road in 1963-64, when all but two of his 30 Division Three outings were made on the right wing. His season at Meadow Lane ended at senior level in March in the midst of a goal drought that was addressed by the reintroduction of John Beresford at inside-left. Tony's son, Paul Moulden, won an entry into the Guinness Book of Records by scoring 289 goals in 40 matches for Bolton Lads' Club in season 1981-82. He won England Schools and Youth caps and a Second Division championship medal with Oldham Athletic in 1991. By strange coincidence his League career ended in the same way as his father's – in a free transfer from Rochdale.

Appearances: FL: 23 apps 1 gl FLC: 1 app 0 gls
Total: 24 apps 1 gl

---○---

MOULSON, Cornelius 'Con'
Centre-half/Full-back   6' 0"   12st 6lbs
b. Cashel, near Fethard, Tipperary, 3rd September 1906
d. Lincoln, 27th October 1989
CAREER: Royal Military College (Dublin)/Cleethorpes Town/Grimsby Town am, signing pro Oct 1929/Bristol City May 1931/Lincoln City June 1932/NOTTS Sept 1936, fee £2,000 (WW2 guest Grimsby Town, Lincoln City and Mansfield Town); retired during WW2/Lincoln City trainer-coach Jan to Mar 1965, trainer until Dec 1965 when he retired and took up employment with a Lincoln engineering firm.
Debut v Walsall (h) 1.10.36, drawn 3 – 3

Con Moulson was Notts' second big signing within a week when he followed Hughie Gallacher to Meadow Lane. The recruitment of the two international players enabled the Magpies to launch a serious bid for promotion from the Third Division South. Sadly, this ended in a second-place finish, Luton Town taking the title by a margin of just two points, and with it the one promotion spot available.

Moulson was originally an inside-forward but developed as a centre-half with Lincoln City. His versatility was put to good use by Notts who initially fielded him at centre-half in place of George Wyness. In the following season he had a lengthy run at left-back, where he made an excellent partner for Percy Mills.

In the close season of 1938 he underwent an operation for cartilage trouble but happily made a full recovery, appearing in 40 senior matches in 1938-39.

Appearances: FL: 97 apps 0 gls FAC: 6 apps 0 gls Other: 3 apps 0 gls Total: 106 apps 0 gls
Honours: Republic of Ireland International, 5 caps

---o---

MOWL, William John

Goalkeeper   6' 1"   12st 6lbs
b. Bulwell, Notts, 23rd June 1922
CAREER: RAF football/NOTTS Oct 1944/Mansfield Town July 1949/Grantham Town late in season 1949-50 to cs 1951.
Debut v Port Vale (h) 13.11.48, won 2 – 1

During wartime season 1944-45 local product John Mowl, an ideally proportioned last line of defence, appeared in eight consecutive League North First Championship matches and a further two in the Second Championship that commenced on Boxing Day 1944. As reserve to Harry Brown in 1948-49 he was brought into the side for four consecutive matches when it was decided that Brown was in need of a rest – he was said to have played 500 club and Army games, without a break, since 1942. Having conceded nine goals in his four outings a further change was deemed necessary, Roy Smith being signed from Sheffield Wednesday. The newcomer was destined to appear in 70 consecutive League matches, a total that included 42 in the 1949-50 championship season. John Mowl meantime was transferred to Mansfield Town, but he did not appear at senior level with the Stags.

Appearances: FL: 3 apps 0 gls FAC: 1 app 0 gls
Total: 4 apps 0 gls

---o---

MUIR, Robert Bruce

Outside-right   5' 8"   11st 0lbs
b. Kilmarnock, 14th April 1878
d. Toronto, Canada, 1953
CAREER: Kilmarnock Deanpark/Clyde June 1896/ Kilmarnock July 1897/Bristol Rovers June 1901/Glasgow Celtic May 1903/NOTTS Apr 1904, fee £400/Norwich City May 1905 to 1908/Toronto Eatonia, Canada, player & secretary-manager.
Debut v Everton (h) 3.9.04, lost 1 – 2

Colourfully described as "A bewilderer with clean and clever footwork" after one stunning display for Celtic in 1903, Bobby Muir's arrival in Nottingham was expected to supply a long-felt want for a really top class outside-right. His collection of medals from all competitions numbered twelve and he was a Scottish junior international cap against England. Despite the excellent credentials his season at Trent Bridge was not distinguished. Operating in a very poor side who won only one home match all season, his inviting centres from the right wing were generally squandered by a shot-shy trio of inside forwards. The Magpies, incidentally, were extremely fortunate not to be relegated from the top flight after finishing at the foot of the table. They were saved by the decision to increase the number of clubs in the First Division to 20. Liverpool and Bolton Wanderers, first and second in Division Two, were promoted, Notts and Bury retaining their top-flight status despite finishing at the foot of the table.

Appearances: FL: 19 apps 0 gls FAC: 1 app 0 gls
Total: 20 apps 0 gls
Honours: Scotland Junior International. (Celtic) Scottish Cup winner 1904. (Kilmarnock) Scottish Cup finalists 1898. Scottish League Division 2 champions 1898 and 1899

---o---

MUNRO, David

Outside-left   5' 10"   11st 2lbs
b. Most probably in Scotland, circa 1885
CAREER: Third Lanark 1904/NOTTS May 1907 to cs 1908
Debut v Woolwich Arsenal (a) 2.9.07, drawn 1 – 1 (scored)

The departure to Reading of Ellis Gee, for seven seasons virtually unchallenged on the Magpies left wing, was expected to be filled by the incoming David Munro, Third Lanark's outside-left in the Scottish Cup finals of 1905 and 1906. As the 'Scottish Referee' reported in August 1907: "Many old and familiar faces will be absent from the ranks of the Warriors next season." A disappointing season in both league and cup leading the Third's directorate to make sweeping changes, Munro being among the players released. His start in the Magpies colours was promising, with a goal at Woolwich Arsenal on his debut, but he had a strong challenge throughout the season from the emerging Tom Waterall.

Five different players occupied the outside-left berth during a campaign that seemed certain to end in relegation, but was salvaged by victories in the final two matches, both away from home, against Bolton Wanderers and Chelsea.

Appearances: FL: 12 apps 1 gl FAC: 2 apps 0 gls
Total: 14 apps 1 gl
Honours: (Third Lanark) Scottish Cup winners 1905, finalists 1906

MURPHY, Francis John

Inside-forward
b. Edinburgh, 16th August 1949
CAREER: Edina Juniors/NOTTS Aug 1967/St Johnstone trial during late stages of season 1968-69
Debut v Rochdale (h) 21.10.67, won 2 – 0

Handily versatile young Scot, who although billed as an inside-forward, made his debut on the left wing. Reintroduced at left-half he scored his first League goal, and the only goal of the match, in the Christmas holiday game against Chesterfield. From his more accustomed position of inside-left he scored Notts' first goal in their 2 – 1 victory against Brentford on 2nd March 1968. Although retained for a second season, he appeared only once in 1968-69 in the home game against Aldershot on 31st August. Later in the same season he was reported to be on trial with St Johnstone, but this did not lead to a contract at Muirton Park.

Appearances: FL: 17(2) apps 2 gls Total: 17(2) apps 2 gls

MURPHY, James Barrie

Inside-forward 5' 9" 11st 4lbs
b. Glasgow, 29th November 1942
CAREER: Larkhall Academy/Larkhall Vics/Lesmahagow Juniors/Burnbank Athletic/Stonehouse Violet/Larkhall Thistle/Alloa Athletic Dec 1962/Heart of Midlothian Nov 1963, fee £2,750/Raith Rovers Aug 1967, fee £4,000/NOTTS Feb 1968, fee £3,000/Motherwell Mar 1969/Hamilton Academical cs 1970/East Stirling June 1971 to 1974
Debut v Brentford (h) 2.3.68, won 2 – 1 (scored one)

One of a pair of Scottish-born Murphy's – not related – on the Magpies' books in the late 1960s. Jim was the most experienced, and was drafted straight into the first team following his arrival from Raith Rovers. Despite a scoring debut his presence failed to lift a struggling side who finished 17th and 19th in Division Four in the seasons that spanned his one-year spell at Meadow Lane. New forward recruits during 1968-69 included Masson, Barker and Butlin, the trio effectively ending Murphy's involvement at first team level. By mutual consent his contract was cancelled in early February, and one month

later he was back in Scottish football with Motherwell who stormed to the championship of the Scottish League Division Two, with an eleven-point margin over runners-up, Ayr United.

Appearances: FL: 33 apps 7 gls FLC: 2 apps 0 gls
Total: 35 apps 7 gls

MURPHY, John

Inside-left 5' 72" 10st 8lbs
b. Ireland
CAREER: Hucknall St John's/NOTTS Mar 1896/Bristol City May 1898/Doncaster Rovers Nov 1900
Debut v Loughborough (h) 5.9.1896, won 3 – 1

An early Notts sharp shooter, John Murphy was born in Ireland but bred in Nottingham. When quite a youngster he was discovered with the Hucknall St. John's club. A wily customer who was a fine dribbler with an original style, he became a great favourite, typically Irish in method and popularly known as 'Taters.' Murphy knew his way to goal with the best of inside forwards, and probably netted more goals from corners and scrimmages in front of goal than any other forward in the team. He had the invaluable knack of rushing the ball through, and some contended that he fisted as many goals as he kicked. He was, however, a fine player, lacking only in speed. He had various clubs after leaving Nottingham, amongst the most successful engagements being one at Doncaster Rovers, where he met up again with his old Magpies colleague, Langham, the pair making a remarkably clever wing.

Appearances: FL: 37 apps 24 gls FAC: 2 apps 0 gls
Other: 4 apps 0 gls Total: 43 apps 24 gls
Honours: (NOTTS) FL Division 2 champions 1897

MURPHY, Shaun Peter

Defender/Midfield 6' 1" 12st 0lbs
b. Sydney, Australia, 5th November 1970
CAREER: Perth Italia, Australia/NOTTS Sept 1992/West Bromwich Albion Dec 1996, fee £500,000/Sheffield United July 1999 (Crystal Palace loan Feb 2002)/Perth Glory, Australia Aug 2003.
Debut as sub v Barnsley (h) 5.9.92, lost 1 – 3

In May 1996 Shaun became the first–ever winner of the 'Player of the Year' award for a second, successive season. A strong tackling central defender equally good in the air and on the ground, he was first noted by manager Neil Warnock when playing for Australia in the 1992 Barcelona Olympics.

Although he took some time to win a regular first team place, outstanding displays at reserve level earned him his chance from 1994-95 onwards, when he became a key member of the side. Born of an Irish father and an Indian mother, Shaun had qualifications to play for the Republic, but at the time of his return to Australia in the summer of 2003, he had won 20 caps for the country of his birth.

Appearances: FL: 100(9) apps 5 gls FAC: 6 apps 0 gls
FLC: 5(2) apps 0 gls Other: 9(1) apps 2 gls
Total: 120(12) apps 7 gls
Honours: Australia Youth, U-23 and full International.
(NOTTS) Anglo Italian Cup winners 1995

MURRAY, Adam David

Midfield   5' 8"   10st 10lbs
b. Birmingham, 30th September 1981
CAREER: Derby County trainee, signing pro Oct 1998 (Mansfield Town loan Feb 2002) (Kidderminster Harriers loan Aug 2003)/Solihull Borough 12th Nov 2003/Burton Albion 22nd Nov 2003/NOTTS nc 27th Nov 2003/Kidderminster Harriers Jan 2004/Mansfield Town July 2004/Carlisle United Mar 2005.
Debut v Oldham Athletic (a) 29.11.2003, won 1 – 0

Despite a League debut at 17 years of age and a 'Young Player of the Year' award in the same season, Adam did not fulfil his potential at Pride Park. Loaned to Mansfield Town in February 2002 he scored twice in his second appearance and totalled seven in 13 matches to help take the Stags to promotion from Division Three. A second loan to Kidderminster Harriers was cut short and his Derby County contract cancelled following widely publicised personal problems. Initially joining the Magpies on a non contract basis, he did enough to warrant an offer of a deal to the end of the season. A longer-term deal offered by Kidderminster Harriers was accepted, however, but within a matter of months Adam returned to the scene of earlier triumphs when joining Mansfield Town.

Appearances: FL: 1(2) apps 0 gls FAC: 0(1) apps 0 gls
Total: 1(3) apps 0 gls
Honours: England Youth International

MURRAY, Shaun

Midfield   5' 8"   11st 2lbs
b. Newcastle-on-Tyne, 7th December 1970
CAREER: Northumberland Schoolboys/Tottenham Hotspur trainee, signing pro Dec 1987/Portsmouth June 1989, fee £100,000 (Millwall loan Aug 1993)/Scarborough Nov 1993, fee £25,000/Bradford City Aug 1994, fee £200,000/NOTTS Aug 1998 (Kettering Town loan Mar 2001)/Kettering Town July 2001/Hinckley United June 2003/Gedling Town Aug 2004.
Debut v Oldham Athletic (a) 8.8.98, won 3 – 1

Capped by England at Schools and youth levels, Shaun had excellent ball skills and a good range of passing, utilised mainly from the left side of midfield. He began as a trainee with Spurs but made his League debut with Portsmouth. Voted 'Player of the Year' during a relatively brief spell with Scarborough, he netted the Third Division club a substantial profit when he moved up a Division to join Bradford City. He assisted the Bantams to promotion in 1995-96, but missed out on the Wembley Play-off Final and 2 – 0 victory against the Magpies. After appearing in most matches in the season following his move to Meadow Lane, he played little first team football thereafter and in late season 2000-01 was loaned to Kettering Town. His arrival came too late to prevent their relegation from the Conference, but he was signed by the Poppies when released from Meadow Lane in the summer.

Appearances: FL: 43(12) apps 3 gls FAC: 9(1) apps 1 gl
FLC: 3 apps 0 gls Other: 1 app 0 gls
Total: 56(13) apps 4 gls
Honours: England Schoolboy International, 3 caps 1987.
England Youth International

NEEDHAM, David William

Central defender   6' 1"   12st 7lbs
b. Leicester, 21st May 1949
CAREER: City Boys Grammar School/Leicester Schoolboys/Blaby Boys' Club/Leicester City associate schoolboy/NOTTS amateur Aug 1965, pro July 1966/Queens Park Rangers June 1977, fee £90,000/Nottingham Forest Dec 1977/Toronto Blizzard, NASL, June 1982/Kettering Town Aug 1983, appointed player-manager Nov 1983 to 1986
Debut v Hartlepool United (h) 30.4.66, won 1 – 0

Born close to Leicester City's ground at Filbert Street, David signed schoolboy forms with the Foxes. When approaching school leaving age he was asked to sign an amateur form, to enable his progress to be monitored. Offered a trial at Meadow Lane, he was immediately offered a place on the ground staff. In the same season he made his League debut as a 16 year-old and retained his place in the side for the final six fixtures of the season. Blessed with natural ability and an ideal physique, although young in the game he displayed the coolness of a veteran.

Tackling with great determination in defence, he was quick to exploit the long pass out to the wings and his effectiveness in the air made him a danger when going forward to corners and set piece plays. He starred in County's Division Four championship season, marsh-alling a miserly defence that conceded only 36 goals in 46matches. He was similarly outstanding in 1972-73 when promotion from Division Three was secured as runners-up to Bolton Wanderers. A desire to further his career led to a transfer request and a £90,000 transfer to Queens Park Rangers, but within a matter of months he was back in Nottingham and made his Forest debut in a crushing 4 – 0 victory at Manchester United. Championship and League Cup medals followed during his successful stay at the City Ground, where he passed the milestone of 500 League appearances. A spell in Toronto preceded his three-year spell at Kettering Town. David's son Ben signed schoolboy forms for the Magpies in 1991 but failed to graduate to senior level.

Appearances: FL: 428(1) apps 32 gls FAC: 17 apps 2 gls FLC: 20(1) apps 1 gl Other: 4 apps 0 gls
Total: 469(2) apps 35 gls
Honours: England 'B' International. (NOTTS) FL Division 4 champions 1971. (Nottingham Forest) FL Division 1 champions 1978. FLC winners 1979, finalists 1980

NELSON, Garry Paul

Forward   5' 10"   11st 4lbs
b. Braintree, Essex, 16th January 1961
CAREER: Essex Schoolboys/Colchester United trial/ Southend United 1978, signing pro July 1979/Swindon Town Aug 1983, fee £10,000/Plymouth Argyle July 1985, fee £15,000/Brighton & Hove Albion July 1987, fee £72,500 (NOTTS loan Nov 1990)/Charlton Athletic Aug 1991, fee £50,000/Torquay United player-coach Aug 1996, retired 1997.
Debut as sub v West Bromwich Albion (h) 10.11.90, won 4 – 3

One of football's wanderers, and usually first choice wherever he went. As either wingman or forward his game featured unselfish running, stamina, enthusiasm and an eye for goal. Career aggregate figures of 564(83) League matches and 136 goals called into some doubt the title of his best-selling book "Left Foot Forward: A year in the Life of a Journeyman Footballer."

Appearances: FL: 0(2) apps 0 gls Total: 0(2) apps 0 gls
Honours: (Southend United) FL Division 4 champions 1981

NEWSHAM, Stanley

Inside or centre-forward   5' 9"   11st 7lbs
b. Farnworth, Lancs, 24th May 1931
d. Portsmouth, 4th May 2001
CAREER: Daubhill Athletic/Blackburn Rovers am/Bolton Wanderers am/Bournemouth & Boscombe Athletic June 1952/NOTTS Aug 1957, fee £10,000/Wellington Town Dec 1961/Burton Albion/Ringwood Town manager for two seasons/Returned to NOTTS in Jan 1964 to assist in the development of the Midland Intermediate League team.
Debut v Sheffield United (h) 24.8.57, lost 0 – 1

Manager Tommy Lawton's first signing for Notts. A fast and forceful attack leader who headed Bournemouth's scoring charts for three consecutive seasons and starred in their FA Cup run in 1956-57 when they reached the sixth round, beating Wolves and Spurs along the way. His time at Meadow Lane was something of a roller-coaster ride, with two relegations and one promotion ensuing from his first three seasons. He eventually lost his place to the emerging talents of eighteen year-old Tony Hateley in the latter stages of the 1959-60 promotion campaign. Subsequently plagued by cartilage and ligament injuries, he was given a free transfer at the end of season 1960-61. A proposed move to Oxford United fell through and he began the season in the Magpies Reserve team, scoring twice against Forest Reserves. In mid term he joined Wellington Town. At the time of his return to Meadow Lane, to assist in the development of the club's younger players, he was a Carlton licensee.

Appearances: FL: 99 apps 44 gls FAC: 4 apps 0 gls
Total: 103 apps 44 gls

NEWTON, Adam Lee

Midfield   5' 10"   11st 6lbs
b. Ascot, Berks, 4th December 1980
CAREER: West Ham United trainee 1998, pro July 1999 (Portsmouth loan July 1999) (NOTTS loan Nov 2000 to May 2001) (Leyton Orient loan Mar 2002)/Peterborough United July 2002
Debut as sub v Oxford United (a) 25.11.2000, won 3 – 2 (scored one)

Adam was a member of the West Ham United Youth team that won the FA Youth Cup against Coventry City in May 1999. He scored a goal in each leg of the final, convincingly won by the Hammers with an aggregate score of 9 – 0. His loan spell with the Magpies featured a dream start, his late goal earning an excellent away victory at Oxford United. Mainly from the right side of midfield his game featured searing pace, combined with an ability to swerve past an opponent. If at times inclined to run the ball too far, he nevertheless seemed an excellent prospect during his spell at Meadow Lane.

Appearances: FL: 13(7) apps 1 gl FAC: 2 apps 0 gls
Total: 15(7) apps 1 gl
Honours: St. Kitts & Nevis International. England U-21 International, 1 app 2001. (West Ham United) FA Youth Cup winners 1999

―――――――――o―――――――――

NEWTON, John

Full-back/Wing-half   5' 8**2**" 11st 8lbs
b. Canongate, Edinburgh, 19th January 1940
CAREER: Edinburgh Schoolboys/ Craiglea Thistle (Sunderland trial Sept 1957)/NOTTS Oct 1957/York City Aug 1961 to cs 1962
Debut v Reading (a) 4.4.59, lost 1 – 3

Utility defender John Newton was signed from the Edinburgh based junior club, Craiglea Thistle. One month earlier, he had undertaken trials with Sunderland, but was not offered a contract. His League debut was memorable, but for all the wrong reasons. John had the cruel misfortune to break his leg at Reading. Ironically, he had replaced John Butler after the first-team right-back had been injured at Queens Park Rangers one week earlier. It was not until a year later that he returned to first-team action when he played, at right-half, in the final three matches of the Division Four promotion season. Aside from a single outing in Division Three, he spent 1960-61 in the Reserves. He did not appear in League football with York City.

Appearances: FL: 5 apps 0 gls Total: 5 apps 0 gls

―――――――――o―――――――――

NICHOLSON, Kevin John

Left-back   5' 8"   11st 5lbs
b. Derby, 2nd October 1980
CAREER: Sheffield Wednesday trainee, signing pro Oct 1997/Northampton Town nc Jan 2001 (Forest Green Rovers loan Jan 2001)/NOTTS Mar 2001 (Scarborough loan Mar 2004)/Grimsby Town trial July 2004/Scarborough Aug 2004.
Debut v Bury (a) 17.3.2001, drawn 1 – 1

Kevin arrived at Meadow Lane in the late stages of season 2000-01. The former England schoolboy and Youth international made his League debut in Division One with Sheffield Wednesday, with an appearance from the bench in a 1 – 1 draw against Blackburn Rovers at Hillsborough. It proved to be his only senior outing for the Owls. In mid term he joined Northampton Town on a non-contract basis and was immediately sent out on loan to Forest Green Rovers. He played only once for the Conference side before being recalled to Sixfields, but he was on his way again when he accepted the offer of a contract with the Magpies. Kevin rounded off an eventful season by scoring twice in 9(2) matches, his first League goal coming against Peterborough United in a 3 – 3 draw at Meadow Lane in March. He was to score just one more goal for Notts. His fine individual goal in the final match of season 2001-02 against Huddersfield Town ensuring Division Two safety. Kevin was out of the first team picture at the time of his initial loan move to Scarborough and, following his release in the summer, he joined the Conference side on a permanent basis.

Appearances: FL: 74(21) apps 3 gls FAC: 2(2) apps 1 gl FLC: 4(1) apps 0 gls Other: 4 apps 0 gls
Total: 84(24) apps 4 gls
Honours: England Schoolboy International. England Youth International

―――――――――o―――――――――

NICOL, Stephen 'Steve'

Midfield   5' 10" 12st 8lbs
b. Irvine, Ayrshire, 11th December 1961
CAREER: Ayr United Boys' Club/Ayr United 1979/Liverpool Oct 1981, fee £300,000/NOTTS player-coach Jan 1995, was briefly joint caretaker manager Apr to June 1995/ Sheffield Wednesday Nov 1995 (West Bromwich Albion loan Mar 1998)/Doncaster Rovers June 1998/New England Revolution, USA, head coach.
Debut v Sunderland (a) 21.1.95, won 2 – 1

Steve Nicol tackled hard and distributed accurately from midfield and won virtually every honour in the game during his thirteen years with Liverpool. He began with Ayr United and had a fair grounding of experience for a teenager, making 70 League appearances for the Scottish club. In a period when Liverpool dominated the English game Steve appeared in 328(15) League matches for the Reds, scoring 38 goals.

He was to eventual total a fraction over 500 English and Scottish League matches in a distinguished career that included his 'Player of the Year' award in 1989. His glittering spell with Liverpool ended when he joined the Magpies, initially as player-coach, during Howard Kendall's brief period as manager. Steve became one of three joint-caretakers following Kendall's dismissal, but was relieved of coaching duties when the Murphy/Thompson duo took over in June. He left for Sheffield Wednesday in November of the new season. Despite his senior professional status at Meadow Lane, Steve did not escape the usual dressing room banter. His specially made football boots (size 13) were christened QE2s by the lads!

Appearances: FL: 32 apps 2 gls FAC: 1 app 0 gls FLC: 1 app 0 gls Other: 3 apps 0 gls Total: 37 apps 2 gls
Honours: Scotland International, 27 caps. Scotland U-21 International, 14 apps. (Liverpool) European Cup winners 1984, finalists 1985. FL Division 1 champions 1984, 1986, 1988 and 1990. FA Cup winners 1986, 1989, 1992, finalists 1988. Footballer of the Year 1989.

———————————○———————————

NIXON, Jonathan Charles 'Jon'

Winger   5' 6"   10st 0lbs
b. Ilkeston, Derbyshire, 20th January 1948
CAREER: Derby County app, signing pro Sept 1965/Ilkeston Town July 1967/Long Eaton United cs 1968/NOTTS trial Oct 1969, pro Jan 1970/Peterborough United Sept 1974, fee £15,000/Shrewsbury Town Aug 1977/Barnsley Mar 1978/Halifax Town June 1978/Long Eaton United/Burton Albion 1979/Grantham Town player-manager cs 1981/Shepshed Charterhouse manager cs 1983/Kettering Town assistant-manager cs 1984
Debut v Exeter City (a) 10.1.70, drawn 1 – 1

Jon spent two years as a professional with Derby County but was released at 19, not having reached League level. He then joined his hometown club, Ilkeston United of the Midland League, managed at that time by former Notts player David Agnew. Despite winning the championship he left after one season to join Long Eaton United.

In October he wrote to Meadow Lane to ask for a trial, scored on his first appearance for the Midland League side, and early in the New Year made his League debut. His rapid progress was all the more creditable, as he was able to spend little time in training, as his days were spent at Bishop Lonsdale College at Mickleover, training to be a teacher. A fleet-footed wingman who centred with nice judgement, Jon was a key member of two promotion sides, being particularly impressive in 1972-73 when he blossomed as a scorer on his own account with 17 goals in 44 League matches. After leaving Meadow Lane Jon spent three seasons with Peterborough United, scoring 16 goals in 104(6) League matches. On leaving senior football he was associated with former colleague David Needham at Kettering Town, and in 1984 was still turning out in the Poppies back four, alongside his managerial partner.

Appearances: FL: 167(12) apps 32 gls FAC: 13 apps 2 gls FLC: 8 apps 3 gls Other: 1 app 0 gls
Total: 189(12) apps 37 gls
Honours: (NOTTS) FL Div 4 champions 1971

———————————○———————————

NOGAN, Lee Martin

Forward   5' 10"   11st 0lbs
b. Cardiff, 21st May 1969
CAREER: Cardiff Schoolboys/Port Talbot/Oxford United trainee Aug 1986, pro Mar 1987 (Brentford loan Mar 1987) (Southend United loan Sept 1987)/Watford Dec 1991, fee £350,000 (Southend United loan Mar 1994)/Reading Jan 1995, fee £250,000 (NOTTS loan Feb 1997)/Grimsby Town July 1997/Darlington July 1999/Luton Town Nov 2000/York City Feb 2001/Harrogate Town Feb 2005.
Debut v Blackpool (h) 15.2.97, drawn 1 – 1

York City's player and assistant manager led the Minstermen's scoring charts in 2003-04 but could not prevent his team's relegation to the Conference. In a League career spanning nine different clubs, Lee scored 128 goals in 550(76) League and Cup matches. He won his first full Wales cap against Austria in 1992, and his second against Moldovia in 1996. He scored Reading's first goal in the 1995 Division One Play-off Final against Bolton Wanderers at Wembley, but a two-goal advantage at half-time ended in disappointment and defeat, Bolton winning 4 – 3 after extra time. A second Wembley appearance in 2000 again ended in disappointment, Darlington losing to Peterborough United in the Division Three Play-off Final. A younger brother, Kurt Nogan, also won Wales Under-21 and 'B' international honours and scored 129 League and Cup goals for six different League clubs between 1989-2001.

Appearances: FL: 6 apps 0 gls Total: 6 apps 0 gls
Honours: Wales International, 2 caps 1992-96. Wales 'B' International. Wales U-21 International, 1 app. (Grimsby Town) Auto Windscreens Shield winners 1998

NOON, Harry

Full-back   5' 9½"   10st 11lbs
b. Mansfield, 6th October 1937
d. Sydney, Australia, September 1996
CAREER: Nottinghamshire Schoolboys/Kirkby Co-op/
Bentinck Methodists/NOTTS am 1954, signing pro May
1955/Bradford City July 1962/Wisbech Town Feb 1963
Debut v Doncaster Rovers (a) 7.12.57, lost 0 – 4

Long serving utility defender Harry Noon finally secured
a settled position at left-back during the 1959-60
promotion season. Probably too versatile for his own
good, he had previously figured on both flanks as either
half-back or full-back without winning a regular place in
the side. He held the number three shirt for two years
until superseded by the youngest player in County's
history, Tony Bircumshaw, who took over in mid season
1961-62. At the start of what proved to be his final season
at Meadow Lane, the 'Football Post' concisely summed
up Harry Noon's virtues: "At all times a highly intelligent
and constructive full-back who never resorts to unfair
methods."

Appearances: FL: 122 apps 0 gls FAC: 6 apps 0 gls FLC:
3 apps 1 gl Total: 131 apps 1 gl

NORRIS, Steve Mark

Forward   5' 9"   10st 8lbs
b. Coventry, 22nd September 1961
CAREER: Tolly Lane F.C./Coventry Sporting/Bedworth
United/Tolly Lane F.C./Long Buckby/V.S. Rugby 1983/
Telford United cs 1987, fee £6,500/Scarborough July 1988,
fee £50,000 (NOTTS loan Nov 1989)/Carlisle United Dec
1989, fee £40,000/Halifax Town Oct 1990/Chesterfield
Jan 1992, fee £33,000 (Halifax Town loan Dec 1994)
(Scarborough loan Jan 1995) (V.S. Rugby loan Mar 1995)/
Worcester City Aug 1995
Debut v Doncaster Rovers, FAC 1 (a) 18.11.89, lost 0 – 1

A lightweight forward with the invaluable knack of being
in the right place at the right moment, Steve Norris had
the briefest association with the Magpies. Elsewhere, he
scored goals with commendable regularity, his final
aggregate in League football being exactly 100 goals in
204(32) appearances.

Appearances: FL: 0(1) app 0 gls FAC: 1 app 0 gls
Total: 1(1) apps 0 gls
Honours: England Semi-Professional International

NORTON, David Wayne

Midfield/Defender   5' 7"   11st 5lbs
b. Cannock, Staffs, 3rd March 1965
CAREER: Redhill School/ Halesowen & Stourbridge
Schoolboys/ West Midlands Schoolboys/Aston Villa app June
1981, pro Mar 1983/NOTTS Aug 1988 (Rochdale loan Oct

1990) (Hull City loan Jan 1991)/Hull City Aug 1991/
Northampton Town Aug 1994/Hereford United Aug 1996/
Cheltenham Town Aug 1998/Yeovil Town Aug 1999/Forest
Green Rovers Dec 1999/Tamworth/Nuneaton Borough
assistant-manager cs 2002/Grantham Town assistant-
manager Feb to Sept 2004.
Debut v Bristol City (h) 27.8.88, drawn 0 – 0

An England Schools trialist and Youth international who
broke into Aston Villa's first team in season 1985-86,
after an initial couple of appearances in the previous
season when aged 19. An injured hip joint halted his
progress and he had spent most of season 1987-88 in
reserve as Villa won promotion from Division Two. His
time at Meadow Lane was blighted by pelvic injuries,
two serious operations were followed by specialist's
advice to retire, but he bravely battled back to figure in
the run-in to promotion from Division Three in 1989-90.
Two loan spells in 1990-91 preceded his eventual transfer
to Hull City where he enjoyed the best spell of his career,
appearing in 163 League and Cup matches in a stay of
three years. He was later to experience the bitter
disappointment of relegation from the Football League
with Hereford United in 1996-97, but assisted
Cheltenham Town to win League status in 1999.

Appearances: FL: 22(5) apps 1 gl FLC: 3(1) apps 0 gls
Other: 4(1) apps 0 gls Total: 29(7) apps 1 gl
Honours: England Youth International. (Cheltenham
Town) Football Conference champions 1999

NOTLEY, Wilfred Samuel

Centre-forward
b. Bourne, Lincs, 25th May 1913
d. Bourne, Lincs, 26th November 1972
CAREER: Bourne Town/Stamford Town May 1932/Lincoln
City trial/Tottenham Hotspur trial 1934-35/NOTTS am
Oct, pro Nov 1935/Boston United Aug 1936
Debut v Queens Park Rangers (h) 19.10.35, won 3 – 0
(scored two)

The son of a Bourne miller, Wilf Notley was a target for
several League clubs but the calls of the family business
initially prevented his joining the paid ranks. A centre-
forward with a good physique and powerful shot he made
the most of his chance on his debut for the Magpies,
scoring twice within the space of a minute against Queens
Park Rangers. Despite limited appearances he was joint
leading scorer in League matches in his only season of
senior football. All of his sons played football,
Christopher had trials with Forest at 16 years of age and
Michael, who often figured in Bourne Town's Midland
League side, appeared at Wembley for Oxford University
v Cambridge in 1962.

Appearances: FL: 20 apps 9 gls FAC: 3 apps 0 gls
Total: 23 apps 9 gls

NUGENT, John
Goalkeeper
CAREER: NOTTS Feb 1905
Debut v Derby County (h) 18.2.05, drawn 0 – 0

Notts fielded four different goalkeepers in Division One matches in season 1904-05. In a promising start the youthful Nugent kept a 'clean sheet' against Derby County, the 'Football Post' commenting: "Nugent was alert and clever and showed to distinct advantage." Subsequently, however, he was described as "Promising, but not the finished article." In the month following his senior bow, Notts legend Albert Iremonger made his first appearance. The rest - as they say - was history, the giant newcomer eventually totalling a record 564 League appearances for the Magpies.

Appearances: FL: 3 apps 0 gls Total: 3 apps 0 gls

———————o———————

O'BRIEN, Raymond Christopher
Left-back   5' 9"   10st 10lbs
b. Dublin, 21st May 1951
CAREER: Shelbourne/Manchester United May 1973/ NOTTS Mar 1974 (Derby County loan Sept 1983)/Boston United player-coach and assistant-manager June 1984, manager Jan 1986/Corby Town manager Nov 1987/Arnold Town manager Aug 1991 to Jan 1994.
Debut v Preston North End (a)
16.3.74, won 2 – 0

An early exponent of the 'bent' free kick round a defensive wall, Ray O'Brien scored many of his goals from dead ball situations in the opponent's third of the field. In season 1979-80 he was the club's leading goalscorer with eleven in League and Cup. Eight of his goals came from the penalty spot, his tally including two 'doubles,' against Shrewsbury Town and Newcastle United. Adept in both defence and attack, he was a fixture in Notts' rearguard, forming memorable full-back pairings with Bill Brindley, Pedro Richards and Tristan Benjamin along the way. Having succeeded one Worthington (Bob) in the number three jersey, he was finally succeeded by another (Nigel) in season 1982-83.

Appearances: FL: 323 apps 31 gls FAC: 11 apps 0 gls
FLC: 25 apps 4 gls Other: 27 apps 4 gls
Total: 386 apps 39 gls
Honours: Republic of Ireland International 4 caps, 1975-77. Republic of Ireland U-23 International 2 apps. (Boston United) FA Trophy finalists 1985

———————o———————

O'DONNELL, Dennis
Centre-forward 5' 10" 10st 12lbs
b. Willington Quay, Northumberland, January Quarter 1882
CAREER: Willington Athletic April 1901/Lincoln City Sept 1901/Sunderland May 1905, fee £350/QPR May 1906/ NOTTS May 1907/Bradford P.A. June 1908/North Shields July 1909
Debut v Woolwich Arsenal (a) 2.9.07, drawn 1 – 1

Prior to signing for the Magpies Dennis O'Donnell had starred for Sunderland when they overcame Notts in the first round of the FA Cup in January 1906. In his third appearance after signing from Queens Park Rangers he was opposed to Sunderland at Roker Park. Despite having the supreme satisfaction of scoring twice against his former colleagues, his efforts were unrewarded as Sunderland won the match 4 – 3. A useful forward with the ability to occupy all attack positions, his record of 31 goals in 118 matches for Lincoln City resulted in his upward move to Sunderland, netting the Imps a club record fee. His brother, Magnus O'Donnell, an inside-forward, also played for Lincoln City between 1904-06 and for Barnsley in 1906-07.

Appearances: FL: 18 apps 4 gls FAC: 1 app 0 gls
Total: 19 apps 4 gls

———————o———————

O'GRADY, Christopher James "Chris"
Forward   6' 1"   12st 8lbs
b. Nottingham, 25th January 1986
CAREER: Nottingham Forest associate schoolboy/Leicester City scholar July 2002 (NOTTS loan Sept 2004)
Debut as sub v Rochdale (a) 25.9.2004, won 3 – 0

Chris O'Grady made his debut in the Magpies' best early season performance at Rochdale. A hat-trick by Glynn Hurst bringing a welcome three points after a dreadful start to the campaign. The young Leicester City striker, signed on loan only days before, was brought on to replace Sofaine (himself a substitute introduced at half time) when the Frenchman suffered a head injury. A very promising 19 year-old, with the bearing of a guardsman, Chris had earned his first taste of League action in April 2003, with an appearance from the bench for Leicester City in a 2 – 0 win against Grimsby Town.

Appearances: FL: 3(6) apps 0 gls FAC: 0(1) app 0 gls
Other: 1 app 0 gls Total: 4(7) apps 0 gls
Honours: England Youth International

O'NEILL, Martin Hugh Michael O.B.E.

Midfield   5' 10"   11st 3lbs
b. Kilrea, County Derry, 1st March 1952
CAREER: St Malachy's College/Distillery Aug 1969/
Nottingham Forest Oct 1971, fee £15,000/Norwich City
Feb 1981, fee £250,000/Manchester City June 1981, fee
£275,000/Norwich City Jan 1982, fee £125,000/NOTTS
Aug 1983, fee £40,000; retired Feb 1985/Grantham Town
manager Aug 1987/Shepshed Charterhouse manager Jul
1989/Wycombe Wanderers manager Feb 1990/Norwich City
manager June 1995/Leicester City manager Nov 1996/Celtic
manager June 2000 to May 2005.
Debut v Leicester City (a) 27.8.83, won 4 – 0 (scored one)

For many years Martin O'Neill was Forest's most capped
player, until his total of 36 was surpassed by Stuart
Pearce. Shortly after helping Distillery beat Derry City
in the Irish Cup Final of 1971 he joined Forest and in ten
seasons scored 62 goals in 348(23) matches as an all action,
attacking central midfielder with an artistic style and the
ability to see the move beyond the next. Two spells with
Norwich City, separated by an unsuccessful sojourn with
Manchester City, preceded his return to Nottingham
where his playing days ended because of a knee injury.
Despite a goal on his debut and an emphatic opening day
victory at Leicester City, Martin's time with the Magpies
featured successive demotions from Division One and
Division Two. Considering his subsequent successes in
the field of management, it was surprising that it took
him over two years to get started, his first foot on the
ladder being with Grantham for three days a week. This
despite a pedigree of European Cup and championship
medals, and having captained his country in the World
Cup quarter-final of 1982. Once into his managerial stride,
the honours came thick and fast. He took Wycombe
Wanderers from the Conference to Division Two before
taking Leicester City into the Premier League and to
victory in two FL Cup Finals. A Scottish domestic treble
with Celtic in his first season at Parkhead and subsequent
entry into the European Champions League and UEFA
Cup competitions has further enhanced his already
outstanding reputation.

Appearances: FL: 63(1) apps 5 gls FAC: 7 apps 0 gls
FLC: 10 apps 2 gls Total: 80(1) apps 7 gls
Honours: Northern Ireland International 64 caps 1972-
85. (Distillery) Irish Cup winners 1971. (Nottingham
Forest) FL Division 1 champions 1978. FL Cup winners
1978 and 1979, finalists 1980. European Cup winners
1980.

O'RIORDAN, Donald Joseph

Central defender/Midfield   6' 0"   11st 12lbs
b. Dublin, 14th May 1957
CAREER: Derby County app, signing pro May 1975
(Doncaster Rovers loan Jan 1978)/Tulsa Roughnecks, NASL,
Apr to Aug 1978/Preston North End Oct 1978/Carlisle
United Aug 1983/Middlesbrough Aug 1985, fee £40,000/
Grimsby Town player assistant-manager Aug 1986/NOTTS

July 1988, fee £16.000 (Mansfield Town loan
Sept 1989)/Torquay United Feb 1993, player-
manager Mar 1993/Scarborough nc Dec 1995/
Eire non-league national manager/Sligo Rovers
manager.
Debut v Bristol City (h) 27.8.88, drawn 0 – 0

Notts' first summer signing by manager Barnwell in 1988,
Don O'Riordan had turned down the opportunity to
become player-manager of Grimsby Town in order to
join the Magpies. An independent tribunal was called in
to decide the transfer fee that was set at £16,000. Equally
at home in a variety of positions, the tall Dubliner was a
lovely passer of the ball from midfield, and played a key
role in taking the team into Division One. It was something
of a fairy tale for the 33 year-old Irishman, who at the
start of the season had accepted an offer to run the
Reserves, with the obvious feeling that his first team
days were behind him. In the event he enjoyed a new
lease of life, playing on the winning side at Wembley in
the Play-off Final against Brighton, having earlier scored
a stunning goal in the 6th round FA Cup tie at Tottenham
Hotspur. Sadly, his First Division career ended in the
curtain-raiser at Manchester United when he injured an
Achilles tendon, an abortive comeback requiring surgery.
The popular Irishman departed Meadow Lane in the
following season; rewarded with a free transfer he followed
Neil Warnock to Torquay United.

Appearances: FL: 102(7) apps 5 gls FAC: 6 apps 2 gls
FLC: 5(1) apps 1 gl FLC: 16(2) apps 1 gl
TOTAL: 129(10) apps 9 gls
Honours: Republic of Ireland U-21 International, 1 app.
Republic of Ireland Schoolboy and Youth International.

OAKES, Dennis Raymond

Wing-half   5' 10"   10st 5lbs
b. Bedworth, Warwickshire, 10th April 1946
CAREER: Coventry City app, signing pro Aug 1964/NOTTS
June 1967/Peterborough United May 1971/Chelmsford City
1973/Nuneaton Borough/Tamworth
Debut v Chester (h) 19.8.67, lost 1 – 2

An excellent free transfer signing from Coventry City,
who accompanied Michael Cartwright to Meadow Lane.
A hard working, constructive wing-half, he did not
establish himself immediately but from mid season 1968-
69 was rarely absent in a two-year spell. A talented all-
round sportsman, Dennis played in five County
Championship matches for Warwickshire in 1965. His
younger brother, Keith Brian Oakes, was a central
defender who played for four different League clubs,
appearing in 535(17) League matches and scoring 48 goals
between 1972-90

Appearances: FL: 108(12) apps 0 gls FAC: 1(2) apps 0
gls FLC: 2(1) apps 0 gls Total: 111(15) apps 0 gls
Honours: (NOTTS) FL Division 4 champions 1971

OAKES, Stefan Trevor

Midfield   5' 11" 12st 4lbs
b. Leicester, 6th September 1978
CAREER: Leicester City trainee, signing pro July 1997 (Crewe Alexandra loan Mar 2003)/Walsall July 2003/ NOTTS Feb 2004
Debut v Stockport County (h) 21.2.2004, won 4 – 1

Stefan followed his elder brother Scott to Filbert Street, and was voted Leicester City's 'Young Player of the Year' in 1999. An attacking mid-fielder, he enjoyed his best season with the Foxes in 1999-2000, appearing at Wembley in City's third FL Cup triumph, a 2 – 1 victory against Tranmere Rovers. Stefan found few opportunities during an unhappy sojourn with Walsall – he was red carded in the first half of his initial starting appearance - but he quickly proved an influential member of the Magpies' midfield. His strengths are to be found in the quality and range of his left-foot distribution, thunderous free kicks, and spectacular long-range shooting. At the time of writing, it is reported that Stefan will be departing Meadow Lane when his contract expires, to sign a two-year contract with Wycombe Wanderers, effective from July 2005.

Appearances: FL: 42(3) apps 5 gls FAC: 2(1) apps 1 gl FLC: 0(1) app 0 gls Total: 44(5) apps 6 gls
Honours: (Leicester City) FL Cup winners 2000

OLDERSHAW, Harry James

Outside-left
b. Logged at Basford, Nottingham, October quarter 1895
CAREER: Notts Magdala Amateurs/NOTTS am Nov 1921/ Boston Town June 1922/West Norwood Nov 1925
Debut v Stoke (h) 26.11.21, drawn 0 – 0

Harry Oldershaw was one of three players from the local Magdala club who played for the North versus the South, Amateur Trial at West Ham United's ground on 19th January 1920. When he made his debut for Notts Reserves against Hull City Reserves in early November 1921, the 'Football Post' praised his accurate centering, and the unerring precision with which he placed his corner kicks. A run out in the first team, later in the same month, was less enthusiastically reported:

"Oldershaw failed to reproduce the admirable form that he exhibited with the Reserves. He never really settled down and evidently needs more time to get accustomed to a style of football that is so utterly different to the amateur game."

Appearances: FL: 1 app 0 gls Total: 1 app 0 gls

OLIVER, Thomas Andrew

Outside-left
b. Nottingham, 13th September 1857
CAREER: NOTTS (first app) Oct 1876 to (final app) Dec 1881
Debut v Sheffield, FAC 1, (h) 3.11.1877, drawn 1 – 1

In the season that Thomas Oliver commenced with the Magpies football was in its infancy although a step forward was made in February 1877 when the Sheffield and London rules finally came into alignment. The need for argument over the rules being put aside, a wider programme of fixtures resulted, including the Notts club's debut in the FA Cup in the following season. Oliver appeared in the initial match against Sheffield and the replay which ended in a 0 – 3 defeat. He also played in the following season's first round against the Forest at the Beeston Cricket Ground, won 3 – 1 by the Reds. In addition to his FA Cup outings, his recorded appearances in other friendly matches amounted to 33 games and four goals.

Appearances: FAC: 3 apps 0 gls Total: 3 apps 0 gls

ORGILL, Harold

Goalkeeper   5' 11" 13st 0lbs
b. Hucknall, Notts., 1st October 1920
d. Nottingham, 21st September 1979
CAREER: Basford F.C./ Nottingham Forest Apr 1947/ NOTTS June 1947 to July 1948
Debut v Bournemouth & Boscombe Athletic (a) 3.9.47, lost 0 – 2

In addition to his debut at Bournemouth, Harry Orgill played in the 1 – 1 draw at Swansea Town on 27th December 1947. For this game he was a late call-up and caught the midnight train from Hucknall, arriving at his destination at 11a.m. He had had no sleep, and just over a couple of hours later was on the receiving end as Swansea forwards gave him a severe examination. As the 'Football Post' commented: "Orgill rendered his team a marvellous service, which included the saving of a penalty." Despite his outstanding display, as reserve to the other Harry (Brown) for the senior goalkeeping position, he remained unemployed. In April and May of the previous season he appeared in seven consecutive Division Two matches for Forest, being one of no fewer than six different goalkeepers fielded by them in the first post-war season.

Appearances: FL: 2 apps 0 gls Total: 2 apps 0 gls

OSBORNE, Archibald W

Right-half   5' 9"   11st 2lbs
b. Lanarkshire, circa 1869
CAREER: Vale of Leven Athletic/Vale of Leven F.C./NOTTS
Aug 1890/Clyde 1894
Debut v Bolton Wanderers (a) 6.9.1890, lost 2 – 4

Archie Osborne represented Lanarkshire County before crossing the border to join the Magpies for their third season as a Football League club. In a season when third place in the League was achieved plus an appearance in the FA Cup Final, Osborne was a key member of a fine team, appearing in all League and Cup matches during the season. His role in today's parlance would be that of a midfield ball winner. An 1891 appraisal revealing that: "He clings on with persistency to an opponent from one end of the field to the other, always endeavouring to hamper his progress."

Appearances: FL: 46 apps 1 gl FAC: 7 apps 0 gls Other: 5 apps 0 gls Total: 58 apps 1 gl
Honours: (NOTTS) FA Cup finalists 1891

OSWALD, James

Centre-forward 5' 6**2**" 10st 10lbs
b. Greenock, 3rd January 1868
d. Cathcart, Glasgow, 26th February 1948
CAREER: Clydebank/Govan Hill/Kilbirnie/Third Lanark R.V. 1888/NOTTS Aug 1889/St Bernard's 1893/Rangers Aug 1895/Leith Athletic Nov 1897/Morton Aug 1899/Leith Athletic June 1900/Raith Rovers Aug 1901/Morton Sept 1901/Raith Rovers May 1902/Leith Athletic Aug 1902.
Debut v Wolverhampton Wanderers (a) 7.9.1889, lost 0 – 2

Notts captain and centre-forward, widely credited as the man whose tuition, knowledge of the game and generalship brought the Magpies much success during his period at Trent Bridge. Originally a full-back, he developed into an outstanding attack leader, short in stature but extremely effective in both positional play and shooting.

Although a boiler maker by trade, he learned the art of cricket bat manufacture during his time in Nottingham, working for William Gunn (q.v.), co-founder of Gunn and Moore, the sports outfitters. Brother of John Oswald (below) and Joe, a Scottish League representative, who was a playing colleague during his spell with Morton.

Appearances: FL: 95 apps 55gls FAC: 13 apps 10 gls Other: 1 app 0 gls Total: 109 apps 65 gls
Honours: Scotland International 3 caps 1889-97. Scottish League representative, 3 apps. (Third Lanark R.V.) Scottish Cup winners 1889. (St Bernard's) Scottish Cup winners 1895. (NOTTS) FA Cup finalists 1891

OSWALD, John

Inside-left
b. Greenock
CAREER: Third Lanark R.V./NOTTS Aug 1889/Burnley 1890 to Jan 1891/Sunderland Albion
Debut v Wolverhampton Wanderers (a) 7.9.1889, lost 0 – 2

Along with his brother James (above), John Oswald received a winners' medal when Third Lanark beat Celtic in the Scottish Cup Final replay at Hampden Park, Glasgow, on 2nd February 1889 by 2 – 1. The Rifle Volunteers were worthy victors, having led by 3 – 0 in the original meeting on 26th January, when a snowstorm caused the game to be abandoned. Despite appearing in all but one of the season's League and Cup matches for the Magpies he was allowed to leave in the close season. Joining Burnley, he found himself cast in the unusual role of outside-right and was released in late January after playing in 15 League and one FA Cup match, scoring two goals.

Appearances: FL: 22 apps 6 gls FAC: 5 apps 4 gls
Total: 27 apps 10 gls
Honours: (Third Lanark R.V.) Scottish Cup winners 1889

OTTO, Ricky Junior

Winger   5' 10"   11st 10lbs
b. Hackney, London, 9th November 1967
CAREER: Clapton Rangers/Puma F.C./Haringey Borough/Dartford/Leyton Orient Nov 1990/Southend United July 1993, fee £100,000/Birmingham City Dec 1994 to Dec 1997, fee £800,000 (Charlton Athletic loan Sept 1996) (Peterborough United Feb 1997) (NOTTS loan Sept-Oct 1997)Tamworth Jan 2001/Halesowen Town Mar 2001/ Romalus F.C./Bloxham United/Rhyl.
Debut v Scunthorpe United (h) 7.9.97, won 2 – 1

A serious knee ligament injury, sustained in a reserve team match during his loan spell at Meadow Lane, effectively ended Ricky's involvement in first class football.

A dread locked wingman, perky and elusive, he was a late starter in senior football after serving a three-year jail sentence for armed robbery. He was Birmingham City's record signing at £800,000 in December 1994 and marked his Boxing Day debut against Cambridge United in unusual fashion, scoring both goals in the 1 – 1 draw. His career aggregate figures were 153(39) FL appearances and 40 goals.

Appearances: FL: 4 apps 0 gls FLC: 2 apps 0 gls
Total: 6 apps 0 gls
Honours: (Birmingham City) FL Division 2 champions 1995; Auto Windscreens Shield winners 1995

OWEN, Hugh Glendwr Palmer

Goalkeeper
b. Bath, Somerset, 19th May 1859
d. Landwick, Dengie, Essex, 20th October 1912
CAREER: Corpus Christi College, Cambridge/NOTTS am Nov 1888/Nottingham Forest am 1889
Debut v Preston North End (h) 3.11.1888, lost 0 – 7

It was unfortunate that Hugh Owen's solitary League appearance for the Magpies occurred when the opponents were Preston North End. Despite home advantage, a crushing 7 – 0 defeat ensued, North End completing the first season of the Football League undefeated, securing 40 points out of a possible 44. Another of the early footballing cricketers, Owen was an opening right-hand bat and right-arm medium paced bowler. He played for Cambridge University and Essex, and was the first player to score a century for the county side, scoring 109 and 86 not out against Oxford University at Leyton. He captained Essex from 1895 until his retirement in 1902. At the time of his debut for the Magpies he was a master at Trent College.

Appearances: FL: 1 app 0 gls Total: 1 app 0 gls

OWEN, (Revd.) John Robert Blaney

Forward
b. Reading, January quarter, 1848
d. Dorset Square, London, 11th June 1921
CAREER: Queen's College, Oxford/Sheffield Club/ NOTTS season 1878-79/Maldon F.C., Essex/Also represented the Sheffield Association, Nottinghamshire & Essex.
Debut v Nottingham Forest, FAC 1, (h) 16.11.1878, lost 1 – 3 (scored)

A scorer in his sole appearance for the Magpies, made when he was Second Master of Trent College. John Owen lived up to his billing in 'Alcock's Annual' who observed in 1875: "Very fast and a great goal-getter."

He was capped by England in their third international against Scotland at the West of Scotland Cricket Ground at Partick on 7th March 1874, a match won by the Scots 2 – 1. Owen was ordained in 1876 and held the following scholastic appointments: Second Master of Trent College 1872-81, Master of Hawkshead Grammar School 1881-83 and Headmaster of Trent College 1883-90. He then gave up academic life and was Vicar of Toftrees, Norfolk, 1890-1905 and Rector of Bradwell-on-Sea, Essex, 1905-21.

Appearances: FAC: 1 app 1 gl Total: 1 app 1 gl
Honours: England International, 1 cap 1874

OWERS, Gary

Midfield   5' 11"   12st 7lbs
b. Newcastle, 3rd October 1968
CAREER: Lord Lawson Comprehensive School (Birtley)/ Chester-le-Street Schoolboys/Sunderland app 1985, pro Oct 1986/Bristol City Dec 1994, fee £250,000/NOTTS July 1998/Forest Green Rovers Aug 2002/Bath City player-manager Dec 2003/Forest Green Rovers manager May 2005.
Debut v Oldham Athletic (a) 8.8.98, won 3 – 1

Gary Owers collected a championship medal after making 37 appearances for Sunderland in his debut season and remained a familiar fixture in the team, completing in excess of 300 appearances, scoring 27 goals. He appeared in the 1990 Play-off Final and the 1992 FA Cup Final before joining Bristol City, just prior to Christmas 1994. He helped them reach the Play-off semi-final in 1997, and to automatic promotion, as runners-up to Watford, in 1998. He arrived at Meadow Lane where his all-action style in central midfield, and later at right-back, safely guided the Magpies through a difficult first season back in Division Two. A measure of his consistency is reflected in his appearance figures. These averaged 45 per season during his four-year stay, and he additionally completed a personal career milestone of 500 League appearances, achieved during season 2000-01.

Appearances: FL: 147(7) apps 12 gls FAC: 13 apps 2 gl
FLC: 10(1) apps 0 gls Other: 2 apps 0 gls
Total: 172(8) apps 14 gls
Honours: (Sunderland) FL Division 3 champions 1988. FA Cup finalists 1992

PACE, Derek John 'Doc'
Centre-forward 5' 10" 11st 7lbs
b. Easington, Staffs, 11ᵗʰ March 1932
d. Easington, Staffs, 17ᵗʰ October 1989
CAREER: Bloxwich Strollers/Aston Villa Sept 1949/
Sheffield United Dec 1957, fee £12,000/NOTTS Dec 1964,
fee £7,000/Walsall July 1966/Walsall Wood F.C. manager.
Debut v Wrexham (h) 12.12.64, lost 1 – 3

Popularly know as 'Doc' Pace, a nickname that originated
during his National Service days, when he served in the
Army Medical Corps. Despite approaching the veteran
stage when he arrived at Meadow Lane, 'Doc' led the
Notts attack with skill and dash, scoring 12 goals in 24
consecutive League matches. His total included a hat-
trick against Doncaster Rovers in January 1965 in a 5 – 2
victory. An abdominal operation sidelined him for much
of season 1965-66, after he had scored three goals in his
first four matches. His career began with Aston Villa,
where he made a scoring debut against Burnley in the
week following his nineteenth birthday. He subsequently
netted 140 goals for Sheffield United, assisting them to
promotion to Division One in 1961 and to the semi-final
of the FA Cup a year later. He narrowly missed a career
total of 200 League goals, his final figures being 384(1)
appearances and 196 goals.

Appearances: FL: 29 apps 15 gls FLC: 1 app 0 gls
Total: 30 apps 15 gls

PACEY, Herbert Cornelius
Left-half
b. Nottingham, January quarter 1890
CAREER: Beeston Ericssons/ NOTTS Nov 1910 to Mar
1914
Debut v Bury (a) 26.11.10, drawn 0 – 0

Described in the 'Nottingham Post Handbook' for 1911-
12 as: "A promising young half-back who has, so far,
been seen mostly with the Reserves, but made his debut
against Bury, and showed some promise." His debut came
about when both Craythorne and Griffiths were
indisposed. On a frost-bound, treacherous Gigg Lane
surface he displayed some artistic touches in the goal less
encounter that featured a spectacular penalty save by
Albert Iremonger from a spot kick taken by Bury's
England international forward, Billy Hibbert.

Appearances: FL: 3 apps 0 gls Total: 3 apps 0 gls

PALMER, Charles Anthony
Right-back   5' 11"   12st 5lbs
b. Aylesbury, Bucks, 10ᵗʰ July 1963
CAREER: Watford app Oct 1979, pro July 1981/
Derby County July 1984/Hull City Feb 1987, fee
£30,000 (NOTTS loan Feb 1989)/NOTTS Mar 1989,
fee £24,000/Walsall July 1994/Burton Albion July 1996
(Moor Green loan Dec 1997)/Hinckley United assistant
manager.
Debut v Chester City (a) 18.2.89, lost 0 – 1

A purposeful
defender and a
model of con-
s i s t e n c y ,
considered by
manager Neil
Warnock to be
one of his best
ever investments
at a modest
£24,000. Char-
lie's lengthy
League career
began with
Watford, but he
had to move on in
search of regular
first team foot-
ball. This came with Derby County, and in season 1985-
86 he assisted the Rams to promotion from Division
Three. He joined the Magpies after two years with Hull
City and embarked on the best spell of his career,
consecutive promotions – via Wembley Play-offs – lifting
the Magpies from Division Three into the top flight.
After leaving Meadow Lane he guided Walsall to
promotion from Division Three in his first season at the
Bescot Stadium. In more recent times Charlie has enjoyed
success as assistant to ex-Magpie Dean Thomas at
Hinckley United.

Appearances: FL: 178(4) apps 7 gls FAC: 10 apps 0 gls
FLC: 9 apps 0 gls Other: 20 apps 2 gls
Total: 217(4) apps 9 gls
Honours: (NOTTS) Anglo Italian Cup winners 1994

PALMER, Christopher Louis 'Chris'
Midfield   5' 6"   11st 0lbs
b. Derby, 16ᵗʰ October 1983
CAREER: Derby Schoolboys/Aston Villa 1994-97/Derby
County scholar, app and pro (Hereford United loan Jan-Feb
2004)/NOTTS July 2004
Debut v Macclesfield Town (a) 10.10.2004, won 2 – 1

For a young player, without League experience when he
arrived at Meadow Lane, Chris has made an excellent
contribution in his first season.

A lively, creative midfielder or wingman with two good feet, he controls the ball well, and is not slow to shoot when the opportunity arises. An injured ankle curtailed his excellent pre-season spell of three goals in friendly matches, and it was late October when he scored his first-ever League goal. An occasion that brought celebrations and much relief, as the 2 – 1 win against Boston United ended a lengthy wait for the Magpies' first home win of the season.

Appearances: FL: 23(2) apps 4 gls FAC: 4 apps 0 gls Total: 27(2) apps 4 gls

---

PALMER, Samuel
Half-back
CAREER: NOTTS (first app) Oct 1880 to (final app) Mar 1881
Debut v Derbyshire, FAC 1, (h) 4.11.1880, drawn 4 – 4

Samuel Palmer played in most matches during 1880-81, aside from the FA Cup matches listed, he missed only one of the friendly matches played during the season. It was the club's first term at the Castle Cricket Club Ground, and the first occasion (11th December 1880) on which they sported their new playing colours of Cambridge blue and chocolate halves. Highlights of the season included a 15 – 1 hammering of Newark, and an 8 – 1 drubbing of Sheffield, on the day that the new colours were first paraded.

Appearances: FAC: 3 apps 0 gls Total: 3 apps 0 gls

PAPE, Albert Arthur
Inside forward 5' 10" 12st 2lbs
b. Elsecar, near Wath-on-Dearne, 13th June 1897
d. Doncaster, 18th November 1955
CAREER: Wath Athletic/Army football with the Yorks Light Infantry during WW1/Bolton upon Dearne F.C./Rotherham County Dec 1919/NOTTS May 1923, fee £1,000/Clapton Orient June 1924/Manchester United Feb 1925/Fulham Oct 1925/Flint Town United June 1927/Rhyl Athletic Aug 1927/Hurst F.C. Jan 1928/Darwen player-coach Sept 1928/Manchester Central Feb 1929/Hartlepools United June 1929/Halifax Town July 1930/Burscough Rangers Sept 1931/Horwich RMI Aug 1932/Nelson Nov 1933.
Debut v Birmingham (h) 24.11.23, drawn 1 – 1 (scored)

Albert Pape was a bustling forward, equally at home in any of the three inside positions. He was also an opportunist of some account, having scored 41 goals in 113 appearances for Rotherham County prior to joining the Magpies.

Sadly, his season at Meadow Lane proved to be his most unproductive, although a return of three goals in eight matches suggested that he, and the team, might well have benefited had he been afforded more opportunities. Of his many subsequent moves, the transfer from Clapton Orient to Manchester United was the most unusual. He had travelled with his Orient colleagues to Old Trafford, fully expecting to play against United. Just 90 minutes before the game was due to kick off, United successfully concluded negotiations for his transfer. There was just sufficient time to wire all the necessary details to the Football League and Football Association to allow him to make his United debut against his former colleagues. He then scored one of United's goals in a 4 – 2 win! Albert Pape scored 103 League goals in his career of 266 matches spanning seven different League clubs.

Appearances: FL: 6 apps 2 gls FAC: 2 apps 1 gl Total: 8 apps 3 gls

---

PARIS, Alan David
Left-back   6' 0"   11st 10lbs
b. Slough, Bucks, 15th August 1964
CAREER: Slough Town/Watford Nov 1982/Peterborough United Aug 1985/Leicester City July 1988/NOTTS Jan 1991 to July 1994 fee £80,000/Slough Town player-coach cs 1994/Stevenage Borough Mar 1996/Harrow Borough player-coach Dec 1996, subsequently appointed player-manager/Boreham Wood player-coach cs 2000/Flackwell Heath (Ryman League Div 2)
Debut as sub v Portsmouth (a) 2.2.91, lost 1 – 2

Alan Paris failed to reach senior level with his first League club Watford, so his winning goal against the Hornets in April 1991 was undoubtedly a sweet moment for the classy full-back who had joined Notts a little over two months earlier. Alan appeared in 15 League matches in 1990-91, his winner against Watford marking the start of a run of seven straight wins that took the soaring Magpies into the Division Two Play-offs. Victory against Brighton secured promotion for the second consecutive season, but the stay in the top flight lasted for just one season and Alan's career was cruelly curtailed by a knee injury. Despite a two-year fight to regain full fitness, he was forced to announce his retirement in the summer of 1994. In earlier days, three excellent seasons with Peterborough United brought an upward move to Leicester City in a player-exchange deal that took Nick Cusack to London Road.

Appearances: FL: 39(3) apps 1 gl FAC: 4 apps 0 gls FLC: 2 apps 0 gls Other: 5 apps 0 gls Total: 50(3) apps 1 gl

---

PARKE, J

Right-half   5' 8 2" 11st 0lbs
b. Scotland circa 1871
CAREER: Jordanhill/NOTTS July 1892, released Jan 1893.
Debut v Sheffield Wednesday (h) 3.9.1892, lost 0 – 1

A Scottish import afforded just one outing in the relegation season 1892-93. After failing to shine in the season's opening fixture he was replaced by local product Charlie Bramley. Parke was probably unfortunate to be directly opposed to Fred Spiksley, dubbed the "Sprinting Sheffielder" by the 'Football News.' Parke was too slow to contain the Wednesday's England international, who was a prize-winning runner as well as a footballer. In late January 1893 both Parke and fellow Scot E. Docherty were released, and were reported to have returned homewards to Scotland. Perhaps Parke's first appearance before the Nottingham public, in a pre-season practice at the Castle Grounds, had dented his confidence. He played in this match without his football boots on. As the 'Football News' commented: "Parke had several falls to commence with so did not attempt to run after the ball, but contented himself with an occasional kick when near it."

Appearances: FL: 1 app 0 gls Total: 1 app 0 gls

PARKER, Albert

Outside-left
b. Most probably at Derby
CAREER: NOTTS during wartime seasons 1944-45 and 1945-46
Debut v Bradford City, FAC1, (A) 24.11.45, won 2 – 1

Described in a wartime match report as "The tall Derby lad," Albert Parker first appeared at inside-left against Derby County on 11th November 1944, a match lost 3 – 6. Late in the same season he played at centre-forward in three matches, scoring his first goal for the club at Grimsby Town on 5th May 1945. Aside from the FA Cup outing above, he played just twice in 1945-46, but his goal against Bradford City put Notts into the second round. The victory earned much needed revenue in the form of a two-legged tie against Northampton Town that attracted 10,000 spectators in the away leg and 18,000 at Meadow Lane for the return.

Appearances: FAC: 1 app 1 gl Total: 1 app 1 gl

PARKIN, Brian

Goalkeeper   6' 4"   14st 2lbs
b. Birkenhead, 12th October 1965
CAREER: Oldham Athletic am Dec 1982, Pro Mar 1983/ Crewe Alexandra Nov 1984/Crystal Palace June 1988/Bristol Rovers Nov 1989/Wycombe Wanderers July 1996/ Shrewsbury Town trial Sept 1998/NOTTS Oct 1998/ Wimbledon Mar 1999/Yeovil Town cs 1999/Bristol Rovers pro Oct 1999, nc Aug 2000
Debut v Lincoln City (h) 10.10.98, lost 2 – 3

Brian Parkin was working in an Ellesmere Port oil refinery when his football career began with Oldham Athletic. Scotland international Andy Goram barred his progress at Boundary Park, and it was not until he moved to Crewe Alexandra that he featured regularly in League football. His career ultimately covered 398 League matches, 241 of them with Bristol Rovers, including 30 in their Division Three championship winning side of 1990. He was due to celebrate his 33rd birthday two days after his debut for the Magpies, which was made as cover for Darren Ward who was absent on international duty with Wales.

Appearances: FL: 1 app 0 gls Total: 1 app 0 gls
Honours: (Bristol Rovers) FL Division 3 champions 1990

PARKINSON, Andrew 'Andy'

Midfield/Forward   5' 8"   10st 12lbs
b. Liverpool, 27th May 1979
CAREER: Liverpool trainee/Tranmere Rovers Apr 1997/ Sheffield United July 2003 (NOTTS loan Jan and Mar 2004)/ Grimsby Town July 2004.
Debut v Wrexham (a) 17.1.2004, won 1 – 0 (scored)

Shaven-headed midfielder Andy spent two separate loan spells at Meadow Lane, in the course of which he became the first Notts player to score on his debut since Marcel Cas did so at Port Vale on 11th August 2001. With a good turn of speed and an enthusiastic approach, he buzzed around to some purpose, and would have made a very worthwhile addition to the permanent staff, had funds been in place to secure his services.

Appearances: FL: 10(4) apps 3 gls
Total: 10(4) apps 3 gls

PARKS, Albert

Outside-left   5' 3"   10st 8lbs
b. Lurgan, Northern Ireland, 9th February 1926
CAREER: Glenavon/NOTTS Nov 1945/Glenavon Aug 1948.
Debut v Bournemouth & Boscombe Athletic (h) 31.8.46, won 1 – 0

If the heights and weights of the 1947-48 playing staff, given in an August 1947 issue of the 'Football Post', were correct, there would be some claim for Albert Parks to share the record of the shortest player to appear in a League match for the Magpies. The other candidate, also measured at 5'3", being Steve Holder (q.v.). Described as "A capital foraging forward of the type who gives opposing defenders no peace," Parks was the first outside-left fielded by the Magpies when normal peacetime League football recommenced in 1946-47.

Later utilised in both inside-forward berths, he was somewhat disappointing as a goal-getter but was a clever initiator who rarely wasted a pass.

Appearances: FL: 30 apps 4 gls Total: 30 apps 4 gls

———o———

PARRY, Cyril

Outside-right   5' 9"   10st 12lbs
b. Derby, 13th December 1937
CAREER: Derbyshire Schoolboys/Derby County am/NOTTS May 1955 to June 1959/Bourne Town/Lockheed Leamington/Matlock Town/Long Eaton United Mar 1967
Debut v Rotherham United (h) 14.12.57, won 1 – 0

One of a family of footballing brothers that included Ray (Bolton Wanderers and England), Jack (517 appearances for Derby County) and Glyn (Derby County staff without reaching senior level). Cyril was capped by England Schools against Ireland and made some outstanding displays in the Magpies Reserves. Initially hampered by a back injury that required surgery he recovered to feature at senior level in seasons 1957-58 and 1958-59 without establishing a regular place in either campaign, both of which ended in relegation.

Appearances: FL: 12 apps 2 gls Total: 12 apps 2 gls
Honours: England Schoolboy International, 1 cap 1952

———o———

PAXTON, John William

Left-back   5' 9½"   12st 0lbs
b. Wolverhampton, 24th March 1928
CAREER: Wolverhampton Wanderers am/NOTTS May 1950/Kidderminster Harriers Sept 1951
Debut v Queens Park Rangers (a) 24.8.50, lost 0 – 1

In the final season of football played under wartime conditions, John Paxton played in seven Football League (South) matches for the Wolves, being one of a club record of 42 players who played in first team football during season 1945-46. He was unable to break into the Wolves' highly successful Division One side in the immediate post-war period, but featured regularly in their reserve team. A similar situation occurred during his season at Meadow Lane. Newly promoted from Division Three South the Magpies struggled to survive in their first season in Division Two and Paxton did not appear at senior level after playing twice in early season defeats at Q.P.R. and Cardiff City.

Appearances: FL: 2 apps 0 gls Total: 2 apps 0 gls

———o———

PEACOCK, Ernest Gilbert

Left-half   5' 10½"   11st 7lbs
b. Bristol, 11th December 1924
d. Bristol, 12th February 1973
CAREER: Barleyfields F.C./Syston Town/NOTTS Mar 1945/Bristol City Oct 1946/Weymouth Town June 1959
Debut v Bradford City, FAC 1, (h) 17.11.45, drawn 2 – 2

A red-haired, combative half-back, Ernie Peacock returned homewards to Bristol when normal peace-time football was a matter of weeks old. He had been noted by the Magpies during war-time season 1944-45 and had appeared in all four of the FA Cup matches contested in 1945-46 but had not made a FL appearance when recruited by Bristol City. At Ashton Gate he became a great crowd favourite, clocking up a total of 366 first team appearances and eight goals in thirteen seasons, his total including 44 out of a possible 46 appearances in the Robins 1954-55 Third Division South championship side.

Appearances: FAC: 4 apps 0 gls Total: 4 apps 0 gls
Honours: (Bristol City) FL Division 3 South champions 1955

———o———

PEAD, Craig George

Defender   5' 9"   11st 6lbs
b. Bromsgrove, 15th September 1981
CAREER: Coventry City trainee, signing pro Sept 1998 (NOTTS loan Sept 2004)/ (Walsall loan Mar 2005)/Walsall May 2005.
Debut v Northampton Town (a) 11.9. 2004, drawn 0 – 0

An early season loan signing from manager Mills' previous club, Coventry City, England Youth international Craig Pead graduated through the Sky Blues' Youth team to make his League debut at Burnley in the final match of season 2001-02. In the following season he claimed a regular place from mid-term, and scored his first senior goals with two second half strikes in the 2 – 2 draw at Preston North End. Thereafter, his progress stalled, and at the time of his loan to the Magpies he had been mainly operating at reserve level.

Appearances: FL: 4(1) app 0 gls Other: 1 app 0 gls
Total: 5(1) apps 0 gls
Honours: England Youth International

———o———

PEARCE, Dennis Anthony

Left-back   5' 10"   11st 0lbs
b. Wolverhampton, 10th September 1974
CAREER: Aston Villa trainee, signing pro June 1993/Wolverhampton Wanderers July 1995/NOTTS July 1997/Peterborough United May 2001 to Dec 2003, when reported to be training with Lincoln City/Stafford Rangers Aug 2004/Northwich Victoria Sept 2004.
Debut v Rochdale (h) 9.8.97, won 2 – 1

A free transfer signing from Wolverhampton Wanderers, where he had played in little first team football, Dennis swiftly established himself at Meadow Lane. Speedy, comfortable on the ball, and increasingly effective in the left wing-back role, he scored his first two senior goals in the final month of the run in to the championship. His season was rewarded, along with three other Notts players, with a place in the PFA's Nationwide Division Three team. Without quite reproducing the fireworks of his first season he remained for a further three seasons as the Magpies established themselves in Division Two. Sadly, his spell with Peterborough United was marred by a succession of injuries, his release coming after almost two and a half years and just 13(3) League and Cup matches.

Appearances: FL: 108(10) apps 3 gls FAC: 12(1) apps 0 gls FLC: 7(1) apps 0 gls Other: 3 apps 0 gls
Total: 130(12) apps 3 gls
Honours: (NOTTS) FL Division 3 champions 1998

PEARSON, Alfred Hetley
Playing position unknown
b. Shardlow, Derbyshire, October quarter 1851
d. Lowdham, Notts, 29th August 1930
CAREER: NOTTS (first app) Oct 1877 to (final app) Mar 1879
Debut v Sheffield, FAC 1, (h) 3.11.1877, drawn 1 – 1

In his youth Alfred Pearson was better known as an athlete. In addition to running 100 yards in even time he was a fine hurdler and high jumper, and won many prizes in athletic meetings throughout the Midlands. He was a senior partner of J.R. Pearson & Sons Ltd., nurserymen, of Lowdham, and in 1911 was awarded the Victoria Medal of Honour in Horticulture. His speciality was the cultivation of fruit trees, and he was regarded as a pomologist of no mean order. He was the brother of Sir Louis F. Pearson, C.B.E., of Lenton Grove, Beeston.

Appearances: FAC: 1 app 0 gls Total: 1 app 0 gls

PEART, John George 'Jack'
Centre-forward 5' 11" 12st 7lbs
b. South Shields, 3rd October 1888
d. Paddington, 3rd September 1948
CAREER: South Shields Adelaide 1905/Durham/Northumberland/Treharris am 1906/Sheffield United Apr 1907/Stoke Sept 1911/Newcastle United Mar 1912, fee £600/Notts Feb 1913, fee £600 (WW1 guest Leeds City, Rochdale, Barnsley & Croydon Common)/Birmingham Nov 1919/Derby County Jan 1920, fee £2,000/Ebbw Vale player-manager Aug 1920/Port Vale Jan 1922/Norwich City July 1922/Rochdale player-manager Mar 1923; retired from playing May 1924/Bradford City manager July 1930/Fulham manager May 1935 to his death.
Debut v Tottenham Hotspur (h) 15.2.13, lost 0 – 1

Despite the sterling efforts of Jack Peart, Notts were relegated from Division One in season 1912-13. Having only joined in February, his return of seven goals from eleven matches – including a hat-trick against Liverpool – made him leading scorer for the season, the next highest being Billy Flint with four in 35 matches. In Division Two Jack led the Magpies line with power and penetration, scoring 28 League goals in 30 matches and was honoured by the League, appearing against the Scottish League at Turf Moor, Burnley on 21st March 1914. Back in Division One in 1914-15, goals did not come as freely, but he again led the scorers with 11 in 32 matches. When normal League football resumed after World War One, Notts transferred Jack to Birmingham in November, after he had scored five goals in nine matches. They probably regretted their decision, as the season ended in relegation from the top flight. Despite suffering a catalogue of injuries throughout his lengthy career, Jack scored goals in every division of the Football League. To quote from the caption on a 1914 Wills "Scissors" cigarette card: "A strong, bustling leader who is to be feared in front of goal."

Appearances: FL: 82 apps 51 gls FAC: 2 apps 1 gl
Total: 84 apps 52 gls
Honours: FL representative, 1 app 1914. Southern League representative, 3 apps 1911. (NOTTS) FL Div 2 champions 1914. Awarded the FL Long service medal in 1945.

PEMBLETON, Arthur
Half-back 5' 10" 11st 8lbs
b. Palterton, Derby, 25th January 1895
d. Luton, 20th February 1976
CAREER: Woodhouse Exchange/Mansfield Mechanics/Woodhouse Exchange/NOTTS May 1919/Millwall July 1922/Norwich City May 1927/Luton Town trainer (One playing app for Luton in wartime season 1940-41)
Debut v Burnley (h) 30.8.19, won 2 – 0

The 'Notts. Post Annual' for 1919-20 considered Arthur Pembleton to be "A diamond in the rough," and he polished up nicely in his first season, appearing regularly in the intermediate line.

A strong, totally committed player with a big reserve of energy, he had first earned a reputation with Mansfield Mechanics before the war. In four years with the Royal Field Artillery he served in Gallipoli, Egypt and France. On demobilisation he played a few games with Woodhouse Exchange before joining the Magpies. In 1921-22, despite appearing in the semi-final of the FA Cup, Notts seemed unable to settle on their best eleven, constant team changes throughout the side saw Arthur largely out of favour and restricted to just 13 Second Division outings. A move to Millwall and five years at the Den took his total of senior appearances to a figure beyond 200. An injury in his final season with Norwich restricted him to 18 League outings. A brother, Thomas, was also with the Canaries in 1928 but did not appear at senior level.

Appearances: FL: 71 apps 0 gls FAC: 9 apps 0 gls
Total: 80 apps 0 gls

---o---

PENNANT, Jermaine
Midfield   5' 6"   10st 0lbs
b. Nottingham, 15th January 1983
CAREER: NOTTS associate schoolboy Apr 1997/Arsenal trainee Jan 1999, pro Mar 2000, fee £1.5million (Watford loan Jan 2002) (Watford loan Nov 2002) (Leeds United loaned for the 2003-04 season) (Birmingham City loan Jan 2005, for the remainder of the season.)/Birmingham City Apr 2005, fee £3 million.
Debut as sub v Hull City, Auto Windscreens Shield 1 (h) 22.12.98, lost 0 – 1

Considered an outstanding prospect as a youngster, Jermaine's dream move to Highbury at sixteen years of age has not worked out as planned. Despite scoring a sensational hat-trick against Southampton in his first starting appearance for the Gunners, he was quickly back in the Reserve side. A series of loan moves have provided the majority of his senior experience to date, with an initial two-month loan to Leeds United being extended to cover the whole of the 2003-04 season that ended in relegation from the Premier League. Having again failed to win a regular place with the Gunners in 2004-05, Jermaine was loaned to Birmingham City. With his Arsenal contract ending in the summer of 2005, it seemed highly unlikely that he would be offered an extension. In March 2005 he was jailed for three months after admitting drink-driving when already banned. Released on parole after serving a month of his sentence, he returned to action at St. Andrews in the game against Spurs on 2nd April. Thus becoming the first footballer to appear in the Premier League while wearing an electronic tag, concealed under his left stocking.

Appearances:
FAC: 0(1) app 0 gls Other: 0(1) app 0 gls
Total: 0(2) apps 0 gls
Honours: England U-21 International. England Schoolboy & Youth International. (Arsenal) FA Youth Cup winners 2000, 2001.

PENNINGTON, Harry
Goalkeeper   6' 0"   13st 8lbs
b. Farnworth, Lancashire, 1st September 1875
CAREER: Chorley Aug 1899/Brentford/NOTTS May 1900/ Atherton Church House Aug 1905 to cs 1906
Debut v Derby County (a) 8.9.00, lost 1 – 2

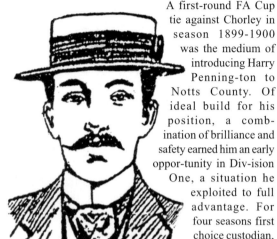

A first-round FA Cup tie against Chorley in season 1899-1900 was the medium of introducing Harry Penning-ton to Notts County. Of ideal build for his position, a comb-ination of brilliance and safety earned him an early oppor-tunity in Div-ision One, a situation he exploited to full advantage. For four seasons first choice custodian, he assisted Notts to third place in Division One in 1900-01. In the early stages of season 1903-04 he saved four penalty kicks, two in succession against Derby County, taken by the legendary Steve Bloomer. Harry was a talented all-round sportsman, during his four years of service with the Scots Guards he made just two short of a thousand runs for the Household Brigade in 1896. As a wicket-keeper/batsman both Middlesex and Lancashire offered him terms. Being a Lancashire man, he elected to join the Old Trafford ground staff, and appeared in four first-class matches in 1900.

Appearances:
FL: 126 apps 0 gls FAC: 10 apps 0 gls
Total: 136 apps 0 gls

---o---

PEPPER, Frederick W
Right-half
b. Details have proved extremely elusive, although it is known that he lived at Netherfield.
CAREER: Netherfield Rangers/NOTTS from season 1906-07 to 1912/Hamilton Lancashire, Canada/Bethlehem Steel/ Harrison Soccer Club/Fall River Marksmen/New York Giants
Debut v Aston Villa (h) 16.4.10, lost 2 – 3

Described in the 'Nottingham Post Annual' as "A local player" and "A plucky half-back of the worrying type", Fred Pepper was a sprightly performer in defence but his distribution proved a drawback at the highest level.

Aside from his debut in the final Division One fixture of 1909-10, his only other first team involvement was a four-match run as deputy for Teddy Emberton in March 1912. Later in the same year he emigrated to Canada. During two seasons with the Hamilton club, who fielded him at centre-forward, he was the league's leading goalscorer. He subsequently went over to the States, joined the Bethlehem Steel F.C., and helped them become the foremost team in the USA. In 1919 their six-year record was 149 games won, 7 lost, goals for 718, against 120. In a letter to the 'Football Post' in December 1921 a Mr. C.M. Stacey, a locally born man, wrote from Pennsylvania. He was player-manager of the Webster Club and had recently come across Fred Pepper who was still playing in States-side football.

Appearances: FL: 5 apps 0 gls Total: 5 apps 0 gls

PERRY, Josiah 'Joe'

Full-back   5' 11"   13st 6lbs
b. Kingswinford, West Midlands, January quarter 1893
CAREER: Brockmoor St John's/Pensnett Victoria/Brierley Hill Associates/Newport County/Stourbridge 1913-14/NOTTS May 1914/Ebbw Vale Aug 1920.
Debut v Blackburn Rovers (h) 10.10.14, drawn 1 – 1

Considered to be one of the most promising full-backs in the Birmingham League in 1913-14. Joe Perry began with Brockmoor St. John's, champions of the Brierley Hill League. Subsequently a finalist in the Dudley Cup with Pensnett Victoria, after a brief spell with Brierley Hill Associates he went to South Wales to work and was signed up by Newport County. After appearing in 58 consecutive Southern League Division Two games he was transferred to Stourbridge, from where Notts obtained him. He created a favourable impression in his first season with the Magpies as a back with courage and resource. He did not appear at senior level after WW1 and in August 1920, along with Richard Allsebrook, joined Ebbw Vale, managed at that time by former Notts County centre-forward Jack Peart.

Appearances: FL: 18 apps 0 gls Total: 18 apps 0 gls

PIKE, Geoffrey Alan

Midfield   5' 6"   11st 0lbs
b. Clapton, 28th September 1956
CAREER: Gidea Park Rangers/West Ham United app, signing pro Sept 1974/NOTTS July 1987, fee £35,000/Leyton Orient Sept 1989, appointed youth & reserve coach June 1991 to July 1993/Hendon player-coach
Debut v Wigan Athletic (h) 15.8.87, drawn 4 – 4 (scored two)

An early signing by new manager John Barnwell, Geoff Pike was a vastly experienced midfielder with 367 appearances in all competitions for West Ham United. The diminutive midfielder made an excellent start, scoring twice on his debut in the amazing 4 – 4 opener to season 1987-88. Three weeks later he scored the only hat-trick of his senior career in the 6 – 2 demolition of Southend United at Meadow Lane. Geoff skippered the Magpies to fourth spot in Division Three in his first season, scoring 14 goals from midfield, by far and away his best seasonal return. Sadly the end of season Play-offs ended in disappointment, and in his second season the team's lack of fire - power resulted in a disappointing ninth place finish. Geoff returned to East London to wind up his playing career with Leyton Orient before taking a coaching position at Brisbane Road.

Appearances: FL: 80(2) apps 17 gls FAC: 5 apps 2 gls FLC: 6 apps 1 gl Other: 8 apps 0 gls
Total: 99(2) apps 20 gls
Honours: (West Ham United) FA Youth Cup finalists 1975. FA Cup winners 1980. FL Division 2 champions 1981. FL Cup finalists 1981.

PIMBLEY, Douglas William

Left-half   5' 11**2**"   12st 0lbs
b. Birmingham, 19th June 1917
d. Wollaton, Notts, 28th January 1988
CAREER: King's Norton YMCA/Northfield/Stourbridge (WW2 guest Manchester City and Nottingham Forest) Leicester City am Dec 1945/Birmingham City July 1946/NOTTS Mar 1948 to 1950
Debut v Swindon Town (h) 6.3.48, won 2 – 1

Doug Pimbley assisted three different League clubs during the transitional season, 1945-46, scoring on his debut for both Leicester City and Nottingham Forest. First noted during wartime Army football with the RAOC at Chilwell, he signed a professional form with Birmingham City in July 1946, but spent his time at St Andrews as a regular in the Blues London Combination side. The powerfully built wing-half fitted in well at Meadow Lane, appearing in all matches during March and April immediately following his arrival. Thereafter he was sparingly used, and appeared only once, as Tommy Lawton's deputy, in the Third Division South championship season, 1949-50.

Appearances: FL: 23 apps 1 gl Total: 23 apps 1 gl

PIPE, David Ronald

Defender/Midfield   5' 9"   12st 4lbs
b. Caerphilly, 5th November 1983
CAREER: Coventry City trainee, signing pro Nov 2000
(NOTTS loan Jan 2004)/NOTTS Apr 2004
Debut v Wrexham (a) 17.1.2004, won 1 – 0

On the right side of defence or at right wing-back, David
Pipe's all-action style has made him a popular figure in
the Magpies' line-up. A combination of pace, commitment
and skill first impressed during his extended loan spell in
the 2003-04 relegation season. Shaven-headed and
muscular, David has become a great favourite of the club's
young supporters, reflected in his selection as 'Player of
the Year' by the Junior Magpies.

Appearances: FL: 56(3) apps 2 gls FAC: 4 apps 0 gls
FLC: 2 apps 0 gls Other: 1 app 0 gls
Total: 63(3) apps 2 gls
Honours: Wales International, 1 cap 2003. Wales U-21
International

―――――――○―――――――

PLACKETT, Sydney

Left-half   5' 11"   11st 4lbs
b. Sawley, 21st September 1898
d. Whitwick, near Coalville, May 1950
CAREER: Sawley United Church/Sawley Discharged Soldiers'
Federation Mar 1919/Derby County Jan 1921/NOTTS Feb
1927 to cs 1930.
Debut v Clapton Orient (a) 12.2.27, lost 1 – 2

The son of a Long Eaton and Loughborough player, Syd
Plackett was a member of a Derbyshire family who excelled
at both football and cricket. Six years of excellent service
to Derby County included an ever-present record when
the Rams won promotion from the Second Division in
1925-26. Originally a centre-forward he found his best
position in the half-back line, where his constructive and
leadership qualities proved invaluable. Aside from a spell
on the injured list he was a regular at Meadow Lane until
season 1929-30 when he played in just ten matches in the
Division Two relegation season. A brother, Ernest, was
also on the Magpies' books, but he did not reach senior
level.

Appearances: FL: 84 apps 0 gls FAC: 1 app 0 gls
Total: 85 apps 0 gls

―――――――○―――――――

PLATNAUER, Nicholas John

Left-back/Midfield   5' 10"   12st 12lbs
b. Leicester, 10th June 1961
CAREER: Northampton Town app/Bedford Town/Bristol
Rovers Aug 1982/Coventry City Aug 1983, fee £50,000/
Birmingham City Dec 1984, fee £55,000 (Reading loan Jan
1986)/Cardiff City Sept 1986/NOTTS July 1989, fee
£50,000 (Port Vale loan Jan 1991)/Leicester City July 1991/

Scunthorpe United Mar 1993/Kettering Town trial July
1993/Mansfield Town nc Aug 1993/Lincoln City Feb 1994/
Bedworth United Sept 1995/Hinckley United Aug 1997/
Rothwell Town manager 2000/Kettering Town caretaker
manager Nov-Dec 2003/Bedford Town manager Jan 2004.
Debut v Leyton Orient (a) 19.8.89, won 1 – 0

Nicky began as a forward with Bedford Town, and was a
Southern League Cup winner in season 1980-81. In a
nomadic League career he featured in all Divisions as an
enthusiastic left-sided midfielder or full-back with
excellent passing and positional skills that invariably found
him in the right spot at the right moment. He enjoyed an
excellent first season with the Magpies, missing only
two matches during the 1989-90 season when promotion
from Division Three was secured, via a Wembley Play-
off victory against Tranmere Rovers. Commenting on his
most memorable match in a 1989 interview, he selected
the Coventry City v Liverpool encounter at Highfield
Road in December 1983. The eventual League champions
never recovered from an early goal from Nicky, followed
by a hat-trick from Terry Gibson, in a famous 4 – 0
victory, all witnessed by 'Match of the Day' cameras.

Appearances: FL: 57 apps 1 gl FAC: 1 app 0 gls FLC: 6
apps 0 gls Other: 10 apps 0 gls Total: 74 apps 1 gl
Honours: (Cardiff City) Welsh Cup winners 1988

―――――――○―――――――

PLATT, Clive Linton

Forward   6' 4"   13st 0lbs
b. Wolverhampton, 27th October 1977
CAREER: Walsall trainee, signing pro July 1996 (Rochdale
loan Aug 1999)/Rochdale Sept 1999, fee £70,000/NOTTS
Aug 2003/Peterborough United Jan 2004/MK Dons Jan
2005.
Debut v Bristol City (a) 9.8.2003, lost 0 – 5

A Wolves supporter as a youngster, Clive began with
nearby Walsall and showed sufficient promise to prompt
Rochdale to pay £70,000 for him after a month spent on
loan at Spotland at the start of season 1999-2000. In four
years with the Dale he played in 168(18) League and Cup
matches and scored 36 goals. Turning down the club's
offer of a new contract he joined the Magpies on a free
transfer. Ideally built for his role as attack leader and with
the necessary attributes of pace, aerial prowess and the
ability to hold the ball up well, the only missing ingredient
in his repertoire was a regular supply of goals. Despite
the offer of an eighteen-month contract to remain with
the Magpies he departed in mid season, following manager
Billy Dearden out of Meadow Lane, to sign a two-and-a-
half year deal with Peterborough United. One year on he
was transferred to MK Dons.

Appearances: FL: 19 apps 3 gls FAC: 3 apps 3 gls FLC:
3 apps 0 gls Total: 25 apps 6 gls

PLATTS, Robert

Outside-right 5' 9" 11st 5lbs
b. Anston, Yorkshire, January quarter 1900
CAREER: Anston United/NOTTS am May, pro Sept 1920/
Southend United May 1925/Heanor Town Sept 1927/British
Celanese am Aug 1928/Nottingham Co-operative Dairy am
Sept 1929
Debut v Bury (a) 7.5.20, won 1 – 0

A wingman with a long raking stride and admirable ball
control who was considered one of Notts' best discoveries
in the immediate post-WW1 period. Platts was said to
prefer the outside-right berth but was equally capable on
the opposite flank. Despite undoubted ability he
nevertheless often found himself cast in the role of stand
in on either flank, his best seasonal return being 17 First
Division outings in 1923-24. In the previous promotion
season he appeared in ten Division Two matches, including
the final eight fixtures which concluded with the
championship clinching 1 – 0 win against West Ham
United. He did not appear at senior level with Southend
United after suffering a severe knee injury in his first pre-
season practice match at the Kursaal.

Appearances: FL: 50 apps 3 gls FAC: 3 apps 0 gls
Total: 53 apps 3 gls
Honours: (NOTTS) FL Div 2 champions 1923

POLLITT, Michael Francis

Goalkeeper 6' 4" 14st 0lbs
b. Farnworth, Lancs, 29th February 1972
CAREER: Manchester United associate schoolboy Oct
1987, trainee July 1988, pro July 1990 (Oldham Athletic
loan Oct-Nov 1990)/Bury July 1991 (Lincoln City loan
Sept 1992)/Lincoln City Dec 1992/Darlington Aug 1994/
NOTTS Nov 1995, fee £75,000 (Oldham Athletic loan
Aug-Nov 1997) (Gillingham loan Dec 1997) (Brentford
loan Jan 1998)/Sunderland Feb 1998, fee £75,000/
Rotherham United July 1998/Chesterfield Aug 2000/
Rotherham United May 2001, fee £75,000
Debut v Scarborough, Auto Windscreens Shield 1 (a) 9.12.96,
won 1 – 0

An extremely capable goalkeeper whose opportunities at
Meadow Lane were restricted due to the outstanding form
of Darren Ward. Mike's excellent form with Darlington
led to his recruitment by County, but he remained on the
bench throughout his first season at Meadow Lane. He
began season 1997-98 on loan to Oldham Athletic, the
first of four moves during the season. Eventually reaching
a settled phase in his career, he helped Rotherham United
to win promotion from Division Three in 1999-2000,
appearing in all 46 League matches. He repeated the feat
with Chesterfield in 2000-01, who won promotion from
Division Three despite having nine points deducted for a
breach of rules.

Appearances: FL: 10 apps 0 gls Other: 2 apps 0 gls
Total: 12 apps 0 gls

POOLE, William

Inside-right
b. Keyworth, Notts, 16th September 1900
CAREER: Boots Athletic/Basford United/NOTTS Apr 1920/
Coventry City 1920/Boston Town Feb 1922
Debut v Middlesbrough (a) 5.4.20, lost 2 – 5

For the Meadow Lane brigade the 1919-20 season could
accurately be described as a term of two halves. From
New Year's Day 1920 the goals dried up and the Magpies
plummeted to relegation from the top flight. Only 15
League goals were scored in the second half of the season,
whereas 41 goals had been registered from the opening 21
fixtures. In early April a trial was given to teenaged inside-
right William Poole. Although the Magpies scored twice
they were heavily defeated and the young trialist from
Basford United was not called upon again. He did not
appear at senior level with Coventry City.

Appearances: FL: 1 app 0 gls Total: 1 app 0 gls

POPE, Francis James L. 'Frankie'

Centre or Inside-forward 5' 10 2" 12st 6lbs
b. Brierley Hill, October quarter 1884
d. Stourbridge, April quarter 1953
CAREER: Cradley Heath Sept 1900/Wolverhampton
Wanderers Sept 1900/Stourbridge/Wolverhampton
Wanderers May 1905/NOTTS Apr 1906/Walsall June 1907/
Stourbridge Jan 1909/Netherton.
Debut v Everton (h) 13.10.06, lost 0 – 1

In two separate spells with the Wolves Frankie Pope
scored four goals in 13 League matches. One of his most
enterprising displays came against the Magpies, when he
scored two of the Wolves' goals in their 6 – 1 win at
Molineux on 16th April 1906. Despite winning the
following, and final fixture of the season, by 7 – 0 against
Derby County, the Wolves had 'woken-up' too late, and
were relegated from Division One. Signed by Notts as
understudy to their Wales international centre-forward,
Arthur Green, Pope had only two senior outings, both
ending goal less for himself and the team. Commenting on
his debut against Everton, the 'Weekly Express' stated
that "Pope showed commendable judgement in opening
out the game." On a rather wry note, however, they
concluded: "Smith (the Everton goalkeeper) had mighty
little to do under the visitor's woodwork."

Appearances: FL: 2 apps 0 gls Total: 2 apps 0 gls

POPPITT, James

Forward 5' 8 2" 11st 7lbs
b. Oakengates, April quarter 1875
d. Swindon, 17th June 1930
CAREER: Wellington Town May 1899/Wolverhampton
Wanderers May 1900/Swindon Town Aug 1902/Reading May
1903/Swindon Town May 1904/NOTTS May 1905/Lincoln
City June 1907 to cs 1908.
Debut v Sheffield Wednesday (a) 28.10.05, lost 1 – 3

Joining the Wolves from Birmingham League football, Poppitt made 20 First Division appearances in his first season, but failed to maintain his progress in a second term at Molineux. He joined the Magpies after three seasons of Southern League football, but failed to realise expectations. Nine appearances and one goal in his first season, however, was considered promising enough to warrant a contract for a further term. Praised for the accuracy of his passing, his speed and accuracy of shooting were less impressive. Despite scoring against Stoke in his first outing in 1906-07, he appeared in only six first team matches. His season with Lincoln City saw the Imps finish at the foot of Division Two. Mainly operating from the inside-right position, he appeared in 23 matches and scored three goals. At the time of his death in 1930 he was landlord of the Whale Inn at Swindon.

Appearances: FL: 15 apps 2 gls Total: 15 apps 2 gls

PORIC, Adem
Midfield   5' 9"   11st 13lbs
b. Kensington, 22nd April 1973
CAREER: St George's Budapest (Australia)/Sheffield Wednesday Oct 1993 (Southend United loan Feb 1997)/ Rotherham United Feb 1998/NOTTS Mar-May 1998
Debut as sub v Leyton Orient (h) 28.3.98, won 1 – 0

A transfer deadline-day signing, released by Rotherham United after completion of a one-month contract. The stocky, tenacious midfielder arrived at Meadow Lane and – however briefly – shared in momentous events. Two days after signing he came off the bench to make his debut in the match that made promotion a mathematical certainty. The Magpies went on to lift the Division Three championship trophy in record style with a club record 99 points, 17 ahead of runners-up Macclesfield Town. Poric's final appearance, on 2nd May, was in the 5 – 2 victory that rounded off the season, and was against Rotherham United, the team who had released him just two months earlier. His euphoria proved short lived, however, as he was released by the Magpies later in the same month.

Appearances: FL: 3(1) apps 0 gls Total: 3(1) apps 0 gls

POSKETT, Thomas William
Goalkeeper   6' 0"   12st 0lbs
b. Esh Winning, 26th December 1909
d. Crewe, 19th December 1972
CAREER: Chopwell Institute/Crook Town/Grimsby Town Dec 1928/Lincoln City May 1932/NOTTS May 1934/ Tranmere Rovers May 1935/Crewe Alexandra July 1937/ Northwich Victoria Oct 1947
Debut v Sheffield United (a) 13.10.34, lost 0 – 3

Statistically speaking, there was little to chose between Notts' two goalkeepers, Knox and Poskett, in season 1934-35. Tom Poskett had a run of eight first team outings in the early stages, but failed to stem the avalanche of goals against. Neither goalkeeper was afforded any favours by a leaky defence that conceded 101 goals in 43 League and Cup matches. The Second World War took a large slice out of Tom's League career. Having missed only one match in two seasons for Crewe Alexandra prior to the outbreak, he was well into the veteran stage at 37 years of age when he recommenced in season 1946-47.

Appearances: FL: 10 apps 0 gls Total: 10 apps 0 gls

POTTER, Arthur
Inside or Outside-right   5' 8"   11st 4lbs
b. Nottingham, 1877
CAREER: Army football/NOTTS am, signing pro Jan 1898/ Bristol City May 1898 to Apr 1900
Debut v Sunderland (a) 5.2.1898, lost 0 – 1

The son of a hosiery factory overlooker, Arthur Potter was bought out of the Army after a series of promising displays as an amateur outside-right in the Magpies Reserves. He was first given a run out with the seniors in the Boxing Day friendly against Forest in 1888, a match won 4 – 1 by the Magpies. After the briefest of stays at Trent Bridge Arthur joined Bristol City who were runners-up for the Southern League championship in 1898-99. Their team included two other former Notts players, Billy Langham and John Murphy. Arthur made one appearance as emergency goalkeeper at Tottenham Hotspur in February 1899, but he proved better at scoring goals that stopping them, Spurs winning by 3 – 2

Appearances: FL: 2 apps 0 gls Total: 2 apps 0 gls

POVEY, Victor Richard "Vic"
Outside-right   5' 8"   12st 0lbs
b. Wolverhampton, 16th March 1944
CAREER: Wolverhampton Wanderers pro July 1961/ NOTTS Aug 1963 to cs 1965, fee £2,500/Pan Hellenic, Sydney (Australia)
Debut v Brentford (a) 24.8.63, lost 1 – 4

Vic Povey was without League experience when signed by Notts' new manager Eddie Lowe in the summer of 1963. After appearing in the first five matches of season 1963-64 – all of which ended in defeat – he lost his right wing spot to Keith Fry. A spell on the injured list further disrupted his first season that ended with him still waiting for his first goal in League football. In the Division Four campaign that followed, new signing Eddie Kavanagh started as first team outside-right.

Povey's first opportunity coming on the opposite flank when he deputised for Tony Flower on 3rd October 1964. A goal in the 3 – 1 home win against York City was followed, one week later, by his scoring the only goal of the game against Newport County. He ended the season with a record of three goals in 19 matches, but was one of several players released, following the late-season removal of manager Eddie Lowe, and the appointment of Tim Coleman as his successor.

Appearances: FL: 35 apps 3 gls Total: 35 apps 3 gls

PRASKI, Josef
Outside-right   5' 6 2" 10st 7lbs
b. 22nd January 1922 (See note below)
d. Mansfield, January 1998
CAREER: Jeanfield Swifts/NOTTS Mar 1949/Sutton Town Aug 1950/South Normanton 1961
Debut v Millwall (h) 19.3.49, lost 1 – 3

Signed from the same Scottish club, Jeanfield Swifts, near Perth, who had earlier supplied Henry Adamson to the Magpies. Joe Praski came with an imposing scoring record, having no fewer than 22 goals to his credit in Scottish junior football in 1948-49. He was one of two new players (Harry Chapman being the other) who made their Magpies debut against Millwall. Sadly, Praski did not come up to expectations and Notts were beaten at home for the first time in six months. Moving on to Sutton Town in the close season, his unorthodox style proved extremely effective over a very long period in non-League circles. Ten years after leaving Meadow Lane his last minute penalty kick against Frickley Colliery put Sutton Town into the First Round of the FA Cup after a lapse of 27 years.
NOTE: At the time of writing, his birthplace remains a mystery. When signed by the Magpies he was described in the local press as 'Belgian born.' Subsequently, and more generally, he was said to be Polish. 'Hugman's Players Records' give France as his birthplace. The author would be grateful for any enlightenment!

Appearances: FL: 3 apps 0 gls Total: 3 apps 0 gls

PRESCOTT, Thomas George
Right-back   5' 9"   10st 12lbs
b. Attercliffe, Sheffield, 8th January 1875
d. Nottingham, 26th November 1957
CAREER: Liverpool East End/Hamilton Athletic/Crosse F.C. 1892/Liverpool South End 1893/NOTTS May 1896 to 1904 when playing career ended following an operation for appendicitis. He was appointed club trainer Apr 1905 and resigned in Aug 1917.
Debut v Loughborough (h) 5.9.1896, won 3 – 1

Among the very best of early Notts full-backs, Tommy Prescott was born at Attercliffe but moved to Liverpool as an infant. Joining Crosse F.C. at 17 years of age he represented the Liverpool Junior League. He became a professional at 18 and won the Liverpool Senior League championship with the South End Club. The last match of the football year 1896 was a friendly against the Magpies at Toxteth. South End won 4 – 0 and Prescott gave such a fine exhibition that Notts at once signed him up. Although considered on the light side for his position he was an accomplished back, his powers of recovery often catching a fugitive wingman by surprise. At a time when he was being widely tipped as a candidate for full international honours, he was unfortunate to be injured in the Inter-League match against Scotland on 1st April 1899. Subsequently, his knee was apt to give way under heavy strain and this was a contributory factor to his relatively early retirement. Appointed club trainer in succession to George Swift in 1905, he held the position until failing eyesight enforced his retirement from the post in 1917.

Appearances: FL: 212 apps 1 gl FAC: 14 apps 0 gls Other: 4 apps 0 gls Total: 230 apps 1 gl
Honours: FL representative, 1 app 1899. North v South, International trial, 1 app 1899. (NOTTS) FL Division 2 champions 1897

PRICE, Llewellyn Palmer 'Lew'
Outside-left   5' 9 2" 12st 6lbs
b. Caersws, Monmouthshire, 12th August 1898
CAREER: Barmouth/Hampstead Town/Mansfield Town/Aston Villa Feb 1921/NOTTS June 1922, fee £250/Queens Park Rangers May 1928/Grantham Town Feb 1929/Basford United Jan 1935
Debut v Coventry City (a) 26.8.22, won 2 – 1

As understudy to the celebrated England international wingman Arthur Dorrell at Aston Villa, Lew Price distinguished himself when called upon, but requested a move due to restricted opportunities.

Quick off the mark, very accurate in centering and an opportunist marksman, he had an excellent start with the Magpies, collecting a Division Two championship medal at the close of his first season. After appearing in 24 First Division matches in 1923-24, he played only infrequently thereafter as Len Barry, the England amateur international, dominated the position. After six seasons at Meadow Lane he was given a free transfer and moved to Queens Park Rangers where he appeared in only three first team matches before dropping into non-League football.

Appearances: FL: 66 apps 6 gls FAC: 4 apps 1 gl
Total: 70 apps 7 gls
Honours: (NOTTS) FL Division 2 champions 1923

PRING, Keith David

Winger 5' 8"   10st 12lbs
b. Newport, Monmouthshire, 11th March 1943
CAREER: Newport Grammar School/Newport County am May, pro Nov 1961/Rotherham United Oct 1964, fee £7,000/NOTTS Dec 1967, in part exchange for Dave Watson/Southport July 1969 to Oct 1971/Wigan Athletic coach 1974-76
Debut v Bradford City (h) 30.12.67, won 1 – 0

Despite attending a rugby-playing secondary school and representing Cardiff Boys in the handling code, Keith Pring became a professional soccer player with Newport County at the age of 18. After three years with Rotherham United, and three Wales caps, he was part of the deal that took Dave Watson to Millmoor at the mid-point of season 1967-68. Joining a Notts side struggling in the lower reaches of Division Four he took some time to settle but ended the season on a high note, scoring the winner at Halifax Town in the season's final fixture. In 1968-69 he shared wing duties with Elliott and Bates, appearing in 27 of the season's League engagements, being released on a free transfer in the close season. Southport was his final move and he marked his home League debut with a rare goal. Sadly, after 48 consecutive games he suffered a broken leg in the opening month of season 1970-71, and did not appear at senior level again. He did, however, recover sufficiently to play rugby for Southport RUFC in season 1973-74, and posted a record total of 253 points for the club.

Appearances: FL: 41(3) apps 2 gls FAC: 1 app 0 gls
FLC: 2 apps 0 gls Total: 44(3) apps 2 gls
Honours: Wales International, 3 caps 1966-67. Wales Youth international. (Newport County) Welsh Cup finalists 1963

PRITCHARD, Roy Thomas

Left-back   5' 9"   10st 4lbs
b. Dawley, Shropshire, 9th May 1925
d. Walsall, March 1993
CAREER: Dawley & District Schoolboys/Wolverhampton Wanderers, from school May 1942/Aston Villa Feb 1955, fee £6,000/NOTTS Nov 1957/Port Vale Aug 1958/Wellington Town Aug 1960, retired 1964
Debut v Cardiff City (h) 2.11.57, won 5 – 2

Roy Pritchard joined Wolves straight from school, worked in the mines as a 'Bevan Boy' during the war, and completed over 200 League games as a cool, crisp tackling left-back. He was a member of the Wolves' 1949 FA Cup winning side and was unfortunate not to add a League championship in the following season, Wolves being runners-up to Portsmouth on goal average. Aston Villa paid £6,000 for him as cover for either Peter Aldis or Stan Lynn, but both players enjoyed such remarkable form and freedom from injury that it was not until a year after signing that he made his first team debut. When he did, he broke his jaw and was out for the remainder of the season! He was approaching the veteran stage when he joined the Magpies in a season that ended in relegation from Division Two. He marked his sojourn at Meadow Lane by scoring the only senior goal in his long career against Bristol City in round four of the FA Cup in January 1958.

Appearances: FL: 18 apps 0 gls FAC: 1 app 1 gl
Total: 19 apps 1 gl
Honours: (Wolverhampton Wanderers) FA Cup winners 1949

PROBERT, Eric William

Midfield   5' 8"   11st 5lbs
b. South Kirkby, 17th February 1952
d. September 2004
CAREER: Yorkshire Schoolboys/Huddersfield Town trial/Leeds United trial/Burnley associate schoolboy, app 1967, signing pro Feb 1969/NOTTS July 1973, fee £30,000/Darlington July 1978, fee £20,000/Rochdale July-Sept 1980.
Debut v Crystal Palace (a) 25.8.73, won 4 – 1

A starring appearance for Yorkshire Schoolboys against Lancashire at Turf Moor led the Clarets to snap up Eric Probert on schoolboy forms. In season 1967-68 he helped Burnley to win the FA Youth Cup for the first time in the club's history, and made his League debut in the following season against Arsenal in Division One. After 67(5) matches and 11 goals he joined the newly promoted Magpies for a club record fee of £30,000. A regular in County's midfield during a period when the club consolidated their place in Division Two, his drive and ball-winning qualities were badly missed in his final two seasons when injuries enforced his absence and severely dented promotion aspirations. Two seasons with Darlington and a brief spell with Rochdale wound up his career, and he later became license of The Ship Inn at Aldborough in North Yorkshire.

Appearances: FL: 122 apps 13 gls FAC: 3 apps 0 gls FLC: 9 apps 0 gls Other: 3 apps 0 gls
Total: 137 apps 13 gls
Honours: England Youth international, 4 appearances 1969-70

---------------o---------------

PROTHEROE, Sidney
Outside-left   5' 9"   11st 4lbs
b. Dowlais, 16th December 1910
d. Chilwell, Notts, 19th February 1982
CAREER: Merthyr Town/Machynilleth/Merthyr Town/Charlton Athletic am June 1931/Wolverhampton Wanderers May 1933/Torquay United May 1934/Rochdale June 1936/NOTTS June 1938 to 1939.
Debut v Swindon Town (a) 27.8.38, lost 1 – 4

Sid Protheroe was hardly able to do himself justice in the Magpies' colours. Injured on his debut at Swindon Town, he was out for almost a month. Returning in the 2 – 0 win against Newport County on 17th September, he was given a further run-out in a friendly match at Boston just two days later and suffered a cracked fibula. Earlier in his career, he made his League debut with Torquay United at Gillingham in August 1934. In two seasons at Plainmoor he appeared in 41 League and Cup matches, scoring four goals. A similar stint with Rochdale was more productive (66 League and Cup matches and 14 goals). Regarded as an exceptionally good capture when signed by Magpies manager Harry Parkes, the unfortunate wingman was denied the opportunity to realise expectations and the subsequent outbreak of war effectively terminated his career.

Appearances: FL: 2 apps 0 gls Total: 2 apps 0 gls
Honours: Wales Amateur International

---------------o---------------

PROUDFOOT, James
Inside-forward 5' 9"   11st 9lbs
b. Usworth Colliery, Washington, 31st January 1906
d. Chester-le-Street, 8th September 1963
CAREER: Washington Higher Grade School/Fatfield Juniors/Usworth Juniors/Washington Colliery/Usworth Colliery/(Aston Villa trial Jan 1925)/Barnsley Nov 1927/NOTTS

June 1932, fee £700/Southend United Aug 1933/Southport June 1934/Ashington July 1936/Murton Colliery Welfare Jan 1937/Blue Bus Co 1937-38.
Debut v Lincoln City (h) 27.8.32, drawn 1 – 1

Aston Villa rejected the youthful Jimmy Proudfoot following a month's trial, but he eventually made good with Barnsley, accumulating 147 League and Cup appearances and scoring 29 goals in a stay spanning five seasons. By contrast, his stay at Meadow Lane lasted only one season and it was marred by injury. In his fifth appearance he suffered damage to his knee in the game against Forest on 8th October 1932. The injury necessitated at cartilage operation and he did not return to first team duty until 11th March, an absence of six months. His move to Southport in June 1934 reunited him with Jimmy Commins, his former manager at Barnsley, who successfully fielded Proudfoot at right half-back for much of his stay at Haig Avenue.

Appearances: FL: 10 apps 0 gls Total: 10 apps 0 gls

---------------o---------------

PURVIS, Bartholomew
Left-back
b. Gateshead, 15th October 1919
d. Gateshead, June 2001
CAREER: North Shields/Everton Jan 1946/Gateshead Oct 1946/Plymouth Argyle June 1947/NOTTS May 1948/Carlisle United Aug 1951
Debut v Torquay United (h) 18.12.48, won 5 – 0

Despite his earlier association with three League clubs, Purvis had only one senior outing to his name (with Gateshead) prior to joining the Magpies. Initially in reserve, he took over the left-back position from Bert Howe just prior to Christmas 1948 and retained it for the remainder of the season. In the promotion season that followed he was deposed by Norman Rigby in the first month of the season, and was restricted to just three senior outings. He appeared in only four League matches for his final League club, Carlisle United.

Appearances: FL: 25 apps 0 gls FAC: 2 apps 0 gls
Total: 27 apps 0 gls

---------------o---------------

PYE, Jessie
Inside-forward 5' 10"   11st 7lbs
b. Treeton near Rotherham, 22nd December 1919
d. Blackpool, 19th February 1984
CAREER: Catliffe/Treeton F.C./Sheffield United Dec 1938/NOTTS Aug 1945/Wolverhampton Wanderers May 1946, fee £10,000/Luton Town July 1952, fee £9,000/Derby County Oct 1954, fee £5,000/Wisbech Town July 1957, appointed player-manager Mar 1960, resigned managership Dec 1966.
Debut v Bradford City, FAC 1 (h) 17.11.46, drawn 2 – 2

At either centre or inside-forward, the dark-haired, swarthy complexioned Jesse Pye was an elegant performer, mixing subtlety and incisiveness to telling effect. He had an excellent season with the Magpies in 1945-46, in addition to the four FA Cup matches noted below he appeared in 30 other fixtures in the transitional season and scored 17 goals. He was still a Notts player when selected to play for England in a Victory International against Belgium at Wembley in January 1946 and scored one of England's goals in a 2 – 0 win. Wolves paid substantially to take him to Molineux, and he proved to be an excellent capture, netting a hat-trick to mark his debut and going on to score 90 League goals in 188 matches. Additionally, he scored five goals in FA Cup ties, his total including two in the 1949 Final victory over Leicester City. Considered unfortunate to have received just one full England cap, he maintained an excellent strike rate throughout his career, totalling 146 goals in 310 League matches.

Appearances: FAC: 4 apps 0 gls Total: 4 apps 0 gls
Honours: England International, 1 cap 1950. England Wartime International, 1 app 1946. England 'B' International, 3 apps. Football League representative, 1 app. (Wolverhampton Wanderers) FA Cup winners 1949

QUAYLE, Mark Leslie
Forward   5' 9"   10st 6lbs
b. Liverpool, 2nd October 1978
CAREER: Everton trainee, signing pro Oct 1995/NOTTS June 1998 (Grantham Town loan Feb to Mar 1999)/Grimsby Town trial June 1999/Leigh RMI/Ilkeston Town/Altrincham/ Morecambe Aug 2000/Telford United/Nuneaton Borough May 2002/Chester City late season 2002-03/Scarborough Aug 2003, fee £2,000/Northwich Victoria July 2004.
Debut as sub v Wigan Athletic (h) 5.9.98, lost 0 – 1

Released by Everton manager Howard Kendall after failing to make the breakthrough at Goodison Park, the lightly-built and speedy striker performed well in the Magpies Reserves without mounting a serious challenge for a first team place. Loaned out to Grantham Town he scored four goals in six matches and following his release from Meadow Lane moved rapidly around the non-League circuit. In January 2004 Mark scored the goal against Southend United that earned Scarborough a money-spinning fourth round FA Cup tie against Premiership Millionaires Chelsea at the McCain Stadium.

Appearances: FL: 2(3) apps 0 gls FAC: 0(2) apps 0 gls Other: 0(1) app 0 gls Total: 2(6) apps 0 gls

---

QUINN, Stephen James "Jimmy"
Forward   6' 1"   12st 10lbs
b. Coventry, 15th December 1974
CAREER: Birmingham City trainee July 1991/Blackpool July 1993, fee £25,000 (Stockport County loan Mar 1994)/ West Bromwich Albion Feb 1998, fee £500,000 (NOTTS loan Nov-Dec 2001) (Bristol Rovers loan Mar 2002/Willem 11, Holland, June 2002/Sheffield Wednesday Jan 2005.
Debut v Bristol City (a) 1.12.2001, lost 2 – 3 (scored one)

Despite having made his debut in League football while still on YTS forms at Birmingham City, Jimmy declined a professional contract with the Blues, opting to join the paid ranks with Blackpool. In a stay of almost five years at Bloomfield Road he appeared in 143(28) League and Cup matches and scored 46 goals. A big money signing by West Bromwich Albion, he was a regular until the appointment of Gary Megson as manager in March 2000. In 2001-02 as the Baggies were winning a place in the Premiership, Jimmy was loaned to both Notts and Bristol Rovers during the season. Despite having played little first team football for over a year, his height and pace made him a handful for Division Two defenders, three goals in his first four matches for the Magpies being a valuable mid-term contribution.

Appearances: FL: 6 apps 3 gls Other: 1 app 0 gls
Total: 7 apps 3 gls
Honours: Northern Ireland International, 25 caps 1996-2002. Northern Ireland 'B' International, 2 apps . Northern Ireland U-21 International, 1 app. Northern Ireland Youth International

---

RABAT, Didier
Forward   6' 1"   13st 0lbs
b. Noumea, New Caledonia, 2nd August 1966
CAREER: Toulon/Paris St Germain/NOTTS trial Dec 1998 to Jan 1999
Debut v Hull City, Auto Windscreens Shield, (h) 22.12.98, lost 0 – 1

Briefly on trial with the Magpies, with the view to a possible free transfer signing, the powerfully built veteran striker was not sufficiently impressive in his single outing to warrant a permanent contract.

Appearances: Other: 1 app 0 gls Total: 1 app 0 gls

RAMAGE, Craig Darren
Midfield   5' 9"   11st 8lbs
b. Derby, 30th March 1970
CAREER: Derby Schoolboys/Chesopeke/Derby County associate schoolboy Nov 1984, trainee Feb 1987, pro July 1988 (Wigan Athletic loan Feb 1989)/Watford Feb 1994, fee £90,000 (Peterborough United loan Feb 1997)/Bradford City June 1997/NOTTS Aug 1999 to July 2001
Debut v Luton Town (h) 7.8.99, drawn 0 – 0

Knee ligament and cartilage problems blighted both the beginning and the end of Craig Ramage's career. Despite a series of operations that severely restricted his League appearances with Derby County, his potential was recognised by the award of three England Under-21 caps. He had an excellent first season at Meadow Lane as an all-action midfielder with grit, vision and no mean ability. A knee injury in November of the following season brought a premature end to his season and he was released in the summer.

Appearances: FL: 50(5) apps 7 gls FAC: 2 apps 0 gls FLC: 7 apps 2 gls Total: 59(5) apps 9 gls
Honours: England U-21 International, 3 apps 1991-92

RAMSDEN, Simon Paul

Defender   6' 0"   12st 4lbs
b. Bishop Auckland, 17th December 1981
CAREER: Sunderland trainee, signing pro Aug 2000 (NOTTS loan Aug 2002 to May 2003)/Grimsby Town Aug 2004.
Debut as sub v Wigan Athletic (h) 24.8.2002, lost 0 – 2

Joined the Magpies on loan for season 2002-03 and took his opportunity well, appearing regularly throughout the Second Division campaign. Mainly from right full-back he exhibited good distributive skills, a strong right foot and the ability to get forward in support of the attack. Having made only one substitute appearance for Sunderland, he opted for a move to Grimsby Town when his contract expired.

Appearances: FL: 21(11) apps 0 gls FAC: 1 app 0 gls FLC: 1 app 0 gls Total: 23(11) apps 0 gls

---

RANDALL, Dean

Central defender   6' 1"   12st 0lbs
b. Nottingham, 15th May 1979
CAREER: NOTTS trainee July 1995, pro July 1997 to July 1998
Debut as sub v Burnley, Auto Windscreens Shield, (a) 27.1.98, lost 0 – 2

Dean graduated through the youth ranks to become a valued member of the reserve team. His performances winning him the accolade of 'Reserve Team Player of the Year.' He failed to graduate to senior level, however, his only first team involvement being his Auto Windscreen Shield outing from the bench. He was released at the end of the same season.

Appearances: Other: 0(1) app 0 gls Total: 0(1) app 0 gls

RANDALL, Kevin

Forward   5' 10 **2**"   12st 9lbs
b. Ashton-under-Lyne, Lancs, 20th August 1945
CAREER: Manchester United trial/ Droylsden//Bury Oct 1965/Chesterfield July 1966/NOTTS Aug 1972, fee £20,000/Mansfield Town Nov 1975, fee £10,000/York City Oct 1977, fee £8,000/Burton Albion 1982/Alfreton Town player-manager Oct 1982/ Goole Town player-manager Jan 1983/Chesterfield coach 1984, appointed manager June 1987 to Oct 1988/Mansfield Town youth development officer/Chesterfield assistant manager Feb 1993/Sheffield United scout.
Debut v York City, FLC 1 (h) 16.8.72, won 3 – 1 (scored one)

After a faltering start to his football career when a trial at Manchester United led to nothing, and a season with Bury ended with a free transfer after only four outings, Kevin eventually prospered with Chesterfield. In six seasons at Saltergate he scored 96 League goals in 258 matches and was leading scorer on three occasions. He joined the Magpies just prior to the 1972-73 season, scored on his debut and totalled 23 goals in League and Cup, a major contribution to the team's promotion from Division Three. He scored twice at Crystal Palace in the opening Division Two fixture as the Magpies quickly found their feet in higher company with a 4 – 1 victory. He was leading scorer for a second, consecutive season, with 15 goals in League and Cup. A strong and skilful striker, he continued to score regularly throughout his career, finishing with 182 League goals in 539(17) matches. An expert from the penalty spot, he converted ten such awards in 1972-73, six in consecutive matches during November and December, and two in the final match of the season against Tranmere Rovers that ensured promotion.

Appearances: FL: 119(2) apps 39 gls FAC: 7 apps 4 gls FLC: 7 apps 4 gls Total: 133(2) apps 47 gls
Honours: (Chesterfield) FL Division 4 champions 1970. (Mansfield Town) FL Division 3 champions 1977

RANKIN, John Patterson

Inside-forward 5' 8½" 11st 0lbs
b. Coatbridge, Lanarkshire, 10th May 1901
CAREER: Bellshill Athletic/Hamilton Academical Nov 1922/ Doncaster Rovers Nov 1924/Dundee Jan 1925/Charlton Athletic Sept 1925, fee £250/Chelsea May 1930/NOTTS May 1934/Burton Town Aug 1936
Debut v Swansea Town (a) 25.8.34, lost 1 – 2

In footballing terms, John Rankin had been around a long time when he arrived at Meadow Lane. A clever player with years of experience, it was felt that even if he was not required by the first team, his experience would be of value in aiding the development of younger reserve team players. In the event, the former Glasgow fruit merchant appeared in more than half of first team matches in his initial season before stepping down to reserve level. In a career spanning Scottish and English League clubs, his best spell was with Charlton Athletic where he played in 204 League and Cup matches and scored 37 goals.

Appearances: FL: 25 apps 2 gls FAC: 1 app 0 gls
Total: 26 apps 2 gls
Honours: (Dundee) Scottish Cup finalists 1925. (Charlton Athletic) FL Division 3 South champions 1929

RAPLEY, Kevin John

Forward   5' 9"   10st 8lbs
b. Reading, 21st September 1977
CAREER: Brentford trainee, signing pro July 1996 (Southend United loan Nov 1988)/NOTTS Feb 1999, fee £50,000 (Exeter City loan Nov 2000) (Scunthorpe United loan Mar 2001)/Colchester United Aug 2001/Chester City July 2003 (Forest Green Rovers loan Jan 2005) (Droylsden loan Mar 2005)
Debut v Luton Town (a) 23.2.99, won 1 – 0 (scored)

Meadow Lane was Kevin's third port of call in season 1998-99, a term that opened for him on a high note when he scored twice for Brentford against Mansfield Town in the initial fixture. In a successful loan spell with Torquay United he scored four goals in nine matches, and he was equally popular at Meadow Lane when he scored on his debut at Luton Town. His second half strike giving the Magpies a much-needed win after a barren spell of seven matches had yielded just a single point. To round off a memorable campaign, Kevin was awarded a championship medal for his early-season efforts at Brentford. He added a Nationwide Conference championship medal to his collection in 2003-04, and was a member of the newly-promoted Chester City side who opened their League Two campaign with a 1 – 1 draw at Meadow Lane. Kevin scoring City's equalising goal three minutes from time.

Appearances: FL: 21(31) apps 4 gls FAC: 1(1) apps 1 gl
FLC: 0(3) apps 0 gls Other: 1 app 0 gls
Total: 23(35) apps 5 gls
Honours: (Brentford) FL Division 3 champions 1999. (Chester City) Nationwide Conference champions 2004

RATCLIFFE, Patrick

Right-back   5' 8½" 11st 8lbs
b. Dublin, 31st December 1919
CAREER: Bohemians/NOTTS Nov 1945/Wolverhampton Wanderers June 1946/Plymouth Argyle June 1947, retired 1956.
Debut v Northampton Town, FAC 2 (a) 8.12.45, lost 1 – 3

Paddy Ratcliffe served in R.A.F. Bomber Command as an air-gunner during WW2, was shot down over Essen and spent two years as a prisoner of war. He returned to Bohemians after liberation but shortly afterwards joined Notts. In the transitional season 1945-46 he appeared in 15 regional matches in addition to the two FA Cup ties noted below. Before the resumption of League football he was transferred to the Wolves, but played only twice in the First Division before moving on to Plymouth Argyle. He remained at Home Park for nine seasons as a cool and efficient back with distribution to match. Ever-present in Argyle's championship season, he clocked up 246 League and Cup appearances and scored ten goals. On retiring from the game he emigrated to the U.S.A.

Appearances: FAC: 2 apps 0 gls Total: 2 apps 0 gls
Honours: (Plymouth Argyle) FL Division 3 South champions 1952

RAWSON, Kenneth

Centre-half   5' 10½"   11st 7lbs
b. Ripley, Derbyshire, 31st March 1931
d. Belper, Derbyshire, June 1986
CAREER: Ripley/NOTTS May 1953/Ilkeston Town player-manager June 1961 to Jan 1964
Debut v Bury (a) 27.11.54, won 2 – 1

Strong and commanding with a keen sense of positional play, Ken Rawson's initial League baptism came as deputy for the injured Leon Leuty in season 1954-55. It was to be a further three years before he enjoyed an extended run in the first eleven, when he contested the centre-half berth with Peter Russell. Season 1959-60 opened with much promise, but after starring in the first 10 matches of the campaign he suffered a broken leg at Hartlepool and did not appear again that season. Subsequently, he was unable to oust Bert Loxley and left Meadow Lane on a free transfer to take over as player-manager of Ilkeston Town. Throughout his time at Meadow Lane Ken was a part time professional and worked as a mining surveyor at Cossall Colliery.

Appearances: FL: 34 apps 0 gls Total: 34 apps 0 gls

RAYNER, James Patrick

Inside-forward 5' 9**2**" 11st 6lbs
b. Cornsay, County Durham, 31ˢᵗ March 1935
CAREER: Langley Park Juniors/Grimsby Town May 1952/
Bury May 1954/Hartlepools United Nov 1954/Bury June
1955/Barrow Sept 1955/Corby Town 1956/Grantham Town
Oct 1957/Peterborough United cs 1958/Grantham player-
manager July 1963/NOTTS Sept 1964, fee £2,500/Ilkeston
Town player-manager June 1966 to January 1967/Boston
United/Durham City.
Debut v Darlington (h) 10.9.64, won 4 – 2 (scored one)

Jimmy Rayner's career commenced at 17 years of age
with Grimsby Town as a budding centre-forward. He
failed to settle anywhere initially but finally blossomed
with Peterborough United. In the final two Midland
League championship seasons he scored better than a
goal-a-game, recording 70 in 65 matches. After such form
it was a total surprise when, upon entry into the Football
League, he was switched to play at right-half. His goals
were not missed, however, as the Posh rattled up a record
134 goals in winning the Division Four title, Terry Bly
being the chief marksman with 52 in 46 League matches.
Returning to Grantham as player-manager Jimmy led the
Gingerbreads to their first Midland League championship,
scoring a club record 71 goals during the successful
campaign. For his season at Meadow Lane he was fielded
at inside-forward and quickly showed that his eye for
goal had not diminished when he netted a hat-trick against
Chesterfield within a month of his arrival.

Appearances: FL: 32 apps 13 gls FAC: 2 apps 1 gl FLC:
2 apps 0 gls Total: 36 apps 14 gls
Honours: (Peterborough United) FL Division 4 champions
1961

READ, Charles William 'Chick'

Left-half 5' 7**2**" 12st 0lbs
b. Holbeach, Lincs, 21ˢᵗ March 1912
d. Holbeach, Lincs, 28ᵗʰ July 1964
CAREER: Little London Vics/Spalding Institute/Spalding
United cs 1929/Sheffield United Oct 1930, fee £50/Lincoln
City Aug 1932, fee £125/Southport Mar 1935/Chesterfield
Feb 1936, fee £200/Spalding United May 1937/Mansfield
Town Dec 1937/NOTTS May 1938, fee £250/Spalding
United 1946/Pinchbeck/Crowland/Spalding United
committeeman 1950s
Debut v Swindon Town (a) 27.8.38, lost 1 – 4

After just two outings at inside-left for the Magpies,
Chick Read was switched to left-half and was immediately
at home in the middle line, retaining the position for much
of the season. His footballing career was interrupted by
the outbreak of WW2 during which he served in the Royal
Army Service Corps in North Africa, and was mentioned
in despatches for bravery. He also managed to play some
soccer, appearing for Stan Cullis's Xl in Italy and for a
Services Xl against the FA.

He was demobilised in November 1945 and reappeared
for the Magpies on December 1ˢᵗ, in the 1 – 0 home win
against Clapton Orient. **Note:** Although known as 'Read'
throughout his career, and registered as such in the Football
League's records, birth and death details confirm that he
was actually named Reed.)

Appearances: FL: 36 apps 2 gls FAC: 3 apps 0 gls
Total: 39 apps 2 gls
Honours: (Chesterfield) FL Division 3 North champions
1936

REDMILE, Matthew Ian

Central defender 6' 3" 14st 10lbs
b. Nottingham, 12ᵗʰ November 1976
CAREER: NOTTS trainee July 1993, pro July 1995
(Shrewsbury Town loan Nov 2000)/Shrewsbury Town Jan
2001, fee £30,000/Scarborough June 2003/Barnet Feb 2004/
Tamworth July 2004
Debut v Chesterfield, Auto Windscreens Shield 1 (a)
17.10.95, lost 1 – 2

A central
defender of col-
ossal proport-
ions, Matt broke
into the first team
in season 1996-
97 showing a high
degree of skill and
composure for
one so young. In
his second season
early goals
against Rochdale
and Hull City
helped secure
maximum points
from the opening
two fixtures in
what proved to be
an outstandingly successful season. At various points
during his five years as a professional with the Magpies
Matt attracted the attention of Premiership scouts, but
in 2000-01 he lost his first team place following a 1 – 5
defeat at Walsall. Loaned to Shrewsbury Town in
November, the move was made permanent in the following
January. After 70 League and Cup appearances and five
goals for the Shrews, Matt moved into non-League
football, initially with Scarborough.

Appearances: FL: 140(7) apps 7 gls FAC: 13 apps 1 gl
FLC: 11 apps 0 gls Other: 4 apps 0 gls
Total: 168(7) apps 8 gls
Honours: (NOTTS) FL Division 3 champions 1998

REECE, Paul John

Goalkeeper   5' 10" 12st 7lbs
b. Bulwell, Nottingham, 16th July 1968
CAREER: NOTTS associate schoolboy/Stoke City app,
signing pro July 1986/Kettering Town cs 1987/Grimsby
Town July 1988, fee £10,000/Kettering Town/Doncaster
Rovers nc Sept 1992/Oxford United Oct 1992/NOTTS Aug
1994/West Bromwich Albion Aug 1995 (Ilkeston Town loan
Mar 1996)/Ilkeston Town July 2003.
Debut v Derby County (h) 23.10.94, drawn 0 – 0

Locally born goalkeeper who began in the Magpies' youth
team but then moved to Stoke City to serve his
apprenticeship. Understudy to Peter Fox at the Victoria
Ground, he played in only two League matches. He found
more opportunities with Grimsby Town (62 League and
Cup matches) and with Oxford United (44 League and
Cup matches). Returning to Meadow Lane as replacement
for the departed Bob Catlin, Paul impressed as a brave a
competent last line of defence, providing cover and real
competition to Steve Cherry for the first team spot. Paul
celebrated his one hundredth League appearance in the
Magpies 3 – 2 win against Sunderland on 5th November
1994, and he also made a Wembley appearance, as
substitute, in the Anglo-Italian Cup Final victory against
Ascoli.

Appearances: FL: 11 apps 0 gls FLC: 1 app 0 gls Other:
2(1) app 0 gls Total 14(1) apps 0 gls
Honours: (NOTTS) Anglo Italian Cup winners 1995

REEVES, David Edward

Forwar 6' 0"   12st 6lbs
b. Birkenhead, 19th November 1967
CAREER: Heswall/Sheffield Wednesday Aug 1988
(Scunthorpe United loan Dec 1986 and again Oct 1987)
(Burnley loan Nov 1987/Bolton Wanderers Aug 1989, fee
£80,000/NOTTS Mar 1993, fee £80,000/Carlisle United
Oct 1993, fee £121,000/Preston North End Oct 1996,
player exchange/Chesterfield Nov 1997, part exchange for
Tony Lormor plus £100,000 (Oldham Athletic loan Dec
2001)/Oldham Athletic Jan 2002 to Dec 2002/Chesterfield
Aug 2002 to June 2004/Scarborough Jan 2005.
Debut as sub v Bristol City (h) 3.4.93, drawn 0 – 0

The twin brother of Alan, the Swindon Town central
defender, David Reeves is a widely travelled striker of
ripe experience who passed the milestone of 500 League
appearances in Chesterfield's colours in March 2001.
Rated as one of the best strikers in the lower divisions,
his stay at Meadow Lane, however, was not distinguished
and he moved on to Carlisle after a stay of seven months.
He captained the Cumbrians to promotion in season
1994-95, scoring 21 of their 67 League goals during the
successful campaign.

He later assisted Chesterfield to promotion from Division
Three in 2000-01 when they finished third in the table,
despite having nine points deducted for financial
irregularities.

Appearances: FL: 9(4) apps 2 gls FLC: 1(1) apps 0 gls
Total: 10(5) apps 2 gls
Honours: (Carlisle United) FL Division 3 champions 1995

REGIS, David

Forward   6' 1"   13st 8lbs
b. Paddington, London, 3rd March 1964
CAREER: Dunstable/Fisher Athletic/Windsor & Eton/
Barnet Mar 1989, fee £8,000/NOTTS Sept 1990, fee
£200,000/Plymouth Argyle Nov 1991, fee £200,000 (AFC
Bournemouth loan Aug 1992)/Stoke City Oct 1992, fee
£100,000/Birmingham City Aug 1994, fee £200,000/
Southend United Sept 1994/Barnsley Feb 1996
(Peterborough United loan Sept 1996) (NOTTS loan Feb
1997) (Scunthorpe United loan Aug 1997)/Leyton Orient
nc Oct 1997/Lincoln City nc Dec 1997/Scunthorpe United
nc Feb to Mar 1998 when he retired/Working with NOTTS
youngsters 2003-04.
Debut as sub v Bristol Rovers (h) 29.9.90, won 3 – 2

Strong running striker with excellent aerial abilities, he
first hit the headlines in non-League football when helping
Fisher Athletic to win the Southern League championship
in 1986-87. He arrived at Meadow Lane from Barnet, a
combined fee of £260,000 bringing both Dave and Paul
Harding to the Magpies. In a stay of a little over a year,
his crowning moment came in May 1991 when he scored
Notts third goal in their 3 – 1 victory at Wembley, in the
Play-off Final against Brighton, that returned the Magpies
to the First Division after an absence of seven years. Of
many subsequent moves, his spell with Stoke City was
his best as he featured in the Potters' Second Division
championship campaign. A second spell at Meadow Lane,
on loan from Barnsley, featured a goal on his first
appearance in a 1 – 2 defeat at Shrewsbury Town, but he
was unable to halt the Magpies slide towards relegation
from Division Two. Hailing from a sporting family, Dave
is the younger brother of Cyril Regis, the former England
centre-forward, and cousin of John Regis, the international
sprinter.

Appearances: FL: 38(18) apps 17 gls FLC: 0(2) apps 0
gls Other: 6 apps 2 gls Total: 44(20) apps 19 gls
Honours: (Stoke City) FL Division 2 champions 1993

REID, James 'Jimmy'
Inside-left   5' 10" 12st 0lbs
b. Bellshill, Lanarkshire 18th November 1879
CAREER: Petershill/Hibernian/Burslem Port Vale Aug 1899/
West Ham United June 1900/Gainsborough Trinity June
1901/Worksop Town July 1902/NOTTS May 1903/Watford
May 1905/Tottenham Hotspur May 1906/New Brompton
Aug 1908/Worksop Town cs 1910.
Debut v Stoke (h) 12.9.03, won 1 – 0

Jimmy Reid's goal scoring feats with Worksop Town, for
whom he netted 35 Midland League goals in season 1902-
03, brought him to the attention of the Magpies, who
added him to their ever-growing list of Scottish recruits
in May 1903. With a varied experience before joining
Notts, the strong-running and forceful Reid was showing
great promise when he was injured in October of his first
season and was incapacitated for the remainder of the
campaign. Pronounced fit in the close season he was
retained for a second term. Despite scoring against Everton
in the season's opening fixture he failed to command a
regular place in the side. He enjoyed more success with
Watford (16 goals in 35 matches) and with the Spurs, for
whom he scored a hat-trick on his debut, and in all
competitions netted 35 goals in 59 matches.

Appearances: FL: 16 apps 2 gls FAC: 1 app 0 gls
Total: 17 apps 2 gls

---o---

REID, Peter
Midfield   5' 8"   10st 7lbs
b. Huyton, Liverpool, 20th June 1956
CAREER: Huyton Schoolboys/Bolton Wanderers app July
1971, pro May 1974/Everton Dec 1982, fee £60,000,
player-coach June 1987/Queens Park Rangers Feb 1989/
Manchester City player-coach Dec 1989, player-manager
Nov 1990 to Aug 1993/Southampton nc Sept 1993/NOTTS
nc Feb 1994/Bury nc July 1994/Sunderland manager Mar
1995/Leeds United caretaker manager Mar 2003, manager
May 2003 to Nov 2003/Coventry City manager May 2004
to Jan 2005.
Debut v Portsmouth (a) 5.2.94, drawn 0 – 0

At 37 years of age, Peter Reid was reaching the end of his
distinguished playing career when signed on a pay-as-
you-play basis by Magpies' manager Mick Walker. He
began with Bolton Wanderers as a 15 year-old apprentice,
and made his League debut at 18. For some three and a
half years he was rarely absent, but a horrendous catalogue
of injuries including two broken legs, a broken kneecap
and a cartilage operation blighted his later seasons at
Burnden Park. At a cut-price £60,000, however, Everton's
manager Howard Kendall effected one of his best-ever
deals when he took the gritty, workaholic midfielder to
Goodison Park. A vital link in the heart of Everton's engine
room, he was voted 'Player of the Year' in 1985.

His first England cap came in the same year and he later
played in the England team that reached the World Cup
quarter-finals. He carried the same verve and enthusiasm
into his managerial career, enjoying considerable success
with Sunderland, although subsequent posts have fallen
into the category of "Call in the fire brigade
appointments," will little realistic hope of success.

Appearances: FL: 5 apps 0 gls Total: 5 apps 0 gls
Honours: England International, 13 caps 1985-88. England
U-21 International, 6 caps 1977-78. (Everton) FL Div 1
champions 1985 & 1987. FA Cup winners 1984, finalists
1985, 1986. FL Cup finalists 1984. European Cup
Winners Cup winners 1985.(Bolton Wanderers) FL
Division 2 champions 1978

---o---

REILLY, Matthew Michael 'Gunner'
Goalkeeper   5' 11**2**"   13st 9lbs
b. Donnybrook, Ireland, 22nd March 1874
d. Dublin 9th December 1954
CAREER: Benburb, Glasgow/Royal Artillery, Portsmouth/
Portsmouth F.C. 1893 (Southampton St Mary's loan Dec
1895) (Freemantle loan)/Portsmouth May 1899/Dundee
cs 1904/NOTTS June 1905/Tottenham Hotspur Oct 1906,
fee £100/Shelbourne Aug 1907.
Debut v Stoke (a) 2.9.05, lost 0 – 3

Popularly known as 'Gunner' Reilly throughout his
career, and described in the 'Post Annual' for 1905 as: "A
custodian who built up a reputation in the Army and later
played for Portsmouth and Dundee. He has represented
the Army, Hampshire, and Forfarshire." He lost his place
in the Magpies' goal to the emerging Albert Iremonger,
after playing in most matches up to the Christmas period
and moved on to the Spurs before ending his career back
in Ireland. The former Gaelic footballer was Portsmouth's
first goalkeeper and assisted them to win the Southern
League championship in 1902.He had qualified for a benefit
game in 1901, and when Portsmouth celebrated their fiftieth
anniversary after playing against Arsenal on 27th
November 1948, Matt Reilly was amongst the guests.

Appearances: FL: 16 apps 0 gls Total: 16 apps 0 gls
Honours: Northern Ireland international, 2 caps 1900-02

---o---

RHODES, Christopher Kyle "Chris"
Midfield   5' 9"   10st 12lbs
b. Mansfield, 9th January 1987
CAREER: NOTTS scholar Aug 2003
Debut as sub v Peterborough United (a) 6.1.04, lost 2 – 5

Handed an unexpected opportunity at League level whilst
still a first-year scholar at Meadow Lane.

Chris ranks amongst talented youngsters Kelvin Wilson, Emmet Friars, Shaun Harrad and Shane McFaul who have all graduated through youth ranks and sampled first team football. A member of the youth team who won the Midlands Youth Cup in 2003-04, Chris' became the 1,000th player to appear in a League or Cup match for the Magpies since 1877, when the first eleven players on the list contested the initial FA Cup tie against Sheffield F.C.

Appearances: FL: 0(1) app 0 gls Total: 0(1) app 0 gls

―――――――――○―――――――――

RICHARDS, Lloyd George
Midfield   5' 8"   11st 12lbs
b. Jamaica, West Indies, 11th February 1958
CAREER: Derby Schoolboys/NOTTS app, signing pro Feb 1976/York City June 1980, contract cancelled Apr 1981
Debut as sub v Newcastle United, FLC 5, (a) 3.12.75, lost 0 – 1

Born in Jamaica, one of eight children, Lloyd Richardson lived in England from the age of six. He starred for Derby Schoolboys and was taken onto the Meadow Lane staff after writing in for a trial. Lacking nothing in speed, skill and confidence, he made his senior debut at the age of seventeen, but despite the club's highest hopes, after he appeared in several early-season matches in 1977-78, he was injured and did not appear again at senior level. Transferred to York City, his contract was cancelled in late season for disciplinary reasons after he had played in 21(1) matches and scored two goals.

Appearances: FL: 7(2) apps 0 gls FLC: 1(1) apps 0 gls
Other: 1(1) apps 0 gls Total: 9(4) apps 0 gls

―――――――――○―――――――――

RICHARDS, Peter 'Pedro'
Full-back   5' 8"   10st 8lbs
b. Edmonton, Middlesex, 11th November 1956
d. Nottingham, 23rd December 2001
CAREER: Nottingham City Schoolboys/Nottinghamshire County Schoolboys/NOTTS app May 1972, pro Nov 1974/Boston United 1986
Debut v Sunderland (a) 23.11.74, lost 0 – 3

Pedro certainly fulfilled all expectations after joining the Magpies straight from Nottingham Schools football. An England Youth trialist, he was voted 'Reserve team player of the Year' by the Supporter's Club at the end of season 1973-74 after an ever-present return in the North Midlands championship winning team. He made his League debut in the month of his 18th birthday against a very strong Sunderland side at Roker Park and was widely praised for his performance. After four years as regular right-back he was successfully switched into central defence, initially teamed with Brian Kilcline in a slightly

deeper role as sweeper. Whatever Pedro's role in the side, his performances were marked by his measured and constructive use of the ball, and the skill evident in the timing of his tackles. Seldom on the score sheet, his strike against Bolton Wanderers in the FL Cup in October 1984, brought a tongue-in-cheek comment from pundit Jimmy Greaves: "The only time he crosses the half way line is when the teams turn round!" Pedro's untimely death, at only 45 years of age, came as a result of pneumonia, from which he died in the Queen's Medical Centre, Nottingham.

Appearances: FL: 397(2) apps 5 gls FAC: 19 apps 0 gls
FLC: 39 apps 1 gl Other: 28 apps 0 gls
Total: 483(2) apps 6 gls

―――――――――○―――――――――

RICHARDS, Samuel
Inside-left   5' 5 2"   11st 4lbs
b. Bulwell, Notts, April quarter 1889
CAREER: Bulwell Forest Villa/NOTTS July 1909 to 1922.
Debut v Manchester City (a) 10.9.10, won 1 – 0 (scored)

A small but sturdy inside-forward with admirable ball control, Sam Richards was a skilful dribbler whose footwork often took him into goal scoring positions. Having reached the danger area, however, his finish did not always match the approach work. He was nevertheless sorely missed in the relegation season 1919-20. On January 24th 1920 the Magpies lost their unbeaten home record against Preston North End after Richards had seriously injured his knee and had to carried off the field on the trainer's back. He was out of action until October of the following season, by which time Notts were operating in Division Two. His best season was undoubtedly 1913-14, when he scored 21 goals from inside-left in 36 League matches. The Magpies took the championship of Division Two, greatly helped by a trio of inside-forwards (Flint, Peart and Richards) who between them scored 63 of the 77 goals recorded during the season.

Appearances: FL: 179 apps 69 gls FAC: 6 apps 2 gls
Total: 185 apps 71 gls
Honours: (NOTTS) FL Division 2 champions 1914

RICHARDSON, Ian George

Defender   5' 10"   11st 1lb
b. Barking, 22nd October 1970
CAREER: Dagenham & Redbridge/Birmingham City Aug 1995, fee £60,000/NOTTS Jan 1996, fee £200,000, caretaker-manager Nov 2004, manager Jan 2005 to May 2005.
Debut v Wrexham (h) 20.1.96, won 1 - 0

Despite being restricted by injury to just 12 appearances in 2004-05, the Magpies' popular player/ caretaker-manager was voted 'Player of the Year' for the third time in his long and distinguished career at Meadow Lane. It was a cruel misfortune for both club and player when his season was ended in September by a knee injury that ultimately required surgery. Certainly his courage, drive and 100% displays in midfield or defence have been sadly missed. One has the feeling that if it were possible to field a team of eleven Richardsons, the County would soon be operating at a much higher level. Ian dropped down a Division when he joined Notts from Birmingham City in mid season 1995-96, but came within a whisker of returning to Division One with the Magpies who reached the Division Two Wembley Play-off Final, only to lose against Bradford City on the big day. With a club appearance tally just short of the 300 mark, all will hope that Ian will be free of injury problems and fully fit to resume his playing career in 2005-06.

His stint as caretaker-manager will no doubt have prepared the ground, should he decide to stay in the game when his playing days are over. Handed something of a thankless task when taking over, he quickly won the respect of the players and, ably assisted by John Gaunt, successfully steered the side clear of relegation.

Appearances: FL: 237(16) apps 21 gls FAC: 20 apps 2 gls FLC: 18 apps 2 gls Other: 5 apps 1 gl
Total: 280(16) apps 26 gls
Honours: England Semi-Professional International, 1 cap. (NOTTS) FL Division 3 champions 1998

RICHARDSON, John

Right-back   5' 8"   9st 12lbs
b. Worksop, 20th April 1945
CAREER: Derby County app, signing pro Apr 1962/NOTTS July 1971/King's Lynn July 1973
Debut v Leyton Orient, FL Cup 1 replay (h) 25.8.71, won 3 – 1

Derby County's first apprentice professional, John Richardson spent over a decade at the Baseball Ground, appearing in 133 League and Cup matches and scoring five goals. He was a regular first team player until 1968-69 when he lost his place after appearing in the first two matches of the Division Two championship season. At Meadow Lane, the well established Brindley/Worthington full-back pairing continued to dominate, the unfortunate Richardson's League outings from the bench amounting to less than ten minutes. He then broke his leg in a reserve team match.

Appearances: FL: 0(2) apps 0 gls FLC: 1 app 0 gls
Total: 1(2) apps 0 gls

RICHARDSON, Leam Nathan

Defender/Midfield   5' 7"   11st 4lbs
b. Leeds, 19th November 1979
CAREER: Leeds City Schoolboys/Leeds United Juniors/ Blackburn Rovers trainee, signing pro Dec 1997/Bolton Wanderers July 2000, fee £50,000 (NOTTS loan Nov 2001) (Bradford City trial Nov 2002) (Blackpool loan Dec 2002)/ Blackpool June 2003, released May 2005.
Debut v Blackpool (a) 20.11.2001, drawn 0 – 0

Leam captained the Blackburn Rovers Youth team that reached the final of the FA Youth Cup in 1998 and in the following year made his senior debut with the Rovers. Fittingly, this came in his hometown, the former Leeds United junior returning to Elland Road for the third round Worthington Cup match, won 1 – 0 by Leeds thanks to a 90th minute goal from full-back Danny Mills.

Transferred to Bolton Wanderers, he was subsequently loaned to the Magpies, having failed to establish himself at the Reebok Stadium. A determined, hard tackling defender, he became a key member in the season memorable for the escape from relegation, thanks to a final flourish, capped by a 2 – 1 victory against Huddersfield Town in the season's final fixture.

Appearances: FL: 20(1) apps 0 gls FAC: 1 app 0 gls Total: 21(1) apps 0 gls
Honours: (Blackburn Rovers) FA Youth Cup finalists 1998. (Blackpool) LDV Vans Trophy winners 2004

RICKARDS, Charles Thomas 'Tex'
Forward   5' 8"   11st 10lbs
b. Giltbrook, Notts, 19th February 1915
d. Peterborough, 10th July 1980
CAREER: Giltbrook Villa/Johnson & Barnes/NOTTS am May 1932, pro Apr 1933/Cardiff City May 1938/Scunthorpe & Lindsey United June 1939 (WW2 guest Leicester City, NOTTS, Crewe Alexandra, Stockport County, Chesterfield, Mansfield Town and Derby County)/Peterborough United cs 1946 to cs 1949
Debut v Burnley (a) 22.4.33, lost 1 – 2

When 'Tex' Rickards made his League debut at 18 years of age, the 'Football Post' commented: "He showed a knowledgeable idea of the game and will improve with experience." He was allowed to develop in the reserves and made the breakthrough into regular League football during 1935-36. Replacing Len Featherby at  inside-left against Clapton Orient in September 1935 he scored after 15 minutes and was praised for his infectious energy and clever play. A fortnight later he blotted his copybook when he was sent off the field for striking a Northampton Town player, and a period of suspension ensued. In the following season a switch of roles saw him moved to outside-right, a position that he retained until his transfer to Cardiff City in May 1938. He assisted a variety of clubs during wartime football including a brief spell with the Magpies comprising 18 matches and eight goals in 1942-43 and two matches and one goal in 1943-44.

Appearances: FL: 112 apps 22 gls FAC: 7 apps 3 gls Other: 5 apps 2 gls Total: 124 apps 27 gls

RIDEOUT, Paul David
Forward   5' 11"   12st 2lbs
b. Boscombe, Bournemouth, 14th August 1964
CAREER: Priestlands School/Southampton & Hampshire Schoolboys/Lawrence Boys' Club/Lymington/Swindon Town app June 1980, pro Aug 1981/Aston Villa June 1983, fee £200,000/Bari, Italy, July 1985, fee £400,000/Southampton July 1988, fee £430,000 (Swindon Town loan Mar 1991)/NOTTS Sept 1991, fee £250,000/Glasgow Rangers Jan 1992, fee £500,000/Everton Aug 1992, fee £500,000/Huan Dao Vanguards, China, Apr 1997, fee £250,000/Shengzhen, Shanghai/Tranmere Rovers July 2000, retired June 2002/Kansas City Wizards USA, coaching appointment 2002/Huan Dao Vanguards, China.
Debut v Sheffield United (a) 17.9.91, won 3 – 1 (scored one)

Paul Rideout brought class and experience during his brief stay at Meadow Lane. He scored on his debut and was on the mark again four days later against Norwich City in his first home appearance. Sadly, he was to stay for only four months, the Magpies netting a handsome profit when he moved on to Glasgow Rangers. Relegation from the top flight became inevitable as the side failed to win in a run of 15 League matches that commenced on New Year's Day with a 0 – 1 defeat at Crystal Palace. In English League football Paul scored 115 goals in 354(48) matches. He was an unused substitute when Rangers beat Airdrie 2 – 1 in the Scottish Cup Final of 1992, but he scored the only goal of the 1995 FA Cup Final for Everton against Manchester United.

Appearances: FL: 9(2) apps 3 gls FAC: 1 app 0 gls FLC: 2 apps 0 gls Other: 2 apps 0 gls Total: 14(2) apps 3 gls
Honours: England Schoolboy International, 12 caps 1979-80. England Youth International. England U-21 International, 5 apps 1985-86. (Rangers) Scottish Premier League champions 1992. (Everton) FA Cup winners 1995.

RIDGWAY, Ian David
Midfield/Winger   5' 8"   10st 6lbs
b. Reading, Berks, 28th December 1975
CAREER: Toothill Comprehensive School (Bingham)/South Notts. and Nottinghamshire Schoolboys/Balderton Juniors/NOTTS trainee July 1992, pro July 1994 to July 1997/Kettering Town
Debut as sub v Swindon Town (a) 3.5.95, lost 0 – 3

A notable schoolboy footballer who, in a Magpies' programme interview in January 1993, recorded his 'Claim to Fame' as winning the League and Cup double with Balderton Juniors! Despite a considerable amount of natural ability, and a lengthy association with the Magpies, Ian remained on the fringes of the first team squad. Ironically, his best season in regard to League action proved to be his last.

Under new manager Sam Allardyce in the late stages of the relegation season 1996-97 he played in four consecutive Second Division matches, but was released in the summer.

Appearances: FL: 3(4) apps 0 gls Other: 0(2) apps 0 gls
Total: 3(6) apps 0 gls

RIGBY, Norman

Centre-half/Left-back   6' 1"   11st 8lbs
b. Warsop, 23rd May 1923
d. Newark, 21st August 2001
CAREER: Newark Town/NOTTS am Apr 1943, pro Sept 1944/Peterborough United cs 1951/Boston United Aug 1962/ Peterborough United assistant trainer May 1964, later trainer, appointed manager Sept 1967 to Jan 1969.
Debut v Ipswich Town (h) 15.4.48, lost 0 – 1

Norman Rigby succeeded Brian Purvis at left full-back in the championship season 1949-50, playing alongside stars of the calibre of Tommy Lawton, Frank Broome and Jackie Sewell. A little over a year later he was transferred to Peterborough United, having lost his place in the first team. He had many years of frustration at London Road as the Posh were repeatedly ignored by the Football League when re-election matters came around. This despite their winning of five consecutive Midland League championships, and their ability to attract gates better than many Third Division sides. Finally, in May 1960 they were elected and in their first season took Division Four by storm, scoring an all-time record of 134 goals to secure the championship. At the end of the following season, one month short of his 39th birthday Norman Rigby played his final match and was given a free transfer. He had been awarded two benefits and appeared in 328 Midland League matches, plus 97 League and Cup matches. A joiner by trade, Norman operated as a part-time professional throughout his very long and successful playing career.

Appearances: FL: 46 apps 0 gls FAC: 3 apps 0 gls
Total: 49 apps 0 gls
Honours: (NOTTS) FL Division 3 South champions 1950. (Peterborough United) FL Division 4 champions 1961

RILEY, Harold

Inside-forward   5' 6 2"   10st 8lbs
b. Hollinwood, near Oldham, 22nd November 1909
d. Lincoln, 12th April 1982
CAREER: Altrincham/Hurst F.C./Manchester United trial Oct 1928/Birmingham am Dec 1928/Ashton National season 1929-30/Accrington Stanley June 1930/Lincoln City June 1931/NOTTS June 1933, in part exchange for T.Feeney/Cardiff City June 1934/Northampton Town June 1936/Exeter City June 1938/Newark Town Oct 1939 (WW2 guest Lincoln City & Nottingham Forest)/Ruston Bucyrus 1945-46.
Debut v Hull City (a) 26.8.33, won 1 – 0

Harold Riley had an excellent season with Accrington Stanley in 1930-31, scoring 18 goals in 32 matches. He ended with a flourish, scoring a hat-trick against Lincoln City in the final match of the season. Obviously impressed, the Imps signed him two months later. In a season that was almost a carbon copy of his Accrington term he scored 18 goals in 33 matches to take Lincoln City to the championship. Despite a lack of inches he was a fine exponent of the art of goal scoring, his career aggregate figures being 74 in 214 League matches. He was also a talented cricketer, representing Lincolnshire in the Minor Counties Championship.

Appearances: FL: 16 apps 3 gls Total: 16 apps 3 gls
Honours: (Lincoln City) Division 3 North champions 1932

RILEY, Joseph

Centre-forward
b. Sheffield, April quarter 1910
CAREER: Conisbrough Welfare/Huddersfield Town trial/Hull City trial Jan 1928/Denaby United Apr 1929/Goldthorpe United/Bristol Rovers May 1931/Bristol City May 1933/ Bournemouth & Boscombe Athletic May 1935, fee £2,000/ NOTTS Dec 1937, in exchange for Harry Mardon/ Gloucester City cs 1938/Cheltenham Town July 1939/ Subsequently Bristol City scout
Debut v Gillingham (h) 27.12.37, won 1 – 0

Joe Riley scored the last of his career total of 83 League goals in the Magpies' colours, when he netted from a penalty against one of his former clubs, Bristol City, in the final fixture of season 1937-38. His career began with Bristol Rovers where, despite scoring a hat-trick on his debut in League football, he had appeared in only nine first team games when he moved to local rivals Bristol City in May 1933. His record with the Robins was 21 goals in 59 League appearances, a highlight being his scoring of all five goals in a match against Brighton & Hove Albion on 7th February 1934. A fee of £2,000 – sizeable at that time – took him to Bournemouth where he netted a very impressive total of 58 League goals in 97 matches. In a season when the Magpies fielded such famous international centre-forwards as Hughie Gallacher and Dixie Dean, Joe Riley was afforded few opportunities at first team level.

Appearances: FL: 7 apps 1 gl Total: 7 apps 1 gl
Honours: (Bristol City) Welsh Cup winners 1934

RILEY, Paul Anthony

Defender/Midfield   5' 9"   10st 7lbs
b. Nottingham, 29th September 1982
CAREER: NOTTS associate schoolboy Aug 1997, trainee July 1999, pro Dec 2001/Grimsby Town trial July 2004/ Ilkeston Town trial Oct 2004.
Debut v Oldham Athletic, LDV Vans Trophy quarter-final, (h) 4.12.2001, lost 0 – 1

Wholesale changes in the wake of the appointment of Gary Mills as manager saw Paul Riley promptly reduced to reserve team football. The fair-haired, left-sided midfielder/defender lacked nothing in honest endeavour, and had been a fairly regular performer in early season under Billy Dearden. An initial approach for his services came from former Magpies manager, Russell Slade, but a trial at Grimsby Town did not lead to the offer of a contract.

Appearances: FL: 18(10) apps 3 gls FAC: 2 apps 0 gls FLC: 1(1) apps 0 gls Other: 1 app 0 gls
Total: 22(11) apps 3 gls

RIMMER, Stuart Alan

Forward   5' 7"   11st 0lbs
b. Southport, 12th October 1964
CAREER: Everton associate schoolboy Feb 1979, app May 1981, pro Oct 1982 (Hamilton, New Zealand loan)/Chester City Jan 1985, fee £10,000/Watford Mar 1988, fee £205,000/NOTTS Nov 1988, fee £200,000/Walsall Jan 1989, fee £150,000/Barnsley Mar 1991, fee £150,000/ Chester City Aug 1991, fee £150,000 (Rochdale loan Sept 1994) (Preston North End loan Dec 1994)/retired June 1998.
Debut v Southend United (h) 12.11.88, drawn 1 – 1

Chester City's record holder for the most goals scored in total aggregate, Stuart Rimmer totalled 135 in two separate spells, and accumulated an overall career total of 169 goals in 437(49) League appearances. His two spells with Chester and his two years with Walsall were responsible for almost the whole of his career figures. His time with Notts was not untypical of his experiences elsewhere. Signed by manager John Barnwell, he was released by new manager Neil Warnock three months later. Notts recouped some part of their outlay when he moved to Walsall, signed by the Saddler's new manager, John Barnwell!

Appearances: FL: 3(1) apps 2 gls FAC: 2 apps 0 gls Other: 3 apps 0 gls Total: 8(1) apps 2 gls
Honours: England Youth International

ROBERTS, Dennis

Centre-half   5' 11**2**"   12st 12lbs
b. Monk Bretton, Yorkshire, 5th February 1918
d. Huddersfield, 8th April 2001
CAREER: NOTTS Aug 1937/Bristol City May 1938 (WW2 guest NOTTS 1943-44); retired cs 1954
Debut v Watford, Div 3 South Cup, semi-final replay (a) 13.9.37, lost 3 – 8

The important role of pivot was shared by three experienced campaigners during season 1937-38 – Hugh McLennahan, Con Moulson and Joe Gallagher. Nineteen year-old Dennis Roberts was restricted to just one outing in the Third Division South Cup. Never a competition that aroused much interest amongst the sporting public, Roberts' debut match was a semi-final replay that had been held over from the previous season, after the sides had drawn 1 – 1 at Meadow Lane before an attendance of 1,300 in April 1937. Even fewer (about 500) bothered to turn up for the replay when a 'scratch' Magpies XI were soundly defeated 3 – 8. Roberts moved after a season at Meadow Lane and made his League debut with Bristol City. Throughout the war years and beyond he was a fixture in their defence until his retirement in 1954. In terms of League and Cup matches his totals were 331 and two goals. In terms of overall matches, he finished just four short of 600, his total including 205 in wartime regional football.

Appearances: Other: 1 app 0 gls Total: 1 app 0 gls

ROBERTSON, Samuel

Right-back   5' 8**2**"   11st 9lbs
b. Possibly at Cowdenbeath, Fifeshire circa 1882
CAREER: Dundee/NOTTS July 1905
Debut v Stoke (a) 2.9.05, lost 0 – 3

Although Sam Robertson began season 1905-06 as first team right-back, he lost out to Arthur Griffiths after just two matches, his debut above and a 3 – 3 draw against Bolton Wanderers at Trent Bridge. Said on his debut to be "A quiet, unostentatious player, but non the less effective," his neat playing style seemed ripe for development but he did not graduate beyond Midland League football in his season with the Magpies.

Appearances: FL: 2 apps 0 gls Total: 2 apps 0 gls

ROBINSON, David Alan

Central defender   6' 1"   12st 3lbs
b. Middlesbrough, 14th January 1965
CAREER: Billingham Town/Hartlepool United Aug 1983/ Halifax Town Aug 1986/Peterborough United July 1989, fee £100,000/NOTTS Sept 1992, fee £425,000; retired due to knee injury Mar 1994.
Debut v Millwall (a) 19.9.92, lost 0 – 6

An experienced central defender with excellent headwork, Dave Robinson was a seasoned pivot with in excess of 200 League appearances at the time of his signing. He had cost Peterborough United a club record fee when signed and began impressively, being voted 'Player of the Year' at the end of his first season. In 1991-92 he starred at Wembley in the Division Three Play-off Final, won 2 – 1 by the Posh against Stockport County. Signed as a replacement for Craig Short, he had a desperately unhappy time at Meadow Lane, figuring in just two games before sustaining a serious knee injury. Despite surgery, he never regained full match fitness and finally conceded defeat after eighteen months spent battling to overcome the injury.

Appearances: FL: 3 apps 1 gl FLC: 1 app 1 gl
Total: 4 apps 2 gls

ROBINSON, George Frederick
Left-back   5' 8 **2**" 10st 10lbs
b. Melton Mowbray, 17th June 1925
d. Leicester, February 2000
CAREER: Holwell Works/NOTTS Aug 1944, pro Mar 1945/ Grantham Town Aug 1948
Debut v Bradford City, FAC 1, (h) 17.11.45, drawn 2 – 2

A mixture of youth and experience combined to form the Magpies last line of defence as football returned to normal after World War Two. Alongside the pre-war stalwart Bill Corkhill, George Robinson hardly put a foot wrong, showing excellent mobility and a valuable faculty for being in the right place at the right moment. He missed only one of the first 27 Third Division South matches, and this in highly unusual circumstances. He was unavailable for the trip to Watford on 21st September 1946 on account of his having gained a diploma in the works where he was employed at Melton Mowbray and had to attend for the presentation!

Appearances: FL: 29 apps 0 gls FAC: 5 apps 0 gls
Total: 34 apps 0 gls

ROBINSON, Leonard James
Left-back   5' 9" 10st 7lbs
b. Nottingham, 1st October 1946
CAREER: Nottingham Forest am/NOTTS ground staff Mar 1964
Debut v Bristol Rovers (h) 9.4.64, lost 3 – 4

Within the space of a single season Len Robinson graduated through Forest's third team and Football Combination side. He was then allowed to cross the Trent to Meadow Lane where he made his League debut as a 17 year-old left-back in the closing month of the 1963-64 relegation season, holding his place for a three-match run.

Sadly, his meteoric rise was not sustained as he played only once more at senior level, an outing at right back at Darlington in September 1964 resulting in a crushing 5 – 1 defeat.

Appearances: FL: 4 apps 0 gls Total: 4 apps 0 gls

ROBINSON, Mark Jeffrey
Forward   5' 10" 10st 8lbs
b. Basford, Notts, 26th November 1960
CAREER: Ilkeston Town/NOTTS Jan 1985/Shepshed Charterhouse cs 1986
Debut as sub v Middlesbrough (a) 9.2.85, won 1 – 0

Mark Robinson was signed by manager Ritchie Barker from non-League football and within two weeks appeared at Middlesbrough in Division Two. Before the season closed he was operating under new manager Jimmy Sirrel, returning for his third spell in charge. Notts were relegated in 1984-85, and Mark made only three starting appearances and nine from the bench in the following term, scoring his only League goal at Wigan Athletic in a 1 – 3 defeat. His career was tragically cut short by cancer, and in March 1988 the Magpies played a fund raising game against Shepshed Charterhouse for his benefit.

Appearances: FL: 12(14) apps 1 gl FAC: 0(1) apps 0 gls
FLC: 1 app 0 gls Other: 0(1) apps 0 gls
Total: 13(16) apps 1 gl

ROBINSON, Marvin Leon St Clair
Forward   6' 0" 12st 9lbs
b. Crewe, 11th April 1980
CAREER: Derby County trainee, signing pro July 1998 (Stoke City loan Sept 2000) (Tranmere Rovers loan Nov 2002)/Chesterfield Sept 2003/NOTTS Sept 2004/Rushden & Diamonds nc Nov 2004/Walsall Dec 2004/Stockport County Mar 2005.
Debut v Southend United (h) 18.9.2004, lost 1 – 2

One of three signings made in one day by manager Gary Mills (the others were loan signings, Craig Pead and Youssef Sofiane.) The trio made little impact at Meadow Lane. Marvin had been training with Mansfield Town after being released by Chesterfield, and he played only twice during his short term contract, appearing some way from match fitness. An unfortunate player in the way of injuries, Marvin suffered a badly broken leg in September 2000, during a brief loan spell with Stoke City.

Appearances: FL: 1(1) apps 0 gls Total: 1(1) apps 0 gls
Honours: England Schoolboy International

ROBINSON, Peter

Right-half   5' 9"   11st 0lbs
b. Manchester, 29th January 1922
d. Manchester, 9th September 2000
CAREER: Urmston/Manchester City Oct 1941 (WW2 guest
Aldershot & Queens Park Rangers)/Chesterfield Oct 1947/
Buxton Aug 1949/NOTTS Feb 1950/King's Lynn 1955-56/
Macclesfield Town manager/Hyde United manager/
Manchester City youth coach/Preston North End youth
coach/Manchester City scout.
Debut v Port Vale (a) 10.4.50, lost 1 – 3

Former captain of Chesterfield who left Saltergate to play
in non-League football with Buxton after failing to agree
terms for the 1949-50 season. Notts manager Houghton
brought him back into League football and, on a purely
personal note, his move to Meadow Lane linked him
again with his great friend Tommy Capel, who had joined
Forest in November 1949. Robinson and Capel attended
the same junior and senior school, went together to their
first League club, Manchester City, were together in the
services during the war, and both joined Chesterfield in
an exchange deal for Billy Linacre in October 1947.
Robinson enjoyed two excellent playing seasons with
the Magpies when he was considered one of the
outstanding wing half-backs operating in Division Two.
He was deposed by Alex Simpson in 1952-53, appearing
in just four first team matches in what proved to be his
final season in League football.

Appearances: FL: 82 apps 1 gl FAC: 2 apps 0 gls
Total: 84 apps 1 gl

ROBINSON, Philip John

Midfield   5' 10"   10st 10lbs
b. Stafford, 6th January 1967
CAREER: Stafford Schoolboys/Aston Villa app June 1983,
pro Jan 1985/Wolverhampton Wanderers July 1987, fee
£5,000/NOTTS Aug 1989, fee £67,500 (Birmingham City
loan Mar 1991)/Huddersfield Town Sept 1992, fee £75,000
(Northampton Town loan Sept 1994)/Chesterfield Dec
1994, fee £15,000/NOTTS Aug 1996, fee £80,000/Stoke
City June 1998/Bamber Bridge June 2000/Hereford United
player-coach 2001/Stafford Rangers player-manager.
Debut v Leyton Orient (a) 19.8.89, won 1 – 0

After winning three trophies within the space of two
seasons with the Wolves, it was somewhat surprising
that they were prepared to part with their inspirational
midfielder. Certainly his move to Meadow Lane proved
to be an unqualified success with two promotions in
successive seasons, both via Wembley Play-off Finals.
During his second spell at Meadow Lane Phil combined
playing with studies at Salford University for a degree in
physiotherapy. He was still able to feature prominently
in a third promotion campaign, the 1998 elevation being
achieved without involvement in the Play-offs. It would

be difficult to
name a more
successful
footballer in the
lower divisions,
considering his
record of six
promotion
triumphs and
three Wembley
visits for Ass-
ociate Members
Cup Finals.
Phil's career
aggregate figures
totalled 451(36)
League and Cup
appearances and
46 goals.

Appearances: FL: 128(15) apps 10 gls FAC: 7(2) apps 1
gl FLC: 10 apps 2 gls Other: 10(1) apps 0 gls
Total: 155(18) apps 13 gls
Honours: (Wolverhampton Wanderers) FL Division 4
champions 1988; FL Division 3 champions 1989; Sherpa
Van Trophy winners 1988. (NOTTS) FL Division 3
champions 1998. (Birmingham City) Leyland Daf Cup
winners 1991. (Huddersfield Town) Autoglass Trophy
finalists 1994.

ROBLEDO, Edward Oliver 'Ted'

Wing-half   5' 9"   11st 6lbs
b. Iquique, Chile, 26th July 1928
d. Persian Gulf, 6th December 1970
CAREER: Barnsley 1943/Newcastle United Jan 1949, fee
£3,500/Colo-Colo (Chile) May 1953/NOTTS Sept 1957
to 1958
Debut v Bristol Rovers (a) 28.9.57, lost 2 – 5

The early stages of Ted's career were spent in tandem
with his better - known brother George, who won fame
as Newcastle United's sharp shooting inside–forward who
was leading scorer in Division One in 1951-52 with 39
goals. Ted earned a regular run in the first team during
1951-52, appearing in 32 Division One matches and seven
FA Cup matches that included the Wembley final against
Arsenal, won by a single goal scored by brother George.
Both brothers returned to Chile in 1953. Ted returned to
England, but his spell with Notts was not distinguished
and he retired from the game to work in the oil industry.
His death occurred when he was lost overboard from an
oil tanker in the Persian Gulf, en route from Dubai to
Lowestoft. Murder charges were brought against the ship's
captain, but he was tried and found not guilty. Ted
Robledo's body was never found.

Appearances: FL: 2 apps 0 gls Total: 2 apps 0 gls
Honours: (Newcastle United) FA Cup winners 1952

ROBSON, Mark Andrew

Winger   5' 7"   10st 2lbs
b. Newham, 22nd May 1969
CAREER: Exeter City app Aug 1985, pro Dec 1986/
Tottenham Hotspur July 1987, fee £50,000 (Reading loan
Mar 1998) (Watford loan Oct 1989) (Plymouth Argyle
loan Dec 1989) (Rosenburg, Norway, loan summer 1991)
(Exeter City loan Jan 1992)/West Ham United Aug 1992/
Charlton Athletic Nov 1993, fee £125,000/NOTTS June
1997 (Wycombe Wanderers loan Oct 1999)/Boreham Wood
Sept 1999/Hornchurch F.C.
Debut v Rochdale (h) 9.8.97, won 2 – 1 (scored one)

Mark Robson scored on his debut for Exeter City in a 2 – 0
victory against Lincoln City on 11th October 1986 and
two months later was awarded a professional contract.
Seven goals in 27 matches in his first season of League
football earned him a rapid upward move to the Spurs,
but until his transfer to West Ham United the bulk of his
first team football had occurred in a number of loan spells
from White Hart Lane. Regular first team football with
both the Hammers and Charlton Athletic preceded his
free transfer to the Magpies in June 1997. Mark would
probably qualify as one of the lightest players to appear
for the Magpies in relatively recent times, but he certainly
made a big impact on the field. Commencing with a goal
from the penalty spot on his debut, he also made the
other in the 2 – 1 win against Rochdale. Much later in the
season he scored against his old club, Exeter City, in a 5 –
2 away victory on March 3rd. On the 28th of the month
his class finish, when he chipped Leyton Orient's
goalkeeper from the edge of the penalty area, proved to
be the goal that clinched promotion.

Appearances: FL: 26(6) apps 4 gls FAC: 3 apps 0 gls
FLC: 3 apps 0 gls Other: 1 app 0 gls
Total: 33(6) apps 4 gls
Honours: (NOTTS) FL Division 3 champions 1998

ROBY, Donald

Outside-right   5' 7"   10st 0lbs
b. Billinge near Wigan, 15th November 1933
CAREER: Orrell Bisphan Methodists/NOTTS am 1949,
signing pro Feb 1951/Derby County Aug 1961, fee £10,000/
Burton Albion June 1965/Loughborough United July 1967
Debut v Sheffield United (h) 24.2.51, won 3 – 0

The Magpies signed the youthful Don Roby in the face
of stiff competition from the likes of Manchester United,
Bolton Wanderers and Everton. He was fixed up with a
job on the ground staff at Meadow Lane until able to sign
as a professional. An excellent ball player, equally at home
as wingman or inside-forward, he was a bundle of energy,
extremely quick and elusive if lacking something as a
marksman. He did prosper in this department in the 1959-
60 promotion campaign, however, scoring 11 in 42 League
matches as outside-right in a virile attack that totalled

107 League goals
in 46 matches.
Later in the
following season
he requested a
transfer and in
the summer
moved on to
Derby County
where he enjoyed
two good
seasons before a
cartilage injury
effectively ended
his involvement
at first team
level. He was
still playing in
Sunday League
soccer at the age of 50, and later coached Radcliffe Olympic
Under-14s.

Appearances: FL: 226 apps 37 gls FAC: 6 apps 0 gls
FLC: 1 app 0 gls Total: 233 apps 37 gls

RODDIE, Andrew Robert

Winger   5' 102"   11st 6lbs
b. Glasgow, 4th November 1971
CAREER: Glasgow United/Aberdeen Apr 1988/Motherwell
Aug 1994, fee £100,000/NOTTS nc trial Jan 1997/
Ljungskile (Sweden)/St Mirren Oct 1997/Stranraer Oct 1999
to Jan 2000/Arbroath/Peterhead Aug 2002
Debut v Scunthorpe United, Auto Windscreens Shield, (a)
28.1.97, drawn 1 – 1 (Scunthorpe won 4 – 2 on penalties)

When Alex McLeish left Aberdeen to take over as manager
of Motherwell, he went back to his old club for his first
signing, Scotland U-21 winger Andy Roddie. Without
fully establishing himself at Pittodrie, the willowy flank
man had featured in the Dons' line up in 1992-93 and
1993-94, when they consecutively finished as runners-
up for the Scottish Premier League title. Motherwell
occupied a similar position in Roddie's first season at Fir
Park, his involvement amounting to four starts and 15
appearances from the bench. In mid season 1996-97 he
was released by Motherwell after 24(31) appearances.
He accepted the offer of a trial on non contract forms at
Meadow Lane, but his sole appearance in the Auto
Windscreens Shield competition did not result in a
permanent contract.

Appearances: Other: 1 app 0 gls Total: 1 app 0 gls
Honours: Scotland Schoolboy, Youth and U-21
International

ROEDER, Glenn Victor

Midfield   6' 2"   12st 8lbs
b. Woodford, Essex, 13th December 1955
CAREER: Gidea Park Rangers/Essex & London Schoolboys/
Arsenal associate schoolboy Dec 1969/Orient app Aug 1972,
pro July 1974/Queens Park Rangers Aug 1978, fee £210,000
(NOTTS loan Nov 1983)/Newcastle United Dec 1983, fee
£125,000/Watford player & reserve-team coach June 1989
to Aug 1991/Millwall Reserves/Leyton Orient Jan to May
1992/Purfleet Oct 1992/Gillingham manager Nov 1992/
Watford manager July 1993 to Feb 1996/England scout/
Burnley assistant manager July 1997/England coach 1998/
West Ham United coach Feb 1999, caretaker manager May
2001, manager June 2001 to Aug 2003/Newcastle United
Academy manager June 2005
Debut v West Bromwich Albion (a) 5.11.83, lost 0 – 2

Glenn Roeder had lost his place at Queens Park Rangers
following an injury when he joined the Magpies on a one-
month loan. He joined a team struggling in the relegation
zone in Division One and without a victory in nine
matches. Wins at Southampton, and a crushing 5 – 2
victory against Aston Villa were included in Glen's seven-
match run that featured two wins, four draws and one
defeat. There was no doubt that his inspiring character
had rubbed off on the team. He was available at a transfer
fee of £150,000 and a 'Buy Glenn Roeder' fund was
raised with chairman Dunnett promising to match
whatever the club's supporters could raise. Sadly, a figure
of £30,000 fell well short of what was necessary, and
Glen moved on to Newcastle United where he remained
for six seasons, helping them to return to the top flight in
1984. As a ball playing midfielder and later centre-half he
made in excess of 550 League appearances. Several
coaching and managerial posts, and a brief spell as Paul
Gascoigne's 'chaperone' in Italy, concluded at West Ham
United. He was sacked just three matches into the season
in August 2003 following the Hammers relegation from
the Premier League in 2002-03.

Appearances: FL: 4 apps 0 gls FLC: 3 apps 0 gls
Total: 7 apps 0 gls
Honours: England 'B' International, 6 apps 1978-82.
(Queens Park Rangers) FA Cup finalists 1982. FL Division
2 champions 1983

ROGERS, Paul Anthony

Midfield   6' 0"   12st 0lbs
b. Portsmouth, 21st March 1965
CAREER: Chipstead/Sutton United July 1983/Sheffield
United Jan 1992, fee £35,000/NOTTS Dec 1995 (Wigan
Athletic loan Dec 1996)/Wigan Athletic Mar 1997, fee
£50,000/Brighton & Hove Albion July 1999, retired May
2003 and joined the clubs' commercial department.
Debut v Middlesbrough, FAC 3 (h) 6.1.96, lost 1 – 2 (scored)

A relatively latecomer to League football, fair-haired Paul
Rogers joined County in mid season 1995-96 and scored
in his first two matches. He retained a first team place
through to the end of the season and into the Wembley
Play-off Final, lost 0 – 2 to Bradford City. By contrast,
he had made only one substitute appearance in a League
match in 1996-97 when he was loaned to Wigan Athletic.
In March the move was made permanent and Paul
collected a Third Division championship medal at the
end of the season. Although well into the veteran stage
when joining Brighton on a free transfer in July 1999, he
captained the Seagulls to successive promotions, leading
by example from his role in central midfield.

Appearances: FL: 21(1) apps 2 gls FAC: 1 app 1 gl Other:
3 apps 0 gls Total: 25(1) apps 3 gls
Honours: England Semi-Professional International, 6 caps.
(Wigan Athletic) FL Division 3 champions 1997. Auto
Windscreens Shield winners 1999. (Brighton & Hove
Albion) FL Division 3 champions 2001. FL Division 2
champions 2002.

ROSE, Michael John

Goalkeeper   6' 2"   13st 8lbs
b. New Barnet, Herts, 22nd July 1943
CAREER: Herts. County Grammar School/Leicester City
trial/Barnet/St Albans City 1962/Charlton Athletic am May,
pro July 1963, for a £200 donation/NOTTS Mar 1967, fee
£2,000 (Mansfield Town loan Aug 1970)/East London F.C.
(South Africa) Mar 1971
Debut v Barnsley (a) 18.3.67, drawn 0 – 0

One week into his appointment as team manager, Billy
Gray beat the transfer deadline by a matter of hours when
he signed 23 year-old Charlton Athletic goalkeeper, Mike
Rose. His difficult task was to follow the splendidly
loyal and consistent George Smith in the Magpies' goal,
and he made the best of starts on his debut at Oakwell,
marking the occasion with a 'clean sheet.' Well-built, daring
and often brilliant, he was generally first choice until
Barry Watlin took over in January 1970. Mike Rose was
retained for season 1970-71 but placed on the transfer
list. A brief loan spell with Mansfield Town, as cover for
their injured first team goalkeeper Graham Brown, featured
three League appearances, but did not result in a
permanent engagement.

Appearances: FL: 109 apps 0 gls FAC: 3 apps 0 gls FLC:
4 apps 0 gls Total: 116 apps 0 gls

ROSS, Ian

Central defender   5' 8"   10st 8lbs
b. Milton, Glasgow, 26th January 1947
CAREER: Glasgow Schoolboys/Liverpool app 1963, pro
Aug 1965/Aston Villa Feb 1972, fee £60,000 (NOTTS loan
Oct 1976) (Northampton Town loan Nov
1976)(Peterborough United loan Dec 1976)/Peterborough
United cs 1977, fee £20,000/Santa Barbara FC (USA)/
Wolverhampton Wanderers Aug 1979, subsequently
appointed coach/Hereford United player and assistant-
manager Oct 1982/Oman coach 1982-83/Birmingham City
reserve team coach 1983/Valur, Iceland, manager-coach
1984-88/Huddersfield Town manager Mar 1992-93/
Sunderland reserve team manager. Additionally held coaching
appointments in South Africa and Australia in the 1980s.
Debut v Leyton Orient (a) 16.10.76, lost 0 – 1

Despite his obvious talent, particularly in a man-marking
role, Ian Ross was restricted to just 42(6) League
appearances during six seasons in the Liverpool first team
squad. He left Anfield to captain Aston Villa, leading them
to the championship of Division Three, a FL Cup success
against Norwich City, and promotion from Division Two
in 1975. Meadow Lane was just one of his three different
loan spells in the first half of season 1976-77, before
Peterborough United signed him on a permanent basis. In
1977-78 the Posh narrowly missed out on promotion to
Division Two, despite having the best defensive record in
the Division – 33 goals against in 46 matches. He captained
the side in his final season, before embarking on a globe
trotting coaching career.

Appearances: FL: 4 apps 0 gls Total: 4 apps 0 gls
Honours: (Aston Villa) FL Division 3 champions 1972.
FL Cup winners 1975

ROSS, William

Centre-forward 5' 11"   11st 8lbs
b. Kiveton Park, Sheffield, January quarter 1874
CAREER: Chesterfield Town Aug 1894/Sheffield United
May 1895 (Gainsborough Trinity loan May 1897)/Lincoln
City Nov 1897/Gravesend United May 1898/Reading May
1899/NOTTS May 1900/Grimsby Town June 1904, fee £25/
Glossop May 1905 to 1907.
Debut v Sunderland (h) 1.9.00, drawn 2 – 2

In September 1903 the 'Football Post' commented: "If
Ross had preserved the accuracy and brilliance of
marksmanship that characterised his first season at Trent
Bridge, his position in the team would never have been in
doubt." Certainly it was a case of diminishing returns in
the goal scoring department, as twelve of his League goals
came in his first season, followed by totals of nine, four
and three. In mitigation his value as a team player was
illustrated in season 1902-03 when he strove to fill the
vacancy at outside-left when Ellis Gee was injured, and
similarly took over at inside-left when Jack Morris was
dropped.

In addition to his soccer prowess, Ross was also a cricketer, good enough to join the Nottinghamshire C.C.C. ground staff in 1902. He was a Derbyshire licensee in 1914 when attempting to join the board of Glossop, but the governing body would not allow it. Former professionals were invariably refused permission to become club directors at this time.

Appearances: FL: 110 apps 28 gls FAC: 8 apps 1 gl
Total: 118 apps 29 gls

ROY, John Robin "Jack"

Winger 5' 9"   10st 4lbs
b. Southampton, 23rd March 1914
d. Bournemouth, 24th November 1980
CAREER: Sholing/Norwich City am July pro Aug 1933/
Mansfield Town Apr 1936/Sheffield Wednesday Feb 1937,
fee £1,750/NOTTS Mar 1938/Tranmere Rovers Dec 1938/
Yeovil & Petters United May 1939 (WW2 guest
Southampton, Yeovil and Petters United & Aberaman)/
Ipswich Town Feb 1946/Gravesend Oct 1947.
Debut v Gillingham (a) 16.3.38, lost 1 – 2

A lively performer on the wing, Jack Roy appeared in
League football both before and after the Second World
War. He was signed by Notts and ex-Mansfield Town
manager Harry Parkes who, when in charge at Field Mill,
had sold him at a handsome profit to Sheffield Wednesday.
No doubt recalling the winger's ability to supply accurate
crosses to centre-forward Ted Harston at Field Mill,
Parkes was anticipating that he would perform a similar
service to his other new signing, 'Dixie' Dean. Hartson
had scored a staggering 55 League goals in 41 matches for
the Stags, but Roy was unable to link up with Dean in
similar fashion. Sadly, the former England centre-forward
fought an unsuccessful battle against injury during his
time at Meadow Lane and was restricted to just nine
League appearances.

Appearances: FL: 15 apps 0 gls FAC: 1 app 0 gls
Total: 16 apps 0 gls

RUSHTON, Brian William Eric

Full-back   5' 10"   9st 3lbs
b. Sedgley, 21st October 1943
CAREER: Brierley Hill Schoolboys/Dudley Schoolboys/
Birmingham City am 1959, pro Oct 1960/NOTTS June
1967/Stourbridge Jan 1968.
Debut v Chester (h) 19.8.67, lost 1 – 2

Brian Rushton joined the Magpies on a free transfer from
Birmingham City, but with an agreement to pay the Blues
£5,000 if he was retained for two years. In the event, he
did not stay for one season, his lightweight physique
being hardly suited to the rigours of Division Four football.
Released in mid season he joined Stourbridge, who were
fined ten guineas by the FA, for playing him only five
days after signing him from Notts, and before registration
formalities had been completed.

Appearances: FL: 2(1) apps 0 gls FLC: 1 app 0 gls
Total: 3(1) apps 0 gls

RUSSELL, David

Half-back
b. Airdrie, 8th April 1868
d. Glasgow, 26th November 1918
CAREER: NOTTS June 1895-96
Debut v Newcastle United (a) 21.9.1895, lost 1 – 5

Versatile Scot who occupied all three half-back positions
after making his League debut at inside-right. In a season
of heavy scoring – both for and against – Russell was
unable to establish a regular place in the middle line, a
well-established triumvirate comprising Bramley,
Calderhead and Alf Shelton.

Appearances: FL: 9 apps 0 gls Total: 9 apps 0 gls

RUSSELL, Edward Thomas

Half-back   6' 0"   13st 7lbs
b. Cranwell, Lincs, 15th July 1928
CAREER: St Chad's College/Wolverhampton Wanderers Apr
1946/Middlesbrough Dec 1951, fee £10,000/Leicester City
Oct 1953, fee £8,000/NOTTS Aug 1958 to Apr 1960, fee
£1,000
Debut v Halifax Town (a) 30.8.58, drawn 1 – 1

Ted Russell made a somewhat unusual entry into football.
When a pupil at St. Chad's Catholic College he was
recommended to Wolverhampton Wanderers by a soccer-
minded brother. He was given a trial, immediately
impressed, and was signed on the eve of his entering the
R.A.F. He did not enjoy regular first team football at
either Molineux or subsequently at Ayresome Park, but
his move to Leicester City provided more opportunities.

The tall, strong-tackling schoolteacher completing 101
League and Cup appearances before his £1,000 transfer
to Notts. Initially lining up alongside his namesake Peter
Russell, Eddie struggled to adjust to life in Division Three
and after just nine matches was placed on the transfer list
in December 1958. He was subsequently retained for
season 1959-60, but did not reappear at first team level.
A part-time professional, Ted also worked as a
schoolteacher in Leicester.

Appearances: FL: 9 apps 0 gls Total: 9 apps 0 gls
Honours: England Youth International. FA Tour to Canada
June 1950. (Leicester City) FL Division 2 champions
1954

RUSSELL, Kevin John 'Rooster'

Forward   5' 9"   10st 12lbs
b. Portsmouth, 6th October 1966
CAREER: Brighton & Hove Albion app/Portsmouth pro
Oct 1984/Wrexham July 1987, fee £10,000/Leicester City
June 1989, fee £175,000 (Peterborough United loan Sept
1990) (Cardiff City loan Jan 1991) (Hereford United loan
Nov 1991) (Stoke City loan Jan 1992)/Stoke City July
1992, fee £95,000/Burnley June 1993, fee £140,000/AFC
Bournemouth Mar 1994, fee £125,000/NOTTS Feb 1995,
fee £60,000/Wrexham July 1995, fee £60,000, player-
coach Oct 2001, player-assistant manager later in the same
season, retired from playing June 2003
Debut v Reading (h) 25.2.95, won 1 – 0

An early member of the shaven-headed brigade of
footballers whose career lasted long enough to make his
style the norm rather than the exception. In early days an
out-and-out striker he later occupied a midfield role, but
in whatever position he was called upon to fill,
"Rooster's" enthusiasm and exceptional work rate made
him a great crowd favourite. He passed the milestone of
500 League and Cup appearances in his second spell with
Wrexham, his final totals amounting to 447(70) matches
and 97 goals.

Appearances: FL: 9(2) apps 0 gls Total: 9(2) apps 0 gls
Honours: England Youth International, 6 apps. (Stoke
City) FL Division 2 champions 1993. (Wrexham) Welsh
Cup finalist 1988

RUSSELL, Robert Inglis 'Bobby'

Wing-half   5' 7½"   10st 10lbs
b. Aberdour, Fife, 27th December 1919
d. Edinburgh, 2004
CAREER: Airdrieonians/Chelsea Dec 1944, fee £3,500/
NOTTS Aug 1948/Leyton Orient Oct 1948
Debut v Torquay United (a) 21.8.48, lost 1 – 3

Bobby Russell was a star in Chelsea's half-back line during wartime football, appearing in two Football League (South) Cup Finals at Wembley in 1944 and 1945. High hopes were centred upon him when the full League programme was resumed. Sadly, he fractured his leg in the very first match that he played after returning from overseas Army service. At Meadow Lane he renewed friendship with manager Arthur Stollery, former Chelsea trainer, but Russell's attempted 'comeback' ended in disappointment after just two first team outings. A move to Leyton Orient was similarly unrewarding as he failed to reach senior level at Brisbane Road.

Appearances: FL: 2 apps 0 gls Total: 2 apps 0 gls

RUSSELL, William Peter

Centre-half   6' 0"   12st 2lbs
b. Sedgley, 16th January 1935
CAREER: Wolverhampton Wanderers pro Oct 1952/ NOTTS Mar 1956 to Apr 1960, fee £5,000
Debut v Plymouth Argyle (a) 17.3.56, drawn 1 – 1

A powerfully-built young centre-half, with few superiors as a defensive pivot, who cost £5,000 despite having played in only three League matches for the Wolves. Restricted as understudy to the great Billy Wright at Molineux, Peter settled immediately at Meadow Lane, his first 64 League appearances being made consecutively. He was the only player to make maximum appearances in 1956-57, his five goals during the campaign being an added bonus. In the following two seasons, when successive relegations took the side from Division Two to football's basement, his form suffered along with that of the team, and he twice requested a transfer. Although remaining on the club's books, he did not feature in the 1959-60 promotion winning side. Two years later it was reported that he was intending to emigrate to South Africa to play football.

Appearances: FL: 106 apps 6 gls FAC: 4 apps 0 gls Total: 110 apps 6 gls

---

RYAN, John Oliver

Outside-right   5' 10"   12st 6lbs
b. Liverpool, 28th October 1944
CAREER: Tranmere Rovers Aug 1964/Wigan Athletic/ Luton Town Oct 1967/NOTTS May 1969, contract cancelled Oct 1970/Altrincham.
Debut v Oldham Athletic (h) 9.8.69, drawn 0 – 0

The first new signing of the 1969 close season, after a 'clear-out' of epic proportions – 14 free transfers – in the wake of the 19th place finish in Division Four in 1968-69.

John Ryan had his first taste of League football with Luton Town, after following his former manager, Allan Brown, from Wigan Athletic to Kenilworth Road in October 1967. He appeared in 10 League matches and scored one goal in his first season, when the Hatters were promoted as champions of Division Four. He added only a further 7(1) appearances to his total in the following campaign and was released at its close. At Meadow Lane he held the outside-right position until mid season before losing out to a combined challenge from new signings Jon Nixon and Charlie Crickmore.

Appearances: FL: 22(2) apps 1 gl FAC: 1 app 0 gls FLC: 1 app 0 gls Total: 24(2) apps 1 gl

---

SAMUELS, Jerome Livingston

Defender   5' 11"   12st 2lbs
b. Jamaica, 8th March 1976
CAREER: Lightning SC (USA)/NOTTS Nov 1998 to Feb 1999/Grantham Town Mar to cs 1999
Debut as sub v Hull City, Auto Windscreens Shield, (h) 22.12.98, lost 0 – 1

Recommended to the Magpies by their former central defender, Michael Johnson, Jerome showed sufficient promise to earn an extension to his initial monthly contract. Despite being comfortable on the ball he failed to progress at senior level beyond his appearance from the bench in the Auto Windshields Shield first round defeat by Hull City. He played in five matches for Grantham Town in the final stages of season 1998-99.

Appearances: Other: 0(1) app 0 gls Total: 0(1) app 0 gls

SANDERSON, Edgar

Wing-half
b. Elkington, Lincs, 16th March 1874
CAREER: Stoke/ Jarrow/NOTTS Mar 1898
Debut v Liverpool (a) 12.3.1898, lost 0 – 2

A recommendation from the Magpies' outside-left John Fraser brought Edgar Sanderson to County in the same week that Bill Gibson had been transferred to Bristol City. The newcomer played in most of the concluding matches of the season at right half-back. Although said to be a little lacking in experience, he was a very active, hard-working player with dribbling skills not normally associated with a half-back. In the following season he was seriously injured at Stoke in the penultimate fixture of the campaign. He turned out again in the practice matches prior to season 1899-1900 but unfortunately broke down again. As a result of his second injury, his case was taken up by the Player's Union and the FA.

This action following a disagreement over the terms of his contract with Notts. A London specialist advised the FA that he was confident that he could cure Sanderson within ten days if he had the player under treatment and in his care. In the following month the FA ruled that once a club had signed a player they were responsible for his wages, even though injured, so long as the incapacity was incurred in their service. Even though that service (in Sanderson's case) was only in practice for a season yet to be inaugurated. Sadly, the specialist's optimism regarding the player's recovery proved unfounded, as the unfortunate Sanderson had to retire after his knee gave way again when exercising, just prior to Christmas 1899.

Appearances: FL: 34 apps 0 gls FAC: 2 apps 0 gls
Total: 36 apps 0 gls

―――――――――○―――――――――

SANDS, Joseph Irving B

Outside-left   5' 8"   11st 3lbs
b. Nottingham, April quarter 1882
d. Nottingham, July quarter 1960
CAREER: Lawrence Athletic (Nottingham)/NOTTS Jan 1904/Nottingham Forest Nov 1904.
Debut v Sheffield Wednesday (a) 22.2.04, lost 0 – 2

Recruited locally from the Notts. & District League, Sands was given his first run out in a friendly match against the Corinthians in late December 1903. Some two months later he appeared in consecutive Division One fixtures, Ellis Gee switching wings to accommodate the newcomer. Without addition to his senior outings Sands crossed the Trent in November 1904, but did not reach senior level with Forest. In the 1901 Census his occupation was given as a wood carver.

Appearances: FL: 2 apps 0 gls Total: 2 apps 0 gls

―――――――――○―――――――――

SCANLON, John 'Ian'

Outside-left   5' 8"   10st 11lbs
b. Uddingston, Lanarkshire, 13th July 1952
CAREER: Viewpark Boys' Guild/East Stirling/NOTTS July 1972/Aberdeen Apr 1978/St Mirren cs 1981
Debut v Sheffield United, Watney Cup round 1 (a) 29.7.72, lost 0 – 3

Ian Scanlon took some time to establish himself at Meadow Lane, playing little first team football in his first two seasons, in part due to a troublesome leg injury sustained in 1973-74. Dark-haired, quick and direct in style he burst onto the scene in season 1974-75. Leading goalscorer by a very wide margin, his total of 14 in 32 League matches included a hat-trick in two and three-quarter minutes against Sheffield Wednesday at Meadow

Lane on 16th November 1974. Surprisingly, on consulting the record books, it was discovered that his feat had earlier been bettered by Jimmy Scarth of Gillingham who scored a hat-trick in two and a half minutes against Leyton Orient on 1st November 1952. Returning homewards to Scotland, he scored on his debut for Aberdeen at Hibernian on 29th April 1978 and, one week later, made a substitute appearance in the Scottish Cup Final against Rangers. It marked the start of a very successful run at Pittodrie under manager Alex Ferguson, Ian's 130(18) appearances for the Dons including 10(2) in European Cup matches. A severe Achilles tendon injury finished his career at St Mirren, and he then became a Glasgow licensee.

Appearances: FL: 99(12) apps 31 gls FAC: 1 app 0 gls
FLC: 9(1) apps 3 gls Other: 9 apps 1 gl
Total: 118(13) apps 35 gls
Honours: (Aberdeen) Scottish Premier League champions 1980. Scottish Cup finalists 1978. Scottish League Cup finalists 1980

―――――――――○―――――――――

SCOFFHAM, Stephen 'Steve'

Forward   5' 11"   11st 10lbs
b. Germany, 12th July 1983
CAREER: Gedling Town/NOTTS Feb 2004, for an initial fee of £5,000
Debut as sub v Brentford (a) 28.2.2004, won 3 – 2

A historic Notts signing, in that the initial £5,000 down payment for his transfer was provided by the Notts' Supporters' Trust. Recruited from Gedling Town of the Northern Counties East League, Steve left his employment in the building trade to embark on a professional football career. He celebrated his first senior goal, against Grimsby Town, in most spectacular fashion with a forward somersault in front of the fans in the County Road stand. Sadly, however, a broken leg marred the conclusion of his first season. After some eleven months out of the first team picture, Steve was welcomed back against Bristol Rovers in late March, having worked extremely hard to regain full fitness.

Appearances: FL: 7(15) apps 2 gls
Total: 7(15) apps 2 gls

―――――――――○―――――――――

SCULLY, Anthony Derek Thomas 'Tony'

Winger   5' 7"   11st 12lbs
b. Dublin, 12th June 1976
CAREER: Crystal Palace trainee, signing pro Dec 1993 (AFC Bournemouth loan Oct 1994) (Cardiff City loan Jan 1996)/Manchester City Aug 1997, fee £80,000 (Stoke City loan Jan 1998)/Queens Park Rangers Mar 1998, fee £155,000 (Walsall loan Mar 2000)/Cambridge United July 2001 (Southend United loan Nov 2002) (Peterborough

United loan Mar 2003)/Peterborough United Sept 2003/ Dagenham & Redbridge/Barnet/Tamworth/NOTTS Feb 2004 and re-signed May 2004.
Debut v AFC Bournemouth (a) 14.2.2004, lost 0 – 1

On form, a rare handful for any full-back. The stocky wingman's direct style and explosive shooting has produced some memorable goals, none more so than his first long range strike for the Magpies in their 4 – 1 victory against Blackpool in April 2004. His performances in an initial trial period led to a short-term contract, and three goals in six starts and four substitute appearances earned him a further engagement for season 2004-05. Certainly, Tony's League career has been resurrected at Meadow Lane, after he had drifted into non-League football, following a brief spell with Peterborough United. Capped at every level apart from full international, Tony's best spells in the colours of other clubs have occurred with Queens Park Rangers and Cambridge United.

Appearances: FL: 26(16) apps 5 gls FAC: 2(2) apps 1 gl
FLC: 2 apps 0 gls Other: 0(1) app 0 gls
Total: 30(19) apps 6 gls
Honours: Republic of Ireland Schoolboy and Youth International; U-21 International, 10 apps; "B" International 1 app.

———————o———————

SEALS, George
Centre-forward (but played twice as goalkeeper)
b. Radford, Notts, July quarter 1850
CAREER: NOTTS (first appearance Dec 1872 to (final appearance) Mar 1880
Debut v Sheffield, FAC 1, (h) 3.11.1877, drawn 1 – 1

George Seals began with the Magpies in the days when their home matches were played at the Meadows Cricket Ground. In the season prior to his debut (1871-72) only five Notts players had turned up to play against Lincoln, but attitudes were improving by the time he made his debut in 1872-73. In this season the first official international between England and Scotland was contested and a London representative side visited the city to play the Magpies at Trent Bridge. League football was still nine years away when George Seals made his final appearance, as emergency goalkeeper in a 3 – 3 draw against Grey Friars in March 1880. The 1901 Census listed him as a Life Insurance Superintendent.

Appearances: FAC: 4 apps 0 gls Total: 4 apps 0 gls

———————o———————

SEWELL, John 'Jackie'
Inside-forward 5' 8½" 10st 6lbs
b. Kells, near Whitehaven, Cumberland, 24th January 1927
CAREER: Whitehaven Schoolboys/Kells Miner's Welfare U-18/ Whitehaven Town (WW2 guest Carlisle United & Workington)/NOTTS am May 1942, pro Oct 1944/Sheffield Wednesday Mar 1951, fee £34,500, a record at that time/ Aston Villa Dec 1955, fee £18,000/Hull City Oct 1959, fee £5,000/Lusaka City (Zambia) Sept 1961, subsequently coach to Zambia's national team.
Debut v Norwich City (h) 14.9.46, won 3 – 0 (scored one)

In a little over four years Jackie Sewell broke the Magpies individual League scoring record, surpassing Tom Keetley's total of 94. A Major Buckley wartime discovery the former Bevan Boy was a quick thinker and even quicker mover. Possessing plenty of craft and commendable ball control, he was never-theless devoid of fancy tricks and was a supreme opportunist. There is no doubt that his development was greatly assisted by playing alongside the great Tommy Lawton, but it was obvious before the advent of England's centre-forward that Sewell was a special talent, instanced by his record of 21 League goals in 1946-47. He was a star in the FA side that toured Canada in 1950, and towards the close of season 1950-51 Sheffield Wednesday splashed out a record fee of £34,500 to take him to Hillsborough. He was unable to halt Wednesday's downward slide into Division Two, but his contribution of 23 goals in 1951-52 was a vital element in the championship success that returned Wednesday to the top flight. In a little over four years at Hillsborough he won six England caps and toured Australia with the FA. After 175 matches and 92 goals he joined Aston Villa, and though his strike rate declined (40 goals in 144 matches) he added to his already impressive haul of trophies when he collected a winners' medal in the 1957 FA Cup Final against Manchester United. A final move in League circles took him to Hull City (9 goals in 50 matches,) before a coaching appointment in Zambia led to his appointment as coach to their national team. He also coached in Northern Rhodesia before returning to Nottingham where he was employed in car sales.

Appearances: FL: 178 apps 97 gls FAC: 15 apps 7 gls Total: 193 apps 104 gls

Honours: England International, 6 caps 1952-55. FL Representative, 5 apps. (NOTTS) FL Division 3 South champions 1950. (Sheffield Wednesday) FL Division 2 champions 1952 & 1956. (Aston Villa) FA Cup winners 1957

SHARMAN, J
Goalkeeper

CAREER: Beeston Humber/NOTTS Aug 1897 to Oct 1899
Debut v Everton (h) 15.1.1898, won 3 – 2

As understudy to the Magpies England international goalkeeper George Toone, Sharman saw little first team action. His first opportunity came following the suspension of Toone, which came about due to a misunderstanding regarding his request for time off to attend to his new business. A second opportunity was a long time in coming, the 4 – 1 defeat against Aston Villa on 14th October 1899 also being his last. By this time he was a soldier with the Royal Scots, and on the Tuesday following the Villa match he was recalled to the Glencorse Barracks in Edinburgh to prepare for imminent embarkation to South Africa. **Note:** No trace of this player's forename has been found, although the Football League's records confirm the initial "J." It is interesting to note, however, that the 'Football Post' issue of 1st April 1933 published a picture of four Sharman brothers and their father. All the brothers were players with Loughborough Corinthians, while their father – known as "Dick" was said to be a former Notts County player.

Appearances: FL: 2 apps 0 gls Total: 2 apps 0 gls

SHARPE, John William
Outside-left

b. Ruddington, Notts, 9th December 1866
d. Ruddington, Notts, 19th June 1936
CAREER: NOTTS Aug 1889/West Herts.
Debut v Derby County (h) 28.9.1889, lost 0 – 2

John Sharpe was much better known as a cricketer than as a footballer. His father, Samuel Sharpe, also reached County level, playing twice for Nottinghamshire in 1868. John Sharpe played in five matches for Nottinghamshire in 1894, and in 59 matches for Surrey 1889-93. He played in three Test Matches for England and toured Australia in 1891-2. As a right-arm medium fast bowler he took 338 career wickets @ 16.06 with a best performance of 9 for 47 for Surrey against Middlesex at the Oval in 1891.

Appearances: FL: 3 apps 0 gls Total: 3 apps 0 gls

SHAW, Arthur Frederick
Inside-forward

b. Basford, Notts, 1st August 1869
d. Woodborough, Notts, 11th March 1946
CAREER: Notts Rangers/NOTTS am Dec 1888/Nottingham Forest Oct 1889 to Mar 1897/Loughborough June 1897
Debut v Aston Villa (h) 8.12.1888, lost 2 – 4

After playing in four Football League matches for the Magpies as a youthful amateur, Arthur Shaw transferred his allegiance to the Forest. The Reds were operating in the Football Alliance at the time, but after winning the championship of that competition in 1891-92 they were elected to the Football League. Appearing in eight seasons of football with the Forest, Shaw recorded 42 Alliance matches and nine goals and 98 League and Cup matches, fifteen goals. For Loughborough he scored three goals in eleven matches. At the time of his death he was mine host of the Nags Head Inn at Woodborough.

Appearances: FL: 4 apps 0 gls Total: 4 apps 0 gls

SHAW, Thomas Frederick 'Fred'
Inside-forward   5' 9½" 10st 8lbs

b. Hucknall, Notts, 27th March 1909
d. Mansfield, November 1994
CAREER: Annesley Colliery/Norwich City trial Sept 1931/ Darlaston/Birmingham am Sept, pro Oct 1932 (NOTTS loan Dec 1934)/NOTTS Oct 1935/Mansfield Town July 1937/Bournemouth & Boscombe Athletic June 1938/ Ollerton Colliery Aug 1939, retired 1943.
Debut v Swansea Town (h) 29.12.34, won 4 – 0 (scored a hat-trick)

Despite Fred Shaw's outstanding contribution (12 goals in 20 matches including two hat-tricks), the Magpies slide down the Second Division table continued unabated. Signed during the Christmas period, he made an immediate impact when he scored a hat-trick on his debut and his live-wire performances made him a great favourite in an otherwise depressing season. Regret was naturally expressed when he returned to Birmingham at the end of his loan period, but he was welcomed back, on a permanent basis, in October of the new season. Twelve months later he lost his first team place after failing to impress as inside partner to the Magpies star signing, Scottish international centre-forward, Hughie Gallacher. The 'Football Post's' correspondent commented: "I am sorry about Shaw, because he is a hard worker, but all that goes for nought when he is unable to keep the ball under control. With Gallacher leading the line there needs to be inside men with sharpened wits to take full advantage of the Scottish international's astute moves."

Appearances: FL: 56 apps 21 gls FAC: 1 app 0 gls Other: 2 apps 1 gl Total: 59 apps 22 gls

SHELTON, Alfred

Left-half 5' 8½" 11st 7lbs
b. Nottingham, 11th September 1865
d. Nottingham, 24th July 1923
CAREER: St. Nicholas School/Notts Rangers/NOTTS Aug
1888/Loughborough Dec 1896/Ilkeston Town July 1897
Debut v Everton (a) 15.9.1888, lost 1 – 2

Alf Shelton was one of three brothers – Harry and Charlie the others – who did so much for Nottingham football. Alf was educated at St. Nicholas School, which he left to join Notts Rangers. When the club collapsed in 1888 he, along with other members, threw in their lot with the Magpies. A wing half with exceptional stamina, he was a difficult man to pass. He also excelled in headwork, often getting his head in the way of goal-bound shots. He appeared in both of Notts two FA Cup Finals and won six England caps, and in 1892 was offered the opportunity to captain the newly formed Liverpool club. Despite what constituted a most generous offer at the time (£250 per annum) he was not tempted to leave the Magpies. When his playing days were over he became a director of the club, serving from 1900 to 1910. He lost his life in tragic circumstances, killed by a collapsing crane at the works of Cammell Laird in Nottingham.

Appearances: FL: 195 apps 4 gls FAC: 29 apps 1 gl
Other: 10 apps 0 gls Total: 234 apps 5 gls

SHELTON, Charles

Centre-half
b. Nottingham, 22nd January 1864
d. Hampton Hill, Middlesex, 7th February 1951
CAREER: Notts Rangers/NOTTS (first appearance) Dec
1887 to (final appearance) Feb 1892
Debut v Stoke (a) 22.9.1888, lost 0 – 3

A somewhat misleading article in the local press in 1899 quoted Alf Shelton (above) as referring to his brother Charlie "Of blessed memory."

Happily Charlie lived to the ripe old age of 87, so Alf must have been recalling his brothers' footballing skills, not his demise. Certainly Charlie was an outstanding footballer, a robust half-back with infectious enthusiasm, possessing sufficient stamina to carry him through the most gruelling match. His elder brother, Harry, assisted Forest in the 1870s and on the eve of the twentieth century had taken up refereeing.

Appearances: FL: 20 apps 1 gl FAC: 3 apps 1 gl
Total: 23 apps 2 gls
Honours: England International, 1 cap 1888

SHELTON, Gary

Midfield 5' 7" 10st 2lbs
b. Carlton, Nottingham, 21st March 1958
CAREER: St. Bernadette's School/Nottingham Schoolboys (trial with Nottingham Forest)/Walsall app June 1974, pro Mar 1976/Aston Villa Jan 1978, fee £60,000 (NOTTS loan Mar-Apr 1980)/Sheffield Wednesday Mar 1982, fee £50,000/Oxford United July 1987, fee £150,000/Bristol City Aug 1989 (Rochdale loan Feb 1994)/Chester City July 1994
Debut v Bristol Rovers (h) 15.3.80, drawn 0 – 0

Gary Shelton made his League debut as a 17 year-old apprentice on Walsall's left wing, and went on to accumulate in excess of 500 League appearances in the colours of eight different League clubs. As a local boy he had not escaped the attention of the Magpies, but Walsall were the first to offer him an apprenticeship, and they netted a handsome fee when Aston Villa signed him after two years at Fellows Park. Seven goals in 19 First Division matches in 1978-79 included a hat-trick against Arsenal, but at the time of his loan move to Meadow Lane he was out of the first team picture at Villa Park. He enjoyed his best spell with Sheffield Wednesday, assisting the Owls to promotion to the First Division in season 1983-84.

Appearances: FL: 8 apps 0 gls Total: 8 apps 0 gls
Honours: England U-21 International, 1 app 1985 (As over-age representative)

SHEPPERSON, George

Inside-right
CAREER: Nottingham Forest/Northwich Victoria 1892/ NOTTS (first appearance) Mar 1894 to (final appearance) Mar 1896.
Debut v Woolwich Arsenal (a) 24.3.1894, won 2 – 1

One week before the Magpies successful appearance in the FA Cup Final of 1894 – when they beat Bolton Wanderers 4 – 1 – George Shepperson made his debut in the penultimate Division Two fixture of the season.

The 2 – 1 victory against Woolwich Arsenal secured the Magpies' place in the Test Match against Preston North End, but the 4 – 0 defeat condemned them to remain in Division Two. Shepperson remained almost exclusively a reserve team player throughout his career, his five appearances for the Magpies being his only taste of League football.

Appearances: FL: 5 apps 0 gls Total: 5 apps 0 gls

--------------------------------o--------------------------------

SHERIDAN, John

Wing-half   5' 10½"   11st 8lbs
b. Ramsgate, 25th May 1938
CAREER: Linby Colliery/NOTTS July 1955/Hartlepool United July 1966 to 1969/Derby County coach/Brighton & Hove Albion coach/Nottingham Forest coach to Sept 1983/ Lincoln City coach and assistant manager/Shepshed Charterhouse manager 1988.
Debut v Huddersfield Town (h) 14.9.57, drawn 1 – 1

John was still a National Serviceman in his debut season, when the Magpies were relegated from Division Two. His first three seasons were a roller coaster ride, featuring two relegations and one promotion, but he went on to complete over 300 appearances as an exceptionally strong, fast and forceful right-half or inside-forward. He was Notts longest serving player at the time of his transfer to Hartlepool United, where Brian Clough and Peter Taylor gave him the opportunity to start again, following a serious ankle ligament injury. In 1967-68 John played in 34 Division Four matches to assist his team to promotion, for the first time in the club's history. He left during the 1969-70 season, to serve as a coach under Clough and Taylor at Derby County. He also followed the duo to Brighton and Forest, departing the City Ground in September 1983.

Appearances: FL: 287 apps 9 gls FAC: 11 apps 1 gl FLC: 10 apps 2 gls Total: 308 apps 12 gls

--------------------------------o--------------------------------

SHERLOCK, Paul Graeme

Left-back/Midfield   5' 10"   11st 9lbs
b. Wigan, 17th November 1973
CAREER: Newark & Sherwood Schoolboys/ Nottinghamshire Schoolboys/NOTTS trainee July 1990, pro July 1992/Mansfield Town Mar 1995 to June 1997, fee £15,000
Debut v Birmingham City (h) 11.1.94, won 2 – 1

Paul's senior debut came when the club's resources were severely taxed by injuries and suspensions. A regular in the Pontins League Division One, he stepped up to the first team and acquitted himself well, being one of three locally-produced players to take the step up from the reserves (Michael Simpson & Tommy Gallagher also graduating during the season.) An unfamiliar Magpies line-up for his debut against Birmingham City included loan signings Colin Foster (Forest) and John Gannon (Stockport County). Despite opening his goal scoring account with a spectacular strike against Portsmouth on the opening day of the 1994-95 season, he departed to Mansfield Town in March, having added only a further 2(3) League appearances to his total. Paul appeared from the bench for Mansfield in the Play-off semi-final, second leg, against Chesterfield, the eventual winners of the Division Three Final at Wembley. Injuries marred his progress at Field Mill, his record for the Stags being restricted to 29(10) League appearances and two goals.

Appearances: FL: 8(4) apps 1 gl FAC: 2 apps 0 gls FLC: 1 app 0 gls Other: 2(1) apps 0 gls Total: 13(5) apps 1 gl

--------------------------------o--------------------------------

SHERWIN, Mordecai

Goalkeeper
b. Kimberley, Notts, 26th February 1851
d. Nottingham, 3rd July 1910
CAREER: NOTTS (first appearance) Sept 1883 to (final appearance) Dec 1888. Appointed "to help with training" Aug 1890.
Debut v Sheffield Heeley, FAC 1, (h) 10.11.1883, won 3 – 1

'Mordy' Sherwin was an agile and reliable goalkeeper, if somewhat eccentric. Proving that today's over-exuberant celebrations on scoring are nothing new, 'Mordy' was given to treating the spectators behind his goal to a cart-wheeling performance when the Magpies scored! Whether he gave a similar performance in his summer role as a wicket-keeper is not recorded but seems unlikely as he caught 611 and stumped 225 in his career as Nottinghamshire C.C.C. captain and wicket-keeper. He played in three Test Matches for England and toured Australia in 1886-87. In later years he was mine host of the Craven Arms, Woodborough Road, Nottingham.

Appearances: FL: 1 app 0 gls FAC: 19 apps 0 gls Total: 20 apps 0 gls

SHIELS, Dennis Patrick

Inside-forward 5' 8" 11st 1lb
b. Belfast, 24th August 1938
CAREER: Distillery 1956/Sheffield United Dec 1958, along with H. Orr, for a combined fee of £9,000/Peterborough United July 1964, fee £6,000/NOTTS July 1965/Retford Town July 1966/Sligo Rovers Feb 1967
Debut v Stockport County (a) 23.8.65, won 3 – 1 (scored one)

Despite a lengthy association with Sheffield United, Dennis Shiels was afforded few first team opportunities, his best seasonal return coming in 1959-60 when he played in 18 Division Two matches and scored five goals. He joined the Magpies after a season with Peterborough United for whom he scored four goals in 13 League and Cup matches. He began at Meadow Lane alongside a former Sheffield United colleague, 'Doc' Pace, but the promising partnership proved short lived, due to Pace's early season injury. 1965-66 was the first season that the Football League allowed the use of substitutes. The initial ruling allowed only one substitute to be used, and this only to replace an injured player. Dennis Shields became the first Magpie to come off the bench when he replaced Brian Bates after 75 minutes in the Lincoln City match at Meadow Lane on 5th February 1966.

Appearances: FL: 28(1) apps 6 gls FAC: 1 app 0 gls FLC: 1 app 0 gls Total: 30(1) apps 6 gls
Honours: Northern Ireland Amateur International, 1 cap 1958. Northern Ireland 'B' International, 1 app 1960. (Distillery) Ulster Cup winners 1958. County Antrim Shield finalists 1958

SHOOTER, Francis Arthur

Centre-forward
b. Ilkeston, Notts, 21st January 1906
d. Warsop, Notts, 4th January 1980
CAREER: Ilkeston Town/Ransome & Marles/Newark Town/NOTTS Nov1930/Mansfield Town July 1931/Matlock Town
Debut v Luton Town (h) 20.12.30, won 1 – 0

Aptly-named attack leader despite the fact that he failed to find the mark in his two League outings with the Magpies. Attempting to fill the boots of the injured Tom Keetley was never going to be easy, as, at the time of Shooter's debut, County's ace marksman had scored 23 goals in 19 League matches. His total including hat-tricks against Clapton Orient, Newport County and Torquay United, plus a four-goal blast against Fulham. Shooter's second and final outing was on Christmas Day 1930 at Queens Park Rangers. The Magpies were beaten 4 – 1, but one day later, with Keetley restored to the attack, they won the return fixture at Meadow Lane 2 – 0 and eventually clinched the championship of Division Three South.

Appearances: FL: 2 apps 0 gls Total: 2 apps 0 gls

SHORT, Christian Mark

Defender 5' 10" 12st 2lbs
b. Munster, Germany, 9th May 1970
CAREER: Pickering Town/Scarborough July 1988/NOTTS Sept 1990, fee £100,000 (Huddersfield Town loan Dec 1994)/Sheffield United Dec 1995/Stoke City Jul 1998, retired Aug 2000 but returned to play for Scarborough in 2001-02/Hinckley United 2003-04.
Debut as sub v Charlton Athletic (h) 30.10.90, drawn 2 – 2

Born in Germany but raised in North Yorkshire, Chris followed in brother Craig's footsteps, joining Scarborough as an eighteen-year old full-back, and arriving at Meadow Lane two years later. Mainly at right-back his game featured strength in the tackle and dangerous forays down the right wing. Chris was carrying a knee injury when he arrived from Scarborough and it was not until March that he enjoyed an eight-match run in the first team, he did not, however, feature in the Wembley Play-off Final against Brighton. Chris was troubled by a post-viral infection and played little first team football in his final three seasons. He recovered sufficiently to complete a career total of 230(2) League and Cup appearances, which included useful spells with Sheffield United and Stoke City. Chris now runs a sport and leisure centre in York.

Appearances: FL: 77(17) apps 2 gls FAC: 4(1) apps 0 gls FLC: 7 apps 0 gls Other: 10(1) apps 1 gl
Total: 98(19) apps 3 gls
Honours: (NOTTS) Anglo Italian Cup winner 1995

SHORT, Craig Jonathan

Central defender 6' 1" 12st 4lbs
b. Bridlington, 25th June 1968
CAREER: Pickering Town/Scarborough Oct 1987/NOTTS July 1989, fee £100,000/Derby County Sept 1992, fee £2.5million/Everton July 1995, fee £2.7million/Blackburn Rovers Aug 1999, fee £1.7million
Debut v Blackpool (h) 26.8.89, lost 0 – 1

Craig embarked on a lengthy career in League football with Scarborough, making his debut from the bench against Hereford United on 21st October 1987. Scarborough, managed by Neil Warnock, had won the G.M. Vauxhall Conference in the previous season and were contesting their first season in Division Four. In 1988-89 brother Chris (above) joined Craig at The Athletic Ground, but their partnership proved short lived as Craig followed manager Warnock to Meadow Lane in July 1989. A tall, commanding central defender, Craig featured in two promotion triumphs during his three years with the Magpies. He memorably scored against Tranmere Rovers at Wembley in the Play-off Final of season 1989-90 to clinch the 2 – 0 victory, and was at Wembley again, twelve months later, when a 3 – 1 win against Brighton took Notts back to the top flight after an absence of seven years. Derby County set a new transfer record to take him to the Baseball Ground, and he later helped Blackburn Rovers to win promotion to the Premier League in season 2000-01.

Appearances: FL: 128 apps 10 gls FAC: 8 apps 1 gl FLC: 6 apps 1 gl Other: 16 apps 2 gls Total: 158 apps 14 gls

---

SHREWSBURY, Philip

Wing-half
b. Heanor, Derbyshire, 25th March 1947
CAREER: NOTTS ground staff Jan 1964, pro Sept 1965/ Long Eaton Feb 1968
Debut as sub v Port Vale (a) 31.12.66, drawn 0 – 0

Phil Shrewsbury won England Youth caps against Ireland and Scotland in January and February 1965 alongside David Nish (Leicester City) and Colin Suggett (Sunderland). He did not, however, appear in the subsequent International Youth Tournament (won by East Germany), held in West Germany over the Easter period. The local interest in the tournament surrounded 'Bill' Brindley, at that time on Forest's books, who appeared at centre-half in all five matches.

Appearances: FL: 1(1) apps 0 gls Total: 1(1) apps 0 gls
Honours: England Youth International

SHUFFLEBOTTOM, John

Centre-half   5' 9"   11st 6lbs
b. Macclesfield, 11th April 1885
CAREER: Hanley Town 1901-03/Loughborough Corinthians 1903-04 (Aston Villa am 1903-04)/ NOTTS am Sept 1904/Small Heath Mar 1905/Oldham Athletic June 1907/Portsmouth May 1909/Southport Central cs 1911, fee £15
Debut v Bury (h) 5.11.04, lost 0   1

A very promising junior, Jack Shufflebottom was only nineteen when he made his debut as an amateur for the Magpies.

This followed an outstanding season with Loughborough Corinthians, for whom he scored ten goals from centre-half and won medals for the Loughborough Charity Cup and the championship of the Leicestershire League. Among later professional engagements he was a reserve defender with Oldham Athletic in their first two seasons in the Football League, scoring one goal in seven League matches. He found more opportunities with Portsmouth, appearing in 21 Southern League matches, four Cup matches, and scored four goals. By October 1914 he had retired from the game and was working as a timber merchant's agent in the Birmingham district.

Appearances: FL: 1 app 0 gls Total: 1 app 0 gls

SIMCOE, Kenneth Edward

Centre-forward 5' 10" 11st 3lbs
b. Nottingham, 14th February 1937
CAREER: Central Y.M.C.A./Nottingham Forest am season 1955-56, pro Dec 1956/Coventry City May 1959/NOTTS July 1960 to Apr 1961/Heanor Town/Loughborough United cs 1963/Ilkeston Town Dec 1963/Heanor Town July 1964; retired due to knee injury Feb 1967
Debut v Queens Park Rangers (a) 29.8.60, lost 0 – 2

Ken Simcoe scored 14 goals in 22 matches for Forest's Football Combination side in 1958-59, but he played only twice at League level, leaving after undergoing a cartilage operation, shortly after the 1959 FA Cup Final against Luton Town. He did a little better with Coventry City (Eight matches, one goal in the Third Division South). He was never likely to challenge his best friend Tony Hateley as attack leader at Meadow Lane, but scored 36 goals for the reserve team. Ken subsequently prospered in non-League circles, particularly during separate spells with Heanor Town, where his tally of goals was approaching the 200 mark when a knee ligament injury curtailed his career. Despite having missed the boat in terms of a first class career in football, there cannot have been too many locally born men with the proud record of having worn both the red and the black-and-white shirt in League football.

Appearances: FL: 2 apps 0 gls Total: 2 apps 0 gls

SIMPSON, Alexander

Wing-half   5' 10"   11st 11lbs
b. Glasgow, 24th November 1924
CAREER: Benburb (Glasgow)/Wolverhampton Wanderers Jan 1947/NOTTS Oct 1949, fee £7,500/Southampton Nov 1952, in part exchange for Jack Edwards/Shrewsbury Town July 1955/Nuneaton Borough July 1958
Debut v Rochdale, FAC 2, 10.12.49 (a) won 2 – 1

When figuring regularly in the Wolves Reserve side Alex Simpson requested a transfer to a Scottish Club. He was rarely called upon at senior level at Molineux and had set his heart on a return to Scotland, planning to make progress in his original profession as a weights and measures inspector. Approaches from Airdrie and Third Lanark were rejected by the Wolves and a £12,000 offer from Preston North End was similarly turned down. Proof that things do not always work out as planned came when Notts stepped in with an offer and both the Wolves and player gave assent. With the benefit of regular first team football Alex quickly developed into a strong, forceful centre or wing-half with a perfect sense of ball control. He made his Magpies debut, replacing the injured Bill Baxter, on a snow covered pitch at Spotland, Rochdale, before a crowd of 24,231, an all-time record attendance for the ground. In a rousing cup-tie played in difficult conditions, Simpson won praise from the 'Football Post' whose reporter commented: "Simpson has a stamp of class about him and never wasted a ball, but always tried to use it to advantage." After leaving Meadow Lane he captained Southampton, completing 68 League appearances before joining Shrewsbury Town on a free transfer in the summer of 1955. He played in exactly 100 League matches for the Shrews, taking his final career aggregate figures to 244 League matches and 11 goals.

Appearances: FL: 74 apps 6 gls FAC: 2 apps 1 gl
Total: 76 apps 7 gls
Honours: (NOTTS) FL Division 3 South champions 1950

----------------o----------------

SIMPSON, Michael

Midfield   5' 9"   10st 8lbs
b. Nottingham, 28th February 1974
CAREER: Alderman Derbyshire School (Bulwell)/ Nottingham Schoolboys/Nottinghamshire Schoolboys at U-15 & U-16 levels/Nottingham Forest associate schoolboy/ NOTTS associate schoolboy Feb 1990, trainee July 1990, pro July 1992 (Plymouth Argyle loan Oct 1996)/Wycombe Wanderers Dec 1996, fee £50,000/Leyton Orient July 2004.
Debut as sub v Hull City, FLC 1 (a) 24.8.93, lost 1 – 3

Locally-born midfielder with a high work-rate and good attacking ideas, both from open play and free kicks and corners. Michael had a lengthy association with Forest as a schoolboy, but when they failed to offer him a Y.T.S. place he joined Notts. He announced his arrival at senior level as a nineteen year-old with an excellent debut performance in League football in the 1 – 0 victory against Sunderland on 28th August 1993. In the following week he opened his goal scoring account with a spectacular long-range volley at Tranmere Rovers. He subsequently enjoyed a lengthy spell as captain of Wycombe Wanderers (326 League matches, including substitute appearances, and 21 goals.)

Released following their relegation in 2004, he was quickly fixed up with Leyton Orient. In October 2004 he returned to Meadow Lane, and with a typically busy display assisted his team to come from behind to secure a 2 – 1 victory.

Appearances: FL: 39(10) apps 3 gls FAC: 2(1) apps 0 gls
FLC: 4(1) apps 0 gls Other: 7(3) apps 0 gls
Total: 52(15) apps 3 gls
Honours: (NOTTS) Anglo Italian Cup winners 1995

----------------o----------------

SIMPSON, Thomas

Outside-left   5' 9"   10st 3lbs
b. Keyworth, Notts, July quarter 1877
d. Oldham, Lancs, 19th December 1961
CAREER: Keyworth F.C. 1893/NOTTS Jan 1899/Leicester Fosse Oct 1902/Everton May 1903, in exchange for John Barlow plus a fee of £175/Nelson Sept 1904
Debut v Burnley (a) 3.3.1900, lost 0 – 3

While working as a framework-knitter Tom Simpson commenced in football at sixteen with his local team, Keyworth F.C., members of the Nottinghamshire Amateur League. Coming to the attention of the Magpies, he was first tried at outside-left in the Reserves and after a satisfactory debut against Arnold was quickly signed as a professional. Lacking opportunities during a lengthy spell as understudy to Ellis Gee, he enjoyed his best season in football with Leicester Fosse, appearing in 27 League matches and scoring five goals. His subsequent move to Everton proved unrewarding as he was again cast in the role of understudy, on this occasion to Harold Hardman the celebrated England Amateur international outside-left. In summer months Tom Simpson played cricket as a left-handed batsman and left-arm medium paced bowler. He reached County level with Nottinghamshire (five matches, 1903-05) and also played in Minor Counties cricket with Cheshire.

Appearances: FL: 7 apps 0 gls Total: 7 apps 0 gls

----------------o----------------

SIMS, John

Forward   5' 11"   12st 6lbs
b. Belper, Derbyshire, 4th August 1952
CAREER: Derby County app, signing pro Aug 1970 (Luton Town loan Nov 1973) (Oxford United loan Sept 1974) (Colchester United loan Jan 1975)/NOTTS Dec 1975, fee £10,000/Exeter City Dec 1978/Plymouth Argyle Oct 1979, fee £22,000/Torquay United Aug 1983/Exeter City Feb 1984/Torquay United player-coach Nov 1984, manager Aug-Sept 1985/Saltash United 1985/Waldon Athletic player-manager
Debut v Charlton Athletic (h) 20.12.75, won 2 – 0 (scored one)

In a span approaching seven years John Sims played in only 2(1) League matches for Derby County.

But amongst other appearances for the Rams was a substitute outing in the semi-final of the European Cup against Juventus. His move to Meadow Lane in December 1975 gave him his first taste of regular League football, and despite the relatively late start he went on to record career figures of 323(22) League matches and 86 goals. Heavily built and not the quickest of attack leaders his qualities were those of a target man with the ability to control, shield, and lay off the ball. He also won most aerial encounters. After leaving Notts he assisted all three of Devon's professional clubs and was very briefly manager of Torquay United, who dismissed him after two months of season 1985-86, following a record of one win and eight defeats in their first nine League matches.

Appearances: FL: 48(13) apps 13 gls FAC: 1 app 0 gls FLC: 4 apps 1 gl Other: 7(1) apps 3 gls
Total: 60(14) apps 17 gls

SIMS, Steven Frank

Centre-half   6' 1"   13st 9lbs
b. Lincoln, 2nd July 1957
CAREER: Lincoln Schoolboys/Lincoln United/Leicester City app Aug 1973, pro July 1974/Watford Dec 1978, fee £175,000/NOTTS Sept 1984, fee £50,000/Watford Oct 1986, fee £50,000/Aston Villa June 1987, fee £40,000/ Burton Albion Sept 1990/Lincoln City nc Oct 1990/AFC Bournemouth nc Feb 1991/Boston assistant-manager cs 1991/Port Vale coach 1991/Stafford Rangers nc Dec 1991/ Shepshed Albion Jan 1992/Aston Villa football in the community officer 1992/Coventry City youth development officer July 1994/Leicester City youth development officer Oct 1996
Debut v Middlesbrough (h) 8.9.84, won 3 – 2

The son of a former Lincoln City centre-half, the Imps missed out on Steve although he did make a handful of appearances for them at the end of his senior career. A formidable defensive pivot and long-throw specialist, he made his League debut with Leicester City in August 1975 and completed 86(1) matches, scoring three goals, before his £175,000 transfer to Watford. A key member of the Hornets' rapid ascent, he enjoyed two seasons in Division One, which included the 1982-83 term when they finished runners-up for the League championship. By complete contrast, his first season with the Magpies ended in relegation to Division Three, and he returned to Watford, and First Division football, in October 1986. His second spell at Vicarage Road ended when his former manager, Graham Taylor, took him to Aston Villa and in his first season he helped Villa to promotion from Division Two as runners-up to Millwall for the title. Steve's career in League football ended painfully when he suffered a broken jaw in his fifth match with his hometown club, Lincoln City. His career aggregate figures totalled 378(3) League appearances and 13 goals.

Appearances: FL: 85 apps 5 gls FAC: 7 apps 0 gls FLC: 9 apps 1 gl Other: 3 apps 0 gls Total: 104 apps 6 gld
Honours: England U-21 International, 10 apps. England 'B' International, 1 app

---

SISSON, Thomas

Left-back   5' 10"   12st 0lbs
b. Basford, Notts, 19th October 1894
d. Nottingham, 11th August 1976, age 81
CAREER: Players Athletic, Nottingham/NOTTS am Apr 1914/Hucknall Byron Nov 1919/Gillingham July 1920/ Barrow trial Nov 1923/Lincoln City Dec 1923/ Peterborough & Fletton United cs 1926/Sutton Town July 1927
Debut v Everton (h) 14.11.14, drawn 0 – 0

Spotted in local junior football, Tom Sisson was considered an excellent prospect and was signed after trials. Before the outbreak of WW1 he had deputised at left-back for Alf West in three First Division matches. He was back in non-League football at the end of hostilities but was signed by Gillingham in 1920 and made 73 Southern League appearances. A trial spanning two League matches and one FA Cup outing with Barrow did not lead to a permanent contract, but a similar trial with Lincoln City proved more successful. Appearing in both full-back berths, at left-half and even at centre-forward, he played in 75 League matches and scored one goal. In May 1925 he obtained a professional contract with the Lindum Cricket Club at Boston.

Appearances: FL: 3 apps 0 gls Total: 3 apps 0 gls

SISSONS, Henry Peter

Inside-left
b. Worksop, April quarter 1874
d. Kilton Hill, Worksop, 8th February 1961
CAREER: Burton Swifts/Worksop Town/NOTTS Jan 1894/ Mansfield Town
Debut v Derby County (Test Match) 27.4.1895, lost 1 – 2

When a Second Division of the Football League was inaugurated for season 1892-93, automatic promotion and relegation was still five years away. A system of 'Test Matches' – not dissimilar to today's play-offs – was introduced. Considering the brevity of the system, Notts were involved on four occasions. They were relegated after losing to Darwen in 1893, and failed to gain promotion from Division Two after losing to Preston North End in 1894 and Derby County in 1895. For the latter game, played at Filbert Street, Leicester, the injury-hit Magpies fielded Henry Sissons, a former Burton Swifts and Worksop Town player, at inside-left. Two years later Notts finished top of Division Two and won the Test Match series against Sunderland and Burnley to regain their top-flight status.

Appearances: Other: 1 app 0 gls Total: 1 app 0 gls

SLAWSON, Stephen Michael

Forward   6' 0"   12st 6lbs
b. Nottingham, 13th November 1972
CAREER: NOTTS trainee July 1989, pro July 1991
(Burnley loan Feb 1993) (Shrewsbury Town loan Oct 1994)/
Mansfield Town July 1995/Rotherham United July 1996/
Kettering Town Jan 1997
Debut as sub v Sheffield United, Zenith Data Systems Cup
2, (a) 22.10.91, drawn 3 – 3 (scored one goal)

A member of the Magpies all-conquering youth team who
won the League and Cup double in season 1990-91, Steve
Slawson was still a month away from his 19th birthday
when he earned his first chance at senior level. The fact
that he departed to Mansfield Town on a free transfer
after four years as a professional at Meadow Lane was a
disappointing outcome. He possessed youth, physique,
and lots of early potential, but was hampered by a serious
knee ligament injury that sidelined him for almost a year.

Appearances: FL: 16(22) apps 4 gls FAC: 0(3) apps 0 gls
FLC: 1(1) apps 0 gls Other: 3(4) apps 1 gl
Total: 20(30) apps 5 gls

SMALLEY, Paul Thomas

Right-back   5' 11"   11st 0lbs
b. Nottingham, 17th November 1966
CAREER: South Notts. Schoolboys/Nottinghamshire
Schoolboys/ NOTTS app, signing pro Nov 1984/Scunthorpe
United Sept 1988 (Blackpool loan Oct 1990)/Leeds United
nc Dec 1990/Doncaster Rovers nc Mar to cs 1991/New
Zealand FA director of football/Sutton Town/Hucknall Town
player-coach Aug 1992
Debut as sub v Doncaster Rovers, FLC 1, (h) 20.8.85, won
1 – 0

Paul represented England U-16 as a central defender
against Switzerland and Hungary in July 1983. Two years
later he made his first senior appearance for the Magpies
and in November 1985 embarked on lengthy run of first
team action at right-back, following injury to the long-
serving Pedro Richards. After an ever-present record in
League matches for the following two seasons, he was
similarly consistent in recording exactly 100 League and
Cup during his spell with Scunthorpe United. He also
scored his only goal in League football, in the 3 – 3 draw
against Darlington at the Feethams on 3rd December 1988.
Scunthorpe finished fourth in Division Four in the same
season, but lost in the Play-off semi-finals by an aggregate
score of 1 – 5 against Wrexham.

Appearances: FL: 113(5) apps 0 gls FAC: 10 apps 0 gls
FLC: 3(1) apps 0 gls Other: 11(1) apps 0 gls
Total: 137(7) apps 0 gls
Honours: England Youth International, 2 apps 1983

SMITH, Albert

Right-half
b. Nottingham, 23rd July 1869
d. Nottingham, 18th April 1921
CAREER: Notts. Rangers/Long Eaton Rangers/Derby
County 1884/Nottingham Forest Oct 1888/NOTTS Feb
1890/Nottingham Forest again later in 1890/Blackburn
Rovers Nov 1891/Nottingham Forest for a third spell early
1892; retired April 1894
Debut v Blackburn Rovers (h) 18.2.1890, drawn 1 – 1

In contrast to his fleeting association with the Magpies,
Albert Smith had three separate spells with the Forest,
assisting them to win the championship of the Football
Alliance in season 1891-92. An amateur throughout his
career, the Nottingham boot factor was described in 1893
as "One of the most forcible half-backs. Always working,
and is a heavy but fair tackler." Albert was capped three
times by England whilst on Forest's books, appearing
against Scotland, Wales and Ireland.

Appearances: FL: 4 apps 0 gls Total: 4 apps 0 gls
Honours: England International, 3 caps 1891-93.
(Nottingham Forest) Football Alliance champions 1892

SMITH, David Alan

Winger 5' 10"   11st 4lbs
b. Sidcup, Kent, 25th June 1961
CARRER: Charlton Athletic associate schoolboy/Orpington
Eagles, Welling 1981/Welling United/Dartford/Welling
United Dec 1984/Oxford United trial/Gillingham Aug 1986,
fee £3,000/Bristol City July 1989, fee £75,000/Plymouth
Argyle Dec 1991, fee £200,000/NOTTS July 1992, fee
£150,000; retired due to knee injury Apr 1994 and emigrated
to Norway.
Debut v Birmingham City (a) 16.8.92, lost 0 – 1

A late starter in League football, Dave Smith made his
debut with Gillingham at 25 years of age. He had resigned
his employment with HM Stationery Office, and taken a
substantial reduction in salary – said to be in the region of
£100 per week - in order to fulfil his ambition to play in
senior football. A skilful winger, able to occupy either
flank, he had an excellent first season at Meadow Lane,
winning the 'Player of the Year' award. Sadly, a serious
knee injury required an operation in the close season and
he was never sufficiently recovered to resume at senior
level. He moved with his family to Norway, where he
opened a fitness centre.

Appearances: FL: 37 apps 8 gls FAC: 1 app 0 gls FLC: 2
apps 0 gls Other: 2 apps 0 gls Total: 42 apps 8 gls

SMITH, David Frederick

Midfield   5' 5"   10st 6lbs
b. Nottingham, 11th March 1956
CAREER: NOTTS app, signing pro Mar 1974/Torquay
United June 1979, contract cancelled Jan 1981
Debut v Sunderland (h) 3.4.76, drawn 0 – 0

"Diminutive, but brave and industrious" commented the 'Post Annual' for season 1974-75, when David was still an apprentice and waiting for his chance at first team level. One of the smallest men in the game during his career, he played regularly in Division Two during season 1976-77, but much less frequently following Jimmy Sirrel's second spell in charge, from October 1975. David's first class career wound up with Torquay United, and in 1984 he was reported to be running a local side in Torquay. Twelve months later he was managing a hostelry on the Devon coast.

Appearances: FL: 45(5) apps 0 gls FAC: 2 apps 0 gls
FLC: 5 apps 0 gls Other: 6 apps 1 gl
Total: 58(5) apps 1 gl

SMITH, David Wilson

Right-half   5' 11"   14st 0lbs
b. Lochgelly, 7th July 1875
d. Middlesbrough, 23rd January 1947, age 71
CAREER: Lochgelly United 1891-92/Cowdenbeath 1893-94/Lochgelly United 1894-95/Bolton Wanderers Feb 1896/Third Lanark trial 4 Sept 1897/Grimsby Town trial 26 Sept 1897/Chatham Oct 1897/Millwall Athletic May 1899/NOTTS May 1900/Middlesbrough Dec 1900 to 1905, subsequently a club director.
Debut v Sunderland (h) 1.9.00, drawn 2 – 2

The 'Football News' of August 1900, commenting on Smith's performance in the pre-season practice match, stated: "The former Millwall captain is a broadly-built, burly fellow who though not quite so nimble as could be desired is capable of performing very creditably." For a player who had led the Millwall team, who sensationally reached the semi-final of the FA Cup in season 1899-1900, his lack of success with the Magpies was a disappointment. Having lost his place after appearing in the opening two matches of the season he was unable to regain it as the team enjoyed their best-ever season in the top flight, finishing in third position in the table. He enjoyed much greater success after moving to Middlesbrough, captaining the side to promotion in 1902 and completing 114 League and Cup appearances and scoring 12 goals before retiring. He became a successful businessman and served as a Middlesbrough director and vice-chairman. During World War One he was interned in Germany.

Appearances: FL: 5 apps 0 gls Total: 5 apps 0 gls

SMITH, George

Right-back   5' 11"   12st 2lbs
b. Glasgow 20th May 1901
CAREER: Strathclyde/NOTTS June 1924/West Ham United June 1928
Debut v Bury (h) 28.2.25, drawn 1 – 1

George Smith attracted the attention of Notts' scouts whilst representing Scotland in a junior international match against Ireland, and on the strength of his performance was signed from Strathclyde. Fearless and resourceful, he deputised most successfully for Ashurst in nine League matches in his first season at Meadow Lane. He injured an ankle so badly in the practice match preceding season 1925-26 that he was unable to kick a ball for half of the season and when recovered appeared to have lost some of his speed off the mark. Ironically, his best season in terms of first team action – 38 League games in 1927-28 – proved to be his last. Moving in the close season to West Ham United, he failed to win a first team place.

Appearances: FL: 83 apps 0 gls FAC: 3 apps 0 gls
Total: 86 apps 0 gls
Honours: Scotland Junior International, 1 app 1923

SMITH, George Henry

Goalkeeper   5' 11½"   12st 8lbs
b. Nottingham, 13th April 1936
CAREER: St. Bernadette's School/Dale Rovers/NOTTS, initially on am forms, July 1953/Hartlepool United July 1967/Arnold 1970.
Debut v Lincoln City (a) 26.11.55, lost 0 – 2

George Smith first played soccer as an outside-right for his school team, and switched to goalkeeping with Dale Rovers in an emergency, when the regular 'keeper failed to turn up. He never played anywhere else subsequently. As a youthful Magpies' fan he was a regular spectator behind the goals, always looking for tips to improve his own performance.

He was signed by Notts in 1953, just prior to his call-up for National Service with the R.A.F., and gained useful experience in representative football in Germany. He establish himself as first choice in 1959-60, a term in which the Magpies won promotion from Division Four. A goalkeeper with a good sense of anticipation and particularly clean ball handling skills, he played in every match during the successful campaign, and repeated the feat in 1960-61. Injury ended the sequence in September 1961after 102 consecutive appearances. He was the first winner of the 'Player of the Year' award, presented by the Supporter's Club in season 1964-65. After an exemplary fourteen years of service he joined Hartlepool United and helped them win promotion in his first season at the Victoria Ground with a third place finish in Division Four. Sadly, they were relegated in the following season and in his final term they had to apply for re-election after finishing 23rd in Division Four. After retiring from the game George and his family emigrated to Perth, Australia.

Appearances: FL: 323 apps 0 gls FAC: 15 apps 0 gls FLC: 14 apps 0 gls Total: 352 apps 0 gls

---

SMITH, Graham William Charles

Goalkeeper   5' 11"   12st 0lbs
b. Liverpool, 2nd November 1947
CAREER: England Grammar Schools/Tranmere Rovers am/ Liverpool am/Loughborough College/Loughborough United/ NOTTS Aug 1968, fee £1,000/Colchester United June 1969/ West Bromwich Albion Dec 1971/Cambridge United Jan 1973, retired June 1976 due to back injury.
Debut v Aldershot (h) 31.8.68, lost 0 – 2

A physical training student at Loughborough College, Graham Smith gained Midland League experience with Loughborough United before joining the Magpies. After a season spent mainly in reserve at Meadow Lane, he joined Colchester United and was destined to be a key player in the shock result of season 1970-71: Colchester United (of Division Four) 3, Leeds United (of Division One) 2, in the fifth round of the FA Cup. Later in the same year he earned an upward move to West Bromwich Albion. This followed an outstanding performance for Colchester United against the Baggies in the pre-season Watney Cup competition of July and August 1971. Colchester took the trophy after drawing 4 – 4 against W.B.A. in the final, going on to win the penalty shoot out by 4 – 3. A final move in League circles took him to Cambridge United where he assisted them to promotion from Division Four in his first season at the Abbey Stadium. When his playing days were brought to a premature end by a serious back injury, he worked in sports management, and in 1992 was instrumental in bringing goalkeeper Bob Catlin to Meadow Lane.

Appearances: FL: 10 apps 0 gls Total: 10 apps 0 gls

SMITH, Harold Roberts

Centre-half   6' 0"   11st 13lbs
b. Watford, 12th March 1907
d. Peterborough, October quarter 1979
CAREER: Wealdstone/NOTTS Nov 1930/Cardiff City July 1935 to 1937
Debut v Crystal Palace (h) 6.12.30, drawn 2 – 2

Just a fortnight before his debut for the Magpies, Harold Smith was working as a railway porter at Harrow. He joined Notts from Wealdstone of the Athenian League and immediately took over the centre-half berth from Frank Froggatt. Smith lost his place to the Scottish international George Walker in 1933-34 but quickly adjusted to the role of wing-half. He remained in this position following his transfer to Cardiff City, making 53 League appearances (three goals) in two seasons at Ninian Park.

Appearances: FL: 117 apps 0 gls FAC: 5 apps 0 gls Total: 122 apps 0 gls

---

SMITH, James Terence

Centre-forward 5' 11" 12st 7lbs
b. Old Kilpatrick, Dunbartonshire, 12th March 1902
d. Bridgepoint, USA, 1975
CAREER: Dumbarton Harp Juniors/Clydebank July 1925/ Glasgow Rangers Apr 1926/Ayr United May 1927/Liverpool Sept 1929, fee £5,500/Tunbridge Wells Rangers July 1932/ Bristol Rovers May 1933/Newport County May 1935/ NOTTS June 1936/Dumbarton player-manager Aug, manager Jan 1939, director June 1941 to 1943
Debut v Exeter City (h) 29.8.36, won 3 – 1

After four matches and one goal for the Magpies at the commencement of season 1936-37, Jim Smith was dropped. Later in the same month, he was replaced by another Scottish centre-forward in the shape of the celebrated Hughie Gallacher. Earlier in his career Smith had hit the headlines with a remarkable 66 goals in Ayr United's runaway championship season of 1927-28 – a British seasonal scoring record. In all matches, including cup ties and friendlies, his total for the season was 72. He retained his goal touch with Liverpool with 38 in 61 League matches, and in his spell in Division Three South added a further 24 in 59 matches. Smith later emigrated to America and settled at Bridgepoint, some sixty miles from New York.

Appearances: FL: 4 apps 1 gl Total: 4 apps 1 gl
Honours: (Ayr United) Scottish League Division 2 champions 1928. Smith is holder of the British seasonal goal scoring record with 66 goals in Ayr's championship season, 1927-28.

SMITH, John 'Jack'

Forward   5' 11"   12st 0lbs
b. West Hartlepool, 24th April 1936
CAREER: Hartlepools United pro May 1953/Watford July 1960, fee £3,000/Swindon Town June 1961/Brighton & Hove Albion Jan 1964, fee £6,000/NOTTS Sept 1966, fee £5,000/Margate Dec 1968/Ramsgate Athletic player-manager 1971/Bath City manager/Portsmouth youth team coach
Debut v York City (a) 16.9.66, lost 1 – 4

Jack Smith joined a Magpies team in deep trouble in September 1966. Defeats in his first two matches stretched a dismal run to nine matches without a win, and the season ended with the side in 20th place in Division Four. Despite a return of eight goals in 32 League matches his form was at times disappointing, and in mid season he was given additional responsibilities as youth team coach, suggesting that his playing career was drawing to a close. In the event, he remained a first team squad member, more increasingly used in defensive roles. A spate of new signings in 1968-69, including Masson, Worthington, Butlin and Stubbs, necessitated a pruning of staff, a club skipper Jack Smith was allowed to move to Margate. In 398(4) League appearances overall, he scored 139 goals, his total including 17 in 35 League matches in Brighton's Division Four championship side in 1964-65.

Appearances: FL: 74(4) apps 12 gls FAC: 2 apps 0 gls FLC: 3 apps 0 gls Total: 79(4) apps 12 gls
Honours: (Brighton & Hove Albion) FL Division 4 champions 1965

SMITH, Joseph William "Jack"

Right-half   5' 10"   11st 8lbs
b. Blackheath, Worcs.
CAREER: Halesowen Town/Aston Villa May 1925/Halesowen Town/Barnsley July 1928/NOTTS July 1932, in exchange for H. Andrews/Scunthorpe United trial Aug 1933
Debut v Bradford City (h) 24.9.32, won 2 – 0

Jack Smith had failed to reach senior level with Aston Villa, but he spent four seasons as a regular performer for Barnsley, accumulating 124 League and Cup appearances and scoring one goal. He left Oakwell in the summer of 1928 following Barnsley's relegation from Division Two – the first time in the club's history that it had suffered a demotion. He arrived at Meadow Lane in an exchange deal that took Harold Andrews to Barnsley, and there is little doubt that the Yorkshire side had the better bargain. While Jack Smith failed to hold down a first team place during his season with the Magpies, Andrews scored 42 goals in 110 League matches for Barnsley, and starred in their 1933-34 Third Division North championship side.

Appearances: FL: 23 apps 1 gl FAC: 1 app 0 gls
Total: 24 apps 1 gl

SMITH, Keith Wilson

Half-back/Full-back   5' 9"   10st 10lbs
b. Woodville, Derbyshire 15th September 1940
CAREER: Ashby Grammar School/Coalville Schoolboys/West Bromwich Albion am Apr 1957, pro Jan 1958/Peterborough United June 1963, in exchange for T. Simpson/Crystal Palace Nov 1964, fee £12,000/Darlington Nov 1966/Leyton Orient May 1967/NOTTS July 1967/Kidderminster Harriers Aug 1970/Tamworth 1971/Bromsgrove Rovers player-manager 1972, retired 1975
Debut v Chester (h) 19.8.67, lost 1 – 2

In his first season at Meadow lane Keith Smith missed only one first team match. Beginning at inside-left, he subsequently moved to left-half, finally settling at left-back, partnering Geoff Ball and Mick Cartwright. In a disappointing season that ended with a final placing of 17th in Division Four, Keith was undoubtedly the most consistent performer and deserved recipient of the 'Player of the Year' award. Injuries disrupted his final two seasons, he nevertheless completed just four short of a century of appearances in his three years with the club. In earlier days a centre-forward, Keith scored 30 goals in 63 League matches for West Bromwich Albion and 28 in 55 matches for Peterborough United. His aggregate career figures were 270(7) League appearances and 81 goals. Keith subsequently spent twelve years as promotions manager at Aston Villa and later joined the West Midlands Police force.

Appearances: FL: 85(4) apps 7 gls FAC: 3 apps 0 gls FLC: 4 apps 0 gls Total: 92(4) apps 7 gls

---

SMITH, Mark Craig

Central defender   6' 2"   13st 11lbs
b. Sheffield, 21st March 1960
CAREER: Sheffield Schoolboys/Sheffield Wednesday from school in 1976, signing pro Mar 1978/Plymouth Argyle July 1987, fee £170,000/Barnsley Nov 1989, fee £145,000/NOTTS Oct 1992, fee £70,000 (Port Vale loan Jan 1993) (Huddersfield Town loan Feb 1993) (Chesterfield loan Mar 1993)/Lincoln City Aug 1993, player-coach Mar 1994, youth team coach cs 1994/NOTTS reserve team coach 1997-98/Barnsley coach/Sheffield Wednesday U-19 Academy coach cs 2003
Debut v Bristol Rovers (h) 3.10.92, drawn 3 – 3

Mark Smith appeared in ten seasons of football with Sheffield Wednesday, assisting them to promotion from Division Three in 1979-80, and into the top flight in 1983-84. Captain for many seasons, he was awarded a testimonial in 1986. He completed 351(1) League and Cup matches for the Owls and scored 20 goals. Spells with Plymouth Argyle and Barnsley preceded his move to Meadow Lane, when his career aggregate of League games alone was little short of 500 matches.

He joined a side in deep trouble in the league and with almost half of the professional playing staff on the casualty list. As results failed to improve, manager Warnock and assistant Jones were sacked. Team affairs were taken over by Mick Walker, initially on a temporary basis, and he immediately took steps to trim staff and reduce the average age of the team. Mark Smith spent the remainder of the season out on loan and joined Lincoln City on a free transfer in the close season.

Appearances: FL: 4(1) apps 0 gls Total: 4(1) apps 0 gls
Honours: England U-21 International, 5 apps

SMITH, Royston L. 'Roy'

Goalkeeper   5' 10½"   11st 9lbs
b. Shirebrook, 22nd September 1916
CAREER: Selby Town/Sheffield Wednesday Feb 1936/NOTTS Dec 1948 to 1953
Debut v Torquay United (h) 18.12.48, won 5 – 0

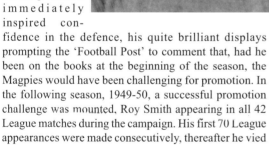

Roy Smith, in common with many of his generation, lost a lengthy spell of his career due to the war. Prior to the conflict he had appeared in 45 League and Cup matches for Sheffield Wednesday, followed by a further 52 in peacetime football. At Meadow Lane he proved a worthy successor to Harry Brown. The prematurely balding Smith immediately inspired confidence in the defence, his quite brilliant displays prompting the 'Football Post' to comment that, had he been on the books at the beginning of the season, the Magpies would have been challenging for promotion. In the following season, 1949-50, a successful promotion challenge was mounted, Roy Smith appearing in all 42 League matches during the campaign. His first 70 League appearances were made consecutively, thereafter he vied with Gordon Bradley for the first team jersey.

Appearances: FL: 110 apps 0 gls FAC: 5 apps 0 gls
Total: 115 apps 0 gls
Honours: (NOTTS) FL Division 3 South champions 1950

SMITH, Stuart George

Outside-right
b. Lenton, Nottingham, October quarter 1858
b. CAREER: NOTTS (first appearance) Oct 1882 to (final appearance) Nov 1983
Debut v Sheffield, FAC 1, (h) 4.11.1881, won 6 – 1 (Scored one)

Stuart Smith played regularly in season 1882-83, scoring nine goals in 16 friendly matches in addition to two goals in five FA Cup ties, which included an appearance in the semi-final at Kennington Oval, lost 1 – 2 to Old Etonians. Switched to inside-right in the following season he was less successful, disappearing from the scene in November after playing in six friendlies (one goal) and the first round of the FA Cup against Sheffield Heeley.

Appearances: FAC: 6 apps 2 gls Total: 6 apps 2 gls

SMITH, Walter

Centre-forward
CAREER: South Liverpool/NOTTS Mar-Apr 1900
Debut v Glossop (h) 24.3.00, drawn 0 – 0

Three months into the twentieth century Walter Smith left Dingle Park, the home of South Liverpool F.C., for a short-term engagement with the Magpies. He joined a club in trouble at the wrong end of Division One, and failed to impress in two outings as deputy for Joe McMain. A business in Kettering was occupying much of McMain's attention and he left in the close season to join Kettering Town. Notts' directors did not offer Walter Smith a contract, but four new forward recruits included William Ross from Reading, who capably filled the centre-forward position for the following three seasons.

Appearances: FL: 2 apps 0 gls Total: 2 apps 0 gls

SMITH, William Alfred

Full-back   5' 11"   12st 6lbs
b. Corsham, Wilts, 22th September 1900
d. Trowbridge, January 1990
CAREER: Corsham F.C./Bath City/NOTTS Feb 1923, fee £300/West Ham United May 1927-28
Debut v West Ham United (h) 1.3.24, drawn 1 - 1

A full-back built on generous lines, resolute in the tackle and with a powerful kick. He made his name as one of the most reliable defenders in the Southern League with Bath City. Despite a lack of speed he had all other necessary qualifications, and was a sure penalty kicker. Ashurst and Cope were the Magpies' first team backs, and Smith had to wait patiently for an extended run in the seniors, his best seasonal return coming in 1926-27 when he played in 21 Division Two matches and scored three goals. He appeared only twice for West Ham United in 1927-28.

Appearances: FL: 41 apps 4 gls FAC: 4 apps 0 gls
Total: 45 apps 4 gls

SMITH, William 'Tich'
Inside/Outside-right   5' 6"   12st 4lbs
b. Sawley, Derbyshire, 10th November 1868
d. Nottingham, 27th September 1907
CAREER: Long Eaton Rangers (Derby County am) Long Eaton Rangers/Notts Rangers/NOTTS cs 1889/Long Eaton Rangers/Nottingham Forest June 1890/Long Eaton Rangers/NOTTS May 1896/Loughborough Aug 1897/Lincoln City July 1898/Burton Swifts 1899
Debut v Wolverhampton Wanderers (a) 7.9.1889, lost 0 – 2

'Tich' Smith was Long Eaton Rangers' centre-forward when they won the Birmingham Cup in 1887, beating West Bromwich Albion 1 – 0 at Perry Bar. They were also runners-up for the Derbyshire Cup in the same year. The son of Mr. William Smith senior, a Long Eaton Lace manufacturer, he represented England (and scored four goals in a 6 – 1 victory) against Canada in an unofficial international match played at The Oval, Kennington, on 19th December 1891. In the same season he assisted Forest to win the championship of the Football Alliance, and was inside-right in the first Forest team to contest a Football League match, at Everton on 3rd September 1892. At about the same time he was a reserve for a place in the England team to meet Scotland, but he did not win a full cap. His first spell with the Magpies was his best, despite it being restricted by an ankle injury after 17 League and Cup games and eight goals. In his second spell at Trent Bridge he scored four goals in eight matches in the Division Two championship season, 1896-97.

Appearances: FL: 23 apps 11 gls FAC: 2 apps 1 gl
Total: 25 apps 12 gls
Honours: (Nottingham Forest) Football Alliance champions 1892

SMYTHE, E. M.
Half-back
CAREER: NOTTS Nov 1879
Debut v Nottingham Forest, FAC 1, (a) 8.11.1879, lost 0 – 4

According to available records, it appears that Smythe played only twice for Notts. Both matches came in 1879-80, in what was very much a foreshortened season, running from 11th October '79 to 12th March '80. It was also a singularly unsuccessful campaign. Aside from the bitter pill of defeat by Forest in the first round of the FA Cup, the programme of friendly fixtures produced only one win, two draws and five defeats.

Appearances: FAC: 1 app 0 gls Total: 1 app 0 gls

SNOOK, Frederick William
Full-back
b. Nottingham, 10th July 1864
d. Nottingham, 9th December 1904
CAREER: NOTTS (debut) Jan 1884 to (final app) Jan 1886
Debut v Sheffield, FAC 3 (h) 3.1.1885, won 5 – 0

A member of the Notts club for over twenty years, and a playing member for three seasons, Frederick Snook was an all-round sportsman who held the championship of the Notts. Lawn Tennis Association for fourteen years. A director of the textile warehousing and wholesale clothing manufacturers, James Snook and Co. of Hounds-gate, Nottingham. Living latterly at Castle-grove, The Park, Nottingham, he left an estate of £11,597 0s 6d when he died at the untimely age of 40.

Appearances: FAC: 5 apps 0 gls Total: 5 apps 0 gls

SNOOK, Herbert Durrant
Full-back
b. Nottingham, 23rd December 1867
d. Lenton, Notts, 13th October 1947
CAREER: High School, Nottingham/Trent College/NOTTS Jan to Dec 1888
Debut v Eckington, FAC 1 Q, (h) 6.10.1888, won 4 – 1

Herbert Snook was a businessman, sportsman and Liberal politician who occupied a prominent position in Nottingham for many years, being appointed a Justice of the Peace of the city in 1911. He completed 62 years with the firm founded by his father, James Snook, of which he was chairman and managing director for forty years. A member of Notts. Tennis and Golf Clubs, he was a County representative with each. With his brother F.W. (above) he established much more than a local reputation in tennis doubles, winning the open mens' doubles tournament on five occasions between 1887 and 1897. Herbert also served as chairman of the Notts. Golf Club, with a spell as club captain, and was a committee member for many years.

Appearances: FL: 1app 0 gls FAC: 3 apps 0 gls
Total: 4 apps 0 gls

SNOOK, James Bracher
Centre-forward
b. Nottingham, 15th November 1859
d. Mapperley Park, Nottingham, 4th April 1943
CAREER: NOTTS (first appearance) Feb 1883 to Apr 1885 (final appearance)
Debut v Grantham, FAC 3, (a) 20.12.1883, won 4 – 1

The elder of the Snook clan, and a wholesale draper by trade, James was an infrequent playing member but got off to a good start when he scored in his first friendly appearance for the Magpies, a 3 – 0 victory against Derby Midland in February 1883. In his first outing in the following season he scored Notts last goal in their 6 – 1 win against a South of England X1. His handful of appearances concluded with an outing in the unaccustomed position of right-back, in a 3 – 0 defeat at the hands of the crack Scottish amateur combination, Queen's Park. The match at the Castle Ground on 3rd April 1884 was a benefit match for Notts' England international forward, Arthur W.Cursham, and raised a sum of £284. Sadly, the beneficiary was dead by Christmas, succumbing to yellow fever after emigrating to Florida.

Appearances: FAC: 1 app 0 gls Total: 1 app 0 gls

SNOOK, Walter Percy 'William'
Forward
b. Nottingham, 23rd October 1869
d. Mapperley, Nottingham, 3rd June 1955
CAREER: Trent College/NOTTS 1888-89
Debut v Old Brightonians, FAC 1 (h) 2.2.1889, won 2 – 0

William Percy Snook was a well-known local solicitor, practising in the city with his own firm in Park-row. He was educated at Trent College and trained as a solicitor in London. He was also an outstanding amateur sportsman, representing the county at golf, tennis and football. He was also a member of Notts. Amateurs Cricket Club. As a golfer, he was one of the oldest members of the Hollinwell Club, and a founder member of the Rushcliffe Club. His involvement with the Magpies was fleeting, but he scored once in two FA Cup appearances. In addition to his debut (above) he scored against Sheffield Wednesday in the 2 – 3 defeat sustained in the second round proper on 16th February 1889. **Note:** Details from his obituary in the 'Nottingham Guardian Journal' indicate that he was known as <u>William</u> Percy, whereas details from both birth and death records indicate that he was actually <u>Walter</u> Percy.

Appearances: FAC: 2 apps 1 gl Total: 2 apps 1 gl

SOFIANE, Youssef
Forward   5' 8"   11st 0lbs
b. Lyon, France, 8th July 1984
CAREER: Auxerre (France)/West Ham United June 2002 (Lille, France, loan Dec 2003) (NOTTS loan Sept 2004)
Debut v Northampton Town (a) 11.9.2004, drawn 0 – 0

Loan signing Youssef Sofiane showed touches of Gallic flair with his neat ball control and the occasional fancy step-over. Whether he was really suited to life in soccer's basement division was not answered in his brief spell at Meadow Lane, but the physical nature of the game and lack of time on the ball appeared at odds with his preferred style of play. He did, however, open his goal scoring account in English football, in the Magpies 2 – 3 defeat against Wrexham in the LDV Vans tie at Meadow Lane on 28th September 2004.

Appearances: FL: 2(2) apps 0 gls Other: 1 app 1 gl
Total: 3(2) apps 1 gl
Honours: France Youth International

SOUTAR, Henry William 'Harry'
Goalkeeper   5' 10½"   11st 12lbs
b. Invergowrie, Dundee, 18th September 1902
CAREER: Dundee Violet (Dundee 'A' loan Mar 1926) Dundee Violet/Rhyl June 1926/Accrington Stanley June 1929/NOTTS May 1930/Rotherham United July 1931/Rhyl May 1932/Shelbourne Nov 1932/Dartford Aug 1933/ Brechin City.
Debut v Queens Park Rangers (h) 26.12.30, won 2 – 0

Harry Soutar made his English League debut with Accrington Stanley, the Reds recruiting the Scotsman after three seasons in Welsh football. He played in only seven League matches for Accrington, and a similar amount when he joined Notts. He did, however, assist in maintaining the best defensive record in the four Divisions, as County won the Third Division South championship during his season at Meadow Lane. Harry wound up his League career with 25 appearances for Rotherham United in 1931-32.

Appearances: FL: 7 apps 0 gls FAC: 2 apps 0 gls
Total: 9 apps 0 gls
Honours: Scotland Junior International. (Rhyl) Welsh Cup finalists 1927

SOUTHWELL, Aubrey Allen
Right-back   5' 9½"   11st 6lbs
b. Grantham, Lincs, 21st August 1921
d. Nottingham, 9th February 2005
CAREER: Grantham St John's/Grantham Town Sept 1939/ Nottingham Forest am/NOTTS Dec 1944/Boston United 1957/Grantham Town cs 1958 to 1959.
Debut v Bradford City, FAC 1, (h) 17.11.45, drawn 2 – 2

Considered one of the speediest defenders of his day, Aubrey Southwell began as an amateur centre-half with Forest.

In the month prior to his debut in the FA Cup, he was a member of the Magpies Xl that beat an all-star British Army international side at Cologne. During thirteen seasons at Meadow Lane the strong tackling full-back played under six different managers and found favour with them all. Previous to an injury on 26th March 1949 he had appeared in 118 consecutive matches, and he remained a loyal, reliable club man throughout, qualifying for two benefits along the way. Interviewed in 1957, he recalled the greatest goal he had ever seen, scored by Tommy Lawton against Forest in the Magpies promotion season 1949-50. From a corner taken by Frank Broome, Lawton's thunderous header, from outside of the penalty area, flashed into the net with the velocity of a bullet – no doubt delighting the majority of the all-ticket Meadow Lane crowd of 37,903!

Appearances: FL: 328 apps 2 gls FAC: 30 apps 0 gls
Total: 358 apps 2 gls
Honours: (NOTTS) FL Division 3 South champions 1950

---o---

SPENCER, Fred

Outside-right   5' 5"   10st 8lbs
b. Nottingham
CAREER: Nottingham Forest July 1895/NOTTS Sept 1900/
St Andrew's (Nottingham) Sept 1903
Debut v Manchester City (a) 10.11.00, lost 0 – 2

Fred Spencer began with Forest, making his debut at Small Heath on 9th November 1895. Without ever winning a permanent place in the side he was an extremely useful utility forward with a record of 19 League goals in 44 matches at the time of his move to the Magpies. Fielded exclusively at outside-right by Notts, his role was one of deputy to Arthur Hadley, and later to Dickie Joynes. As the 'Football Post' commented in September 1903: "Fred Spencer will play in Notts. Alliance football with St Andrew's this season. He has never quite realised expectations in League football."

Appearances: FL: 15 apps 2 gls FAC: 1 app 0 gls
Total: 16 apps 2 gls

STABB, George Herbert

Centre-forward 5' 8½" 12st 0lbs
b. Paignton, Devon, 26th September 1912
d. Bradford, Yorks, 11th December 1994
CAREER: Paignton Town/Dartmouth United/Torquay United Sept 1931/NOTTS Oct 1934/Port Vale July 1935/Bradford P.A. Sept 1936 to 1946 when he was appointed assistant-trainer (WW2 guest Torquay United, Bradford City, Huddersfield Town & Barnsley.)
Debut v Fulham (h) 27.10.34, drawn 1 – 1

Fulham provided the opposition when George Stabb made his debut for the Magpies. Some three years previously George had made his first appearance in League football at Craven Cottage. In a memorable debut, he scored one of Torquay's goals in the 2 – 0 win against a Fulham team, destined to win the championship of Divison Three South in the same season. In 1932-33 he was Torquay's leading goal scorer with 26 League and Cup goals in 45 matches, and when he left Plainmoor to join the Magpies his record stood at 47 goals in 101 matches. He was probably unfortunate to join Notts during one of their worst-ever seasons, when they crashed out of Division Two with only 25 points from their 42 matches. Moving on to Port Vale, he scored on his debut at Barnsley, but in the second month of the season suffered a cartilage injury that required surgery. After 35 League and Cup matches and 11 goals, his final move took him to Bradford Park Avenue where he was quickly converted from a forward role to that of right half-back. In addition to 99 League and Cup matches and 6 goals, George played regularly throughout the war years, adding another 204 matches to his total.

Appearances: FL: 24 apps 6 gls FAC: 1 app 0 gls
Total: 25 apps 6 gls

---o---

STALLARD, Mark

Forward   6' 0"   13st 6lbs
b. Derby, 24th October 1974
CAREER: Derby Schoolboys/Derby County trainee, signing pro Nov 1991 (Fulham loan Sept 1994)/Bradford City Jan 1996, fee £110,000 (Preston North End loan Feb 1997)/Wycombe Wanderers Mar 1997, fee £100,000/NOTTS Mar 1999, fee £10,000/Barnsley Jan 2004 (Chesterfield loan Oct 2004)(NOTTS loan Feb 2005)
Debut as sub v York City (h) 13.3.99, won 4 – 2

Mark Stallard began with Derby County and was still a trainee when he made his League debut, as a substitute, against Oxford United. In the following month, when two days away from his 17th birthday, he scored his first senior goal at Middlesbrough, in a Zenith Data Systems Cup tie. Despite the early promise, he failed to establish himself at the Baseball Ground. He was, however, immediately successful with Bradford City. Leading scorer in League matches, despite having joined in mid season, his goals helped the Bantams to sixth place in Division Two and a place in the end of season Play-offs.

At Wembley Stadium he scored the second goal that ended the Magpies hopes of promotion. Transferred to Wycombe Wanderers in March 1997, he was their leading scorer in 1997-98 with 17 goals in 43 matches. A medial ligament injury sidelined him for a little over three months in the following season, and with his contract due to run out at the end of the season, he proved an absolute bargain buy for the Magpies at just £10,000. Apart from a frustrating season in 2001-02 when he struggled with a hernia injury that eventually required surgery, Mark proved an excellent attack leader, clever and strong on the ball, and not easily shaken off when heading for goal. His outstanding return of 24 League goals in 43(2) matches in 2002-03 saw him voted supporters' 'Player of the Year.' At the time of his transfer to Barnsley, Mark was the second highest paid player at the club and with a contract until June 2005. His departure, brought about by the prevailing financial situation, was still an unpleasant shock to the club's supporters. He was as surprise - but very welcome - loan signing from Barnsley in February 2005.

FL: 184(17) apps 70 gls FAC: 10 apps 3 gls FLC: 13(1) apps 7 gls Other: 2 apps 0 gls Total: 209(18) apps 80 gls

---

STANCER, Leslie B

Left half-back
b. Grantham, April quarter 1925
CAREER: NOTTS during WW2 period/Grantham Town Jan 1946 to March 1953.
Debut v Bradford City, FAC 1, (h) 17.11.45, drawn 2 – 2

Les Stancer first appeared for the Magpies during wartime season 1942-43, playing in two away matches at Northampton Town and Lincoln City in December. The team had not competed in the previous season because of bomb damage at Meadow Lane. Wartime football contained few regular players, as most were serving in the forces, and the Magpies fielded an amazing total of 129 players in season 1943-44 to complete a programme of 38 matches. Les Stancer with eight appearances was one of the more familiar faces!

His one appearance in the FA Cup was made out of position on the left wing and it proved to be his last. Two months later he made his debut for Grantham Town and scored a goal against Mansfield Town Reserves. He went on to play in 43 matches for the Gingerbreads, scoring 13 goals, a highlight being his appearance in the Lincolnshire Senior Cup Final against Boston United in 1946-47. He settled in Grantham and for many years was mine host of the Cherry Tree public house on Harrowby Lane.

Appearances: FAC: 1 app 0 gls Total: 1 app 0 gls

STANIFORTH, Archer Christopher 'Chris'

Centre-forward 5' 10" 11st 7lbs
b. Carrington, Nottingham, 26th September 1897
d. Creswell, Chesterfield, 24th December 1954
CAREER: Nottingham Schoolboys/NOTTS am 1913/Creswell Athletic cs 1913/Chesterfield Municipal 1919/Creswell Colliery/Mansfield Town Mar 1921/Oldham Athletic May 1922, fee £400/Mansfield Town May 1924/NOTTS Dec 1924, fee £800/Mansfield Town May 1926/NOTTS May 1927, fee £800/Mansfield Town May 1928/Shirebrook player-coach June 1930/Grantham Mar 1931/Mansfield Town player-coach Sept 1931/Sutton Town Aug 1932/Worksop Town Aug 1933/Creswell Colliery player-manager cs 1934.
Debut v Tottenham Hotspur (a) 3.1.25, drawn 1 – 1

Chris Staniforth had the unique record of signing for Mansfield Town on no fewer than five separate occasions. He was without doubt one of the best players in the Stags long history, despite the fact that the bulk of his Field Mill career was spent in Midland League and Combination soccer. His overall record was 152 goals in just 160 matches. In two separate spells with the Magpies, his second was his best, as he finished as second highest goalscorer in season 1927-28 with 14 in 27 Division Two matches. What should have been a big moment in 1925-26 – a hat-trick at Newcastle United – was ruined by the fact that Newcastle scored six goals in reply. Outside of the game Chris worked at Cresswell Colliery, also as a publican, and in an Ordnance stores during the Second World War. He and his wife raised a family of twelve children, all eight sons being named after footballers. An item in the 'Football Post' in 1949 mentioned one of his sons. Obviously one whose footballing talents were centered at the opposite end of the field: "J. Staniforth, son of Chris, saved two penalties in Creswell Colliery's 3 – 0 win against Maltby Main Colliery in an extra preliminary round of the FA Cup on 9th September 1949."

Appearances: FL: 66 apps 22 gls FAC: 1 app 0 gls
Total: 67 apps 22 gls

STANT, Philip Richard

Forward   6' 1"   12st 7lbs
b. Bolton, 13th October 1962
CAREER: Army football/Camberley Town/Reading Aug 1982/Hereford United Nov 1986/NOTTS July 1989, fee £175,000 (Blackpool loan Sept 1990) (Lincoln City loan Nov 1990) (Huddersfield Town loan Jan 1991)/Fulham Feb 1991, fee £60,000/Mansfield Town July 1991, fee £50,000/Cardiff City Dec 1992, fee £120,000 (Mansfield Town loan Aug 1993)/Bury Jan 1995, fee £90,000 (Northampton Town loan Nov 1996)/Lincoln City Dec 1996, fee £30,000, appointed assistant-manger Mar 1998, manager May 2000 to Feb 2001/Brighton & Hove Albion Mar 2001/Worcester City Aug 2001/Dover Athletic Jan 2002/Hayes Mar 2002/Hinckley United Mar 2002/Gainsborough Trinity manager May 2002 to cs 2003/Ilkeston Town manager Oct 2003.
Debut v Leyton Orient (a) 19.8.89, won 1 – 0 (scored)

One of soccer's happy wanderers (and a Bolton Wanderers fan as a youngster,) Phil did not progress beyond a trial game in the Trotters' 'A' Team when on leave from the Army. He nevertheless went on to enjoy a long and successful career, representing twelve different League clubs and totalling 188 goals in 405(71) League and Cup matches. He first hit the headlines by scoring 29 League and Cup goals in a struggling Hereford United side in season 1988-89, finishing as leading scorer in Division Four. The Magpies won the race for his signature, and although he scored on is debut, he lost his first team place in mid season and did not feature in the Wembley Play-off Final against Tranmere Rovers. At the age of 38 Phil rounded off his League career with seven late season appearances from the bench, and a final goal against Hull City, to assist Brighton to promotion as champions of Division Three in season 2000-01.

Appearances: FL: 14(8) apps 6 gls FAC: 0(1) apps 0 gls
FLC: 2 apps 1 gl Other: 3(2) apps 0 gls
Total: 19(11) apps 7 gls
Honours: (Cardiff City) Division Three champions and Welsh Cup winners 1993

---○---

STEELE, Ernest

Outside-right   5' 11"   11st 0lbs
b. Leigh, Lancs, 28th October 1911
d. Tiverton, Devon, 16th April 1997
CAREER: Middleton/Rochdale am Mar 1931/Mossley am cs 1931/Rochdale pro Aug 1931/Oldham Athletic Aug 1932/Torquay United May 1933/NOTTS Oct 1934, fee £750/Bath City July 1936/Millwall Dec 1936/Crystal Palace Sept 1938/Stockport County Sept 1939 (WW2 guest Rochdale, Carlisle United, Sheffield United, Chesterfield, Leicester City and Swansea Town)/Barry Town 1946/Hurst F.C. Dec 1946/Northwich Victoria 1947-48/Ossett Town/Barnsley groundsman 1954-67.
Debut v Fulham (h) 27.10.34, drawn 1 – 1

A genuine all-rounder, Ernie was East Lancashire's cross country champion when a member of Middleton Harriers. Additionally, he reached Minor Counties level as a cricketer, representing Lancashire and serving as professional to a number of league clubs. Success in football arrived rather late in his career, as his early associations tended to be with struggling sides, most notably Rochdale who finished at the bottom of Division Three North with only eleven points in 1931-32. It was a pattern repeated with Torquay United (20th in Division Three South in 1932-33) and the Magpies (relegated from Division Two in 1934-35). By contrast, his Third Division South championship medal with Millwall was followed by a runners-up position with Crystal Palace just twelve months later. Ernie died, aged 85, while watching a football match between Tiverton and Taunton.

Appearances: FL: 54 apps 9 gls FAC: 4 apps 1 gl Other: 1 app 0 gls Total: 59 apps 10 gls
Honours: (Millwall) FL Division 3 South champions 1938

---○---

STEELE, Murray Arthur

Goalkeeper   6' 0"   12st 3lbs
b. Mansfield, July 1891
d. Mansfield, 19th April 1922
CAREER: Queen Elizabeth's Grammar School (Mansfield)/Mansfield Wednesday 1908/Mansfield Amateurs 1909-10/Mansfield Mechanics Dec 1910/NOTTS cs 1912 to Apr 1919/Mansfield Mechanics
Debut v Sunderland (a) 26.10.12, lost 0 – 4

Murray Steele assisted Mansfield Mechanics to the championship of the Notts. & Derbyshire League in his first season, and in 1911-12 was beaten only 28 times in Central Alliance matches. His task on joining County was always going to be a difficult one, operating in the giant shadow of Albert Iremonger who, at that point, had already appeared in over 200 consecutive first team matches. Nevertheless, Steele was afforded an early opportunity. He could have wished for a less taxing introduction, but his debut at League champions elect Sunderland proved a stern examination, and in the following week he suffered a broken collar-bone at Manchester United. Later in the season, in what proved to be his final appearance at senior level, he had the satisfaction of helping Notts defeat Sunderland by 2 – 1 at Meadow Lane. Off the field he was a talented baritone singer who featured in amateur operatics.

Appearances: FL: 3 apps 0 gls Total: 3 apps 0 gls

---○---

STEVENS, Samuel

Centre-forward 5' 8"   12st 7lbs
b. Netherton, near Cannock, Staffs, 18th November 1890
d. Dudley, October quarter 1948, age 58
CAREER: Cradley Heath St Luke's/Hull City Jan 1912 (WW1 guest Cradley Heath and Birmingham F.C.)/NOTTS July 1920, fee £1,750/Coventry City Mar 1921, fee £1,300/ Dudley Bean July 1923/Lichfield City cs 1924/Dudley Bean Oct 1925, appointed trainer cs 1926
Debut v Bristol City (a) 28.8.20, won 1 – 0

A scoring sensation during his time with Hull City, Sammy Stevens was a centre-forward of the strong, bustling type. Not particularly tall for his position but well built and quick he was a terror to opposing defences, instanced by his return of 116 goals in 191 matches for the Tigers. Prolonged negotiations and a record fee were required to obtain his signature, as the player was due to receive a benefit at Anlaby Road in season 1920-21. Despite scoring five goals in his first six outings in the black and white jersey a perceived lack of cohesion in the forward line led to his transfer to Coventry City in March 1921. Despite the early exit, he finished as joint leading scorer for the season with eleven goals, and he subsequently became Coventry City's leading marksman with 21 in 42 League matches in 1921-22. In season 1914-15 he was on the fringe of international honours when selected as travelling reserve for the England v Scotland match.

Appearances: FL: 22 apps 9 gls FAC: 3 apps 2 gls
Total: 25 apps 11 gls

———————o———————

STEVENS, Theodore Harold Victor

Forward
b. Nottingham, 21st December 1866
d. West Bridgford, Nottingham 22nd January 1958
CAREER: NOTTS (first appearance) Apr 1887 to (final appearance) Oct 1888
Debut v Eckington, FAC 1 Q, (h) 6.10.1888, won 4 – 1

Harold Stevens was the middle brother of five, all of whom were in business in Nottingham. His father founded the firm of Stevens & Robinson Ltd, locally based Coal Merchants. In his youth he played Football, cricket and golf and was a pioneer motorist. His driving licence was numbered in the nineties, and he was one of the first locals to own a motorcycle. He was a member of the Rushcliffe Golf Club and Nottinghamshire C.C.C. and was past president of the Coal Merchants Benevolent Association. He died a widower, aged 91, leaving a daughter.

Appearances: FAC: 2 apps 0 gls Total: 2 apps 0 gls

———————o———————

STEVENS, Shaun Delano

Forward   5' 7"   10st 4lbs
b. London, 28th September 1978
CAREER: Millwall trainee/NOTTS Aug to Oct 1997
Debut as sub v Tranmere Rovers, FLC 2 (a) 23.9.97, won 1 – 0

Following his release from Millwall, Shaun Stevens was given a trial period of two months at Meadow Lane, but this did not lead to a permanent engagement. His only involvement at senior level came one week before his 19th birthday in the second round, second leg Coca Cola Cup match at Tranmere. He appeared as substitute for Craig Dudley, whose 43rd minute goal won the match. It did not secure victory, however, as Tranmere had won at Meadow Lane by 2 – 0 in the first leg.

Appearances: FLC: 0(1) app 0 gls Total: 0(1) app 0 gls

———————o———————

STEVENSON, Alfred Edward

Centre-forward 5' 8"   11st 6lbs
b. Broughton, Northants, April quarter 1902
d, Ashfordby, Leics, 4th September 1960
CAREER: Keyworth/Carlton Athletic/Worksop Town/ NOTTS am June, pro Aug 1926/Chatham Town Dec 1927/ Rothwell Town Oct 1929/Melton Mowbray Army Remount Depot Aug 1932/Ashfordby Old Boys, Melton Mowbray Oct 1934.
Debut v Southampton (a) 27.12.26, lost 0 – 2

The Magpies were very poor travellers in season 1926-27, and Stevenson's trio of appearances give a glimpse of the team's shortcomings in away fixtures. In addition to his debut at Southampton, above, his other matches were at Portsmouth (lost 1 – 9) and at Fulham (lost 0 – 3.) Scoring goals was less of a problem, with the usual inside-forward trio of A.G.Davis, Neil Harris and P.Kelly totalling 16, 14 and 16 goals respectively. Defensively, however, the team leaked 106 goals in League and Cup. Stevenson's involvement at reserve level brought him a Notts. Senior Cup medal in 1927 and a new contract, but lack of opportunities led to his departure midway through his second term.

Appearances: FL: 3 apps 0 gls Total: 3 apps 0 gls

———————o———————

STEWART, Alexander 'Alec'

Wing-half   5' 8½" 11st 12lbs
b. West Greenock, Renfrewshire, 1868
CAREER: Morton/Burnley Dec 1889/Everton Dec 1892/ Nottingham Forest cs 1893/NOTTS Mar 1897/Bedminster May 1898/Northampton Town Oct 1899/Burnley Sept 1901/Leicester Fosse trainer Dec 1902 to 1905
Debut v Blackpool (h) 20.3.1897, won 3 – 1

Alec Stewart joined the Magpies in their run-in to promotion in season 1896-97. He played at right half-back in the final five League matches, and at left-half in the successful four games in the Test matches. As the team battled to consolidate their hard-earned place in the top flight, he was one of only two players to make maximum appearances during a season when the Magpies finished in thirteenth place (in a division of sixteen clubs.) They finished with 24 points, as did all of the clubs occupying the bottom five positions in the table. None were relegated, however, as the League increased the First Division to eighteen clubs for the following season, promoting Burnley and Newcastle United from Division Two. Alec appeared in 97 League matches for Forest, and totalled 211 (14 goals) in his career. His last appearance, and final goal, being scored for Leicester Fosse when, as club trainer, he turned out in an emergency at Glossop on 10th April 1903 and helped his team to a 2 – 1 victory.

Appearances: FL: 35 apps 3 gls FAC: 1 app 0 gls Other: 4 apps 0 gls Total: 40 apps 3 gls
Honours: (Everton) FA Cup finalists 1893

STILL, Ronald George
Centre-forward 6' 2"   12st 4lbs
b. North Aberdeen, 10th June 1943
CAREER: Woodside Boys' Club/Arsenal am, signing pro Aug 1961/NOTTS July 1965/Brentford July 1967/Margate trial Sept-Oct 1967
Debut v Darlington (h) 21.8.65, drawn 0 – 0

In four years with Arsenal, from the age of 18, Ron Still had gained considerable Combination experience but was still to make his bow in League football when he joined the Magpies on a free transfer in July 1965. Although signed as a centre-half or left-back, Notts' manager Tim Coleman, himself a former centre-forward with Grimsby Town and Arsenal, felt that Still's height and weight would be of more benefit in the forward line. His judgement was proved correct as the new attack leader finished the season as leading scorer with 13 in 34 Division Four matches.

Appearances: FL: 46 apps 15 gls FLC: 3 apps 0 gls Total: 49 apps 15 gls

---

STIMPSON, George Henry
Full-back   5' 11" 12st 0lbs
b. Giltbrook, Notts, 25th January 1910
d. Nottingham, 31st January 1983
CAREER: Ainsworth United Methodists/Kimberley Amateurs/NOTTS am, signing pro cs 1929/Derby County trial cs 1935/Rhyl 1935/Exeter City May 1936/Mansfield Town May 1937/Gilbrook Villa, reinstated am, 1942/In Nov 1945 reported to be playing for Brinsley in the Notts. And Derby Senior League.
Debut v Bristol Rovers (a) 7.2.31, drawn 2 – 2

A strong, square-shouldered and challenging back, sure in the tackle and with good headwork, George Stimpson had some time to wait for a senior debut, as the Percy Mills/Charlie Bisby back line was very well established. When he did break into the side, it was initially as deputy at left-half for Haydn Kemp in the promotion season 1930-31. He had made great progress at right-back when he was taken ill at the mid-point of season 1933-34. He was re-signed in the close season in the hope of a complete recovery, but did not appear at senior level again. A season in non-League football with Rhyl was obviously beneficial, as he returned refreshed to assist Exeter City (29 matches) and Mansfield Town (85 matches.)

Appearances: FL: 90 apps 0 gls FAC: 3 apps 0 gls
Total: 93 apps 0 gls
Honours: (NOTTS) FL Division 3 South champions 1931

STOAKES, James Henry
Outside-right   5' 9"   11st 9lbs
b. Newark, Notts, 17th December 1895
d. Newark, Notts, 5th February 1979
CAREER: Newark Athletic/Army football (North Staffordshire Regiment)/NOTTS am May 1919/Norwich City am Apr, pro May 1921/Newark Town Sept 1926/Ransome & Marles Jan 1928.
Debut v Chelsea (h) 13.3.20, lost 0 – 1

Jimmy Stoakes was much better known on the running tracks of Nottingham rather than the Meadow Lane enclosure, where he featured only twice at senior level during two years with the Magpies. An Olympic Games trialist, his blistering pace and inviting centres were fully utilised in the service of Norwich City. Operating at outside-left for the Canaries he was rarely absent in a four-year stay, maintaining his place despite his poor record as a marksman – just six goals scored in 150 League and Cup matches.

Appearances: FL: 2 apps 0 gls Total: 2 apps 0 gls

STOKES, Alfred 'Fred'
Right-half   5' 9½" 11st 10lbs
b. West Bromwich, Staffs, Oct quarter 1904
d. West Bromwich, July quarter 1960
CAREER: Allan & Everett F.C. (Birmingham)/NOTTS Nov 1926/Coventry City May 1929/Watford May 1931 to cs 1933
Debut v Grimsby Town (a) 29.1.27, won 4 – 1

A recruit from Birmingham works league football, Fred Stokes was a vigorous tackler whose distribution improved dramatically during his spell with the Magpies.

Generally considered a reserve team man, he enjoyed his best season in 1927-28 appearing in eight League matches as deputy for Haydn Kemp. Released in the 1929 close season, he joined Coventry City whose manager at that time was former Notts player, James McIntyre. After 52 League and Cup appearances he was released by new manager Harry Storer and joined Watford on a free transfer. He made 42 League and Cup appearances in two seasons at Vicarage Road.

Appearances: FL: 13 apps 0 gls Total: 13 apps 0 gls

STONE, Daniel John Cooper 'Danny'
Defender   5' 11" 12st 4lbs
b. Liverpool, 14th September 1982
CAREER: Blackburn Rovers trainee/NOTTS Aug 2001/ Southport Aug 2003/Burscough Aug 2004/Lancaster City Sept 2004 (Had left by December and was linked with a possible move to Marine)
Debut as sub v Bury, LDV Vans Trophy 1 (a) 30.10.2001, won 3 – 2

Danny had a taste of League fare in 2001-02 following his debut in the LDV Trophy tie at Bury, making five starts and one substitute appearance in Division Two. In 2002-03 he began as first choice at right-back, but the team's faltering start to the season brought team changes. Deposed after playing in the first seven League matches he never regained a regular berth in the side. He returned north in the close season, joining Southport, the team who humbled the Magpies in the first round of the FA Cup by 4 – 2 at Haig Avenue.

Appearances: FL: 16(5) apps 0 gls FAC: 2(1) apps 0 gls Other: 2(1) apps 0 gls Total: 20(7) apps 0 gls

---

STONE, Geoffrey
Centre-half   6' 2"   13st 0lbs
b. Mansfield, 10th April 1924
d. Nottingham, August 1993
CAREER: Beeston Boys' Club/NOTTS am, signing pro Sept 1948/Darlington Aug 1950 to 1952.
Debut v Swindon Town (a) 23.4.49, lost 0 – 3

An ideally proportioned centre-half who graduated through the Magpies' Colts side to make his first League appearance in the final fixture of season 1947-48. Despite the fact that the centre-half position remained a cause for concern throughout the following season, Stone did not appear at senior level until the final month, when he played in the final three fixtures. Transferred to Darlington in the summer of 1950 he played in 26 League matches in 1950-51 but failed to maintain a first team place in 1951-52, appearing in five League matches and one FA Cup tie during the season. He became a storekeeper in the North East before joining the Notts. Police Force.

He served for 26 years, retiring in December 1980. Geoff played for the Police football team until the age of forty and then became their trainer.

Appearances: FL: 4 apps 0 gls Total: 4 apps 0 gls

STONE, Michael
Goalkeeper   5' 9½" 10st 13lbs
b. Hucknall, Notts, 23rd May 1938
CAREER: Basford Hall Boys' Club/Linby Colliery/NOTTS am, signing pro July 1958 to June 1960
Debut v Queens Park Rangers (h) 30.3.59, lost 0 – 1

Signed on amateur forms after just three appearances with Linby Colliery, Mick Stone's seven League appearances came consecutively, after he had replaced Jimmy Linton for the Easter Monday fixture against Queens Park Rangers. A plumber by trade, he found himself operating behind a leaky defence and conceded 17 goals in his seven outings, the Magpies sustaining a second, consecutive relegation. In the following season newly signed George Smith dominated, being one of only two players to appear in maximum League and Cup matches when promotion from Division Four was achieved.

Appearances: FL: 7 apps 0 gls Total: 7 apps 0 gls

STOTHERT, James
Full-back
b. Blackburn, April quarter 1870
CAREER: Braeside/Bohemians (Blackburn) 1888/Blackburn Rovers Oct 1891/Darwen Dimmocks 1891/Knuzden Rovers Feb 1892/Brierfield/Lincoln City Dec 1893/NOTTS Nov 1894/Bacup F.C. June 1896/Barnsley July 1897/Crewe Alexandra Aug 1898 to 1899.
Debut v Burton Wanderers (a) 8.12.1894, lost 0 – 1

Said to have been plucked from the crowd to make his debut for Blackburn Rovers when a player turned up for the game with an injury that prevented him from playing. Despite the unique start, he scored a goal in a 4 – 4 draw with Bolton Wanderers, but his goal was said to have been registered "More through good luck than good management." He did not play at League level again for the Rovers, but they held his registration and Stothert was twice suspended for playing for Darwen Dimmocks and Knuzden. The later suspension was sine die but it was subsequently lifted to allow him to sign for Brierfield and later for Lincoln City. In his first season with the Magpies he occupied both full-back berths, but six of his nine appearances were at left-half. He established a more settled role at right-back in 1895-96, partnering Jack Hendry for the first fourteen matches before being replaced by Jack Connor in early December.

Appearances: FL: 23 apps 0 gls Total: 23 apps 0 gls

STREETS, George Henry

Goalkeeper   5' 9"   11st 12lbs
b. Nottingham, 5th April 1893
d. Nottingham, 25th July 1958
CAREER: Nottingham St. Margaret's/Raleigh Athletic/
Mansfield Mechanics/Sheffield Wednesday 1913/NOTTS
July 1919 to 1928
Debut v Sheffield Wednesday (a) 13.9.19, drawn 0 – 0

George made the best possible start to his Magpies career
when he made his debut against his former club, Sheffield
Wednesday, and starred in a 0 – 0 draw at Hillsborough. A
goalkeeper with good anticipation, who was especially
good in dealing with low shots, he was restricted by Albert
Iremonger's consistency, enjoying just one season as
undisputed first choice in 1926-27. The opportunity
arising following Iremonger's transfer to Lincoln City.

Appearances: FL: 133 apps 0 gls FAC: 9 apps 0 gls
Total: 142 apps 0 gls
Honours: (NOTTS) FL Division 2 champions 1923

———————————○———————————

STRODDER, Gary John

Central defender   6' 1"   13st 3lbs
b. Cleckheaton, 1st April 1965
CAREER: Yorkshire Amateurs/Lincoln City associate
schoolboy Jan 1980, app July 1981, pro Apr 1983/West
Ham United Mar 1987, fee £150,000/West Bromwich Albion
Aug 1990, fee £190,000/NOTTS July 1995, fee £145,000
(Rotherham United loan Jan 1999)/Hartlepool United Feb
1999, fee £25,000/Guiseley July 2001
Debut v Wrexham (a) 12.8.95, drawn 1 – 1

The son of Colin Strodder, a full-back with Huddersfield
Town and Halifax Town in the early Sixties, Gary followed
in his father's footsteps, beginning with Lincoln City on
schoolboy forms. He made his League debut while still an
apprentice and completed 122(10) League appearances
and scored six goals before joining West Ham United in
the season that the Imps dropped out of the Football
League. Gary made 59(6) League appearances and scored
two goals for the Hammers, followed by 127(17) League
appearances and eight goals for West Bromwich Albion.
An early signing by the new Murphy/Thompson
management duo at Meadow Lane, Gary was installed as
captain and proved a tremendously popular, hard
defender, of the never-say-die stamp. He missed only
seven matches in the 1997-98 season, scoring four goals
in the title winning side and was one of four players
selected in the Division Three team in the PFA's Divisional
Awards. Gary left Meadow Lane in 1998-99 after losing
his first team place. A short loan period with Rotherham
was followed by a permanent move to Hartlepool United.
After a 2000-01 season plagued by injuries he was released
and moved into non-League football. In terms of League
matches alone, Gary's impressive career aggregate figures
totalled 481(41) matches and 26 goals.

Appearances: FL: 116(5) apps 10 gls FAC: 10(1) apps 0
gls FLC: 9 apps 0 gls Other: 4 apps 0 gls
Total: 139(6) apps 10 gls
Honours: (NOTTS) FL Division 3 champions 1998

———————————○———————————

STUBBS, Brian Henry

Central defender   6' 2"   12st 0lbs
b. Keyworth, Notts, 8th February 1950
CAREER: Rushcliffe Schoolboys/Loughborough United/
Nottingham Forest trial/NOTTS Sept 1968/Grantham Town
Nov 1981 to Dec 1982/Calverton Miners' Welfare player-
manager/Keyworth United player-manager.
Debut v Swansea Town (h) 21.9.68, lost 0 – 3

The youngest of
four soccer-
playing brothers,
Brian was working
as an apprentice
printer and
playing for Lough-
borough United in
season 1967-68
when he was
offered a trial by
Nottingham
Forest. In the
following season
he signed for the
Magpies and in the
same month found
himself under
different management, as Billy Gray vacated the 'hot
seat' to be replaced by caretaker boss Jack Wheeler. Brian
made his debut at inside-right, but was successfully
converted into a powerful and dominating central defender
who became a key figure in the team's rise from Division
Four to Division Two. Whole-hearted and consistent,
Brian tackled with great determination and was extremely
effective in the air, at both ends of the pitch. A popular
player throughout his long career, he was voted 'Player
of the Year' at the end of the 1970-71 season as the
Magpies celebrated the championship of Division Four.
Having averaged around 39 League matches per season
for past eleven campaigns, Brian did not figure in a single
match in the 1980-81 promotion season as the Magpies
reached the heady heights of Division One. He departed
Meadow Lane to link up again with former colleagues
Jon Nixon and Bill Brindley at Northern Premier League
Grantham. David McVay also linked up with them. A
tongue-in-cheek comment by assistant-manager Brindley
at the time suggested that Brian and David had only been
signed to boost takings in the social club!

Appearances: FL: 423(3) apps 21 gls FAC: 21 apps 1 gl
FLC: 24 apps 5 gls Other: 15 apps 1 gl
Total: 483(3) apps 28 gls
Honours: (NOTTS) FL Division 4 champions 1971

SULLIVAN, James Henry

Centre-forward 5' 9½" 11st 6lbs
b. Burnley, 14th November 1904
CAREER: Burnley Grammar School/Burnley am/Barrow am 1922/Crewe College/Crewe Alexandra Aug 1924/NOTTS Oct 1925, fee £1,500/Grantham Town June 1928/Loughborough Corinthians Sept 1931/Gainsborough Trinity.
Debut v Bury (h) 17.10.25, won 4 – 1

Jimmy Sullivan was in the final stages of a college course of scholastic training when he joined Notts, and on qualifying took up a teaching post at Southwark Street School. As an amateur centre-forward he scored 23 goals for Barrow Reserves, and continued in similar vein when he entered League football with Crewe Alexandra. In his first season at Gresty Road he netted 16 goals in 27 Northern Section matches, and had added another six in 10 matches before joining the Magpies in October 1925. At the time of his signing, Notts had lost six of their first eleven engagements, winning only three. They were also the lowest scorers in Division One. The new centre-forward made an immediate impact, scoring twice against Sheffield United on his third appearance. One week later he netted a hat-trick against West Bromwich Albion at the Hawthorns to earn the Magpies a share of the points after they had been three goals down inside a quarter of an hour. Shortly afterwards, in a bruising encounter against Everton, he injured his collar-bone and shoulder ligaments and was out of action for several weeks. The Magpies were relegated from Division One in the same season. Sullivan had scored seven goals in nine matches and one is left with a feeling that the season's outcome might well have been different had their sharp-shooting schoolteacher steered clear of injury. In his first season with Grantham Town Jimmy scored 44 goals, and averaged exactly a goal-a-game in 97 matches spread over just three seasons.

Appearances: FL: 22 apps 10 gls FAC: 2 apps 0 gls
Total: 24 apps 10 gls

SUTER, Ernest Robert 'Bob'

Goalkeeper 6' 0" 12st 6lbs
b. Epperstone, Notts, 10th July 1880
d. Halifax, 1st December 1945
CAREER: Southwell Church Lads' Brigade/Southwell St. Mary's 1897(Also played twice for Nottingham Park F.C. in 1897) NOTTS am May 1898, pro Apr 1899/Alnoea FC 1903/Newark Town cs 1903/NOTTS 2 May 1906/Goole Town cs 1912/Halifax Town cs 1913, trainer April 1929/ Warley Circuit FC trainer Aug 1934.
Debut v Derby County (a) 18.2.1899, lost 2 – 4

At the time of his FL debut Bob Suter had conceded only three goals in 12 matches for Southwell St. Mary's who had taken maximum points from all their fixtures in the Notts. Alliance League.

The teenage custodian was born at Epperstone but raised in Southwell, described in 1899 as "That modest little cathedral city of 3,000 inhabitants." Suter initially justified the high hopes placed upon him. A string of brilliant displays keeping George Toone, for so many years a fixture in the side, out of the first team picture. After holding the position for much of 1899-1900, a shaky opening to the following season resulted in the introduction of Harry Pennington, who dominated the position for the best part of four seasons. Some 30 years after making his League debut for the Magpies Bob Suter was pressed into action to appear in a League match for Halifax Town, when injuries had left his side without a goalkeeper. He set aside his bucket and sponge, donned the obligatory flat cap and polo-neck sweater, and at the age of 48 years and 9 months was beaten only twice, Gateshead winning 2 – 0 at the Shay. His son, Francis Robert Suter, also a goalkeeper, played in three League matches for Halifax Town in season 1932-33.

Appearances:FL: 42 apps 0 gls FAC: 5 apps 0 gls
Total: 47 apps 0 gls

SWIFT, George

Full-back 5' 9" 12st 8lbs
b. Oakengates, Shropshire, October quarter 1870
d. Wembley, Middlesex, 1st January 1956
CAREER: St George's Swifts/Wellington Town 1885/ Wellington St George's 1886/Stoke, trial 1886/Crewe Alexandra 1889/Wolverhampton Wanderers cs 1891/ Loughborough cs 1894/Leicester Fosse Aug 1896, fee £100/ NOTTS June 1902, engaged as trainer May 1903 to Apr 1905/Leeds City trainer/Chesterfield Town trainer, then secretary-manager Sept 1907 to 1910/Southampton manager Apr 1911 to Apr 1912
Debut v Middlesbrough (h) 27.9.02, won 2 – 0

George Swift rounded off a fine playing career with a season at Trent Bridge before taking the place of Joe Goode as Notts' trainer. A defender built on hefty lines, he commenced in the Football Alliance with Crewe Alexandra. Joining Wolves, he was the only ever-present player during season 1892-93 when they reached the FA Cup Final, beating Everton 1 – 0 at Fallowfield, Manchester. Later with the Loughborough club he became the only player in their relatively brief history to be recognised by the international selectors when he was chosen to play for the Football League against the Irish League at the Victoria Ground, Stoke, on 9th November 1895. Prior to joining the Magpies he enjoyed an excellent six - year spell with Leicester Fosse, completing exactly 200 League and Cup appearances and scoring six goals.

Appearances: FL: 16 apps 0 gls Total: 16 apps 0 gls
Honours: FL representative, 1 app 1895.
(Wolverhampton Wanderers) FA Cup winners 1893

TAIT, Barry Stuart

Inside-forward 5' 6"   10st 3lbs
b. York, 17th June 1938
CAREER: Manor School (York)/Doncaster Rovers am/York City Sept 1958/Peterborough United trial/Bradford City Nov 1961/Halifax Town July 1962/Crewe Alexandra Sept 1963/NOTTS July 1964/Scarborough July 1965/York City assistant-coach & scout Mar 1990 to Sept 1994/Sunderland youth coach & scout July 1995
Debut v Tranmere Rovers (a) 31.8.64, lost 0 – 4

The Magpies attack lacked a cutting edge in 1964-65 although the mid-term signing of 'Doc' Pace brought about some welcome improvement. Barry Tait, a free transfer signing from Crewe Alexandra, appeared twice at centre-forward and once at inside-right during the season but on each occasion both he, and the team, failed to score. Two years earlier, his spell with Halifax Town resulted in a return of 21 League goals in 36 matches, and his overall career aggregate was highly respectable, 38 goals accruing from his 83 League appearances.

Appearances: FL: 3 apps 0 gls Total: 3 apps 0 gls

TAIT, Robert James

Inside-forward 5' 8"   9st 10lbs
b. Edinburgh, 4th October 1938
CAREER: Aberdeen 1960/NOTTS July 1962/Barrow July 1964/Chesterfield July 1966/Arnold July 1967/Long Eaton United player-manager.
Debut v Coventry City (a) 18.8.62, lost 0 – 2

Bobby Tait began with Notts as an outside-left, lost his first team place in mid season, but was then re-introduced at inside-left, a move that proved an outstanding success. Hard working and constructive but not the best of finishers, he blossomed as a marksman after leaving Meadow Lane. In two seasons with Barrow he netted 14 goals in 1964-65 and 15 in 1965-66, his total in the latter season including a goal within a minute of the kick-off against Hartlepools United. Moving into non-League football after a season with Chesterfield he assisted Arnold to a record - breaking season in which they reached the first round proper of the FA Cup for the first time. They were also finalists in the Notts. Senior Cup and finished in third place in the Midland Counties League.

Appearances: FL: 60 apps 11 gls FAC: 4 apps 2 gls FLC: 5 apps 2 gls Total: 69 apps 15 gls

---

TARPLIN, Walter

Inside-forward 5' 8"   10st 10lbs
b. Small Heath, 30th March 1879
d. Birmingham, April quarter 1937
CAREER: Small Heath Albion/Coventry City Sept 1902/NOTTS Apr 1904/Reading May 1908
Debut v Small Heath (a) 23.4.04, lost 0 – 2

The Magpies scouting system unearthed no fewer than five new players from Birmingham League football, all within the space of two months, in April and May 1904. Four of the newcomers proved to be real 'gems' and were to total in excess of 1,000 first team appearances between them, their Notts career figures as follows: Emberton (382), Craythorne (296), Dean (268) and Walter Tarplin (103). Only Tom Wainwright failed to make the grade, spending two seasons in reserve and appearing in just eight League matches. Walter Tarplin was a versatile forward, at home in all three inside positions. His best season was 1905-06 when he scored 13 goals in 36 First Division matches to finish as joint leading scorer for the season.

Appearances: FL: 97 apps 25 gls FAC: 6 apps 2 gls Total: 103 apps 27 gls

---

TASKER, Ernest

Right-back
b. Logged at Basford, Nottingham, January quarter 1898
CAREER: Hucknall Byron/NOTTS am July 1919/Shirebrook Mar 1920
Debut v West Bromwich Albion (a) 25.10.19, lost 0 – 8

It was rather unfortunate timing that saw amateur full-back Ernest Tasker pressed into action, as deputy for George Charlesworth, when the Magpies visited the Hawthorns and were routed 8 – 0 by the eventual League champions. The Albion left-wing pair had a field day, England international Fred Morris scoring five goals, his outside partner Howard Gregory netting one. The return fixture was one week later, and with changes that included a return of George Charlesworth and a change in goal, the Magpies turned the tables and won 2 – 0. The scorer of the two goals, Harold Hill, being carried shoulder high from the field by enthusiastic supporters.

Appearances: FL: 1 app 0 gls Total: 1 app 0 gls

TAYLOR, George Arthur

Goalkeeper   5' 11"   12st 7lbs
b. Grimsby, January quarter 1916
CAREER: Grimsby junior football/Boston United Apr 1934/NOTTS May 1938 to May 1939, fee £150.
Debut v Cardiff City (a) 15.4.39, drawn 1 – 1

Considered to be the best goalkeeper operating in the Midland League at the time of his signing, George Taylor was unable to oust Tom Flowers as first choice despite glowing reports gained from his performances at reserve level. Agile, confident and sound, he finally obtained his chance when an injury to Flowers, late in the campaign, gave Taylor a six-match consecutive run that rounded-off season 1938-39.

Appearances: FL: 6 apps 0 gls Total: 6 apps 0 gls

TAYLOR, George Thomas

Outside-right   5' 8½"   11st 4lbs
b. Walsall, 12th December 1907
CAREER: Croft Street School/Walsall Schoolboys/Talbot Stead/Walsall Wood/Bloxwich Strollers/Stourbridge/NOTTS May 1925/Bolton Wanderers Dec 1933, fee £3,500/ Coventry City Oct 1937, fee £2,250 (WW2 guest Leicester City, retired 1943)
Debut v Newcastle United (a) 5.9.25, lost 3 – 6

George Taylor had an outstanding career after winning schoolboy international honours and graduating to become the best outside-right in the Birmingham League. He began with Notts in Division One and played in 38 League and Cup matches in his first season. His full development was probably hindered by his selection at inside-right and centre-forward, when outside-right was clearly his best position. His game featured exhilarating dash and tenacity, his terrier-like methods often responsible for the collapse of opposing defences. After leaving Meadow Lane he helped Bolton Wanderers back into Division One in season 1934-35 and additionally to the semi-final of the FA Cup in the same season. After completing 170 League and Cup appearances for the Trotters, he passed the milestone of 500 career appearances in Coventry City's colours during season 1938-39. As his fine career was drawing to a close, his younger brother, Tom (q.v.) joined the Magpies in December 1938.

Appearances: FL: 265 apps 46 gls FAC: 12 apps 3 gls
Total: 277 apps 49 gls
Honours: England Schoolboy International, 2 caps 1921.
(NOTTS) FL Division 3 South champions 1931

TAYLOR, John Ephraim 'Jack'

Inside-right   5' 9"   11st 6lbs
b. Chilton, 11th September 1924
CAREER: Stockton/Luton Town Feb 1949/ Wolverhampton Wanderers June 1952/NOTTS Feb 1954/Bradford P.A. July 1957
Debut v Lincoln City (h) 20.2.54, drawn 1 – 1

"Forceful, progressive, and very much where the work is" was an early appraisal of Jack Taylor who scored five goals in his first dozen appearances as the 1953-54 season drew to a close. Sadly, in October of the new season he was injured and was out of action for six months. Coincidentally, Notts other former Wolverhampton Wanderers player, Ray Chatham, was injured two weeks later and was out for five months. Under the circumstances the Magpies did well to finish seventh in Division Two, and they also enjoyed a good run in the FA Cup, beating Middlesbrough, Sheffield Wednesday and Chelsea before going down 1 – 0 in the sixth round to the season's 'giant killers' York City. Jack Taylor's total career figures were 160 League appearances and 55 goals.

Appearances: FL: 53 apps 19 gls FAC: 1 app 0 gls
Total: 54 apps 19 gls
Honours: England 'B' International

TAYLOR, Thomas

Outside-right
b. Possibly at Walsall, circa 1916
CAREER: Streetly Works/NOTTS Dec 1938/Walsall June1939
Debut v Brighton & Hove Albion (h) 17.12.38, won 4 – 3

Tom Taylor, brother of George, who was such a great servant of the Magpies, was signed as a professional on the recommendation of his elder brother. Considering the fact that he was drafted straight into the first team, having only previously played in junior football, he showed no sign of nerves and played with an intelligence that would have done credit to an older player. As the 'Football Post' commented: "Taylor knew how to beat his man and was astute enough to put over centres at the most favoured moment." Having missed only one first team match – the last one of the season against Bristol City – he was rather surprisingly transferred to Walsall. Due to the outbreak of WW2, his involvement with the Saddlers amounted to just nine matches and two goals in the Regional League (Midland Division.)

Appearances: FL: 25 apps 1 gl FAC: 3 apps 0 gls
Total: 28 apps 1 gl

TEWKESBURY, Kenneth Cyril

Goalkeeper   6' 3"   12st 0lbs
b. Steyning, Sussex, 10th April 1909
d. Worthing, 20th November 1970
CAREER: Birmingham University/Birmingham am Oct 1929/Aston Villa am Dec 1931/NOTTS am Aug 1932/Aston Villa pro Jan 1933/Bradford P.A. July1935/Walsall May 1936, retired Aug 1939
Debut v Lincoln City (h) 27.8.32, drawn 1 – 1

Rather surprisingly took over the captaincy of the Magpies when he arrived from Aston Villa. At the time, the Aston Villa secretary was quoted as saying: "If Tewksbury will sign a professional form, he can come back to Villa tomorrow." In a matter of months he was back at Villa Park as a professional but he played only one first team match for them. The holder of a Bachelor of Science degree and an amateur international, the towering goalkeeper had some unusual opinions on the subject of goalkeeper's attire. In January 1938 he was reported as saying that goalkeepers should wear a waterproof jacket over a sweater, ankle-length trousers and light boots. At least the light boots came to pass!

Appearances: FL: 7 apps 0 gls Total: 7 apps 0 gls
Honours: England Amateur International, 3 caps 1931-32

THOMAS, Dean Ronald

Midfield/Full-back   5' 10"   11st 8lbs
b. Bedworth, 19th December 1961
CAREER: Exhall Minors/Nuneaton Borough/Wimbledon July 1981, fee £8,000/Alemania Aachen (Germany)/Fortuna Dusseldorf (Germany)/Northampton Town Aug 1988/ NOTTS Mar 1990, fee £175,000, was joint caretaker manager, Apr to June 1995/Bedworth United manager/ Hinckley United manager 1997.
Debut v Bristol City (h) 24.3.90, drawn 0 – 0

A midfielder with dete-rmination and ability, Dean made his debut with Wimbledon in season 1981-82, a term in which they were relegated from Division Three. In complete contrast the Dons bounced straight back in the following season as champions of Division Four, commencing a meteoric rise that saw them established in the top flight just four years later.

Dean, however, departed Plough Lane in the summer of 1983 and spent the next five years playing in the German Bundesliga, eventually reaching Meadow Lane after two seasons with Northampton Town. He left a team heading towards relegation from Division Three, to one moving in the opposite direction, the Magpies winning the Wembley Play-off Final against Tranmere Rovers by a 2 – 0 score line in May 1990. Twelve months later and another Wembley visit saw the Magpies earn a second, successive promotion. The 3 – 1 victory against Brighton returning them to Division One after an absence of seven years. Sadly, they were unable to consolidate their hard-won place in the top flight, suffering relegation in 1991-92. Dean left Meadow Lane in 1995; during his Magpies career he expressed an ambition to stay involved in the game, polishing coaching and managerial skills in Sunday league football. More recently, as manager of Hinckley United, he has guided them to two promotions and raised the profile of his team thanks to excellent performances in the FA Cup in 2001-02 and 2004-05.

Appearances: FL: 129(5) apps 8 gls FAC: 6 apps 0 gls
FLC: 10(1) apps 0 gls Other: 11(3) apps 0 gls
Total: 156(9) apps 8 gls
Honours: (Wimbledon) FL Division Four champions 1983

THOMAS, Geoffrey Robert

Midfield   6' 1"   13st 2lbs
b. Manchester, 5th August 1964
CAREER: Ashe Labs.(Littleborough)/Rochdale Aug 1982/ Crewe Alexandra Mar 1984/Crystal Palace June 1987, fee £50,000/Wolverhampton Wanderers June 1993, fee £800,000/Nottingham Forest July 1997/Barnsley July 1999/ NOTTS Mar 2001/Crewe Alexandra Aug 2001 to June 2002.
Debut v Walsall (h) 3.3.2001, won 2 – 0

Geoff Thomas began in League football with Rochdale. He scored his first League goal against Crewe Alexandra, and later in the same season joined the Railwaymen. He finally quit football some eighteen years later after a second spell at Gresty Road. A strong-tackling central midfielder, Geoff starred with Crystal Palace, captaining their 1990 FA Cup Final team against Manchester United. He became an England international under manager Graham Taylor, and later helped Forest win the First Division championship. He retired with career aggregate figures of 462(60) League and Cup matches and 73 goals. Geoff was diagnosed with leukaemia in July 2003, a condition he continues to battle with bravery and determination.

Appearances: FL: 8 apps 1 gl Total: 8 apps 1 gl
Honours: England International, 9 caps, 1991-92. England 'B' International, 3 apps. (Crystal Palace) FA Cup finalists 1990. Zenith Data Systems Cup winners 1991. (Nottingham Forest) FL Division 1 champions 1998

THOMPSON, David Stephen

Winger   5' 11"   12st 4lbs
b. Manchester, 27th May 1962
CAREER: North Withington/Rochdale Sept 1981/NOTTS
Aug 1986, in part exchange for Alan Young plus £10,000/
Wigan Athletic Oct 1987/Preston North End July 1990/
Chester City Aug 1992/Rochdale Aug 1994, fee £6,000/
Southport Aug 1997/Marine Aug 1999 to Jan 2005.
Debut v Wigan Athletic (h) 23.8.86, won 2 – 0

Dave Thompson began and ended his League career with
Rochdale, in two spells clocking up in excess of 250
League matches, becoming only fourth player in the club's
history to reach such a total. He had an excellent first
season at Meadow Lane, being the only player to appear
in all of the season's fixtures. Released by new manager
John Barnwell in the following season, he went on to
total 551(57) League and Cup matches and 61 goals in a
sixteen-year career. Proving to be anything but a spent
force, he then played in all but 14 of Southport's 120
games in two seasons at Haig Avenue. His association
with Marine, first as a player and later as a coach, lasted
for almost six years. Dave's son Daniel now plays for
Southport Reserves.

Appearances: FL: 52(3) apps 8 gls FAC: 3 apps 0 gls
FLC: 3(1) apps 0 gls Other: 2 apps 0 gls
Total: 60(4) apps 8 gls

THOMPSON, Terence William

Full-back/Wing-half   5' 10"   11st 2lbs
b. Barlestone, Leics, 25th December 1946
CAREER: Wolverhampton Wanderers app, signing pro Jan
1964/NOTTS Mar 1966 to 1968
Debut v Aldershot (a) 9.3.66, drawn 0 – 0

Terry Thompson became a professional with
Wolverhampton Wanderers at the age of seventeen, but
was without senior experience when he joined the Magpies
some two years later. He was given an early baptism in
Division Four, and after four games as right-half was
transferred to inside-right were he proved to be a clever
and dangerous tactician. The Notts managerial position
underwent a series of rapid changes during Thompson's
period at Meadow Lane, and this was doubtless a
contributory factor in the constant team and positional
changes effected. Certainly Thompson's versatility was
stretched to the limit, as he spent much of his second
season in the left full-back berth.

Appearances: FL: 66 apps 3 gls FAC: 2 apps 0 gls FLC:
3 apps 0 gls Total: 71 apps 3 gls

THORNE, Terence

Wing-half   5' 10½"   11st 2lbs
b. Boston, Lincs, 2nd February 1947
CAREER: Lincoln City am/Ipswich Town Aug 1964/NOTTS
June 1966/Sydney F.C. (Australia) Apr 1967/Pan Hellenic,
Sydney (Australia) Oct 1971/Holbeach F.C. player-coach.
Debut v Crewe Alexandra (a) 3.9.66, lost 1 – 4

Terry Thorne had a brief association with the Magpies as
a teenage half-back. Finding few opportunities at senior
level he took the decision to emigrate to Australia, and in
April 1967 obtained a playing contract with Sydney F.C.
He had planned to stay for two years, but in the event
remained for five before returning to the UK to work in
the family business in Nottingham. He retained an
involvement in the game as player-coach with Holbeach,
the United Counties League side.

Appearances: FL: 2 apps 0 gls Total: 2 apps 0 gls

THORPE, Adrian

Forward   5' 8"   11st 6lbs
b. Chesterfield, 25th November 1963
CAREER: Mansfield Town nc Aug 1982/Heanor Town Sept
1983/Bradford City Aug 1985 (Tranmere Rovers loan Nov
1986)/NOTTS Nov 1987, fee £50,000/Walsall Aug 1989,
fee £75,000/Northampton Town Mar 1990/Instant Dict
(Hong Kong)/Kettering Town cs 1993/Arnold Town cs
1994/Grantham Town Jan 1998/Arnold Town Apr 1998.
Debut as sub v Brentford (h) 7.11.87, won 3 – 0

A speedy wingman with a go-for-goal style who began
with Mansfield Town but was released without having
made a League debut. He joined the Magpies from
Bradford City in search of first team football, and for
two seasons enjoyed the best spell of his career, despite
the disappointment of defeat in the Play-off semi-final
against Walsall in May 1988. Including substitute
appearances Adrian played in a total of 160 League
matches for five clubs, scoring 20 goals.

Appearances: FL: 48(11) apps 9 gls FAC: 4 apps 1 gl
FLC: 3 apps 1 gl Other: 7(1) apps 2 gls
Total: 62(12) apps 13 gls

THORPE, Albert Edward

Full-back   5' 10"   10st 8lbs
b. Pilsey, Derbyshire, 14th July 1910
d. Langwith, Notts, 3rd January 1971
CAREER: East Derbyshire Schoolboys/Langwith Colliery/
Shirebrook am 1926/Coventry City trial Apr 1928/
Wolverhampton Wanderers May 1928/Mansfield Town July
1929/NOTTS Sept 1930/Norwich City May 1932/Crystal
Palace Oct 1935, in exchange for Frank Manders/Scunthorpe
& Lindsey United/Hereford United
Debut v Bristol City (h) 7.5.32, won 3 – 0

Teddy Thorpe began with the Wolves as a 17 year-old but was allowed to leave after just one League appearance. The Magpies signed him from Mansfield Town, (a non-League club at that time,) but he made little progress at Meadow Lane, failing to break into the 1930-31 championship winning side. Norwich City provided his first experience of regular first team football. He played in 20 matches in the Canaries' Third Division South championship winning side of 1934, completing 62 League and Cup matches before joining Crystal Palace. He served with the Sherwood Foresters Regiment during the war, and served with the Control Commission in Germany in 1951. For a short time he was coach and manager of Langwith Welfare F.C.

Appearances: FL: 1 app 0 gls Total: 1 app 0 gls
Honours: (Norwich City) FL Division 3 South champions 1934

THRAVES, James
Goalkeeper   5' 6"   11st 4lbs
b. Darley Dale, Derbyshire, January quarter 1868
d. Bramcote, Notts, 29th May 1936
CAREER: Notts. St. John's/NOTTS Aug 1889/Leicester Fosse July 1892/Long Eaton Rangers Sept 1897/Elected to NOTTS board Apr 1927
Debut v Burnley, FAC 2, (h) 31.1.1891, won 2 – 1

Injury to George Toone gave James Thraves his chance in the Magpies goal and his form following promotion to first class football was quite outstanding. In his first eight matches only eight goals were scored against him, the opposing clubs including Blackburn Rovers and Sunderland (twice each) and the crack amateurs, the Corinthians. At the time of his appearance in the 1891 FA Cup Final he was living in Stapleford and, in the words of the 'Evening News' correspondent: "engaged in agricultural pursuits." After leaving the Magpies he enjoyed a five-year spell with Leicester Fosse, making 148 consecutive appearances and qualifying for a benefit match in 1896. His earlier 'agricultural pursuits' again came in useful, as for two years he combined his playing career with that of groundsman for the Fossils. Subsequently he was in business as a road contractor and returned to the Magpies for an eleven-year stint on the board of directors.

Appearances: FL: 4 apps 0 gls FAC: 5 apps 0 gls
Total: 9 apps 0 gls
Honours: (NOTTS) FA Cup finalists 1891

THURMAN, Arthur John
Right-half
b. Radford, Nottingham, 8th May 1874
d. Boshof, South Africa, 30th May 1900
CAREER: Gedling Grove/NOTTS am May 1897
Debut v Stoke (a) 17.12.1898, drawn 1 – 1

In September 1889 the 'Football News' reported that: "The amateur, Thurman, again captains the reserve team." Commenting on his value to the club, they considered "His disappearance from the ranks of the 2nd Xl would cause a blank very similar to that which would be created should Calderhead sever his connection with the first team." Sadly, the former railway clerk lost his life in the following year after enlisting for service in the Boer War.

Appearances: FL: 2 apps 0 gls Total: 2 apps 0 gls

TIERNEY, Francis 'Fran'
Midfield   5' 10"   11st 0lbs
b. Liverpool, 10th September 1975
CAREER: Crewe Alexandra trainee, signing pro Mar 1993/ NOTTS July 1998 to May 2000/Altrincham trial/ Chesterfield trial/Witton Albion/Exeter City Nov 2000/ Witton Albion Jan 2001/Doncaster Rovers Mar 2001 to December 2004.
Debut as sub v Preston North End (h) 12.12.98, lost 2 – 3

From the right-side of midfield Fran Tierney starred for Crewe Alexandra as a player with skill on the ball and a wide range of passing skills and constructive moves. At one time linked with a move to Liverpool, which failed to materialise, he departed Gresty Road after five years, having played little first team football in his final two seasons. Lack of match fitness and an early injury combined to keep him out of the picture at Meadow Lane until mid season, and in following term he again struggled to make any kind of impact at senior level. More recently, Fran has tasted success with Doncaster Rovers. He scored the extra-time goal that won the Conference Play-off Final in May 2003 against Dagenham & Redbridge, and was a member of the squad who took Doncaster to a second consecutive promotion in 2003-04. In December 1904 he announced his retirement from full time soccer due to injury.

Appearances: FL: 19(14) apps 4 gls FAC: 1(4) apps 1 gl
FLC: 0(1) app 0 gls Other: 2 apps 0 gls
Total: 22(19) apps 5 gls
Honours: England Youth International. (Doncaster Rovers) FL Division 3 champions 2004.

TOMLINSON, Thomas

Outside-left 5' 8" 10st 10lbs
b. Sheffield circa 1890
CAREER: Newbold United Oct 1905/Birdholme Rovers June 1906/Chesterfield Town Mar 1907/Worksop Town May 1908/Chesterfield Town Dec 1908/Bradford P.A. season 1909-10/Mexborough Town cs 1910/NOTTS May 1912, fee £150/Newport County Aug 1913.
Debut v Manchester City (h) 2.9.12, lost 0 – 1

Tommy Tomlinson was part of a double swoop by Notts directors who took both of Mexborough Town's extreme wingmen in the close season of 1912. The other recruit was Frank Wathey, both stayed for just one season, and their playing records were identical: 7 matches, no goals. Tomlinson was a noted track athlete, but his football career was rather less distinguished, including both Football League and Southern League totals, his career aggregate was 57 matches and 14 goals.

Appearances: FL: 7 apps 0 gls Total: 7 apps 0 gls

He would doubtless have won more international caps had his progress not been hampered by a severe broken leg injury sustained at Sunderland in January 1891. This injury also cost him his place in the FA Cup Final against Blackburn Rovers. One of the leading writers of the day reported his display for England against Scotland at Ibrox Park, Glasgow, on 2nd April 1892 as follows: "Shots poured in upon Toone, and these were saved in splendid style. His display was one of the features of the match, and I have no hesitation in saying that he is one of the best goalkeepers that ever played for England." Despite being an international, he did not devote all of his time to sport, working as a twist hand in the local textile industry. He was also, for many years, a member of the local licensing trade. His son, George junior (below,) followed his father's footsteps, also playing for the Magpies.

Appearances: FL: 265 apps 0 gls FAC: 25 apps 0 gls
Other: 18 apps 0 gls Total: 308 apps 0 gls
Honours: England International, 2 caps 1892. (NOTTS)
FA Cup winners 1894. FL Division 2 champions 1897.

TOONE, George

Goalkeeper 5' 7½" 11st 2lbs
b. Nottingham, 10th June 1868
d. Nottingham, 1st September 1943
CAREER: Forest Olympic (Nottingham)/St Saviour's (Nottingham)/Lincoln City (briefly)/Notts. Rangers/NOTTS 1889/Bedminster Aug 1899/Bristol City May 1900/NOTTS Dec 1901; retired 1902; re-signed Aug 1903 but made no further FL apps.
Debut v Wolverhampton Wanderers (a) 7.9.1899, lost 0 – 2

George Toone first made his debut in football as a half-back with a small local club, Forest Olympic. He then joined St Saviour's, a rising junior team, and helped them win the Notts. Junior Cup. After a brief association with Lincoln City he joined Notts. Rangers, and at this time he first shone as a goalkeeping star of the future. Remarkably agile, he gave some wonderful exhibitions of the art of goalkeeping. He played for Nottinghamshire versus Staffordshire in 1889 and for the North versus the South in 1891.

TOONE, George (junior)

Centre-half 5' 8½" 11st 6lbs
b. Nottingham, 6th September 1893
d. Nottingham, 21st July 1950
CAREER: Northvale F.C./Sneinton Institute/Sherwood F.C./Sneinton Institute/NOTTS Aug 1913/Watford July 1919/Sheffield Wednesday Aug 1924, in exchange for G. Prior plus £240/Ilkeston United Sept 1925/Scarborough Penguins Oct 1928
Debut v Clapton Orient (a) 4.10.13, lost 0 – 1

Fair-haired George Toone was a plumber by trade and son of the famous George senior (above). Unlike his goalkeeping father he played in most positions on the field before settling down at centre-half. After army service in Mesopotania during WW1 he joined Watford for a small fee and played in every one of their first 159 Football League matches, totalling 190 senior outings before joining Sheffield Wednesday. His League career ended after a season at Hillsborough during which he played in 19 League and two FA Cup matches In late August 1925 he was reported to be "not fixed up," doubtless not helped by the fact that the Wednesday had placed a fee of £750 on him. In the following month he represented a fine capture for Ilkeston United who, as a non-League club, were not required to pay a fee for his services.

Appearances: FL: 1 app 0 gls Total: 1 app 0 gls

TORPEY, Stephen David James

Forward   6' 3"   14st 6lbs
b. Islington, 8th December 1970
CAREER: Cloparco U-10s/Bedford Park School/Coventry City trial/Millwall trainee, signing pro Feb 1989/Bradford City Nov 1990, fee £70,000/Swansea City Aug 1993, fee £80,000/Bristol City Aug 1997, fee £400,000 (NOTTS loan Aug 1998)/Scunthorpe United Feb 2000, fee £175,000
Debut as sub v Oldham Athletic (a) 8.8.98, won 3 – 1

Loaned to Notts at the start of season 1998-99, Steve Torpey was working his way back to match fitness after injury had brought a premature end to his first season with Bristol City. After two outings from the bench, he scored in his following two matches, against Manchester City in the League Cup, and at Northampton Town in Division Two. Although not a prolific goalscorer throughout his career, his all-round ability, physical presence and ability to win most balls in the air made him an outstanding 'target man,' and focal point for his team's attack. At the start of the 2004-05 season, Steve's impressive career figures totalled: 553(55) League and Cup matches and 152 goals.

Appearances: FL: 4(2) apps 1 gl FLC: 1(1) apps 1 gl
Total: 5(3) apps 2 gls
Honours: (Swansea City) Auto Glass Trophy winners 1994

TOSER, Ernest William

Centre-half   6' 0"   12st 0lbs
b. Old Ford, Bow, London, 30th November 1913
d. Hastings, 25th March 2002
CAREER: Smeed Road Junior School/Bow Central School/East London Schoolboys/Eton Manor/Luton Town am Feb 1931/ Dulwich Hamlet Apr 1931/Southampton am June 1931/Crystal Palace am Jan 1934/Millwall May 1937 (WW2 guest Clapton Orient, Bradford City, Rochdale, Fulham and Aldershot)/NOTTS Sept 1946/Bognor Regis Town Dec 1947/Dulwich Hamlet trainer 1948
Debut v Bristol City (h) 11.9.46, lost 0 – 3

An England Schoolboy international against Scotland in 1927 who went on to enjoy an outstanding career in top class amateur circles. Despite association with a number of Football League clubs, his appearances at this level amounted to just two for Millwall in the 1937-38 Division Three South championship season, and two for Notts. His involvement with the Magpies came when Bill Fallon, pressed into service at centre-half, was injured in both of the season's first two matches. It was hoped that Toser would fill the pivotal role and enable Fallon to revert to his normal outside-left berth. The 'Football Post', commenting on Toser's debut stated: "Nobody could say that Toser had a really good game in his first appearance at Meadow Lane.

He appeared to be on the slow side and rather ungainly in action and was unable to dominate the middle, the Bristol City centre-forward being much too quick for him." Sadly, he was given little opportunity to redeem himself, as a swift move into the transfer market brought in the ex-Sunderland pivot, Alex Lockie.

Appearances: FL: 2 apps 0 gls Total: 2 apps 0 gls
Honours: England Schoolboy International, 1 cap 1927. (Dulwich Hamlet) FA Amateur Cup winners 1934 & 1937

TOWLER, Bernard Edward

Outside-left   5' 8"   11st 4lbs
b. Ipswich, 13th March 1912
d. Bassingham, Lincs, 19th May 1992
CAREER: Lincoln Corinthians/Lincoln City am Aug, pro Sept 1932/NOTTS Aug 1938 (WW2 guest Lincoln City)/ Ruston Bucyrus (Lincoln) 1945-46/Boston United Oct 1946
Debut v Northampton Town (a) 24.9.38, lost 1 – 2

"Has plenty of pluck, and knows how to take a chance" was the 'Post Annual' verdict on Bernard Towler. He began in the reserve team at Meadow Lane but an early hat-trick against Hull City Reserves resulted in his being given a run in the first team. His best form came late in the season and he was retained for 1939-40 but returned to Lincoln City to assist them in wartime football. Subsequently he worked at the crane makers, Ruston Bucyrus, and was then a partner in a plant hire business.

Appearances: FL: 22 apps 9 gls Total: 22 apps 9 gls

TUCKER, Kenneth

Outside-left   5' 10"   11st 7lbs
b. Poplar, London, 2nd October 1925
CAREER: East Ham Schoolboys/Finchley/West Ham United Aug 1946/NOTTS Mar 1957 to 1958, fee £3,000/Margate
Debut v Port Vale (h) 9.3.57, won 3 – 1

Ken Tucker scored a hat-trick on his debut for West Ham United against Chesterfield in October 1947, but it proved insufficient to win him a regular berth in the side. This was finally achieved in season 1955-56 when he scored 14 goals in 37 League matches. He left the Hammers in March of the following season with a record of 31 goals in 93 League and Cup matches. He scored three goals in 11 appearances at the close of the 1956-57 season, when a late run of five wins and five draws pulled the Magpies out of the relegation zone. There was no such late rally in the following term when relegation from Division Two resulted, Ken Tucker being one of the players released in the close season. The 'Empire News Annual' for 1956-57 revealed that he had branched out as a businessman, and had two confectionery shops.

Appearances: FL: 28 apps 5 gls FAC: 2 apps 1 gl
Total: 30 apps 6 gls

TURNER, George William

Outside-left   5' 10½"   12st 0lbs
b. Mansfield, 5th May 1910
d. Luton, 17th April 1996
CAREER: Mansfield Athletic/Sneinton/NOTTS am Feb, pro May 1930/Luton Town June 1931/Everton Mar 1932/Bradford City June 1934/Luton Town June 1935/Northampton Town Mar 1936/Newark Town Aug 1938
Debut v Bournemouth & Boscombe Athletic (a) 28.1.31, lost 1 – 2 (scored)

Described in the 'Post Annual' for 1930-31 as: "A young, speedy outside-left, who performed well with the reserves last season. He was sought by other League clubs before he signed a professional form for Notts at the close of last season." When injury curtailed Sam Haden's lengthy run of consecutive appearances in January 1931, Turner was called upon. He deputised in three consecutive matches, scoring on his debut, as the Magpies progressed to win promotion as champions of the Third Division South. Turner left Meadow Lane in the close season and his subsequent career covered three divisions of the League, but he failed to fully establish himself anywhere, his career aggregate figures being 63 matches, 11 goals. Outside of the game he worked as a mechanic in the motor industry.

Appearances: FL: 3 apps 1 gl Total: 3 apps 1 gl

TURNER, Philip

Midfield   5' 8"   11st 0lbs
b. Sheffield, 12th February 1962
CAREER: Sheffield Rangers/Lincoln City associate schoolboy Oct 1976, app July 1978, pro Feb 1980/Grimsby Town Aug 1986, in exchange for G. Lund/Leicester City Feb 1988, fee £42,000/NOTTS Mar 1989 to June 1996, fee £125,000/Grantham Town assistant-manger to Sept 2004.
Debut v Reading (a) 4.3.89, won 3 – 1

A key player in Notts' rise from the Third Division to the First in successive seasons, Phil Turner led by example, grafting long and hard in midfield and equally able to operate in defence or attack if required. Valued at £125,000 when he joined the

Magpies as part of the deal that took Gary Mills to Filbert Street, he captained Notts to two consecutive promotions via Wembley Play-off victories. Considering his misfortunes in the shape of a catalogue of injuries and operations during his seven years at Meadow Lane, his return of over 300 appearances was a testament to his bravery, resilience, and total commitment to the cause. Phil announced his retirement in June 1996 with a career total of 538(26) League matches and 44 goals.

Appearances: FL: 219(18) apps 16 gls FAC: 15 apps 3 gls FLC: 17(3) apps 0 gls Other: 33(1) apps 3 gls
Total: 284(22) apps 22 gls
Honours: (NOTTS) Anglo Italian Cup winners 1995, finalists 1994

TURNER, Robert Peter "Robbie"

Forward   6' 3"   13st 11lbs
b. Gateshead, 18th September 1966
CAREER: Sunderland associate schoolboy/ Huddersfield Town app July 1983, pro Sept 1984/Cardiff City July 1985 (Hartlepool United loan Oct 1986)/Bristol Rovers Dec 1986/Wimbledon Dec 1987, fee £15,000/Bristol City Jan 1989, fee £45,000/Plymouth Argyle July 1990, fee £150,000 (NOTTS loan Nov 1992)/NOTTS Dec 1992, fee £90,000 (Shrewsbury Town loan Mar 1993) (Burnley trial Jan 1994)/Exeter City Feb 1994/Cambridge United Dec 1995 to Jan 1997 (Hull City loan Oct 1996)/Taunton Town early in 1997
Debut v Southend United (a) 21.11.92, lost 1 – 3

Robbie assisted a round dozen of League clubs in a nomadic career. Muscular, hard working and good in the air, his goal trail began with Cardiff City. His first appearance for the Bluebirds was made at Meadow Lane on the opening day of season 1985-86. The 4 – 1 victory proved an isolated success, however. Relegated at the end of the season, he had the dubious honour of scoring Cardiff's first-ever goal in Division Four. Robbie arrived at Meadow Lane on loan from Plymouth Argyle and was sufficiently impressive to warrant a £90,000 fee being paid for his transfer. Mainly used as a central defender, he was unfortunate to lose his place due to injury. His League career ended with aggregate figures of 244(41) appearances and 54 goals.

Appearances: FL: 7(1) apps 1 gl FAC: 1 app 0 gls
Total: 8(1) apps 1 gl

TWIGG, Richard Lance

Goalkeeper   6' 0"   12st 0lbs
b. Barry, 10th September 1939
CAREER: Barry Town/NOTTS Oct 1957 to 1959/Sutton United/Barry Town Nov 1961 to May 1965
Debut v Plymouth Argyle (h) 14.3.59, lost 1 – 2

At the age of 19 Richard had a trial for the Welsh Under-23 side. He joined the Magpies from Barry Town and was considered an exceptional prospect after performing with brilliance in his 17 appearances for the Magpies' Reserves in his first season. Stern competition was nevertheless provided by Jimmy Linton, with the equally experienced Gordon Bradley as back up. Richard was restricted to just two consecutive League outings in March 1959 and linked up with Sutton Town on his release. In November 1961 he had returned to live in his hometown, and rejoined Barry Town, having found the marathon journeys to Sutton "a bit much."

Appearances: FL: 2 apps 0 gls Total: 2 apps 0 gls

ULLATHORNE, Robert

Left-back   5' 8"   11st 3lbs
b. Wakefield, 11th October 1971
CAREER: Goole Grammar School/Norwich City associate schoolboy Oct 1986, trainee July 1988, pro July 1990/CA Osasuna (Spain) July 1996/Leicester City Feb 1997, fee £600,000/Huddersfield Town trial Oct 1999/Real Zaragoza (Tenerife) trial/Newcastle United trial Sept 2000/Sheffield United Dec 2000 to May 2003/Stoke City trial/Walsall trial/ Derby County trial/Northampton Town Feb 2004/NOTTS July 2004.
Debut v Chester City (h) 7.8.2004, drawn 1 – 1

A left sided midfielder or full-back of ripe experience, Rob began with Norwich City as a 15 year-old on schoolboy forms and went on to win two England U-18 caps. After almost ten years with the Canaries, he enjoyed a spell in northern Spain with Osasuna, coached at that time by current Liverpool manager and European Cup winner, Rafa Benitez. A sizeable fee took Rob to Leicester City, but within eleven minutes of his debut against Wimbledon he suffered a broken leg and missed out on a trip to Wembley for the FL Cup Final victory against Middlesbrough. Two years on, he featured in the 1999 FL Cup Final against the Spurs, but in the following month suffered another broken leg when in collision with his own goalkeeper, Kasey Keller. Spells with Sheffield United and Northampton

Town preceded his arrival at Meadow Lane, where his experience, class and ball skills on the left flank have made him a real asset in a difficult season for the club.

Appearances: FL: 34(2) apps 0 gls FAC: 1 app 0 gls
FLC: 2 apps 1 gl Total: 37(2) apps 1 gl
Honours: England Youth International, 2 apps. (Leicester City) FL Cup finalists 1999

UPTON, Frank

Left-half   6' 0"   13st 4lbs
b. Ainsley Hill, 18th October 1934
CAREER: Nuneaton Borough/Northampton Town Mar 1953/Derby County June 1954/Chelsea Aug 1961, fee £15,000/Derby County Sept 1965/NOTTS Sept 1966/Worcester City July 1967/Workington player-manager Jan 1968, fee £1,650/Northampton Town coach Oct 1969/Aston Villa coach Jan 1970/Chelsea coach Aug 1977, caretaker manager Dec 1978/Randers Freja coach Feb 1979 to Feb 1980/Dundee coach Aug 1980/Al Arabi coach 1981/Wolverhampton Wanderers youth coach Oct 1982/Bedworth United coach Oct 1984/Coventry City assistant manager Dec 1984 to Apr 1986/IBK Keflavik May 1987/Aston Villa scout/youth development/Borneo national coach May 1989/Burton Albion caretaker manager Jan-Feb 1990/Northwich Victoria youth development officer Apr 1990/Sabah, Malaysia, coach/Cheltenham Town YTS officer to Nov 1990/India national coach Jan 1994 to June 1995/Aston Villa chief scout 1998.
Debut v Lincoln City (h) 24.9.66, won 2 – 1

Two separate spells with Derby County accounted for a large part of Frank Upton's total of 389(2) League appearances and 24 goals. Although he did not figure regularly in the Rams' Third Division North championship in 1956-57, he subsequently gained a regular place. The strongly-built wing-half completed a little over 250 League matches for Derby in two spells, broken by a successful four-year stint with Chelsea. He assisted the Pensioners to promotion from Division Two in 1962-63, and to victory in the 1965 FL Cup, played over two legs in those days, in a 3 – 2 aggregate victory over Leicester City. The Magpies narrowly avoided a re-election application in his season at Meadow Lane. Fielded at both left-half and later at centre-forward, his best return as a scorer came within three weeks of his arrival, two goals in the 5 – 2 home win against Luton Town in Oct 1966 coming from his midfield berth. Thirteen appearances as attack leader later in the season failed to add to the teams' fire power, as Frank managed to score only once from his unaccustomed position.

Appearances: FL: 33(1) apps 3 gls FAC: 1 app 0 gls
Total: 34(1) apps 3 gls
Honours: (Chelsea) FL Cup winners 1965

VALLANCE, Robert

Left-half   5' 9"   11st 8lbs
b. Stanley Common, Ilkeston 19th September 1901
d. Stanley Common, Ilkeston, 28th February 1980
CAREER: Heanor Town/Ilkeston Town Aug 1925/Grantham
Town May 1927/NOTTS May 1929, fee £100/Grantham
Town cs 1930/Gainsborough Trinity Sept 1931/Stanley
Common Miners Welfare Aug 1932/Smalley United, Derby,
Sept 1934/Stanley Excelsior July 1936
Debut v Cardiff City (a) 16.9.29, lost 1 – 3

The month of April 1930, in which Bob Vallance played
in his final League match, yielded just one point from
seven Division Two matches. Unsurprisingly, the
Magpies were relegated and Vallance returned to Grantham
Town after a season when he failed to establish himself
beyond reserve team football, interspersed with infrequent
call-ups for senior duty as deputy for Haydn Kemp.

Appearances: FL: 8 apps 0 gls Total: 8 apps 0 gls

VASEY, Robert Henry 'Bob'

Left-half   5' 8"   11st 0lbs
b. Annfield Plain, Co Durham, 16th December 1907
d. Dipton, County Durham, 4th December 1979
CAREER: Annfield Plain/Consett/Nottingham Forest Jan
1932/NOTTS June 1936/Brighton & Hove Albion Aug 1938
(WW2 guest Chester 1941-42)
Debut v Exeter City (h) 29.8.36, won 3 – 1

After filling a reserve team role for much of his spell with
the Forest, Bob Vasey played in a little over half of the
season's matches during his first term in the Black &
White jersey. Whilst 26 League and Cup appearances
constituted an improvement in terms of first team action,
he would probably have fared even better had his stamina
levels improved. As the 'Football Post' commented in
October 1936: "What a pity it is that Vasey is not stronger
physically! He has put up some excellent first-half
performances, but rarely is able to last out a game at top
speed." He played in only five first team matches in
1937-38, but had done sufficient in one of them, a 1 – 0
win at Brighton, to win a contract with them following
his release from Meadow Lane.

Appearances: FL: 27 apps 1 gl FAC: 1 app 0 gls Other: 3
apps 0 gls Total: 31 apps 1 gl

VINCENT, Robert

Centre-forward
b. Leicester, 29th May 1949
CAREER: NOTTS am Jan 1966
Debut v Port Vale (a) 19.3.66, won 1 – 0

In his solitary League outing, as
deputy for Dennis Shiels,
amateur centre-forward Vincent
had the satisfaction of appearing
in a winning side, a single goal from
Tony Flower deciding the outcome in the
Magpies' favour. An eighth place finish in
Division Four in 1965-66 was a frustrating
outcome, inconsistent form at home ruining
the benefit of an excellent away record. With
ten wins and four draws on their travels, the
Magpies had the best away record in the division, but
they won only nine of their 23 League matches at Meadow
Lane.

Appearances: FL: 1 app 0 gls Total: 1 app 0 gls

VINTER, Michael 'Mick'

Forward   5' 9"   11st 0lbs
b. Boston, Lincs, 23rd May 1954
CAREER: Boston United/NOTTS Mar 1973, fee £2,000/
Wrexham June 1979, fee £150,000/Oxford United Aug
1982, fee £30,000/Mansfield Town Aug 1984, fee £15,000/
Newport County Aug 1986/Gainsborough Trinity cs 1987/
Boston United cs 1988/Matlock Town cs 1989/Oakham
United player-coach cs 1990/Hucknall Town player-coach
June 1991/Sutton Town player-coach Sept 1992/Sneinton
1994
Debut as sub v Shrewsbury Town (a) 12.8.72, drawn 0 – 0

Mick Vinter starred as a quick thinking, spirited front
runner, alive to every possibility, and an arch snapper-up
of the half chance. He scored the bulk of his 63 goals in
his final three seasons at Meadow Lane, 1977-78 being a
vintage year with 25 goals in 49(1) League and Cup
outings, rewarded by his selection as 'Player of the Year.'
Highlights during his spell with Wrexham included
appearances in the European Cup Winners Cup, and a
goal against the Forest in Wrexham's shock 3 – 1 FA Cup
victory at the City Ground in season 1981-82. During
two years with Oxford United he was a member of their
Division Three championship side in 1983-84, scoring
11 goals in 25(1) League matches. Mick's League career
concluded with spells at Mansfield Town and Newport
County, his career aggregate figures being 373(49) League
appearances and 113 goals.

Appearances: FL: 135(31) apps 54 gls FAC: 7(1) apps 5
gls FLC: 8(2) apps 1 gl Other: 9(1) apps 3 gls
Total: 159(35) apps 63 gls
Honours: (Oxford United) FL Division 3 champions 1984.
(Wrexham) Welsh Cup finalist 1981

WADE, Allen

Full-back/Half-back   5' 10"   12st 4lbs
b. Scunthorpe, 19th July 1926
CAREER: Scunthorpe United am/ NOTTS July 1952/
Grantham July 1956/FA director of coaching Oct 1962
Debut v Bury (a) 13.9.52, won 1 – 0

At either full-back position or centre-half Allen Wade
played regularly for the reserve team, and occasionally
for the first team, with a break in service when he obtained
a scholastic appointment in Manchester. He returned to
the City of Nottingham Education Authority in time to
resume at Meadow Lane, and made his final three League
appearances in late season 1955-56. Released by Notts
in the close season he joined Grantham. Six years later, at
the age of 40, he was appointed the FA's director of
coaching.

Appearances: FL: 9 apps 0 gls Total: 9 apps 0 gls

―――――――――o―――――――――

WAINWRIGHT, Thomas

Centre-half   5' 11½"   11st 2lbs
b. Nantwich, April quarter 1879
CAREER: Church School Boys/Nantwich F.C./Crewe
Carriage Works/Burslem Port Vale Nov 1900/Crewe
Alexandra May 1902/Wellington Town 1903/NOTTS May
1904/Wellington Town June 1906.
Debut v Aston Villa (a) 12.11.04, lost 2 – 4

A tall and slimly-built reserve centre-half, Thomas
Wainwright had previous League experience with Burslem
Port Vale in Division Two, but struggled in Division One
with Notts. His eight senior outings, split over two
seasons, yielded one win, one draw and six defeats. In
non-League circles he collected six gold and one silver
medal. These included one awarded during his spell with
Crewe Alexandra, who were runners-up in the
Birmingham & District League in season 1902-03.

Appearances: FL: 8 apps 0 gls Total: 8 apps 0 gls

―――――――――o―――――――――

WAITT, Michael Hugh

Forward   6' 4"   12st 0lbs
b. Hexham, 25th June 1960
CAREER: Green Dragon Athletic 1978/Calverton Rangers/
Arnold Kingswell 1982/Keyworth United Aug 1984/NOTTS
trial Oct, pro Dec 1984, fee £500/Lincoln City June 1987,
fee £17,500/Boston United Dec 1989/Lai Sun (Hong Kong)
Dec 1989/Nuneaton Borough Mar 1990/Spalding United
Dec 1990/Nuneaton Borough Jan 1991/Grantham Town
Mar 1991/Gedling Town Sept 1991/Ilkeston Town/Napier
City (New Zealand) player-coach Jan 1992/New Zealand
national team coach 2002.
Debut v Wimbledon (a) 26.12.84, lost 2 – 3

Towering striker who struggled initially in a poor Magpies
1984-85 side that finished 20th in Division Two and were
relegated, despite the efforts of three different managers
to halt the slide. In Jimmy Sirrel's third spell in charge,
Notts consolidated in Division Three and Waitt, who
employed his height to great advantage in set piece
situations, enjoyed two successful seasons, scoring 18
League and Cup goals in 1985-86 and 13 in his final season,
1986-87. Signed by Lincoln City's manager Colin Murphy
as the Imps attempted to win back their place in Division
Four, Waitt got them off to an excellent start by scoring
eight goals in 18 matches before a broken leg in October
1987ended his involvement in the ultimately successful
campaign. **Note:** When first brought to the Magpies for
trials, Mick was working night shifts as an electrician at
Plessey's. His hours were midnight to 8 a.m. Two hours
later he had to report for fitness training at Meadow
Lane!

Appearances: FL: 71(11) apps 27 gls FAC: 8(2) apps 4
gls FLC: 4(1) apps 1 gl Other: 5 apps 0 gls
Total: 88(14) apps 32 gls
Honours: (Lincoln City) GM Vauxhall Conference
champions 1988

―――――――――o―――――――――

WALKER, Albert

Outside-left   5' 9"   10st 12lbs
b. Ripley, August 1888
CAREER: South Wingfield/Ripley Athletic/Nottingham
Forest Dec 1906/Queens Park Rangers May 1907/Notts
May 1908/Croydon Common Sept 1912.
Debut v Woolwich Arsenal (h) 5.9.08, won 2 – 1

Lightweight centre-forward who graduated in Forest's
Reserve team and enjoyed a successful season in the South
before returning to Nottingham to join the Magpies. The
scorer of 16 goals in 30 League and Cup matches for
Q.P.R., he was nevertheless considered too light for the
position of a First Division attack leader. Given an
extended run at outside-left he proved a good auxiliary,
figures of seven goals in 34 League matches constituting a
satisfactory first season in the top flight. He took part in
the Magpies' first overseas tour to Denmark in June 1910
and figured in the half-back line with surprisingly good
results. The additional string to his bow did not enhance
his prospects at senior level, however, much of his final
two terms being spent in the Midland League.

Appearances: FL: 53 apps 9 gls FAC: 3 apps 0 gls
Total: 56 apps 9 gls
Honours: (Queens Park Rangers) Southern League
champions 1908

―――――――――o―――――――――

WALKER, George

Centre-half 5' 11" 11st 10lbs
b. Musselburgh, Midlothian, 24th May 1909
CAREER: Rosslyn Juniors/St Mirren Nov 1926/NOTTS June 1933, fee £2,600/Crystal Palace June 1936, fee £1,000/ Watford June 1939
Debut v Hull City (a) 26.8.33, won 1 – 0

In August 1933 Notts players were left to elect their own captain for the season. Their unanimous choice was for George Walker, who had joined the club only a few weeks earlier. The team's selection proved to be an excellent one, as the 24 year-old newcomer proved to be a captain in the true sense, directing operations on the field and impressing as a pivot off all-round competence, equally able in both attack and defence. When the outbreak of WW2 suspended League football, George had recorded an aggregate of 412 appearances. George was a nephew of the Hearts and Scotland celebrity, Bobby Walker, who won 29 Scotland caps between 1900-13.

Appearances: FL: 100 apps 1 gl FAC: 4 apps 0 gls Other: 1 app 0 gls Total: 105 apps 1 gl
Honours: Scotland International, 4 caps 1930-31. Scottish League representative, 2 apps

---

WALKER, James Henry 'Harry'

Left-half 5' 7½" 10st 12lbs
b. Wirksworth, Derbyshire, January quarter 1890
d. Doncaster, January quarter 1934
CAREER: Wirksworth Boys' Brigade/Wirksworth F.C./Clay Cross/Derby County May 1910/NOTTS June 1920/Fulham Mar 1921/Aberdare Athletic May 1923/Bournemouth & Boscombe Athletic Mar 1924/Chesterfield June 1924/Derby County am May 1925
Debut v Bristol City (a) 28.8.20, won 1 – 0

Harry Walker began as an inside-forward with Derby County, making his FL debut at Clapton Orient in September 1911 in a forward line that included the legendary Steve Bloomer. Walker played in only three League matches in his debut season, when the Rams won the championship of Division Two.

Three years and one relegation later he was established at right-half when a second title win restored the Rams to Division One. He joined the Magpies having appeared in 88 League and Cup matches for Derby, but he was unable to secure a regular place at Meadow Lane. After appearing in four out of the five opening fixtures of season 1920-21, he subsequently made only one other senior appearance, leaving before the end of the season to join Fulham. His involvement at senior level from then onwards was minimal, totalling 14 League matches for three different clubs before a return, an amateur forms, to his first love Derby County at the age of 35.

Appearances: FL: 5 apps 0 gls Total: 5 apps 0 gls
Honours: (Derby County) FL Division 2 champions 1915

WALKER, John Allsop

Inside-left
b. Plumtree, Notts. 30th November 1871
CAREER: Shrewsbury School/Magdalen College (Oxford)/ Derby Junction/Derby County 1889/NOTTS Oct 1891 (Last FL app 24.9.1892)
Debut v Aston Villa (h) 2.1.1892, won 5 – 2

In the season prior to the formation of the Football League, John Walker appeared in the FA Cup semi-final for Derby Junction who were defeated 3 – 0 by West Bromwich Albion, the eventual winners of the trophy. He first appeared for Derby County on 28th September 1889, his debut being made against the Magpies, the team he was to join some two years later. He had not appeared regularly for Derby (13 senior matches over two seasons) and he failed to establish himself with the Magpies. This despite his bright start in splendid 5 – 2 victory against Aston Villa.

Appearances: FL: 4 apps 0 gls Total: 4 apps 0 gls

WALKER, Richard Neil

Defender 6' 0" 12st 0lbs
b. Derby, 9th November 1971
CAREER: NOTTS trainee July 1988, pro July 1990 to June 1997 (Mansfield Town loan Mar 1995)
Debut v West Ham United (h) 13.3.93, won 1 – 0 (scored)

Following an injury to Charlie Palmer, manager Mick Walker drafted in his namesake, Richard, for the visit of high-flying West Ham United, unbeaten in their last fifteen matches. In true 'Roy of the Rovers' style, the debut-boy headed the only goal of the match. He retained his place for the remainder of the season, scoring a further two priceless goals.

Deep into injury time he headed the equaliser at Brentford in a 2 – 2 draw, and on May 1st netted against Oxford United at the Manor Ground in a 1 – 1 draw. Relegation averted, Richard began the following season as an established first team man. Sadly, he was injured at Grimsby Town in late December, and played only once more that season. Eventually crowded out by new signings he was released in the summer of 1997.

Appearances: FL: 63(4) apps 4 gls FAC: 1(2) apps 0 gls FLC: 10 apps 0 gls Other: 8(1) apps 0 gls Total: 82(7) apps 4 gls

---

WALKERDINE, Garnet Coxon

Inside-left
b. Nottingham, October quarter 1882
d. Nottingham, October quarter 1965, age 82
CAREER: Notts. League amateur football/NOTTS Jan 1904/ Gainsborough Trinity Aug 1904/Sutton Town Sept 1905/ Mansfield Mechanics June 1907
Debut v Manchester City (a) 23.1.04, lost 0 – 3

A younger brother of Harry (below) who was first tried in senior football against the crack amateur side, the Corinthians, in a friendly match played on 28th December 1903. Playing in the same inside-left position so successfully occupied by his elder brother, he showed sufficient promise in the 3 – 5 defeat to warrant a run out against Manchester City in a First Division match at Hyde Road some three weeks later. Without adding to his solitary senior outing he was transferred in the close season to Gainsborough Trinity, at that time a Football League club operating in Division Two.

Appearances: FL: 1 app 0 gls Total: 1 app 0 gls

WALKERDINE, Henry 'Harry'

Inside-left
b. Nottingham circa 1870
d. Mansfield, 7th November 1949
CAREER: NOTTS 1889/Gainsborough Trinity 1890/ NOTTS 1891-93
Debut v West Bromwich Albion (a) 4.1.1890, lost 2 – 4

In his first spell with Notts Harry Walkerdine scored four goals in one friendly match against Dumfries at Trent Bridge on 28th December 1889. He returned after a season with Gainsborough Trinity, who he assisted to the championship of the Midlands League in season 1890-91. Lightly-built, consistent and adaptable, he had an excellent season in 1891-92, appearing in all but one of the season's 28 League and Cup matches. Mainly from inside-left he scored 13 goals, his total including a hat-trick in the 9 – 0 defeat of Accrington in November 1891.

A bright start to the following season was not maintained, however, six consecutive League defeats in late season resulting in relegation from the top flight. Harry was said to be living in Mansfield in 1893, but he later moved to Gainsborough were he worked as editor of a local newspaper from around 1900.

Appearances: FL: 38 apps 16 gls FAC: 3 apps 1 gl Other: 1 app 0 gls Total: 42 apps 17 gls

---

WALL, Tom Henry

Goalkeeper
b. Nottingham, 29th May 1909
d. Nottingham, 8th June 1989
CAREER: Ripley Town/Clifton Colliery/NOTTS am May 1932/Tottenham Hotspur June 1933/Nottingham Forest trial Sept-Oct 1934/Ripley Town Sept 1935
Debut v Southampton (h) 17.4.33, lost 1 – 2

A reserve goalkeeper whose involvement in League football amounted to just four matches. Three appearances for the Magpies, and one opposed to them. He did not appear at senior level for Tottenham Hotspur, and his one outing during a trial period with Forest was made at Meadow Lane. Although beaten three times, it was Forest who took the points with a 5 – 3 victory. His lack of success at senior level was revealed in the 'Football Post' who, in April 1933, stated: "Wall is good in anticipation and shot stopping, but his goal kicking and general clearing is a big weakness."

Appearances: FL: 3 apps 0 gls Total: 3 apps 0 gls

WARBURTON, Benjamin Frederick

Centre-half
b. Worksop, July quarter 1864
d. West Bridgford, 22nd September 1943
CAREER: NOTTS Sept 1888 to 1889
Debut v Everton (a) 15.9.88, lost 1 – 2

Once described as "A sterling half-back," Warburton's brief involvement included an appearance in County's first ever fixture in the Football League at Everton. His second outing was at West Bromwich Albion in the following month. In the New Year he accepted a Government appointment with the telegraph service in South Africa. As a young man he played cricket for Notts. Castle C.C.

Appearances: FL: 2 apps 0 gls Total: 2 apps 0 gls

WARD, Alfred

Outside-right   5' 10"   12st 0lbs
b. Eastwood, Notts, 1883
d. Burton-on-Trent, August 1926, age 42
CAREER: Clowne White Star (Derbyshire)/NOTTS Oct 1903/Brighton & Hove Albion May 1904/Aberdeen May 1905/Bradford P.A. cs 1907/Southampton May 1908, retired cs 1909
Debut v Middlesbrough (h) 31.10.03, won 3 – 2

Although with a record of eleven seconds for the 100 yards sprint, Ward was said to be a little short of training when he joined the Magpies. Nevertheless, his well-judged centres marked him as an outside right of exceptional promise. One of six different players to contest the outside-right spot during 1903-04, he departed in the close season to Brighton & Hove Albion. He failed to fulfil expectations at the Goldstone but in two seasons with Aberdeen scored 10 goals in 26 Scottish Division One matches, operating at this point at inside-right or centre-forward. His premature retirement from the game was caused by a cartilage injury, sustained at Leipzig when he was a member of Southampton's continental touring party in May 1908.

Appearances: FL: 7 apps 0 gls FAC: 1 app 0 gls
Total: 8 apps 0 gls

WARD, Darren

Goalkeeper   5' 11"   12st 9lbs
b. Costhorpe, near Worksop, 11th May 1974
CAREER: Langold Boys/Bassetlaw Schoolboys/Nottinghamshire Schoolboys/Mansfield Town associate schoolboy Aug 1988, trainee July 1990, signing pro July 1992/NOTTS June 1995, fee £160,000/Nottingham Forest May 2001/Norwich City Aug 2004.
Debut v Wrexham (a) 12.8.95, drawn 1 – 1

Darren Ward made his League debut in Division Two for Mansfield Town against Hartlepool United on 16th February 1993. The 18 year-old goalkeeper starred in a 2 – 0 victory and held his place for a run of eleven consecutive matches that coincided with an upturn in results.

Born of an English father and a Welsh mother, he was first included in the Wales U-21 squad in March 1995. Out of contract at Field Mill in June of the same year, he joined the Magpies for an initial £100,000 fee with a further £60,000 based on appearances. In almost six years at Meadow Lane a measure of Darren's consistency can be found in his appearance figures which average almost 50 matches per season. Selected for the award winning PFA team following the Magpies Third Division championship success in 1997-98, Darren won his first full Wales cap and established himself as club captain before moving across the Trent to join Forest on a 'Bosman' free transfer. In terms of League matches alone, his career figure totalled 455 appearances before the start of season 2004-05.

Appearances: FL: 251 apps 0 gls FAC: 23 apps 0 gls
FLC: 18 apps 0 gls Other: 7 apps 0 gls
Total: 299 apps 0 gls
Honours: Wales International 5 caps. Wales 'B' International, 1 app. Wales U-21 International, 2 apps. (NOTTS) FL Division 3 champions 1998

WARD, John

Right-back
b. Mansfield, 18th January 1948
CAREER: NOTTS app, signing pro July 1965
Debut v Bradford City (h) 27.4.66, won 4 – 0

One of a trio of Notts apprentices to sign a professional form in July 1965. The others were Richard Stead, who failed to graduate to senior level, and Bob Woolley who had burst into League football as a 16 year-old while still on apprentice forms. John Ward spent most of the 1965-66 season as reserve right-back until an injury to Ivan Hampton afforded him an opportunity in late season. His five consecutive appearances spanned a little over a fortnight, his sojourn in the spotlight beginning well with three consecutive wins, but ending with two defeats.

Appearances: FL: 5 apps 0 gls Total: 5 apps 0 gls

WARDLE, Edwin Silvester

Outside-right
b. Nottingham, 11th January 1870
CAREER: NOTTS 1888-89
Debut v Everton (a) 15.9.1888, lost 1 – 2

Edwin Wardle's two League appearances spanned the first and last matches of County's first season as a Football League club. He found more involvement in the season's FA Cup matches, appearing at outside right in qualifying rounds one to four.

The Magpies' Cup opponents in those far-off days being Eckington, Beeston St. John's, Derby Midland and Staveley. Wardle scored one of the goals in the 3 – 1 win against Staveley that took the Magpies into the first round proper. At this stage they beat Old Brightonians 2 – 0, but exited the competition in the next round, losing 2 – 3 at Sheffield Wednesday.

Appearances: FL: 2 apps 0 gls FAC: 4 apps 1 gl
Total: 6 apps 1 gl

WARNER, Alfred Cragg

Inside-forward   5' 8"   10st 10lbs
b. Nottingham circa 1880
CAREER: Notts. Rangers/Notts. Olympic/St Andrew's/Weal F.C./NOTTS am during season 1898-99, pro Aug 1899/Tottenham Hotspur May 1902/Luton Town May 1905/NOTTS Oct 1907- cs 1908.
Debut v Glossop (a) 18.11.1899, drawn 0 – 0

On the light side and of medium height, Alf Warner was a Nottingham man and an excellent local player who commenced with County's Reserves during season 1898-99. At times accused of a little selfishness and a bit of 'gallery play' he was on balance a talented forward with clever ball control and a great shot. In season 1900-01 he scored 12 League goals to assist the Magpies to third place in Division One. After three years with Tottenham Hotspur and two with Luton Town he had announced his retirement as a player but was persuaded to make a come back to assist his old club who were struggling in the lower reaches of Division One. By the narrowest of margins the relegation trapdoor was avoided, and Alf Warner signed off for a second time in the close season.

Appearances: FL: 56 apps 15 gls FAC: 3 apps 1 gl
Total: 59 apps 16 gls

WARREN, Mark Wayne

Defender   6' 0"   12st 2lbs
b. Hackney, London, 12th November 1974
CAREER: Essex Schoolboys/Leyton Orient trainee July 1991, pro July 1992 (Oxford United loan Dec 1998)/NOTTS Jan 1999/Colchester United Aug 2002/Southend United June 2003
Debut v Reading (h) 30.1.99, drawn 1 – 1

A former England Youth international who made his League debut with Leyton Orient at the age of seventeen in May 1992 and went on to complete 147(20) League and Cup appearances, scoring seven goals. He refused terms for a new contract and was snapped up by Magpies' manager Sam Allardyce, who had long admired Mark's assets of pace, tenacity and outstanding aerial ability.

His totally fearless approach inevitably brought a catalogue of injuries, much of his final season at Meadow Lane being spent on the sidelines. Mark appeared with Southend United at the Millennium Stadium in March 2004 for the LDV Vans Trophy Final. Having overcome his previous club, Colchester United, in the semi-finals, the Shrimpers were then beaten 2 – 0 by Blackpool in the final.

Appearances: FL: 76(8) apps 1 gl FAC: 1 app 0 gls FLC: 9 apps 0 gls Other: 4 apps 0 gls Total: 90(8) apps 1 gl
Honours: England Youth International. (Southend United) LDV Vans Trophy finalists 2004.

WATERALL, Albert

Inside-forward   5' 7"   10st 10lbs
b. Radford, Nottingham 1st March 1887
d. Nuthall, Nottingham 8th March 1963 age 76
CAREER: Radford Institute/Sneinton/NOTTS May 1909/Stockport County June 1913/Queens Park Rangers trial Sept 1926/Clapton Orient Oct 1926/Grantham Town Nov 1926 to circa 1929
Debut v Aston Villa (h) 15.4.11, lost 1 – 2

The fourth member of the Waterall family to assist Radford Institute. Albert had a crop of goals to his credit while playing in the Notts. Junior League, and success followed after his move to Sneinton, leading to his recruitment by the Magpies. He made rapid progress in the Midland League side, and was soon appearing alongside his brother "Ike" in First Division matches. Eventually seeking pastures new, he joined Stockport County where he clocked up exactly 300 League and Cup appearances and 36 goals. He was awarded two benefits for his thirteen years of outstanding service, which also included 97 wartime appearances and nine goals. On retirement from the game he returned to Nottingham and became a licensee.

Appearances: FL: 26 apps 1 gl FAC: 1 app 0 gls
Total: 27 apps 1 gl

WATERALL, Isaac 'Ike'

Winger   5' 8½"   10st 6lbs
b. Radford, Nottingham, 3rd October 1888
d. Sherwood, Nottingham, 25th December 1970 age 82
CAREER: Radford Woodhouse/Heanor United/NOTTS am Sept 1906/Doncaster Rovers May 1907/Rotherham County Aug 1907/Rotherham Town May 1908/NOTTS July 1909/Millwall June 1920/Ebbw Vale July 1921, manager Feb 1923
Debut v Middlesbrough (a) 17.11.06, lost 0 – 2

County's popular right winger was probably the most successful of the quintet of Waterall brothers. At the age if sixteen he was chosen to represent the Notts. Junior

League against the Irish Junior League, and shortly afterwards was signed by Heanor United. His initial stay with the Magpies was brief, but he was induced to return after a term in the Midland League with Rotherham Town. He subsequently developed into one of the finest wingmen in the country. Able to play on either wing, he possessed a rare turn of speed. An added advantage was his ability to centre on the run with either foot. A cricketer, too, of above average ability, summers were spent as coach to the Blundell School, Tiverton, Devon.

Appearances: FL: 184 apps 13 gls FAC: 7 apps 1 gl
Total: 191 apps 14 gls

WATERALL, Tom
Outside-left   5' 8"   10st 6lbs
b. Radford, Nottingham, 24th October 1884
d. Nottingham, 8th November 1951, age 67
CAREER: Radford Institute 1904/Heanor United 1905/
NOTTS am March, pro April 1906/Bradford P.A. June 1908/
Mansfield Mechanics cs 1909/Leicester Fosse July 1913,
fee £10/Watford July 1914 (WW1 guest Stockport County
Sept 1915)/Gillingham July 1921/Sheppey United May 1922/
Sittingbourne (by Mar 1926)/Sheppey United May 1926/
Canning Town Glass Works Oct 1930
 Debut v Wolverhampton Wanderers (a) 16.4.06, lost 1 – 6

Dark-haired and handsome, Tom Waterall succeeded Ellis Gee on the Magpies left wing. In the opening month of season 1907-08 he scored in consecutive Division One matches against Sunderland and Woolwich Arsenal, but in the same month he lost his inside partner, Aaron Jones, to an injury that brought an untimely end to the former Birmingham player's career. Without a regular inside partner thereafter, Waterall's form suffered and he left Nottingham for Bradford P.A. at the end of the season. Watford was the scene of his greatest success, beginning with ten goals in the Southern League championship season 1914-15. He was still with the Hornets in August 1920, when they won 2 – 1 at Queens Park Rangers in their first-ever FL fixture.

In the inter-war period he was a licensee in Sheerness, returning to Nottingham during the WW2 period as landlord of the Old Cricket Players at Hyson Green.

Appearances: FL: 28 apps 5 gls FAC: 4 apps 0 gls
Total: 32 apps 5 gls
Honours: (Watford) Southern League champions 1915

WATHEY, Frank
Outside-right   5' 8"   10st 8lbs
b. Barnsley, January quarter 1888
CAREER: Denaby United/Conisburgh Swifts/Mexborough/
NOTTS Apr 1911 to 1913.
Debut v Sheffield Wednesday (h) 21.9.12, lost 1 – 2

Listed in the 1901 Census as "A coal miner pony driver." (One is struck by the thought that life was anything but a picnic for a 13 year-old at the turn of the twentieth century.) At sixteen Frank Wathey joined Denaby United, and was operating in the Midland League with Mexborough at the time of his signing by Notts. Unfortunately, there was no happy ending for the young Yorkshire man, or for the Magpies, who were relegated from Division One, having only just celebrated their fifty-year Jubilee. As the 'Athletic News' unkindly commented: "No club has made a more thorough acquaintance with the bottom positions."

Appearances: FL: 7 apps 0 gls Total: 7 apps 0 gls

WATLING, Barry John
Goalkeeper   5' 9"   11st 12lbs
b. Walthamstow, 16th July 1946
CAREER: Leyton Orient app, signing pro July 1964/Bristol City July 1965/NOTTS July 1969/Hartlepool United July 1972 (Chester loan Sept 1975) (Rotherham United loan Dec 1975)/Sheffield Wednesday Jan 1976/Maidstone United July 1977
Debut v Exeter City (A) 10.1.70, drawn 1 – 1

In a defence comprised mainly of strapping six-footers, Barry Watling seemed almost diminutive by comparison, but despite his short, stocky build he was an extremely agile and accomplished last line of defence. In the championship season 1970-71 he conceded just 35 goals in 43 League matches, his record including the saving of five penalty kicks during the successful season. He had played in only two League matches when he arrived at Meadow Lane on a free transfer from Bristol City, and took over as first team goalkeeper, replacing Mike Rose, in January 1970. Transferred to Hartlepool United in July 1972 he had the remarkable record of appearing in all but one of League and Cup matches for three consecutive seasons, 156 matches out of a possible 157.

His League career ended with a single appearance for Sheffield Wednesday against Swindon Town in January 1976.

Appearances: FL: 66 apps 0 gls FAC: 4 apps 0 gls FLC: 1 app 0 gls Total: 71 apps 0 gls
Honours: (NOTTS) FL Division 4 champions 1971

————————o————————

WATSON, Arthur Edwin Cooke

Outside-right
b. Hucknall Torkard, April quarter 1870
d. Mansfield, 29th January 1937
CAREER: University College/Mansfield Greenhalgh's/Mansfield Town/NOTTS May 1893/Mansfield Town/West Bromwich Albion Aug 1896, fee £25/Lincoln City 1899
Debut v Crewe Alexandra (a) 2.9.1893, won 2 – 1 (scored one)

Said to possess the faculty of bothering, and altogether upsetting the defenders opposed to him, Arthur Watson possessed rare speed, and the deadly combination of graceful dribbling and a splendid shot. He appeared at League level with Notts and West Bromwich Albion, and scored on his debut for both clubs. He starred for the Magpies in his first season, scoring 13 goals from outside-right in League matches. He was also a goal scorer in the FA Cup final of 1894 when the Magpies lifted the trophy, beating Bolton Wanderers by 4 – 1 at Goodison Park.

Appearances: FL: 22 apps 13 gls FAC: 5 apps 1 gl Other: 2 apps 0 gls Total: 29 apps 14 gls
Honours: (NOTTS) FA Cup winners 1894

————————o————————

WATSON, Charles Richard

Goalkeeper   5' 10"   11st 0lbs
b. Newark, Notts, 10th March 1949
CAREER: Southwell City/NOTTS Feb 1967 (Dunstable Town loan Aug 1968)/Rainworth Miners' Welfare.
Debut v Doncaster Rovers (h) 1.5.68, lost 0 – 2

Although considered a highly promising youngster, Charlie Watson was just one of four goalkeepers on the Magpies' books, Mike Rose and Mick Gadsby were the main contenders for the first team jersey, with Phil Williams and Charlie Watson in reserve. At the commencement of season 1968-69, Watson was loaned to Southern League club Dunstable Town, managed at that time by the former Leicester City and Notts full-back, Len Chalmers. In season 1981-82 Charlie appeared in the FA Vase Final, at Wembley, for Rainworth Miners' Welfare who lost 3 – 0 to Forest Green Rovers.

Appearances: FL: 1 app 0 gls Total: 1 app 0 gls

WATSON, David Vernon

Centre-half/Centre-forward   6' 0"   12st 0lbs
b. Stapleford, Notts, 5th October 1946
CAREER: Nottingham Schoolboys/Stapleford Old Boys/NOTTS am June 1966, pro Jan 1967/Rotherham United Jan 1968, fee £8,000 plus Keith Pring/Sunderland Dec 1970, fee £100,000/Manchester City June 1975, fee £175,000 plus Jeff Clarke/Werder Bremen (Germany) June 1978, fee £200,000/Southampton Oct 1979, fee £200,000/Stoke City Jan 1982, fee £50,000/Vancouver Whitecaps (Canada) Apr 1983/Derby County Sept 1983/Fort Lauderdale (USA) May 1984/NOTTS player-coach Sept 1984/Kettering Town Aug 1985
Debut v Chester (h) 28.3.67, won 3 – 0

Dave Watson was among the outstanding centre-halves of the post World War Two era: cool, superb in the air, with an imperious stabilising influence. He was also extremely durable, his League career approaching two decades and 657 League appearances, beginning and ending at Meadow Lane. A younger brother of Peter Watson, the former Forest and Southend United centre-half, Dave had been a professional for only a year when he was recruited by Rotherham United's manager, Tommy Docherty, in a cash plus player deal that brought Keith Pring to Meadow Lane. Subsequent career highlights included Sunderland's lifting of the FA Cup in 1973, and his first taste of First Division football with Manchester City when two months short of his 29th birthday and with 14 international caps already in his locker. A League Cup winners' medal was the highlight of his four years with Manchester City. His final total of 65 England caps, spread over a period of eight years with five different clubs, established a record, subsequently equalled by Peter Shilton. Sadly, his fine career ended in disappointment as his first love, the Magpies, crashed out of Division Two in season 1984-85. His wife Penny wrote a most interesting book about his career entitled 'My Dear Watson.'

Appearances: FL: 48(2) apps 2 gls FAC: 1 app 0 gls FLC: 2 apps 0 gls Total: 51(2) apps 2 gls
Honours: England International, 65 caps 1974-82. (Sunderland) FA Cup winners 1973. (Manchester City) FL Cup winners 1976.

WATSON, Joseph

Left-back   5' 9"   11st 10lbs
b. Most probably at Derby
CAREER: St. Chad's/Theatre Gospel Hall/ Derby
Wednesday/NOTTS am June 1932, pro Mar 1933
Debut v Port Vale (a) 20.3.33, lost 0 – 4

Amateur left full-back Joe Watson was first tried in a friendly match against Airdrieonians in January 1933. Two months later he made an impressive debut in League football, when it was noted in the local press that he had been operating in a junior team in Derby only six months ago. At the outset of his career he represented the Derbyshire Sunday School League against their Nottingham counterparts and had taken part in two S.S.L. Cup finals. In November 1934 the 'Football Post' revealed that Watson feared retirement, due to illness. It seems likely that this unhappy event did in fact take place as his final Magpies appearance came at Oldham Athletic on November 11th, 1934.

Appearances: FL: 10 apps 0 gls Total: 10 apps 0 gls

WATSON, Norman

Half-back   5' 8"   12st 0lbs
b. Sunderland, 21st December 1899
CAREER: Hylton Colliery/Southwick/Chester-le-Street/ Leicester City May 1922/NOTTS June 1932, fee £400/ Workington Aug 1933/Wigan Athletic Aug 1934/Horwich RMI/Wigan Athletic Feb 1937
Debut v Lincoln City (h) 27.8.32, drawn 1 – 1

A strongly built and versatile half-back with the benefit of a decade's service in Divisions One and Two with Leicester City, covering 178 League and Cup appearances. Well into the veteran stage when he arrived at Meadow Lane, Norman appeared in only five League matches in a season blighted by illness. Moving to Workington, at that time a North Eastern League club, he assisted them to reach round four of the FA Cup, eliminating three Football League clubs along the way. He enjoyed further success with Wigan Athletic, captaining them to consecutive Cheshire League championships in 1935 and 1936. Summer months were spent playing cricket for the Sunderland based Hendon club.

Appearances: FL: 5 apps 0 gls Total: 5 apps 0 gls

WATSON, William James Boyd 'Jimmy'

Inside-forward   5' 10½"   11st 7lbs
b. Govan, Glasgow, 14th August 1910
CAREER: Glasgow St Anthony's/Tunbridge Wells Rangers July 1932/Bristol Rovers May 1933/Northampton Town June 1934/Gillingham July 1935/NOTTS May 1938, fee £350/Bristol Rovers July 1939 (WW2 guest Tunbridge Wells Rangers, Blackpool and Bradford City)/Brighton & Hove Albion 1945
Debut v Swindon Town (a) 27.8.38, lost 1 – 4

Ginger-haired Jimmy Watson arrived at Meadow Lane with good credentials. In three seasons with Gillingham he had scored 38 goals in 110 appearances, and his skilful play had often been admired by the Magpies' directors when Gillingham provided the opposition at Meadow Lane. Sadly, for a player of ripe experience he was slow to settle. Lack of a regular wing partner did not help his game, but he was given an extended run, appearing in the first 13 League matches, before being dropped in favour of schoolteacher Stan Clayton.

Appearances: FL: 17 apps 4 gls Total: 17 apps 4 gls

WATTS, Ernest A

Right-half   5' 10"   12st 9lbs
b. Woolhampton, Berkshire, circa 1874
CAREER: Reading Apr 1896/NOTTS May 1898/Reading May 1899/West Ham United cs 1903/New Brompton cs 1904/Reading/Clapton Orient Dec 1906 to May 1907
Debut v Liverpool (h) 27.12.1898, drawn 1 – 1

Commenting on the performance of the season's signings in April 1899, the 'Football News' stated: "Watts proved beyond all question a capable half-back, though his earlier displays were anything but promising." Five months later the local correspondent was bemoaning the defection of Watts, who had rejoined his first love, Reading. He became a familiar figure on Southern League grounds, and was selected for an International trial, South v North in 1903. A 'Who's Who' publication of the period described him as: "A sterling centre-half and captain. An old soldier but a grand football exponent." Outside of football Ernie played for Berkshire County Cricket Club, and held the R.H.S. certificate for life saving.

Appearances: FL: 17 apps 0 gls FAC: 1 app 0 gls Total: 18 apps 0 gls

WATTS, T. H.

Centre-forward
b. Most probably in Scotland
CAREER: Magdala Amateurs/NOTTS am Feb 1906 to 1911
Debut v Sheffield Wednesday (h) 27.10.06, drawn 2 – 2

Commenting on the League debut of the young schoolmaster, the 'Football News' revealed that he had turned out in borrowed boots that fitted where they touched. Nevertheless, he had proved useful in many ways: "Getting the ball out to the wings and letting the opponents know that he was knocking about." A tall and well-built young fellow, well able to hold his own in a good shoulder charge, he had collected a rich harvest of goals for Notts. Magdala, the crack local amateurs.

Had Watts been able to get away for regular training he was considered promising enough to be a very suitable understudy for Arthur Green, the Magpies Welsh international centre-forward. Although he remained registered on amateur forms up to and including season 1910-11, Watts did not add to the three League outings made in his debut season.

Note: As an amateur, Watts was able to retain a foot in both camps, assisting both the Magpies and Magdala during his term of association with both clubs. In season 1906-07, Magdala reached the final of the Notts. Senior Cup for the first time, eliminating the Magpies in the semi-final. They were beaten by Forest in the final at the City Ground by 4 – 1.

Appearances: FL: 3 apps 0 gls Total: 3 apps 0 gls

WEAVER, Eric

Winger   5' 7"   11st 13lbs
b.Rhymney, 1st July 1943
CAREER: Trowbridge Town/Swindon Town Dec 1961/ NOTTS Aug 1967/Northampton Town Dec 1967 to cs 1970/Boston United
Debut v Chester (h) 19.8.67, lost 1 – 2

Eric Weaver sampled both promotion and relegation during five and a half years with Swindon Town. By contrast, he had hardly had time to unpack his bags in his brief association with the Magpies. In the month following an excellent run of form – he scored in four consecutive League matches in November – he moved up a Division when transferred to Northampton Town. He scored in his second appearance for the Cobblers and played in 23 consecutive matches, scoring five goals to conclude a successful season 1967-68. Without a win in their last ten League matches in the following term the Cobblers were relegated, and Eric departed the County Ground at the end of the 1969-70 season with a record of nine goals in 71 League and Cup matches.

Appearances: FL: 16(1) apps 4 gls FAC: 1 app 0 gls Total: 17(1) apps 4 gls

---

WEBSTER, Adam Paul

Forward   6' 1"   12st 5lbs
b. Leicester, 3rd July 1980
CAREER: Thurmaston Town/Barwell F.C./NOTTS Feb 1999 (Grantham Town loan Sept 1999) (Bedworth United loan Jan 2000)/Bedworth United Mar 2000/Worcester City Dec 2001
Debut as sub v Scunthorpe United (a) 22.1.2000, lost 0 – 1

A tall young striker, discovered in Leicestershire junior football and signed on a professional form towards the close of season 1998-99.

In the following term Adam spent loan spells with two Dr Martens League clubs and had a brief substitute appearance at Scunthorpe United. He then joined Bedworth United on a permanent basis.

Appearances: FL: 0(1) app 0 gls Total: 0(1) app 0 gls

WEIGHTMAN, Frederick Hugh

Inside-forward
b. Newark, Notts, January quarter 1863
d. Nottingham, 2nd May 1897
CAREER: Notts. Rangers/Nottingham Forest Feb 1888 / Notts. Wanderers/NOTTS Dec 1888/Nottingham Forest to Apr 1890
Debut v Aston Villa (h) 8.12.1888, lost 2 – 4

In what little has been traced of Fred Weightman's football career, it can nevertheless be stated that he certainly knew where the goals were. A scorer in his solitary Football League outing for the Magpies, in the following season he played in four Football Alliance matches for Forest, and was a scorer against Sheffield Wednesday and Long Eaton. At the time of his death, at the tragically early age of 34, he was working as a railway clerk.

Appearances: FL: 1 app 1 gl Total: 1 app 1 gl

WELLS, Mark Anthony

Midfield   5' 9"   11st 2lbs
b. Leicester, 15th October 1971
CAREER: NOTTS trainee Aug 1988, pro July 1990/ Huddersfield Town Aug 1993/Scarborough July 1994 to June 1997/Worcester City Aug 1998/Hinckley United.
Debut as sub v Sheffield United, Zenith Data Systems Cup 2 (a) 22.10.91, drawn 3 – 3 a.e.t., Notts won 2 – 1 on penalties.

A strong-tackling left side midfielder who was five days beyond his 20th birthday when making his senior debut as a substitute in the ZDS Cup at Sheffield United. He exhibited a marked lack of nerves when successfully converting a penalty in the shoot-out that decided the tie in the Magpies favour. A further two substitute appearances in the League side was his only other involvement at senior level prior to his release, on a free transfer, to Huddersfield Town. He made the best possible start with his new club, scoring the winner at Rotherham United on his debut, but he played in only half of the seasons Division Two matches and joined Scarborough on a free transfer in the close season. Injury blighted much of his spell at the McCain Stadium, restricting his League appearances to just 26(6) prior to his release in June 1997.

Appearances: FL: 0(2) apps 0 gls Other: 0(1) app 0 gls Total: 0(3) apps 0 gls

WEST, Abraham Kendall

Goalkeeper
b. Cockermouth, July quarter 1887
d. Nottingham, 23rd May 1952
CAREER: NOTTS trial Nov 1912
Debut v Tottenham Hotspur (a) 4.11.12, won 3 – 0

The first 'clean sheet' of season 1912-13 was in no small way thanks to trialist goalkeeper Abe West, but in the days when Albert Iremonger ruled supreme beneath the Magpies' crossbar, West did not add to his solitary League outing. Something of a mystery man (to the football researcher that is), West was also known by the surname Kendall. Details in Probate revealing that he had died at Nottingham General Hospital under the name of Abraham Kendall West – also known as Furniss.

Appearances: FL: 1 app 0 gls Total: 1 app 0 gls

———————o———————

WEST, Alfred

Left-back   5' 8"   12st 0lbs
b. Nottingham, 15th December 1881
d. Nottingham, April quarter 1944
CAREER: Nottinghamshire Schoolboys/Notts. Jardines/ Radford Congregational/Ilkeston United 1900/Barnsley May 1902/Liverpool Nov 1903/Reading June 1909/Liverpool May 1910/NOTTS July 1911/Mansfield Town Aug 1919/ Shirebrook Dec 1919 to Jan 1920
Debut v West Bromwich Albion (a) 2.9.11, lost 1 – 2

Alf West completed a career total of exactly 300 League appearances when he played his final match for the Magpies against Aston Villa in April 1915. Although a Nottingham man, he began in senior football with Barnsley, his first association with the Yorkshire club coming when he captained the Rest of the Midland League against Barnsley in 1900. Although never a showy back, West was consistently cool and reliable and it was almost three years before he missed a single League or Cup game for the Magpies, making 116 consecutive appearances before injury curtailed his record. During his Meadow Lane spell he collected a Second Division championship medal to add to the First Division championship he had won with Liverpool eight years earlier. The 'Post Annual' for 1914-15 revealed that Alf was also "Hot stuff at golf, which keeps him in fine condition."

Appearances: FL: 130 apps 4 gls FAC: 4 apps 0 gls Total: 134 apps 4 gls
Honours: (Liverpool) FL Division 1 champions 1906. (NOTTS) FL Division 2 champions 1914

———————o———————

WHITCOMBE, George Charles

Centre-half   5' 10½"   13st 0lbs
b. Cardiff, 21st January 1902
d. Cardiff, 30th April 1986
CAREER: Cardiff & District League football/Cardiff City cs 1922/Stockport County May 1925/Port Vale Aug 1926/ NOTTS Dec 1930, fee £375/Ashton National May 1931/ Colwyn Bay United Sept 1932
Debut v Queens Park Rangers (a) 25.12.30, lost 1 – 4

George Whitcombe, a powerfully-built defender, enjoyed his best spell of League football with Port Vale who signed him following injury to their regular pivot, Bob Connelly. Although selected intermittently, he appeared in 51 League matches and three FA Cup ties before his mid-season transfer to the Magpies. He was expected to succeed Frank Froggatt at centre-half, but his involvement at senior level lasted for just seven consecutive matches before he lost out to the former Wealdstone amateur, H.R. Smith. When released by Notts, a trio of League clubs (Q.P.R., Norwich City and Bristol Rovers) expressed an interest in him, but the player opted for a move to Ashton National. In May 1930 George played for Wales in an international baseball match against England held at Port Vale's ground at Bryan Street, Hanley.

Appearances: FL: 7 apps 0 gls FAC: 1 app 0 gls Total: 8 apps 0 gls

———————o———————

WHITE, Devon Winston

Forward   6' 3"   14st 0lbs
b. Nottingham, 2nd March 1964
CAREER: Radford Olympic/Arnold F.C. Sept 1984/Lincoln City Dec 1984/Boston United Oct 1986 (Naxxar Lions, Malta, loan)/Grantham Town Aug 1987 (playing in one match only)/Bristol Rovers Aug 1987/Cambridge United Mar 1992, fee £100,000 plus John Taylor/Queens Park Rangers Jan 1993, fee £100,000/NOTTS Dec 1994, fee £110,000/Watford Feb 1996, fee £100,000/NOTTS Mar 1997, fee £20,000/Shrewsbury Town Sept 1997, fee £35,000/Ilkeston Town June 1999/Stafford Rangers.
Debut v Millwall (a) 26.12.94, lost 0 – 1

A former electrician, Devon was born within sight of Meadow Lane and had trials with Notts as a youngster. He was to return as a seasoned professional with ten years League experience when County manager Russell Slade paid £100,000 to bring him from Queens Park Rangers. His return brought both joy and disappointment. His spectacular headed goal clinched victory in the Anglo-Italian Cup Final against Ascoli at Wembley, but two months later Notts were relegated from Division One. Despite starting the following season in a blaze of scoring glory with 14 League and Cup goals in his first 20 matches, he was transferred to Watford in February and the promotion drive faltered. A fourth place finish was followed by a Play-off Final defeat by Bradford City. Brought back to Meadow Lane a little over a year later, he was unable to lift a side heading for relegation into Division Three. Devon scored his final Magpies goal in August of the following season against Lincoln City, the club who had launched his League career.

Appearances: FL: 45(10) apps 17 gls FAC: 2(2) apps 0 gls FLC: 7 apps 7 gls Other: 4(2) apps 2 gls
Total: 58(14) apps 26 gls
Honours: (Bristol Rovers) FL Division 3 champions 1990. Leyland DAF Cup finalists 1990. (NOTTS) Anglo Italian Cup winner 1995

WHITELAW, Andrew

Right-back   5' 7½" 10st 10lbs
b. Jamestown, Dunbartonshire, 19th May 1865
d. Mansfield, 2nd January 1938
CAREER: Vale of Leven/Heanor Town/NOTTS June 1891/ Heanor Town cs 1893/Leicester Fosse July 1894/Heanor Town July 1895/Ilkeston Town Aug 1897
Debut v Preston North End (h) 5.9.1891, won 2 – 0

Andrew Whitelaw captained Vale of Leven for five years, and represented Dunbartonshire in 15 county matches. He also appeared in the Scottish Cup final of 1890 when Vale of Leven were defeated, in a replay, by Queen's Park 2 – 1. A team-mate, and scorer in the final, was Daniel Bruce and the two were reunited in the Magpies ranks in season 1892-93. A cool but resourceful tackler with excellent mobility, he contested the first team right-back position with Tommy McLean in his first season but was unchallenged in 1892-93 when he appeared in all League and Cup matches. After a season with Heanor Town he returned to League action with Leicester Fosse, who were contesting their first season as a Football League club. After a shaky start the Fossils rallied to finish fourth in Division Two, Whitelaw appearing in 16 League matches and 5 FA Cup ties.

Appearances: FL: 41 apps 0 gls FAC: 4 apps 0 gls Other: 1 app 0 gls Total: 46 apps 0 gls
Honours: Scotland International, 2 caps 1887-90. (Vale of Leven) Scottish Cup finalists 1890

WHITLEY, Jeffrey 'Jeff'

Midfield   5' 8"   11st 2lbs
b. Zambia, 28th January 1979
CAREER: Manchester City trainee, signing pro Feb 1996 (Wrexham loan Jan 1999) (NOTTS loan Mar 2002 and again Oct 2002)/Sunderland Aug 2003/Cardiff City June 2005
Debut v Brighton & Hove Albion (a) 23.3.2002, drawn 2 – 2

Jeff Whitley made his League debut with Manchester City at the age of 17 in September 1996. An industrious midfield ball-winner who came up through City's youth development programme, he appeared at Wembley in the 1999 Division Two Play-off Final against Gillingham, despite having made only one starting appearance during the season. The in-and-out nature of his City career saw him play in 42 League matches in the following season. The twin brother of James (Wrexham,) Jeff had also seemed certain to be moving to the Racecourse on a permanent basis, but stayed with City to record 107(30) League and Cup appearances and eight goals before his permanent move to Sunderland in August 2003. Between times, his two loan spells with the Magpies were most impressive. He would have made an excellent signing had finances been in place. With a Belfast-born father, Jeff qualified to play for Northern Ireland and he received his first call-up by Bryan Hamilton's full international squad in January 1997.

Appearances: FL: 18 apps 0 gls FAC: 1 app 0 gls Other: 1 app 0 gls Total: 20 apps 0 gls
Honours: Northern Ireland International, 6 caps. Northern Ireland 'B' International, 2 apps N Ireland U-21 International, 17 apps

---

WHITLOW, Michael 'Mike'

Defender   6' 0"   12st 12lbs
b. Northwich, 13th January 1968
CAREER: Witton Albion/Leeds United Nov 1988, fee £100,000/Leicester City Mar 1992, fee £250,000/Bolton Wanderers Sept 1997, fee £500,000/Sheffield United July 2003/NOTTS July 2004
Debut v Chester City (h) 7.8.2004, drawn 1 – 1

A former playing colleague of manager Gary Mills during Leicester City days, Mike was signed to captain his new-look team, a combination hoping for a fresh start and some success after the memories of near extinction and relegation in 2003-04. A seasoned campaigner with a career total in excess of 450 senior appearances, Mike's spirited defensive play, timely headed interventions and coolness under pressure have been a great source of strength to the side. Rugged and extremely capable in defence, his influence was sadly missed when injury problems curtailed his season.

Appearances: FL: 22(2) apps 0 gls FAC: 4 apps 0 gls FLC: 1 app 0 gls Other: 1 app 0 gls
Total: 28(2) apps 0 gls

WHITTAKER, Frederick

Centre-forward
b. Canada, 12th October 1923
CAREER: Vancouver (Canada)/NOTTS Aug 1946 to June 1947 when he returned to Canada.
Debut v Bournemouth & Boscombe Athletic (h) 31.8.46, won 1 – 0

The Magpies commenced the first season back in League football after WW2 with a Canadian centre-forward, Fred Whittaker. Sadly, he was not physically fit and in the second month of the new season was receiving specialist treatment for a sciatic nerve problem. He appeared very infrequently, but in April and May scored his first two goals for the club and, more unusually, played twice as goalkeeper when regular custodian Harry Brown was unavailable. If a little unorthodox in method, Fred won high praise on both occasions, starring in a 1 – 1 draw at Bristol City and in a 1 – 0 victory against Reading at Meadow Lane.

Appearances: FL: 10 apps 2 gls
Total: 10 apps 2 gls

WHYTE, Peter

Outside-right
CAREER: Scottish junior football/NOTTS June 1902/ Renton Oct 1903
Debut v Middlesbrough (a) 24.1.03, lost 1 – 2

Recruited from Scottish junior football, Peter Whyte spent a season in reserve, finding little profit as understudy to the ever-consistent Dickie Joynes. Aside from his Division One debut, Whyte appeared against Newcastle United and Liverpool. Upon his return to Scotland, however, he faced more modest opposition – his debut for Renton being made against Greenock Morton's 'A' team!

Appearances: FL: 3 apps 0 gls FAC: 4 apps 0 gls
Total: 7 Apps 0 gls

WIDDOWSON, Albert

Outside-right
CAREER: Nottingham Forest/NOTTS Mar 1892
Debut v Bolton Wanderers (a) 26.3.1892, lost 0 – 2

A late-season try out failed to result in a permanent engagement for Albert Widdowson. On his debut he deputised for England cap, Harry Daft, at outside left. In the last two fixtures of the 1891-92 campaign he appeared on the opposite flank, the Magpies Lancashire tour ending pointless, defeats by 1 – 0 at Burnley being followed one day later by a 4 – 0 reverse against Everton.

Appearances: FL: 3 apps 0 gls Total: 3 apps 0 gls

WIDDOWSON, Alfred

Centre or Inside-forward   5' 7"   10st 10lbs
b. Keyworth, Notts, 16th September 1900
d. Nottingham, January quarter 1970
CAREER: Army football/NOTTS Dec 1919/Coventry City Mar 1928, with N. Dinsdale for a combined fee of £500/ Newark Town Aug 1932/Heanor Town July 1933
Debut v Newcastle United (h) 27.3.20, drawn 0 – 0

Considered one of the best representatives of the younger school of players at Meadow Lane Alf Widdowson led the attack of the reserve team with considerable skill, following his demobilisation from the Army. He first appeared regularly at senior level during 1921-22 and was reckoned to have played the best game of his career in the replayed fourth round FA Cup tie against Aston Villa at Villa Park. Notts won a rousing encounter by 4 – 3 to reach the semi-final but at that stage went under by 3 – 1 against the eventual winners of the trophy, Huddersfield Town. Without fully realising the highest hopes brought on by his early promise, Widdowson was an undoubted talent who dribbled well and shot strongly with either foot. He was a keen supporter of the Magpies and a regular on the Meadow Lane terraces right up until his death in 1970. **Note:** At the time of his League debut, the 'Football Post' pointed out that Alfred Widdowson had already been confused with the Widdowson who played at centre-half for the reserves after joining from Boots Athletic.

Appearances: FL: 141 apps 39 gls FAC: 16 apps 7 gls
Total: 157 apps 46 gls

WIDDOWSON, Sam Weller

Centre-forward 5' 8½" 11st 7lbs
b. Hucknall Torkard, Notts, 16th April 1851
d. Beeston, Nottingham, 9th May 1927
CAREER: Notts. schoolboy & junior football/NOTTS Jan 1873 to Nov 1878/Nottingham Forest 1878-85 & was that club's chairman 1879-84. Twice served on the FA Committee, 1888-92 & 1893-94
Debut v Sheffield, FAC 1 (h) 3.11.1877, drawn 1 – 1

Adjudged by Alcock's Annual to be "A capital centre-forward, very quick and a sure goal-getter." Widdowson was also a talented cricketer who appeared for Nottinghamshire C.C.C. and was also a noted track athlete. He captained Nottingham Forest for many seasons, and was the first man to devise and wear shin guards in 1874, originally worn buckled over the stockings. The son of an avid Dickensian, he was named after Sam Weller of Charles Dickens' 'Pickwick Papers.'

Appearances: FAC: 1 app 0 gls Total: 1 app 0 gls
Honours: England International, 1 cap 1880

WIDDOWSON, Thomas Haslam
Goalkeeper
b. Hucknall, Notts, January quarter 1862
d. Kimberley, Nottingham, 20th June 1944
CAREER: Nottingham Forest/NOTTS Dec 1888/ Nottingham Forest/Kimberley F.C. Sept 1898
Debut v Aston Villa (h) 8.12.1888, lost 2 – 4

Tom Widdowson had an unfortunate start in the Magpies' goal, his debut against Villa at Trent Bridge being contested in terrible weather. The slippery ball was blamed for his diversion of a right wing centre through his own goal, but otherwise he had a sound game and retained his place for the remainder of Notts first season in the Football League. An interesting point from the match report was the fact that the two teams had not provided distinguishing colours and "only some" of the Notts team had white shirts!

Appearances: FL: 12 apps 0 gls FAC: 2 apps 0 gls
Total: 14 apps 0 gls

WILDER, Christopher John 'Chris'
Defender   5' 11"   12st 8lbs
b. Stocksbridge, 23rd September 1967
CAREER: Southampton app Sept 1984, pro Sept 1985/ Sheffield United Aug 1986 (Walsall loan Nov 1989) (Charlton Athletic loan Oct 1990) (Leyton Orient loan Feb 1992)/Rotherham United July 1992, fee £50,000/ NOTTS Jan 1996, fee £150,000/Bradford City Mar 1997, fee £150,000/Sheffield United March 1998, fee £150,000 (Northampton Town loan Nov 1998) (Lincoln City loan Mar 1999)/Brighton & Hove Albion July 1999/Halifax Town Oct 1999/Alfreton Town Sept 2001, player-manager Oct 2001/Halifax Town manager July 2002
Debut v Wrexham (h) 20.1.1996, won 1 – 0

A highly experienced and versatile defender, able to occupy any position along the back four. An additional bonus being his ability as a free-kick and long-throw specialist.

Chris made League appearances for eleven different clubs, totalling in excess of 400 League appearances, these included over 100 for both Sheffield United and Rotherham United. His lengthy senior career was ended following a back injury, and he then made an excellent start to his managerial career, winning no fewer than four trophies during his brief association as player-manager of Alfreton Town.

Appearances: FL: 46 apps 0 gls FAC: 4 apps 0 gls FLC: 2 apps 0 gls Other: 1 app 0 gls Total: 53 apps 0 gls

---

WILEMAN, Richard Andrew
Outside-left   5' 9½"   10st 10lbs
b. Breedon on the Hill, Leics, 4th October 1947
CAREER: NOTTS July 1966/Loughborough United 1967
Debut v Chester (a) 24.3.67, won 2 – 1

One of three close season recruits from Leicestershire – David Needham and Tim Crispin completing the trio – Richard Wileman was initially listed as a wing-half on joining the Meadow Lane staff. In the event, his two FL outings were made at outside-left, a position that saw seven different players used during the course of the season. A move to Loughborough United linked him with ex-Notts favourites Don Roby, Alan Withers and manager Ronnie Mann.

Appearances: FL: 2 apps 0 gls Total: 2 apps 0 gls

WILKES, Timothy Craig 'Tim'
Forward   6' 0"   12st 0lbs
b. Nottingham, 7th November 1977
CAREER: NOTTS trainee July 1994, pro July 1996 (Grantham Town loan Feb 1997)/Kettering Town Mar 1997/ Telford United/Gainsborough Trinity (Rothwell Town loan)/ Grantham Town cs 1999/Hinckley United cs 2002/Barwell Sept 2002/Coalville Town 2003/Shepshed Dynamo Jan 2004/Coalville Town.
Debut v Plymouth Argyle (a) 7.9.96, drawn 0 – 0

Local product whose displays at reserve team level earned him an opportunity in Division Two whilst still a teenager. In a season when the Magpies scored just 33 League goals in 46 matches and finished at the foot of the table, Tim was allowed to move on loan to Grantham Town before joining Kettering Town. His first spell in non-League football with the Poppies produced figures of 33(27) appearances and 10 goals. With Grantham Town his figures were 93 matches and 22 goals.

Appearances: FL: 3 apps 0 gls Other: 1(1) apps 0 gls
Total: 4(1) apps 0 gls

WILKIE, Lee

Central defender   6' 4"   13st 4lbs
b. Dundee, 20th April 1980
CAREER: Downfield Juniors/Dundee Sept 1998 (Plymouth Argyle loan Jan 2001) (NOTTS loan Aug 2001) (Falkirk loan Nov 2001)
Debut v Port Vale (a) 11.8.2001, lost 2 – 4

Briefly associated with the Magpies when appearing in the opening two matches at the start of season 2001-02. The strapping central defender spent a second loan spell from Dundee in November of the same season, appearing in nine Scottish League matches for Falkirk, scoring against St Mirren and Ross County. Returning to Dens Park, he appeared in the final eight Scottish Premier League fixtures. In the close season he joined the Scotland squad and won the first two of his international caps in the matches against South Africa (as a substitute) and a Hong Kong League X1.

Appearances: FL: 2 apps 0 gls Total: 2 apps 0 gls
Honours: Scotland International, 11 caps 2002-04.
Scotland U-21 International, 6 caps 2000-01

WILKINSON, Frank

Half-back
b. Radcliffe-on-Trent, Notts, 8th January 1867
CAREER: Wilkinson's F.C. (Beeston)/NOTTS am Aug 1889, pro May 1892 to 1894
Debut v Bolton Wanderers (h) 11.1.1890, lost 3 – 5

First called up as emergency cover for David Calderhead, local amateur Frank Wilkinson suffered a severe baptism in League football, Bolton Wanderers gaining an unexpected success in a high scoring encounter at Trent Bridge. In the less demanding circles of the Notts. League, he captained his team to the championship, and to the final of the Notts. Senior Cup in 1891-92. Although associated with the Magpies as amateur and professional for a lengthy period he did not graduate beyond reserve team level, his best seasonal return in League terms being four matches in the 1892-93 relegation season.

Appearances: FL: 9 apps 0 gls FAC: 1 app 0 gls Other: 5 apps 0 gls Total: 15 apps 0 gls

---

WILKINSON, John William

Left-back   5' 8"   12st 5lbs
b. Hucknall Torkard, Notts, October 1883
CAREER: Hucknall White Star/NOTTS am Apr, pro May 1904/Tottenham Hotspur May 1906 to May 1907
Debut v Newcastle United (h) 8.10.04, lost 0 – 3

Said to be the first player from the Bulwell & District League to appear for a local First Division club, Wilkinson was first given a run out by Notts in a friendly match against Clapton F.C. in April 1904. Described as "Nippy and industrious" he was a valuable member of the reserve ranks, particularly accomplished in headwork, despite his modest stature. Recommended to Tottenham Hotspur by ex-Notts stalwart Walter Bull, his season with the Spurs was mainly spent at reserve level.

Appearances: FL: 7 apps 0 gls Total: 7 apps 0 gls

WILLIAMS, Andrew

Midfield   6' 0"   11st 9lbs
b. Birmingham, 29th July 1962
CAREER: Dudley Town/Solihull Borough/Coventry City July 1985/Rotherham United Oct 1986/Leeds United Nov 1988 (Port Vale loan Dec 1991) (NOTTS loan Feb 1992)/NOTTS Mar 1992, fee £115,000 (Huddersfield Town loan Sept 1993)/Rotherham United Oct 1993/Hull City July 1995/Scarborough nc Aug 1996/Gainsborough Trinity Sept 1996/Matlock Town Feb 1997/Guiseley Feb 1998
Debut as sub v Arsenal (h) 8.2.92, lost 0 – 1

Andy Williams was a late starter in League football, leaving his employment as an accountant to join Coventry City at the age of 23. It was not until he joined Rotherham United that his career took off, his form at Millmoor leading to an upward move to Leeds United. It was from Elland Road that Andy joined Notts, initially on loan, a move made permanent on the eve of transfer deadline-day. He joined a desperate, and ultimately unsuccessful, battle to avoid relegation, a 2 – 0 defeat at Manchester City on 25th April finally sealing the Magpies fate. In the following season he was injured after heading a fine goal at Peterborough United to record the season's first victory, and his steadying influence was sadly missed during his two months on the sidelines. A second, successive, relegation was narrowly avoided following the mid-term departure of managerial duo Neil Warnock and Mick Jones. Andy, however. featured little in the plans of new manager Mick Walker

.

Appearances: FL: 30(9) apps 2 gls FAC: 1 app 0 gls FLC: 3 apps 0 gls Total: 34(9) apps 2 gls
Honours: (Leeds United) FL Division 2 champions 1990

WILLIAMS, David H

Inside-forward   5' 8"   11st 10lbs
b. Liverpool
CAREER: St Helens Recreation/Glossop Sept 1912/NOTTS
Nov 1912, fee £750 /Belfast Celtic 1914/Cliftonville Nov
1914/Liverpool Apr 1915 (WW1 guest Arsenal Sept 1916)/
Luton Town July 1919/Brighton & Hove Albion Feb 1920,
fee £200/Maidstone United May 1921
Debut v Manchester United (a) 2.11.12, lost 1 – 2

The 'Post Annual' for 1913-14, commenting on Dave
Williams' first season at Meadow Lane, stated that: "He
came to the Magpies from Glossop with a reputation as
a thrusting centre and a fine shot, and if he did not quite
come up to expectations was always a genuine trier."
Considering the £750 fee paid – hefty by the standards of
the day – his return of three goals in 24 matches was
extremely disappointing, although an all round lack of
fire power was the chief reason behind the team's relegation
from Division One (only 28 goals being scored in 38
matches). In the Division Two promotion season that
immediately followed Williams scored twice in seven early
season matches. After Army service during WW1 he
assisted both Luton Town and Brighton & Hove Albion,
costing the Goldstone club their then record transfer fee
of £200.

Appearances: FL: 31 apps 5 gls FAC: 1 app 0 gls
Total: 32 apps 5 gls

WILLIAMS, John Nelson

Forward   6' 1"   13st 12lbs
b. Birmingham, 11th May 1968
CAREER: Cradley Town/Swansea City Aug 1991, fee
£5,000/Coventry City July 1992, fee £250,000 (NOTTS
loan Oct 1994) (Stoke City loan Dec 1994) (Swansea City
loan Feb 1995)/Wycombe Wanderers Sept 1995, fee
£150,000/Hereford United Feb 1997/Walsall July 1997/
Exeter City Aug 1997/Cardiff City Aug 1998/York City
Aug 1999, fee £20,000/Darlington Dec 2000/Swansea City
July 2001/Kidderminster Harriers Aug 2003 to cs 2004.
Debut as sub v Port Vale (h) 8.10.94, drawn 2 – 2 (scored
one)

One of soccer's happy wanderers, briefly associated with
the Magpies in the early stages of the 1994-95 Division
One relegation season. In three starts and two appearances
from the bench the powerfully-built former postman
scored goals against Port Vale and Watford, showing a
fine turn of speed and the ability to get past his marker.
In his final League season, and nearing his 36th birthday,
John was a minute away from FA Cup glory. Against
Premier League opponents in Wolverhampton Wanderers,
his 77th minute strike, after coming off the bench, seemed
all set to become the season's 'giant killing' story.

Kidderminster hearts were broken, however, when Alex
Rae equalised after 89 minutes. The Wolves were winners
by 2 – 0 in the replay at Molineux. John was released by
the Harriers in the summer of 2004. In terms of League
matches alone, his career aggregate figures were 312(112)
matches and 70 goals.

Appearances: FL: 3(2) apps 2 gls Total: 3(2) apps 2 gls

WILLIAMS, Matthew "Matty"

Forward   5' 8"   9st 11lbs
b. St. Asaph, 5th November 1982
CAREER: Manchester United trainee July 1999, pro Feb
2000/NOTTS Mar 2004
Debut v Chesterfield (h) 20.3.2004, drawn 1 – 1

A member of Manchester United's Reserve team who
won the championship of the FA Premier Reserve League
North in 2001-02, and second highest scorer for the Reds'
Reserves in 2002-03, Matty has yet to fully establish
himself at Meadow Lane. Lightweight but skilful on the
ball, he scored his first senior goal for the Magpies in
November 2004. A brave diving header against relegation
rivals Cambridge United, followed by a stunning strike
from Chris Palmer, gave the ten-men Magpies the points,
despite being without red-carded Paul Bolland for much
of the second half.

Appearances: FL: 13(12) apps 1 gl FAC: 2(1) apps 0 gls
FLC: 1(1) apps 0 gls Total: 16(14) apps 1 gl
Honours: Wales U-21 International. Wales Youth
International

WILLIAMSON, Albert

Outside-right
b. Sawley, Derbyshire, April quarter 1866
CAREER: Sawley Rangers/Derby County 1884/NOTTS July
1891/Nottingham Forest
Debut v Accrington (h) 28.11.1891, won 9 – 0

Albert Williamson could have been forgiven for feeling
hard done by after being dropped immediately following
his FL debut – a stunning 9 – 0 victory against Accrington.
Perhaps the selection committee considered him short of
experience for the following week's daunting trip to the
season's eventual champions, Sunderland, who ran out
comfortable winners by 4 – 0. Williamson's second, and
final League outing was a 3 – 1 defeat by Everton,
County's only home defeat of the season. Outside of the
game Albert was employed in the lace making industry.

Appearances: FL: 2 apps 0 gls Total: 2 apps 0 gls

WILLS, Gordon Francis

Winger 5' 10" 10st 7lbs
b. West Bromwich, 24th April 1934
CAREER: West Bromwich Albion am/Wolverhampton Wanderers Dec 1951/NOTTS Aug 1953/Leicester City May 1958, fee £9,000/Walsall June 1962/Sankeys cs 1964/Dudley Town cs 1965
Debut v Everton (a) 23.9.53, lost 2 – 3 (scored one)

During Notts' manager George Poyser's earlier post as coach to Wolverhampton Wanderers he had given much attention to the development of a young Gordon Wills, little realising that both of them would reap the benefits with another club. Without League experience when he arrived at Meadow Lane, he was quickly knocking on the first team door. On either wing, and on occasions inside, his deft footwork enabled him to find a way through the most compact defences. In his last two seasons he was operating in a poor side and when relegation from Division Two occurred at the close of season 1957-58 the Magpies lost their most effective marksman when First Division Leicester City paid £9,000 to take him to Filbert Street. A regular on City's left flank until the advent of Mike Stringfellow, Gordon scored 30 goals in 111 League matches, and was unfortunate to miss the 1961 FA Cup Final against Tottenham Hotspur after sustaining an injury in the semi-final against Sheffield United.

Appearances: FL: 154 apps 45 gls FAC: 8 apps 1 gl
Total: 162 apps 46 gls

WILSON, Andrew Philip

Outside-right   5' 8½" 10st 0lbs
b. Maltby, 13th October 1947
CAREER: Rotherham United June 1967 (NOTTS loan Aug 1968)/Scunthorpe United Sept 1968/Corby Town.
Debut v Halifax Town (h) 28.8.68, lost 1 – 2

Aside from his single appearance for the Magpies, Andy Wilson made 12 starts for Rotherham United in his first season as a professional. A total of 23 Division Four outings (four goals) for Scunthorpe United were made in

the face of stiff competition from an up-and-coming Kevin Keegan. The 1968-69 season proved to be Wilson's last in League football, during the course of which he played once for the Magpies and twice against them in Division Four fixtures.

Appearances: FL: 1 app 0 gls Total: 1 app 0 gls

WILSON, Kelvin

Defender   6' 2" 12st 3lbs
b. Nottingham, 3rd September 1985
CAREER: Notts. Schoolboys/NOTTS scholar July 2002, pro July 2004.
Debut as sub v Hartlepool United 17.4.2004, lost 0 - 4

After an unfortunate beginning, when he scored an own goal in his first starting appearance at Brighton, Kelvin has enjoyed a season of outstanding progress in 2004-05. A local boy, he seems set to follow the likes of Jermaine Pennant, Leon Best and David McGoldrick, all of whom graduated through the Magpies' School of Excellence and were snapped up by top flight teams. At either full-back or in central defence, Kelvin has shown a maturity beyond his years and has developed into a classy, unflappable defender with enough close control to create plenty of attacking moves. Undoubtedly a special talent with a real future in the game.

Appearances: FL: 38(6) apps 2 gls FAC: 4 apps 0 gls
FLC: 1(1) apps 0 gls Other: 1 app 0 gls
Total: 44(7) apps 2 gls

WILSON, Kevin James

Forward   5' 8" 11st 4lbs
b. Banbury, 18th April 1961
CAREER: Ruscote Sports/Banbury United 1978/Derby County Dec 1979, fee £20,000/Ipswich Town Jan 1985, fee £100,000/Chelsea June 1987, fee £335,000/NOTTS Mar 1992, fee £225,000 (Bradford City loan Jan 1994)/Walsall player-coach Aug 1994/Northampton Town July 1997, player-assistant manager midway through season 1998-99, player-manager Oct 1999 (retired from playing July 2001) to Sept 2001/Bedford Town manager Oct 2002/Aylesbury United manager Oct 2003/Kettering Town manager Dec 2003.
Debut v Crystal Palace (h) 28.3.92, lost 2 – 3 (scored one)

A transfer deadline-day signing from Chelsea, Kevin was unable to save his new team from relegation from the top flight. Despite scoring on his debut, a 2 – 0 lead against Crystal Palace was squandered, Mark Draper failing to score from the penalty spot, and Notts went under by 2 – 3.

Things didn't get very much better for the team, or for Kevin, who - in the goal scoring department - experienced the leanest time of his career at Meadow Lane. Probably too versatile for his own good, he was fielded as much in midfield and at right-back as in the attack. In retrospect, considering his outstanding record as a striker, with in excess of

100 League goals to his credit when signed, he would have been of more value to the side in a forward role. Kevin was still scoring goals in his 40th year, chasing an overall total of 200 senior goals. Qualifying for Northern Ireland through parentage, he was first capped during his spell with Ipswich Town, and won 15 of his total of 42 caps whilst at Meadow Lane, qualifying him as the club's most capped player. In earlier days, he scored 13 League goals for Chelsea when they won the championship of the Second Division in 1988-89. Much later in his career he assisted Walsall to promotion from Division Three in 1994-95, and as player-manager of Northampton Town he led them to promotion from Division Three in 1999-2000.

Appearances: FL: 58(11) apps 3 gls FAC: 2 apps 0 gls FLC: 3(1) apps 0 gls Other: 5(1) apps 0 gls
Total: 68(13) apps 3 gls
Honours: Northern Ireland International, 42 caps 1987-95. (Chelsea) FL Division 2 champions 1989. Zenith Data Systems Cup winners 1990. (NOTTS) Anglo Italian Cup finalists 1994

———————o———————

WITHE, Christopher
Left-back   5' 8½" 11st 3lbs
b. Liverpool, 25th September 1962
CAREER: Nottingham Forest (trial)/Liverpool associate schoolboy/Newcastle United app 1978, pro Sept 1980/ Bradford City June 1983/NOTTS Oct 1987, fee £20,000/ Bury July 1989, fee £40,000 (Chester City loan Oct 1990) (Mansfield Town loan Jan 1991)/Mansfield Town Mar 1991, in exchange for Mark Kearney/Shrewsbury Town Aug 1993/ Boston United Aug 1996.
Debut v Chester City (a) 3.10.87, won 2 – 1

The younger brother of England international Peter Withe, Chris was on Newcastle United's books at the same time as his brother, but he played only twice at League level before leaving on a free transfer to Bradford City. Lacking his brother's physical advantages, Chris obtained his effects by sheer skill and judgement and enjoyed a successful career totalling 402(21) League appearances and 13 goals. He missed only two matches in his first two seasons at Valley Parade, and for a fee of just £20,000 proved a real bargain when he moved to Meadow Lane in October 1987. Rarely absent for the best part of two Third Division campaigns, the first of which ended in the disappointment of defeat in the Play-offs, Chris was voted 'Player of the Year' in the following season, in which he missed just one of the season's 55 League and Cup matches. As recently as season 2003-04, Chris was turning out in Sunday football with Spot-On F.C. (Hucknall.)

Appearances: FL: 80 apps 3 gls FAC: 5 apps 0 gls FLC: 4 apps 0 gls Other: 12 apps 1 gl Total: 101 apps 4 gls
Honours: (Bradford City) FL Division Three champions 1985. (Shrewsbury Town) FL Division Three champions 1994

———————o———————

WITHERS, Alan
Outside-left   5' 6½" 10st 10lbs
b. Bulwell, Nottingham, 20th October 1930
CAREER: Aspley Boys' Club/Blackpool July 1949/Lincoln City Feb 1955/NOTTS Jan 1959, fee £3,500/Wisbech Town July 1963/Boston F.C. cs 1966/Lockhead Leamington Aug 1967/Loughborough United Nov 1967
Debut v Halifax Town (h) 3.1.59, drawn 4 – 4

Despite a dream start to his Football League career, when he scored a hat-trick on his debut for Blackpool against Huddersfield Town in November 1950, Alan Withers was unable to hold a first team place at Bloomfield Road. He had a season to wait before establishing himself on Lincoln City's left wing, but had made 98 League appearances and scored 18 goals when he joined the Magpies at the mid-point of season 1958-59.

Unlike his much earlier dream debut for Blackpool, he had the misfortune to miss from the penalty spot on his Magpies debut. Experiencing both relegation and promotion in his first two seasons, he remained a popular and accomplished wingman with a career aggregate of 46 goals in 234 League matches.

Appearances: FL: 121 apps 22 gls FAC: 6 apps 2 gls FLC: 4 apps 0 gls Total: 131 apps 24 gls

———————————○———————————

WOOD, Gary Terence
Full-back   5' 10"   11st 3lbs
b. Corby, Northants, 2nd December 1955
CAREER: Rothwell Town/Kettering Town/NOTTS Dec 1977/Kettering Town cs 1982
Debut v Sunderland (a) 15.4.78, lost 1 – 3

Despite a lengthy spell at Meadow Lane, fair-haired Gary Wood found few first team opportunities. Operating in the shadows of Ray O'Brien, Pedro Richards and Nigel Worthington, it was a spate of injuries and suspensions that finally afforded him a brief mid-season spell of first team action in the Second Division promotion season of 1980-81.

Appearances:FL: 7(4) apps 0 gls FAC: 1 app 0 gls FLC: 1(2) apps 0 gls Other: 3(1) apps 0 gls
Total: 12(7) apps 0 gls

———————————○———————————

WOODFIELD, Terry
Right-half   5' 11"   11st 0lbs
b. Nottingham, 21st January 1946
CAREER: NOTTS pro July 1963
Debut v Bristol Rovers (h) 9.4.64, lost 3 – 4

Local discovery Terry Woodfield had a lengthy wait for an opportunity at first team level following his signing as a professional in July 1963. It was not until the final month of the relegation season 1963-64 that he was introduced at right-half and showed sufficient promise to hold his place for the final five matches. He was only eighteen years old at the time.

Appearances: FL: 5 apps 0 gls Total: 5 apps 0 gls

———————————○———————————

WOODFORD, Robert Michael
Right-half   5' 9"   11st 0lbs
b. Keyworth, Notts, 6th December 1943
CAREER: Keyworth United/NOTTS pro Mar 1961
Debut v Southend United (h) 23.4.62, won 2 – 0

Bobby Woodford's trio of FL appearances came consecutively, covering the final three matches of season 1961-62. He was only eighteen years old at the time, and had been a professional for a little over a month. Rather unusually, he had played very little football when he arrived at Meadow Lane as he had attended a school where soccer wasn't played.

Appearances: FL: 3 apps 0 gls Total: 3 apps 0 gls

———————————○———————————

WOODLAND, Arthur
Half-back   5' 8"   11st 8lbs
b. Mount Pleasant, Liverpool, 3rd August 1889
d. Dalton, Rotherham, 17th December 1941
CAREER: St Polycarps/Kirkdale/Zingari/St Helens Town/Norwich City May 1912 (WW1 guest NOTTS)/Royal Field Artillery/NOTTS Jan 1920/Southend United June 1922/Pontypridd Aug 1923/Leamington Town May 1924
Debut v Bradford P.A. (h) 7.2.20, lost 0 – 2

A catalogue of injuries to key players resulted in the recruitment of Arthur Woodland in late January 1920. Just released from Army service the experienced centre-half was reported to show a good knowledge of the game, but was lacking pace and match fitness. A strong tackler who made use of his weight and was especially good in the air, he battled gamely in what ultimately proved to be an unavailing fight against relegation from Division One. Earlier in his career he had captained Norwich City in the period up to the outbreak of WW1, appearing in 90 Southern League and Cup matches, scoring two goals. Some ten years later, in season 1923-24, he assisted Pontypridd to the championship of the Welsh National League (South.)

Appearances: FL: 48 apps 1 gl FAC: 1 app 0 gls Total: 49 apps 1 gl

———————————○———————————

WOOLLEY, E
Forward
CAREER: NOTTS (first app) Oct 1883 to (final app) Oct 1885
Debut v Sheffield Heeley, FAC 1, (h) 10.11.1883, won 3 – 1

Reserve forwards were afforded few opportunities in season 1883-84, as the team boasted four international front men, the brothers Cursham, William Gunn and John Dixon. C.F. Dobson was the odd man out, but he still managed to score 14 goals in 30 matches. In the season when Notts moved to play at Trent Bridge, Wooley made his debut against Attercliffe on 4th October 1893, and played in six friendly matches plus the one FA Cup game, his debut as above.

He was less involved in 1884-85 but scored in one of his three matches, at Bolton Wanderers in a 2 – 4 defeat on 14th March 1885. His final outing was in the following season, against Walsall Town Swifts, on 6th October 1885.

Appearances: FAC: 1 app 0 gls Total: 1 app 0 gls

WOOLLEY, Jim Horobin
Full-back   5' 9½" 11st 4lbs
b. Kegworth, Leics, 24th October 1889
d. Nottingham, April quarter 1980
CAREER: Kegworth/NOTTS July 1911 to 1915
Debut v Manchester City (a) 2.1.13, lost 0 – 4

Time ran out for Jim Woolley, a reserve back from the Kegworth club. The 'Post Annual' for season 1914-15 said of him: "The Kegworth youth develops slowly but surely, and is only awaiting the opportunity for a long trial with the seniors to show the stuff he is made of as a left-back." Although the pairing of Morley and West as first team backs was less of a foregone conclusion than in earlier seasons, Woolley appeared only once more, in a 0 – 0 draw at Burnley in December 1914. With the suspension of normal League football at the close of season 1914-15, Woolley's potential in the top flight sadly remained an unknown quantity.

Appearances: FL: 3 apps 0 gls Total: 3 apps 0 gls

WOOLLEY, Robert Alan
Inside-forward
b. Nottingham, 29th December 1947
d. Arnold, Nottingham 2nd October 1971
CAREER: Nottingham Schoolboys/NOTTS app, signing pro July 1965
Debut v Millwall (a) 4.4.64, lost 1 – 6

Bob Woolley, a 16 year-old apprentice from the Clifton district, received a surprise baptism in League football. Less than an hour prior to kick-off he was drafted into the Magpies team at Millwall. He had travelled as twelfth man and was called up when Ivan Hampton developed influenza on reaching London. On a muddy pitch, the soon to be relegated Magpies were thrashed 6 – 1, but young Woolley revealed potential with several bursts of speed and some nice ball control, despite the sticky conditions.

Appearances: FL: 9 apps 2 gls Total: 9 apps 2 gls

WORTHINGTON, Nigel
Left-back/Midfield   5' 11" 12st 6lbs
b. Ballymena, Northern Ireland, 4th November 1961
CAREER: Ballymena United (Linfield loan June 1981)/ NOTTS July 1981, fee £100,000/Sheffield Wednesday Feb 1984, fee £125,000/Leeds United July 1994, fee £325,000/ Stoke City July 1996/Blackpool player-manager July 1997, manager Nov 1997 to Dec 1999/England U-21 coach/N Ireland U-21 assistant-manager/Norwich City caretaker manager, then manager Jan 2001
Debut v Wolverhampton Wanderers (a) 26.9.81, lost 2 – 3

The former Northern Ireland Youth international captain became only the second six-figure signing in the Magpies' history, and the £100,000 fee made him the costliest player ever to come out of Northern Ireland. Nigel was playing as a guest for Linfield in a youth competition in Amsterdam when spotted by Jimmy Sirrel, who brought him to Meadow Lane in the following month. Destined for a big future in the game, he nevertheless had an unfortunate start, appearing in only two League matches in his first season, being injured and having to undergo a cartilage operation. Fully recovered, he missed only one match in the following season, and in 1983-84 he left the Magpies' relegation battle to join Sheffield Wednesday, linking up again with former boss Howard Wilkinson at Hillsborough. He assisted Wednesday to promotion from Division Two in his first season and shortly afterwards won the first of his Northern Ireland caps. In ten years with the Owls he amassed 334(4) League appearances and scored 12 goals, totals that constituted a high proportion of his final career figures of 445(29) League matches and 17 goals.

Appearances: FL: 62(5) apps 4 gls FAC: 4 apps 0 gls FLC: 11apps 0 gls Other: 3 apps 0 gls
Total: 80(5) apps 4 gls
Honours: Northern Ireland International, 66 caps, 1984-96. Northern Ireland Youth International. (Sheffield Wednesday) FL Cup winners 1991

WORTHINGTON, Peter Robert 'Bob'
Left-back   6' 1" 12st 7lbs
b. Halifax, 22nd April 1947
CAREER: Halifax Town app, signing pro May 1965/ Middlesbrough Aug 1966/NOTTS Sept 1968, with Don Masson for £5,000/Southend United Aug 1974 (Hartlepool United loan Mar 1975)
Debut v Darlington (a) 14.9.68, lost 2 – 3

Fondly remembered by Magpies' supporters as a fixture in a back four along with Bill Brindley, David Needham and Brian Stubbs. The four comprising the defensive bedrock of a team that enjoyed great success in the early 1970s.

Beginning with promotion from Division Four, with 69 points when it was two points for a win, a second promotion followed two years later, coupled with a run to the fifth round of the FL Cup in the same season. Eventually succeeded by Ray O'Brien, Bob spent only one of his two years contract with Southend United before retiring from League football. He was part of a remarkable family of footballers. His father Eric was a forward with Halifax Town, and he proved a splendid tutor to sons Bob, Frank (England International) and David, also a full-back, with almost 500 League appearances, 293 with Grimsby Town. A nephew, Gary, won England Youth honours and assisted seven different League clubs, totalling 176(32) appearances and 56 goals.

Appearances: FL: 230(2) apps 1 gl FAC: 15 apps 0 gls FLC: 10 apps 0 gls Total: 255(2) apps 1 gl
Honours: (NOTTS) FL Division 4 champions 1971

---○---

WREN, John Edward 'Jack'
Half-back   5' 8½" 11st 12lbs
b. St Werburghs, Bristol, 30th January 1894
d. Ashley Hill, Bristol, 30th July 1948
CAREER: Greenbank F.C./Bristol Rovers Reserves/Army football, Grenadier Guards (WW1 guest Millwall)/Bristol City July 1919/NOTTS Aug 1922, fee £1,100/Southport Aug-Nov 1926
Debut v Coventry City (a) 26.8.22, won 2 – 1

The 'Post Annual' for 1923-24, commenting on Jack Wren's first season at Meadow Lane, considered that: "He knows every move on the board and tackles fearlessly." An opinion upheld by his fine captaincy and industrious approach. The eldest of a family of nine children, he began in League football with Bristol City and in his second season took over the centre-half berth from the celebrated England international 'Fatty' Wedlock. After 104 matches, and an appearance in a FA International trial match, he joined the Magpies and led them to promotion in his first season.

His League career ended after a brief spell with Southport and he returned to Bristol and became licensee of the Station Hotel at Ashley Hill. He also raced greyhounds at the Eastville Stadium.

Appearances: FL: 63 apps 0 gls FAC: 4 apps 0 gls
Total: 67 apps 0 gls
Honours: (NOTTS) FL Division 2 champions 1923

---○---

WRIGHT, Bernard A. W
Goalkeeper
b. Walthamstow, 19th September 1923
CAREER: NOTTS Feb 1946, pro Oct 1946 to June 1947
Debut v Torquay United (h) 23.1.47, lost 0 – 2

One of five players to don the goalkeeper's jersey in 1946-47 as normal League football resumed in a season memorable for the arctic conditions and numerous rearranged fixtures. Notts' engagements concluded on May 29th with centre forward Fred Whittaker making his second appearance as goalkeeper. Aside from regular custodian Harry Brown (36 League appearances), outfield player Bill Corkhill guarded the breach once, as did J.A. Dewick. Bernard Wright's second League appearance, at Bristol Rovers on 22nd March 1947, resulted in a 4 – 1 defeat despite what was described as "A magnificent display of goalkeeping." This on an Eastville pitch that had had over nine million gallons of water pumped off it, and resembled a sea of mud when further torrential rain fell as the match got underway.

Appearances: FL: 2 apps 0 gls Total: 2 apps 0 gls

---○---

WRIGHT, Frederick
Left-back   5' 8"   11st 0lbs
b. Ruddington, Notts, October quarter 1908
CAREER: Ruddington/NOTTS am Mar 1926/Grantham Town Sept 1929/Hull City Nov 1930, fee £350/Loughborough Corinthians Sept 1931/Leicester City Police Oct 1931
Debut v Stoke (a) 27.5.29, lost 0 – 5

Described as: " A sturdy left-back, showing much promise," Fred Wright was paired with Harold Childs for his League debut in the final Second Division fixture of season 1928-29. Notts sustained their heaviest defeat of the season, losing 5 – 0, and both of the reserve backs departed Meadow Lane within a matter of months. Wright spent a little over a year in Midland League football before joining Hull City, where he played only twice at League level.

Appearances: FL: 1 app 0 gls Total: 1 app 0 gls

WRIGHT, John E

Centre-forward 5' 11" 12st 7lbs
b. North Wingfield, Derbyshire
CAREER: Alfreton Town/Staveley Town cs 1927/Matlock Town (trials with Birmingham & Luton Town)/NOTTS May 1931/Ilkeston United Aug 1932/Sutton Town/Grantham Town Aug 1934 to Feb 1935.
Debut v Oldham Athletic (h) 23.9.31, won 1 – 0 (scored)

There can be few 'one appearance' men who scored on their debuts, but this was the case with John Wright, a schoolteacher who otherwise spent a season in reserve at Meadow Lane. His goal after 38 minutes play was sufficient to give Notts the points and some revenge for their 5 – 2 defeat at Oldham's Boundary Park just nine days earlier.

Appearances: FL: 1 app 1 gl Total: 1 app 1 gl

———o———

WYLIE, Ronald Maurice

Inside-forward 5' 8" 10st 4lbs
b. Kelvin, Glasgow, 6th August 1933
CAREER: Clydesdale Juniors/NOTTS am Apr 1948, pro Sept 1950/Aston Villa Nov 1958, fee £9,500/Birmingham City June 1965, retired Apr 1970/Aston Villa coach June 1970 to May 1972/Coventry City coach July 1975, assistant-manager 1978-81/Cyprus F.C. coach/Bulova (Hong Kong) coach 1982/West Bromwich Albion manager July 1982 to Feb 1984/Aston Villa reserve team manager-coach Feb 1984 to May 1987.
Debut v Doncaster Rovers (h) 13.10.51, won 1 – 0

Ron Wylie started his career with a Scottish schoolboy cap, and was discovered by the Magpies in the ranks of Clydesdale Juniors. Shrewd and slick, and a wonderful ball player despite his youth, he began in League football as an eighteen year-old and in the final home match of his debut season scored four goals in a 5 – 0 win against Birmingham City. Although subsequently noted as a provider rather than a goalscorer on his own account his clever and purposeful play made him a target for bigger clubs.

A broken ankle, suffered at the beginning of season 1957-58 kept him sidelined for a little over six months. Lacking his inspirational play the Magpies season ended in relegation from Division Two. Returning to his brilliant best in the following term he was plucked from Division Three by Aston Villa, were he was voted 'Midlands Footballer of the Year' in 1965. In a stay of seven years he appeared in 244 matches and scored 28 goals in the famous claret and blue colours. He added a further 125(3) appearances and two goals in five seasons with Birmingham City, leading the Blues to the semi-finals of the FL Cup in 1967 and the FA Cup in 1968.

Appearances: FL: 227 apps 36 gls FAC: 11 apps 3 gls
Total: 238 apps 39 gls
Honours: Scotland Schoolboy International, 2 caps. (Aston Villa) FL Division 2 champions 1960. FL Cup winners 1961

———o———

WYLIE, John

Left-half 5' 9" 11st 0lbs
b. Maybole, Ayrshire, circa 1914
CAREER: Glenafton Athletic/Partick Thistle (provisional) Oct 1933/Ayr United Feb 1936/Partick Thistle pro May-Oct 1936/Bury trial Jan 1937/Lincoln City Aug 1937/NOTTS June 1938-39
Debut v Ipswich Town (h) 22.10.38, won 2 – 1

John Wylie was a younger brother of the free-scoring George, who headed Partick Thistle's goal scoring lists in 1935-36 with 21 in 30 matches. John shared the inside-right berth with Peter McKennan in 1935-36, appearing in 12 First Division matches for Thistle and scoring one goal. This came against Dundee in a 3 – 3 draw in November 1935, brother George scoring in the same match. John's attempts to establish himself in English football were not successful, his solitary appearance at senior level being his debut, and sole appearance for the Magpies.

Appearances: FL: 1 app 0 gls Total: 1 app 0 gls

———o———

WYNESS, George Dow

Centre-half 5' 9" 11st 4lbs
b. Monkwearmouth, Sunderland, 12th August 1907
d. Sunderland, 26th June 1993
CAREER: Sunderland Schoolboys/Tyzack F.C. 1925/Jarrow am July 1926/Houghton Colliery Welfare 1927/Leicester City 1928/Falkirk Sept 1928/Southport Aug 1929/Chester July 1933/Rochdale June 1934/NOTTS May 1936/Gateshead Aug 1937/Jarrow Oct 1937-38
Debut v Exeter City (h) 29.8.36, won 3 – 1

In the 1936-37 season, when the Magpies finished in second place in Division Three South, George Wyness lost his regular berth in the side after appearing in the first eight matches.

His replacement was Irish international 'Con' Moulson a £2,000 signing from Lincoln City. George was recognised as one of the finest centre-halves in the Northern Section of Division Three prior to his move to Meadow Lane, the former shipyard riveter was speedy, not afraid of work, and particularly effective in the air. A younger brother, William Dow Wyness was associated with Southport, Aldershot and Wrexham in the 1930s.

Appearances: FL: 10 apps 0 gls Total: 10 apps 0 gls

————————o————————

YATES, Dean Richard
Central defender   6' 2"   12st 6lbs
b. Leicester, 26th October 1967
CAREER: Syston Juniors/ NOTTS app Aug 1984, pro June 1985/Derby County Jan 1995, fee £350,000/Watford July 1998 to 1999.
Debut v Wimbledon (h) 6.4.85, lost 2 – 3

At the age of fourteen Dean hoped to be a centre-forward, and dreamt of emulating the feats of his hero, Frank Worthington. With Syston Juniors, however, he was moved back to midfield and later to central defence, in which position he subsequently starred for Notts. In September 1988 he became the first Notts player to win England recognition for six years when he was named in the Under-21 squad to meet Denmark. He played in the last seventeen minutes of the match, as substitute for Forest's Steve Chettle, in a 0 – 0 draw. He had made his first team debut as a seventeen year-old some three years earlier, lining up at right-back alongside Steve Sims, Dave Watson and Pedro Richards. Dean quickly became recognised as the best central defender outside of Division One and for six seasons hardly missed a League or Cup match, winning the 'Player of the Year' award in 1987 and successive promotions in 1990 and 1991. His progress was halted in 1992 with a severe knee injury that required a 'total rebuild' and kept him on the sidelines for a little over two years. Moving on to Derby County, he assisted the Rams to promotion from Division Two in 1996 and was named their 'Player of the Year.'

A final move to Watford ended when a knee injury, again requiring surgery, ended his season in October 1998, his final League outing coming just three days after his 31st birthday. Dean's career figures totalled 437(5) League and Cup appearances and 37 goals. He currently works as a match summariser for Radio Nottingham.

Appearances: FL: 312(2) apps 33 gls FAC: 20 apps 0 gls FLC: 24 apps 0 gls Other: 36 apps 4 gls
Total: 392(2) apps 37 gls
Honours: England U-21 International, 5 apps 1989

————————o————————

YEOMANS, Kelvin
Right-back
b. Nottingham, 25th August 1947
CAREER: Beeston/NOTTS am June 1967
Debut v Workington (a) 23.9.67, lost 1 – 5

The Magpies were not at their best throughout the Sixties and season 1967-68 commenced on a typical note with only one victory in the opening ten matches. For the visit to Workington on 23rd September, amateur right-back Kelvin Yeomans was introduced in place of the injured Len Chalmers. He was partnered by another relatively inexperienced back in Tim Crispin, also making his first senior appearance of the season. It proved to be their only senior pairing, and the team's fortunes did not improve until the arrival of Les Bradd in the following month. His goals helping pull the side clear of a re election application.

Appearances: FL: 1 app 0 gls Total: 1 app 0 gls

————————o————————

YOUNG, Alexander Forbes 'Alan'
Forward   6' 0"   12st 0lbs
b. Kirkcaldy, Fife, 26th October 1955
CAREER: Kirkcaldy High School/Kirkcaldy YMCA/Oldham Athletic July 1974/Leicester City July 1979, fee £250,000/ Sheffield United Aug 1982, fee £160,000/Brighton & Hove Albion Aug 1983, fee £140,000/NOTTS Sept 1984, fee £55,000/Rochdale Aug 1986, fee £10,000 plus D. Thompson/Shepshed Charterhouse player-coach Mar 1988/ Ilkeston Town 1989-90/NOTTS coach and subsequently Community Officer/Chesterfield Youth Development Officer 1998/Leeds United Academy coach.
Debut v Middlesbrough (h) 8.9.84, won 3 – 2

Alan Young won Scotland Schoolboy honours and was later selected twice in the Scotland squad, without winning a full cap. The tall and rangy striker made rapid strides on joining Oldham Athletic, his form attracting a bid of £250,000 from Leicester City after his hat-trick had removed them from the FA Cup in the previous season.

He scored 14 goals in 42 matches in his first season with the Foxes, spearheading their promotion into Division One. Spells with Sheffield United and Brighton preceded his arrival at Meadow Lane, manager Larry Lloyd paying £55,000 for him in September 1984. Seven goals in 24 Division Two matches in his first season proved insufficient to prevent the Magpies suffering a second, consecutive relegation, and after an injury plagued second season Alan left to join his former Oldham team-mate Vic Halom at Rochdale. When a back injury enforced his retirement at the age of 32, Alan took a business management course; the sports injury course at Lilleshall and the FA coaching badges. He later returned to Meadow Lane to run the PFA Football in the Community programme, and to assist in the running of the Magpies Under-16 side.

Appearances: FL: 39(4) apps 12 gls FAC: 5 apps 1 gl FLC: 6 apps 2 gls Total: 50(4) apps 15 gls
Honours: Scotland U-18 Schoolboy International, 2 caps 1974. (Leicester City) FL Division 2 champions 1980

In season 1986-87 the Magpies lacked nothing in height and weight up front, with Mick Waitt and Richard Young in contention for the role of attack leader alongside Charlie McParland who enjoyed a vintage season with 27 goals in League and Cup. Young departed after just one season of first team involvement. He had a poor season with Torquay United, goal less in just 5(4) matches, before switching to Devon rivals, Exeter City. Season 1989-90 marked the high point of his career, the Grecians, managed by former England full-back Terry Cooper, winning the championship of Division Four with a margin of ten points. In excellent Cup runs they held Sunderland to a draw in the FL Cup and Norwich City to a draw in the FA Cup. As the Grecians stormed to their first-ever championship, Richard scored five goals in the final six matches of the historic campaign.

Appearances: FL: 18(17) apps 5 gls FAC: 2(1) apps 1 gl FLC: 0(2) apps 0 gls Other: 1(1) apps 0 gls
Total: 21(21) apps 6 gls
Honours: (Exeter City) FL Division Four champions 1990

YOUNG, Archibald
Right-half   5' 9"   11st 7lbs
b. Paisley, 1st January 1915
CAREER: Clydebank Juniors/Portsmouth Jan 1935/NOTTS June 1938 to May 1939, fee £315.
Debut v Swindon Town (a) 27.8.38, lost 1 – 4

Archie Young spent a lengthy period with Portsmouth after joining them from Clydebank Juniors as a twenty year-old wing half-back. Despite the fact that he had played in only two League matches for Pompey, they were not anxious to part with him and negotiations for his transfer to the Magpies proceeded over a lengthy period. After appearing in the opening two fixtures of season 1938-39, both of which ended in defeat, he was replaced at right-half by John Hindmarsh. After five months of reserve team football he was reintroduced, but his 'comeback' lasted for only six matches before he again stepped down into the Midland League side.

Appearances: FL: 11 apps 0 gls Total: 11 apps 0 gls

YOUNG, Richard Anthony
Forward   6' 3"   13st 7lbs
b. Nottingham, 18th October 1968
CAREER: NOTTS trainee, signing pro Aug 1986/Southend United Aug 1987/Exeter City Mar 1989 to Apr 1991.
Debut as sub v Wigan Athletic (h) 23.8.86, won 2 – 0

ZADKOVICH, Ruben Anton
Midfield   5' 11"   11st 7lbs
b. Wollongong, Australia, 23rd May 1986
CAREER: Bulli F.C. (Australia)/Wollongong Wolves (Australia)/Queens Park Rangers Sept 2004/NOTTS Mar 2005
Debut as sub v Chester City (a) 19.3.2005, lost 2 – 3 (scored one goal)

In a season of few highlights at Meadow Lane, the signing of the youthful Australian midfielder certainly introduced some much needed energy and drive into midfield. Lacking nothing in enthusiasm and stamina, Ruben marked his arrival with a crisp left-foot finish to record his first League goal, after replacing Shane McFaul as a second half substitute at Chester. With confidence and maturity well in advance of his years, he possesses all the attributes necessary to progress to the highest level in the game. Ruben faces a hectic and challenging summer as he has been selected to represent his country in their tour of South Korea and for the World Youth Championships in Holland.

Appearances: FL: 6(2) apps 1 gl Total: 6(2) apps 1 gl
Honours: Australia U-20 International

NOTTS COUNTY MANAGERS
compiled by Keith Warsop

Notts County's first manager in the modern sense was Albert Fisher, appointed on 1st August 1913. Before then, in common with many other Football League clubs, members of the board of directors ran team affairs. Albert's title was secretary-manager and this was standard procedure in the game until around the time of World War Two. Charlie Jones, appointed on 5th May 1934, was the first Magpies manager given complete authority to select the team. Previously this was done at board meetings though at these input from the manager was considerable.

The season-by-season details which are included in each manager's entry show how Notts County performed in the Football League during his period in charge. The figure in parentheses after the season indicates the tier in which the club competed ignoring changes from 1992 which successively converted Division IV into III and now League II, Division III into II and Division II into I. 3S is the old Division III South. The 'P' and 'R' after the seasonal results line indicates a promotion or relegation campaign.

Note: † Indicates this manager appears in the players' section, where full career details can be found.

ALLARDYCE, Samuel 'Sam'
b. Dudley, Worcestershire, 19th October 1954

Manager: 16th January 1997 to 14th October 1999.

Central defender Sam played for Bolton, Sunderland, Millwall, Coventry, Tampa Bay, Huddersfield, Bolton again, Preston, West Bromwich and a final stint at Preston before moving into management at Blackpool. After losing his job there he came to Meadow Lane too late to turn round a relegation campaign but won immediate promotion with the record-breaking 1997-98 season. He resigned from County in controversial fashion in order to take the vacant manager's post at Bolton, the club where his heart always lay and has since established them as a competitive Premiership side.

	P	W	D	L	F	A	Pts	
1996-97 (3)	21	2	6	13	15	30	12	R
1997-98 (4)	46	29	12	5	82	43	99	P
1998-99 (3)	46	14	12	20	52	61	54	
1999-00 (3)	10	6	2	2	18	10	20	
Total	123	51	32	40	167	144	185	

---

†BARKER, Richard Joseph 'Richie'
b. Loughborough, Leicestershire, 23rd November 1939
Manager: 5th November 1984 to 19th April 1985.

	P	W	D	L	F	A	Pts	
1984-85 (2)	24	5	5	14	22	36	20	R

BARNWELL, John
b. Newcastle-upon-Tyne, 24th December 1938

Manager: 7th June 1987 to 2nd December 1988. John's League career was as a midfielder with Arsenal, Forest and Sheffield United before injury curtailed his progress. He coached at Hereford and Peterborough where he stepped up to manager but resigned after accusing the Posh of lack of ambition. He then managed Wolverhampton and AEK Athens, then came to Meadow Lane to take the Magpies to an unsuccessful 1987-88 play-off. Later he managed Walsall and Northampton but in 1996 he was appointed chief executive of the League Managers Association where he has proved an active and successful leader.

	P	W	D	L	F	A	Pts
1987-88 (3)	46	23	12	11	82	49	81
1988-89 (3)	16	2	8	6	16	19	14
Total	62	25	20	17	98	68	95
1987-88 Play-offs	2	0	1	1	2	4	—

BEATTIE, Andrew 'Andy'

b. Kintore, Aberdeeenshire, 11th August 1913
d. Nottingham, 20th September 1983

Managerial adviser with Peter Doherty: 10th December 1965 to 18th March 1966. He became acting manager on 6th December 1966 when Jack Burkitt was granted leave of absence through ill health and general manager when Jack resigned on 23rd February 1967. When Billy Gray was appointed team manager on 13th March 1967 he stayed on as general manager but gave up team selection duties though he resumed these responsibilities from the start of the 1967-68 season until he resigned on 28th September 1967. As a player Andy was a full-back who spent 12 years with Preston and also won seven Scottish caps. He had a lengthy list of clubs on his managerial CV: Barrow, Stockport, Huddersfield, Carlisle, Forest, caretaker boss at both Plymouth and Wolves, then after ending his links with Notts he became assistant manager at Sheffield United. Later he scouted for the Magpies. He was Scotland manager in 1954, 1959 and 1960.

	P	W	D	L	F	A	Pts
1965-66 (4)	13	4	5	4	14	10	13
1966-67 (4)	12	5	2	5	13	13	12
1967-68 (4)	8	1	2	5	6	18	4
Total	33	10	9	14	33	41	29

BRAZIL, Gary Nicholas

b. Tunbridge Wells, Kent, 19th September 1962

Caretaker-manager: 14th October 1999, then manager from 26th October 1999 to 28th June 2000, and again from 10th October 2001 to 7th January 2002. Gary's clubs as a forward were Sheffield United, Port Vale (on loan), Preston, Newcastle, Fulham, Cambridge and Barnet. He joined the Magpies as Sam Allardyce's assistant, took over as youth development coach, then became assistant-manager to both Jocky Scott and Billy Dearden before reverting to his youth role. Since leaving Notts he has been supervising FA Premiership academy schemes.

	P	W	D	L	F	A	Pts
1999-00 (3)	36	12	9	15	43	45	45
2001-02 (3)	14	1	5	8	18	26	8
Total	50	13	14	23	61	71	53

---

†BROOME, Frank Henry

b. Berkhamsted, Hertfordshire, 11th June 1915
d. Bournemouth, Hampshire, 5th September 1994

Acting manager: 7th January 1957 to 7th May 1957. He was appointed assistant-manager to Tommy Lawton on 7th May 1957 and resigned on 27th December 1957 to become manager of Exeter City.

	P	W	D	L	F	A	Pts
1956-57 (2)	17	6	8	3	28	18	20

BUCKLEY, Major Frank Charles

b. Urmston, Lancashire, 9th November 1883
d. Walsall, Staffordshire, 22nd December 1964

Manager: 1st March 1944 to 11th May 1946. After a career with Aston Villa, Brighton, Manchester United, Manchester City, Birmingham, Derby and Bradford City, centre-half Frank made a big managerial impact with Wolverhampton following earlier spells at Norwich and Blackpool. During two years at Meadow Lane Frank gave chances to many young players including Jackie Sewell and Aubrey Southwell. Moving on, he later managed Hull, Leeds and Walsall. Frank, who won one England cap, reached the rank of major in the Footballers' Battalion in World War One.

BURKITT, John Orgill 'Jack'

b. Wednesbury, Staffordshire, 19th January 1926
d. Brighouse, West Yorkshire, 12th September 2003

Manager: 18th March 1966 to 23rd February 1967 after taking leave of absence through ill health (nervous exhaustion caused by overwork) from 6th December 1966. Wing-half Jack's only League club was Forest and he capped a long career by lifting the FA Cup as skipper at Wembley in 1958-59. Meadow Lane was his first and only managerial job. Later he joined Brian Clough and Peter Taylor at Derby as club trainer then spent several years as a sub postmaster on Oakdale Road in Nottingham.

	P	W	D	L	F	A	Pts
1965-66 (4)	15	8	2	5	25	16	18
1966-67 (4)	20	4	6	10	28	41	14
Total	35	12	8	15	53	57	32

COLEMAN, Ernest 'Tim'

b. Blidworth, Notts, 4th January 1908
d. University Hospital, Nottingham, 20th January 1984

Joint caretaker-manager with Jack Wheeler: 1st July 1958 to 17th October 1958; then team manager 31st October 1961 to 31st June 1963; and again from 12th April 1965 to 10th December 1965 when he continued as assistant to managerial advisers Andy Beattie and Peter Doherty until 18th March 1966.

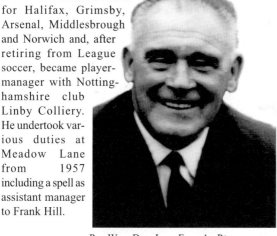

Tim was an effective striker for Halifax, Grimsby, Arsenal, Middlesbrough and Norwich and, after retiring from League soccer, became player-manager with Nottinghamshire club Linby Colliery. He undertook various duties at Meadow Lane from 1957 including a spell as assistant manager to Frank Hill.

	P	W	D	L	F	A	Pts	
1958-59 (3)	15	2	6	7	16	27	10	R
1961-62 (3)	29	11	6	12	35	43	28	
1962-63 (3)	46	19	13	14	73	74	51	
1964-65 (4)	5	2	2	1	7	3	6	
1965-66 (4)	18	7	5	6	22	27	19	
Total	113	41	32	40	153	174	114	

DEARDEN, William 'Billy'
b. Oldham, Lancashire, 11th February 1944

Manager: 7th January 2002 to 7th January 2004. Billy's playing career was a northern one as a goal-scoring winger with Oldham, Crewe, Chester, Sheffield United, Chester again and Chesterfield. He had a long spell as coach and assistant manager of Mansfield Town (1984-94) but after acting as a successful caretaker boss in 1993-94 he was rejected for the full-time post and moved on as John Rudge's assistant at Port Vale. Billy returned to Field Mill as manager in 1999 but quit when offered the Meadow Lane job where he masterminded 'the great escape' from relegation in 2001-02 with 23 points out of the last 33. He resigned at a point when he felt he could take his squad of players no further and financial constraints ruled out his bringing in new blood. Later he joined Blackpool as assistant manager.

	P	W	D	L	F	A	Pts
2001-02 (3)	21	8	3	10	27	28	27
2002-03 (3)	46	13	16	17	64	70	55
2003-04 (3)	25	5	6	14	24	44	21
Total	92	26	25	41	115	142	103

DOHERTY, Peter Dermont
b. Magherafelt, Ireland, 5th June 1913
d. Fleetwood, Lancashire, 6th April 1990

Managerial adviser with Andy Beattie: 10th December 1965 to 18th March 1966. He was called in to help by his friend Andy Beattie. After a successful playing career at inside-forward with Coleraine, Glentoran, Blackpool, Manchester City, Derby and Huddersfield, Peter was player-manager at Doncaster and manager at Bristol City. Following his brief spell helping Notts he became Aston Villa chief scout and then assistant manager at both Preston and Sunderland. He won 16 caps for Northern Ireland and was an outstanding manager of his country from 1951-62 which included reaching the quarter-finals of the World Cup in 1958.

FENTON, Ronald 'Ron'
b. South Shields, Co.Durham, 21st September 1940

Manager: 16th October 1975 to 6th October 1977. Inside-forward Ron's playing career involved stays at Burnley, West Bromwich, Birmingham and Brentford before joining Notts as youth coach in July 1970. He then stepped up to club coach and took over as manager when Jimmy Sirrel moved to Sheffield United. After his dismissal he immediately switched to the Forest coaching staff and stayed there until Brian Clough resigned in May 1993.

	P	W	D	L	F	A	Pts
1975-76 (2)	31	13	8	10	49	32	34
1976-77 (2)	42	19	10	13	65	60	48
1977-78 (2)	9	0	4	5	10	21	4
Total	82	32	22	28	124	113	86

FISHER, Albert
b. Glasgow, June 1879
d. Birkland Avenue, Nottingham, 4th December 1937

Secretary-manager: 1st August 1913 to 31st May 1927 (absent in the Armed Forces 17th July 1917 to 29th January 1919).

After a playing career as a striker with Aston Villa, Fulham, Bristol City, Brighton, Manchester City and Bradford Park Avenue, he managed Merthyr Town before joining the Magpies. Albert saw County to two promotions as Division II champions in 1913-14 and 1922-23. Also led Notts to the FA Cup semis in 1921-22.

	P	W	D	L	F	A	Pts	
1913-14 (2)	38	23	7	8	77	36	53	P
1914-15 (1)	38	9	13	16	41	57	31	
1919-20 (1)	42	12	12	18	56	74	36	R
1920-21 (2)	42	18	11	13	55	40	47	
1921-22 (2)	42	12	15	15	47	51	39	
1922-23 (2)	42	23	7	12	46	34	53	P
1923-24 (1)	42	14	14	14	44	49	42	
1924-25 (1)	42	16	13	13	42	31	45	
1925-26 (1)	42	13	7	22	54	74	33	R
1926-27 (2)	42	15	5	22	70	96	35	
Total	412	155	104	153	532	542	414	

FISHER, Wilfred 'Wilf'
b. 13th February 1913
d. Comery Ave., Carlton, Nottingham, 22nd November 1985

Secretary-manager: 15th February 1949 to 25th May 1949. He held the post at the request of the directors while a successor was sought for Arthur Stollery. Wilf was the club secretary from 14th July 1942 to 4th November 1956 after being assistant-secretary from 1935.

	P	W	D	L	F	A	Pts
1948-49 (3S)	14	6	1	7	24	23	13

GRAY, William Patrick 'Billy'
b. Dinnington, Co. Durham, 24th May 1927

Manager: 13th March 1967 to 23rd September 1968. From the start of the 1967-68 season (1st August 1967) he relinquished team selection responsibilities to Andy Beattie and resumed them on 28th September 1967. Billy crowned a fine playing career on the wing with Leyton Orient, Chelsea and Burnley by helping Forest to win the FA Cup in 1958-59. He came to Meadow Lane after managerial stints at Millwall and Brentford. Later he spent time as Fulham coach and returned to Notts as groundsman. He won one England 'B' cap.

	P	W	D	L	F	A	Pts
1966-67 (4)	14	4	3	7	13	18	11
1967-68 (4)	38	14	9	15	47	61	37
1968-69 (4)	9	1	2	6	9	21	4
Total	61	19	14	28	69	100	52

---

†HENSHALL, Horace Vincent
b. Hednesford, Staffordshire, 14th June 1889
d. Trent Navigation Inn, Meadow Lane, Nottingham, 7th December 1951

Secretary-manager: 1st June 1927 to 5th May 1934, continuing as secretary only to 17th April 1935.

	P	W	D	L	F	A	Pts	
1927-28 (2)	42	13	12	17	68	74	38	
1928-29 (2)	42	19	9	14	78	65	47	
1929-30 (2)	42	9	15	18	54	70	33	R
1930-31 (3S)	42	24	11	7	97	46	59	P
1931-32 (2)	42	13	12	17	75	75	38	
1932-33 (2)	42	15	10	17	67	78	40	
1933-34 (2)	42	12	11	19	53	62	35	
Total	294	105	80	109	492	470	290	

HILL, Frank Robert
b. Forfar, Angus, 21st May 1906
d. Lafayette, California, United States, 28th August 1993

Manager: 17th October 1958 to 31st October 1961 when his contract expired and was not renewed. 'Tiger' Hill, a wing-half, earned three Scottish caps during a playing career which took in Forfar, Aberdeen, Ar-senal, Black-pool and Southampton. He was manager at Crewe, Burnley and Preston before taking on the Notts job. He helped the Magpies to promotion from Division IV in 1959-60. From Meadow Lane he went on to manage Charlton and then scouted for Manchester City.

	P	W	D	L	F	A	Pts	
1958-59 (3)	31	6	7	18	39	69	19	R
1959-60 (4)	46	26	8	12	107	69	60	P
1960-61 (3)	46	21	9	16	82	77	51	
1961-62 (3)	17	6	3	8	32	31	15	
Total	140	59	27	54	260	246	145	

---

†HOUGHTON, William Eric
b. Billingborough, Lincolnshire, 29th June 1910
d. Birmingham, 1st May 1996

Manager: 25th May 1949 to 1st September 1953.

	P	W	D	L	F	A	Pts	
1949-50 (3S)	42	25	8	9	95	50	58	P
1950-51 (2)	42	13	13	16	61	60	39	
1951-52 (2)	42	16	7	19	71	68	39	
1952-53 (2)	42	14	8	20	60	88	36	
1953-54 (2)	5	2	1	2	9	15	5	
Total	173	70	37	66	296	281	177	

JONES, Charles 'Charlie'

b. Troedyrhiw, Glamorgan, 12th December 1899
d. Brentwood, Essex, April 1966

Manager: 5th May 1934 to 6th December 1934. Charlie, who won seven Welsh caps, played once for Cardiff, then had successful stays as a winger at Stockport, Oldham and Forest. From there he joined Arsenal where he was converted to a fine wing-half by the great Herbert Chapman. Charlie arrived at Meadow Lane promising to run County using the Arsenal methods developed by Chapman but after 17 disastrous games he resigned when the directors took complete control away from him. From 1935 to 1939 he was secretary-manager of Essex works side Crittalls Athletic and later worked in a hospital.

	P	W	D	L	F	A	Pts	
1934-35 (2)	17	1	4	12	15	42	6	R

JONES, Philip Wayne

b. Treorchy, Glamorgan, 20th October 1948
Caretaker-manager with Steve Nicol and Dean Thomas: 1st April 1995 to 5th June 1995. A midfielder or forward, Wayne played more than 200 matches for Bristol Rovers and was capped once for Wales but a serious injury ended his career at the age of 24 and he turned to coaching, first with Rovers and then at Shrewsbury. He returned to Rovers as assistant boss, qualified as a physiotherapist, went into Saudi Arabian football and then succeeded John Short as the Notts physio in 1986. He had a spell as Huddersfield physio then returned to Meadow Lane. More recently he has been physio at Gillingham.

	P	W	D	L	F	A	Pts	
1994-95 (2)	7	1	3	3	3	9	6	R

KENDALL, Howard

b. Ryton-on-Tyne, Co.Durham. 22nd May 1946

Manager: 12th January 1995 to 1st April 1995. Midfield man Howard played for Preston, Everton, Birmingham and Stoke where he filled the role of player-coach, then went to Blackburn as player-manager. After retiring as a player he successfully managed Everton, went to Spain to boss Athletic Bilbao then returned home for managerial spells with Manchester City, Everton again, a brief stay at Meadow Lane followed by Sheffield United and Everton for a third time.

	P	W	D	L	F	A	Pts	
1994-95 (2)	14	4	4	6	20	21	16	R

---

†LAWTON, Thomas 'Tommy'

b. Bolton, Lancashire, 6th October 1919
d. Nottingham 6th November 1996

Manager: 7th May 1957 to 1st July 1958.

	P	W	D	L	F	A	Pts	
1957-58 (2)	42	12	6	24	44	80	30	R

LLOYD, Laurence Valentine 'Larry'

b. Bristol, 6th October 1948

Manager: 7th July 1983 to 21st October 1984. Larry won four England caps and two European Cups with Forest, in 1979 and 1980. He was a central defender who played for Bristol Rovers, Liverpool, Coventry, Forest and Wigan as player-manager. He led Wigan to promotion but was sacked the next season and then moved to County to replace Howard Wilkinson.

	P	W	D	L	F	A	Pts	
1983-84 (1)	42	10	11	21	50	72	41	R
1984-85 (2)	11	2	0	9	11	28	6	R
Total	53	12	11	30	61	100	47	

---

†LOWE, Edward 'Eddie'

b. Halesowen, Worcestershire, 11th July 1925

Player-manager: 1st July 1963 to 12th April 1965.

	P	W	D	L	F	A	Pts	
1963-64 (3)	46	9	9	28	45	92	27	R
1964-65 (4)	41	13	12	16	54	70	38	
Total	87	22	21	44	99	162	65	

McMULLAN, James 'Jimmy'

b. Denny, Stirlingshire, 26th March 1895
d. Carrville Drive, Sheffield, 27th November 1964

Secretary-manager: 10th November 1936 to 29th December 1937. Jimmy played at wing-half for Third Lanark, Partick and Manchester City before switching to management with Oldham and Aston Villa. Just missed leading the Magpies to promotion from Division III South in 1936-37, then resigned halfway through the following season in order to take over at Sheffield Wednesday. Jimmy gained 17 Scottish caps and was captain of the immortal 'Wembley Wizards' of 1928.

	P	W	D	L	F	A	Pts
1936-37 (3S)	28	18	5	5	51	30	41
1937-38 (3S)	21	11	5	5	32	15	27
Total	49	29	10	10	83	45	68

---

†MILLS, Gary Roland

b. Northampton, 11th November 1961

Manager: 9th January 2004 to 4th November 2004.

	P	W	D	L	F	A	Pts	
2003-04 (3)	21	5	6	10	26	34	21	R
2004-05 (4)	16	4	5	7	17	22	17	
Total	37	9	11	17	43	56	38	

MURPHY, Colin

b. Croydon, Greater London, 21st January 1944

General manager: 5th June 1995 to 23rd December 1996. Colin never played League soccer but was with Wimbledon in their pre-League days, then injury put paid to his active career. He went as coach to Charlton followed by the job of youth team manager at Forest, then coach at Derby where he stepped up to full manager but was eventually sacked. He was then Jimmy Sirrel's assistant at Meadow Lane from October 1977 to November 1978 before moving to manage Lincoln, Stockport and Lincoln again. Next Colin was youth coach with Leicester, assistant manager at Luton and Southend manager. He came back briefly to Meadow Lane, sharing managerial duties with Steve Thompson who was responsible for the playing side. Since then he has been assistant manager at Hull City. Colin achieved a cult reputation for his eccentric and flowery programme notes!

NEWMAN, John Henry George

b. Hereford, 13th December 1933

Acting manager: 2nd December 1988 to 5th January 1989. John represented Birmingham, Leicester, Plymouth and Exeter as a wing-half before taking the managerial reins at the last of these. He then took charge at Grimsby, Derby and Hereford before his appointment as assistant boss to John Barnwell in July 1988. After Neil Warnock arrived at Meadow Lane John had spells as York chief scout and Mansfield coach/chief scout (1990-94).

	P	W	D	L	F	A	Pts
1988-89 (3)	5	3	0	2	7	7	9

---

†NICOL, Stephen 'Steve'

b. Irvine, North Ayrshire, 11th December 1961

Caretaker-manager with Wayne Jones and Dean Thomas: 1st April 1995 to 5th June 1995.

	P	W	D	L	F	A	Pts	
1994-95 (2)	7	1	3	3	3	9	6	R

PARKES, Harry Arnold

b. Gorstey Hill, Halesowen, Worcestershire, September 1888

d. Station Hotel, Station Road, Hucknall, Notts., 11th March 1947

Secretary-manager: 11th January 1938 to 13th July 1939. Winger Harry played for West Bromwich and Coventry, then went on to manage Newport, Chesterfield, Lincoln and Mansfield before joining the Magpies.

	P	W	D	L	F	A	Pts
1937-38 (3S)	20	5	4	11	18	34	14
1938-39 (3S)	42	17	9	16	49	54	43
Total	62	22	13	27	67	88	57

POYSER, George Henry

b. Mansfield, Notts, 6th February 1910

d. Notts, 30th January 1995

Manager: 22nd October 1953 to 7th January 1957. As a full-back he had spells at Wolverhampton, Mansfield, Port Vale, Brentford and Plymouth before joining Dover Town as manager. Then he was appointed chief coach at Wolverhampton from where he came to Meadow Lane.

He had an outstanding season in 1954-55 with the Magpies reaching the quarter-finals of the FA Cup and challenging for promotion but after the tragic death of star centre-half Leon Leuty at the start of the following season, things went downhill. A Cup defeat by non-League Rhyl Athletic was the final straw and George was dismissed, going on to spend six years as deputy boss at Manchester City, then stepping up as manager there.

	P	W	D	L	F	A	Pts
1953-54 (2)	28	11	11	6	41	36	33
1954-55 (2)	42	21	6	15	74	71	48
1955-56 (2)	42	11	9	22	55	82	31
1956-57 (2)	25	3	4	18	30	68	10
Total	137	46	30	61	200	257	122

PRATT, David

b. Lochore, Fife, 5th March 1896

d. Not found

Secretary-manager: 29th April 1935 to 28th June 1935. David was a wing-half with Celtic, Bradford City, Liverpool and Bury, then managed Yeovil and Clapton Orient. He took over at Meadow Lane for the final match of 1934-35 with the club already doomed to relegation. After a 5-1 defeat he quit two months later in order to manage Hearts. David went on to become a well-known BBC sports commentator. He was appointed manager of Port Vale in 1944 but could not obtain his discharge from the RAF so was unable to take up the post.

	P	W	D	L	F	A	Pts	
1934-35 (2)	1	0	0	1	1	5	0	R

---○---

†RICHARDSON, Ian

b. Barking, Essex, 22nd October 1970

Player-caretaker-manager 4th November 2004, then full player-manager to 17th May 2005.

	P	W	D	L	F	A	Pts
2004-05 (4)	30	9	8	13	29	40	35

---○---

SCOTT, John 'Jocky'

b. Aberdeen 14th January 1948

Manager: 28th June 2000 to 10th October 2001. Before coming to Meadow Lane Jocky's playing and managerial career was in Scotland except for a couple of spells with Seattle Sounders. After being on the Chelsea ground staff aged 15, he turned out for Dundee, Aberdeen and Dundee again as well as winning two Scottish caps as an inside-forward. Towards the close of his second period at Dundee he became player-coach then stepped up as manager before switching to boss Aberdeen, another of his former clubs. Further appointments took him to Dunfermline and Arbroath followed by a return to Dundee. His departure from Notts was an abrupt one which came after he had reacted angrily to barracking from fans and the board decided he had to go. Since then he has been first team coach at Plymouth Argyle.

	P	W	D	L	F	A	Pts
2000-01 (3)	46	19	12	15	62	66	69
2001-02 (3)	11	4	3	4	14	17	15
Total	57	23	15	19	76	83	84

---○---

SIRREL, James 'Jimmy'

b. Glasgow, 2nd February 1922

Manager: 19th November 1969 to 16th October 1975; then again from 6th October 1977 to 28th August 1982 when he became general manager and then a paid director from June 1984. He was caretaker-manager from 21st October 1984 to 5th November 1984 and resumed full team managerial duties from 20th April 1985 to 2nd June 1987.

Jimmy was without doubt County's greatest manager who oversaw promotions from Division IV to Division I via seasons 1970-71, 1972-73 and 1980-81. The war cut into his playing career as an inside-forward but he had spells with Celtic, Bradford Park Avenue, Brighton and Aldershot where he was appointed trainer and then managed Brentford before coming to Meadow Lane. He left the Magpies to take charge of Sheffield United but an unsuccessful time there saw him ousted and quickly on his way back to Notts. After retiring in 1987 he had a spell as a Derby County scout under Arthur Cox.

Two points for a win

	P	W	D	L	F	A	Pts	
1969-70 (4)	28	15	5	8	53	40	35	
1970-71 (4)	46	30	9	7	89	36	69	P
1971-72 (3)	46	25	12	9	74	44	62	
1972-73 (3)	46	23	11	12	67	47	57	P
1973-74 (2)	42	15	13	14	55	60	43	
1974-75 (2)	42	12	16	14	49	59	40	
1975-76 (2)	11	6	3	2	11	9	15	
1977-78 (2)	33	11	12	10	44	41	34	
1978-79 (2)	42	14	16	12	48	60	44	
1979-80 (2)	42	11	15	16	51	52	37	
1980-81 (2)	42	18	17	7	49	38	53	P
Total	420	180	129	111	589	486	489	

Three points for a win

	P	W	D	L	F	A	Pts	
1981-82 (1)	42	13	8	21	61	69	47	
1984-85 (2)	7	3	2	2	12	9	11	R
1985-86 (3)	46	19	14	13	71	60	71	
1986-87 (3)	46	21	13	12	77	56	76	
Total	141	56	37	48	221	194	205	
Grand total	561	236	166	159	810	680	694	

---○---

SLADE, Russell Mark

b. Wokingham, Berkshire, 10th October 1960

Manager: 14th September 1994 to 12th January 1995, then he became assistant-manager. Russell was a schoolmaster who was involved with coaching youngsters after earning his FA badges. He then helped Mick Walker in running County's youth team and reserves before his elevation to manager. Four months of struggle led to his reverting to the assistant's role for a while.

Since leaving Meadow Lane he has helped out at Sheffield United and moved back into full management with Scarborough and Grimsby.

	P	W	D	L	F	A	Pts	
1994-95 (2)	18	3	4	11	14	25	13	R

SMITH, Percy James
b. Burbage Spring, Hinckley, Leicestershire, 1880
d. The Manor House, High Road, Leavesden, Watford, 18th April 1959

Secretary-manager: 19th July 1935 to 31st October 1936. As a player he had long spells with Preston and Blackburn, first as centre-forward and later at wing-half, then managed Fleetwood, Nelson, Bury and Tottenham before joining County. After 15 months Percy moved on and took charge at Bristol Rovers.

	P	W	D	L	F	A	Pts
1935-36 (3S)	42	15	12	15	60	57	42
1936-37 (3S)	13	5	4	4	21	20	14
Total	55	20	16	19	81	77	56

STOLLERY, Arthur William
b. Woolwich, London, July/September, 1889
d. Thornton Heath, Surrey, 4th February 1955

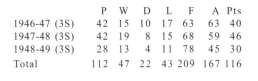

Manager: 12th June 1946 to 15th February 1949. He made his name as a PE expert in the RAF and joined Chelsea as trainer in 1939. He left Stamford Bridge for Notts but returned there to sign Tommy Lawton for the Magpies for the then record transfer fee. Ill-health brought about Arthur's resignation.

	P	W	D	L	F	A	Pts
1946-47 (3S)	42	15	10	17	63	63	40
1947-48 (3S)	42	19	8	15	68	59	46
1948-49 (3S)	28	13	4	11	78	45	30
Total	112	47	22	43	209	167	116

---

†THOMAS, Dean Robert
b. Bedworth, Warwickshire, 19th December 1961

Caretaker-manager with Wayne Jones and Steve Nicol: 1st April 1995 to 5th June 1995.

	P	W	D	L	F	A	Pts	
1994-95 (2)	7	1	3	3	3	9	6	R

THOMPSON, Steven Paul 'Steve'
b. Sheffield, 28th July 1955
Team manager: 5th June 1995 to 23rd December 1996. Central defender Steve had a playing career which took in Lincoln, Charlton, Leicester, Sheffield United and a second spell with Lincoln where he succeeded Colin Murphy as manager in 1990 and led the Imps for three years. He had a brief stay in charge at Southend before joining the Magpies in a joint role with Colin who became general manager while Steve controlled on-the-field affairs. He was recently manager at Cambridge United until they lost their League place in 2004-05.

	P	W	D	L	F	A	Pts	
1995-96 (3)	46	21	15	10	63	39	78	
1996-97 (3)	23	5	6	12	15	26	21	R
Total	69	26	21	22	78	65	99	
1995-96 Play-offs	3	1	1	1	3	4	—	

THORDARSON, Gudjon
b. Iceland, 14th September 1955

Manager: appointed 17th May 2005. Gudjon came into English football to take charge at Stoke City after managing Iceland's international team. He earned plaudits at Stoke but the managerial merry-go-round saw him on his way and then take over at Barnsley for a short period before moving back to Iceland as manager of Keflavik. He becomes County's first foreign manager in the club's 143-year history.

TOWERS, James Ralph 'Tony'
b. Nottingham, April/June 1895
d. Musters Road, West Bridgford, Nottingham, 16th July 1963

Secretary-manager: 13th July 1939 to 14th July 1942. Began his association with Meadow Lane by running Notts County Colts in the early 1920s, then became a club director on 2nd February 1927. After Harry Parkcs quit as manager in 1939, he took on that role just in time for the start of wartime soccer in 1939-40. Tony resigned as manager on 14th July 1942, and left the board 18 months later

---

WALKER, Michael 'Mick'

b. Belper, Derbyshire, 27th November 1940

Manager: 14th January 1993 to 14th September 1994. Mick played as a teenage amateur right-winger with Forest Reserves, then for Loughborough Colleges, Kettering Town and Matlock Town before foot injuries sidelined him permanently. He took charge of PE at Nottingham's Mundella School, qualified as an FA staff coach, was manager of Ilkeston Town and moved to Singapore to coach the national team. Mick returned to Mundella as maths master, managed Burton Albion and then Boston United. He then came to Meadow Lane to head the youth scheme which produced a crop of fine youngsters such as Brian Kilcline, Mark Draper and Dean Yates. He stayed as coach until promoted to replace Neil Warnock as manager. Mick was sacked after a poor start to 1994-95 and then ran Sheffield Wednesday's youth scheme before moving to coach at Leeds United.

	P	W	D	L	F	A	Pts	
1992-93 (2)	22	8	8	6	31	26	32	
1993-94 (2)	46	20	8	18	65	69	68	
1994-95 (2)	7	1	2	4	8	11	5	R
Total	75	29	18	28	104	106	105	

WARNOCK, Neil

b. Sheffield, 1st December 1948

Manager: 5th January 1989 to 14th January 1993. Neil made his name by taking Scarborough into the Football League, the first club to win automatic promotion to this level. He had a lengthy roster of clubs during his playing days as a forward with spells at Chesterfield, Rotherham, Hartlepool, Scunthorpe, Aldershot, Barnsley, York, Crewe and Burton Albion. He then managed Gainsborough Trinity and Burton before switching to Scarborough and then to Notts. He took County to two successive promotions via the play-offs but they were relegated after only one season in the top flight.

After his Meadow Lane sacking Neil stayed in management with Torquay (caretaker role, saving them from relegation), Huddersfield, Plymouth, Oldham, Bury and Sheffield United, building up a reputation as a colourful and controversial operator.

	P	W	D	L	F	A	Pts	
1988-89 (3)	25	13	5	7	41	28	44	
1989-90 (3)	46	25	12	9	73	53	87	P
1990-91 (2)	46	23	11	12	76	55	80	P
1991-92 (1)	42	10	10	22	40	62	40	R
1992-93 (2)	24	4	8	12	24	44	20	
Total	183	75	46	62	254	242	271	
1989-90 Play-offs	3	2	1	0	5	1	—	
1990-91 Play-offs	3	2	1	0	5	2	—	

WHEELER, William John 'Jack'

b. Evesham, Worcestershire, 13th July 1919

Joint caretaker-manager with Tim Coleman: 1st July 1958 to 17th October 1958; then care-taker-manager 23rd September 1968 to 19th November 1969. He was club trainer from the start of the 1957-58 season until the end of 1982-83 and never missed a first team match, which numbered well over 1,000.
As a player Jack was a sound goalkeeper with Birmingham and Huddersfield then joined Tommy Lawton at Kettering, coming to Meadow Lane when Tommy was appointed County manager.

	P	W	D	L	F	A	Pts	
1958-59 (3)	15	2	6	7	16	27	10	R
1968-69 (4)	37	11	16	10	39	36	38	
1969-70 (4)	18	7	3	8	20	22	17	
Total	70	20	25	25	75	85	65	

WHITE, Robert Clark 'Bob'

b. 1884
d. Eltham Road, West Bridgford, Nottingham, 17th November 1951

Secretary-manager: 17th July 1917 to 29th January 1919 (during Albert Fisher's absence in the Armed Forces). He was a club director from 9th July 1919 to 22nd April 1925.

WILKINSON, Howard
b. Sheffield, 13th November 1943

Team manager: 28th August 1982 to 24th June 1983. After playing in the forward line for Sheffield Wednesday and Brighton, Howard moved into non-League as player-manager at Boston United, then became County club coach from December 1979, being closely involved with Jimmy Sirrel in the promotion push to Division I.

His success at Meadow Lane tempted him to accept the offer to take charge at Sheffield Wednesday then he moved to Leeds United with whom he won the final Division I title before the formation of the Premiership. Howard had a long involvement with the FA as England semi-pro and Under-21 manager, later being appointed FA Director of Coaching which included a short time as England manager. He made a brief return to League management with Sunderland and in 2004-05 returned to Meadow Lane as a non-executive director.

	P	W	D	L	F	A	Pts
1982-83 (1)	42	15	7	20	55	71	52

WOMACK, Frank
b. Wortley, near Sheffield, 16th September 1888
d. Caister, Lincolnshire, 8th October 1968
Manager: 14th July 1942 to 4th November 1943. A one-club man, he had a lengthy 515-match career at full-back with Birmingham before becoming manager at Worcester City, Torquay, Grimsby and Leicester. Took over at Notts during war-time soccer and post-war managed Oldham and Grimsby.

A selection of Notts players
on Cigarette Cards and the author's caricatures.

G. BLYTH

J. CANTRELL
NOTTS COUNTY F.C.

Joseph Cooper